A Companion to American

BLACKWELL COMPANIONS TO AMERICAN HISTORY

This series provides essential and authoritative overviews of the scholarship that has shaped our present understanding of the American past. Edited by eminent historians, each volume tackles one of the major periods or themes of American history, with individual topics authored by key scholars who have spent considerable time in research on the questions and controversics that have sparked debate in their field of interest. The volumes are accessible for the nonspecialist, while also engaging scholars seeking a reference to the historiography or future concerns.

Published

A Companion to the American Revolution
Edited by Jack P. Greene and J. R. Pole

A Companion to 19th-Century America
Edited by William L. Barney

A Companion to the American South
Edited by John B. Boles

A Companion to American Indian History
Edited by Philip J. Deloria and Neal Salisbury

A Companion to American Women's History
Edited by Nancy Hewitt

A Companion to Post-1945 America
Edited by Jean-Christophe Agnew and Roy Rosenzweig

A Companion to the Vietnam War
Edited by Marilyn Young and Robert Buzzanco

A Companion to Colonial America
Edited by Daniel Vickers

A Companion to 20th-Century America
Edited by Stephen J. Whitfield

A Companion to the American West
Edited by William Deverell

A Companion to American Foreign Relations
Edited by Robert Schulzinger

A Companion to the Civil War and Reconstruction
Edited by Lacy K. Ford

A Companion to American Technology
Edited by Carroll Pursell

A Companion to African-American History
Edited by Alton Hornsby

BLACKWELL COMPANIONS TO HISTORY

Published

A Companion to Western Historical Thought
Edited by Lloyd Kramer and Sarah Maza

A Companion to Gender History
Edited by Teresa Meade and Merry E. Weisner-Hanks

BLACKWELL COMPANIONS TO BRITISH HISTORY

Published

A Companion to Roman Britain
Edited by Malcolm Todd

A Companion to Britain in the Later Middle Ages
Edited by S. H. Rigby

A Companion to Tudor Britain
Edited by Robert Tittler and Norman Jones

A Companion to Stuart Britain
Edited by Barry Coward

A Companion to Eighteenth-Century Britain
Edited by H. T. Dickinson

A Companion to Nineteenth-Century Britain
Edited by Chris Williams

A Companion to Early Twentieth-Century Britain
Edited by Chris Wrigley

BLACKWELL COMPANIONS TO EUROPEAN HISTORY

Published

A Companion to the Worlds of the Renaissance
Edited by Guido Ruggiero

A Companion to the Reformation World
Edited by R. Po-chia Hsia

A COMPANION TO AMERICAN WOMEN'S HISTORY

Edited by

Nancy A. Hewitt

BLACKWELL PUBLISHING
350 Main Street, Malden, MA 02148-5020, USA
108 Cowley Road, Oxford OX4 1JF, UK
550 Swanston Street, Carlton, Victoria 3053, Australia

First published 2002
First published in paperback 2005 by Blackwell Publishing Ltd

Library of Congress Cataloging-in-Publication Data

A companion to American women's history edited by Nancy A. Hewitt.
p. cm.—(Blackwell companions to American history; #5)
Includes bibliographical references (p.) and index.
ISBN 0-631-21252-3 (hb: alk. paper)—ISBN 1-4051-2685-X (pb: alk. paper)
1. Women—United States—History. 2. Feminism—United States—History. I. Hewitt, Nancy A, 1951–. II. Series.

HQ1410. C63 2002

2002020882

A catalogue record for this title is available from the British Library.

Set in 10/12.5 pt Galliard
by Kolam Information Services Pvt. Ltd, Pondicherry, India
Printed and bound in the United Kingdom
by TJ International Ltd, Padstow, Cornwall

The publisher's policy is to use permanent paper from mills that operate a sustainable forestry policy, and which has been manufactured from pulp processed using acid-free and elementary chlorine-free practices. Furthermore, the publisher ensures that the text paper and cover board used have met acceptable environmental accreditation standards.

For further information on
Blackwell Publishing, visit our website:
www.blackwellpublishing.com

To the graduate students who have taught me so much.

Contents

About the Contributors ix
Introduction xii

Part I The Colonial Era, 1600–1760 1

1 The Imperial Gaze: Native American, African American, and Colonial Women in European Eyes 3
Kirsten Fischer

2 Slavery and the Slave Trade 20
Jennifer L. Morgan

3 Contact and Conquest in Colonial North America 35
Gwenn A. Miller

4 Building Colonies, Defining Families 49
Ann M. Little

5 Sinners and Saints: Women and Religion in Colonial America 66
Susan Juster

Part II The Creation of a New Nation, 1760–1880 81

6 A Revolution for Whom? Women in the Era of the American Revolution 83
Jan E. Lewis

7 Gender and Class Formations in the Antebellum North 100
Catherine Kelly

8 Religion, Reform, and Radicalism in the Antebellum Era 117
Nancy A. Hewitt

9 Conflicts and Cultures in the West 132
Lisbeth Haas

10 Rural Women 150
Marli F. Weiner

11 The Civil War Era 167
Thavolia Glymph

12 Marriage, Property, and Class 193
Amy Dru Stanley

13 Health, Sciences, and Sexualities in Victorian America 206
Louise Michele Newman

Part III Modern America, 1880–1990 **225**

14 Education and the Professions 227
Lynn D. Gordon

15 Wage-earning Women 250
Annelise Orleck

16 Consumer Cultures 274
Susan Porter Benson

17 Urban Spaces and Popular Cultures, 1890–1930 295
Nan Enstad

18 Women on the Move: Migration and Immigration 312
Ardis Cameron

19 Women's Movements, 1880s–1920s 328
Kirsten Delegard

20 Medicine, Law, and the State: The History of Reproduction 348
Leslie J. Reagan

21 The Great Depression and World War II 366
Karen Anderson

22 Rewriting Postwar Women's History, 1945–1960 382
Joanne Meyerowitz

23 Civil Rights and Black Liberation 397
Steven F. Lawson

24 Second-wave Feminism 414
Rosalyn Baxandall and Linda Gordon

Bibliography: Selected Secondary Sources 433
Compiled by April de Stefano
Index 481

About the Contributors

Karen Anderson is Professor of History at the University of Arizona. She is the author most recently of *Changing Woman: A History of Racial Ethnic Women in Modern America* (1996) and is currently completing a book on the Little Rock, Arkansas, school desegregation crisis, 1954–64.

Rosalyn Baxandall is Professor and Chair of American Studies at the State University of New York at Old Westbury. She has written widely on working women, reproductive rights, and suburbia. She is co-author of *Picture Windows: How the Suburbs Happened* (2000) and co-editor, with Linda Gordon, of *Dear Sisters: Dispatches from the Women's Liberation Movement* (2000).

Susan Porter Benson is Associate Professor of History at the University of Connecticut. She is the author of *Counter Cultures: Saleswomen, Managers, and Customers in America's Department Stores* (1986) and is at work on *Household Accounts: Working-class Families in the Interwar United States.*

Ardis Cameron is Director of American and New England Studies at the University of Southern Maine. Author of *Radicals of the Worst Sort: Laboring Women in Lawrence, Massachusetts, 1860–1912* (1993), she is currently working on *In Search of Peyton Place: The Biography of a Book.*

April de Stefano is Visiting Assistant Professor at Claremont McKenna College. She is revising her dissertation "'A Freer Existence for Womanhood': Gender, Marital Status and Wage Work in Los Angeles, 1900–1929", for publication.

Kirsten Delegard is an Independent Scholar at Duke University. She is currently revising her dissertation, *Women Patriots: Female Activism and the Politics of Anti-radicalism*, for publication.

Nan Enstad is Associate Professor of History at the University of Wisconsin, Madison. She is the author of *Ladies of Labor, Girls of Adventure: Working Women, Popular Culture, and Labor Politics at the Turn of the Twentieth Century* (1999).

Kirsten Fischer is Associate Professor of History at the University of Minnesota. She is the author of *Suspect Relations: Sex, Race, and Resistance in Colonial North Carolina* (2002).

Thavolia Glymph, Assistant Professor of History and African and African American Studies at Duke University, has co-edited and co-authored several volumes on the Civil War and postbellum South. She has written widely on women's role in war and the struggle for emancipation, including "'This Species of Property': Female Slave Contrabands in the War," in *A Woman's War: Southern Women, Civil War, and the Confederate Legacy* (1996).

Linda Gordon is Professor of History at New York University. Her most recent books are *The Great Arizona Orphan Abduction* (1999), winner of the Bancroft and Beveridge prizes, and *Dear Sisters: Dispatches from the Women's Liberation Movement* (2000), which she co-edited with Rosalyn Baxandall.

Lynn D. Gordon is Associate Professor of Education and History and Chair of the Gender and Society Group at the University of Rochester. Author of *Gender and Higher Education in the Progressive Era* (1990), she is currently working on a biography of the journalist Dorothy Thompson.

Lisbeth Haas is Associate Professor of History at the University of California, Santa Cruz. She is the author of *Conquests and Historical Identities in California, 1769–1936*, awarded the Elliott Rudwick prize, and is currently completing *The Chumash Rafael and Other Histories of Colonial and Mexican California*.

Nancy A. Hewitt is Professor of History and Women's Studies at Rutgers University, New Brunswick. She is the author of *Southern Discomfort: Women's Activism in Tampa, Florida, 1880s–1920s* (2001) and co-author, with Chris Clarke, of *Who Built America?*, volume 1 (2000).

Susan Juster is Associate Professor of History at the University of Michigan. Her articles on gender and prophecy have appeared in the *William and Mary Quarterly* and the *American Historical Review*. She is currently at work on *Prophets of Evil: Millenarian Culture and the Public Sphere in Revolutionary America*.

Catherine Kelly is Associate Professor of History at the University of Oklahoma. She is the author of *In the New England Fashion: Reshaping Women's Lives in the Nineteenth Century* (1999).

Steven F. Lawson, Professor of History at Rutgers University, New Brunswick, has written widely on the civil rights movement and black politics. He is the author of *Debating the Civil Rights Movement* (1998) with Charles Payne and has written an essay on Ruby Hurley for *Notable American Women*, volume 5 (forthcoming).

Jan E. Lewis is Professor of History at Rutgers University, Newark. She is the author of *The Pursuit of Happiness: Family and Values in Jefferson's Virginia* (1983) and co-author, with Jeanne Boydston, James Oakes, Nick Cullather, and Michael McGerr, of *Making a Nation: The United States and Its People* (2001).

Ann M. Little is Associate Professor of History at Colorado State University. She is the author of articles on colonial women's and gender history and the author of *Abraham in Arms: Gender and Power on the New England Frontier, 1620–1760.*

Joanne Meyerowitz is Professor of History at Yale University and past editor of the *Journal of American History*. She is the editor of *Not June Cleaver: Women and Gender in Postwar America* (1994) and author of *How Sex Changed: A History of Transsexuality in the United States* (2002).

Gwenn A. Miller is Assistant Professor of History at College of the Holy Cross. She is currently revising her dissertation, " 'She Was Handsome . . . But Tattooed': Gender, Empire, and Environment in Russian Alaska, 1720–1820."

Jennifer L. Morgan is Associate Professor of History and Women's Studies at Rutgers University, New Brunswick. She is the author of *Laboring Women: Reproduction and Slavery in Early America* (2004).

Louise Michele Newman, Associate Professor of History at the University of Florida, is author of *White Women's Rights: The Racial Origins of Feminism in the United States* (1999). She is currently at work on *See Through the Sixties: Hollywood Histories of Civil Rights and Feminism.*

Annelise Orleck, Associate Professor of History and Women's Studies at Dartmouth College, is the author of *Common Sense and a*

Little Fire: Women and Working-class Politics in the United States (1995) and *Soviet Jewish Americans* (1999). She co-edited *The Politics of Motherhood: Activist Voices from Left to Right* (1997).

Leslie J. Reagan is Associate Professor in the Department of History and the Medical Humanities and Social Sciences Program at the University of Illinois, Urbana-Champaign. She is the author most recently of "Crossing the Border for Abortions: California Activists, Mexican Clinics, and the Creation of a Feminist Health Agency in the 1960s," *Feminist Studies* (Summer 2000) and "From Blessing to Tragedy: Teachings on Miscarriage in Twentieth-century America," *Feminist Studies* (forthcoming).

Amy Dru Stanley, Associate Professor of History at the University of Chicago, has published numerous articles on women, race, property, and citizenship. She is the author of *From Bondage to Contract: Wage Labor, Marriage, and the Market in the Age of Slave Emancipation* (1998).

Marli F. Weiner is Professor of History at the University of Maine, Orono. She is the author of *Plantation Women: South Carolina Mistresses and Slaves* (1998) and editor of *Of Place and Gender: Essays on Women in Maine History* (forthcoming). She is currently at work on *"My House has been an Hospital": Gender, Race, and the Politics of Healthcare on the Antebellum Plantation.*

Introduction

Nancy A. Hewitt

WORK on the history of American[1] women has exploded in recent years, building on and challenging the interpretations and frameworks first developed in the 1960s and 1970s. From the emergence of American women's history as a field, scholars explored the diverse experiences of women. Barbara Welter's "The Cult of True Womanhood" (1966) was joined by Anne Firor Scott's *Southern Lady* (1970), Gerda Lerner's *Black Women in White America* (1972), and Thomas Dublin's *Women at Work* (1979) as hallmarks of the first generation of scholarship.[2] Not until the decade from the mid-1970s through the mid-1980s did studies of white, middle-class women in the northeastern United States come to dominate the landscape. During that period, this single group of women not only received the bulk of scholarly attention, but in addition interpretations based on their lives came to govern scholarship in the field as a whole.

Still, there was no single approach to American women's history. Some scholars focused on prescriptive literature and the way popular discourses reflected and/or shaped behavior; others emphasized material conditions and the way the market economy and industrial capitalism transformed women's lives. A few examined how the breadth and instability of the emergent "middle class" created divisions among white bourgeois women in the early to mid-nineteenth century. These studies, pioneered by Mary Ryan in *The Cradle of the Middle Class* in 1981, highlighted the common concerns of women and men who shared socioeconomic circumstances and kinship ties. This approach challenged more frequent claims that separate sexual spheres distanced women from men experientially as well as rhetorically. Other scholars, most notably Linda Gordon in *Woman's Body, Woman's Rights* (1976), traced ideological differences among women that shaped both the private lives of ordinary women and the public agendas of the far smaller number who participated in movements for social change. Moreover, even amid the outpouring of work on white, middle-class northeastern women, historians continued to pursue studies of working-class, immigrant, African American, southern, and western women.

By the late 1980s, a major transformation in American women's history occurred as the exploration of differences among women took center stage. Research on class, race, ethnicity, and region poured off the presses and exploded into visibility at conferences and in classrooms. Pathbreaking studies such as Deborah Gray White's *Ar'n't I a Woman?* (1985) and Jacqueline Jones's *Labor of Love, Labor of Sorrow* (1985); Joanne Meyerowitz's *Women Adrift* (1988) and Christine Stansell's *City of Women* (1986); Susan Glenn's *Daughters of the Shtetl* (1990) and Evelyn Nakano Glenn's *Issei, Nissei, War Bride* (1986); Susan Armitage and Elizabeth Jameson's *The Women's West* (1987) and Sarah Deutsch's *No Separate Refuge* (1987); and Catherine Clinton's *The Plantation Mistress* (1987) and Jacquelyn Dowd Hall's *Revolt Against Chivalry* (1979) demonstrated vast differences in women's experiences. At conferences and panel discussions as well as in published works, the debate moved from differences and struggles between women and men to hierarchies and power dynamics among women.

The disagreements among women's historians were intense and often painful in this period, but they illustrated the field's growth and vitality. They also inspired provocative new work that used detailed explorations of particular women's experiences to challenge existing interpretations. For example, in "Womanist Consciousness" (1989b), Elsa Barkley Brown wielded a case study of Maggie Lena Walker, a leader in Richmond, Virginia's African American community, to critique concepts of identity and politics derived from white women's experience. Similarly, "Disorderly Women" (1986), Jacquelyn Dowd Hall's investigation of a textile workers' strike in Elizabethton, Tennessee, employed an elegantly crafted local study to question class and regional assumptions about sexuality and modernity.

Throughout this period, the study of specific communities in which the experiences of ordinary women could be studied in fine detail vied with those exploring national associations, movements, and developments. The analysis of social movements, in particular, required both perspectives to explain how change occurred. Yet rarely did scholars combine the two approaches. For the most part, historians of national movements developed general arguments regarding women's efforts on behalf of a cause, while those who pursued local studies used their findings to complicate and challenge that national portrait. For example, in "The Domestication of Politics" (1984), Paula Baker argued that the passage in 1920 of the Nineteenth Amendment granting woman suffrage was a critical turning point because it eliminated the common ground of disfranchisement that had so long formed the centerpiece of a distinct women's political culture. In contrast, studies of political activism among African American women in Richmond, Virginia, immigrant women workers in Tampa, Florida, and female Populists in Kansas, all focused on the late nineteenth century, suggested that women's political culture was deeply fractured (or delightfully diverse) decades earlier. Only recently have scholars like Sarah Barringer Gordon and Gayle Gullet – examining the intersection of debates over suffrage and polygamy and the statewide campaign for women's votes in California, respectively – begun to address the interplay of local, state, and national developments.

As studies that focused on the intersection of local, regional, and national developments began to emerge in the 1990s, those that recognized the intertwined character of "separate" spheres multiplied rapidly. Starting in the 1980s, a number of historians traced the ways that women's public and private activities shaped each other. In *A Midwife's Tale* (1990), Laurel Thatcher Ulrich drew a compelling portrait of the life of eighteenth-century Maine midwife Martha Ballard, demonstrating her critical role not only in the intimate dramas of labor and birth but also in the community-wide exchange of goods and services and the politically charged rituals of trial and judgment. For the nineteenth century, Jeanne Boydston detailed the ways that the most mundane domestic labors contributed to the rise of a market economy and industrial capitalism. And Elaine Tyler May explored the discourse of Soviet containment in the post-World War II period to illuminate the connections between fears of Communism in the arena of national politics and the ideal of the happy homemaker in the domestic realm.

The debates among American women's historians over issues of race, class, and region; local and national perspectives; and private and public spheres unfolded in the midst of larger theoretical controversies among feminist scholars over concepts and categories. Conflicts over the meaning and significance of "experience" and "identity" were especially heated. Joan Scott's "Gender: A Useful Category of Analysis" (1986) became the most-cited reference of the new postmodernist position which challenged the existence of experiences or identities unmediated by language and critiqued grand narratives and fixed identities as largely created, rather than recovered, by scholars. The battle that raged over what we could know and how we could know it engaged a wide array of scholars, but it had a particular intensity for those in emerging fields – African American history and labor history as well as women's history – who were concerned that postmodern challenges to fixed identities and grand narratives would subvert the power of their work just as it was beginning to receive serious attention. It now seems clear, however, that the postmodernist turn has opened up new possibilities for analyzing women's past, including more critical readings of a variety of texts and richer understandings of the multiple and contested identities embraced by individuals and groups. At the same time, it has not diminished the power of other, often more materially based, approaches to the field.

The history of sexuality offers a particularly important example of the ways that modern and postmodern perspectives have contributed simultaneously to scholarship on American women. Early work in this area focused on the experiences and identities of lesbians or the issues surrounding contraception and abortion, that is, on areas defined as outside normative heterosexuality. John D'Emilio and Estelle Freedman's *Intimate Matters* (1988) and Leslie Reagan's *When Abortion Was a Crime* (1997) provide superb examples of how such an approach recast understandings of women's history. Although neither of these studies adopted postmodernist perspectives, both included readings of popular, medical, and legal discourse in their analyses. The development of queer theory, which employed postmodernist perspectives to reconceptualize sexuality and its relation to race, gender, and performance, created alternate narratives. Such recent studies as Siobhan Somerville's *Queering the Color Line* (2000) and Lisa Duggan's *Sapphic Slashers* (2000) highlight the power of work that conceives of sexuality as continually constructed (and reconstructed) and interrogates its relation to discourses of race, violence, and power in particular historical contexts.

One consequence of the debates over postmodernism and the work on sexuality has been increased attention to gender within the context of women's history.

Gender was a critical concern of women's historians from the founding of the field. Joan Kelly's 1976 essay, "The Social Relations of the Sexes," argued that women's circumstances and experiences must be understood in relation to those of men, analyzing both their distinctive and shared histories. Her 1977 essay "Did Women Have a Renaissance?" provided a compelling example of how such comparisons not only illuminated previously hidden aspects of a period, but recast what was already familiar. Although many scholars agreed, it was not until the 1990s that a significant number of American women's historians began framing analyses in terms of gender and analyzing manhood and masculinity as well as womanhood and femininity. A relatively recent development, gender analyses such as Gail Bederman's *Manliness and Civilization* (1995) and George Chauncey's *Gay New York* (1994) have received widespread acclaim and have once again expanded the frameworks of the field.

Perhaps the greatest strength of American women's history, and women's history more generally, has come from the field's ability to take advantage of new approaches, concepts, and theoretical perspectives without abandoning those that came before. Certainly serious debates and disagreements remain among women's historians. In many cases, they are the lifeblood of the field, nurturing new and important work on a vast range of topics from a wide variety of perspectives. Journals, conferences, monograph series, doctoral programs, undergraduate and graduate courses, historic sites, documentaries, museum exhibits, oral history projects, workshops, seminars, and websites – all devoted to women's history and many focused on American women's history – multiply each year. African American women's history, southern and western women's history, Jewish women's history, working-class women's history, and lesbian/queer/transgender history have developed as critical areas of study that are sufficiently large to be considered distinct entities, building upon and transforming American women's history as a whole.

As this book goes to press, the scope and definition of American women's history is again being recast. Attention to the politics and influence of conservative women is gaining increased attention. This is not surprising given the conservative resurgence in American politics from the 1980s on. It has become more and more difficult to ignore the power of women who opposed suffrage and social welfare programs, such as the Sheppard-Towner Act of 1921, or to consider them as mere pawns of male politicians or clerical authorities. Women who joined the Ku Klux Klan and other nativist and racist organizations or who spoke out in favor of increased military spending in the 1920s or those who rallied against racial integration and led anti-abortion campaigns in the post-World War II era were as much activists as those who initiated and supported progressive causes. In addition, the rhetoric of conservative and right-wing movements often wielded tropes of gender, sexuality, and race as an important means of provoking fear and maintaining the status quo. No longer can women's historians interpret the history of progressive social activism without viewing it in relation to conservative and right-wing opponents of change.

At the same time, work on colonial and postcolonial societies around the world, on imperialism, and on the Americas and the Black Atlantic has challenged scholars of the United States to move away from an insular view of their past. Those who study colonial North America have always had to be attentive to a wider world. Yet even they are being pushed to expand their vision beyond the thirteen Atlantic coast colonies and consider issues of conquest and contact across the continent as a whole, recognizing that for many Americans, the colonial era extended deep into the nineteenth century. Indeed, some would now argue that it converged in the 1890s with the United States' first imperial ventures. Women's historians exploring the American West, on the one hand, and American colonial and imperial relations, on the other, have been in the forefront of work that recasts questions and categories of race, gender, and sexuality, and demands attention to a wider array of sources. These include materials in a variety of languages, such as Spanish, French, Russian, and various Native American languages, as well as rituals, photographs, and other artifacts of cultural contact, conflict, and conquest. These initiatives, fueled by the rising tide of globalization in the twenty-first century, assure that American women's history will continue to develop in new and intriguing directions.

This volume in the Blackwell series represents the wide range of American women's histories appearing at the beginning of the twenty-first century while reminding readers of the critical work produced over the past four decades. They address the debates outlined above in the context of specific topics and time periods and introduce as well those most immediate to a particular subject. The chapters are divided chronologically into three sections – colonial, 1760–1880, and 1880–1990. Within each of these sections, essays are arranged thematically, covering areas such as activism, work, family, religion, war, and popular culture that have received significant attention from American women's historians over an extended period. There are not, in general, separate essays on African American, Indian, immigrant, or working-class women. Instead, authors have integrated work on diverse communities of women into their analyses of particular topics, from colonial contact to marriage and property to consumption. Thus African American women appear, for instance, not only in essays on "Slavery and the Slave Trade" and "Civil Rights and Black Liberation," but also in those on "Education and the Professions" and "Urban Spaces and Popular Cultures." A few articles, covering areas where the research is especially rich, are regionally specific, including "Conflicts and Cultures in the West" and "Gender and Class Formations in the Antebellum North." But other topics that are often treated in regional terms – North vs. South or urban vs. rural – such as "The Civil War Era" and "Consumer Cultures," address issues across these conventional divides.

This volume is intended to be expansive but not comprehensive, introductory rather than definitive. Given the voluminous work in the field and the extraordinary amount published every year, authors were asked to provide interpretive essays that addressed what they considered to be the major issues in a particular area of research. Other topics and other interpretive approaches could certainly have been included, but these essays, individually and collectively, illuminate a vast landscape and provide entry to a range of other narratives and arguments. The bibliography at the end of each chapter is supplemented by a more extensive listing of works at the end of the volume. In both, citations to books and articles in fields outside American women's history are included where authors consider them especially important to their argument. Such references are thus eclectic, but they provide a window into the ways that American women's history was constituted and continues to develop as part of the wider world of women's history, American history, and women's studies scholarship. So, too, references to dissertations are included only when individual authors chose to cite them. Here again, however, even these limited references to new work in the field provide a glimpse of future directions. The books and articles cited in the volume are by no means exhaustive, but they will lead readers to a large number of significant works, and attention to footnotes and bibliographies in these as well as to other works published by the presses and journals cited herein, will open up an even more vast terrain. Because of its size, in most cases, the bibliography at the end of the volume lists only anthologies (rather than the individual articles in them), since most contain a number of essays relevant to American women's history. It also focuses primarily on secondary sources and readily accessible printed primary sources.

American women's history, like women's history in general, is a work in progress. With this *Companion* we seek both to provide a sense of the incredible progress already made in the field and to inspire further work. The effort to capture American women's history in a single volume at a particular moment has been daunting. Given the vitality of the field, authors continued to revise essays and add citations until I had to beg them to send their "final" version. My conceptualization of topics and chapters did not always mesh with those of the authors who wrote the essays, which necessitated a continual rearrangement of chapters and of my own thinking about the volume. This has been a tremendous learning experience for me, mostly positive. I could not have survived it, however, without the enthusiastic support and goodwill of Susan Rabinowitz and Kenneth Provencher at Blackwell, and the attention and expertise of Brigitte Lee, who oversaw the production process. I am deeply grateful as well to the authors whose essays appear here. They all took time away from important research of their own to grapple with that of others. April de Stefano, who compiled the massive bibliography at the end of this volume, offered far more than technical assistance, although she offered that as well. Her vision of American women's history, so different and yet so connected to my own, reminded me time and again of why this volume was important; and her good humor and sharp wit helped me over many a hurdle. Steven Lawson not only provided an essay for this volume at a critical moment, but he also suffered through all the anxieties and frustrations that attended the project as a whole. His support of my editorial efforts made the completion of this volume possible, and his willingness to recast his own work through the lens of women's history reminded me of the power of this field to transform history as a whole. Finally, the graduate students with whom I have worked, especially those at the University of South Florida, Duke University, and Rutgers University, have been a constant source of inspiration and insight. In company with their counterparts in programs across the country and increasingly throughout the world, they are transforming the agenda of American women's history. I dedicate this volume to them.

NOTES

1 American is used here in its narrow sense to denote the United States and the territories that came to comprise it. Although there is some attention, particularly in the colonial period, to areas of North America that remained outside the United States, there is no attempt to systematically include work on women in other parts of the continent or the hemisphere.
2 Full citations to works cited in this introduction are in the bibliography at the end of this volume.

Part I

The Colonial Era, 1600–1760

CHAPTER ONE

The Imperial Gaze: Native American, African American, and Colonial Women in European Eyes

KIRSTEN FISCHER

ALGONQUIAN women in New England, wrote William Wood in 1634, were "more loving, pitiful, and modest, mild, provident, and laborious than their lazy husbands." Wood imagined that oppressed Indian women would gladly embrace European gender roles with their presumably lighter burdens of female domesticity. Commenting in 1657 on enslaved African women in Barbados, Richard Ligon remarked that their breasts "hang down below their Navals," and "when they stoop at their common work of weeding, they hang almost to the ground, that at a distance you would think they had six legs." Ligon's vision of nearly deformed African women supported his belief that they, like beasts, were fit for grueling labor. Pennsylvania was a healthy place, one promotional tract claimed in 1698, in which transplanted English women proved remarkably fertile: "Barrenness among women [is] hardly to be heard of," and "seldom any young Married Woman but hath a Child in her Belly, or one upon her Lap." Colonial women who settled there would be as fruitful as the land. Written in three different places at different times, these descriptions did not simply mirror their subjects. Rather, images of women were part of complex and often contradictory efforts by colonizers to understand and control intercultural contact in the "New World." (Wood cited in Smits 1982: 293; Ligon cited in Morgan 1997: 168; Pennsylvania tract cited in Klepp 1998: 919.)

How did Europeans' perceptions of Native American, African, and European women influence the project of settlement and expansion in colonial America? Historians have begun to mine well-known writings of European explorers and settlers in search of something often previously overlooked: representations of women and the role these images played in colonizers' perceptions and practices of conquest. The "linguistic turn" in academia in the 1980s and 1990s, with its attention to language as an aspect of power relations rather than as a transparent and neutral means of communication,

The author thanks Ann M. Little for her excellent comments on this essay.

encouraged the interrogation of primary sources as suspect informants. Along with anthropologists and literary critics, historians have come to understand verbal descriptions as embedded in and constitutive of (rather than apart from and simply descriptive of) social relations between different groups. The critical reassessment of historical sources has in turn boosted research on the perceptions of colonial writers, the cultural predispositions of their "gaze," and the sometimes fantastic images they projected of the would-be colonized. As a result, some historians have focused on the way colonizers deployed images of women in an effort to promote and justify colonial conquest. This line of inquiry is still relatively new, and some of the most relevant scholarship to combine analyses of gender, imperialism, and imagery of colonized women is based on literary analysis or on historical and anthropological examinations of nineteenth- and twentieth-century colonial contexts. This essay, however, focuses on perceptions of women in or migrating to British North America to explore what power relations underlay colonizers' descriptions of "other" women, and the role that particular images of women played in the process of colonization.

Representations of Native American Women

Many English readers first encountered "America" in the form of an allegory. By the 1570s, America appeared in numerous European books and maps as an Indian woman wearing only a feathered headdress. In the famous engraving of "America" by Theodor Galle, for example (ca. 1580 after a drawing by Jan van der Straet), America appears as a native woman on a hammock, aroused from her slumber by Amerigo Vespucci, the Italian explorer whose name, in feminine form, would become attached to the continents of the western hemisphere (see plate 1). The conquistador, fully clad and armed, plants his banner into the ground with the same firm assertion with which he will stake claim to the region and the people in it. As Louis Montrose explains, the representation of America as a semi-nude and reclining woman does much to naturalize the conquest as part of the predictable relations of men to women and of civilized people to "savages." In images such as these, the "New World" is gendered female, and its exploration and conquest is made sexual. The land, like the women in it, is depicted as there for the taking, available to any male colonist intrepid enough to grasp the prize. The scene of cannibalism in the background renders America savage (despite the figure's idealized European looks), suggesting that the pending conquest will banish savagery at the same time that it appropriates both the female figure and the land she represents.

Similarly, as Annette Kolodny has shown, Europeans commonly described the country's physical terrain in gendered terms that conveyed the appropriateness of its annexation. Descriptions of a "virgin land," one untouched by human agency and awaiting its own awakening (and profitable exploitation), did much to erase symbolically the presence of Indians whose agricultural practices and routine forest burnings had long marked the countryside. Portrayals of a sparsely inhabited and entirely "unimproved" land falsely suggested that only small numbers of nomadic Indians roamed the area with merely spurious claims to the region. The descriptions of a land lying in wait, its riches as yet unexplored because Indian men were incapable of the

Plate 1 America. Engraving (ca. 1580) by Theodor Galle after a drawing by Jan van der Straet (ca. 1575). Courtesy of the Burndy Library, Dibner Institute for the History of Science and Technology, Cambridge, Massachusetts.

deed, served as a sexual metaphor that appealed to European men. William Strachey, for example, argued that the English could much better exploit "those benefits... which god hath given unto them [Indian men], but evolved and hid in the bowells and womb of their Land (to them barren, and unprofitable, because unknowne)" (cited in Brown 1996: 57). Sir Walter Ralegh went so far as to describe Guiana as "a countrey that hath yet her maydenhead, never sackt, turned, nor wrought, the face of the earth hath not bene torne, nor the vertue and salt of the soyle spent by manurance... It hath never bene entred by any armie of strength, and never conquered or possessed by any Christian prince" (Montrose 1992: 154). Anne McClintock uses the term "porno-tropics" to describe the "long tradition of male travel as an erotics of ravishment." For centuries, European travel accounts "libidinously eroticized" Africa, the Americas, and Asia as places of male conquest (McClintock 1995: 22). The comments by Strachey and Ralegh can stand in for countless examples that illustrate the point made by Joan C. Scott that forms of social inequality may be modeled on gendered relations of power, whether or not these social relations expressly involve men and women. Justifications of conquest that depicted the land and its indigenous inhabitants as passive and submissive (and hence feminized) implied that colonial relations of domination were as natural, obvious, and appropriate as Europeans presumed hierarchical gender relations to be. Acts of conquest framed in gendered terms served to naturalize relations of power, with Indian peoples and their environment portrayed as the feminized "Other."

Peter Hulme notes, however, that on occasion the feminization could be strategically reversed, as in Samual Purchas's 1625 account of the Indian massacre of Virginia colonists in 1622: "But when Virginia was violently ravished by her owne ruder Natives, yea, her Virgin cheeks dyed with the bloud of three Colonies . . . the stupid Earth seems distempered with such bloudy potions and cries that shee is ready to spue out her Inhabitants" (Hulme 1986: 160). In this case, the "virgin" land was raped by its own natives, and the spilt blood was that of the colonies, which are, in the process, identified with the ravaged land. The colonists have become the natural residents, the passive victims of native violence, while the Indians are spewed out. Gendered relations of colonialism could appear in different forms, but they routinely served to justify the use of colonial force (in this case, as retaliation) against the Indians.

As part of the eroticization of conquest, native women often appeared as figures of deviant and excessive sexuality. Amerigo Vespucci, for example, described a "shameful" custom in which Indian women, "being very libidinous, make the penis of their husbands swell to such a size as to appear deformed." The women accomplish this with the bite of a poisonous snake, he said, though as a result many husbands "lose their virile organs and remain eunuchs" (Montrose 1992: 144). The inversion of a European gender hierarchy, apparent in the image of depraved and sexually violent Indian women and of men willing to tolerate emasculation for the pleasure of their wives, again signaled the "savagery" that to Europeans made moot any native claims to the land and its resources.

Vespucci's account sounds entirely fabricated, but actual gender roles and sexual mores astonished European newcomers and fueled perceptions of Indian incivility. As Kathleen Brown explains, ethnic identities stemmed in part from "the confrontations of culturally-specific manhoods and womanhoods" (Brown 1995: 27). Many Native American groups, for example, provided visitors with female bedfellows. Women mediators offered not only sexual companionship but also rudimentary language skills and lessons in local customs that facilitated trade relations. Because these arrangements served an overtly diplomatic function, Indian leaders debated the merits of such associations before giving their assent. By contrast, European norms defined only marital sex as acceptable for women. Although women often transgressed sexual rules and Europeans in fact accommodated premarital and extramarital sex to a considerable degree, prescriptive mores defined women's nonmarital sexual activity as profligacy. Some Europeans imputed to sexually available Indian women a mercenary nature; others described them as innocents in a precivilized Eden. Whether perceived as calculating or naive, Indian women's sexual relations with outsiders appeared to Europeans as acts of blatant promiscuity. Colonial perceptions of sexual "deviance" contributed to a rhetoric of rightful dispossession: if civilized women were chaste, then lascivious Indian women (and tolerant native men) further proved that Indians in general (often lumped together in European minds) were "uncivilized" and therefore without legitimate claim to the land.

Despite the derisive tone in many accounts of Indian women, a great deal of admiration also infused colonial depictions of their bodies and behavior. Women were described not only as promiscuous creatures, but as gorgeous ones as well, thus "eroticizing the middle ground" between European men and Indian women (Godbeer 1999). Margarita Zamora notes that "eroticization of the feminine implies *both* desire and disdain," and she explains that in the context of a European gender hierarchy, Indian women could be idealized and denigrated at the same time, without contradiction, while reasserting the European male viewer's sense of superiority over the object of his gaze (Zamora 1990/1991: 146). From their first encounter, colonists ogled scantily clad Indians, fantasized about native women as sexual objects, and produced minutely detailed descriptions of their physical appearance. John Lawson, for example, a surveyor in the Carolinas, wrote of Indian women that:

> when young, and at Maturity, they are as fine-shap'd Creatures (take them generally) as any in the Universe. They are of a tawny Complexion; their Eyes very brisk and amorous; their Smiles afford the finest Composure a Face can possess; their Hands are of the finest Make, with small long Fingers, and as soft as their Cheeks; and their whole Bodies of a smooth Nature. They are not so uncouth or unlikely, as we suppose them; nor are they Strangers or not Proficients in the soft Passion. (Lawson 1984 [1709]: 189–90)

By contrast, Lawson (and others) portrayed Indian men as effete and without ardor, and hence unable to satisfy libidinous Indian women. "*Indian* Men are not so vigorous and impatient in their Love as we are," he wrote. "Yet the Women are quite contrary, and those *Indian* Girls that have convers'd with the *English* and other *Europeans*, never care for the Conversation of their own Countrymen afterwards" (Lawson 1984 [1709]: 193). In this depiction, feminized Indian men offered no competition to lusty Englishmen for the sexual interest of native women. This notion of an absent sex drive in Indian men, combined with the belief that they failed to make proper and profitable use of the land, reinforced a colonial masculinity that expressed its manhood in an impulse for sexual as well as geographical conquest.

Karen Kupperman argues that English concerns with gender roles and class relations among Indians initially outstripped an interest in racial difference. Colonial leaders were especially keen on ascertaining that Indians had gender roles and distinctions of status (made visible in posture, gestures, clothing, and hair styles) that affirmed the social hierarchy in England and its supposedly natural underpinnings of gender and class. Such hierarchies among Indians also seemed to suggest that "civilizing" the natives would not be too difficult. Consequently, contradictory images evolved that included not only effete Indian men but also noble, dignified savages who formed a natural aristocracy. Skin color was not yet as important as other markers of difference; only when Indians proved unwilling to assimilate did colonials assert immutable categories of racial difference.

For a long time, in fact, no consensus prevailed among the English as to the cause, permanence, or even precise shade of Indians' complexions. Captain Arthur Barlowe reported in 1585 that Indians on the Carolina coast were "of a colour yellowish," while other travelers described Native Americans as tawny, brown, olive, russet, or copper. Many, like John Smith, believed that Indians "are borne white" and then purposefully darken their skin. James Adair, who lived among the Cherokee and Chickasaw for many decades, proclaimed "that the Indian colour is not natural; but that the external difference between them and the whites, proceeds entirely from their customs and method of living, and not from any inherent spring of nature." North America's "parching winds, and hot sun-beams . . . necessarily tarnish their skins with the tawny red colour," while the constant application of bear's grease "mixt with a certain red root" produces in a few years "the Indian colour in those who are white born." Europeans could change their skin color as well. Adair knew "a Pensylvanian, a white man by birth, and in profession a christian, who, by the inclemency of the sun, and his endeavours of improving the red colour, was tarnished as deep an Indian hue, as any of the camp, though they had been in the woods only the space of four years." In these descriptions, color was only skin deep, the result of exposure to the elements combined with applied color. (Barlowe 1966 [1584–5]: 107; Smith cited in Kupperman 1997: 207; Adair cited in Williams 1930 [1775]: 4.)

Malleable categories of racial difference, however, meant that erotic images of Indian women could create a "dilemma for a male colonist, as expression of the erotic may signal his own lapse into savagery" (Robertson 1996: 561). Some feared that intermarriage with Indians – especially among the lower ranks of colonists – would lead to complete assimilation to Indian ways. Others, hoping instead that Indian women would become anglicized and in the process bring native lands under colonial control, made gendered distinctions of race, depicting Indian women as lighter-skinned than Indian men. William Bartram, for example, believed that Cherokee women had a "complexion rather fairer than the men's." Englishmen fantasized not only that Indian women were paler than native men, but also that they preferred to bear white children. Lawson believed the "handsome" Congaree women of South Carolina "esteem[ed] a white Man's Child much above one of their getting" (Bartram cited in Waselkov and Braund 1995: 150–1; Lawson 1984 [1709]: 35–6). Men like Bartram and Lawson projected not only that native women preferred white children, but also that the descendents of an English–Indian union would eventually approximate the skin color of the white ancestor. Those who promoted intermarriage as a means of infiltrating Indian culture and acquiring land thus downplayed differences between Indian women and English men, racializing Native Americans in ways that served an ideology of conquest.

The discourse about intercultural unions explicitly addressed concerns about class. Lawson, who supported colonial intermarriage with Indians, made it clear that only "ordinary People, and those of a lower Rank" should do so (Lawson 1984 [1709]: 244–5). The well-to-do considered lower-class English people closer to a savage state anyway. In an English culture obsessed with genealogy and bloodlines, the lower orders could hardly claim purity of blood, nor could they necessarily insist on their own "whiteness" as the concept was developing. Some well-heeled colonists assumed that Indians could be no worse than the already crude members of the lower ranks.

Virginia slaveholder William Byrd, for example, compared Indian women favorably with the English women transported (often from workhouses) to the fledgling Virginia colony, and he felt he could "safely venture to say, the Indian women would have made altogether as Honest wives for the first Planters, as the Damsels they us'd to purchase from aboard the Ships" (Byrd 1829: 120–2). But as race gradually took on fixed qualities and "redness" came to connote permanent degradation, English ideas about assimilation also changed, reflecting the shift toward more entrenched assumptions about innate difference. As the balance of power in intercultural relations shifted to colonial advantage, so too did depictions of voluptuous and eager Indian maidens give way to more standard images of primitive and dirty drudges.

Images of African Women

While images of Indian women fluctuated considerably over the colonial era and shifted according to political expediency, European depictions of African women appear to have stabilized earlier into a negative stereotype. Winthrop Jordan details Europeans' interest in Africans from the mid-sixteenth century on, and he notes longstanding assumptions of primitive and oversexed African women and men. Women were described as lascivious and crude, with overheated passions, while African men (in contrast to effete Native American men) were thought to be lustful and endowed with immense sexual organs. These images of African men, Jordan says, reveal European men's anxiety about them as sexual competitors and at the same time implied that white men exercised civilized sexual self-restraint. Other scholars of English culture have developed more explicitly the ways in which images of Africans shaped the identity of English men and women as "white." Kim Hall's examination of English literature, painting, and material culture from 1550 to 1640 reveals the pervasive use of racialized language and "tropes of blackness" by which English people created identities for themselves as white women and men. Felicity Nussbaum shows how eighteenth-century English novels invented the African woman as "inscrutable and sexually amorphous." Nussbaum argues that upper-class English women imagined English servants and prostitutes as aligned with "savage" African women, while their own monogamous and middle-class maternity helped "to consolidate the national cultural identity" (Nussbaum 1995: 3, 74). Eighteenth-century literature thus braided together anxieties about female sexual propriety, racial difference, class distinctions, and national identity.

Historians are beginning to focus on other written sources to explore how images of African women interacted with European culture, identity, and an ideology of colonialism. Travel accounts differ from novels and plays in that they purport to be accurate reports of people and places the author has seen, but as Mary Louise Pratt explains, travelogues, like natural histories, framed other peoples in ways that aided the colonial enterprise as well. The language of natural science employed by European observers encompassed new lands and peoples within a homogenizing scientific framework, giving readers the sense that they could easily control unfamiliar people. Jennifer Morgan's analysis of travel writing from the sixteenth through the late eighteenth centuries demonstrates some of the "negative symbolic work" that representations of black women performed for readers in early modern England. The female African body appeared in travel literature as "both desirable and repulsive, available and untouchable, productive and reproductive, beautiful and black." These contradictory images of black women as both mothers and monsters marked the edges of the familiar (maternity) and the strange (monstrosity), creating a discourse of racial difference that was "deeply imbued with ideas about gender and sexual difference" (Morgan 1997: 169–70). In particular, depictions of women who shamelessly suckled their offspring in public with breasts so long they could be flung over their shoulders evoked images of animal teats (see plate 2). Furthermore, the belief that African women experienced painless childbirth made their reproduction (like their nursing) seem mechanical and effortless. Edward Long wrote in 1774 that black women in Jamaica "are delivered with little or no labour; they have therefore no more occasion for midwifes than the female oran-outang, or any other wild animall" (ibid.: 189). Represented as both sexual and savage, African women appeared perfectly suited for the productive and reproductive labor of slavery. More studies on images of black women in sources purporting to be nonfiction will be a welcome contribution to the field. While there have been great gains in the social history of

Plate 2 Women in Africa, from *Verum et Historicam Descriptionem Avriferi Regni Guineaa*, in Theodor de Bry, *Small Voyages*, vol. 6 (Frankfurt am Main, 1604), plate 3. Courtesy of the John Work Garrett Library of the Johns Hopkins University.

African American women (especially regarding demography, work, culture, and families), there is relatively little scholarship on the way depictions of African and African American women helped shape the development of a British colonial system based substantially on slave labor and the international slave trade.

Also useful would be more research on how Native American, African, and English people were "raced" differently and in ways that took gender and social status into account. For example, the assumption of painless childbirth among African women contributed to the fiction of casual and emotionally detached reproduction on their part. By contrast, the pain-free childbirth projected onto Native American women raised the question of whether they were exempt from "Eve's curse" and therefore existed in a special state untouched by "original sin." When colonial women were said to have "very easy Travail in their Child-bearing," as John Lawson put it, the image described robust, healthy women whose procreation was useful to the imperialist project. Why did the image of painless labor, projected onto different groups of women, create such striking *distinctions* among the women rather than similarities? Furthermore, why did the English imagine – well into the eighteenth century – that physical traits such as skin color among Indians were a matter of cultural (and so reversible) choices and that native women tended to be lighter than their male counterparts, while European assumptions about the fixity of the complexions of African men *and* women gained credence much earlier and despite the vast range in actual appearance of African peoples?

The answers likely reside in the specific and changing social contexts in which intercultural contact took shape. English inclinations to see Native Americans as less markedly or permanently different from themselves may have stemmed from early English dependence on Native Americans for subsistence and military alliances, and from the fact that Europeans initially failed to enslave Indians and so sought trade with them instead. Others, hoping the "New World" would prove a new Eden, found idealized Indians a useful foil against which to critique European corruption. Some Europeans believed Indians were the descendents of a "Lost Tribe of Israel" and thus biblical kin whose conversion and assimilation, they hoped, would come easily. By contrast, the degradation inherent in human bondage and the association of Africans with slavery, as well as centuries of contact between Europeans and Africans and an awareness of African resistance to easy assimilation, probably contributed to the earlier fixing of "blackness" with inferiority in chauvinistic English minds. David Brion Davis suggests, furthermore, that when people in England began to imagine themselves the world's first free people and no longer vilified their own poor to the same degree, Africans were scapegoated and made to represent all that was degraded. Interestingly, the notion persists to this day that the "race" of Native Americans was somehow different (and less) than that of European Americans or, more especially, African Americans. Many scholars still describe white–Indian conflicts in the colonies as the result of cultural clashes, while the mere presence of African Americans transforms social antagonisms into problems of "race." If African Americans still seem to have more "race" than European Americans or Native Americans, it is worth investigating what cultural and national mythologies are at work. Images of women as sexual objects, mothers, and laborers give especially valuable clues about the construction of difference and the culturally specific meanings ascribed to gender, and race, and class.

Colonial Women as Caricatures and Colonizers

Images of white women also played an important part in shoring up colonial rule, although research on white women in the imperial gaze is still underdeveloped for colonial North America. Scholars of the second British Empire have done superb work on the ways in which white women – as rhetorically deployed symbolic figures and as actual persons – participated in the nineteenth- and twentieth-century colonization of Africa and South Asia. There the presence of colonial white women became crucial to the definition and patrol of racial borders, even as they could not hinder the illicit sexual liaisons that became the prerogative of ruling white men. As Ann Stoler and others have shown, contests involving white women's role in the sexual politics of a colonial social order can reveal much about the complex and gendered power relations between indigenous and colonial women and men. Regarding early America, we do know a great deal about the social history of white women and the social and legal regulations that circumscribed their lives. But we can uncover much more about how attempts to control the behavior of colonial women by projecting certain images of them meshed with larger imperialist aims and shaped social relations in the colonies.

English women in British North America had uneven and unstable reputations. From the beginning, many white women were depicted as lowly immigrants of suspect pedigree, often as former convicts and prostitutes. Such labels could effectively target wealthier women as well, calling into question the authority of their husbands to rule in the young colonies. Missionaries were quick to point out the moral flaws of colonial women, and they often despaired at the recalcitrance of would-be converts. In 1711, Reverend John Urmston, a missionary for the Society for the Propagation of the Gospel in Foreign Parts, bitterly described North Carolina as "a nest of the most notorious profligates upon earth . . . Women forsake their husbands come in here and live with other men." Should the husband follow his wayward spouse to North Carolina, "then a price is given to the husband and madam stays with her Gallant," the lovers spread a rumor that the husband is dead, "become Man and Wife make a figure and pass for people of worth and reputation [and] arrive to be of the first Rank and Dignity" (Urmston cited in Fischer 2002: 53). For Urmston, the prevalence of illicit sex in North Carolina served as a measure of the colony's low moral standing and lack of civility. As with Indian and African American women, white women's sexual misconduct became a barometer of social instability in the culture at large.

Unruly women found their most powerful embodiment in the figures of scolds and witches, and accused women were often those whose outspoken or independent behavior transgressed prescribed female deference to men. As Carol Karlsen and others have pointed out, however, allegations of witchcraft also stemmed from altercations over property, longstanding feuds between families, and the anxiety that infused a Puritan culture caught up in political turmoil and engaged in costly

Indian wars. In other words, cracks in colonial rule exacerbated concerns about unruly women and the impact of (real or imagined) female misconduct. Accusations of deviance served to keep women in line, reasserting the patriarchal order and underscoring the crucial links between domestic order and colonial control.

Counterposed images of colonial women appeared in female icons of fecundity and contented productivity. Such depictions sought to encourage the migration of families that would in turn consolidate colonial rule. John Lawson was one of many who promoted colonization by touting the healthful effects of the environment. Second-generation settlers in Carolina "are a straight, clean-limb'd People" whose children are "seldom or never troubled with Rickets; or those other Distempers, that the *Europeans*" endured. Lawson perceived a distinctly gendered pattern in this environment-induced return to a more natural state. European American men soon followed in the footsteps of "idle" male Indians (the "plentiful Country, makes a great many Planters very negligent," Lawson explained), while Anglo women, like their Indian counterparts, "are the most Industrious Sex in that Place." But in contrast to the image of the "squaw drudge," transplanted Anglo women represented happy, healthy laborers. Lest prospective female immigrants worry that along with good health they would turn a few shades darker, Lawson added the following reassurance: the "Vicinity of the Sun makes Impression on the Men, who labour out of doors," but the Anglo-American women who do not expose themselves to the weather are "often very fair" (Lawson 1984 [1709]: 90–1). Here again, skin color was made gender-specific, in the anticipation that immigrants would have concerns about the climate that combined issues of reproduction, class, and color. Images of white women in the imperial gaze were thus multiple and unfixed: depictions of harlots and scolds demanded increased vigilance and social control on the one hand, while portrayals of healthy fertility promised maternity and increase on the other.

White women's reproductive behavior became an important part of the process of colonial settlement and expansion, which is why promotional literature touted women's ability to bear children with ease in the colonies. Ruth Perry has shown that motherhood and breastfeeding in mid-eighteenth-century Britain were "colonized" and made into a service that women provided to the expanding and bellicose state. The growing concern with child mortality, Perry argues, resulted from England's protracted and costly wars against France and the endless need for soldiers. In the American colonies, too, procreation became an imperial imperative, one that merged easily with the biblical mandate to "increase" and "multiply" (see plate 3). On the whole, however, the rather shrill English rhetoric of reproduction for the sake of the state, the movement against wet-nursing (having another woman breastfeed one's child), and the concern to establish foundling hospitals to save the lives of abandoned orphans – these were less characteristic of the eighteenth-century colonies than they were of the London metropole. It would be interesting to know more precisely how colonial ideas about reproduction and the cultural significance of breastfeeding (that Marilynn Salmon explores) tied in with the expanding reach of the colonies, wars against the Indians, and developing ideas about race. How, in other words, did European American understandings of the links between gender and imperialism contrast with those in the "mother" country?

Plate 3 Reproduced by permission of the British Library.

Scholars have described the British experience in Ireland as a laboratory for conquest elsewhere. In the process of colonization, Irish people were depicted as a different and degraded race, with much the same language later applied to peoples in the Americas. It would be interesting to know whether and how images of women, in particular, translated across cultures. The sixteenth-century traveler and artist John White, for example, contrasted "Pict" women with those of tattooed Algonquins on the North Carolina coast, suggesting that "barbaric" Indians could experience the same civilizing process that ancient Britons had once undergone (see plate 4). One wonders how images of Irish women or poorer English women translated into other colonial contexts and were transformed there by local circumstances.

The "imperial gaze" is most easily found in the published perceptions of colonizing men, but Anglo-American women were imperialists as well, and they, too, projected images of African and Native American women. Women's voices are harder to come by than those of men, but scholars have mined women's narratives of Indian captivity for the way the authors positioned themselves *vis-à-vis* Indian "others." Christopher Castiglia, for example, shows that although female authors of captivity narratives participated in a language of Indian "savagery," they also often contradicted that image with examples of considerate and generous Indian hosts who cared for and eventually adopted them. Although framed by male editors as the tale of a helpless woman's redemption through divine providence from uncivilized savages and her return to a superior culture, the narratives themselves, Castiglia argues, subverted that espoused message. They do so by showing the admirable agency of Indian women and of the captive herself, the malleability of cultural identity, and the suffocating limitations of English gender norms for the "redeemed" captives. It is precisely in those moments when the narrative undercuts the moral it is supposed to

Plate 4 Woman Pict, from Thomas Hariot, *A Briefe and True Report of the New Found Land of Virginia*, as translated by Theodor de Bry, in *Occidentalischen Reisen*, volume I, part I, Frankfurt am Main, 1590. Courtesy of the James Ford Bell Library, University of Minnesota.

uphold that we can "hear" the woman's authorial voice, Castiglia says, and this leads him to move beyond literary analysis to make claims about the racial ideology of white women captives. Without denying that profound cultural conflicts existed, Castiglia maintains that the captivity experience enabled colonial women to articulate a positive view of Indian women that subverted essentialist racial thinking and raised questions about aggressive colonial expansionism.

Other scholars emphasize the complicity of white women authors with imperialist renditions of Indians. According to Carroll Smith-Rosenberg, for example, Mary Rowlandson, captured in Massachusetts in 1676 and held for nearly two months before she was ransomed, authorized herself in her bestselling 1682 narrative, *Sovereignty and Goodness of God*, as the symbol of a white and now feminized America. Presenting herself as the victimized and yet still sexually pure icon of the Puritan state,

Rowlandson promoted aggressive colonial expansion against unredeemable Indians. Ann Little focuses less on the symbolic imagery of women and more on the captives themselves to argue that English women imported their norms of orderly households into the captivity experience and judged their captors based on whether they established hierarchical families in the English style. This gave women captives less reason to speak highly of even those native women who cared for and protected them. Clearly, captivity narratives, straddling the line between fiction and nonfiction, provide complex and contradictory evidence of white women's perceptions of Indian women.

White women produced images of Africans as well. One Madam Knight, for example, recorded her daily impressions while traveling from Boston to New Haven in 1704. She found farmers in Connecticut "too Indulgent" with their slaves, "suffering too great familiarity from them, permitting th^{m} to sit at Table and eat with them, (as they say to save time,) and into the dish goes the black hoof as freely as the white hand" (Andrews 1990: 104–5). Traveling to the West Indies and then to the mainland colonies in 1774, Scottish traveler Janet Schaw, self-described as a "lady of quality," was shocked when she first saw the scarred backs of whipped slaves. She rationalized the whippings, however, choosing to believe that Africans' "Natures seem made to bear it,... whose sufferings are not attended with shame or pain beyond the present moment" (Andrews and Andrews 1934: 127). Schaw projected onto enslaved men and women a deficient ability to feel physical and emotional pain; in her construction, the whiplashes induced only a brief physical sensation without deeper emotional impact or meaning. This mindset enabled Schaw to justify the cruelty inherent in slavery and contributed to a racist understanding of enslaved laborers. While there are excellent studies on nineteenth-century travel writings by British women, it would be very useful to have more interpretive scholarship on traveling women in the colonies and their comments on the "other" women they encountered. The results would likely show neither an uncomplicated bonding with Indian and African "sisters," nor the same eroticized images of women so favored by imperialist men.

Looking Back

Some of the most interesting scholarship is also the most difficult: it explores the interaction between the imperial gaze and imperial rule, between the imagination and actual social relations, between the expectations created by a viewer's projections and the human exchange that confirmed or disrupted those views. Can historians use the imperial gaze to write about women's subjectivities? To seek the real women behind the images imposed on them is to explore the relationship between colonial rhetoric and the experience of colonization; it combines textual analysis with social and cultural history. Karen Robertson, for example, argues that in the gaps and silences of John Smith's accounts of Pocahontas we can see the Indian woman's counterpoint to his version of her, an alternative mindset not accommodated by Smith's narrative. Attempts like Robertson's are necessarily cautious and often inconclusive, leaving the reader wishing for more, but *not* to undertake the venture means forfeiting a rare opportunity to go beyond image and convention. Worse, it makes the imperial gaze seem autonomous, as if it existed in a vacuum uninfluenced by the very people it interprets. As Klaus Neumann explains, "a critique of European colonial discourse must not be self-referential, but ought to take into account how European perceptions have been shaped both by what Europeans were conditioned to see and by what there was to be seen" (Neumann 1994: 119). Alice Conklin asks: "How might the gendered and racialized gaze of the colonizer be subverted in our own historical writing?" The trick, she says, is to alternate between accounts of western hegemony and the experience of subalterns (Conklin 1998: 155).

Just how to tack back and forth remains a matter of experimentation, but subaltern women in colonial America most certainly could and did look back at colonizing Europeans with a gaze of their own. Furthermore, women behaved purposefully to alter the images others had of them. Susan Klepp shows how white women reconfigured maternal imagery, distancing themselves from an identification with their pregnant state and focusing instead on the fetus as a separate being. They did so, Klepp says, in an effort to emphasize their rational capabilities over their reproductive ones. Perhaps some day we will have colonial-era accounts akin to Walter Johnson's analysis of the way slaves in nineteenth-century slave markets molded the perceptions of prospective buyers and did what they could to disrupt sellers' stories of an inadvertent or inevitable sale. Or maybe someone will excavate prerevolutionary sources to compare with Mia Bay's discussion of African American ideas about race in the United States. Michael Gomez charts the way with his investigation of an African American ethnogenesis in the early South, and surely it will not be long before gender becomes more integrated into the analysis. Nancy Shoemaker shows how Native Americans co-opted "red" as a descriptive term for themselves even as they maintained alternative understandings of "race," and Theda Perdue and others have demonstrated that with tenacious perseverance and creative adaptation to conditions wrought by colonialism, Native American women countered the image of themselves as "vanishing Indians." Clearly, there is still much to explore regarding the multiple and gendered images of "self" and "other" that shaped intercultural contact and experiences of colonization.

BIBLIOGRAPHY

Andrews, Evangeline W. and Andrews, Charles M. (eds.) (1934) *Journal of a Lady of Quality; Being a Narrative of a Journey from Scotland to the West Indies, North Carolina, and Portugal, in the Years 1774 to 1776*. New Haven, CT: Yale University Press.

Andrews, William (ed.) (1990) *Journeys in New Worlds: Early American Women's Narratives*. Madison: University of Wisconsin Press.

Barlowe, Arthur (1966 [1584–5]) "A New Land like unto That of the Golden Age (1584–85)," in Louis B. Wright (ed.), *The Elizabethans' America*. Cambridge, MA: Harvard University Press, pp. 103–36.

Bay, Mia (2000) *The White Image in the Black Mind: African-American Ideas about White People, 1830–1925*. New York: Oxford University Press.

Brown, Kathleen (1995) "The Anglo-Algonquian Gender Frontier," in Nancy Shoemaker (ed.), *Negotiators of Change: Historical Perspectives on Native American Women*. New York: Routledge, pp. 26–48.

Brown, Kathleen M. (1996) *Good Wives, Nasty Wenches, and Anxious Patriarchs: Gender, Race, and Power in Colonial Virginia*. Chapel Hill: University of North Carolina Press.

Byrd, William (1829) *William Byrd's Histories of the Dividing Line Betwixt Virginia and North Carolina*, with an introduction and notes by William K. Boyd. Raleigh: North Carolina Historical Commission.

Castiglia, Christopher (1996) *Bound and Determined: Captivity, Culture-crossing, and White Womanhood from Mary Rowlandson to Patty Hearst*. Chicago: University of Chicago Press.

Chaplin, Joyce E. (1997) "Natural Philosophy and an Early Racial Idiom in North America: Comparing English and Indian Bodies," *William and Mary Quarterly*, 3rd ser., 54, pp. 229–52.

Conklin, Alice (1998) "From World-systems to Post-coloniality: Teaching the History of European Imperial Encounters in the Modern Age," *Radical History Review* 71, pp. 150–63.

Daunton, Martin and Halpern, Rick (eds.) (1999) *Empire and Others: British Encounters with Indigenous Peoples, 1600–1850*. Philadelphia: University of Pennsylvania Press.

Davis, David Brion (1997) "Constructing Race: A Reflection," *William and Mary Quarterly*, 3rd ser., 54, pp. 7–18.

Derounian-Stodola, Kathryn Zabelle and Levernier, James Arthur (1993) *The Indian Captivity Narrative, 1550–1900*. Boston: Twayne.

Fischer, Kirsten (2002) *Suspect Relations: Sex, Race, and Resistance in Colonial North Carolina*. Ithaca, NY: Cornell University Press.

Godbeer, Richard (1999) "Eroticizing the Middle Ground: Anglo-Indian Sexual Relations along the Eighteenth-century Frontier," in Martha M. Hodes (ed.), *Sex, Love, Race: Crossing Boundaries in North American History*. New York: New York University Press, pp. 91–111.

Gomez, Michael A. (1998) *Exchanging Our Country Marks: The Transformation of African Identities in the Colonial and Antebellum South*. Chapel Hill: University of North Carolina Press.

Hall, Kim F. (1995) *Things of Darkness: Economies of Race and Gender in Early Modern England*. Ithaca, NY: Cornell University Press.

Hulme, Peter (1986) *Colonial Encounters: Europe and the Native Caribbean, 1492–1797*. London: Methuen.

Johnson, Walter (1999) *Soul By Soul: Life Inside the Antebellum Slave Market*. Cambridge, MA: Harvard University Press.

Jordan, Winthrop D. (1968) *White Over Black: American Attitudes Toward the Negro, 1550–1812*. Chapel Hill: University of North Carolina Press. Rpt. (1977), New York: Norton.

Karlsen, Carol F. (1989) *The Devil in the Shape of a Woman: Witchcraft in Colonial New England*. New York: Vintage Books.

Klepp, Susan E. (1998) "Revolutionary Bodies: Women and the Fertility Transition in the Mid-Atlantic Region, 1760–1820," *Journal of American History* 85, pp. 910–45.

Kolodny, Annette (1975) *The Lay of the Land: Metaphors as Experience and History in American Life and Letters*. Chapel Hill: University of North Carolina Press.

Kupperman, Karen Ordahl (1997) "Presentment of Civility: English Reading of American Self-presentation in the Early Years of Colonization," *William and Mary Quarterly*, 3rd ser., 54, pp. 193–228.

Kupperman, Karen Ordahl (2000) *Indians and English: Facing Off in Early America*. Ithaca, NY: Cornell University Press.

Lawson, John (1984 [1709]) *A New Voyage to Carolina*, ed. and with an introduction and notes by Hugh Talmage Lefler. Chapel Hill: University of North Carolina Press.

Little, Ann M. (n.d.) "Abraham in Arms: Gender and Power on the New England Frontier, 1620–1760." Unpublished manuscript.

McClintock, Anne (1995) *Imperial Leather: Race, Gender, and Sexuality in the Colonial Conquest*. New York: Routledge.

Montrose, Louis (1992) "The Work of Gender and Sexuality in the Elizabethan Discourse of Discovery," in Domna C. Stanton (ed.), *Discourses of Sexuality: From Aristotle to Aids*. Ann Arbor: University of Michigan Press, pp. 138–84.

Morgan, Jennifer L. (1997) " 'Some Could Suckle Over Their Shoulder': Male Travelers, Female Bodies, and the Gendering of Racial Ideology, 1500–1770," *William and Mary Quarterly*, 3rd ser., 54, pp. 167–92.

Namias, June (1993) *White Captives: Gender and Ethnicity on the American Frontier*. Chapel Hill: University of North Carolina Press.

Neumann, Klaus (1994) " 'In Order to Win Their Friendship': Renegotiating First Contact," *The Contemporary Pacific* 6, pp. 111–45.

Nussbaum, Felicity A. (1995) *Torrid Zones: Maternity, Sexuality, and Empire in Eighteenth-century English Narratives*. Baltimore: Johns Hopkins University Press.

Perdue, Theda (1998) *Cherokee Women: Gender and Culture Change, 1700–1835*. Lincoln: Nebraska University Press.

Perry, Ruth (1991) "Colonizing the Breast: Sexuality and Maternity in Eighteenth-century England," *Journal of the History of Sexuality* 2, pp. 204–34.

Pratt, Mary Louise (1992) *Imperial Eyes: Travel Writing and Transculturation*. New York: Routledge.

Robertson, Karen (1996) "Pocahontas at the Masque," *Signs* 21, pp. 551–83.

Salmon, Marylynn (1994) "The Cultural Significance of Breastfeeding and Infant Care in Early Modern England and America," *Journal of Social History* 28, pp. 247–70.

Scott, Joan C. (1986) "Gender: A Useful Category of Historical Analysis," *American Historical Review* 91, pp. 1053–75.

Shoemaker, Nancy (1997) "How Indians Got to be Red," *American Historical Review* 102, pp. 625–44.

Smith-Rosenberg, Carroll (1993) "Captured Subjects/Savage Others: Violently Engendering the New American," *Gender and History* 5, pp. 177–95.

Smits, David D. (1982) "The 'Squaw Drudge': A Prime Index of Savagism," *Ethnohistory* 29, pp. 281–306.

Stoler, Ann L. (1989) "Making Empire Respectable: The Politics of Race and Sexual Morality in Twentieth-century Colonial Empires," *American Ethnologist* 16, pp. 634–60.

Stoler, Ann L. (1992) "Sexual Affronts and Racial Frontiers: European Identities and the Cultural Politics of Exclusion in Colonial Southeast Asia," *Comparative Studies in Society and History* 34, pp. 514–51.

Waselkov, Gregory A. and Braund, Kathryn E. Holland (eds.) (1995) *William Bartram on the Southeastern Indians*. Lincoln: University of Nebraska Press.

Williams, Samuel Cole (1930 [1775]) *Adair's History of the American Indians*. New York: Promontory Press.

Zamora, Margarita (1990/1991) "Abreast of Columbus: Gender and Discovery," *Cultural Critique* 17, pp. 127–50.

Chapter Two

Slavery and the Slave Trade

Jennifer L. Morgan

Slave Ships and Forts

ON February 12, 1678, English slave traders loaded three recently purchased women and the same number of men on the *Arthur*, a slave ship anchored in the Callabar River, at the area known as the Bight of Biafra, West Africa. The ship's factor, George Hingston, paid the "kinge of New Callabarr" thirty copper bars for each woman; for each man he paid thirty-six. At most embarkation points, women cost less than men did. The exception was Senegambia, the "only known region where Europeans paid equal prices for males and females" (Geggus 1989: 41). The following day canoes brought eighteen women and fourteen men to the ship. The day after only three canoes approached the *Arthur* and Hingston purchased three men, one woman, and some yams with which to feed them. For the next six and a half weeks this piecemeal loading pattern continued, small numbers of women and men purchased each day from individual canoes. Assuming that the three women who boarded the ship on February 12 survived, they would watch with increasing despair from the cramped cargo bays as more and more women, men, and children joined them in the hold (Hingston Journal, March 1678).

Food was scarce, and at times Hingston turned back canoe-men bringing captives "by reason of their remissing in Bringn't us provision." Without food, he would purchase no men or women. Provisioning remained a constant problem throughout the six weeks during which Hingston loaded the *Arthur* with African women and men. For the three women and their compatriots, the "problem" was dire. Fed only yams as they languished in a ship from which they could see the land they would never again set foot on, they began to "grow Leane." Hingston found this perplexing as he believed that "they want fore nothinge haveinge doely as much provision as they Cann make use of." His confusion must have been matched by their horror as only two weeks after the sale of these three women, the people around them began to die. For the African captives waiting in the rank and stifling hold of the ship, the scarce food, dying men and women, and the three to thirty more people thrown in each day, punctuated the weeks until the *Arthur* finally left the river for the Atlantic Ocean (Hingston Journal, March 1678).

Once the *Arthur* pulled out to sea, the death rate increased. Not a day passed during the voyage without a dead African woman or man, boy or girl, being tossed overboard. On April 22 Hingston noticed that "the winds [were] nott blowinge so fresh" and allowed the 294 women and men out into the open air (Hingston Journal, April 1678). As they emerged from the hold of the ship, a common language might have assisted the men and women in the *Arthur* as they mourned their capture and worried about their future. Although they came in small groups from "Bandy," "Donus," and Callabar, all the points Hingston identified were Ibo-speaking trading centers clustered at the basin of the Niger Delta. But an ability to communicate would not assuage the fears and uncertainties of the captives. Glancing around at the expanse of the Atlantic Ocean, the looks and words of terror exchanged by the three women loaded almost two and a half months before, if they still lived, are difficult to imagine. Returned to their shackles, the survivors would remain below for the remainder of the two-month passage to Barbados. By the end of the voyage, forty-nine men and boys and thirty-three women and girls died. Five more weeks passed before they again breathed fresh air. Having brought the ship to Bridgetown, Barbados during the height of the island's sugar boom, Hingston sold the surviving 144 men, 110 women, nine boys, and nine girls in a mere three days. The island's slaveowners wasted no time relieving Hingston of his cargo and initiating the women and men who had survived the journey aboard the *Arthur* into the demands of sugar cultivation.

In December 1727, Cayoba, a woman enslaved at the Royal African Company's fort on Bence Island at Sierra Leone, escaped from the castle. Cayoba ran with three men, renamed Peter, Dick, and Monday. Five months after their escape the local king, Suphulo, recaptured the runaways and returned them to the Company. Weeks later the Royal African Company agent discovered another escape plot, this time among the men and women destined for transport to the Americas who had, perhaps, been emboldened by Cayoba and her companions. The Royal African Company agent stationed at the castle punished the conspirators publicly. But his authority was demolished five months later when castle slaves and "sale slaves" joined together once again and successfully attacked the whites, drove them out, and burned the castle (Bence Island Diaries, May and October 1728).

The purchasing method used by George Hingston aboard the *Arthur* was one of two employed by European slave traders. The other – to keep enslaved women and men in forts on the coast waiting the arrival of European ships – was used at Bence Island. African slavers brought men and women to the "holes" of European fortresses up and down the Upper Guinea and Gold coasts. There they languished in "damp Trunks" which caused "great Mortality" as they waited to be loaded aboard slaving vessels (Letterbook to Cape Coast Castle, July 1730). Other men and women were brought to the forts to be permanently enslaved therein. The Royal African Company directed agents at distant forts to exchange men and women with one another when obtaining castle slaves so as to remove individuals from familiar landscapes that beckoned runaways. "We have indeed order'd our Agents at Gambia . . . to pick out . . . ten or twenty of the choicest young healthy men and women slaves and to send them down to you . . . and to receive from you in return as many young healthy Gold Coast Negroes as they may have occasion for at Gambia" (Letterbook to Cape Coast Castle, July 1731).

Like those on board ships awaiting departure, women at slave forts were in the midst of a process of understanding the new terms of their identity. The encounter between far-flung ethnic groups that characterized the experience of enslavement throughout the Americas began on the West African coast. No longer did their place in the world grow out of the particularities of family, region, language, and ethnicity. Rather, it became dependent upon imposed racial sameness. However, the frightening implications of how a woman's reproductive life would be mobilized to support perpetual racial slavery would be a realization slow in coming. In the month following Cayoba's return to the fortress, a woman named Moota, another castle slave, gave birth to her third child. Among the myriad images and expectations which African women brought to their New World enslavement, childbirth among women who answered to a white "owner" and whose children accompanied her as she carried out her labors in an alien land was a painful emblem of their future. Through tiny windows or iron doors, while being "provisioned" or "mustered," women waiting for sale at the forts might catch glimpses of other mothers who labored as slaves. As the weeks and months unfolded before them, those who came aboard the same ships or endured the same fortress walls and who continued to see one another on adjoining plantations or in and around port cities must have truly regarded themselves as kin – connected by an unfathomable ordeal of transportation, deprivation, and loss. If their paths crossed, they must have shared a rare and poignant moment of recognition, one full of a tangible past. Months or years later, as African women were led from the holes of ships and into New World plantations, the stories of Moota and Cayoba – the enslaved mother and the resistant woman – continued to resonate. As a newly enslaved African woman contemplated the frightening prospect of sustaining herself in the New World, Moota and the children she bore but did not "own" would stand as powerful portents of all that enslavement in the Americas could mean.

The Parameters of the Trans-Atlantic Slave Trade

In many respects the men and women on board the *Arthur* experienced a demographically normative middle passage. It was far more common for a seventeenth-century slave ship leaving the West or West Central African coast to arrive in the Caribbean or Latin America than in North America. Indeed, those forcibly transported to North America comprised a mere 5 percent of the total number of persons ensnared in the trans-Atlantic slave trade. Between 9.6 and 10.8 million persons survived the middle passage over the course of the 300-year-long trade, of which 481,000 were transported to British North America. Mortality rates were between 10 and 20 percent, bringing the total number of men and women forcibly transported to the Americas to at least 12 million. During the entire period, ships brought a total of some 353,000 Africans to Barbados alone – while close to 4,700,000 enslaved Africans were transported to the British, French, Dutch, and Danish Caribbean.

The proportionally tiny number of Africans transported to British North America seems to conflict with what we know about the economic dependence of the region on slavery and on the enduring social, cultural, and economic impact of African Americans on the American landscape. The situation is clarified by a single crucial factor that differentiated North America from most other slave societies in the hemisphere. Enslaved women and men in North America had children. These children were born and survived in numbers high enough to offset the numbingly high mortality rates; their presence meant a slave society no longer dependent upon African imports to maintain population after the turn of the nineteenth century; and their sale as youngsters and adults to the "deep South" occasioned an ongoing tragedy of familial disruption and instability among enslaved North Americans.

Prior to the 1807 ban on the slave trade to the United States, slaveowners' demand for labor fueled a steady stream of forced migrants to North America. European and American slavers traded up and down the African coast. Enslaved persons embarked from points all along the Western African coast and Southeastern Africa:

> There are seven general regions from which slaves were imported. The first, Senegambia, encompasses that stretch of coast extending from the Senegal River to the Casamance, to which captives from as far away as the upper and middle Niger valleys were transported. The second, Sierra Leone, includes the territory from the Casamance to Assini, or what is now Guinea-Bissau, Guinea, Sierra Leone, Liberia, and the Ivory Coast. Adjoining Sierra Leone is the Gold Coast, occupying what is essentially contemporary Ghana. Further east lay the fourth region, the Bight of Benin, stretching from the Volta to the Benin River and corresponding to what is now Togo, contemporary Benin, and southwestern Nigeria. The Bight of Biafra, in turn, comprised contemporary southeastern Nigeria, Cameroon, and Gabon. West Central Africa includes Congo (formerly Zaire) and Angola, and the seventh region, Mozambique-Madagascar, refers to southeastern Africa, including what is now Mozambique, parts of Tanzania, and the island of Madagascar. (Gomez 1998: 27)

Fully one quarter of all exported persons originated from the Bight of Biafra and another quarter came from West Central Africa. Approximately 15 percent each came from Senegambia, Sierra Leone, and the Gold Coast while only 3 percent came from the Bight of Benin and 2 percent from Mozambique-Madagascar.

Adult men, while the largest group of persons transported, comprised less than half of the total number of people brought to the Americas. Women, boys, and girls combined outnumbered them in the trade. In the last four decades of the seventeenth century, overall, women comprised almost 40 percent of those who crossed the Atlantic, men comprised 50 percent, and children made up the remainder. During the eighteenth century, the proportion of children (those thought by slave traders to be under the age of fifteen) rose to 20 percent, women fell to 30 percent, and men maintained their previous proportion. Not until the nineteenth century would women's numbers fall to almost 15 percent, while men and children equally constituted the remainder (Eltis and Engerman 1993: 256). Moreover, African women comprised four-fifths of all women to make the Atlantic crossing – either voluntarily or involuntarily – prior to 1800 (Eltis 2000). It is thus essential that, when examining the contours of early American slave societies, the perspective of enslaved women occupy a central place. Women entered the trans-Atlantic slave trade in significant numbers and comprised an essential part of the workforce on American plantations.

The connections between ethnicity and gender are fundamental. Regional origins did much to influence the sex ratios for the Africans who comprised the cargoes of slave ships. In the seventeenth century, ships leaving the Upper Guinea Coast or West Central Africa carried 20 to 25 percent more men than those leaving the Bight of Biafra. Although as time passed the disparity between the regions diminished somewhat, in the eighteenth century both the Bight of Biafra and the Bight of Benin continued to supply the highest ratios of women to men, while the Gold Coast, West Central Africa, and the Upper Guinea coast supplied the lowest.

As they oversaw the workings of the slave trade, officials of the Royal African Company in London consistently sent slave ship captains to the West African coast under orders to "view well the Negroes that they may be sound and merchantable[,] between the ages of 15 & 40[,] and that the major part be male" (Royal African Company Instructions, 1678). The injunctions of the Royal African Company have been understood as simply formulaic orders carried out with little difficulty, the conclusion being that European slavers purchased twice as many men as women for labor in the Americas. Yet they occasionally reveal a tone of entreaty rather than authority. "If you are carefull you may have two men for one female," or "endeavour all you can to have your Number of Males exceed the females," or "the number of women Exceeding [men] doeth much disparayes the whole Cargoe" (Royal African Company Instructions, 1692, 1694, 1698). In an attempt to explain to Royal African Company officials the large numbers of women he purchased, George Hingston wrote that "as yett wee find ye women generally Better than the men" (Hingston Journal, March 1678). Their instructions, then, often reflected the Company's inability to dictate the terms of trade.

The causes of shifting sex ratios are still being explored, but it is now clear that we must look to African sociopolitical relations rather than to European demands in analyzing the issue. For example, patrilineal societies appear to have exported more women than societies ordered along matrilineal lines. The value of women in regional African slave trades (to Northern Africa or Asia) affected the willingness of local slavers to make women available to the Atlantic trade where slave traders paid lower prices for women than men. Regions affected by consistent warfare or military upheaval exported fewer women. In rare cases, gendered prohibitions on the trading of slaves worked in the opposite direction. German trader David Van Nyendael wrote at the turn of the seventeenth century "[that in the city of Benin it is not] allow'd to export any Male slaves that are sold in this Country for they must stay there; But females may be dealt with at anyone's pleasure" (Van Nyendael 1967: 462). Van Nyendael referred here to a state policy in place since 1560 whose enforcement only began to dissipate after the second decade of the eighteenth century. This prohibition against trading in men may well be a key to the reluctance of European traders to stop there. While arguments have been made that African women's value as agricultural producers kept them out of the trans-Atlantic trade, women performed agricultural work throughout West Africa, regardless of the ratio at which they were made available to the Atlantic slave trade. Thus neither European interest in male laborers nor African interest in female laborers satisfactorily explains the pattern of sex ratios. Rather, regional issues, rhythms of supply and demand, of warfare and conquest, and of competing markets for slaves worked together to increase the likelihood that those adult men exposed to capture and slavery would be transported to the Americas.

The Life Left Behind: Sketches of West African Cultures

By the time they were purchased by Hingston, the women on the *Arthur* could not have been ignorant of enslavement at the hands of Europeans. Europe's slaving vessels had been visiting the Bights since before the seventeenth century. Economic upheavals and the desire for trade goods cast a wide web of capture and sale for African women, men, and children. As wars and slave raiders disrupted the rhythms of daily life, people would have heard word of their vulnerability to the white man's ships. Women and men on the Upper Guinea Coast too were well aware of the dangers of capture and sale. From the sixteenth century, the invading *Mane* pressed toward the coast creating a cycle of capture and sale to European traders that endured for centuries. As prisoners of war, men – exported at a rate three times that of women – were particularly vulnerable to European slavers. But, as we know from the examples of Cayoba and Moota, women were not invulnerable.

In all regions of West Africa, internal factors could alter sex ratios from year to year. These large demographic patterns should not be seen as static. In response to high demand, for example, slavers sold equal numbers of women and men to European slave ships from the Gold Coast in 1688. Women captured by the European slave trade that year must have found their capture particularly shocking, it being a fate more often befalling men. Traveling to Allada at the Gold Coast, William Snelgrave carefully negotiated sex ratios such that "I should have three Males to one Female, and take none but what I like." He realized he was in a position to set the terms of trade shortly after viewing the devastation at Whydah in the aftermath of Dahomey's successful military campaign against Whydah and Allada on the coast. "People being in a starving condition [are] obliged to sell their servants and children for money and goods" (Snelgrave 1734: 73, 70). Snelgrave's vocation – slave trader and apologist for the slave trade – calls into question the veracity of his claim that people sold their own children. However, the aftermath of Dahomean expansion did cause increased numbers of dependent women, and men, from the immediate area to be offered into the trade. Thus, in the late 1720s and 1730s, more females were likely exported from Whydah than at other periods. Internal factors here, and all down the coast, altered sex ratios from year to year.

The women who found their futures so unthinkably changed must have been beset by fears and uncertainties that built as ships languished on the Callabar River or "holes" filled up at Elmina. As they contemplated the unpredictability of their lives, their thoughts must have turned to the children and families left behind. Perhaps they thought of crops untended and children unfed. As night fell, daily evening markets predominated by women up and down the coast, where they had exchanged wares, gossip, food, or friendship, may have crept into their thoughts of an imminently receding past. If they had been members of polygamous households, perhaps the understanding that they would never again see their relatives would be tempered by the knowledge that another woman would step in to care for their children – a bittersweet confidence indeed. The habits and events that had been so common as to be invisible would be suddenly thrown into sharp relief as the portability of some and the irretrievability of others completely altered their worlds.

By all accounts, Ibo women captured upon the *Arthur* and myriad other slave ships came from communities in which they shouldered important responsibilities. Slave traders watched the way women worked in West and West Central Africa and called these women "slaves" to African men – no doubt an accusation that went some way toward exonerating their own role in the slave trade. All along the area south of Sierra Leone and West of Togo agricultural work fell within the purview of women. While European observers denigrated this essential sphere of women's activity, all members of society depended upon women's agricultural work and compensated for it at the markets.

Agricultural work brought with it particular kinds of social and cultural spaces. The nature of agricultural work on the Upper Guinea Coast required large-scale collective effort, effectively pulling all members of the society into the agricultural sphere. The huge dikes built to accommodate the draining and flooding of fields required the cooperation of hundreds of people. During construction and planting, both men and women moved from their homes to the fields to better tend the crop and manage the waters. Surrounded by numerous rivers and dense mangrove swamps, the peoples who lived in this part of West Africa utilized the waterways for transport and for food. They navigated canoes with as few as one person or as many as sixty people aboard and devised systems of dikes, sometimes miles long, to flood and drain rice fields. Enormous markets took place every eight days bringing thousands to buy and sell, some coming from as far as 60 miles away. In the process they created enduring social networks and utilized canoes and riverways as transport to participate in social, religious, and political gatherings.

At the Gold Coast, prior to European contact, women produced agricultural exports essential to the regional economy. Wilhelm Muller, a German minister who lived at the Gold Coast between 1662 and 1669, noted that "apart from the peasants who bring palm-wine and sugar-cane to market every day, there are no men who stand in public markets to trade, but only women. It is remarkable to see how the market is filled every day with . . . women selling [food]" (Muller 1983: 243). Samuel Brun commented upon the division of labor concerning cultivated crops at the beginning of the seventeenth century. He noted that, at Cape Palmas (Liberia), men traded Malaguetta pepper for money, and traded beads for rice "because the rice is the ware of women, while Malaguetta is that of the men" (Brun 1983: 78). The marketplace was a central place for women to meet and trade; and they did not exchange only goods. Muller wrote: "they strengthen their memories by zealously repeating the old stories . . . young people and children listen to such discourse with avid ears and absorb it in their hearts" (Muller 1983: 154). One wonders how long after their transport to the

Americas men and women gathered to "strengthen their memories." While doing so, they might evoke their memories of the marketplace, of their homes, of the physical landscapes of their former lives. Women here decorated their "clean and tidy [homes]...with white or red earth which they consider... particularly beautiful" (Muller 1983: 201). What beauty did they unearth from American soil?

On the Upper Guinea Coast, the frequent movement of peoples from place to place no doubt influenced their patterns of cultural and economic acquisitions. Women covered themselves with elaborate scarification, an adornment wholly perplexing to Europeans, but certainly an essential component to a girl's coming of age, both physically and spiritually. *Grigri* prayer amulets were worn all along the coast. Women and men carried their belief systems on their persons, offering food and thanks and requesting blessings from a pantheon of gods before eating, stepping into a boat, or going to sleep. As women moved through the work that defined their day, the protective divine would accompany them.

Much has been made of the "matriarchal" origins of West African families. Perhaps more significant for women transported from the Slave Coast would be the experience of having lived, or served, in households headed by male/female pairs who ruled, in tandem, over their lineage. Such was the case for the Fon. Known as the *Taninon*, the female head's responsibilities came from her role as intermediary between the living and the ancestors of each Fon lineage. Even a woman "enslaved" by a Slave Coast family could have no doubt as to the potential authority and responsibility of women in Fon society. Linkages between powerful women and men were inherent to Fon cosmology. Among the Igbo the Creator was *Chineke* – who represented both male (*Chi*) and female (*Eke*) and whose unity and complementarity formed the crux of Igbo cosmology. In the mid-seventeenth century, Allada had been the focus of Christian missionary efforts. African catechisms prepared by the Capuchins allowed "Lisa" to refer to Jesus Christ. In Allada cosmology Lisa, a white man, and Mawa, a black woman, form a paired deity. As agricultural producers, conduits to the ancestors, complements to Jesus Christ, even as armed guards at the king's palace, the memory of women's multiple and pivotal role at all levels of society would travel with both men and women across the Atlantic.

The particularities of how girls' and women's place in the world had been demarcated varied from region to region. In relation to matters of spirit, perhaps the tangibles of home and public space receded. Thinking back on her life before enslavement a woman from the Gold Coast might remember being a child, of seven or eight, called upon to witness a marriage. Apparently a small girl was compelled to "sleep in between [the bride and groom] and watch out that they do not touch each other for seven days" as part of a wedding ritual (Muller 1983: 214). There is no telling what insights a young girl might carry with her, or how her sense of her own importance might be shaped, as a result of her role at the inception of a marriage. Women would carry many different such childhood memories. For many, their girlhood would have been marked by circumcision. Among other things, the rite of circumcision initiated female children into a sisterhood, creating a bond of shared secrets and pain. In modern accounts the rite is deeply laden with traditional imagery that imparts a longstanding connection between girls, their mothers, grandmothers, and ancestors. Once these women found themselves in American slave societies, slave-owners wrenched this most essential site of commonality between mothers and daughters from them. Enslaved mothers would be forced to devise new ritual spaces as substitutes.

Motherhood was a social role carefully prepared for in Africa, as elsewhere. On the Gold Coast after a marriage announcement, the bride's friends ritually prepared her for conception. Once pregnant she would be "brought to the sea-shore in order to be washed," after being ritually dirtied by "a great number of boys and girls" on her way to the water (Bosman 1967: 208). As they had since their first trips to West Africa, Europeans believed childbirth came easily to African women. "In the second or third day [after childbirth] they already go among people and do their housework and business," exclaimed Muller. His awe at the speed of women's recovery on the Gold Coast is perhaps contextualized by the length of time that elite European women spent recuperating from childbirth – the German word for childbed in fact meant "six-week bed" (Muller 1983: 217, n335).

During pregnancy, women and men initiated a sexual distance that extended at least a year and a half after a birth. "Not allowed even the Matrimonial caresses of her husband" from the moment of a discovered pregnancy, men and women cooperated to protect unborn children and to space childbirth (Van Nyendael 1967: 444). Abstinence reflected an understanding of the relationship between intercourse and pregnancy as well as a mutual desire to spare women's energy and health from too frequent pregnancies. Men as well as women, then, acknowledged and understood the physical demands of childbirth and nursing in ways lost on European observers. As they often did, European observers misconstrued birth spacing in their haste to denounce all African women as either enslaved by their men or "inclined to Wantonness." They associated what they saw as sexual freedom with "an absolute sterility [or]... a seldom pregnancy." Thus they believed that the woman who mothered only "two or three [children] in their whole lives" did so as a consequence of sexual promiscuity, not of conscious efforts at birth spacing (Dapper 1670: 466). Some European observers believed the post-delivery period of abstinence lasted three months; others commented upon a two- to three-year period of breastfeeding. Contemporary studies note the evidence that prolonged breastfeeding in tandem with postpartum sexual abstinence was an essential factor in African women and men's ability to regulate fertility. Modern anthropological studies focused on the area of West Africa from Sierra Leone to the Bight of Biafra calculated the average duration of postpartum taboo a year or longer. By abstaining from sexual contact, or practicing coitus interruptus during breastfeeding, parents were able to assure manageable birth spacing and thereby increase the probability that their children would survive infancy.

At the Gold Coast, parents protected newly born children by anointing them with palm-wine, adorning them with safeguarding fetishes, and strapping them to a mother's back until they could walk. At the Upper Guinea Coast, as throughout West Africa, women were accompanied by the infants they carried upon their backs for "as long as they are breast-feeding them" (Barbot 1732: 88). At the Sierra Leone estuary and the Sess River at Cape Palmas, women carried infants "as long as they have them at the breast . . . in a kind of leather box, in which the little one is sat. They also tie it to their body to prevent accident" (Barbot 1732: 272). In many places, protection also took the form of circumcision. Once in America, however, parents would contend with an inability to carry through essential practices associated with birth and childrearing. Faced with permanent exile, women and men left behind much of what defined them as members of specific sociocultural entities. The inability to provide a child "with all kinds of exquisite beads and with elegantly fashioned gold . . . through whose strength the tender child is to be protected against *summan*, the Devil, and against illness, injury and accident" must have cut deep into the hearts of men and women who became parents in the Americas (Muller 1983: 161). It may have been comparable to the inability to circumcise so as to properly initiate boys and girls into their adulthood. The loss of this rite constituted an unbelievable violence to family, ethnic, and religious traditions. The memories and belief systems that dictated female circumcision, or polygamous households, or sexual abstinence as birth control, would live on in the Americas even as men and women's ability to actualize such aspects of their past would be lost and mourned. Over time, these cultural traditions were renegotiated as Africans made sexual connections and gave birth to children whom they guided into an adulthood categorically at odds with their own past.

African Women in the Americas

The traditional beliefs and behaviors that European observers identified as encompassing the worlds of men and women from the Gold Coast, or the Bights of Benin and Biafra, should be seen only as suggestive. It is difficult to know how close these white men, whose reasons for noting black women's lives were heavily laden with their own agendas and fortunes in the slave trade, could come to the heart of women's experiences. Nevertheless, their observations are one means of approaching a more detailed sense of the lives left behind by men and women transported to the Americas. African women who found themselves in the Americas would struggle as the terms and conditions under which they performed agricultural work and tried to maintain traditions of family were drastically and violently altered. Yet they continued to perform agricultural labor and to bring children into the world even as they developed a radically altered vision of the cultural meanings of their pasts and their futures.

Throughout the plantation societies that dominated the seventeenth- and eighteenth-century European colonies in the Americas, women labored in the fields. Despite images of domestic service – cooking, cleaning, and taking care of slaveowners' children – the vast majority of African and African American women spent their entire lives engaged in fieldwork. In some cases, the crops they grew may have tied them to their lives before enslavement. In the early eighteenth century in South Carolina, for example, plantation owners appropriated essential rice cultivation skills from the men and women they enslaved. Indeed, as long as rice was the colony's staple export crop, planters preferred to purchase and enslave persons from the

Upper Guinea Coast over any other West African region. Any sense of continuity for those women from the Upper Guinea Coast would, however, be thwarted in the malaria-infested rice fields of South Carolina. For others, however, surviving the regime of the American colonies included learning to grow less familiar crops. Nonetheless, whether on coffee plantations in Santo Domingo, rice plantations in South Carolina, or sugar plantations in Jamaica, wherever staple crops were grown, women were forced to cultivate them. When we bear in mind that artisanal positions were all but closed to female laborers, women's preponderance in the backbreaking work of the fields begins to make sense. Drivers, boilers, coopers, sailors, blacksmiths, carpenters, herdsmen – all these occupations excluded women. The modicum of increased autonomy, mobility, and release from the violence and violation of slavery that these positions offered was available only to enslaved men. Women who hoped to escape fieldwork had to be resigned to the close confines of domestic work – a space open to only a tiny few and arguably more difficult than fieldwork with the relentless supervision, sexual violation, and retaliatory violence that swirled around women caught up in the immediacy of slaveowners' intimate familial contestations.

Physical and emotional spaces did exist where enslaved women could momentarily escape the violence and drudgery of fieldwork. None was so widely customary as their participation in colonial markets. In many American societies, slaveowners assigned provision grounds to the enslaved. These were small plots of land on which one had to grow food to feed oneself and one's family. Women often were responsible for tending these plots and, subsequently, for selling surplus wares at weekend markets in Charleston, Richmond, Cape Hat, Bridgetown, or St. John's. Even in those colonies where there were no formalized provision grounds, many enslaved women managed to participate in the weekend markets. Outraged at their dependence on black women for produce like eggs and vegetables and the opportunities for covert gatherings that markets and travel to markets provided, but unwilling to shoulder the responsibility for provisioning the labor force themselves, colonial legislators complained bitterly about black women's behavior in the markets. For their part, the women who made the weekly trip to market their goods must have felt fiercely protective of their ability to do so; the market after all was a place for all manner of exchange – financial, informational, and emotional.

Markets were particularly visible places for women to collectively bolster one another against the outrages of enslavement. But marketplaces were not the only sites for subversion. Enslaved women articulated their opposition in many ways to the labor and social system so brutally forced upon them: running away, sometimes with children in tow; establishing Maroon communities; poisoning slaveowners; participating in revolts; feigning illness, pregnancy, or ignorance; breaking tools; working slowly; ministering to the sick; or spitting in the soup. But perhaps the most important opposition to the system of enslavement was the ability and desire to build communities. The regime of plantation work wreaked havoc on the health of all enslaved persons. Although birthrates began to outstrip death rates in North American slave societies in the second half of the eighteenth century, they did not do so until after nineteenth-century emancipations elsewhere in the Americas. Overworked and underfed, enslaved laborers were extremely vulnerable to disease and malnutrition. Infant mortality rates were extremely high. Disease either destroyed women's reproductive ability, or consigned children to early death. Mortality rates were so high in seventeenth-century Barbados, for example, that a typical slaveowner interested in simply maintaining a constant number of laborers over the course of a decade would have to purchase a third again the total number of persons he enslaved. At least some portion of women who had no children while enslaved must have been engaging in an act of withholding this most intimate and emotional form of labor. As an institution, slavery did nothing better than to emphasize the commodification and disposability of a woman and the children she might bear. To have children under slavery was to open oneself up to the inevitability of loss – through sale or death – and to line the pockets of the very person who violated you. On the other hand, to have children was to stake a claim of ownership. It was to stare down the grim future of enslavement and to imagine something different. In the face of a daily existence marked by death, disease, and despair, it is remarkable that among the many legacies of enslavement are enduring traditions of political culture, religion, healing, and arts.

Creating and protecting the spaces in which community could grow was curtailed not only by the physicalities of health and labor. Slaveowners engaged in a constant – albeit fundamentally unsuccessful – struggle to limit women and men's lives to the narrowest of confines. But with or without childbirth, the men and women who crossed the Atlantic became immediately enmeshed in families. Whether the formation of real or fictive family ties was bolstered by shared ethnic antecedents or hindered by the vast cultural divides between far-flung African ethnicities, enslaved women and men created new cultural institutions almost from the moment of their forced arrival. A sense of family emerged from displacement – many persons who shared the middle passage referred to one another as brother or sister. As their own expectations about religion, family formation, or healing intersected with those of other enslaved African or Native American persons, women created communities. These communities, these sites of culture formation, took on meaning in relation to the materialities of work, the market, disease, death, and finally birth.

Cayoba's decision to throw her lot in with "fort slaves" and "sale slaves" was both brave and prophetic. She could have no idea how the kind of cross-status and cross-ethnic alliance she was about to participate in would become the essential component in her descendents' lives in the New World. Nor could she possibly imagine the ways in which her extraordinarily visible expression of revolt might actually be connected to Moota's seeming complacency. As Moota appeared to go about her work oblivious to the rebelliousness percolating around her, her children embodied other possibilities for rebellion and other manifestations of subjugation. They were in complicated relationship to the emerging social power that was personified by the slave fort and the Europeans who inhabited it. As Moota negotiated her status as slave she created culture. Her children personified the irretrievability of her past and the unimaginable trajectory of her future.

BIBLIOGRAPHY

Primary Sources

Barbot, John (1732) *A Description of the Coasts of North and South-Guinea*..., in A. Churchill (ed.), *A Collection of Voyages*. London: n.p.

Bence Island Diaries, 1727–8, Series T70, Volume 1465, Public Record Office, Kew, England.

Bosman, William. *A New and Accurate Description of the Coast of Guinea, divided into the Gold, the Slave, and the Ivory Coasts*, The Netherlands, 1704; first English edition, London, 1705; fourth English edition, London: Frank Cass, 1967.

"Samuel Brun's Voyage of 1611–20," in Adam Jones (ed.), *German Sources for West African History, 1599–1669*. Weisbaden: Franz Steiner, 1983, pp. 44–90.

Copies of Instructions from the Royal African Company of England to the Captains of Ships in their Services 10 December 1685–16 April 1700, Series T70, Volume 61, Folio 38, Public Record Office, Kew, England.

[Dapper, O.] (1670) *Africa. Being an Accurate Description of the Regions*..., ed. John Ogilby. London: n.p.

[Hingston, George.] Journal Aboard the *Arthur*, 5 December 1677–31 March 1678, Series T70, Volume 1213, Public Record Office, Kew, England.

Letterbook to Cape Coast Castle, 1728–40, Series T70, Volume 54, Folio 18, Public Record Office, Kew, England.

"Wilhelm Johann Muller's Description of the Fetu Country, 1662–9," in Adam Jones (ed.), *German Sources for West African History, 1599–1669*. Weisbaden: Franz Steiner, 1983, pp. 132–359.

Snelgrave, William (1734) *A New Account of Some Parts of Guinea, and the Slave Trade*. London: J. J. and P. Knapton.

Van Nyendael, David. "A Description of Rio Formosa or... Benin," in William Bosman, *A New and Accurate Description of the Coast of Guinea*, The Netherlands, 1704; first English edition, London, 1705; fourth English edition, London: Frank Cass, 1967.

Secondary Sources

Bay, Edna G. (1995) "Belief, Legitimacy and the Kpojito: An Institutional History of the 'Queen Mother' in Precolonial Dahomey," *Journal of African History* 36, pp. 1–27.

Boddy, Janice (1997) "Womb as Oasis: The Symbolic Context of Pharaonic Circumcision on Rural Northern Sudan," in Roger N. Macalaster and Micaela di Leonardo (eds.), *The Gender/Sexuality Reader: Culture, History, Political Economy*. New York and London: Routledge, pp. 309–24.

Bush, Barbara (1996) "Hard Labour: Women, Childbirth, and Resistance in British Caribbean Slave Societies," in David Barry Gaspar and Darlene Clark Hine (eds.), *More Than Chattel: Black Women and Slavery in the Americas*. Bloomington: Indiana University Press, pp. 193–217.

Carney, Judith (1996) "Rice Milling, Gender, and Slave Labour in Colonial South Carolina," *Past and Present* 153, pp. 108–34.

Curtin, Phillip (1969) *The Atlantic Slave Trade: A Census*. Madison and London: University of Wisconsin Press.

Dunn, Richard S. (1993) "Sugar Production and Slave Women in Jamaica," in Ira Berlin and Philip D. Morgan (eds.), *Cultivation and Culture: Labor and the Shaping of Slave Life in the Americas*. Charlottesville: University Press of Virginia, pp. 49–72.

Eltis, David (2000) *The Rise of African Slavery in the Americas.* Cambridge: Cambridge University Press.

Eltis, David and Engerman, Stanley (1993) "Was the Slave Trade Dominated by Men?" *Journal of Interdisciplinary History* 23, pp. 237–57.

Fage, J. D. (1989) "African Societies and the Atlantic Slave Trade," *Past and Present* 125, pp. 97–115.

Galenson, David W. (1986) *Traders, Planters, and Slaves: Market Behavior in Early English America.* Cambridge: Cambridge University Press.

Geggus, David P. (1989) "Sex Ratio, Age, and Ethnicity in the Atlantic Slave Trade: Data from French Shipping and Plantation Records," *Journal of African History* 30, pp. 23–44.

Geggus, David P. (1993) "Sugar and Coffee Cultivation in Saint Domingue and the Shaping of the Slave Labor Force," in Ira Berlin and Philip D. Morgan (eds.), *Cultivation and Culture: Labor and the Shaping of Slave Life in the Americas.* Charlottesville: University Press of Virginia, pp. 73–100.

Gomez, Michael A. (1998) *Exchanging Our Country Marks: The Transformation of African Identities in the Colonial and Antebellum South.* Chapel Hill: University of North Carolina Press.

Handler, Jerome S. and Corruccinni, Robert S. (1986) "Weaning among West Indian Slaves: Historical and Bioanthropological Evidence from Barbados," *William and Mary Quarterly*, 3rd ser., 43, pp. 111–17.

Klein, Herbert S. and Engerman, Stanley (1978) "Fertility Differentials between Slaves in the United States and the British West Indies; A Note on Lactation Practices and their Possible Implications," *William and Mary Quarterly*, 3rd ser., 35, pp. 357–74.

Klein, Martin (1983) "Women and Slavery in the Western Sudan," in Claire Robertson and Martin Klein (eds.), *Women and Slavery in Africa.* Madison: University of Wisconsin Press, pp. 67–88.

Law, Robin (1991) *The Slave Coast of West Africa, 1550–1750: The Impact of the Atlantic Slave Trade on an African Society.* Oxford: Clarendon Press.

Lightfoot-Klein, Hanny (1989) *Prisoners of Ritual: An Odyssey into Female Genital Circumcision in Africa.* New York: Herrington Park Press.

Littlefield, Daniel (1991) *Rice and Slaves: Ethnicity and the Slave Trade in Colonial South Carolina.* Urbana: University of Illinois Press.

Mintz, Sidney and Price, Richard (1976) *An Anthropological Approach to the Afro-American Past: A Caribbean Perspective.* Philadelphia: Institute for the Study of Human Issues.

Olwell, Robert (1996) " 'Loose, Idle and Disorderly': Slave Women in the Eighteenth-century Charleston Marketplace," in David Barry Gaspar and Darlene Clark Hine (eds.), *More Than Chattel: Black Women and Slavery in the Americas.* Bloomington: Indiana University Press, pp. 97–110.

Ong, Walter (1982) *Orality and Literacy.* New York: Methuen.

Richardson, David (1989) "Slave Exports from West and West-Central Africa, 1700–1810: New Estimates of Volume and Distribution," *Journal of African History* 30, pp. 1–22.

Robertson, Claire and Klein, Martin (1983) "Women's Importance in African Slave Systems," in Claire Robertson and Martin Klein (eds.), *Women and Slavery in Africa.* Madison: University of Wisconsin Press, pp. 3–28.

Rodney, Walter (1970) *A History of the Upper Guinea Coast, 1545–1800.* London: Oxford University Press.

Schoenmaeckers, R., Shah, I. H., Lesthaeghe, R., and Tambashe, O. (1981) "The Child-spacing Tradition and the Post-partum Taboo in Tropical Africa," in Hilary Page and Ron

Lesthaeghe (eds.), *Child-spacing in Tropical Africa: Traditions and Change.* New York: Academic Press, pp. 25–72.

Thornton, John (1988) "On the Trail of Voodoo: African Christianity in Africa and the Americas," *The Americas* 44, pp. 261–78.

Thornton, John (1992) *Africa and Africans in the Making of the Atlantic World, 1400–1680.* Cambridge and New York: Cambridge University Press.

Wood, Peter H. (1974) *Black Majority: Negroes in Colonial South Carolina, from 1670 through the Stono Rebellion.* New York: W. W. Norton.

Chapter Three

Contact and Conquest in Colonial North America

Gwenn A. Miller

ATTENTION to women in the history of colonial contact and conquest in North America has increased markedly in recent years. New studies that explore the significance of women's actions and their relationships with other family members as mothers, workers, lovers, and pioneers are transforming our understanding of the social relations that sustained and shaped European colonization in the "New World." The scholarly recognition of interethnic relationships among Native Americans, Europeans, and Africans has further highlighted women's central role in shaping early American communities.

The impact of colonial contact and conquest upon various racial and ethnic groups in the Americas has been on the historical agenda for a long time. However, the interpretations that emerged in the 1970s with the ascent of the "new cultural history" tended to emphasize stark delineations and overt conflict between groups. For instance, when scholars examined relations between Pequots and Anglo-New Englanders, or African slaves and British landowners, each group was likely to be treated as a monolithic entity. Such an approach echoed discussions of colonialism for other parts of the world. More recently, the literature has stressed the porous nature of boundaries between different groups, their crossings, and their redefinitions. Increased knowledge of women's specific contributions to burgeoning colonial societies, whether on the frontiers of California, Western Canada, Pennsylvania, or Virginia, has cast doubt on monolithic perceptions of ethnic groups. By bringing these two perspectives together, feminist scholarship on the colonial era has opened up a range of new questions about how colonial boundaries shifted, who crossed them, and why.

In 1995, Gary Nash described colonial American societies as "zone[s] of deep intercultural contacts." By this time Richard White had already defined a colonial "middle ground" in North America and Kathleen Brown had suggested the importance of "gender frontiers." Latin Americanists, such as Irene Silverblatt and Mary Louise Pratt, had been attending to these zones for years; and scholars such as Ann Stoler and Karen Hansen, who study colonialism in other parts of the world, had been declaring the importance of the "intimacies of empire" for almost a decade. However, as many people have noted, Nash's presidential address to the Organization of American Historians, "The Hidden History of Mestizo America," was a landmark for mainstream American history; the field had reached a point where it could no longer ignore the extent and permeability of relationships among people of divergent ethnic backgrounds in colonial communities. The rapid rise in the number of conference papers and panels, edited collections, and monographs dedicated to social and cultural mixing in American history over the past decade confirms that the time for mestizo histories of America has arrived. Feminist scholars have pointed to the centrality of women in this history. They have also opened up seldom used sources such as school records and housekeeping manuals and have encouraged scholars to look at more familiar documents such as marriage and birth records, deeds, court cases, and ships' logs in new ways.

Women in Colonial Societies

One of the most critical contributions of recent studies on early colonial relations has been the recognition of indigenous women's centrality to their own societies and to interactions with Europeans. Economically, native women's behavior often challenged European norms which situated men as the primary arbiters of agricultural affairs and trade. Many Indian women were in charge of planting and cultivating crops or gathering wild vegetation from local areas. Depending on the organization of kinship relations, in some native societies, such as Iroquoian groups, elderly women leaders were also in charge of the distribution of food. Some women participated in trade by preparing skins that were collected in the fur hunt or by selling items that they made.

As Clara Sue Kidwell suggests, native women were often the "first important mediators" when people from divergent cultures met. For example, after initial contact, some Indian women lived with and married European men, such as the French fur traders or *coureurs de bois* of the Great Lakes region, moving frequently across the permeable boundaries of native and European communities. Because of these relationships women such as the fabled *La Malinche* in sixteenth-century Mexico or Isabel Montour on the later Pennsylvania frontier were frequently among the first Indians to learn European languages and thus became interpreters in political negotiations. Not all relations with Europeans were consensual, however. Indian women were often raped by European men who forcibly entered their communities demanding goods, labor, or homage to particular leaders and religions. Such sexual abuse occurred not only in the Southwest, where brutality inflicted by the Spanish is best documented, but also throughout the continent. Accounts left by the notorious Virginia colonist William Byrd and the Carolina traveler John Lawson plainly show that native women were also abused along the Virginia and Carolina frontiers in the Southeast. According to Theda Perdue, the South Carolina Indian trade records are filled with native grievances indicating sexual abuse. Thus, some Native American women willingly chose to live with European men, while others lived in fear of physical abuse from them.

As with social interaction, Native American women had a range of responses to European religions. In some cases they were among the first indigenous people to convert to Christianity, or at least allow themselves to be baptized, so that they could marry European men and thus "legitimize" their children in the eyes of European governments and courts. Some native people, both men and women, converted to Christianity when their populations were devastated by unfamiliar foreign diseases like smallpox, which European missionaries always seemed to survive. At the same time, some women actively resisted any form of Christianity because it promoted a world-view that often ignored or challenged the power they traditionally held over religious rights, childrearing, and economic resources within their own communities.

For their part, European women also exhibited a range of responses to colonial contact. While most early missionaries were men, women such as the Ursuline sisters in New France founded convents and girls' schools open to Indians, thus acting as social mediators in their own right. In other regions, such as New England, European women alternately worked with so-called "praying Indians" and wrote horrific accounts of their contact with "heathen savages."

Early Works

Scholarship on European–native interaction in North America during the colonial period expanded rapidly from the late 1970s to the present. Initially, these analyses left women on the periphery. The few early studies that did attend to women mirrored the state of American women's history in that they focused on economic production and social agency. These studies were especially influenced by feminist anthropologists, who centered on women's experiences of the sexual division of labor and social responsibility. They were also influenced by work on contact and conquest in Latin America.

In 1980, for example, Mona Etienne and Eleanor Leacock edited an important collection entitled *Women and Colonization* that highlighted anthropological perspectives and included articles on women all over the Americas, from the North Atlantic to Peru. Using Montagnais women as an example, Leacock herself argued that colonization, and the attendant spread of both capitalism and Christianity, led to a decline in women's status. She argued that the Jesuits' "civilizing" program which emphasized a European model of women's and children's subordination to men operated together with forced change in the mode of production and the sexual division of labor to destabilize the more egalitarian gender relationships that existed before the arrival of large numbers of Europeans. Meanwhile, Canadian historians reexamined the lives of fur trade families. Sylvia Van Kirk explored relations between men and women in the Canadian West and concluded that the dependence of native women and European male fur traders on one another often developed into affectionate "tender ties" during the earliest phases of colonial contact. For Van Kirk the fur trade, as opposed to missionary and military projects, was distinctive in that it was a staple industry based upon the *mutual* dependence of two diverse cultural groups. Indian women sometimes sought out European men, sometimes guided their travels, and often married them according to the "custom of the country." This type of marriage tended to follow native practices, such as the male suitor obtaining the permission from the woman's family and paying a "bride price" to secure the marriage. The native women who married fur traders were the most important cultural mediators of this contact zone in that they facilitated trade, translated languages, formed families with European men, and shaped those men's lives from day to day. In spite of the attempts by various trading companies to regulate the degree of interaction between native women and European men, the number of sexual relations, marriages, and mixed-race children increased rapidly.

Jennifer Brown attended to the demographics of the Hudson Bay and Northwest Company fur trade. She claimed that men's actions were adaptive responses to the official and unofficial organizational structures of the companies themselves, rather than to their experiences as men in Indian country. Jacqueline Peterson looked specifically at the formation of a distinct fur trade society, the Red River Métis, and the prominence there of women as church founders, traders, and community leaders.

In the mid-1980s Joan Jensen and Darlis Miller edited a volume on the northern reaches of colonial New Spain (particularly the area that is now New Mexico) and included two articles on women and colonial contact during the earliest Spanish Mexican invasions of this region. Cheryl Foote and Sandra Schackel took up the issue of women's status, a theme then current in the history of white women in the early American East, and applied it to Pueblo women. While their analysis emphasized the harsh treatment of native women by Spanish Mexicans as laborers and objects of sexual desire, they also pointed to the "cultural borrowing" that occurred not only between the Spanish and the Pueblos, but also between Pueblos and other native groups. Salome Hernandez also focused on women's status by looking at *mexicanas*, a term which in this case includes settler women of any combination of Indian, African, or European descent who arrived in New Mexico after the first Spanish invasion of the region. In contrast to the previous article, this essay pointed to the harsh treatment of *mexicana* women by Indian men. Both of these studies expanded the parameters of American women's history by recovering the history of women in the Southwest. In doing so, they also illustrated some general effects of interethnic contact and conquest on women.

At the same time that these early works on women, sex, and cultural mixing emerged, feminist work on Anglo-American colonial history sought the roots of women's oppression in America. Scholars questioned whether the period before 1800 constituted a "golden age" during which Anglo-American women had more autonomy than their nineteenth-century counterparts. By the mid-1980s, scholars within the field were beginning to recognize the limits of such a framework that addressed white women only. Although Mary Beth Norton called for a focus on African American and Native American women in her now well-known 1984 overview of the literature, historians of women embarked on this mission tentatively. They remained committed to investigating the lives of Anglo-New England women that were so richly documented in the colonial archives, with little acknowledgment of their interactions with Native Americans.

The treatment of captivity narratives offers an important deviation from this pattern of scholarship. This work stemmed from an American fascination, indeed obsession, with these narratives that reaches back into the seventeenth century. In 1973, Richard Slotkin argued that captivity narratives and "savage wars" were staples of the American frontier myth in that they perpetuated the fears of, and fixation on, an "untamed wilderness" and the subsequent drive to subdue it. Only twenty years later, feminist historians such as June Namias and Carroll Smith-Rosenberg brought the gender component of these narratives to center stage. Namias argued that white women's captivity narratives show that European American ideas about how men and women should act in their own society developed in relation to their experiences of interaction with Native Americans beginning in the formative years of the colonies and extending through the nineteenth century. Smith-Rosenberg suggested that the stories told by white women, such as Mary Rowlandson (1682) and later Susanna Rowson (1798), defined British immigrants as the true Americans and Native Americans as "savage" outsiders, thereby creating an American identity. Yet these works still focused on white women and did not explore similar instances of Native Americans captured by Europeans, a topic that had been touched on decades earlier in the work of Carolyn Foreman.

One of the most provocative analyses was offered by John Demos, who explored the life of Eunice Williams, the captive daughter of the minister John Williams from Deerfield, Massachusetts. Contradicting the notion that white women were always held against their will, Eunice became a Catholic Mohawk at Kahnawake near Montreal and, according to Demos, happily remained there until she died. While studies of captivity narratives gave some indication of what interactions between Native Americans and European Americans might have encompassed, only Helen H. Tanner, in a highly creative essay, managed to use a white captivity narrative to reconstruct the life of a Native American woman. With but few exceptions, treatments of these accounts were skewed toward white women who became part of Indian communities without providing much insight into native communities themselves or the experiences of native captives in European settlements. Still, by reexamining captivity narratives feminist scholars helped to open up new questions about the meaning of social and cultural border crossings in early North America.

The Late 1980s to Early 1990s

One critical aspect of scholarship on women and colonization in North America has been its compartmentalized nature, stemming from divisions within American history overall. Regions such as the Southwest, the Old Northwest, the Southeast, the Northeast, and the Northwest have often been studied in isolation; and the thirteen Anglo colonies in particular have been separated repeatedly from one another and from the rest of the continent. Until the mid-1990s, early American women's history had focused almost exclusively on these British colonies as it sought the roots of white women's condition in New England and, to a lesser degree, in the middle colonies and the Southeast. At the same time, work on the gender component of interethnic and interracial relations primarily centered on studies of Spanish interactions with indigenous Americans in the Southwest and French and British Canadian contacts in the Great Lakes regions. For example, Etienne and Leacock's volume (with the exception of one article by Robert Grumet), and the studies by Van Kirk, Brown, Peterson, and Jensen and Miller, as well as those of Ramón Gutiérrez, Carol Devens, and Karen Anderson, all explored women's experiences of colonial contact outside the thirteen Anglo-American colonies.

By the early 1990s, while still centered on interactions between indigenous peoples in the Southwest and the Old Northwest, scholars turned to domains of women's involvement in colonial contact that addressed questions about these women's identity. In his controversial book, *When Jesus Came, the Corn Mothers Went Away* (1991), Ramón Gutiérrez argued that gendered social constructions were part of the making of colonial identity in the region that is now New Mexico. By showing how age and sex provided organizing markers within Pueblo society before the Spanish invaded the area, Gutiérrez argued that Pueblo women's sexuality gave them power. This power was challenged when Franciscan missionaries aligned themselves with young Pueblo men. The arrival of the Spanish thus recast gender roles for Pueblo women and men. Karen Anderson and Carol Devens looked north to New France. Anderson argued that French Jesuits were able to convert Huron men to Christianity because these missionaries undermined women's economic independence and sexual freedom; until the arrival of the Black Robes, there had been space for relative autonomy within Huron marriages. Devens suggested that women were the ones who delayed missionary efforts in the Great Lakes region, affecting the course of that history differently than did men.

In the early 1990s, there were few comparable studies of women and colonization for the Anglo-American colonies. Most work focused on the perceptions of white Puritan men and on the construction of an Anglo-American community and polity. New Englanders, moreover, appeared to maintain a rigid distance from local Native Americans. Because they often migrated in families, they had less incentive, according to some historians, to mingle with and marry aboriginal Americans than did the French and Spanish. However, as Theda Perdue, John Mack Faragher, and others have noted, by the late eighteenth century in the Southeast, native women – Cherokee and Creek among them – had been marrying and living with deerskin fur traders and trappers for over a century. However, until recently these relationships have received little attention in mainstream American history, in part because the enslavement of Indians has only begun to be explored. The majority of scholars who have studied Anglo–native interactions have focused almost completely on the possibility of Native Americans and European Americans coexisting. They have argued, that is, that while their lives were drastically altered, Native Americans continued to live in regions bordering European settlements long after the establishment of the first English colonies. Even with the rapid rise of the "new Indian history," as late as 1993, Daniel Richter expressed concern that Native American history remained on the periphery of American history. Given these circumstances, there was little room to discuss the gender dynamics of multi-ethnic relations.

Recently, however, attention to women is contributing to the expansion of this area of research. Highlighting specific historical sites, feminist scholars have demonstrated how the control of sex by both men and women, Indian and European, in domains ranging from missions and trade outposts to schools, homes, and courtrooms, became a critical and contested ground of colonial discourse and experience. In this context, the early emphasis on economic production and social status has expanded to include more focused explorations of how women influenced and were influenced by colonial ideas about morality, motherhood, domesticity, and sexuality. By the same token, earlier attempts to identify women's separate spheres have been replaced, or at least amplified, by a focus on gendered systems of knowledge and experience, masculine as well as feminine.

The Mid-1990s to the Present

Women's history has been changed by attention to colonial contact and conquest. This phenomenon is illustrated, for instance, in the revisions to Vicki Ruíz and Ellen DuBois's widely used multicultural reader, *Unequal Sisters*, first published in 1990. Like earlier editions, the 2000 edition tells the parallel stories of women from many different ethnic and racial backgrounds in the United States. However, it also begins to explore multi-ethnic and interracial relationships. Emphasis in the earlier editions on individual heroines and popular images from the colonial era has been replaced by greater attention to ordinary women's participation in colonial exchange. The newer work also turns away from American historians' traditional overemphasis on the East coast. For example, James Brooks's article on women captives in New Mexico and Antonia Castañeda's on gender, race, and culture in frontier California replace Rayna Green's article on European images of eastern Indian women such as Pocahontas and Deena Gonzalez's on the legendary Mexican businesswoman, *La Tules*.

In the past decade historians of early America have begun to consider some of the challenges presented to scholars of colonialism, gender, and native history by those, like Mary Louise Pratt and Richard White, who have proposed that imperial interactions took place in "contact zones" or on "middle grounds." Pratt purposefully distinguished the "contact zone," a space that connotes "copresence" of previously separated people, from the "colonial frontier," which emphasizes a European expansionist perspective. In a similar vein, while exploring the Great Lakes region, White found that relations between indigenous women and white men were "a bridge to the middle ground" (1991: 4). He described the middle ground as a place, as well as a moment in time, that exists between cultures, empires, and people; all those present learn from each other, and all rely on each other for various needs. As long as all parties have sufficient reason to maintain the relationship, they continue to meet in this way.

There has been a surge of new work responding to these more nuanced explanations of colonial interaction. Jennifer Morgan set the stage for such studies by exploring the ways in which European males used their perceptions of African and Native American women's bodies to construct a "naturalized" human hierarchy. In her book on colonial Virginia, Kathleen Brown has argued that gender was completely intertwined with race and class in the construction of a social order that would allow wealthy European men to dominate colonial residents, including all Africans, Indians, and European women as well as poor European men. For North Carolina, Kirsten Fischer has pointed to "unlawful sex" among indigenous, African, and

European peoples as central to political, legal, and social debates about the very structure of colonial authority. At the same time, Nancy Shoemaker's anthology on Native American women seeks to dispel the idea that contact with Europeans had a uniformly negative effect on Native American women. In this volume, for instance, Kathleen Brown argued that both English and Algonquian perceptions about gender roles informed the ways in which people from these groups treated one another when they met on Virginia's coastal plain in the seventeenth century. Shoemaker's own discussion of Kateri Tekakwitha's enthusiastic conversion to Christianity suggested that it is important to look at the range of possible choices that individuals encountered during these periods of tremendous social upheaval. In her most recent work on Cherokee women, Theda Perdue also challenged the simplicities of a declension model of native women's experience, that is, that all native women's lives became uniformly worse with the arrival of Europeans. The diversity of native women's experiences is also evident in a recent volume of profiles of Native American women edited by Perdue.

Other scholars have analyzed native women's roles in New England, where historians have long been resistant to embracing multicultural perspectives. Elaine Breslaw examined Tituba's role in the Salem witchcraft drama at the end of the seventeenth century, suggesting that she may have been Indian rather than African and exploring the significance of that identity in the context of new histories of the Atlantic world. Expanding on earlier articles, in her recent book Ann Marie Plane has focused on Indian marriages in New England, arguing that these relationships reflect major struggles within colonial societies.

In Martha Hodes's collection, *Sex, Love, Race* (1999), which opens with Nash's "Hidden History," scholars have investigated a range of interethnic and interracial relationships across time and across the North American continent. Daniel Mandell explored eighteenth-century marriage between native women and African American men in New England. Here, he brought forth the range of possible motivations behind an Indian woman's consecutive marriages to two men of African descent and concludes that there was never one singular reason behind such choices. In the same volume, Richard Godbeer pointed to sexual relations between Indian women and English men as important elements of the southern colonial frontier. He, too, suggested the significance of a range of choice and motivation for women as he found both forced and willing sex, both stable and fleeting relationships.

In addition to new work on Anglo-America, scholarship on women's experience of colonial contact in Spanish and French regions has expanded. In 1996, James F. Brooks further complicated the colonial story in New Mexico by looking at how the Spanish–Indian trade in human captives affected women during the eighteenth and early nineteenth centuries. As the Spanish Mexicans moved north, they captured people to turn them into laborers, convert them to Christianity, and make them subjects of New Spain. Here Brooks has suggested that women could be "victims" whose lives were ruptured by their initial capture, but it was through this same process that they became valuable as cultural mediators. In his analysis, many women eventually gained power and respect for themselves and their children in the new environments.

In her 1999 dissertation, Juliana Barr looked to the importance of gender in the multiple conquests of Texas by the Apaches, Comanches, and Wichitas, as well as the French and the Spanish. There was little common ground to link these disparate groups, but they all organized themselves according to constructions of both masculine and feminine behavior. It was by paying attention to these cultural markers that they tried to understand one another on a contested terrain where no single group ever held complete power over the others.

Natalie Zemon Davis also stretched the existing canvas by tracing the life of a French woman, Marie de l'Incarnation, who left her young son and became an Ursuline nun. She then headed to North America where, officially, she led a spiritual life of humility within the confines of a closed community. Yet it is clear from Davis's analysis that this woman was an active member of a culturally mixed community. When she became the first Mother Superior of the Ursulines in Quebec, she formed a school where Native American and French girls were educated together. Through her fine-grained narrative, Davis has uncovered the significance of one French woman's contribution as a cultural mediator in early North America.

For the Great Lakes region, Susan Sleeper-Smith expanded Richard White's model of the "middle ground" by focusing on women as "negotiators of change." In doing so, she has challenged both Karen Anderson and Carol Devens's notion that Catholicism caused a subversion of female authority in native communities. Sleeper-Smith looked to the ways that Jesuit recruitment of native women as religious teachers or "catechizers" within their own communities acted in concert with the importance of kinship, rather than nation, within certain societies to form a strong "Catholic kin network" that hinged on the participation of these women. She also stressed the fact that European fur traders were incorporated into native communities when they married native women. These unions usually benefited traders in their quest for furs, and benefited native women in that they often gained authority among their own people; these women did not become outsiders. Thus, Sleeper-Smith found that the Jesuit presence contributed to the centrality of women in the middle grounds of the Great Lakes region during the eighteenth century.

Some recently published anthologies reach beyond earlier collections that simply catalogued the multi-ethnic character of early America. These newer works instead have stressed interethnic relationships and at their best explore how and why people during the seventeenth and eighteenth centuries crossed social boundaries. *The Devil's Lane* (1997), a collection edited by Catherine Clinton and Michele Gillespie, focused on race and gender in the early South and included essays relating to women's complex interactions among European, African, and Indian peoples. Merrill D. Smith's *Sex and Sexuality in Early America* (1998) began with a section entitled "European/Native American Contact, 1492–1710." Martha Hodes's *Sex, Love, Race*, in addition to the articles mentioned above, includes a piece by Jennifer Spear on métissage in colonial Louisiana. Other anthologies, such as *Writing the Range* (1997), edited by Elizabeth Jameson and Susan Armitage, have pointed to the particularities of women's cultural crossings in the American West. *Contact Points* (1998), edited by Andrew Cayton and Fredrika Teute, included articles centering on gender and colonial contact along frontiers east of the Mississippi during the early national period.

The fact that these collections include interethnic colonial contact after 1760 illustrates the point that for many people living on the peripheries of native-European settlement, whether Indian, European, African, or any combination of the three, the American War for Independence and the founding of the United States did not end the period of European colonialism. Historical work that focuses on later periods of contact and conquest benefits from more plentiful sources. And unlike scholars of New England, those examining the West may face less resistance to a multicultural palette; multi-ethnic marriages and cultural mixing have long been recognized as part of the myth of the American frontier. From the earliest written histories, stories of wild, unpolished European newcomers marrying and living near or with Indians complemented the more stolid histories of the original English colonies first written by those who sought to "civilize" and "tame" the American landscape. In addition, native people survived in far greater numbers in the West, a region which also attracted Spaniards, Mexicans, Chinese, Japanese, African Americans, Anglo-Americans, and other European immigrants. Studies on women in this region, including many that reach into the nineteenth century, thus remain central to the field of colonial women's studies more generally.

All of the works mentioned above have reinvigorated our understanding of early North American communities. What is striking about many of these works, however, is their refusal to look beyond the geographical boundaries of their subject. Recently Ann Stoler has suggested the possibilities presented to American historians if they look toward the "tense and tender ties" of colonialism in other parts of the world. Some scholars have indeed realized Kathleen Brown's suggestion that New World "gender frontiers" need to be explored in "connection with the European gender roles that influenced the demographics of migration" (1993: 321). It seems equally important that historians with an interest in colonial interaction engage more directly with scholarship that addresses other regions of North America.

When we cast a narrow net, focusing only on specific locales, the stereotypes of an earlier historiography often cloud our vision. For instance, the "Black Legend" of the Spanish conquest never seems to be completely forgotten in American historiography and brutality toward Indian women has, until recently, been discussed more extensively for the Southwest and Alta California than for any other region. Similarly, stereotypes such as the "equitable" treatment of Native Americans by the French, the benevolence of Puritans, and the contrasting "savagery" of the Pequot and other New England Indians are beginning to be questioned in the broader historiography. The problem of stereotypes is one which greater attention to women's involvement in mixed colonial societies can help redress. Alberto Hurtado's assertion that "the middle ground was fraught with possibilities and perils that ranged from the familiar comforts of family life to violent death" is crucial to our understanding of colonial societies (in Jameson and Armitage 1997: 137). As Hurtado indicates, comparison of different layers of middle grounds is crucial. If scholars continue to expand their explorations of the comfortable contours of Spanish, French, and English colonization in North America in light of the untold stories about women and contact in less familiar regions, then perhaps we will be better able to understand the wide range of women's experiences.

Some possibilities might include consideration of relationships between Native Americans and Europeans in or around Dutch, German, or Swedish settlements, which were not always firmly attached to colonial governments. My own work addresses mixed marriages in the Alaskan Russian fur trade. The story of European and native interaction in Alaska is, in many ways, a recognizable one to scholars of colonial North America. It raises questions about adaptation to unfamiliar environments, the discovery and exploitation of natural resources, the nature of relationships between indigenous peoples and colonizing Europeans, the role of the imperial state in moderating those relations, and the introduction of Christianity. However, colonization in Alaska is also historically specific. The indigenous people are distinct from other aboriginal people on the continent, and the colonizing regime is Russian. From the time of Peter the Great (1682–1725), Russia had been trying to make sense of its economic, political, cultural, and geographic location between Western Europe and Asia. In addition, when Russian expansion moved outward from Kiev, and eventually crossed the Pacific, it moved from West to East, not from East to West. Perhaps by looking at sites of colonial contact that challenge conventional narratives of westward movement in North America we can more easily step outside the bounds of a framework that perpetuates stereotypes of both European and native men and women. Russian America represents only one vantage point from which to rethink ungendered conventions that have pervaded the historiography of North America.

Whatever its chronological and geographical scope, the early period of North American women's history is critical in setting the stage for understanding American society in the nineteenth, twentieth, and twenty-first centuries. To ignore the density and diversity of this complicated early history, to focus only on the East, and to fast forward to the mid-nineteenth century as the first significant era for American women, is to ignore the history of the continent as a whole and the early participation of people from divergent cultural backgrounds in shaping the way we live and interact today.

BIBLIOGRAPHY

Anderson, Karen (1991) *Chain Her By One Foot: The Subjugation of Native Women in Seventeenth-century New France*. New York: Routledge.

Barr, Juliana (1999) "The 'Seductions' of Texas: The Political Language of Gender in the Conquests of Texas, 1690–1803," Ph.D. dissertation, University of Wisconsin-Madison.

Brasseaux, Carl A. (1986) "The Moral Climate of French Colonial Louisiana," *Louisiana History* 27, pp. 27–41.

Braund, Kathleen E. Holland (1990) "Custodians of Tradition and Handmaidens to Change: Women's Role in Creek Economic and Social Life During the Eighteenth Century," *American Indian Quarterly* 14, pp. 239–58.

Breslaw, Elaine G. (1996) *Tituba, Reluctant Witch of Salem: Devilish Indians and Puritan Fantasies*. New York: New York University Press.

Brooks, James F. (1996) "'This Evil Extends Especially... To the Feminine Sex': Negotiating Captivity in the New Mexico Borderlands," *Feminist Studies* 22, pp. 279–309.

Brown, Jennifer S. H. (1980) *Strangers in Blood: Fur Trade Company Families in Indian Country.* Norman: University of Oklahoma Press.

Brown, Judith K. (1975) "Iroquois Women: An Ethnohistoric Note," in Rayna R. Reiter (ed.), *Toward an Anthropology of Women.* New York: Monthly Review Press, pp. 235–51.

Brown, Kathleen M. (1993) "Brave New Worlds: Women's and Gender History," *William and Mary Quarterly* 50, pp. 311–28.

Brown, Kathleen M. (1996) *Good Wives, Nasty Wenches, and Anxious Patriarchs: Gender, Race, and Power in Colonial Virginia.* Chapel Hill: University of North Carolina Press.

Castañeda, Antonia (1996) "Women of Color and the Rewriting of Western History: The Discourses, Politics and Decolonization of History," *Pacific Historical Review* 61, pp. 501–33.

Cayton, Andrew L. and Teute, Fredrika J. (eds.) (1998) *Contact Points: American Frontiers from the Mohawk Valley to the Mississippi, 1750–1830.* Chapel Hill: University of North Carolina Press.

Clinton, Catherine and Gillespie, Michele (eds.) (1997) *The Devil's Lane: Sex and Race in the Early South.* New York: Oxford University Press.

Davis, Natalie Zemon (1995) *Women on the Margins: Three Seventeenth-century Lives.* Cambridge, MA: Harvard University Press.

Demos, John (1994) *The Unredeemed Captive: A Family Story from Early America.* New York: Alfred A. Knopf.

Devens, Carol (1992) *Countering Colonization: Native Women and Great Lakes Missions, 1630–1900.* Berkeley: University of California Press.

Etienne, Mona and Leacock, Eleanor (eds.) (1980) *Women and Colonization: Anthropological Perspectives.* New York: Praeger.

Faragher, John Mack (1988) "The Custom of the Country: Cross-cultural Marriage in the Far Western Fur Trade," in Vicki Ruíz, Janice Monk, and Lillian Schlissel (eds.), *Western Women: Their Land, Their Lives.* Albuquerque: University of New Mexico Press, pp. 199–215.

Fischer, Kirsten (2002) *Suspect Relations: Sex, Race, and Resistance in Colonial North Carolina.* Ithaca, NY: Cornell University Press.

Foreman, Carolyn T. (1943) *Indians Abroad, 1493–1938.* Norman: University of Oklahoma Press.

Green, Rayna (1980) "Native American Women," *Signs* 6, pp. 248–67.

Gutiérrez, Ramón A. (1991) *When Jesus Came, the Corn Mothers Went Away: Marriage, Sexuality, and Power in New Mexico, 1500–1846.* Stanford, CA: Stanford University Press.

Hansen, Karen (1989) *Distant Companions: Servants and Employers in Zambia, 1900–1985.* Ithaca, NY: Cornell University Press.

Harkin, Michael and Kan, Sergei (eds.) (1996) "Native Women's Responses to Christianity," Special Issue, *Ethnohistory* 43.

Hodes, Martha M. (ed.) (1999) *Sex, Love, Race: Crossing Boundaries in North American History.* New York: New York University Press.

Jameson, Elizabeth and Armitage, Susan (eds.) (1997) *Writing the Range: Race, Class and Culture in the Women's West.* Norman: University of Oklahoma Press.

Jensen, Joan M. and Miller, Darlis A. (eds.) (1986) *New Mexico Women: Intercultural Perspectives.* Albuquerque: University of New Mexico Press.

Karttunen, Frances (1994) *Between Worlds: Interpreters, Guides, and Survivors.* New Brunswick, NJ: Rutgers University Press.

Kidwell, Clara Sue (1992) "Indian Women as Cultural Mediators," *Ethnohistory* 39, pp. 97–107.

McCartney, Martha W. (1989) "Cockacoeske, Queen of the Pamunkey: Diplomat and Suzeraine," in Peter H. Wood, Gregory Waselkov, and M. Thomas Hatley (eds.), *Powhatan's Mantle: Indians in the Colonial Southeast*. Lincoln: University of Nebraska Press, pp. 173–95.

Morgan, Jennifer L. (1997) "'Some Could Suckle Over Their Shoulder': Male Travelers, Female Bodies, and the Gendering of Racial Ideology, 1500–1770," *William and Mary Quarterly*, 3rd ser., 54, pp. 167–92.

Mozumbdar, Chandana (1995) "The Role of Mixed Bloods among the Southeastern Indians during the Colonial Period," *New England Journal of History* 51, pp. 2–9.

Namias, June (1993) *White Captives: Gender and Ethnicity on the American Frontier*. Chapel Hill: University of North Carolina Press.

Nash, Gary B. (1995) "The Hidden History of Mestizo America," *Journal of American History* 82, pp. 941–64.

Parmenter, Jon (1999) "Isabel Montour: Cultural Broker on the Frontiers of New York and Pennsylvania," in Ian K. Steele and Nancy L. Rhoden (eds.), *The Human Tradition in Colonial America*. Wilmington, DE: Scholarly Resources, pp. 141–59.

Perdue, Theda (1997) "Pocahontas Meets Columbus in the American South," *Southern Cultures* 3, pp. 4–21.

Perdue, Theda (1998) *Cherokee Women: Gender and Culture Change, 1700–1835*. Lincoln: University of Nebraska Press.

Perdue, Theda (ed.) (2001) *Sifters: Native American Women's Lives*. New York: Oxford University Press.

Peterson, Jacqueline (1985) "Many Roads to Red River: Métis Genesis in the Great Lakes Region, 1680–1815," in Jacqueline Peterson and Jennifer S. H. Brown (eds.), *The New Peoples: Being and Becoming Métis in North America*. Lincoln: University of Nebraska Press.

Plane, Ann Marie (2000) *Colonial Intimacies: Indian Marriage in Early New England*. Ithaca, NY: Cornell University Press.

Pratt, Mary Louise (1992) *Imperial Eyes: Travel Writing and Transculturation*. New York: Routledge.

Richter, Daniel K. (1983) "Whose Indian History?" *William and Mary Quarterly* 50, 3rd ser., pp. 379–93.

Ruíz, Vicki and DuBois, Ellen (eds.) (2000) *Unequal Sisters: A Multicultural Reader in U.S. Women's History*, 3rd ed. New York: Routledge.

Shoemaker, Nancy (ed.) (1995) *Negotiators of Change: Historical Perspectives on Native American Women*. New York: Routledge.

Silverblatt, Irene (1987) *Moon, Sun, and Witches: Gender Ideologies and Class in Inca and Colonial Peru*. Princeton, NJ: Princeton University Press.

Sleeper-Smith, Susan (2000) "Women, Kin, and Catholicism: New Perspectives on the Fur Trade," *Ethnohistory* 47, pp. 423–52.

Slotkin, Richard (1973) *Regeneration through Violence: The Mythology of the American Frontier, 1600–1860*. Middletown, CT: Wesleyan University Press.

Smith, Merrill D. (ed.) (1998) *Sex and Sexuality in Early America*. New York: New York University Press.

Smith-Rosenberg, Carroll (1993) "Captured Subjects/ Savage Others: Violently Engendering the New American," *Gender and History* 5, pp. 177–95.

Smits, David D. (1987) "'We Are Not To Grow Wild': Seventeenth-century New England's Repudiation of Anglo-Indian Intermarriage," *American Indian Culture and Research Journal* 11, pp. 1–31.

Spear, Jennifer Michel (1999) "'Whiteness and the Purity of Blood': Race, Sexuality, and Social Order in Colonial Louisiana," Ph.D. dissertation, University of Minnesota.

Stoler, Ann L. (2001) "Tense and Tender Ties: Intimacies of Empire in North American History and (Post)Colonial Studies," *Journal of American History* 88, pp. 829–65.

Tanner, Helen H. (1979) "Coocoochee: Mohawk Medicine Woman," *American Indian Culture and Research Journal*, 3, pp. 23–41.

Van Kirk, Sylvia (1980) *Many Tender Ties: Women in Fur Trade Society, 1670–1870.* Norman: University of Oklahoma Press.

White, Richard (1991) *The Middle Ground: Indians, Empires, and Republics in the Great Lakes Region, 1650–1815.* New York: Cambridge University Press.

Chapter Four

Building Colonies, Defining Families

Ann M. Little

MARRIAGE, family life, and especially motherhood are intensely political issues today, given the inflammatory rhetoric and pitched battles over abortion rights, day care, "deadbeat dads," working mothers vs. stay-at-home mothers, school vouchers, sex education, and family leave policies. People of all political leanings and ideological camps are obsessed with the relationship between the family and the state, relationships within families, and questions of authority and power in both kinds of relationships. The messiness of colonial family history and its complex relationship with feminist scholarship no doubt reflects the contested relationship between feminism and family life today.

Colonial family history's uneasy relationship with feminism is due in part to the fact that modern scholarship preceded the second-wave feminist movement and the birth of women's history. The field is further divided by the fact that feminist scholars sometimes differ greatly among themselves in their portrayals of colonial family life. For these reasons, it is difficult to present a seamless summary of colonial family history, divided as it is philosophically by historians who emphasize consensus and continuity in the family, and those whose scholarship highlights conflict. Scholarship on colonial families is also divided methodologically between historical demographers and number-crunching social historians, on the one hand, and legal scholars and cultural historians who put more emphasis on qualitative sources, on the other. Furthermore, not all of these differences among historians fall neatly into ideological categories: some women's historians are also consensus historians, and historians who see more conflict in colonial families are not necessarily feminist scholars.

For the purposes of imposing some kind of order on the historiography of colonial families, this essay divides the field into two groups: consensus and feminist family history. Consensus family historians generally assume that colonial European American families were broadly functional, and that they successfully played the role of a great number of social institutions in the primitive wilderness of America. They recognize the hierarchies of sex, age, and status that defined colonial family life, but argue (or at least imply) that these hierarchies were broadly accepted by all family members and that they therefore bred stability and imposed an effective orderliness in colonial households. Where conflict appears, it comes from outside the family.

Consensus historians usually locate conflict between the family and the state or between the family and economic, religious, or cultural forces. Feminist family historians, most of whom were trained in women's history, recognize the same hierarchies within the colonial family as the consensus camp. However, they challenge the notion that these hierarchies were cheerfully accepted by all members, and suspect instead that they bred resentment and conflict not just among women, but among other household dependents like children, servants, and slaves. Feminist historians also tend to believe that political and family history are deeply intertwined. They recognize that sometimes the family and the state were at odds, but generally their work demonstrates how household government and state power reflected and reinforced each other in the colonial period.

Consensus Family History

Through the first half of the twentieth century, colonial families were for the most part ignored by professional historians and left to genealogists and antiquarians, many of whom were women. Some of the best of these researchers, like the prolific Alice Morse Earle, wrote about the social history of colonial America for a general readership. Her books have been reprinted for modern readers as recently as the 1990s, as they are still rich sources of reliable information on the material culture and household and family life of the English colonies.

In 1944, the publication of Edmund Morgan's *The Puritan Family* signaled the beginning of the academy's interest in the history of colonial families. Morgan recognized the political analogy of the family and the state and identified gender complementarity and hierarchy as central to family life in colonial America. But, he argues, the duty to fulfill one's role in the family was balanced by love. Morgan portrays the Puritan family as harmonious and functional, arguing that it was perhaps the strongest institution in early New England and ultimately undercut the purity of New England's religious mission. This is what Morgan calls Puritan Tribalism: faced with a second and third generation that did not share the founding generation's religious zeal, Puritan love and loyalty to their families led them to accept compromise measures like the Half Way Covenant, which extended church affiliation to the children of church members without their having to seek formal church membership. Morgan's thesis provided a neat social historical explanation for the "declension" of the Puritan mission described by Perry Miller in his analysis of Puritan intellectual and political life. Thus, "when theology became the handmaid of genealogy, Puritanism no longer deserved its name" (Morgan 1966: 186). This consensus view – casting all conflict outside of the colonial family, and portraying it as a unit that served to advance the needs of all members – remains influential to this day.

Interest in family history grew slowly over the next two decades, but a provocative essay by Bernard Bailyn in 1960 inspired a generation of young scholars to take the family seriously as a subject for historical inquiry. He argued (along the lines of the Morgan study) that the adaptations Europeans made to adjust to the demands of the frontier resulted in new family forms, and that these new families were central to the process of modernization. In the 1960s and 1970s, American scholars borrowed enthusiastically the research strategies and techniques of analysis advanced by the French *Annales* school and the historical demographers of the Cambridge Group. These scholars, notably Philippe Ariès and Peter Laslett, demonstrated how historians could make use of sources like tax lists, census data, vital records, and marriage and baptismal records to create collective portraits of family and village life among the lower orders of European society.

Morgan's consensus view was still powerfully influential on the generation of historians writing in the late 1960s through the 1980s. Like Morgan, they saw the colonial family as seventeenth-century ministers and magistrates did: as an organic entity represented by a male head of household, one characterized by shared goals and the purposeful strivings of husbands and wives, parents and children, masters and servants. By naturalizing the hierarchies of gender, age, status, and race, these historians minimized conflict within the family. Their research in court records, family papers, and church records was inventive and thorough, and they pushed beyond the borders of Puritan New England to investigate families throughout colonial America. Furthermore, their case studies and arguments set the terms of many of the debates that are still central to family history today.

In *A Little Commonwealth* (1970), John Demos grounds his analysis of family life in seventeenth-century Plymouth colony in the intimate houses and primitive material culture shared by the early English families who settled there. He carefully considers the effects of the life cycle on family dynamics, arguing that the Puritan family successfully negotiated the passages fraught with potential danger – adolescence and marriage for children and the decline into old age for parents – and that conflict within families even at these crisis points was minimal. On the one hand, it is clear that in Demos's view the strict hierarchy of the family is what makes it such a sturdy institution: it serves as a business, a school, a site of vocational instruction, of religious teaching, and of penal correction. According to Demos, this hierarchy does not necessarily translate into the arbitrary or abusive exercise of power. Because he finds little evidence of spousal or child abuse in the written record, he argues that "this does *not* seem to have been a society characterized by a really pervasive, and operational, norm of male dominance" (1970: 95).

Nearly twenty-five years later, Demos's view of the colonial family is unchanged. In the dramatic and thoroughly researched *The Unredeemed Captive* (1994), he tells the story of the family of the Reverend John Williams, rent by the 1704 attack by French-allied Indians on their Deerfield, Massachusetts, home during Queen Anne's War. Here we have a family literally under attack, besieged by wholly external forces. Those family members who were not immediately killed were taken into Indian captivity: Williams's wife died, and his five remaining children were dispersed among different groups of Indians, but all family members were eventually ransomed to the French and redeemed by the English except for daughter Eunice. This "unredeemed captive" of the book's title is adopted by a band of Catholic Indians, marries an Indian man, and chooses to remain with her new family despite her father's entreaties. Demos's account puts Reverend Williams at the center of this family ordeal, detailing his ultimately futile attempts to bring daughter Eunice back to New England and Puritanism, and his heartbreak at his failure. The lesson of Demos's book is the endurance of family ties against the enemies of war, cultural, religious, and language differences, and time itself. In his narrative, the father's disappointment is salved somewhat by his son Stephen's renewed correspondence with the lost sister; throughout, he portrays the loss of Eunice as a fundamentally emotional loss to John and Stephen Williams, rather than a loss of patriarchal or fraternal control over a daughter and a sister. The experience of the Williams family was surprisingly common on the early New England frontier, although most "captivated" English girls took French rather than Indian husbands. Moreover, most families were disgusted by their daughters' and sisters' multiple conversions – to the French language and law, to Indian ways, and to Catholicism – and when they failed to reclaim the girls, they disinherited and disowned them.

Historians of other regions of colonial America outside of strongly patriarchal Puritan New England are even more insistent about the consensus interpretation of family history. Barry J. Levy's *Quakers and the American Family* (1988) is a dense and wide-ranging history of Quaker families, from their origins in a poor region of seventeenth-century England to their grandchildren's and great-grandchildren's prosperous farms and towns in eighteenth-century Pennsylvania. Quakers, he argues, created the first truly child-centered families in America, as their theology rejected the harsh doctrine of original sin and instead cast children as innocent vessels of the inner light in need of protection from the corruptions of the world. Yet like Morgan, Levy notes that a conflict arose between the demands of their religious beliefs and the demands of their child-centered family life. He argues that the Quaker emphasis on endogamy (marriage within the Quaker meeting) worked to punish less well-off families who could not give their children large marriage portions. Less well-off children were then less competitive on the Quaker marriage market and were thus forced to marry outside of the meeting. Levy suggests that it was only economic circumstances that drove Quaker children to insult their parents who were so devoted to their spiritual and economic well-being; Levy sees neither adolescent resentment, individual initiative, nor simple bloody-mindedness at work in these families, and casts all conflict outside of the family. Unlike Morgan's Puritans, however, Levy argues that the Quakers chose doctrinal purity and thus demographic and political marginalization over family solidarity and the preservation of their worldly influence – a choice that was sure to create conflict within families, even if it was not driven by it.

Similarly, Daniel Blake Smith argues that harmonious relations between the sexes and the generations characterized family life on eighteenth-century Chesapeake plantations. He excludes the enslaved families on these plantations and focuses on the elite, white families, a choice that surely makes it easier to present a consensus point of view. In any case, Smith is less interested in family structure than he is in the "family experience": the "personal values, beliefs, and emotions given expression in the daily life of the family, the 'emotional texture' of the household" (1980: 18). He argues that the vestiges of traditional patriarchy that shaped white family life on plantations in the first half of the eighteenth century melted away by mid-century, when families became increasingly affectionate, child-centered, and supportive of children's autonomy. Smith details the strongly gendered aspects of the southern family, arguing that mothers by and large were responsible for raising daughters, while fathers took charge of their sons' education in manhood at an early stage. With this, he suggests that the emotional "separate spheres" identified with bourgeois Victorian family life emerged much earlier among elite southern families.

Despite the dominion of the consensus school of family history in the 1960s and 1970s, one notable scholar of the period charted and analyzed conflict. Philip J. Greven, Jr.'s *Four Generations*, published in 1970, outlines a theory of patriarchy based on his research in seventeenth- and eighteenth-century Andover, Massachusetts. Greven's vision of colonial family life is characterized by the exercise of paternal power apparently unmediated by tenderness and love, and unmindful of the interests or needs of the other members of the family. Unlike the stern but loving (or even indulgent) fathers of the consensus school, who gave their sons their marriage portions when they wanted to marry, Greven's first-generation settlers lived to advanced old ages and held onto their land. This meant that they preserved their patriarchal privileges and delayed their sons' marriages and independence as long as possible. Only when Andover fathers ran out of local land and were unable to satisfy the needs of their sons to establish their own household and farms did their patriarchal control loosen. Forced to look westward to find land, the third and fourth generations enjoyed greater autonomy than their fathers. Since Greven concerns himself only with how patriarchy structured relationships among men, his description of its workings is rather narrow. He is wholly unconcerned, for example, with the wives and daughters caught in the struggle for control between fathers and sons – women whose lives were presumably shaped by this conflict.

In his subsequent work, *The Protestant Temperament: Patterns of Child-rearing, Religious Experience, and the Self in Early America* (1977), Greven suggests that his findings for Andover might be regionally and culturally contingent. He identifies three strands of denominational "temperament" and argues that the key to understanding the persistence of these three habits of mind is found in the distinctive attitudes and beliefs about childrearing found in three subcultures. First, Greven describes the Evangelicals as "dominated by a persistent and virtually inescapable hostility to the self and all its manifestations" (1977: 12). Comprised for the most part of seventeenth-century New England Puritans (like his first- and second-generation Andover residents) and eighteenth-century revivalists, Evangelical parents were devoted to breaking the individual wills of their children. The Moderates, eighteenth-century New England Congregationalists and middle colony Quakers, were concerned for the most part with self-control, "preoccupied with virtue and morality, keeping themselves within fairly narrow boundaries of feeling and behavior" (1977: 14). Accordingly, they attempted to instill this moderation in their children, helping them hew to the path of both duty and love. Finally, the Genteel sensibility was the province of colonial elites of all regions, but perhaps most particularly of wealthy southern slaveholding families. Pride and self-confidence were not sins as they were among the Evangelicals, but the ultimate virtues; children were indulged, encouraged even in their willfulness. "Self-assertion rather than self-control or self-suppression was to be the central theme of many of their lives" (1977: 14).

Greven's research is clearly exhaustive, and he does a convincing job of linking religious beliefs and ideas about the self to the practice of parenthood, but once again his analysis of colonial family life is more useful for explaining the interaction of fathers and sons. After all, the denial of the self expected by Evangelical parents of their children sounds much like the denial of the self expected of all daughters, whatever their region or class or denominational background. For daughters who would (for the most part) never vote or own property, "self-control" and "self-assertion" must be understood in a completely different context from the meanings these values had for sons. While Greven devotes some pages to noting and explaining the gendered expectations parents had for their children, it is clear that he believes the experience of sons is paramount because of their roles as ministers, political leaders, and interpreters of the culture.

New Feminist Scholarship

In the 1970s and 1980s, feminist historians began publishing articles and monographs that challenged the consensus view of family history and all family histories that excluded serious consideration of women and girls. Scholars trained in women's history were understandably skeptical that the patriarchal nuclear family was a unit that served the best interests of all members. They examined the family hierarchy, noting that it was hardly designed to tolerate dissent. Moreover, "household government" was not just custom, but was detailed and enforced by the power of law. The English common law tradition of coverture used in the Anglo-American colonies operated according to the legal fiction that there was only one person in a marriage – the husband – and that as the male head of household, he represented the legal, political, and economic interests of the entire family. Not only wives, but children, servants, and slaves were considered people "under household government," and they had no legal or political standing of their own and only very limited economic rights. The head of household also enjoyed broad liberties to discipline household members, including the use of corporal punishment. Besides critically examining the family hierarchy, feminist scholars also challenged the consensus view by noting that the family was the site at which women's opportunities in particular were determined. Marital status was after all a crucial variable in women's lives: the laws of coverture allowed only unmarried adult women (or *femes soles* according to the common law designation) to own property, conduct business, and appear in court in their own names. A married women was designated *feme covert*, and thus all of her property and wealth was held in the name of her husband.

Accordingly, the work of legal historians has been particularly valuable for setting the terms of feminist analysis of the family. In her careful and detailed study, *Women and the Law of Property in Early America* (1986), Marylynn Salmon charts regional variation within the broadly shared legacy of the common law in America. Puritan New England made more changes from English traditions than other regions, allowing for the possibility of divorce but increasing men's power over their wives' property through changes in the law on conveyancing, dower, and marriage settlements. Massachusetts, Connecticut, and Quaker Pennsylvania also eliminated chancery courts, a decision Salmon calls "the most radical legal change instituted by some of the American colonies." Chancery courts administered trust estates, "the vehicle under which wives owned property separately from their husbands." Thus, "the presence or absence of an equity court virtually determined a colony's position on female separate estates" (1986: 11). By contrast, New York, Maryland, Virginia, and South Carolina preserved chancery and "developed a body of law allowing femes coverts to own separate property. Over time, the degree of independence granted to women in these jurisdictions increased" (1986: 185).

The work of historical demographers was also vitally important for evaluating women's roles and opportunities in colonial families, especially in the southern colonies for which few qualitative primary sources have survived. Following up on Bailyn's thesis in the 1970s, women's historians noted that the stresses the American frontier put on European families presented a chance to learn about the challenges and opportunities available to European American women in America. Was the family more patriarchal, or less so? Did women have greater opportunities for social advancement, like some of their male counterparts? The answers they arrived at varied according to region and period. Lois Carr and Lorena Walsh argued in "The Planter's Wife" (1974) that first-generation women were presented with great opportunities for social and economic advancement, if they survived the rigors of the trans-Atlantic crossing and the ardors of seventeenth-century Chesapeake servitude and seasoning. Contrary to the consensus view of the colonial family, Carr and Walsh portray the family as a rare and fragile institution. Unlike French and Spanish men in North America, English men displayed a strong antipathy to marrying native women. Thus with English women in scarce supply, coupled with high mortality rates due to disease and malnutrition, marriages were hard to come by and short-lived, and the lives of the children born of these unions were even more fragile. But the weak family form in the early Chesapeake presented opportunities for strong English women: because of their low numbers, first-generation women had a high value on the Maryland marriage market, and frequently could marry up the social ladder. The granddaughters of the founders appear to have fulfilled more traditional expectations of women's conduct. As the sex ratio balanced out in the third generation, these women appear to have lost the opportunities for social mobility and property ownership that their grandmothers had. Walsh along with Darrett and Anita Rutman considered the effects of this kind of fractured family life for children; they did not interpret it as potentially liberating for children as it was for some women. They argue that childhood in the seventeenth-century Chesapeake cannot be understood apart from the sad fact that few parents would see their children into adulthood, and that single parenthood and step-parentage were normal, not exceptional.

Scholars of early modern European families informed the views of colonial American historians and pointed to new directions that emphasized the connection between politics and the family. Susan Amussen's *An Ordered Society* argues that because "the family served as a metaphor for the state" in early modern England, historians must interrogate the consequences of these intertwining kinds of authority (1988: 1). Both class and gender hierarchies were built into the family and the state, and they mirrored and reinforced each other. In times of crisis like the English Civil War and Revolution, the family's role in maintaining the social order was of greater importance; after the Restoration, Amussen argues that the analogy between the family and the state began to weaken because the family's importance in maintaining order had declined. Similarly, Lyndal Roper argues that families are seen as key to upholding the social order in tumultuous times in Reformation Augsburg. She asks a question common to Reformation scholars: "How did this revolutionary Evangelicalism become transformed into the consoling, socially conservative pieties of Protestant guildsfolk?" But Roper provides a new answer: first, "the moral ethic of the urban Reformation, both as a religious credo and a social movement, must be understood as a theology of gender" (1989: 1). Women's behavior in particular came under fanatical scrutiny in sixteenth-century Augsburg, notably their sexual behavior both inside and outside of marriage and their activities on behalf of household craft workshops. The Reformation was therefore "domesticated – as it closed convents and encouraged nuns to marry, as it lauded the married state exemplified by the craft couple, and as it execrated the prostitute – so it was accomplished through a politics of reinscribing women within the family" (1989: 3).

In the last ten years, colonial feminist historians have written at length about the mirroring of state and family hierarchies. In an important essay, Carole Shammas proposes that "the formal power structure within households is one of the main elements linking the political development of colonial Anglo-America with that of the United States" (1995: 106). This provides a useful concept for early American historians who teach unwieldy US survey courses that begin with Columbus and end at Appomatox Courthouse, and who want to marry the rich family history scholarship of the last forty years to the traditional political narrative that structures most survey textbooks. But this is a difficult task. She argues that contrary to the traditional political narrative of increasing freedom, "household government most likely expanded over the colonial period" (1995: 120). After early challenges to traditional patriarchal authority on the seventeenth-century frontier like those noted by Chesapeake scholars above, Shammas points to the expansion of both indentured servitude and slavery and the continued existence of coverture. She argues that neither the American Revolution nor the Market Revolution alone deserve the credit (or the blame) for the weakening of traditional patriarchal powers in household government that eventually led to the abolition of both slavery and coverture. She suggests that the opening of western lands and nonagricultural employment, combined with a "weak lineage system" that gave fathers no legal control over their children once they reached the age of majority, meant that adolescents and young people could and did exercise greater autonomy in the nineteenth century. Family history must be considered alongside the traditional political and economic explanations for historical change, she argues, since excluding "patriarchal household government from the political history of the colonial and early national periods leaves out most of the political relationships of the population" (1995: 143).

Mary Beth Norton's *Founding Mothers and Fathers* (1996) also argues that seventeenth-century colonial families both reflected and shaped colonial politics. Her comparative study of New England and the Chesapeake argues that these regions "developed diverse modes of political and judicial behavior as a result of demographic and religious differences" (1996: 12). The traditional English analogy between the family and the state worked well in strongly patriarchal New England, with its family-based migration patterns and demographic stability. However, the Chesapeake regions' servant-based migration, high male-to-female sex ratio within the English population and high mortality rates meant that "the family could not serve as a model for the state – or vice versa – because families were too truncated, anomalous, and unstable by English standards." Contrary to the view that the roots of the democratic republic are found in the Mayflower Compact and in New England town meetings, Norton argues that it was in Maryland and Virginia that "the overwhelmingly numerically dominant men quickly became culturally dominant, and in which the idea of consensual male political interaction assumed a prominence hitherto unknown." Thus, the Chesapeake was a "practical laboratory for the dichotomous theory of authority years before Locke systematically formulated his ideas" (1996: 13–14).

Other historians have explored the relationship between the family and state power and have concluded that women in particular were vulnerable to its intrusions. Although *A Search for Power: The "Weaker Sex" in Seventeenth-century New England* (1980) focuses more on women than families, Lyle Koehler argues that the contradictory cultural expectations of colonial women led almost inevitably to a great deal of family and community conflict. While he does not argue that women like Anne Hutchinson were typical, he gives ample evidence that mundane conflicts like marital breakdown and more spectacular social eruptions like witchcraft accusations and heresy trials must be seen along a continuum as they were all sparked by women who seemed to refuse to fulfill their expected family roles as submissive "goodwives" and mothers. Similarly, Carol Karlsen argues in *The Devil in the Shape of a Woman* (1987) that women's families and their roles within them were crucial variables in determining which women were accused of *maleficium*. Whatever their marital status, women over forty were more vulnerable to witchcraft accusations than women of childbearing age, and widows and never-married women were more vulnerable than their married sisters safely enclosed by the laws of coverture. Perhaps most importantly, Karlsen's research demonstrates that the variable that made women most vulnerable to witchcraft accusations had nothing whatsoever to do with their own behavior or position within their communities, but with inheritance laws. Women without brothers or sons who inherited their families' estates or stood to inherit them blocked the "orderly transmission of property from one generation of males to another" that coverture was designed to protect (1987: 116).

Recently, legal scholars have also begun to show how the law operated in the lives of everyday women, and how their marital status, family life, and position and reputation in their communities further shaped their experiences in colonial courtrooms. Apparently, even if colonial women escaped infamy as accused witches or heretics and played the role of goodwives, they still lost ground with the state over the course of the colonial period. In *Women Before the Bar*, Cornelia Hughes Dayton argues that women's standing before the law declined in eighteenth-century Connecticut as the courtroom changed from "an inclusive forum representative of community to a rationalized institution serving the interests of commercially active men" (1995: 13). Where once *femes soles* had been able to represent themselves in civil cases, the rise of credit networks that excluded women made them marginal to the litigated economy; where once women and men had both been held accountable for fornication and bastardy, eighteenth-century juries and justices were increasingly interested in prosecuting only the women; and where once women's testimony in court had been valued, their words were deemed less reliable at the close of the colonial period.

Feminist scholars' emphasis on the connections between the family and the state led them to question the place of servants and slaves in the family. Borrowing the pioneering scholarship and methodologies of ethnohistory and African American studies, feminist family historians are creating a new historiography on native and African families and their creole descendents. This new scholarship of the 1980s and 1990s argues that for Indians and African Americans, the family was the site of both accommodation and resistance to the insults and pressures of life in a New World characterized by increasingly rigid racial hierarchies. Kathleen Brown illustrates the vast differences between English and native gender roles and family life, and argues that it was a major element in English disdain for the Indians. While we know a great deal about English reactions to Indian ways, we know very little about the ways in which native families adapted to European exploration and settlement, and to the ravages of the ensuing disease and warfare, which were responsible for killing up to 90 percent of the native population of the Americas. Such a demographic disaster was surely devastating to many, if not most, Indian cultures, but historians suggest that the survival of some groups was due to a successful renegotiation of family life. In *Colonial Intimacies: Indian Marriage in Early New England* (2000), Ann Marie Plane argues that Algonquian families in the praying towns of southeastern New England adopted the different expectations of marriage in English culture, religion, and law, and that this reformation of marriage was key to the survival of Indians in this region where the English population overwhelmingly outnumbered the natives.

We know much less about the Indian families who refused to participate in missionary efforts or who lived much farther from areas intensively settled by Europeans. However, we do know that these families were central to the practice of taking and keeping English captives, whether the captives were eventually adopted into their new families, or whether they were taken as prisoners of war meant to be quickly redeemed for cash. Captivity narratives of English people, although written by those who eventually returned to English society, portray English family life as fragile and native families as powerful entities. While these are highly ideological texts, they are very valuable primary sources for learning more about the strategies of the majority of Indian families who resisted conversion and co-optation by the English.

Allan Kulikoff also puts family life at the center of *Tobacco and Slaves* (1986), which locates the emergence of a distinctive African American culture with the creation of stable black families in the mid-eighteenth-century Chesapeake. Ironically, the factors that strengthened the grip of slavery in the colonial South were the same ones that made black family life possible: only when creole slaves outnumbered Africans, and larger plantations requiring the use of large slave populations appeared, did enslaved Virginians and Marylanders have the kind of demographic and environmental conditions necessary for the creation of a reasonably stable family life. However, the evidence is equivocal as to whether or not families made slaves more docile or more prone to run away. Many enslaved on large plantations had a spouse and children living with them, which might have made them more cautious about rebelling or running away. On the other hand, many men and women had family scattered across several plantations; some historians believe that slaves whose families were dispersed might have been more motivated to attempt family reunification by running away.

Feminist scholarship on slavery argues for the central importance of African and African American women both to their families and to the invention of American slavery. In *Good Wives, Nasty Wenches, and Anxious Patriarchs* (1996), Kathleen Brown argues that the hierarchies of gender and status that characterized the seventeenth-century English family were instrumental to the construction and elaboration of racial hierarchies in colonial Virginia. Through her detailed analysis of the evolution of slavery in the law, she examines how the shifting terrain of gender ideology became the means by which racial hierarchies were first imagined and then implemented. Hierarchies of gender and class in the seventeenth century changed to incorporate race as Virginia's labor force shifted from being composed mostly of indentured servants to being composed of enslaved Africans. Where once only class distinctions among women were necessary to tell the "good wives" from the "nasty wenches," the use of African labor created "a racial opposition in which women of English descent embodied the privileges and virtues of womanhood while women of African descent shouldered the burden of its inherently evil, sexual lust" (1996: 2). Brown argues that the bodies of African women were central to this process, as were the interracial families to which they gave birth. Making the identity of children either enslaved or free dependent on the status of their mothers, as Virginia did in 1662, reversed centuries of common law tradition that identified children legally with their fathers. But it accomplished two important things: first, the law helped the colony resolve the difficult problem of how to define its mixed-race children, as most interracial children were the offspring of English fathers and African mothers. Second, it helped establish slavery as a permanent and heritable condition.

Other feminist historians have revealed that colonial families were not just figuratively but sometimes literally of one blood, and have recently begun to consider the questions of interracial sex and family life. Annette Gordon-Reed's *Thomas Jefferson and Sally Hemings* (1997) is not only an analysis of eighteenth- and early nineteenth-century master–slave relationships, but also a compelling exploration of the reasons why nineteenth- and twentieth-century Americans have worked so concertedly to deny the possibility of interracial liaisons at Monticello. The colonial essays in Martha Hodes's *Sex, Love, Race: Crossing Boundaries in North American History* (1999) reach beyond the white master–black slave dynamic, and document the existence of several different family mixtures of Europeans, Africans, and Indians and the social consequences they faced. These scholars agree that the position of these families became increasingly precarious in colonial America. In *Suspect Relations: Sex, Race, and Resistance in Colonial North Carolina* (2002), Kirsten Fischer shows how sexual relationships among and between Anglo-Americans, African Americans, and Native Americans contributed to developing eighteenth-century notions of racial difference. By examining sexual slander among whites, acts of sexualized violence against slaves, and interracial liaisons, Fischer illustrates the increasing politicization of interracial sex and mixed-race families. Over the course of the eighteenth century, as indeterminate ideas about race melded with older notions of gender and class to form a fully biological notion of race, sexual relations became an arena in which people tested and contested these changing ideas.

While marriage and childrearing are understandably central to both consensus and feminist family history, some women's historians remind us that most women spent a portion of their lives as unmarried adults, and that many women never married. In *Not All Wives* (2000), Karin Wulf demonstrates that single women were an important presence in colonial cities. She argues that understanding their experiences outside of marriage and motherhood is crucial to understanding the possibilities and limitations of the lives of colonial women. "Examining the construction of the unmarried woman as marginal can also be highly revealing" because of colonial America's intertwined anxieties about financial and sexual independence for women. Because of the taint of sexual promiscuity attached to women's employment, unmarried women had few options for making a living; most toiled in poverty, and many were ironically forced into sex work. "Thus the woman outside the normative experience of marriage and domesticity faced both an ideological injunction against her existence as well as the practical problems created by that ideology" (2000: 7–8).

Beyond the fragile, shifting borders of English settlement, the ethnic, cultural, legal, and linguistic differences among other American colonial projects created different family histories. Like Wulf, historians of the French and Dutch colonies also remind us that European American family life cannot be entirely understood in the context of coverture. Married women in New Netherland had equal rights of property ownership, according to the tradition of Roman-Dutch law that descended from the Justinian Code. Women could retain their own name after marriage, own real and personal property, own and operate a business or engage in trade without a husband's permission or signature, and sue or be sued in court. In *Women and Property in Colonial New York* (1983), Linda Briggs Biemer argues that women's opportunities declined predictably upon the English conquest and imposition of English law beginning in 1674. David E. Narrett's *Inheritance and Family Life in Colonial New York City* (1992) bears out this thesis with a richer supply of evidence. Narrett also argues that while married women and widows felt the cold grip of patriarchal control in post-conquest New York in ways their Dutch mothers and grandmothers had not, the privatization of family life and child welfare in the eighteenth century served to increase the power and autonomy of widows with dependent children. He argues that the practice of fathers appointing legal guardians for children in their wills ended by 1730, and widows thus had greater power and autonomy for managing their own household affairs. Narrett also demonstrates that New York fathers increasingly granted their children equal portions over the course of the eighteenth century, arguing that this reflects the rise of the child-centered modern family.

The experience of women in New France was even more varied, as Jan Noel argues in *Women in New France* (1998). Native women intermarried much more frequently with French men than in the Dutch or English colonies, becoming the mothers of

Métis families and culture; the sex ratio of French men and women remained imbalanced much longer than in other colonies, putting the value of a French wife at a premium; and many women came to New France not to be wives and mothers, but as brides of Christ to labor as his *dévotes* in the wilderness. Those who did marry earthbound husbands had the advantages of the *Coutume de Paris*, which distinguished itself from the English common law by stipulating that husbands and wives owned marital property equally (except for wealth in land owned by either partner prior to marriage). Although husbands were designated "masters of the community," neither husbands nor wives could sell, mortgage, or alienate their joint property without the written consent of the other. Furthermore, French men had no power to use inheritance law to influence their families as the *Coutume* dictated the disposition of their estates. Upon the death of either spouse, the widow or widower inherited half of all real and personal property, as well as half the debts; the other half of the property and debts went to the children, but widows with minor children had the liberty of managing their children's portions as they saw fit.

While in general women's historians have challenged the stories of benevolent patriarchs told by the consensus school, not all of them take issue with the consensus model for understanding colonial families. Laurel Thatcher Ulrich's vision of colonial family life, for instance, owes much to Edmund Morgan, as she argues that the system of complementary duties for men and women instilled orderliness in most households. Ulrich disagrees that women's history is the "recital of disadvantage and subjection which some historians have made it," as "the notion of male supremacy must not be wrenched from the larger concept of an organic social order in which rights and responsibilities were reciprocal" (1982: 8). Her vision of colonial families is admirably complex, and her analysis of women's lives tries to take account of the sometimes overlapping and contradictory demands of "discrete duties" that cannot be neatly tucked into "a self-consistent and all-embracing 'sphere'" (1982: 8). Her representation of colonial womanhood is nothing short of heroic: Ulrich's subjects struggle mightily to reconcile the many challenges of huswifry, motherhood, community life, and in the case of Martha Ballard, her professional calling as a midwife. But Ulrich seems reluctant to address the conflicts that inevitably arose among these many responsibilities to family and community. For example, when the midwife Martha Ballard was in her seventies, her husband Ephraim was imprisoned for debt at age seventy-nine because of his failures as a tax collector; their impulsive, troublesome son Jonathan exploited his mother's vulnerability and moved his family into her house, relegating her to a single room which she was sometimes forced to heat with wood she gathered and chopped herself. Despite her years of service, she received little assistance from either family or community in the seventeen months of Ephraim's imprisonment. Yet Ulrich describes her in the last years of her life as finding "an eye of peace in a heroic commitment to her neighbors and in a passionate, almost lyrical devotion to the small patch of earth for which she was responsible" (1990: 308).

Similarly, in her study of manhood in New England, Lisa Wilson argues that the family was equally central to men's identities as it was to women's in the colonial period. She explicitly rejects the approach of scholars who analyze power relations, arguing that "men appear in this literature as one-dimensional power brokers rather than flesh and blood people with complex and contested relationships. Studying power does not allow for a nuanced portrait of colonial manhood" (1999: 2). Instead, she uses Ulrich's *Goodwives* "as a model in part to provide opportunity for [the] comparison" of men's and women's domestic roles and responsibilities (1999: 4). Men's lives were structured around these common concerns: finding a "serviceable" profession or calling, courting and marrying a suitable wife, creating a loving marriage and family life, and warding off the specter of dependence in old age. Because she relies almost entirely on her subjects' own words in letters and diaries, she acknowledges that her sources are heavily biased toward elite eighteenth-century urbanites – educated men, political leaders, merchants, and ministers – men who were in fact at the top of colonial society. Wilson paints these men as feeling vulnerable and frequently insecure in their roles in their families and the wider world despite the fact that their authority was supported and enforced by the laws they administered, the religion they preached and promulgated, and the culture they produced.

A Revolution in the Family?

Predictably, feminist and consensus family historians differ greatly in their interpretation of the American Revolution. Consensus historians like Melvin Yazawa in *From Colonies to Commonwealth* (1985) have argued that the American revolt against its father the king and the mother country was necessarily antipatriarchal. Feminist historians have questioned this assumption, pointing to the continued existence of slavery and coverture well after the Revolution. After Carole Pateman, Shammas suggests that the "late eighteenth-century republican revolutions established no more than a fraternal patriarchy of white adult men who spread power more equally among themselves but did little to bring equality to others" (1995: 128–9). As Linda Kerber argues in *Women of the Republic: Intellect and Ideology in Revolutionary America* (1980), questions about women's role as citizens of the new republic were widely discussed and debated, but in the end women were excluded rhetorically and politically from the Jeffersonian declaration that "all men are created equal." Their roles as mothers took on increasing importance, but Kerber describes this Republican Motherhood as something of a booby prize: women found creative ways to express themselves as citizens and patriots, but they became the leaders of the domestic sphere only after men had vacated the position for the greater prestige and public influence of the world of politics and commerce. As Jacqueline Jones has shown, the lives of African American women saw even less change in the wake of the Revolution. Few of them were freed with the abolition of slavery from Pennsylvania northward, so the majority of African American women found their motherhood forcibly enlisted as the slave republic expanded into the new cotton fields of the Old Southwest.

If the Revolution had any consequences on the fates of those under household government, it was the flexibility of its Jeffersonian rhetorical flourish that "all men are created equal." Adopted and reinterpreted by abolitionists, feminists, and civil rights workers in the nineteenth and twentieth centuries, their struggles ended slavery and coveture, secured political and legal equality for all adults, and extended a greater measure of constitutional protection to children. But many questions about the just balance of power between men and women, between parents and children, and between the family and the state remain unanswered today. These concerns will doubtless continue to shape the scholarship of family historians, and the best of this scholarship should inform the political and cultural debates of the twenty-first century.

BIBLIOGRAPHY

Amussen, Susan D. (1988) *An Ordered Society: Gender and Class in Early Modern England.* Oxford: Oxford University Press.

Ariès, Philippe (1962) *Centuries of Childhood: A Social History of Family Life*, trans. Robert Baldick. London: Cape. (Originally published as *L'Enfant et la vie familiale sous l'ancien régime*, Paris: Plon, 1960.)

Bailyn, Bernard (1960) *Education in the Forming of American Society: Needs and Opportunities for Study.* Chapel Hill: University of North Carolina Press.

Biemer, Linda Briggs (1983) *Women and Property in Colonial New York: The Transition from Dutch to English Law, 1643–1727.* Ann Arbor, MI: UMI Research Press.

Brown, Kathleen M. (1995) "The Anglo-Algonquian Gender Frontier," in Nancy Shoemaker (ed.), *Negotiators of Change: Historical Perspectives on Native American Women.* New York: Routledge.

Brown, Kathleen M. (1996) *Good Wives, Nasty Wenches, and Anxious Patriarchs: Gender, Race, and Power in Colonial Virginia.* Chapel Hill: University of North Carolina Press.

Carr, Lois G. and Walsh, Lorena S. (1974) "The Planter's Wife: The Experience of White Women in Seventeenth-century Maryland," *William and Mary Quarterly* 34, pp. 542–71.

Dayton, Cornelia Hughes (1995) *Women Before the Bar: Gender, Law, and Society in Connecticut, 1639–1789.* Chapel Hill: University of North Carolina Press.

Demos, John (1970) *A Little Commonwealth: Family Life in Plymouth Colony.* New York: Oxford University Press.

Demos, John (1994) *The Unredeemed Captive: A Family Story from Early America.* New York: Alfred A. Knopf.

Earle, Alice Morse (1898) *Home Life in Colonial Days.* New York: Macmillan. Rpt. (1989), Williamstown: Corner House.

Earle, Alice Morse (1899) *Child Life in Colonial Days.* New York: Macmillan. Rpt. (1993), Stockbridge: Berkshire House.

Fischer, Kirsten (2002) *Suspect Relations: Sex, Race, and Resistance in Colonial North Carolina.* Ithaca, NY: Cornell University Press.

Gordon-Reed, Annette (1997) *Thomas Jefferson and Sally Hemings: An American Controversy.* Charlottesville: University Press of Virginia.

Greven, Jr., Philip J. (1970) *Four Generations: Population, Land, and Family in Colonial Andover, Massachusetts.* Ithaca, NY: Cornell University Press.

Greven, Jr., Philip J. (1977) *The Protestant Temperament: Patterns of Child-rearing, Religious Experience, and the Self in Early America.* New York: Alfred A. Knopf.

Hodes, Martha M. (ed.) (1999) *Sex, Love, Race: Crossing Boundaries in North American History.* New York: New York University Press.

Jones, Jacqueline (1989) "Race, Sex, and Self-evident Truths: The Status of Slave Women during the Era of the American Revolution," in Ronald Hoffman and Peter J. Albert (eds.), *Women in the American Revolution.* Charlottesville: University Press of Virginia.

Karlsen, Carol (1987) *The Devil in the Shape of a Woman: Witchcraft in Colonial New England.* New York: W. W. Norton.

Kerber, Linda (1980) *Women of the Republic: Intellect and Ideology in Revolutionary America.* Chapel Hill: University of North Carolina Press.

Koehler, Lyle (1980) *A Search for Power: The "Weaker Sex" in Seventeenth-century New England.* Urbana: University of Illinois Press.

Kulikoff, Allan (1986) *Tobacco and Slaves: The Development of Southern Cultures in the Chesapeake, 1680–1800.* Chapel Hill: University of North Carolina Press.

Laslett, Peter (1965) *The World We Have Lost: England Before the Industrial Age.* New York: Charles Scribner's Sons.

Levy, Barry J. (1988) *Quakers and the American Family: British Settlement in the Delaware Valley.* New York and Oxford: Oxford University Press.

Little, Ann M. (n.d.) "Abraham in Arms: Gender and Power on the New England Frontier, 1620–1760," manuscript in progress.

Morgan, Edmund (1944) *The Puritan Family: Religion and Domestic Relations in Seventeenth-century New England.* Boston: Trustees of the Public Library. Rpt. (1966), New York: Harper and Row.

Narrett, David E. (1992) *Inheritance and Family Life in Colonial New York City.* Ithaca, NY: Cornell University Press.

Noel, Jan (1998) *Women in New France.* Ottowa: Canadian Historical Association.

Norton, Mary Beth (1996) *Founding Mothers and Fathers: Gendered Power and the Forming of American Society.* New York: Alfred A. Knopf.

Pateman, Carole (1988) *The Sexual Contract.* Stanford, CA: Stanford University Press.

Plane, Ann Marie (2000) *Colonial Intimacies: Indian Marriage in Early New England.* Ithaca, NY: Cornell University Press.

Roper, Lyndal (1989) *The Holy Household: Women and Morals in Reformation Augsburg.* Oxford and New York: Oxford University Press.

Rutman, Darrett B. and Rutman, Anita H. (1979) "Now-wives and Sons-in-law: Parental Death in a Seventeenth-century Virginia County," in Thad W. Tate and David L. Ammerman (eds.), *The Chesapeake in the Seventeenth Century: Essays on Anglo-American Society.* Chapel Hill: University of North Carolina Press, pp. 153–82.

Salmon, Marylynn (1986) *Women and the Law of Property in Early America.* Chapel Hill: University of North Carolina Press.

Shammas, Carole (1995) "Anglo-American Household Government in Comparative Perspective," *William and Mary Quarterly* 52, pp. 104–44.

Smith, Daniel Blake (1980) *Inside the Great House: Planter Family Life in Eighteenth-century Chesapeake Society.* Ithaca, NY: Cornell University Press.

Ulrich, Laurel Thatcher (1982) *Goodwives: Image and Reality in the Lives of Women in Northern New England, 1650–1750.* New York: Alfred A. Knopf.

Ulrich, Laurel Thatcher (1990) *A Midwife's Tale: The Life of Martha Ballard, Based on Her Diary, 1785–1812.* New York: Alfred A. Knopf.

Walsh, Lorena S. (1979) "'Till Death Us Do Part': Marriage and Family in Seventeenth-century Maryland," in Thad W. Tate and David L. Ammerman (eds.), *The Chesapeake in the Seventeenth Century: Essays on Anglo-American Society.* Chapel Hill: University of North Carolina Press, pp. 126–52.

Wilson, Lisa (1999) *Ye Heart of a Man: The Domestic Life of Men in Colonial New England.* New Haven, CT: Yale University Press.
Wulf, Karin A. (2000) *Not All Wives: Women of Colonial Philadelphia.* Ithaca, NY: Cornell University Press.
Yazawa, Melvin (1985) *From Colonies to Commonwealth: Familial Ideology and the Beginnings of the American Republic.* Baltimore: Johns Hopkins University Press.

Chapter Five

Sinners and Saints: Women and Religion in Colonial America

Susan Juster

"WOMEN are in churches, saints: abroad, angels: at home, devils: at windows, sirens: at doors, magpies: and in gardens, goats" (Mack 1992: 24). This early modern proverb sums up an image of women that shaped Anglo-American religious beliefs and practices on both sides of the Atlantic in the seventeenth and eighteenth centuries. The image of woman as changeling – capable of transforming from saint to sinner with frightening ease – captures an essential truth about the spiritual universe of colonial American women, consigned as they were by science and theology to the nether side of a series of oppositions that pitted reason against emotion, culture against nature, order against disorder, male against female. Our most familiar stories of colonial women – Anne Hutchinson matching biblical verse with biblical verse with the magistrates of Puritan Massachusetts in 1637; Mary Dyer giving birth to a deformed fetus after being whipped by the Puritan authorities for her unauthorized preaching; Rebecca Nurse swinging from the end of the hangman's noose in Salem in 1692 – are tales of heroic piety or of monstrous depravity, of women whose spiritual powers both awed and frightened the colonial authorities.

It is no accident that colonial women's history has been dominated by the twin images of the saint and the witch, for these represent the poles of an ideological continuum along which the many ordinary women of the period were arrayed. Whether as saints or witches, women were believed to have exceptional spiritual power: the power to merge in ecstatic union with Christ or in diabolical union with Satan. Both forms of supernatural connection derived from an image of the female body as especially porous and open to external influences, as easily invaded and conquered by beings of stronger will. The prevailing medical paradigm of the early modern period, the humoral, described women as "wet and spongy" creatures who absorbed the effluvia of the external world through their various orifices and expelled its waste through periodic bleeding and other female secretions. The language of fluids and their movements shaped women's spiritual as well as biological lives, as grace flowed through the veins of holy women while Satan and his familiars sucked blood from the teats of suspected witches.

The metaphors that early modern people used to describe the feeling of being caught up in God's embrace drew upon the humoral model; saints spoke of being "saturated" by the Spirit, of being "inebriated" with the love of God and of being filled to the brim with passion and desire. Men and women both spoke this language – the seventeenth-century Puritan divine Edward Taylor, for example, wrote stunningly erotic poetry that celebrated the metaphorical marriage of blood and wine enacted in the Lord's Supper as a paradigm of spiritual renewal. But women, with their "spongy" bodies and strong passions, were considered (and considered themselves to be) peculiarly open to the Spirit's gifts.

There was, however, a thin line separating ecstasy from disease in the early modern understanding of the humoral body. Any imbalance in the humors was cause for alarm: health (spiritual and physical) was a matter of maintaining a delicate balance within the body and between the body and its environment. The more open the body, the more prone to disease and disorder. And the prime spiritual ailment with which early modern women were afflicted was religious enthusiasm, understood as a rush of passion overwhelming the critical faculties and even the body itself. By the late seventeenth century, religious fanaticism was considered one disease among a larger species of disorder whose origins were fundamentally physiological, that is, rooted in the unstable constitution of the female body and its humors. While the full pathologization of extreme religious behavior would await the medical and cultural revolutions of the Victorian era, seventeenth- and eighteenth-century Anglo-Americans placed religious sensibility in the domain of nerve physiology where it was subject to connotations of mental illness and social debility.

Frequently overwhelmed by their bodies' insatiable desires and weak defenses, early modern women fell prey to a variety of spiritual and nervous maladies as they progressed through life's different stages. They entered into catatonic states where they saw visions of a bleeding Christ, they spoke with angels and other celestial messengers, they fell to the ground in convulsive fits when overpowered by the spirit of God, and some – a tragic few – allowed the devil to enter their bodies.

Women and the Devil

One thing most students know about colonial America is that women were overwhelmingly the victims of witchcraft prosecutions: some 80 percent of all those accused, and some 90 percent of those executed between 1647 and 1692, were women. And, almost without exception, those who were possessed by the devil (with or without their consent) were also women, often young girls. The "devil in the shape of a woman" was a familiar presence in colonial New England, and not only when communities organized to rid themselves of cantankerous old women who muttered strange curses under their breath when mistreated or ignored. The more we have delved into the rich trial records left by witchcraft prosecutions, the more we have come to appreciate the degree to which the witch's vices were those of women writ large. With their "hot tongues" that seared the reputations of godly neighbors and their abrasive personalities, witches reminded the colonial authorities of other women who transgressed social and gender norms: the scold, the gossip, the beggar, the hag. As the work of Carol Karlsen, Jane Kamensky, and John Demos has shown in convincing detail, witchcraft prosecutions (despite their relative infrequency) belong in the realm of the ordinary rather than the exceptional, consisting in most cases of ordinary women performing unremarkable acts in everyday situations. Elizabeth Godman was suspected because she could uncannily detect the figs hidden in her neighbor's pocket; Eunice Cole grumbled her way into court by complaining about the quality of the bread she received from the local poor relief. The element that transformed the ordinary into the tragic was an elusive combination of personal and collective frustration, some alchemical transformation of normal feelings of envy, resentment, anger, and fear into a lethal expression of judicial revenge.

Women themselves understood there was a thin line separating the witch from the ordinary sinner, as they struggled with feelings of innate depravity that led some, at least, to confess to diabolical acts. Elizabeth Reis's most recent contribution to the large literature on colonial witchcraft offers the most disturbing account yet of the sinister association of diabolism with ordinary female capacities and failings, as she traces the theological and psychological roots of witchcraft confessions back to the Puritan association of women with evil – in its ordinary as well as extraordinary manifestations. Puritan women, Reis argues, took to heart what their ministers told them about the ubiquity of female depravity. Tormented by feelings of guilt and inadequacy that afflicted all Puritans to some degree, women were especially vulnerable to suggestions from the pulpit that Satan was attracted by their unstable souls. The theological association of the soul with the female qualities of porosity and insatiability underwrote the intimate association of women with evil that had first received concrete expression in Eve's fatal bargain with Satan in the Garden of Eden. Thus when Alice Lake was about to be hanged in 1651 for witchcraft, she believed she deserved to die even though she "owned nothing of the crime laid to her charge" because "she had when a single woman play'd the harlot, and being with Child used means to destroy the fruit of her body to conceal her sin and shame" (Reis 1997: 125).

Satan haunted the dreams of many colonial women, even those unsuspected of practicing witchcraft. The visceral presence of the devil in women's accounts of their spiritual trials is one of the most striking features of colonial religious memoirs. Hannah Heaton, an eighteenth-century Connecticut farm woman, was tormented regularly by the devil as she embarked on a lifelong quest for religious assurance. Satan "whispered" in her ear, "twitch[ed]" her clothes, and enticed her to commit the unpardonable sin of suicide. Susanna Anthony, another Great Awakening convert, despaired that "satan seemed to have had full power of me . . . I seemed as one really possessed of the devil" (Juster 1994: 60–1).

Colonial men, too, recorded visits by Satan and his agents, but the devil was more an allegorical than a real presence in their spiritual dramas. The relative immunity of men from witchcraft accusations has something to do with their greater invulnerability to Satan and his stratagems that less sensational records reveal. Whether tormented privately in their own spiritual imaginations or more visibly in the public confrontations that gave rise to witchcraft accusations, women were believed to have a special relationship with the devil that was at the root of colonial constructions of female disorder.

Colonists inherited a mixed bag of theological, legal, medical, and cultural attitudes toward women that they fashioned into a flexible and relatively consistent ideology of female depravity (or, rather, of women's greater *susceptibility* to depravity, for like all reformed Protestants, Anglo-American colonists insisted that sin was an act of individual will). What is somewhat surprising about this ideology is its rejection of a biblically based notion of women's inherent evil. It was Puritan divines, in fact, Carol Karlsen tells us, who "mounted the most cogent, most sustained and most enduring attack on the contemporary wisdom concerning women's inherent evil" – even while they were busy ferreting out suspected witches and hanging those whom they believed to have made a pact with the devil (Karlsen 1987: 161). Even if a deeply misogynistic strain of popular belief is still evident in the daily lives and trials of many colonial women, on the level of official discourse, at least, colonial authorities (especially, but not only, in New England) firmly rejected a belief in women's *inherent* or *inherited* evil in favor of a more contingent and instrumental view of sin. Reflecting the evolution of legal and theological discourse away from models of human accountability that stressed generational inheritance ("the sins of the father") toward one which stressed individual initiative and responsibility, colonial magistrates and ministers were less interested in tracing blame back through the centuries than in locating it in the here and now.

Just as New England's magistrates refused to blame Eve for the sinning women in their midst, so, too, did magistrates in Virginia and Maryland find traditional concepts like the "scold" and the "gossip" (and traditional methods of detection and punishment like the ducking stool) less useful in policing unruly women in the early Chesapeake. Historians have spent a lot of energy trying to document the survival of cultural practices associated with the early modern European tradition of popular protest, including compelling models of female disorderliness, in colonial America, and for the most part they have come up empty. Almost no charivaris were recorded in early American communities, the language of insult and counter-insult was thin and unimaginative in comparison, and rituals of shaming and mocking do not seem to have been elaborately developed. Traces of these traditions can be found in colonial trial records of neighborly altercations and domestic disputes, to be sure, but there does not seem to have been a wholesale transplantation of the *cultural system* of early modern misogyny whose roots lie in biblical tales of women's disobedience and aggressive sexuality.

Sin was more an individual act than a cultural tradition, in other words, in colonial America. As such, its history lies in the evolution of historically specific modes of subjectivity and accountability in the early modern era: in the creation of an autonomous, self-knowing, and self-regulating subject whose public apotheosis would come in the democratic revolutions of the late eighteenth century. Habits of communal responsibility and regulation certainly ran deep in colonial America, as settlers struggled to forge new communities in a strange and hostile environment, but they did not in and of themselves constitute a coherent juridical or intellectual system. This retreat from the collective to the individual, what we might call the retreat from typology, had paradoxical consequences for colonial women who, on the one hand, were protected from the worst excesses of early modern popular misogyny and, on the other hand, left to face alone the consequences of their misbehavior without the exculpatory veil of tradition.

We can perhaps see this evolution in attitudes most clearly in the prosecution of slander in the colonies. Slander, along with gossiping, was a peculiarly female vice in early modern England – as, apparently, it was in the colonies. The anthropological literature on slander would suggest that the proclivity to speak disparagingly about one's neighbors was, paradoxically, a function of social power and political marginality; denied access to more legitimate forums for expressing grievances and securing compensation, yet fully embedded in social networks, the disfranchised turn to rumor-mongering as a way to exert informal power within the community. Like another prototypically female crime, fornication, slander was believed to originate in women's inability to contain their naturally hot and moist temperaments. The language used to describe both offenses betrays a common etymology – "hot" words flung in anger resembled nothing so much as the heat of lust. "Heated" speech (the seventeenth-century term for profanity, insults, curses, and other forms of angry speech) was, as the phrase suggests, passionate speech. It was often – literally – sexual speech, or speech about sex, but whatever its content, "heated" speech invariably invoked the dangers of sex to colonial Americans who frequently compared the tongue with that other unruly "member" – the genitalia. "There is the tongue and another member of the body," the famed eighteenth-century evangelist Jonathan Edwards wrote in his private journal, "that have a natural bridle, which is to signify to us the peculiar need we have to bridle and restrain those two members" (Greven 1977: 129).

Colonial American women seemed to have a special knack for "heated" speech. When the Virginia assembly outlawed slander in 1662, they did so because "many brabling women often slander and scandalize their neighbours for which their poore husbands are often brought into chargeable and vexatious suits" (Wall 1990: 46–7). Mary Beth Norton's and Kathleen Brown's studies of the seventeenth-century Chesapeake, Cornelia Hughes Dayton's of eighteenth-century Connecticut, and Helena Wall's survey of the entire colonial era have all shown that women were disproportionately accused of slander by colonial authorities. The resort to hot words was a dangerous gambit – slanderers were as likely to be burned as their unfortunate victims, as the colonial courts were filled with angry plaintiffs trying (often with success) to redeem their reputations. And in some cases women paid the ultimate price for their inability to control their tongues. Jane Kamensky notes the powerful association between "heated" speech and witchcraft. Accused witches, like other discontented women, spoke in "tongues of fire" rather than "tongues of silver." They cursed their neighbors, threatened retribution when crossed, "muttered" and grumbled when dissatisfied, whispered evil words in a cold fury, and generally spoke in ways unbecoming a Puritan goodwife. Indeed, Kamensky goes so far as to suggest that the threat posed by witches was predominantly a linguistic one, for "*what they said came true*" – milk spoiled, cows died, children sickened, all because of the words spoken in anger by the witch (Kamensky 1997: 152–4).

On closer examination, however, the association of women with slander breaks down – or, rather, assumes different shape from what we might expect. In those regions where colonial authorities were most "traditional" in outlook and authority (namely, the Chesapeake and the Carolinas), women were indeed disproportionately accused of slander. But the total number of cases in these communities was small in comparison with English legal custom, and largely inconsequential in the structuring of private and public life. In those regions where notions of individual accountability were most developed (that is, in the Puritan colonies and in Quaker Pennsylvania), women were *not* more likely to find themselves accused of slander. For every woman who appeared as a defendant in a defamation suit in Essex County, Massachusetts, in the years 1640 to 1680, for instance, there were ten men. Slander was every bit as worrisome to nervous Puritan and Quaker magistrates as it was to their Anglican counterparts, but not for the same reasons. When Puritan ministers encountered women who ridiculed their authority, they did not see the ever-present shadow of Eve but the far more urgent problem of subversion. Given women's public invisibility and political impotence, subversion was almost always a male problem, not a female one. More importantly, it was an act of individual defiance, not a mark of an underlying moral or spiritual corruption.

By the eighteenth century, fears of women's "hot" tongues and overheated passions had assumed a more explicitly sexualized form. Seventeenth-century malcontents like Anne Hutchinson "seduced" their weaker neighbors with their "fluent" tongues and grasping minds. Hutchinson's neighbor, the proud and quarrelsome Ann Hibbens, was hanged in 1656 for, in the words of one disgusted magistrate, "having more wit than her neighbors" (Karlsen 1987: 28). Their eighteenth-century counterparts were more likely to be accused of seducing others through their bodies. The sexualization of female nature was the product of several historical trends: the devaluing of female intellectual capacity in the Enlightenment search for a controlling rationality, the decriminalization of fornication for colonial men and the emergence of a sexual double standard in legal practice, the flowering of Pietism with its erotic spiritual economy in the mid-eighteenth century, the consumer revolution of the early eighteenth century in which women's material preferences, rhetorically figured as sexual desire, played a central role, and the creation of a vigorous urban culture centered on the pursuit of pleasure in heterosocial venues.

Critics of the new commercial order betrayed a fascination with women's desires, linking sexual passion to economic expansion and cultural innovation in a single chain of pernicious female influence. The image of the "consuming" woman, immoderate in her desires, emboldened in her reckless pursuit of luxury and pleasure, and unrestrained by obligations of caste or taste, came to exert a powerful cultural influence on both sides of the Atlantic in the eighteenth century. And sex, more than avarice or ambition, lay at the heart of the consuming woman's power and, hence, her danger.

Court and church records also reveal a growing association of women with the dangers of unrestrained sexuality over the course of the eighteenth century. We can perhaps see this most clearly in the records of the dissenting congregations. New England Baptists, for example, displayed a remarkable indifference to sins of the flesh (whether committed by men or women) in the early years of their existence. In sharp contrast to the vigor with which they persecuted sins of the tongue, sexual disorder went largely undetected and unpunished in the years before 1780. Less than 1 percent of the total Baptist membership was excluded in the years 1730 to 1780 for fornication and adultery, a ratio greatly at variance with the demographic reality of steadily rising premarital pregnancy rates that historians have documented for the period. One church, in fact, found to its dismay that a member had actively encouraged her daughter's adulterous behavior. "Our sister," it reported, "had from time to time Knowingly allowed her daughter Ester being a married woman to keep Company with a man who was not her husband" (Juster 1994: 103). Significantly, women who did find themselves premaritally pregnant were more apt to be excluded for lying about their condition than for fornication. Time and again, the evangelical churches made it clear that members who transgressed the verbal codes of the community would pay a higher price than those who had merely indulged their personal desires, however illicit. Sex, in other words, was not yet a problem for the community – only for the individual.

This lax attitude changed rather abruptly in the late eighteenth century, as church records began to be filled with charges of sexual misconduct, leveled almost exclusively at women. And, more significantly, such misconduct was now more likely to be described as a habitual moral failing rather than as a singular lapse of judgment. Women who had sex before marriage or who entertained men at inappropriate times in their homes were accused of sexual "incontinence," a character flaw, rather than "fornication" or "adultery," a specific act. When Betsey March was accused in 1809 of "an unusual fondness for a married man," the church excluded her from membership because it had "lost [its] confidence in her" (Juster 1994: 155). By the end of the century women were being disowned simply for the catch-all offense of "disorderly walking," a loose category that included everything from sexual incontinence to intemperance to frivolity. The message was clear: women were not to be trusted, and the source of this inconstancy of character was their inability or unwillingness to restrain their passions.

Women and the Spirit

Women's spiritual virtuosity, which enabled them to see and converse with God more easily than their male co-religionists, was the flip side of their special talent for evil. If women's hot words could land them in court or on the scaffold, they could also broach the incomparable divide separating humans from God.

Female visionaries have a long and distinguished history in the annals of colonial religion: Lady Deborah Moody, who was excommunicated by the Salem church for rejecting infant baptism; Sarah Keayne, disciplined for "irregular prophesying in mixt Assemblies"; Anne Eaton, the unhappy wife of the governor of New Haven who was banned from the church in 1644 for lying and stubbornness; Mary Dyer, hanged for defying the ban on Quaker preaching in 1659; and, of course, Anne Hutchinson, whose famous banishment in 1637 and later death at the hand of marauding Indians served as a cautionary tale for generations of colonial women. Hutchinson's paradigmatic status as an icon of female disorder derives as much from her claims to have received direct revelations from God as from her assumption of a pastoral and theological authority unbefitting her sex. Marilyn Westerkamp's reading of the

Antinomian crisis highlights the deep-seated ambivalence of the Puritan authorities to women's mystical powers as one explanation for the harshness of their response. According to modern Puritan scholars, Hutchinson sealed her own fate when she declared, in the face of aggressive questioning by a panel of renowned ministers, that her knowledge of God's will came from "an immediate revelation ... By the voice of his own spirit to my soul" (Hall 1968: 336–7). In banishing Hutchinson and her followers from their midst, and later zealously persecuting the Quaker missionaries who arrived from England in the 1650s fired with the same mystical fervor, the Puritan authorities tried to seal off the direct channel between the Spirit and female visionaries that had proved so troublesome in the early decades of the colony's existence. Mary Maples Dunn's survey of Puritan church records after the Antinomian crisis shows just how successful the ministers were in silencing the "spirit of prophesying," as women were no longer allowed to relate their experiences of grace publicly in front of the congregation. Soon they disappeared from the records altogether, either as saints or sinners. By 1660, Dunn concludes, women "had lost not only voice, but also identity" (Dunn 1978: 589).

The evangelical revivals of the eighteenth century saw the resurgence of the mystical strain of Anglo-American Protestantism and its renewed association with female piety. The image of woman being constructed in the disciplinary practices of evangelical congregations – she of strong passion and weak mind – was the counterpart to the secular image of the "consuming" woman of eighteenth-century economic discourse. Indelibly associated with the dangers of sex, the evangelical revivals of the century made passion the centerpiece of their new style of worship and the measure of spiritual renewal. The Grand Itinerant, George Whitefield, devoted himself to the study of passions; only when people had been moved to *experience* the New Birth, viscerally and emotionally, could they be brought to Christ. The physical transports he induced in his listeners were the outward signs of this inner experience. Convulsions, spasms, uncontrollable laughter and weeping, strange contortions of the body – all were signs of souls in distress, or in ecstasy. The more extravagant the physical "agitations," the greater the relief when the soul was finally united with God. Orthodox clergy were appalled at the bodily antics of the converted; Charles Chauncy, perhaps the most vocal (and most articulate) of the Awakening's critics, was disgusted by the "*strange Effects* upon the *Body*" produced by Whitefield's sermons, including "*swooning away* and *falling to the Ground*... bitter *Shriekings* and *Screamings*; *Convulsion-like Tremblings* and *Agitations, Strugglings* and *Tumblings*" (Taves 1999: 22).

Women, as the more passionate of the two sexes, were natural allies in this crusade. Whitefield and, especially, the Wesleys went out of their way to court women as they traveled the backroads of the British Empire in search of converts. And women responded, enthusiastically and in numbers, forming the invisible backbone of the evangelical movement and its most ardent public supporters. Men may have converted in equal numbers in the American colonies, but they did so because of the example and pressure exerted by the women closest to them.

The eclectic band of itinerant preachers and lay exhorters who followed in Whitefield's and Wesley's footsteps, fanning the flames of religious enthusiasm, were far more accepting of mystical behaviors than their seventeenth-century forbears. Women like Mary Reed, whose visions entranced her pastor and held an entire congregation spellbound in Durham, New Hampshire, in the 1740s, were acting out a script that had been in play in sectarian circles since the religious ferment of the English Civil War era, but their performances were now integrated into a new sacred theater of revivalism. Catherine Brekus has suggested that "scores or even hundreds" of women participated in the Great Awakening as lay exhorters, including the "brawling" Bathsheba Kingsley who stole her husband's horse in 1741 to preach to her rural neighbors after receiving "immediate revelations from heaven" (Brekus 1998: 23, 49). Not all visions were as empowering as these examples would suggest; illness and catatonic states frequently accompanied the flight of the soul out of the body. Women like Catherine Livingston, the genteel daughter of a prominent New York family, were simultaneously "ravished" by mystical visions of Christ and afflicted with "cruel conflicts" that tested their physical and emotional strength to the breaking point. "Attacked again and again" by headaches, nausea, and faintness, Livingston confided that she "kn[ew] not what to think! – I am confounded! Seven months I have wandered in a strange land . . . I have been afflicted! tormented! disappointed! deluded! I have been bewildered and almost distracted!" (Juster 2000: 271–2). Only marriage to the Methodist itinerant Freeborn Garrettson and the establishment of her own household quieted Livingston's doubts and, also and perhaps regrettably, her active dream life.

Livingston's example suggests that eighteenth-century women found it difficult to integrate their spiritual virtuosity with their everyday responsibilities. Sarah Osborn somehow found time amidst the burdens of her life as a widow and impoverished schoolteacher to welcome hundreds of seekers into her home each week (including many of Newport's African population) to pray together. But she worried constantly about the propriety of her role as a pastoral teacher and missionary, sharing her doubts with her friend and spiritual mentor, Joseph Fish. While ultimately she rejected Fish's advice to "shut up my Mouth and doors and creep into obscurity," she continued to insist that she had not "mov[ed] beyond my line" in her prayer meetings, which were conducted always with decorum and discretion (Norton 1976: 519, 521). A century earlier, Anne Hutchinson had expressed no such ambivalence about her prophesying and praying in mixed assemblies. An apologetic thread runs through women's accounts of their more extravagant spiritual exercises in the mid-eighteenth century, one which helps makes sense of the images of death and disease that intruded even into the most exuberant accounts of spiritual union.

It is perhaps not surprising that some of our richest and most evocative accounts of female mysticism in the era of the Awakening come not from the pens of white women, but from accounts of enslaved women (left, for the most part, not by the women themselves but by their pastors and, occasionally, their masters). Cynthia Lynn Lyerly notes that, in contrast to white women who were often incapacitated physically and emotionally by the search for God, black women in the slave South pursued ecstatic union in full possession of their faculties. While white women fell into trances from which they emerged with no memory of what had transpired, slave women remembered in vivid detail their often striking visions. The black Shaker visionary Rebecca Jackson recalled in the 1830s that "When my spirit left my body, I was as sensible of it as I would be now to go out of this house and come in it again. All my senses and feeling and understanding was in my spirit" (Humez 1981: 110–12). A slave woman confounded the Methodist itinerant William Colbert by telling him that "she sometimes sees something like milk streaming down her breast; at other times something like a cake of ice or snow, and sometimes something like a young child sitting on her shoulder. She wanted to know what these things meant." Colbert could not tell her (Lyerly 1997: 173). When the Baptists and Methodists began their assault on the spiritual wilderness of the American frontier in the late eighteenth century, they were confronted everywhere by enslaved men and women who welcomed them enthusiastically into their communities and displayed the most powerful "symptoms" of religious enthusiasm (including falling down, convulsions, trances, jerking of heads and limbs, and uncontrollable shouts) they had ever witnessed.

It would not be until the revivals of the Second Great Awakening, in the early decades of the nineteenth century, that slaves – male and female – would convert in significant numbers to European American Christianity. The Africans whom Colbert and his itinerant comrades encountered in the early years of this evangelical assault were, for the most part, isolated examples of a pattern that would become well established by the 1820s. If few in number, however, these early slave converts embodied a peculiar form of spirituality that fused elements of African spirit possession with the participatory rituals of evangelical Protestantism to form a compelling model of somatic piety. Deeply expressive, anchored in what contemporaries called the "animal spirits," this African American brand of ecstatic spirituality was both more physical and more vital than the religion preached and practiced by white ministers. Inescapably marginalized by the double burden of race and bondage, enslaved women had little to lose and everything to gain by embracing a model of spiritual power that located truth in the human body and not in the words of masters or their clerical allies. White women, already moving into a world of bourgeois respectability and Victorian gentility, were hesitant to give full range to their visionary impulses; black women felt no such constraints.

Most women, black or white, never reached the dizzying spiritual heights of Catherine Livingston and Rebecca Jackson. The Spirit remained for them a theological abstraction rather than a visceral presence in their lives. But it is no accident that believers in colonial America called themselves "saints" rather than congregants, for the condition of being saved shared something with the ecstatic piety of certified visionaries. Like Livingston, ordinary women (and men) celebrated the "marriage" with Christ that preachers urged them to consummate in their diaries and letters. Like Jackson, they felt "swallowed up" in God's love even if they were not physically transported to a higher realm of being. The trope of erotic piety that fueled the dream lives of so many early modern visionaries was a commonplace rhetorical formulation in ministers' records and lay diaries throughout the colonial period as ordinary saints recorded their spiritual experiences. The "religious virtuosos" whom Christine Heyrman finds everywhere in the antebellum South included elderly "Mothers in Israel" who opened their homes and their hearts to the dashing young itinerants who showed up unannounced on their doorsteps, female class leaders who continued the work of Methodist organization long after the itinerant had moved on to the next settlement, women who maintained networks of correspondence between preachers and believers scattered across the western landscape, and the countless women who testified publicly to the Spirit within religious meetings and privately in the confines of their own homes.

One of the truisms of colonial religious history is the preponderance of women in church registers from the second generation of settlement to the present day. Throughout Protestant American history, in almost every denomination in every region in every time period, women have joined churches at a greater rate than men. There were exceptions: Anglicans in the colonial South counted families, not individuals, as the building blocks of the church and so drew men and women in equal measure. Some of the less orthodox sectarian movements appealed to men as guardians of the primitive spirit of Christianity (the Gortonists in the 1640s, for example, and the perfectionist circle gathered by Shadrach Ireland in the 1770s), while others appealed largely to women as the more mystical of the two sexes (the Quakers and Shakers, for example). But by and large, the Protestant churches presented a uniformly female face to the outside world.

Women and the Church

Susceptible to fits of religious enthusiasm, charismatic women played key roles in the sectarian challenges that flourished everywhere in colonial America, even in the repressive atmosphere of Puritan New England. With the rupturing of Catholic orthodoxy and the establishment of the local, congregational model of spiritual authority and community after the Reformation, religious life in early modern England and its colonial offshoots became organized around a series of shifting institutional configurations (episcopacies, presbyteries, conventicles) and sectarian challenges. The basic pattern as it emerged by the seventeenth century was one of successive centers establishing themselves and then being fragmented by the emergence of small sects on the fringes, which over time became new centers. The evolution from sect to church is thus one of the classic stories of Anglo-American Protestantism. Women are central to this narrative, as the chief beneficiaries of sectarian energies and the chief victims of the drive for consolidation. As sects matured into churches, in almost every community in every time period, women were pushed to the margins – they lost their political capacities, their intellectual influence, their very voices. On the fringes, women were powerful religious figures: over half the original Quaker missionaries sent to the American colonies in the mid-seventeenth century were women, one of whom was martyred for her faith; the first groups to allow women the right to preach were sectarian offshoots of the Puritan wing of the Reformed tradition (Philadelphians, Shakers, Freewill Baptists, Primitive Methodists). In addition, women voted on an equal basis with men in all the important congregational decisions in the Separate and Baptist churches that sprang up in New England like weeds after the revivals of the 1740s – they elected pastors, admitted new members, expelled deviant ones; and women dominated the holiness and Pentecostal movements of the late nineteenth century as charismatic "speakers in tongues." Every time a new sect popped up on the American frontier in the eighteenth and early nineteenth centuries (and they popped up with frightening regularity), women could be found organizing meetings, speaking in public assemblies, even on occasion serving as the divinely inspired leader of the new sect (Ann Lee and Jemima Wilkinson, to name just two examples).

Within a generation, most of these sects (the Quakers are the big exception) had made the transition to social respectability and, in the process, disfranchised their female members in key ways. The Separate churches of New England, forged in an atmosphere of intense religious enthusiasm, took away women's right to "improve their gifts" (that is, to speak in public meetings) when they merged with the Congregational order at the end of the eighteenth century. Early New England Baptists, long accustomed to allowing women to participate in all important congregational matters from electing pastors to dismissing backsliding members, retreated from this commitment to shared governance after the American Revolution. The Methodists – arguably the most successful and influential evangelical movement of the eighteenth century – initially allowed women to exhort and even preach in public; by 1830, when Sally Thompson was excommunicated from her church in New York for her disturbingly "masculine" style of preaching, not a single female preacher remained in the Methodist church. By 1840, the retreat from female preaching was in full swing in all the evangelical churches, with only a few splinter groups (like the Primitive Methodists) resisting the general trend.

There is a depressing regularity to these histories. Women, it sometimes seems, are destined to forever be "strangers and pilgrims" in their own homelands, to quote Catherine Brekus. But when we speak of sectarian challenges as nurturing female spirituality, we are speaking not so much of numbers but of a peculiar mode of piety. Because women did not in fact usually constitute the majority of the membership of these sects which, in their formative years, needed the political clout and financial resources of men more than the vigorous piety of women. Rather, historians see these sects as offering a feminine version of piety to men and women alike (privileging direct revelation over the printed word, trusting in dreams and visions as sources of revelation, encouraging heterodox forms of communication such as speaking in tongues, faith healing, etc.). One of the most influential formulations of the "feminization" thesis has to do with the binary opposition of spirit to word. More text-centered faiths, it is argued, appeal to men and embody masculine qualities; faiths which privilege direct spiritual communication between this world and the next, on the other hand, appeal to women and represent female qualities. Thus the importance of women to early Quakerism has been linked by Carla Pestana to its embrace of a more "mystical" style of worship, while the biblicism of the early Baptists explains why men were drawn to this community in larger numbers in its formative years.

Not until these sects had made the transition into mainstream respectability, in fact, did women begin to dominate their membership. From almost the beginnings of English settlement in the New World, women's overwhelming presence at worship services and devotional rites was a frequent cause of concern for ministers, who as they looked out over their congregations often saw a sea of female faces with nary a male in sight. Surveying New England's meetinghouses in the 1690s, where two-thirds to three-quarters of the congregants were female, Cotton Mather concluded that there were "far more *godly Women*" than men in the world (Bonomi 1986: 111). Ironically, given that for many of these congregations the push to become part of the mainstream meant a jettisoning of the more "feminized" aspects of their faith, their very success in attracting more members led to what they perceived as a "feminization" of the church. And a feminized church, they all knew, was a diminished one. Historians have traced the pervasive lament about the "declension" of the Puritan faith among ministers in colonial New England to the precise moment when women began to outnumber men as communicants.

So women are associated with marginality in either scenario: the feminized aspects of sectarian movements mark them as outside the mainstream, while the numerical dominance of women in more established churches is taken to be a sign of "declension." Protestant churches, it seems, have been fighting a losing battle for well over three centuries to attract men and manly status to their cause. The battle was first joined in the seventeenth century by Puritan divines anxious to rescue their movement from the taint of heterodoxy, continued by the revivalists of the First Great Awakening who were determined to bring men back into the churches they had been neglecting for at least a half-century, and carried into the very heart of American national and cultural identity by the itinerants of the Second Great Awakening who labored to inject a manly spirit of self-reliance and aggressive piety into the newly settled frontier areas. This drive would reach epic proportions in the late nineteenth and early twentieth centuries as revivalist preachers adopted a form of "muscular Christianity," complete with images of Christ as a rugged carpenter and the church as a kind of business corporation. Throughout the long history of this drive to masculinize the church, women have continued to attend church in large numbers, to organize prayer circles and disburse charity, to write evocatively of their spiritual longings in their diaries and in letters to one another, and occasionally to enter into visionary states where they could see and converse with God directly. Bound together in a tight web of mutual dependence, women and the church have enjoyed a long, fruitful, and sometimes contentious relationship from colonial times to the present. In their capacity as sinners and saints, colonial women embodied the deepest spiritual desires and the darkest spiritual fears of their society – a society that both longed to see the face of God and recoiled from those who did.

BIBLIOGRAPHY

Bederman, Gail (1989) " 'The Women Have Had Charge of the Church-work Long Enough': The Men and Religion Forward Movement of 1911–1912 and the Masculinization of Middle-class Protestantism," *American Quarterly* 41, pp. 432–65.

Bonomi, Patricia (1986) *Under the Cope of Heaven: Religion, Society, and Politics in Colonial America*. New York: Oxford University Press.

Brekus, Catherine A. (1998) *Strangers and Pilgrims: Female Preaching in America, 1740–1845*. Chapel Hill: University of North Carolina Press.

Brown, Kathleen M. (1996) *Good Wives, Nasty Wenches, and Anxious Patriarchs: Gender, Race, and Power in Colonial Virginia*. Chapel Hill: University of North Carolina Press.

Dayton, Cornelia Hughes (1995) *Women Before the Bar: Gender, Law, and Society in Connecticut, 1639–1789*. Chapel Hill: University of North Carolina Press.

DeBerg, Betty (1990) *Ungodly Women: Gender and the First Wave of American Fundamentalism*. Minneapolis: University of Minnesota Press.

Demos, John (1982) *Entertaining Satan: Witchcraft and the Culture of Early New England*. New York: Oxford University Press.

Dunn, Mary Maples (1978) "Saints and Sisters: Congregational and Quaker Women in the Early Colonial Period," *American Quarterly* 30, pp. 582–601.

Greven, Jr., Philip J. (1977) *The Protestant Temperament: Patterns of Child-rearing, Religious Experience, and the Self in Early America*. New York: Alfred A. Knopf.

Hall, David D. (1968) *The Antinomian Controversy, 1636–1638: A Documentary History*. Middletown, CT: Wesleyan University Press.

Heyrman, Christine (1997) *Southern Cross: The Beginnings of the Bible Belt*. Chapel Hill: University of North Carolina Press.

Humez, Jean M. (1981) *Gifts of Power: The Writings of Rebecca Jackson, Black Visionary, Shaker Eldress*. Amherst: University of Massachusetts Press.

Juster, Susan (1994) *Disorderly Women: Sexual Politics and Evangelicalism in Revolutionary New England*. Ithaca, NY: Cornell University Press.

Juster, Susan (1997) "The Spirit and the Flesh: Gender, Language, and Sexuality in American Protestantism," in Harry S. Stout and Daryl G. Hart (eds.), *New Directions in American Religious History*. New York: Oxford University Press, pp. 334–61.

Juster, Susan (2000) "Mystical Pregnancy and Holy Bleeding: Visionary Experience in Early Modern Britain and America," *William and Mary Quarterly*, 3rd ser., 57, pp. 249–88.

Kamensky, Jane (1997) *Governing the Tongue: The Politics of Speech in Early New England*. New York: Oxford University Press.

Karlsen, Carol F. (1987) *The Devil in the Shape of a Woman: Witchcraft in Colonial New England*. New York: W. W. Norton.

Lang, Amy Schrager (1987) *Prophetic Women: Anne Hutchinson and the Problem of Dissent in the Literature of New England*. Berkeley: University of California Press.

Lyerly, Cynthia Lynn (1997) "Passion, Desire, and Ecstasy: Gender and the Opposition to Methodism in the South, 1770–1810," in Catherine Clinton and Michele Gillespie (eds.), *The Devil's Lane: Sex and Race in the Early South*. New York: Oxford University Press, pp. 168–86.

Mack, Phyllis (1992) *Visionary Women: Ecstatic Prophecy in Seventeenth-century England*. Berkeley: University of California Press.

Norton, Mary Beth (1976) "'My Resting Reaping Times': Sarah Osborn's Defense of her 'Unfeminine' Activities, 1767," *Signs* 2, pp. 515–29.

Norton, Mary Beth (1987) "Gender and Defamation in Seventeenth-century Maryland," *William and Mary Quarterly*, 3rd ser., 44, pp. 3–39.

Pestana, Carla (1991) *Quakers and Baptists in Colonial Massachusetts*. New York: Cambridge University Press.

Porterfield, Amanda (1991) *Female Piety in Puritan New England*. New York: Oxford University Press.

Raboteau, Albert (1978) *Slave Religion: The "Invisible Institution" in the Antebellum South*. New York: Oxford University Press.

Reis, Elizabeth (1997) *Damned Women: Sinners and Witches in Puritan New England.* Ithaca, NY: Cornell University Press.

St. George, Robert (1984) "'Heated Speech' and Literacy in Seventeenth-century New England," in David Hall and David Grayson Allen (eds.), *Seventeenth-century New England.* Boston: Colonial Society of Massachusetts, pp. 275–322.

Shields, Richard (1981) "The Feminization of American Congregationalism, 1730–1835," *American Quarterly* 33, pp. 46–62.

Sobel, Mechal (1987) *The World They Made Together: Black and White Values in Eighteenth-century Virginia.* Princeton, NJ: Princeton University Press.

Stout, Harry S. and Brekus, Catherine (1991) "Declension, Gender, and the 'New Religious History,'" in Philip R. VanderMeer and Robert P. Swierenga (eds.), *Belief and Behavior: Essays in the New Religious History.* New Brunswick, NJ: Rutgers University Press, pp. 15–37.

Taves, Ann (1999) *Fits, Visions, and Trances: Experiencing Religion and Explaining Experience from Wesley to James.* Princeton, NJ: Princeton University Press.

Wall, Helena (1990) *Fierce Communion: Family and Community in Early America.* Cambridge, MA: Harvard University Press.

Westerkamp, Marilyn J. (1999) *Women and Religion in Early America, 1600–1850: The Puritan and Evangelical Traditions.* New York: Routledge.

Wood, Betty and Frey, Sylvia (1998) *Come Shouting to Zion: African American Protestantism in the American South and British Caribbean to 1830.* Chapel Hill: University of North Carolina Press.

Part II

The Creation of a New Nation, 1760–1880

Chapter Six

A Revolution for Whom? Women in the Era of the American Revolution

Jan E. Lewis

REVOLUTIONS not only change control of government, but they often replace one form of government with another. Moreover, they inevitably bring into question all social relationships, as people begin to question and remake the bases for authority in their societies. In addition, revolutions are often produced by long-term changes in politics, society, and the economy, and their upheavals, in turn, often accelerate those changes.

All of these generalizations apply to the American Revolution, which represented first and foremost the replacement of a British colonial government with an American representative democracy. Yet this change required a transformation in the way that American men and women thought about the nature of authority. In the attendant discussions and debates, they were compelled to consider the place of women in the new republic, and whether they would participate in it on the same basis as men. Women presented a challenge to the Revolutionary doctrine of equality, one that this generation of Americans was not fully prepared to meet. At the same time, the Revolution was the product of certain long-term changes in society and the economy, which affected different groups of women in different ways. These trends – toward a more complex society, arranged less hierarchically, and with an economy increasingly based upon commerce – continued after the Revolution, changing the context in which women would struggle for the equality that the Revolution failed to deliver.

Women in a Commercial Economy

The American Revolution was but one of several in what the historian R. R. Palmer once called "the age of the democratic revolution." This trans-Atlantic world was increasingly shaped by the forces of an emergent capitalism. American historians continue to debate when the new United States made the transition to capitalism and when it became a consumer society. It is clear, however, that by the middle of the eighteenth century, the American economy was maturing, more people were involved in production for the market, more people were purchasing consumer goods, and more people were susceptible to the upturns and downturns in the market. Over the course of the eighteenth century, there were significant gains in productivity. Although economic historians do not know exactly how these gains were made, they believe that the American colonies, like the nations of western Europe, experienced an "industrious revolution," in which people worked harder. All of these forces both affected women and were shaped by them.

Over the course of the eighteenth century, economic pressures, particularly in long-settled regions, placed increasing economic pressure on families. In New England, for example, population growth led to "land pressure," that is, more people trying to extract a living from farm land than it could support. This land pressure would send many young men into the cities and onto the seas and, during times of war, into the army, to attempt to provide for themselves. Young women went to work in other families' homes or increased production for the market at home. After the Revolution, young women, like their brothers before them, made their way to the cities, there working, as Jeanne Boydston has found, in a wide variety of occupations: "sailors, morticians, day laborers, iron mongers, and money lenders, as well as seamstresses, mantuamakers, and milliners" (1996: 192–3). There they were joined by women whom the Revolution had left widows and freed slaves, the majority of whom were female. These urban women helped to constitute the United States' first working class.

The wealthiest of colonial women, such as the wives of the merchants who traded in new commercial wares, hired poorer women to perform some of their household labor, freeing them to entertain in newly furnished homes, displaying a wide array of just-purchased consumer goods. But even less affluent women eagerly purchased whatever consumer goods they could afford, and the desire for such goods reached even into the slave quarter. Archaeologists digging in late eighteenth-century slave quarters have found buttons and beads, as well as shards of tableware, all castoffs from the big house or purchased from slaves' modest incomes from their own garden plots and other money-making endeavors. The women who purchased such goods did so free from the guilt that Calvinist Protestantism had attached to displays of luxury. When a South Carolina shopkeeper persisted in lecturing a female customer about the vanity of earthly possessions, she responded, "Yes, Sir, but I did not ask you the Virtues of it, I ask'd you the Price" (Breen 1993: 258).

Women were drawn into the market as both consumers and producers, and the Revolution only accelerated their participation in the market in these roles. The land pressures and other dislocations of the late eighteenth-century commercial economy formed the backdrop for the Revolution, and Britain's economic policies in the colonies were one of the immediate causes of that conflict. The tea that was dumped into Boston Harbor, of course, was one of the consumer goods for which colonial women had developed a taste. Once the colonists adopted boycotts of British manufactured goods as a tactic of political resistance, women were called upon explicitly to increase their production, particularly of cloth, and these calls continued throughout the Revolution. These injunctions were coupled with republican declamations against "luxury," which suggested that women's domestic production could lead to the moral regeneration of the American people.

Women enthusiastically participated in the boycotts. They were able to make the connection between their economic activities and political action. Over the course of the war, as shortages drove up the price of food, women not only took part in riots directed against merchants who were hoarding or charging too high a price for food, but they directed one-third of such actions.

Although colonial boycotts of British manufactures before the war were rather effective, neither they nor the republican complaints about excessive consumption that continued throughout the conflict did anything to retard women's increased participation in the market, either as producers or consumers. The Revolution only accelerated the long-term trends in the economy and hence women's reasons for entering the market as both consumers and producers. Alexander Hamilton's *Report on Manufactures* (1791) made explicit the principles of the industrious revolution when it advocated the employment of women and children: "The husbandman ...experiences a new source of profit and support from the encreased industry of his wife and daughters" (Syrett, 10: 252). Although Congress rejected Hamilton's plan for government support of manufacturing, the logic behind it prevailed.

The Enlightenment and the Education of Women

If the increasing complexity of the American economy provided part of the context for the American Revolution, so did that huge intellectual movement known as the Enlightenment. As with the transformation of the economy, the Enlightenment would have an important impact upon women, not because they were its focus, but because they could not help being affected by a force so powerful.

Enlightenment thinkers held that man was a creation of reason, and although, as Linda K. Kerber has suggested, most of the *philosophes* meant the male sex rather than generic humankind, there was enough ambiguity in their formulation to enable eighteenth-century Europeans and Americans to think seriously about the intellectual capacities of women. Some went so far as to argue that women were men's intellectual equals. "Will it be said that the judgment of a male of two years old, is more sage than that of a female's of the same age?" asked the Massachusetts writer Judith Sargent Murray (Murray 1995 [1790]: 5–6). If grown women appeared less intelligent than men, then that was only because their educations were inferior. The remedy was obvious: improve women's education.

Women's education was rarely an end in itself. Instead, women were to be educated to be useful and ornamental members of society. In Enlightenment thought, *society* had a particular meaning. According to John Locke, civil society or government was created when men left the state of nature in order to protect their lives and their property. Feminist scholars such as Carole Pateman have argued that women were not part of this *social contract*, although Locke may have been more ambiguous than they suggest. There is no ambiguity, however, in the Scottish theorists who amplified Locke's work. In the century after Locke wrote his *Two Treatises of Government* (1690), commerce transformed British society, creating in the process a much more vibrant civic life, a world of coffee houses, clubs, schools, theaters, newspapers and magazines, and social gatherings. Scottish philosophers such as Francis Hutcheson,

Thomas Reid, and Adam Smith drew a distinction between society and government, and if they, like Locke, saw little or no place for women in government, they insisted that women were vital to society.

According to the Scots, it was in the family that men were trained for society. There they learned manners and morals and were schooled in affection, with women expected to soften the brutish tendencies that men brought with them when they left the state of nature. Moreover, women played important roles not only in the family, but also in society. Indeed, as Rosemarie Zagarri has shown, the Scots believed that in commercial societies (such as Scotland had become and the American colonies were fast becoming), men and women were equals. And, in another amplification of Locke, they asserted that the purpose of government was not so much to protect property as to protect society. American Revolutionaries developed this line of thinking even further, arguing that society was preferable to government. As Thomas Paine put it in *Common Sense*, "Society in every state is a blessing, but government even in its best state is but a necessary evil" (1976 [1776]: 65). With each amplification of Locke's theory, Scottish thinkers created a more important role for women and a stronger rationale for women's education.

As the companions of men, the mothers of children, and participants in the bourgeois public sphere, women exercised enormous influence. Republican thought warned that uneducated or frivolous women could too easily be seduced, while well-taught and sober women could keep men on the path of virtue. Scottish Enlightenment thought recommended women's education in even more positive terms. Women were the repositories of manners, by which the Scots meant not etiquette but the rules of civilized behavior.

Although an occasional writer such as Judith Sargent Murray would justify women's education as an end in itself, most focused on women's service to others, their usefulness to society. Yet because the primary justification for women's education was its usefulness to others, some worried about the dangers of women who were too educated. Would they neglect their responsibilities to others? Would they lose their femininity? Would they become selfish, that is to say, antisocial? The possibility of overeducating men never prompted the same sorts of fears. Thus, as great as the opportunities that the Enlightenment opened up for women were, they were not, by any means, unlimited.

It was not only that colleges remained closed to women for another half-century, as were most of the professions for even longer, but that Americans (like Europeans) had difficulty imagining a woman who was both learned and attractive, who loved knowledge for itself and who still loved her family. The life of the English feminist Mary Wollstonecraft served as a cautionary tale. At first admired in the United States, both she and her book, *A Vindication of the Rights of Woman* (1792), were repudiated after she bore a child out of wedlock. Intellectual women, it was feared, were necessarily libertines.

This undercurrent of fear notwithstanding, women's education made stunning advances in the decades after the Revolution. More women were educated and they were educated better. Before the Revolution, the gap between male and female literacy was so great that a man as accomplished as Benjamin Franklin could be married to a woman, Deborah Read Franklin, who although quite bright, was barely lettered. By 1850, the literacy gap in New England between men and women had been closed, and significant improvements were made in the South as well. These advances were the result of greatly expanded schooling, both public and private.

The quality and consistency of women's education varied widely, depending upon region and class. Schooling was best for affluent white women in the North and Mid-Atlantic, who could enroll in private academies such as the one run by the novelist Susanna Rowson in Medford, Massachusetts. It was much spottier for poorer women, for women in the South, and, of course, for slave women, who had to learn to read surreptitiously (although it was not until after the Nat Turner Rebellion in 1831 that southern legislatures expressly prohibited teaching slaves to read and write). Facilities were often poor, schedules irregular, and attendance intermittent. Nonetheless, almost all white women learned to read and write, and many became learned. Women themselves became teachers, by the middle of the nineteenth century dominating the profession. In two generations, women's education was transformed.

Revolutionary Thought and Revolutionary Politics

Despite women's changing relation to commerce and education, neither women nor gender were central to the Revolution or Revolutionary thought. Women were by and large excluded from politics – that is, the high politics of government – before the Revolution, and they were by and large excluded after it as well. Nonetheless, the Revolution could not help raising questions about female citizenship. Moreover, because the Revolution altered the relationship of the citizen to the state, reconfiguring the bases for authority, it necessitated a new rationale for excluding women from government, one consistent with democratic theories of government.

Prior to the Revolution, women were only one of several groups that were denied full political rights. In a hierarchical, status-based society, women, slaves, children, and propertyless white men all suffered from a variety of civil disabilities. With each colony setting property requirements for voting, a significant number of white men could not vote or hold elective office. In the new constitutions written after independence was declared, states began to lower or drop property qualifications for voting, although full white manhood suffrage would not be accomplished for more than half a century.

The Revolutionary trend was toward greater democracy, particularly for white men, but that trend was shaped by several political theories, each of which had different implications for women. Consider, for example, the question of women's voting. Affluent women, those who held property, were the first to demand the right to vote, but only for those independent women who met the same property qualifications for voting as men. It is a measure of how uncertain they were of their rights that they did so privately, however, in letters to family members, rather than in petitions or other public acts. (The contrast here is to slaves, who, empowered by Revolutionary ideals, began to petition for their freedom and to sue for it in court.)

In 1778, Hannah Lee Corbin of Virginia asked her brother, the Revolutionary leader Richard Henry Lee, to explain why the vote was withheld from widows who paid taxes. (Under the doctrine of coverture, married women were considered represented by their husbands, and unmarried women living at home, by their fathers.) Significantly, Lee could not see any compelling reason why propertied widows should not vote, "notwithstanding it has never been the practice either here or in England" (Lee 1778).

In the face of a powerful republican political theory that linked political participation to independence, it was difficult to exclude propertied women on the basis of sex alone. Perhaps that is why New Jersey's first state constitution, adopted in 1776, enfranchised all those who had lived in the state for a year and owned £50 in property. Making clear that the gender-neutral language of the state constitution was no accident, a 1790 law making polling places more accessible referred to voters as "he or she" (Klinghoffer and Elkis 1992: 172). Although the constitution did not limit the franchise to propertied single women, that was its effect, for, under the doctrine of coverture, married women, by and large, were precluded from holding property in their own name. All of the other states limited voting explicitly to men. Rather than viewing New Jersey as an exception, it might be more useful to consider the state as representing the furthest reach of the liberating possibilities of republican thought, than the aberration or mistake that historians have usually considered it. Unimpeded by the force of custom, New Jersey followed through on the logic of republicanism.

Unmarried, propertied women voted in New Jersey until 1807. With the development of political parties in the 1790s, in closely contested elections, both parties attempted to mobilize their female supporters. The anomaly of female voters, however, prompted a mixture of pride and consternation. At first, neither party could figure out which benefited more from the enfranchisement of women; in 1800, the Federalists attempted to take away their right to vote, and then, in 1807, the Democratic-Republicans were successful. Both the Federalist attempt and the Democratic-Republican measure were part of broader movements to restrict the franchise. The 1807 law at the same time removed the franchise from free blacks and aliens, as well as property holders who were untaxed. While this measure was being debated, the more radical members of the Republican Party, using Lockean terms, had argued that "a widow's mite is property," as was the life or liberty of a person "black, white, red or yellow" or of "exotic or domestic birth" (Klinghoffer and Elkis 1992: 187). They were defeated, however, by more conservative members of their own party, and with that defeat ended one of the bolder experiments in American political history.

If no other state was prepared to go as far as New Jersey, the question of women's citizenship nonetheless arose, most famously in the correspondence of Abigail Adams and her husband John. In a private letter to John Adams, who was representing his state in the Continental Congress, Abigail Adams asked him and his fellow delegates to "Remember the Ladies" in "the new Code of Laws which I suppose it will be necessary for you to make.... Do not put such unlimited power into the hands of the Husbands. Remember all Men would be tyrants if they could. If perticular care and attention is not paid to the Ladies we are determined to foment a Rebellion, and will not hold ourselves bound by any Laws in which we have no voice, or

Representation." Although Abigail Adams made allusion to the republican doctrine of representation, and although she made her plea humorously and gently, her real concern seemed to be domestic abuse. "Why then," she asked her husband, "not put it out of the power of the vicious and the Lawless to use us with cruelty and indignity with impunity. Men of Sense in all Ages abhor those customs which treat us only as the vassals of your Sex" (Butterfield, 1: 369–70).

In a response that was as condescending as it is famous, John Adams made light of his wife's plea, telling her, "As to your extraordinary Code of Laws, I cannot but laugh. We have been told that our Struggles has loosened the bands of Government every where. That Children and Apprentices were disobedient – that schools and Colledges were grown turbulent – that Indians slighted their Guardians and Negroes grew insolent to their Masters. But your letter was the first Intimation that another Tribe more numerous and powerfull than all the rest were grown discontented" (Butterfield, 1: 382–3). Like the New Jersey legislators who revoked the franchise of women and free blacks, Adams made a connection between the rights of women and racial minorities. To make women full citizens of the new nation threatened anarchy, by removing the ideological justification for the subordination of any group.

This private exchange between a husband and wife would be of little interest to history were not John Adams so powerful a figure or the question he and Abigail Adams discussed so important to women's and political history. Although John Adams dismissed his wife's concern, the issue they discussed came up only a month later when he and James Sullivan, a Massachusetts patriot and Justice, considered the question of representation in the new state constitution. The question was how Lockean theory, which held, as Sullivan put it, that "every member of Society has a Right to give his Consent to the Laws of the Community or he owes no Obedience to them," could be reconciled with the customary disfranchisement of various groups of citizens. While accepting this theory in principle, Adams believed that in practice it must be qualified. "Shall we Say, that every Individual of the Community, old and young, male and female, as well as rich and poor, must consent, expressly to every Act of Legislation? No, you will Say, This is impossible." It was not simply custom that decreed that some must be denied the right to consent, but the republican belief that only those with a stake in society were entitled to run its affairs.

If Adams fell back upon republican thought to limit the role of women in the new government, he raised a question that the Revolution would continually pose: "How then does the Right arise in the Majority to govern the Minority, against their Will? Whence arises the Right of the Men to govern Women, without their Consent?" (Butterfield, 4: 208–13). Republican thought did not require that each member of society give his (or her) consent to government, but liberal thought, which derived from John Locke's *Second Treatise of Government* (1690), did. Once liberalism came to prevail, those who wished to exclude women from government would have to devise a new rationale, one that was consistent with contract theory.

Several rationales were developed, but none was particularly compelling, from a theoretical point of view. Collectively, however, they were effective in keeping women from voting for more than a century and from participating in government in other formal ways. Perhaps the least elegant but most effective rationale was custom: except for the occasional queen, women had never participated in government, and it would seem odd, if not downright ludicrous, if they did. Government was a rough-and-tumble business, and it would taint women and impair their femininity. Women were too occupied with their families to spare the time. None of these ideas was intellectually coherent, but they seemed logical enough to most Americans, even most women, and they were the ideas that were usually offered when occasional women protested their exclusion.

More compelling, at least from a modern viewpoint, was the idea that even if women could not fully participate in government, government would protect them. When the delegates to the Constitutional Convention were debating the question of representation, Pennsylvania's James Wilson proposed that delegates should be apportioned on the basis of "the whole number of white & other free Citizens & inhabitants of every age sex & condition" and three-fifths of the slaves (Farrand 1966 [1911]: 201). Although the language was later edited down, the intent seems clear: all free women (as well as children) were to be represented by the new government. According to liberal theory, women were part of the social compact that created government. Women were part of society, and the purpose of government was to protect society.

Moreover, both republican and liberal thought took great interest in the character of their citizens. Republicanism held that citizens must be *virtuous*; that is, they must be willing to sacrifice their self-interest for the good of the nation. Although classical republicanism had doubted that women were capable of this sort of disinterest, Americans came to assert not only that women were as virtuous as men, but, as Ruth H. Bloch has shown, more virtuous, as virtue itself was redefined as a private rather than public quality. This change was consistent with the emergence of liberalism, which held that morality emanated from the private sphere rather than from the state, and with women's increasing influence over members of their family. Some historians have held that this new notion of women's influence was a sop given women to appease them for not being accorded a direct role in government, while others see it as the foundation for women's moral reform movements in the early nineteenth century.

If historians cannot decide whether the Revolutionary doctrine of influence represented a new opportunity or a new restraint on women, it is probably because the developments in women's political roles in this period were fundamentally ambiguous. Consider the closely related topics of women's rights and obligations. It seems clear, although scholars have not addressed this topic systematically, that the Bill of Rights applied to women as well as men. The First Amendment rights, for example – freedom of religion, speech, press, and assembly – are all expressed in the public sphere, that is, in the social realm that women helped to constitute. At the same time, as Linda K. Kerber has shown, women were generally prevented from exercising the obligations of citizenship. They could not, for example, serve in either the militia or the army, nor could they serve on juries. And although one could argue that women benefited from the Revolution more than they suffered, it is also true that men gained additional advantages through fulfilling the obligations of citizenship, ranging from trial by jury of their (male) peers to veterans' benefits.

Women and the Law

After the Revolution, there were a number of small improvements in women's legal status in a number of states. As Marylynn Salmon has suggested, these changes anticipated the more significant improvements of the 1830s and 1840s. The picture is not entirely clear, however, because each state followed its own course and because a number of the changes were not intended to benefit women in particular. Consider the case of divorce. Before the Revolution, divorce was unusual except in Puritan colonies such as Massachusetts and Connecticut. By 1800, however, it was legal, if not common, in twelve states, as well as the Northwest Territory. If the direct impact of the Revolution on some aspects of American life is often hard to ascertain, such is not the case with divorce. In the years just before the Revolution, Britain's Privy Council disallowed divorces in Pennsylvania, New Hampshire, and New Jersey and instructed colonial governors to do the same. Once independence was declared, the new states could permit divorce, and they did, putting the United States well in advance of Britain.

Moreover, the ideological connections between divorce and the American Revolution are clear. Both Thomas Jefferson and Thomas Paine advocated the legalization of divorce, which they justified in terms of natural rights. When Jefferson said that "no partnership can oblige continuance in contradiction to its end and design" (Basch 1999: 23), he was talking about divorce, but he might as well have been discussing the Revolution.

The legalization of divorce marked an important improvement for women, at least in principle. Consistent with liberal principles, marriage was a contract, one that either party could seek to void, albeit only in exceptional circumstances. Divorce afforded married women one of their rare opportunities to enter court and to sue in their own name. In practice, however, the liberalization of divorce brought few benefits to women. As Norma Basch has shown, the primary practical effect of the new statutes was to bring some legal protection to women whose husbands had already abandoned them. Divorce, however, remained quite rare, and if it afforded the occasional woman some respite from an adulterous or dangerously abusive husband, it did little to redress the imbalance of power under which many more married women suffered.

Women benefited as well from the abolition of primogeniture in those states that had practiced it. As with the liberalization of divorce, the intent was not necessarily to advantage women but to eliminate a practice that now appeared inconsistent with Revolutionary ideals. Once again, the practical effect may have been slight, but the principle – that all children, female and male, should share equally in their parents' estates – was important.

In some of the states, there were other, small improvements. Some states, for example, expanded the rights of married women to enter into business. In 1788, the Connecticut Supreme Court gave married women the right to bequeath real estate, a decision that was so controversial that it was later overruled. In 1808, however, the state legislature reaffirmed the right of women to bequeath real estate, making Connecticut the liberal exception. Advances in women's legal rights came slowly and in a piecemeal fashion, particularly when they singled out women. Moreover, to the extent that changes in the law focused on property and inheritance, they advantaged only those women who had property, that is, relatively affluent free women.

Women, Sexuality, and the Family

The Revolution took place in the middle of several long-term changes in the family and sexual behavior. The Revolution cannot be linked directly to these changes, although some of them were reinforced by challenges to traditional modes of government. Moreover, the social and economic changes of the Revolutionary era probably accelerated certain trends, in particular by breaking up families and sending single women into the cities.

For a number of complex reasons, the control that fathers exercised over their families began to decline by the mid-to late eighteenth century in many regions of the colonies. In New England especially, land pressure meant that increasingly, children would have to provide for themselves because their fathers no longer had enough land to bequeath them farms (if sons) or dowries (if daughters). As a consequence, parents had less leverage over their children. Young women began sometimes to marry before their elder sisters, suggesting that young women were putting their own desires ahead of conforming to their parents' wishes. This change also manifested itself in higher rates of bridal pregnancy. In some New England towns, by the eve of the Revolution, more than a third of the brides were pregnant on their wedding days. Without the promise of an inheritance to hold over their children's heads, parents had less ability to coerce good behavior from them. Any woman who engaged in sexual relations before marriage, however, was taking a considerable risk, for there was always the danger that her partner would refuse to marry her – and that her father would be unable to compel him to. As geographical mobility increased after the Revolution, young men and women in the cities, away from their families, became even freer in the expression of their sexuality. Only the young women suffered, however, if an unwanted pregnancy was the result.

New standards of sexual behavior and doctrines of sexuality appeared, and some historians have judged them a response to the breakdown of patriarchal families: if fathers could not protect their daughters from designing men, then young women would have to learn how to protect themselves. Popular novels such as Susannah Haswell Rowson's *Charlotte Temple* (1794) and Hannah Foster's *The Coquette* (1797), as well as dozens of stories published in magazines (all modeled after Samuel Richardson's *Clarissa*), warned young women of the dire fate that would befall them should they succumb to the enticements of a seducer.

At the same time, ideas about female sexuality changed dramatically. As Nancy F. Cott has shown, in the years just after the Revolution, women, who had once been compared to Eve, the original temptress, were now often thought to be passionless. A combination of forces combined to effect this change, chief among which were: critiques of aristocratic libertinism; polite literature, which reshaped middle- and upper-class female manners; and evangelical Protestantism, which placed an emphasis on women's moral agency and capacity for virtue. It would be foolhardy to deduce a change in behavior from such prescriptive literature, which would have had almost no influence on working-class women in the cities and slave women, in any event. Even so, the standards for female behavior, particularly for middle-class women, changed dramatically, presenting young women with new images of femininity that deemed free expressions of sexuality aberrant.

This change coincided with a redefinition of marriage and the family, especially among affluent and middle-class Americans. The family was increasingly pictured in sentimental terms, and men and women began increasingly to marry – or at least to say they were marrying – for love. Both in private correspondence and in fiction and essays, men and women claimed that private life was the source of true happiness.

By the beginning of the nineteenth century, birthrates for white women began to fall. Once again, a number of factors were responsible for this change, and the Revolution itself played no direct role. As the economy became more complex and, very slowly, more urban, children were less necessary to a family's economic success, and harder to provide for. The economic incentive for large families diminished. At the same time, women's emotional value to their husbands increased, and some husbands began to worry about the physical and psychic toll that bearing large families placed upon their wives. Even before the introduction of modern means of birth control, family size began to fall. Daniel Scott Smith has speculated that husbands were controlling their own sexuality in order to preserve their wives' physical and mental health, suggesting a shift of power within the family toward women.

Women Under Slavery

If the effect of the American Revolution on free women was ambiguous, so was it upon slave women, if in very different ways. The most important change, which affected all slaves, regardless of their sex, was the beginning of the elimination of slavery in every state north of Maryland. During the Revolution itself, slaves in Massachusetts began suing for their freedom, claiming that slavery was contradictory to the egalitarian language of the Revolution. They won, and slavery in Massachusetts was effectively ended. In other states, such as New York and New Jersey, gradual plans for emancipation were adopted, which, incidentally, affected male and female slaves slightly differently. In New York, all children born to slave mothers (slavery always followed the condition of the mother) after July 4, 1799, would be freed, but boys would have to serve their mothers' masters until the age of twenty-eight, while girls would be freed when they became twenty-five. In New Jersey, which passed a gradual emancipation bill five years later, boys were required to serve until they were twenty-five, girls until twenty-one.

The result of such emancipation plans was that, by the antebellum period, a new class of free blacks came to replace slaves in the North. Slavery was challenged, too, in the Chesapeake, and even though Maryland and Virginia refused to eliminate slavery, thousands of slaves were freed by their owners, swelling the free black populations in those states. Before the Revolution, for example, only 4 percent of Maryland's black population was free; by 1810, that number had increased to 20 percent, a trend that would continue until the Civil War.

Throughout the South, slavery was challenged, both by the ideology of the Revolution and the Revolution itself. In 1775, Virginia's Governor Dunmore offered freedom to all slaves who would fight for Britain. Not only did black men and women flee to the British forces, but the word of Dunmore's offer spread, stirring hopes throughout slave territory. In addition, wherever Patriot and British troops fought for control of the countryside, the Revolution disrupted the lives of inhabitants, both slave and free. In the confusion, many slaves left their plantations in search of freedom, whether in cities or with the British. In 1781, Thomas Jefferson estimated that 30,000 slaves had left their masters. In South Carolina, one-fourth of the slave population simply disappeared, while Georgia lost about two-thirds. Runaway rates were high, too, in the region around New York and New Jersey.

Runaway slaves met a variety of fates. Some found freedom with the British, while others met with reenslavement. Untold numbers died, victims to the diseases that often befall people who are crowded into refugee camps in times of war. The disruption to slavery itself and to the lives of the men and women who were trying to escape the institution can hardly be exaggerated.

Despite this disruption, slavery was not eliminated south of Maryland. In fact, in all those states except Maryland that chose to perpetuate the institution, it only became stronger. After the war, with the opening of Kentucky and Tennessee to settlement, and then with the introduction of cotton cultivation in the lower and deep South, the institution spread. Slavery became more entrenched, but as it did, the autonomy of slaves within it increased. Both on plantations and in urban communities, slaves increasingly established strong families and a thriving culture. In general, there was less interaction with whites, but more with other blacks.

These important long-term trends shaped the lives of slave women in particular ways. The changes for women were most visible in the northern states, where freedwomen migrated and enslaved women enjoyed the greatest freedom. In the cities of the North and South, black women found work as domestics, in particular as cooks, seamstresses, and laundresses. The growing white merchant and professional class created a demand for household workers. Smaller numbers of women plied their own trades, sometimes as teachers in large northern cities such as Philadelphia or as vendors in city markets of the South, as in Charleston. A few free black women made it into the middle class (which would grow in the antebellum period), while most struggled with poverty. Still, urban life offered greater opportunities for freedom of movement and association than women could find on plantations or in rural areas.

The urban black population was disproportionately female, for several reasons. Men had greater opportunities elsewhere, such as at sea. Also, in the South in particular, more women than men were emancipated. Those slaves who were freed were most often those with whom white owners had the closest contact. As house servants, female slaves were often better known to their masters and mistresses than were male field hands. In addition, some portion of the emancipated slaves were women with whom white owners had had sexual relations, sometimes fathering children. In the period after the Revolution, sexual relations between white masters and female slaves seem to have increased, creating a mulatto population, a small portion of which was granted freedom.

If free and slave black women in cities generally enjoyed greater freedom, such was not the case on plantations. Such new occupations as developed, for example in the skilled trades, usually went to men. As a result, women were left with an increasing proportion of the drudge work, such as gathering manure. Slave women continued to labor in the fields, performing work that would have been considered degrading for white women. While slave women's work lives generally became more difficult after the Revolution with the entrenchment of slavery, their family lives became somewhat more secure. For every such generalization, there are countless exceptions. Nonetheless, the evening out of sex ratios, the growth of larger plantations (and with them, larger slave populations on them), and even the spread (however shallow) of humanitarian values, meant that more slave women had the opportunity to live in committed relationships, with kin nearby, enjoying a distinctive slave culture.

The Revolution in Indian Country

No group was more adversely affected by the Revolution than Native Americans. When the war was over, the British generally abandoned their former allies, making no provision for them in the Treaty of Paris that ended the war. Indians now found themselves at the mercy of the new American government, which defined them as alien peoples, wholly outside of society. Moreover, because many of them occupied lands that white people coveted, Native Americans, even those who supported the Revolutionaries, were in a precarious position.

As with slave women, the Revolution affected Indian women more as Indians than as women. For example, during the war American troops attacked the villages of Indians who allied themselves with the British – and sometimes those of friendly Indians as well. In 1779 Major John Sullivan and his troops burned forty Iroquois towns in upstate New York, destroying all the crops and orchards, and displacing all the Indian inhabitants. Similar attacks were visited upon the Shawnee in Ohio and the Cherokee in South Carolina, where women and children were slaughtered and burned alive. Richard White has suggested that the mutilation of enemy women's bodies, by both whites and Indians, became "bloody metaphors" for the "denial of common humanity" (1991: 388). More Indian men than women were killed, however, increasing the number of widows. According to one account, after the war, there were ten times as many Cherokee women as there were men.

Historians have yet to describe the full impact of the Revolution on Native Americans, and Native American women in particular. Theda Perdue has suggested that the disproportionate number of male deaths in the Revolution enhanced the status of men in Cherokee society, making it a society dominated by its warriors, now more necessary for the protection of their villages. If that was the case, the war may only have accelerated a trend that had begun before the Revolution, at least among the Creek. As Claudio Saunt has shown, the trade in deerskins had already altered gender relations in that tribe. Traditionally, as among all Eastern Woodlands tribes, women farmed, made clothing, and maintained the homes, while men hunted and engaged in war. In the early years of the deer trade, men hunted for deer, while women dressed the skins. As European demand for undressed deerskins increased in the 1760s, the trade became an exclusively male business; women's work was no longer necessary. And without women's participation, men were able to keep all of the proceeds for themselves, typically spending them on rum and the clothing and other goods that women had once produced.

Official American Indian policy also attempted to alter Indian gender roles. American Indian agents such as Benjamin Hawkins urged Native American women to abandon farm labor and instead to take up spinning and weaving, which would compel native men to start farming, in order to feed their families. Although native women generally welcomed this aspect of the American government's "plan of civilization," native men were more skeptical. Creek men worried that, as Hawkins explained, "if the women can cloathe themselves, they will be proud and not obedient to their husbands" (Saunt 1999: 154). At the same time, native women were less eager to adopt other American customs. They refused, for example, to give up their traditional equality within the family.

In time, American attempts to "civilize" Indians led to conflict, as some Native Americans willingly adopted American gender customs, others adapted them to their own purposes, and others rejected them outright. Some of this conflict was between women and men and some among members of the same tribes. For example, the Cherokee eventually split into a "progressive" group, which even adopted the American custom of slavery, and "traditionalists," who generally rejected American ways. The Seneca religious leader Handsome Lake encouraged his people to farm and make their homes as the Americans did, but he rejected the principles of private property and raising crops for the market. On the other hand, the Shawnee Prophet Tenskwatawa rejected American gender roles and warned that the Americans were "making women of the Indians" (Dowd 1992: 136). Thus, not only was gender – and the attempt to remake gender roles – central to American Indian policy, but it was also at the core of the religious revitalization movements that Indians themselves initiated in response to the upheavals of the Revolutionary era.

Conclusion

The American Revolution affected women quite differently, depending upon their race and their class. In many ways, the Revolution improved the lives of middle-class and affluent white women, or even if it did not, it began a process that eventually would lead to significant improvements. The most important improvements came in women's education, a direct legacy of Enlightenment ideas of equality. Revolutionary thought deemed women members of society, participants in the imaginary social compact that created the nation. The most direct impact here was in the principle that women were rights-bearing individuals, protected by the Constitution and the Bill of Rights. The Revolution also ushered in some improvements in women's legal rights, particularly the right to divorce. Except for increased access to education, many of these improvements in women's status and rights were more abstract than palpable. Few women, for example, availed themselves of divorce; only a few women voted for a brief time in New Jersey; and, although all Americans benefited from the guarantees of the Bill of Rights, it is not clear that there were immediate or dramatic changes in daily life for most women (or for men). Still, the significance of these changes in principle should not be discounted.

The influence of Revolutionary thought can be seen in the family, too, particularly among the middle class and elites. Americans rejected patriarchy as a fit model for government or the family. Although the changes in practice may not have been as dramatic as those in principle, the new premium placed upon affection and on choice may have enhanced equality within marriage, at least to some extent.

If it is hard to point to dramatic changes wrought by Revolutionary ideals in the daily lives of free women, such is not the case for slave women. Slavery was terminated almost immediately in New England and gradually in the Mid-Atlantic, making free women (and men) out of former slaves and creating, particularly in the cities, a new class of free blacks. Yet the development of the market, which enhanced the choices of women with money, also led many women, most notably slaves, to work harder. The opening of the cotton South and the growth of the market for cotton may have allowed for the development of a vibrant slave culture, but the lives of slave women generally became harder.

Indian women were the other great losers in the Revolutionary era, although even here, there is some ambiguity. Many lost their homes and their husbands in the Revolution. Yet Indian communities before the Revolution were hardly stable, and Native Americans' participation in the market in furs had already altered gender roles. After the Revolution, the American government encouraged Native Americans to adopt American gender roles, which some native women were eager to do.

Ultimately, the Revolution was most beneficial to women when it applied directly its doctrine of equality. Slavery was attacked, and thousands of slaves were emancipated. Women were educated. The principle of patriarchy was questioned. Women were deemed members of the social compact. Many of the failures of this era are the result of the incomplete application of the doctrine of equality. Many more women remained in slavery than were freed. Higher education was still off limits to women. Men still retained inordinate powers within their families. Women gained rights in theory but often not in practice.

At the same time, forces other than the Revolution shaped women's lives and neither politics nor political thought was the driving force in most women's lives. The developing market economy affected women very differently, depending upon their race, their ethnicity, and especially their class. Yet these changes were not independent of, or tangential to, the changes wrought by Revolutionary thought. The American Revolution liberated the United States to become a thriving capitalist nation, and hence, the changes wrought by politics and the economy, working in tandem, are what gave the age of the democratic revolution its broadest form, affecting women in sometimes contradictory ways.

BIBLIOGRAPHY

Basch, Norma (1999) *Framing American Divorce: From the Revolutionary Generation to the Victorians.* Berkeley: University of California Press.

Berlin, Ira (1998) *Many Thousands Gone: The First Two Centuries of Slavery in North America.* Cambridge, MA: Harvard University Press.

Berlin, Ira and Hoffman, Ronald (eds.) (1983) *Slavery and Freedom in the Age of the American Revolution.* Charlottesville: University Press of Virginia.

Bloch, Ruth H. (1987) "The Gendered Meanings of Virtue in Revolutionary America," *Signs* 13, pp. 37–58.

Boydston, Jeanne (1990) *Home and Work: Housework, Wages, and the Ideology of Labor in the Early Republic.* New York: Oxford University Press.

Boydston, Jeanne (1996) "The Woman Who Wasn't There: Market Labor and the Transition to Capitalism in the United States," *Journal of the Early Republic* 16, pp. 183–206.

Breen, T. H. (1993) "The Meaning of Things: Interpreting the Consumer Economy in the Eighteenth Century," in John Brewer and Roy Porter (eds.), *Consumption and the World of Goods.* New York: Routledge, pp. 249–60.

Brown, Chandos Michael (1995) "Mary Wollstonecraft, or, the Female Illuminati: The Campaign Against Women and 'Modern Philosophy' in the Early Republic," *Journal of the Early Republic* 15, pp. 389–424.

Butterfield, L. H. et al. (eds.) (1963–) *Adams Family Correspondence.* Cambridge, MA: Harvard University Press.

Cott, Nancy F. (1977) *The Bonds of Womanhood: "Woman's Sphere" in New England, 1780–1835.* New Haven, CT: Yale University Press.

Cott, Nancy F. (1978) "Passionlessness: An Interpretation of Victorian Sexual Ideology, 1790–1850," *Signs* 4, pp. 219–36.

Dowd, Gregory Evans (1992) *A Spirited Resistance: The North American Indian Struggle for Unity, 1745–1815.* Baltimore: Johns Hopkins University Press.

Farrand, Max (ed.) (1911) *The Records of the Federal Convention of 1787.* New Haven, CT: Yale University Press. Rpt. (1966), New Haven, 4 vols.

Kerber, Linda K. (1980) *Women of the Republic: Intellect and Ideology in Revolutionary America.* Chapel Hill: University of North Carolina Press.

Kerber, Linda K. (1998) *No Constitutional Right to Be Ladies: Women and the Obligations of Citizenship.* New York: Hill and Wang.

Klinghoffer, Judith Apter and Elkis, Lois (1992) " 'The Petticoat Electors': Women's Suffrage in New Jersey, 1776–1807," *Journal of the Early Republic* 12, pp. 159–93.

Lee, Richard Henry (1778) Letter to Hannah Corbin, March 17, 1778, DuPont Library, Stratford Hall, Stratford, Virginia.

Lewis, Jan (1987) "The Republican Wife: Virtue and Seduction in the Early Republic," *William and Mary Quarterly*, 3rd ser., 44, pp. 689–721.

Lewis, Jan (1995) " 'Of Every Age Sex & Condition': The Representation of Women in the Constitution," *Journal of the Early Republic* 15, pp. 359–87.

Lewis, Jan and Lockridge, Kenneth (1988) " 'Sally Has Been Sick': Pregnancy and Family Limitation among Virginia Gentry Women, 1780–1830," *Journal of Social History* 22, pp 5–19.

Locke, John (1988 [1690]) *Two Treatises of Government*, ed. Peter Laslett. Cambridge: Cambridge University Press.

McLaughlin, William G. (1986) *Cherokee Renascence in the New Republic.* Princeton, NJ: Princeton University Press.

McMahon, Lucia (2002) "Gender, Education, and Sociability in the Early Republic," Ph.D. dissertation, Rutgers University.

Murray, Judith Sargent (1995) *Selected Writings of Judith Sargent Murray,* ed. Sharon M. Harris. New York: Oxford University Press.

Nash, Margaret A. (1997) "Rethinking Republican Motherhood: Benjamin Rush and the Young Ladies' Academy of Philadelphia," *Journal of the Early Republic* 17, pp. 171–91.

Norton, Mary Beth (1980) *Liberty's Daughters: The Revolutionary Experience of American Women, 1750–1800.* New York: Little, Brown.

Paine, Thomas (1976 [1776]) *Common Sense,* ed. Isaac Kramnick. London: Penguin.

Perdue, Theda (1998) *Cherokee Women: Gender and Culture Change, 1700–1835.* Lincoln: University of Nebraska Press.

Salmon, Marylynn (1989) "Republican Sentiment, Economic Change, and the Property Rights of Women in American Law," in Ronald Hoffman and Peter J. Albert (eds.), *Women in the Age of the American Revolution.* Charlottesville: University Press of Virginia, pp. 447–75.

Saunt, Claudio (1999) *A New Order of Things: Property, Power, and the Transformation of the Creek Indians, 1733–1816.* New York: Cambridge University Press.

Smith, Daniel Scott (1973) "Family Limitation, Sexual Control, and Domestic Feminism in Victorian America," *Feminist Studies* 1, pp. 40–57.

Smith, Daniel Scott (1975) "Parental Power and Marriage Patterns: An Analysis of Historical Trends in Hingham, Massachusetts," *Journal of Marriage and the Family* 35, pp. 419–28.

Syrett, Harold et al. (eds.) (1961–79) *The Papers of Alexander Hamilton.* 26 vols. New York: Columbia University Press.

White, Richard (1991) *The Middle Ground: Indians, Empires, and Republics in the Great Lakes Region, 1650–1815.* Cambridge: Cambridge University Press.

Zagarri, Rosemarie (1992) "Morals, Manners, and the Republican Mother," *American Quarterly* 44, pp. 192–215.

Zagarri, Rosemarie (1998) "The Rights of Man and Woman in Post-Revolutionary America," *William and Mary Quarterly,* 3rd ser., 55, pp. 203–30.

Chapter Seven

Gender and Class Formations in the Antebellum North

Catherine Kelly

IF most historians working in the 1960s and 1970s knew anything about American women's history, outside of the Salem witch trials and the suffrage amendment, they knew something about nineteenth-century domesticity, about the "cult of true womanhood" that confined mothers and daughters to the circumscribed world of parlor sentimentality. The publication of Nancy Cott's *Bonds of Womanhood* in 1977 shed new light on domesticity and women's sphere, while raising a series of questions about the relationship between gender and antebellum society. Most notably, Cott rehabilitated domesticity by suggesting that the elaboration of a "woman's sphere" between roughly 1780 and 1835 led to a heightened gender consciousness that "bound women together even as it bound them down." Just as important, Cott suggested that this female sphere was connected to the emergence of modern, industrial America. Trying to explain the origins of women's sphere, she suggested that it was set off from men's sphere – from the public sphere – by changing experiences of work: while men's work had become increasingly disciplined by the clock and structured by the cash nexus, most of women's work remained somehow "pre-industrial." In other words, whatever "bound women together" was linked to broader social and economic transformations and by extension to the emergence of new class structures and relationships. Cott's arguments about the origins and nature of "woman's sphere" have helped shape more than two decades of research. Scholars exploring the nature of women's paid and unpaid work, the discursive development of gendered spheres, and the extent and meaning of women's "public" presence have enriched our understanding of antebellum life and, at the same time, have fundamentally reshaped our understanding of class formation.

Surveying the terrain of antebellum America today, we no longer see separate spheres, but the broad and sweeping transformation of the household economy – a transformation that encompassed a variety of settings and that was, at the most fundamental level, gendered. Nowhere are the gendered dimensions of this process clearer than in feminist studies of labor. It is no longer possible to imagine that women's work, whether performed in factory or household, whether paid or unpaid, was isolated from the social and economic processes that transformed men's work in the first half of the nineteenth century. An especially rich body of literature has suggested the ways in which this process was marked by a complex interplay of continuity and change. Older forms of labor organization and social relations did not simply give way in the face of industrialization, but neither did they survive unchanged. Instead, they became grounds for contest, between capitalist entrepreneurs and workers, between women and men, between native-born and immigrant, and between black and white. Feminist historians have contributed significantly to understanding the ways in which the development of American capitalism created multiple divisions in American society and the extent to which those divisions were mediated by gender.

Most obviously, women's historians have done much in the last twenty years to uncover the complex, contradictory world of wage work. Drawing inspiration not only from women's history, but also from the work of labor historians working on both sides of the Atlantic, scholars including Thomas Dublin, Christine Stansell, and Mary Blewett moved far beyond writing women into the narrative of work to show how capitalist transformations of labor were shaped by gender. Early accounts, like Dublin's pioneering study of the Lowell "mill girls," stressed a break between older traditions of family labor and women's factory work. A stint at Lowell offered farmers' daughters peer-based camaraderie and perhaps even identities as wage workers; most notably, it seemed to offer them a sense of autonomy which derived both from their income and their freedom from the confines of rural households. And indeed, the autonomy that Lowell "mill girls" enjoyed extended to some women working in less salubrious factory settings. Mary Blewett found that the sewing machine drew sizable numbers of women shoe binders into factories in Lynn, Massachusetts, in the 1850s. There they played a pivotal role in the strike of 1860, using their position as industrial workers to fight for better wages for all women employees. Although only a small percentage of New York City's antebellum working women ever found employment in factories, Stansell suggests that they were in the forefront of efforts to organize their sisters into trade unions. Significantly, that same independence earned them a reputation for immodesty and unseemly pride among middle-class reformers and at least some male artisans.

Blewett and Stansell moved beyond a fascination with the innovations of the factory to demonstrate how the sexual division of labor that obtained in artisanal shops and the household economy shaped women's work and the process of industrialization. Both scholars emphasized the importance of outwork, or the putting-out system, for the development of antebellum manufacturing. Among shoemakers, outwork developed out of women's roles as helpmeets within the artisanal economy. Over time, the shoemaker's wife who had once sewed shoe uppers under her husband's tutelage began to take orders from a manufacturer who paid her in credit, then in goods, and finally in wages. At the same time, her husband found himself working as a wage earner in a shoe factory. In New York City, the triumph of outwork seemed to have less to do with the persistence of the artisanal household than with its collapse. In the metropolitan context, outwork emerged in industries that were feminized early on. There, entrepreneurs in the garment industry seized upon outwork because of its low overhead and expendable labor pool, just as they seized upon desperately poor women as a source of scandalously cheap labor.

Outwork allowed women to draw on traditions of family cooperation by assigning easier tasks to children and younger siblings. It enabled women to earn wages while attending to domestic concerns, though to be sure this arrangement more closely resembled a grueling double shift than idealized descriptions of modern "flex time." In other words, outwork allowed women to supplement the family income while seeming to minimize the disruptions and the potential threat posed by female wage earning. By submerging women's wage earning within households, outwork undercut women's ability to fight for higher wages or better working conditions and made it all but impossible for men to see them as fellow workers. As Blewett has observed, when Lynn's militant factory women argued for a strike on behalf of *all* female workers, regardless of where they worked, they were opposed by male workers (along with some home workers), who insisted on the primacy of a family wage paid to the male head of household. Stansell, in particular, has demonstrated how outwork created new opportunities for exploitation by appropriating the gender hierarchies that had characterized the family economy while abandoning the mutual obligation that ideally served to mitigate those hierarchies. In this context, the political economy of outwork is significant not only because it helps us to understand women's experiences of industrialization, but also because it illuminates both the dynamics of industrial expansion and the ways in which an emergent working class understood and articulated its gendered interests. Where earlier generations of labor historians had cast outwork as the stunted prologue to "real" industrialization, it now figures as a central element in capitalist development.

The rural North was hardly exempt from the kinds of changes that transformed antebellum towns and cities. Indeed, within the last fifteen years, the northern countryside has moved much closer to the center of historians' questions about the "market revolution," including the timing and nature of the American transition to capitalism. If historians of rural capitalism have been somewhat slow to recognize fully the gendered dimension of that transition, they have still provided abundant evidence of it. As we have seen, farmers' daughters supplied the initial labor for the nation's first large-scale textile factories. And as Jonathan Prude has pointed out, for every respectable Yankee young woman who wound up at Lowell, many more, blessed with fewer opportunities and fewer resources, wound up working in smaller rural mills characterized by family labor. After 1820, large numbers of rural women were also drawn into the industrial economy through outwork, making buttons and palm-leaf hats as well as shoes for wages or credit with local merchants. These women seem to have turned to outwork partly in response to the availability of cheap factory-made cloth; Christopher Clark, for instance, has found that Connecticut River Valley outworkers spent the lion's share of their earnings on fabric and notions. Not surprisingly, then, rural outwork was an overwhelmingly female activity. Married women turned to hatmaking, for example, to supplement their household income while single women used it to help pay for their support in the years before marriage.

Rural women shaped the transition to capitalism not only by taking up new forms of labor, but also by intensifying older ones. Through the first half of the nineteenth century, women took cloth, yarn, butter, eggs, and vegetables to market. In her important study of Pennsylvania butter making, Joan Jensen described how one variety of "women's work" figured in that transition. Farm families in the Philadelphia region initially stepped up their commercial butter production during the hard times of the 1820s and 1830s, hoping to insulate themselves from the instability of the market. But by the 1840s, the product's profitability sparked a reorientation of farming as families increased both their commitment to dairying and their butter output. As Jensen argues, this reorientation depended on women's ability to produce more butter more efficiently. Women instigated the technological innovation necessary for increased efficiency; they stopped making cloth in order to devote more time to butter; and they turned increasingly to hired help, both to free them up from housework and to assist them with butter making. Indeed, Jensen credits women's dairying with bringing both security and relative economic equality to the region's (white) households. But these contributions did not necessarily translate into a renegotiation of power between women and men. Men owned the land; and land, not butter, was seen as the source of the region's wealth.

Jensen's dairying women were remarkable, both in the profitability of their market involvement and in their Quaker faith, which often nurtured more egalitarian gender arrangements, so it is probably unwise to generalize from her findings. Sally McMurry, for example, has found that with the commercialization of New England dairying, men assumed control of production. Still, Jensen's arguments about the ways in which farm women transformed their labor become all the more suggestive when considered alongside other evidence from New England. As Christopher Clark has pointed out, Massachusetts families responded to market penetration by driving themselves to increase their productivity and cut costs. This burden fell disproportionately on women. In part, these inequities derived from the sexual division of labor that characterized Anglo-American agriculture; men's work, however intensified, retained its seasonal character while women's work remained far more constant through the calendar year. But more than a time-honored sexual division of labor was at work. Clark found that in the first decades of the nineteenth century, Connecticut River Valley families briefly reversed the downward trend in fertility rates, increasing women's reproductive labor at precisely the moment they were intensifying their productive labor. Presumably, the expansion of household production promised parents the resources to provide for their children at the same time that it put a premium on family labor. Clark also documents the extent to which rural women restructured their production and consumption strategies – most notably purchasing cloth rather than making it – in order to earn extra income. In Jensen's telling, dairying wives snatched up opportunities; in Clark's analysis, weary rural women had new burdens thrust upon them. But both accounts testify to the ways in which rural women manipulated the quantity, kind, and pace of labor to buttress their households' position in a precarious economy. Just as important, they document the ways in which women shaped the development of rural capitalism. Women's decisions to reorder production and consumption played a critical role in increasing the density of market relations throughout the northern countryside.

We should not assume that wage work was confined to working-class or rural women. Contrary to the assumption of many social and women's historians through the 1970s, middle-class women, married and single, performed their share of work for cash. Indeed, in her 1981 study of middle-class formation in Utica, New York, Mary P. Ryan was among the first to insist that gender was not merely affected by industrialization but that it was instead a constituent part of that transformation. She argued that women's wage labor was central to their families' economic strategies and class aspirations. Middle-class parents took great pains to fashion their sons into the "self-made" men of nineteenth-century myth by delaying their entry into the workforce and investing in their education and vocational training. They kept adolescent and adult sons within the parental household far longer than immigrant, working-class, or earlier generations of Uticans did. But such preparation was expensive, often demanding additional income as well as careful savings. That income was furnished by wives who took in boarders and daughters who went out to work. As Ryan points out, Utica's middle-class families substituted the labor of wives and daughters for that of their sons; a good number of young men enjoyed the opportunity to become self-made precisely because of the income generated by their mothers and sisters.

This general process was hardly confined to upstate New York. Even where the importance of middle-class women's wage work for the careers of sons and brothers is less well documented, it is clear that they worked – for money if not for wages narrowly defined – to a far greater extent than historians had earlier imagined. Throughout the antebellum North, the seeming contradiction between "lady" and "worker" often collapses upon close examination. The most genteel lady could augment her family's income as long as she labored at tasks that seemed to replicate the unpaid labor that middle-class women performed within their homes. Accordingly, scores of middle-class women took in boarders and plain sewing and produced fancy work for sale. They also sent their daughters out to teach.

The rapid expansion of public and private education in the North, coupled with the dismal wages that teachers received, all but guaranteed the early feminization of teaching. Then, too, this profession could be construed as an extension of women's domestic responsibilities. By 1860, one quarter of the nation's teachers were female, and in New England that percentage was much, much higher. Indeed, reading the diaries and letters of New England women, teaching registers less as an occupational choice than as a rite of passage. Most teachers were haphazardly trained, serving relatively brief stints in common schools. And even within that context, teaching provided something less than a vocation. It was typically one form of work among many that a young woman might piece together to help support herself in the years before marriage. Still, the growing number and increasing quality of private female academies and seminaries enabled a few women, like Sarah Pierce, Emma Willard, and Mary Lyon, to carve out careers as educators and women of letters. By founding schools, testifying before state legislatures, publishing textbooks, and training scores of teachers, to say nothing of generations of elite women, such women exerted a powerful influence on American culture.

Historians have generally cast these pioneering professionals as spectacularly ambitious and successful teachers, notwithstanding the pronounced differences between their lives and careers and those of most schoolteachers. It may make more sense to consider them among the growing numbers of women and men who attempted to forge careers in America's fledgling culture industry. American culture was increasingly commercialized over the course of the antebellum period. While historians have begun to trace that process, they have yet to tease out either the full extent or meaning of women's participation in it.

We know most about the connections between gender and the development of the literary marketplace. As literary historians and historians of the book have shown, the exponential expansion of the reading public in the antebellum era created markets for a wide variety of literature, ranging from newspapers and magazines to pamphlets and tracts to novels and poetry. Much of this demand was met by women. As early as 1984, Mary Kelley offered a rich and nuanced analysis of the difficulties encountered by those female writers famously damned by Nathaniel Hawthorne as a "pack of scribbling women." They confronted deeply entrenched cultural prescriptions that made it difficult to claim an authorial identity, much less a public one. And even a novelist as successful as Harriet Beecher Stowe struggled to find a balance between the clamor of domestic responsibilities and the time and concentration that writing demanded. But Kelley also documented the remarkable popularity that many women writers attained. Indeed, it is this success that most distinguishes Kelley's subjects. For every woman who managed to sell her writing, there were hundreds who drafted poetry, stories, and novellas but were unsuccessful in forging careers or even earning a bit of cash with their pens. Since the publication of Kelley's pioneering work, feminist scholars working from a variety of perspectives have complemented and complicated her depiction of literary women. In particular, they have further illuminated the ways in which gender helped shape both the literary marketplace and the American canon. They have also offered rich studies of particular writers and genres.

But for all that we have learned about the intersection of gender, reading, and writing, we still know very little about women's other paid cultural work. After all, publishing was only one sector of the antebellum culture industry, which included the lyceum lecture circuit and the visual arts along with the theater and music hall. And just as small numbers of educated, middle-class women earned money as writers, so too did they earn money lecturing and painting. Anne Laura Clarke, for example, abandoned teaching in the 1840s to pursue a highly respectable if not highly profitable career lecturing on literature and philosophy. And as art historian David Lubin has demonstrated, painter Lillie Martin Spencer supported herself and her family by creating visual counterparts to domestic fiction on canvas. Other women, including miniaturists Sarah Goodridge and Eliza Goodridge, managed not only to support themselves but also to gain national reputations as portrait painters. This is not to suggest that scores of antebellum women fashioned lucrative careers as speakers and artists; they did not. But historians have yet to trace fully women's attempts to turn the culture industry to their own ends or the extent to which the production and marketing of culture was shaped by gender. At the very least, scholars should hesitate before recapitulating truisms about widespread prohibitions on women's public speaking or the outright exclusion of women from the arts.

Regardless of the surprising range of middle-class women's paid work, it would be a mistake to romanticize it. Like the labor performed by working-class women, it was radically undervalued in the world of cash transactions. Despite the very real differences between the teenaged schoolteacher and the academy headmistress, between the middle-class wife who took in boarders and the professional novelist, all found themselves disadvantaged in a wage economy. Women's limited access to cash bore very real consequences. On the one hand, as Mary P. Ryan suggested, the money women earned might go a long way toward helping establish a young man's middle-class career; the same money might help a family maintain its middle-class status during hard times. On the other hand, when families found themselves especially short of cash, women's most Herculean efforts could not provide – much less guarantee – financial stability. In other words, if women's income often contributed to their families' middle-class status, it could neither ensure nor protect that status.

Antebellum economic development was thus both reflected in and shaped by women's work when that work resulted in a saleable product or drew women beyond the confines of their households. But housework, whether paid or unpaid, also serves as a register of these changes. The transformation of domestic service provided women's historians with the earliest and clearest index of this development. Few middling households could manage without some form of help, and over the first half of the nineteenth century, this help was increasingly proletarianized. As Faye Dudden pointed out, in the eighteenth and early nineteenth centuries, young women routinely worked in the homes of neighbors and kin as part of broader patterns of exchange among households. The hierarchy that distinguished mistress from help derived more from age and marital status than from class. After all, the help would one day assume command of her own household and the mistress could look back on the day when she, too, had served as help. By the 1820s in urban areas and later in the hinterland, this system of domestic "help" gave way to a form of domestic "service" that required servants to perform increasingly specialized tasks for an increasingly distant mistress. Not coincidentally, this shift took place at the same time that native-born women abandoned household service in order to pursue outwork, mill work, or teaching, leaving immigrants, especially the Irish, and African Americans to dominate the ranks of servants. The transformation of domestic work entailed more than a change in the race and ethnicity of the labor pool. Carol Lasser has argued that the elaboration of middle-class domesticity increased the number of household tasks and raised the standards against which housekeeping was measured, making it necessary for urban middle-class households to hire more, and more specialized, help. By mid-century, domestic service had become the one feminized labor market where demand exceeded supply. To mistresses' dismay, even Irish and African American servants could and did turn this situation to their own advantage, bargaining hard for better wages and working conditions and switching jobs at will. Lasser's analysis of this "servant problem," ubiquitous across the North, illuminates the ways in which market relations and market negotiations penetrated even "unproductive" households.

Despite the expansion of paid work for both middle- and working-class women, the majority of labor performed by the majority of women was uncompensated domestic labor: housework. Arguably the most important recent study of women's antebellum labor, Jeanne Boydston's *Home and Work* (1990) took full measure of housework, which she described as labor that had value but not price. Rejecting the rigid distinctions that some historians and economic theorists have drawn between productive and reproductive labor, Boydston carefully calculated the value of northern women's unpaid domestic work and explored how gender ideology shaped perceptions of it. Building upon earlier studies by Ruth Schwartz Cowan and Susan Strasser, Boydston offered the fullest description to date of the range of housework performed by laboring and middle-class women in rural areas and cities alike. She found that working-class women made critical contributions to their households' subsistence regardless of whether or not they earned wages. Women's unpaid labor, saving, and scavenging often meant the difference between survival and catastrophe for laboring households. But in an economy that turned on the cash nexus, this crucial labor was largely invisible. By failing to recognize the value of housework, capitalists could point to the survival of working-class households to demonstrate that they did indeed pay male workers a living wage; ironically, the same blindness precluded male workers from understanding exactly what constituted a living wage.

For middle-class families, women's unpaid efforts helped insure a measure of stability. And in participating in the support of a relatively prosperous sector of society, one that generally aligned itself with capitalist development, housework contributed to the cultural construction of the middle-class family as a symbol of the security ideally available to all Americans. But, as Boydston argues, the ascendance of the market and the cash nexus turned middle-class housework into something other than labor. In the middle-class imagination, household labor was recast first as women's duty and eventually as an act of magical transformation. In fiction and didactic literature, writers created a pastoral fantasy of women's nonlabor by describing homes that were maintained not through women's physical exertions but through their feminine sensibilities. This fantasy moved beyond the printed page to shape the women's own vision of the tasks that consumed their time; whatever they were doing, it surely was not *work*.

The remarkably rich and wide-ranging scholarship on antebellum women's work has made several things clear. First, female labor was decisively shaped by industrialization, regardless of whether it garnered a wage or where it was performed. More to the point, the labor that women performed, and the meaning that women and men ascribed to that labor, shaped the development of capitalism. Indeed, the flexibility of women's work, both paid and unpaid, made it central to this development and to the emergence of the working and middle classes alike. Clearly, there was little about antebellum women's work that remained "pre-industrial," as Cott had initially suggested; accordingly, it is now difficult to see the special nature of women's work as the material out of which a "woman's sphere" could be fashioned. And yet, it is just as clear that an emergent domestic ideology shaped the meaning ascribed to antebellum women's work as well as the conditions under which it was performed. Housework was invisible not simply because it did not command a wage, but because of antebellum gender ideologies that privileged the male breadwinner of all classes and the fictive leisured lady of the middle class. My own work has shown that after the

1840s, rural women increasingly drew upon the language of domesticity to describe the most "productive" of household labor.

Thus the discursive construction of separate spheres extended well beyond the white middle-class home. Stansell succinctly characterized the assumptions that undergirded the outwork system as "the language of woman's sphere – working class version." Indeed, studies of outwork reveal just how easily the sexual division of labor and the gender ideologies that structured the artisanal family economy could be reconceptualized through the rhetoric of separate spheres in order to meet the needs of an industrial economy. Even the Boston Associates, founders of the famous Lowell mills, claimed respectability for their operation and their operatives by casting the factory as an innovative extension of the domestic sphere.

Even more telling were the efforts of an emerging black middle class to adopt and adapt the gender roles prescribed for its white counterpart. The sustained struggles to create African American communities in the North were shaped by middle-class gender conventions as well as by the structure of economic and political inequality, as James Oliver Horton and Lois Horton have pointed out. In the African American press, men were celebrated for their strength, ambition, and judgment while women were celebrated for their delicacy, taste, and mercy. Men were exhorted to succeed in business; women were encouraged to wield influence within their families. But these prescriptions, which never completely registered the complex realities of white households, proved an even poorer match for African American ones.

Most obviously, as many labor and social historians have observed, racism placed extraordinary constraints on black men's opportunities to become "self-made." Skilled men found it all but impossible to secure suitable employment in the trades. Similarly, African Americans were all too frequently denied access to the business licenses necessary for entrepreneurship; those men – and women – who did start businesses often found themselves serving an undercapitalized African American community. Because very few black households could expect to survive on the earnings of a male head of household, married black women, even those from the middle class, could expect to work for wages, most often as domestic servants or by taking in some combination of laundry, sewing, and boarders. While the occupations available to black men were dogged by seasonal unemployment, the demand for black women's services remained relatively constant, insuring a steady income. Paid domestic work allowed black women to care for their children while earning an income, which contributed to their authority within their households. It played a crucial role in the economic and social strategies of many African American families and enabled a smaller number to forge a black middle class. But it also guaranteed that black women performed two jobs at once. The African American press added yet more pressure to this already doubled burden by repeatedly expressing the expectation that black women remain models of domesticity regardless of their role as wage earners.

Horton and Horton's examination of northern black communities reveals more than the contradictions between white middle-class prescription and African American practice. The language that described masculine and feminine ideals and codified class aspirations took on added meaning in the context of northern racism and southern slavery. The discursive idealization of black men as breadwinners, husbands, and fathers was framed in the context of antebellum slavery, which stripped enslaved men of all those roles; the language of manhood resonated with the language of freedom. Similarly, prohibitions against displays of female sexuality registered more than middle-class propriety. African American women who worked in the homes of white families were especially vulnerable to sexual harassment and assault. Prevailing class and racial stereotypes undermined their hopes of protection, much less legal recourse. In this context, modesty offered some measure of invisibility and self-protection.

As Horton and Horton have trenchantly argued, African Americans appropriated the conventions of middle-class culture and discourse as part of a broader strategy of racial uplift. By advancing a politics of respectability based on white middle-class conventions, black men and women unwittingly articulated a vision of freedom predicated upon the gender inequality that obtained within middle-class culture exacerbated by the special problems confronting free blacks. It is not yet clear whether this argument can be extended beyond the African American middle class. Joan Cashin, for example, has suggested that blacks in the Old Northwest, while poorer and more vulnerable to slave catchers than those in the urban Northeast, may have developed more egalitarian gender roles than those described by Horton and Horton. We will need to know far more about the dynamic intersection of race, class, and gender in the lives of free African Americans before we can assess fully the extent to which blacks appropriated the conventions of "separate spheres," to say nothing of the meaning they ascribed to those values and practices. Still, it seems clear that for blacks as well as whites, the ideology of separate spheres provided a language that could alternately reinforce and challenge a variety of hierarchies.

The argument that gendered "spheres" served largely as a trope which simultaneously stood in for and obscured a variety of power relations was persuasively advanced by historian Linda K. Kerber in an influential 1988 essay. For historians, she argued, both the explanatory power and the analytical weaknesses of "separate spheres" depend on their metaphoric nature. The metaphoric character of "woman's sphere" was especially clear to historians who focused on the breadth of women's activism beyond the home. Especially in northern cities, middle-class women caught up in the fervor of the Second Great Awakening hit the streets in order to circulate temperance pledges, campaign for moral reform, dispense charitable aid, fret over the fate of seamstresses and prostitutes, and work for the conversion of the unsaved; toward the end of the antebellum period, many of these same women turned their energies to antislavery causes. The rich history – and historiography – of women's activism testifies to antebellum women's public presence.

Having established women's presence in the public sphere, historians were less sure what to make of it. Initially, studies of middle-class women's activism seemed to reflect a female critique of male society, a more-or-less covert condemnation of the values and practices that stood at the center of bourgeois culture. Several historians, notably Barbara Berg, Keith Melder, and Carroll Smith-Rosenberg, suggested that antebellum women's reform turned the ideology of a separate female sphere on its head, attempting to remake the public in the image of the private. To be sure, much of middle-class women's activism was couched in terms of women's special domestic sensibility. It was precisely the virtue of woman's sphere, its remove from the corruptions of politics and the market, that provided the platform for a wide range of social activism and social criticism. Paradoxically, an ideology aimed at confining women to the home seemed to offer many women the impetus for leaving it.

But as feminist labor historians were quick to point out, this accounting ignored the noisy presence of laboring women in the antebellum public, casting them only as objects of middle-class women's activism rather than agents in their own right. Urban working-class women, in particular, helped shape a rich public culture. In New York City, for example, they paraded the Bowery, gossiped and scrutinized their neighbors from tenement porches, frequented oyster bars and theaters. In New York and Philadelphia, splendidly dressed African American women and men staged formal balls and availed themselves of commercial establishments like New York City's African Grove, which offered ice cream, tea, and music. Less frequently, working-class women deployed their publicity in strikes and protests, challenging the exploitive conditions of the female trades. Clearly, working-class women's experience of the public sphere had little to do with domesticity. And as Christine Stansell observed, even when New York City's radical working women began in the 1850s to represent themselves and their cause in the language of domestic sentiment and feminine victimization, the shift owed more to strategy than self-identity. At best, it was an awkward fit, one that failed to account for the great variety of working women's experiences. Moreover, as a strategy, it was singularly unsuccessful during the antebellum period.

If analyses that derived from separate spheres ideology could not explain the presence of working-class women in the public sphere, neither could they explain most of middle-class women's public activity. For one thing, there was little about women's reform and benevolent activism that was particularly domestic. As Lori D. Ginzberg has demonstrated, despite the persistence of rhetoric that cast female benevolence as a function of femininity, women's charitable societies bore a pronounced resemblance to modern corporate culture. Benevolent societies were complex institutions, responsible for raising and disbursing large sums of money and mediating between local governments and welfare recipients. Their professional and volunteer staffs manifested order, efficiency, and punctuality in equal measures with compassion and generosity. Indeed, the conflation of female benevolence and the domestic sphere was itself part of what Ginzberg has aptly termed the business of benevolence. Most obviously, the purportedly voluntary nature of women's benevolence enabled municipal governments to obtain much-needed social welfare services at rock-bottom prices. If this perception guaranteed that female staff members would be woefully underpaid, it also worked to the advantage of women's charitable organizations. Both Ginzberg and Beverly Gordon have suggested that women's organizations deployed the language of domesticity to preserve their autonomy, to ensure that the business of benevolence would remain *women's* business.

Moreover, despite its historiographical prevalence, benevolence does not begin to account for the range of middle-class women's political activism. Despite their exclusion from suffrage, many antebellum women were deeply interested and involved in politics. Indeed, one of the most exciting discoveries in recent studies is just how involved they were. African American women, for example, were strikingly visible in antebellum political struggles for racial equality. They participated passionately in every aspect of the abolition movement, and many proved successful speakers on the antislavery lecture circuit. And middle-class women's political activism extended well beyond abolition to include participation in a variety of state and local conventions aimed at securing civil and political rights and economic opportunities for free northern blacks. Indeed, antebellum African American women were such dynamic and contentious activists that James Oliver Horton has identified politics as the single instance in which middle-class blacks willingly deviated from the gender norms that undergirded dominant conceptions of domesticity.

There is no denying black women's contributions to the fight for racial equality. But recent work on the political engagements of middle-class white women suggests that they, too, deviated from gender conventions that would have banished them from politics. White women appeared in costume at partisan events as personifications of Liberty, or Columbia, or Virtue, fed and entertained convention delegates, and made banners for rallies and processions. But they also participated in political parades, attended rallies, debates, and Congressional deliberations as knowledgeable partisans, and helped convey political information through formal and informal communication networks. In short, politically minded white women – and there were many of them – did everything short of casting ballots and running for office. Indeed, it now seems likely that the critical differences between antebellum black and white women's political activism derived less from black women's greater participation than from the causes and parties that black and white women championed, the special urgency of black women's partisanship, and the political constraints faced by all African Americans, regardless of gender.

Our growing awareness of women's role in shaping partisan socialization is reshaping the ways in which we view antebellum political culture. In an influential 1984 essay, Paula Baker cast the antebellum period as the high watermark of masculinist politics. She argued that faced with the task of mobilizing large and divergent constituencies, national parties increasingly emphasized forms of political socialization that drew men together *as men*, leaving women behind. Other historians, notably Mary P. Ryan and Michael McGerr, claimed that middle-class women were quite visible in antebellum politics, but suggested that they served only as decorations for male pageantry. More recently, historians have offered subtler readings of women's political activity, readings that acknowledge both their committed partisanship and the ways in which national parties deployed it. David Waldstreicher has argued that if Republicans and Federalists took pains to conceal women's outright partisanship, both parties made public use of female support to buttress legitimacy and to represent themselves as *the* party of the new nation. Important essays by Jan Lewis and Fredrika Teute have traced women's influence on Washington's elite political circles. Elizabeth Varon's fine study of Virginia Whigs showed that by the 1840s, the party actively courted female supporters; the support of "true women" seemed to temper the worst aspects of male partisanship and trumpet Whig virtue.

And in a study of New England Whig women, Ronald Zboray and Mary Saracino Zboray found that while gender shaped the precise form of women's participation in electoral politics, it did not bear on their political sensibilities; for them, partisanship resulted from local affiliation, deeply held party loyalty, and a close reading of current events rather than from any particularly domestic perspective.

Recent work on gender and politics thus suggests that we can no longer simply cast middle-class women's public activism as an extension of their domestic roles. Instead, it seems clear that middle- as well as working-class women's active and varied participation in the public sphere did as much to shape the tumultuous culture of democratic capitalism as did the pervasive domestic ideology that confined women to a "sphere." Certainly, political culture contributed significantly to the "separate spheres" ideology of the nineteenth century. When the Whig Party cast itself as the inheritor of republican statesmanship and exemplar of republican virtue, it invoked distinctly masculine notions of republicanism. Similarly, the antebellum Democratic Party was notable for its bellicose defense of the prerogatives of white manhood against the incursions of women and African Americans. Nevertheless, recent studies suggest that gender ideology likely shaped men's *and* women's partisanship, even if in contradictory ways.

These studies also suggest that the connections between politics and class might be yet more complicated than we had imagined. Historians have long associated the masculinity of antebellum politics with the mediation of class relations. Indeed, it has become a historiographical commonplace that political parties helped mitigate class tensions by emphasizing – albeit in different ways – the political equality and unity of all (white) men as citizens. But standing alongside their partisan wives and daughters may well have allowed some men to claim power not simply on the basis of their sex but as members of particular communities and, especially, classes. Women's political participation, especially their remarkable visibility within the ranks of the Whig Party, and their contributions to political socialization more generally, suggest that antebellum political culture, like antebellum gender politics, might have shaped and registered class identities in multiple and contradictory ways.

Studies that underscore women's visibility in the public sphere suggest further questions about the intersection of gender, class formation, and selfhood. Many historians have suggested that the separation of spheres, whether conceived as prescription or practice, shaped individual identities to conform with the norms of a distinctively middle-class selfhood. Scholars since the early 1970s have been struck especially by the intimacy and affection that marked the friendships of many middle-class women. Carroll Smith-Rosenberg provided the most influential analysis of these relationships, arguing in an early essay that women's social separation from men fostered a distinct women's culture, a "female world of love and ritual." Smith-Rosenberg's arguments were buttressed by pioneering studies of nineteenth-century masculinity which found similar relationships among a broad cross-section of middle-class men. Following these studies, historians cast homosociability as the emotive analogue to the social and spatial separation of spheres. Homosociability, separate spheres, and middle-class formation have been so closely associated that some scholars have construed the presence of heterosociability as evidence of a de facto challenge to bourgeois culture. In their respective studies of New York farm families and New England's working class, Nancy Grey Osterud and Karen V. Hansen argued that heterosociability subverted middle-class values by threatening the separation of spheres. But middle-class women and men also partook of a rich heterosocial culture that extended well beyond reform and politics to include singing schools, literary societies, and dancing schools – associations that owed less to political partisanship or social reform than to bourgeois self-fashioning.

It now seems likely that antebellum middle-class culture was defined less by homosociability per se than by the intersection of self-fashioning and interiority, the highly self-conscious cultivation of sentiment and sensibility. Recent work on the history of the emotions has suggested that the culture of democratic capitalism was constituted in no small measure by patterns of feeling that prized affection and sensibility as well as self-discipline and self-restraint in both women and men. To be sure, these qualities were gendered; affection and restraint figured differently in the idealized masculine and feminine subjectivities of the early nineteenth century. Nevertheless, middle-class Americans sought simultaneously to craft and then reveal a true, inner self that transcended the conventions of market, polis, and parlor. Paradoxically, this pursuit of authentic selfhood was itself a constituent element of the very conventions it aimed to transcend. As numerous historians and literary scholars have observed, constructions of selfhood that claimed to counter the market in fact depended on it. The performance of middle-class sensibility depended upon clothing, manners, conversation, reading, writing, and all the social rituals that drew these elements together. In other words, sensibility depended upon consumption.

More than twenty years ago, Ann Douglas explored the relationship between gender, subjectivity, consumption, and class formation. She provocatively argued that the narcissistic consumer culture that characterized late twentieth-century America originated in the ornamental leisure of nineteenth-century middle-class women and, especially, in the sentimental fiction they devoured. Douglas's work has been roundly criticized for underestimating both the complexities of women's lives and their literary productions. But if women's historians have demonstrated the problems with Douglas's formulation, they have not yet fully untangled the complex and contradictory connections between gender, class, and consumption. For all we have learned about consumption in the eighteenth and twentieth centuries, we know surprisingly little about the discursive and social practices that constituted antebellum consumption. We know still less about the connections between consumption and the social, economic, and cultural dimensions of class formation.

This is unfortunate, for scholarship thus far has suggested that an emergent consumer culture offered free women and men unprecedented opportunities for self-invention at the same time that it helped articulate distinctions of class, race, and gender. Fashionable consumption was central to both bourgeois discourse and self-presentation. Gaining membership in the antebellum middle class surely required thrift, diligence, and savings, but it also required display. At the same time, the longstanding association between femininity, luxury, and consumption became a commonplace. Over the course of the antebellum period, strident descriptions of profligate wives and daughters appeared with increasing frequency in didactic literature and fiction as well as diaries and letters.

The significance of fashion and consumption extended well beyond the middle class. In New York City, for example, young working-class women and men used fashion and sociability to set themselves apart both from older artisan traditions and from an emergent middle class. As Christine Stansell observed, the gender roles and sexual mores that characterized Bowery "b'hoys and gals" depended as much upon the commercialization of style and leisure as upon the transformation of work. Fashion also played a significant role in antebellum racial politics, according to recent work by Shane White and Graham White. For free blacks, clothing and appearance more generally provided a vehicle for furthering both a gendered politics of respectability and a distinctive African American aesthetic. At the same time, an increasingly racist discourse depicted African American fashion as one more proof of blacks' misguided attempts to mimic the conventions of middle-class white society, attempts that proved threatening and laughable by turns. The sheer range of fashion, to say nothing of the contradictory meanings that Americans imputed to it, suggests that far more was at stake than Veblenesque social emulation. Antebellum consumers were engaged in a contested process of invention and reinvention that was dynamically and inextricably bound up with the construction of race, class, and gender. Women's historians would thus do well to consider consumption as a constituent element of gendered class formation rather than invoking it merely as proof of the emergence of a middle class.

Since the publication of Cott's pioneering *Bonds of Womanhood*, scholars have moved well beyond analyses that cast women's experiences as simply the outcome of industrialization and modernization. Indeed, it is now clear that the experiences and expectations of a variety of women, black and white, middle- and working-class, critically shaped the process of class formation. Even more important, we have begun to understand just how deeply gender was embedded in the social, economic, and cultural structures of democratic capitalism. In 1977, it would not have been possible to predict the outlines and complexities of this capacious body of scholarship; accordingly, it is difficult to see how future historians will amend and expand it. Still, several questions seem especially pressing. Recent work on the close association between whiteness and working-class masculinity raises several questions about women. How did whiteness shape working-class femininity? And how did it figure in the identities of middle-class women, especially those who did not involve themselves in the antislavery movement? The growing literature examining race in general and whiteness in particular – to say nothing of the literature on slavery – only serves to underscore the dearth of scholarship on free black women. We need to know far more about their experiences as workers, churchgoers, neighbors, wives, and activists. We surely need to know more about the ways in which they constructed race. Finally, as I have already suggested, nineteenth-century women's historians might supplement the rich literature on the capitalist transformation of work and production with studies of consumption, exploring how antebellum Americans developed the gendered dichotomies of making and spending.

BIBLIOGRAPHY

Baker, Paula (1984) "The Domestication of Politics: Women and American Political Society, 1780–1920," *American Historical Review* 89, pp. 620–47.

Blewett, Mary H. (1998) *Men, Women, and Work: A Study of Class, Gender, and Protest in the Nineteenth-century New England Shoe Industry, 1780–1910*. Urbana: University of Illinois Press.

Boydston, Jeanne (1990) *Home and Work: Housework, Wages, and the Ideology of Labor in the Early Republic*. New York: Oxford University Press.

Cashin, Joan E. (1995) "Black Families in the Old Northwest," *Journal of the Early Republic* 15, pp. 449–75.

Clark, Christopher (1990) *The Roots of Rural Capitalism: Western Massachusetts, 1780–1860*. Ithaca, NY: Cornell University Press.

Cott, Nancy F. (1977) *The Bonds of Womanhood: "Woman's Sphere" in New England, 1780–1835*. New Haven, CT: Yale University Press.

Cowan, Ruth Schwartz (1983) *More Work for Mother: The Ironies of Household Technology from the Open Hearth to the Microwave*. New York: Basic Books.

Douglas, Ann (1977) *The Feminization of American Culture*. New York: Alfred A. Knopf.

Dublin, Thomas (1979) *Women at Work: The Transformation of Work and Community in Lowell, Massachusetts, 1826–1860*. New York: Columbia University Press.

Dublin, Thomas (1994) *Transforming Women's Work: New England in the Industrial Revolution*. Ithaca, NY: Cornell University Press.

Dudden, Faye E. (1983) *Serving Women: Household Service in Nineteenth-century America*. Middletown, CT: Wesleyan University Press.

Ginzberg, Lori D. (1990) *Women and the Work of Benevolence: Morality, Politics, and Class in the Nineteenth-century United States*. New Haven, CT: Yale University Press.

Gordon, Beverly (1998) *Bazaars and Fair Ladies: The History of the American Fundraising Fair*. Knoxville: University of Tennessee Press.

Hansen, Karen V. (1994) *A Very Social Time: Crafting Community in Antebellum New England*. Berkeley: University of California Press.

Horton, James Oliver (1986) "Freedom's Yoke: Gender Conventions among Antebellum Free Blacks," *Feminist Studies* 12, pp. 51–76.

Horton, James Oliver and Horton, Lois E. (1997) *In Hope of Liberty: Culture, Community, and Protest among Northern Free Blacks, 1700–1860*. New York: Oxford University Press.

Jensen, Joan M. (1986) *Loosening the Bonds: Mid-Atlantic Farm Women, 1750–1850*. New Haven, CT: Yale University Press.

Kelley, Mary (1984) *Private Woman, Public Stage: Literary Domesticity in Nineteenth-century America*. New York: Oxford University Press.

Kelly, Catherine E. (1999) *In the New England Fashion: Reshaping Women's Lives in the Nineteenth Century*. Ithaca, NY: Cornell University Press.

Kerber, Linda K. (1988) "Separate Spheres, Female Worlds, Woman's Place: The Rhetoric of Women's History," *Journal of American History* 75, pp. 9–39.

Lasser, Carol (1987) "The Domestic Balance of Power: Relations between Mistress and Maid in Nineteenth-century New England," *Labor History* 28, pp. 5–22.

Lewis, Jan (1999) "Politics and the Ambivalence of the Private Sphere: Women in Early Washington, D.C.," in Donald R. Kennon (ed.), *A Republic for the Ages: The United States Capitol and the Political Culture of the Early Republic*. Charlottesville: United States Capitol Historical Society and University of Virginia Press, pp. 122–51.

Lubin, David M. (1994) *Picturing a Nation: Art and Social Change in Nineteenth-century America*. New Haven, CT: Yale University Press.

McGerr, Michael (1990) "Political Style and Women's Power, 1830–1930," *Journal of American History* 77, pp. 864–85.

McMurry, Sally Ann (1995) *Transforming Rural Life: Dairying Families and Agricultural Change, 1820–1885*. Baltimore: Johns Hopkins University Press.

Osterud, Nancy Grey (1991) *Bonds of Community: The Lives of Farm Women in Nineteenth-century New York*. Ithaca, NY: Cornell University Press.

Prude, Jonathan (1985) *The Coming of the Industrial Order: Town and Factory Life in Rural Massachusetts, 1810–1860*. New York: Cambridge University Press.

Ryan, Mary P. (1990) *Women in Public: Between Banners and Ballots, 1825–1880*. Baltimore: Johns Hopkins University Press.

Ryan, Mary P. (1981) *The Cradle of the Middle Class: The Family in Oneida County, New York, 1780–1865*. New York: Cambridge University Press.

Smith-Rosenberg, Carroll (1985) *Disorderly Conduct: Visions of Gender in Victorian America*. New York: Alfred A. Knopf.

Stansell, Christine (1986) *City of Women: Sex and Class in New York City, 1789–1860*. New York: Alfred A. Knopf.

Stearns, Peter and Lewis, Jan (eds.) (1998) *An Emotional History of the United States*. New York: New York University Press.

Strasser, Susan (1982) *Never Done: A History of American Housework*. New York: Pantheon.

Teute, Fredrika J. (1999) "Roman Matron on the Banks of Tiber Creek: Margaret Bayard Smith and the Politicization of Spheres in the Nation's Capital," in Donald R. Kennon (ed.), *A Republic for the Ages: The United States Capitol and the Political Culture of the Early Republic*. Charlottesville: United States Capitol Historical Society and University of Virginia Press, pp. 89–121.

Varon, Elizabeth R. (1998) *We Mean to be Counted: White Women and Politics in Antebellum Virginia*. Chapel Hill: University of North Carolina Press.

Waldstreicher, David (1997) *In the Midst of Perpetual Fetes: The Making of American Nationalism, 1776–1820*. Chapel Hill: University of North Carolina Press.

White, Shane and White, Graham (1998) *Stylin': African American Expressive Culture from its Beginnings to the Zoot Suit*. Ithaca, NY: Cornell University Press.

Zboray, Ronald J. and Zboray, Mary Saracino (1997) "Whig Women, Politics, and Culture in the Campaign of 1840: Three Perspectives from Massachusetts," *Journal of the Early Republic* 17, pp. 277–315.

Chapter Eight

Religion, Reform, and Radicalism in the Antebellum Era

Nancy A. Hewitt

THE cult of domesticity, the fires of evangelicalism, and the crusade for woman's rights marked the antebellum era as the harbinger of modern America. Foundational studies in US women's history, published in the late 1960s and 1970s, grappled with these seemingly contradictory impulses. Some focused on the distinctive configurations of family, church, and politics in the mid-nineteenth century; others searched for historical routes that would link the emergence of woman's rights in that era to its sister movements in the twentieth century. This work was complicated and challenged in the 1980s and 1990s by women's historians' increased attention to differences of race, region, religion, and class. At the beginning of the twenty-first century, changing definitions of politics and a growing interest in globalization have recast these narratives once again. This essay highlights research on women active in reform and radical movements in the early to mid-nineteenth century and on the ways that diverse cultural traditions and social circumstances shaped, curtailed, or nurtured the particular forms of social activism they pursued. The literature in this field is rich, provocative, and filled with contestation. The critical themes and debates sketched out here do not exhaust its possibilities. Instead, they suggest the powerful hold that religion and activism had on antebellum women and on the scholars who have sought to reclaim and explain their histories.

The decades between the American Revolution and the Civil War have attracted the attention of women's historians since the emergence of the field. Barbara Welter's classic 1966 essay, "The Cult of True Womanhood, 1820–1860," explored the complex ways in which a carefully constructed ideal sought to stabilize gender relations in the midst of rapid economic, social, political, and technological change. Here and in her 1973 article, "The Feminization of American Religion," both reprinted in *Dimity Convictions*, Welter sketched out a portrait of white, middle-class women relegated to home and church by Jacksonian men eager to embrace materialism and secularism but wary of overthrowing traditional ties to family and spirituality. She also suggested the power that some women gained through their embrace of new gender ideals and the possibility, because of those ideals' inherent contradictions, to wield them in pursuit of a wider sphere. In "Beauty, the Beast, and the Militant Woman," Carroll Smith-Rosenberg traced the development of female moral reform campaigns in the 1830s, demonstrating how notions of female domestic authority and spiritual superiority could, indeed, provide an entrée to the public sphere. In this case, the battle against the sexual double standard was possible because women activists could wrap themselves in the mantle of maternal piety. Clearly the cult of true womanhood was a double-edged sword, confining women to a separate and subordinate sphere, on the one hand, and nurturing an incipient feminism, on the other.

In her brilliant biography of Catharine Beecher, Kathryn Kish Sklar offered a third path for nineteenth-century true women. Beecher used women's supposed moral superiority to create a public career for herself and to expand educational opportunities for her sisters, all in the name of promoting domestic and maternal ideals. Although similar in many respects to moral reformers (and to female abolitionists) who justified their activities as pious interventions on behalf of abused women and children, Beecher and her followers retreated from direct attacks on male privilege and abjured involvement in overtly political movements. In this, they embraced the double-edged character of antebellum gender ideals, seeking to promote their influence and authority but only within the limited spheres marked out for them by a patriarchal culture.

Most of this early work highlighted the lives of women in the northeastern United States, where the first substantial publishing companies poured out reams of magazines, sermons, gift and prayer books, advice manuals, housekeeping guides, and other materials that were bought and read by the region's highly literate population. Literacy also assured the existence of a voluminous correspondence among women while rapid urbanization nurtured the formation of women's voluntary associations. The records of organizations like the American Female Moral Reform Society and its many local branches combined with women's letters to each other and to husbands, brothers, and ministers allowed historians to test admonitions and ideals against experiences and behavior. Although such materials were most available for white, urban, middle-class women, scholars did document northern women's lives more broadly by seeking out diaries, letters, and organizational papers for rural and small-town women and by utilizing church, poorhouse, and school records that illuminated the lives of women across the class spectrum. These materials also provided glimpses into the experiences of immigrant women and, less often, of African American women.

Southern white women in this period were, on the whole, less literate than their northern counterparts, less urbanized, and far less likely to launch public campaigns. Plantation mistresses did leave extensive diaries and letters, detailing their private thoughts and family experiences, and they did have access to a small number of women's magazines published in the South as well as those available from the North. Yet they often lived in isolated circumstances with little chance, or desire, to engage in collective ventures. Nonetheless, as pioneer women's historian Anne Firor Scott showed in *The Southern Lady*, tensions between the ideals of southern womanhood and the harsh realities of daily life could nurture critiques of patriarchal power and now and then a collective consciousness among some white women. In the crucible of Civil War and its aftermath, she argued, these would be transformed into public organization and action. During the antebellum era, only the church offered southern women an arena in which to express communal concerns. For white women, it provided a few opportunities for social activism in the form of missionary and charitable endeavors. For black women, slave and free, the church offered more complicated prohibitions and possibilities, but only rarely did women's historians explore the character of their lives for a decade after Scott's work appeared.

Early explorations of the intimate links among domesticity, religion, and social activism among white women inspired a profusion of scholarship in the late 1970s. Much of this work, directly or indirectly, focused on the emergence of the middle class as a discrete entity and its meaning for women's private and public roles. In *The Bonds of Womanhood*, Nancy Cott explored the construction and deployment of a "discourse of domesticity," tracing its emergence amid rapid economic and social development and its significance for work, religion, education, and "sisterhood." Although not the main focus of her work, Cott did, in her conclusion, tie the "flowering of women's associational activities" in the 1830s to "the revival movement of the early nineteenth century" (Cott [1977] 1997: xv, 133). These revivals, known collectively as the Second Great Awakening, had played a critical role for antebellum moral reformers and in the educational campaigns of Catharine Beecher. They were a response in part to Protestants' growing concerns about secularization, rationalism, and the influx of Catholic immigrants. Shifting away from traditional emphases on predestination and personal prayer, evangelical ministers like Charles Grandison Finney highlighted public conversions and good works as a sign of grace. Women flocked to the protracted meetings and prayer vigils that characterized this wave of revivals, reinforcing the feminization of religion that helped to make such techniques effective in the first place. They then served as conduits to conversion within their families and communities. It was only a small step from these individual efforts at promoting religion to collective movements aimed at creating a broader moral order.

A number of historians built on Cott's logic, tracing northern women's early involvement in charitable and missionary efforts through the Second Great Awakening to the explosion of moral reform, temperance, and antislavery efforts that followed in its wake. Even scholars who unearthed alternate paths to activism continued to view domestic ideals and evangelical fervor as the mainspring of antebellum women's public campaigns. Blanche Glassman Hersh, for example, explored the transition from abolitionism to woman's rights. She found that "emancipation from religious orthodoxy was a crucial element in the development of a feminist leadership" in this period. Yet she concluded that the ideology her abolitionist-feminists "bequeathed to future generations" was grounded in "evangelicals' concept of a woman's 'proper' sphere" and in their "romantic faith in the perfectibility of the race" (1978: ix, 205).

At the same time, the limits of evangelicalism as a stimulus to political action, first suggested by Welter and Sklar, were also probed more deeply. In *The Cradle of the Middle Class*, Mary Ryan linked men's pursuit of new mercantile, industrial, and professional careers in Oneida County, New York, to their wives' embrace of domestic ideals, evangelical religion, and civic responsibility. Here domesticity and revivalism converged with social activism, but only to bolster the emergence of a new urban bourgeoisie. For the families who saw themselves as advocates of a white, middle-class, Protestant, and ultimately patriarchal, agenda, women's public efforts solidified rather than challenged dominant gender ideals. Ellen DuBois's work on the emergence of an independent women's movement followed a similar logic. Earlier studies had suggested that the campaign against the sexual double standard by female moral reform societies pointed to the protofeminist possibilities of evangelically inspired activism. In DuBois's analysis of the woman's rights movement, the constraints became more visible. Indeed, DuBois argued that adherents of the radical notion that women deserved equal political rights with men had "a tendency to outgrow" their "evangelical origins." She still assumed that Protestant revivalism nurtured abolitionism initially; and that Quakers, Unitarians, and other religious liberals were drawn to the movement later, in part by William Lloyd Garrison's attacks on conservative clergy. Nonetheless, DuBois made clear that evangelical tenets could only carry women activists so far.

For mid-nineteenth-century women to embrace truly revolutionary visions seemed to demand either a break from revivalistic Protestantism or immersion from childhood in more progressive spiritual/political communities. Linda Gordon was among the first to make this case. In her sweeping social history, *Woman's Body, Woman's Right*, she analyzed the campaign for "voluntary motherhood," an early form of birth control based on a woman's right to say no to sexual intercourse. The movement only emerged fully in the 1870s, but the idea was born from three distinct strands of antebellum activism: moral reformers, women suffrage advocates, and "come-outers," that is, radical abolitionists and utopian communalists who rejected established churches and governments. Only members of the last group, who formed small circles of free lovers in the post-Civil War period, "could offer intellectual leadership in formulating the shocking arguments that birth control in the nineteenth century required" ([1976] 1990: 94). Most moral reformers, although they believed in a single sexual standard and in women's right to set that standard, focused their attention on prostitution and other forms of "deviant" behavior, not on "normal" marital relations. Suffragists included both radical theoreticians, such as Elizabeth Cady Stanton, and more moderate reformers; but their need to win mass support demanded that they all maintain a certain social respectability. The come-outers accepted no such constraints. Many embraced spiritualism and other liberal religious doctrines, and they followed the gender role experiments of utopian communalists with great interest. Some enhanced their freedom from mainstream expectations by moving to the Midwest. A large group settled in Lawrence, Kansas, for example. Once a hotbed of radical abolitionism, in the post-Civil War period, it became a center of the free love movement.

Scholars who studied groups outside the white, middle class also found that evangelical religion played an ambiguous, even contradictory, role in women's activism. Among Lowell mill operatives, for instance, church attendance was high; religion was embraced by many workers and attendance was mandated by factory owners, who supported the town's ministers. Yet laboring women's participation in strikes and other forms of collective action was nurtured elsewhere, in the dense kinship networks and communal living arrangements that characterized early factory life. Similarly, although religion was central to the lives of those rare southern women, like Sarah and Angelina Grimké, who pursued activist careers, it was the brutality of the slave system and the egalitarian principles of their adopted Quakerism – not the evangelical Protestant doctrines with which they were raised – that inspired their move north and their embrace of abolition and woman's rights. In utopian communities that brought together working-class and middle-class women and men and that experimented with more egalitarian gender roles, conventional religion in any form was eschewed. Although most of these experiments failed, they nonetheless demonstrated the possibilities of reconceiving domestic roles, spiritual commitments, social activism, and the relations among all three. For women, like Mary Paul – the daughter of a Vermont farmer, a one-time mill operative, and a resident of the Red Bank Fourierist Phalanx in 1855 – even a brief experience of receiving equal pay and of sharing in decision making with men opened up previously unimagined vistas.

The efforts of historians to reclaim a wider expanse of women's experiences intensified during the 1980s. Scholars continued to address issues of religion, reform, and radicalism, but they delved more deeply into the lives of southern, African American, and working-class women. Suzanne Lebsock's study of southern women in antebellum Petersburg, Virginia, for instance, both echoed and challenged work on their northern counterparts. She found that free women, black and white, organized charitable and missionary societies, established orphan asylums, and contributed to church-building funds. Many were moved to action by religious revivalism, and they dominated local benevolent efforts and individual congregations throughout most of the antebellum era. In the South, however, women's activism did not gradually expand to include moral reform and abolitionism, much less woman's rights. Instead, during the 1850s, men, especially white men, wrested control of benevolence from women. At the same time, white women and men joined together in the cause of temperance, the establishment of a public library, and the promotion of agricultural modernization and southern nationalism. Paralleling Ryan's analysis of Oneida County, New York, Lebsock found middle-class and affluent wives and daughters wielding a specifically women's culture in efforts that benefited their class and race as a whole. At the same time, poorer and African American women also sought to improve their families and communities by sharing scarce resources. Neither white or black women had the power to challenge patriarchal authority openly, but they did find in the construction of a distinct women's culture the possibility for some level of autonomy and collective action.

Theda Perdue offered another perspective on southern women's activism by introducing Cherokee women as central players in tribal politics and in negotiations between Indians, missionaries, and US government agents. In this context, domestic ideals and religious zeal offered women some relief from backbreaking labor and greater opportunities for formal education, but only at the cost of losing both property rights and communal authority. Yet as Perdue shows, Cherokee women retained sufficient power to advance or hinder missionary efforts, to challenge or support tribal leaders and government agents engaged in land sales, and to sustain or transform traditional rituals and customs.

African American women played equally important roles in their communities. Only among free blacks in the North, however, did they have the resources to establish voluntary societies and participate in religious and reform movements. In *We Are Your Sisters* (1984), Dorothy Sterling documented the efforts of black women North and South, in slavery and freedom. She was particularly attentive to the contributions free women made to building and sustaining families and communities, dispensing charity, promoting religion, and eradicating slavery. Focusing on mutual aid, black women founded benevolent, educational, and missionary societies in Philadelphia, Boston, New York, Newport, Rhode Island, Newburyport, Massachusetts, and other cities in the 1820s and 1830s. Literary clubs and antislavery societies also burgeoned in this period with African American women often setting the pace for their white sisters.

The community efforts of African American women were not confined to the middle class, which was often a small and fragile circle within the larger black community. In Philadelphia, 200 working-class African Americans established the Daughters of Africa in 1821 to provide funds for the sick and loans for funerals. Like the Daughters of Africa, many black women managed their own institutions; others formed associations under the umbrella of the African Methodist Episcopal church, the African Baptist church, and other religious organizations. They also joined mixed-sex associations with African American men and, more rarely, interracial societies with white women. This last connection was made mainly in the service of the antislavery movement, with men and women, black and white, serving as conductors on the underground railroad to help slaves escape to the North and fugitives maintain their freedom.

It was through their work with fugitives that free black women, and men, extended the patterns of southern slave resistance into northern climes. Documented by Gerda Lerner, Angela Y. Davis, and other pioneer scholars of African American women's history, daily resistance formed a critical weapon in the hands of women held in bondage. Although men outnumbered women among those who escaped slavery by running North, several women who made the journey successfully – including Harriet Tubman, Harriet Jacobs, and Ellen Craft – became significant figures in antislavery circles. The more common ways that slave women challenged white domination included initiating work slowdowns, confiscating food or other items from the white household, feigning pregnancy or illness, breaking tools, and in more extreme cases, using arson or poison to punish cruel masters and mistresses. Those fugitive women who found safe haven in the northern United States, Canada, or Great Britain publicized both the horrors of the slave system and the myriad ways that women protested its brutalities. Their testimonies were critical to recruiting other women to the abolitionist cause, particularly white women whose own experiences were far distant from those of their slave "sisters."

Like resistance in slave communities, many free black women's organizations were linked to religion. The activism of African American women in the North was rooted in black churches or fostered by a variety of spiritual commitments. Religion offered solace and hope to people abused and exploited, whether slave or free; and it provided some with an entrée to a wider world. In the early nineteenth century, newly established black churches hosted the largest number of women's missionary, charitable, literary, and antislavery societies. Unconventional spiritual journeys opened the doors for other women. The Society of Friends, for example, although a predominantly white institution, encouraged the activities of journalist Mary Ann Shadd Cary, abolitionist and suffragist Harriet Purvis, and educator and activist Sarah Douglass. Others, like Isabella Van Wagenen (Sojourner Truth), embraced ecstatic religions that inspired both public speaking and political advocacy. In addition, some women initially moved by traditional religious beliefs, such as Jarena Lee and Maria Stewart, were forced to reconsider their spiritual commitments when confronted by hostile ministers and elders. Jarena Lee was eventually recognized as an important lay preacher by the African Methodist Episcopal church; Maria Stewart made her name as a lecturer, but was driven from her Boston home by the condemnations heaped upon her by black civic leaders, especially ministers. For black as well as white women, then, conventional religious beliefs and institutions could only carry activism so far; certainly for many radical activists, a break with the mainstream churches seemed a necessary part of their political evolution.

The establishment of interracial movements among women also occurred largely outside mainstream religious circles. In 1833, just five years after the Hicksite Quakers split from the Orthodox members of the Society of Friends, a group of Hicksite women in Philadelphia met with a circle of local African American women to form the Philadelphia Female Anti-Slavery Society. This organization, the most important interracial association in the antebellum era, brought together radical Quakers, black and white, with members of some of the city's most affluent African American families. Radical Quakers also played central roles in interracial abolitionist efforts in western and central New York and in Michigan and other parts of the Midwest. In Rochester, Amy and Isaac Post and other white Hicksites helped convince Frederick Douglass to move to the city and publish his antislavery paper, the *North Star*, there. Douglass and the Posts were active in the interracial and mixed-sex Western New York Anti-Slavery Society and were among the circle that welcomed Harriet Jacobs to Rochester after her escape from slavery. Interracial groups, such as those in Rochester and Philadelphia, were also active in providing aid to fugitive slaves, campaigning for integration of public school systems, sustaining boycotts against slave-produced goods, and protesting the Mexican–American War, which threatened to expand significantly the size of slave territory in the United States.

Many of the most radical white Quakers involved in these efforts eventually left the Society of Friends altogether. Their advocacy of abolition, utopian communalism, peace, land reform, health reform, anti-tobacco and anti-capital punishment campaigns, Indian rights, and woman's rights, all in the company of non-Quakers, assured that those who did not leave the Society of their own accord would be dismissed. Some banded together to form more progressive religious groups – the Congregational Friends, the Progressive Friends, and the Friends of Human Progress – welcoming women and men, blacks and whites, to participate equally in governance and worship services. Ann Braude traced an important circle of early woman's rights advocates, including radical Quakers, into spiritualism in the late 1840s and 1850s. Embracing a religion that eliminated the need for ministers, elders, or any mediators between individuals and higher authorities, including God, feminist spiritualists found, at least in the early years of this movement, a kind of autonomy that institutionalized religions lacked. Other radicals found a home with the Unitarians, Universalists, and Free Will Baptists, or among Fourierists, or in the company of other come-outers in the New England Non-Resistant Society. Adopting an agenda of universal rights – in both religious and secular arenas – these activists brought together radical religious visions with radical political activism.

Yet the links between spiritual commitments and social causes was never simple. As Judith Wellman has shown, the Seneca Falls Woman's Rights Convention of July 1848 attracted not only radical Quakers but also more evangelically minded political abolitionists and more secularly oriented legal reformers. The last group had led the fight for a married women's property rights law in New York State, which passed in the spring preceding the convention. In other cases, evangelical religion promoted radical thinking and inspired many women to actions well beyond those imagined, and approved, by clergy. One particularly intriguing example involves the church trial of Rhoda Bement, analyzed by Glenn Altschuler and Jan M. Saltzgaber. Set in the village of Seneca Falls in 1843, the trial illuminates one woman's path from religious conviction to social activism. Bement was disciplined for "unchristian and unladylike" conduct after challenging her minister at the local First Presbyterian church for refusing to read her announcement of an antislavery lecture by Abby Kelley. She was then excommunicated for attending the neighboring Wesleyan Methodist church, an antislavery congregation that became the site of the woman's rights convention five years later. In nearby Rochester, two leading woman's rights advocates had been members of evangelical churches, including Abigail Bush, who presided over the Rochester Woman's Rights Convention in August 1848. Like Bement, they were excommunicated for their abolitionist activities in the early 1840s.

As women's historians explored more radical social movements – including not only abolitionism and woman's rights, but also nonresistance, utopian communalism, health reform, spiritualism, and labor organizing – the links between mainstream Protestantism and women's activism appeared increasingly frayed. Indeed, Christine Stansell's *City of Women*, which documented the lives of laboring women in late eighteenth- and early nineteenth-century New York City, critiqued rather than applauded the activities of white, middle-class, evangelical women. Her heroines were the native-born and immigrant working women who tried by various means to assure their own survival and that of their community. Middling, and meddling, women reformers only made their lives harder by intruding into family relations, demanding bourgeois standards of domesticity and childrearing, and demonizing the few leisure pursuits that liberated women from the drudgery of their daily lives. Among the desperate mothers, streetwise children, and Bowery gals, Stansell brought to life women like Elizabeth Gray, the chairwoman of the Ladies' Industrial Association. The members of the organization staged a strike in 1845, declaring themselves independent women who needed to earn a living. Echoing the republican ideals voiced by laboring men and women in the 1820s and 1830s, Gray declared of the turnout, "we know it to be our duty, and that of every female who wishes to earn an honest livelihood." Her confederates agreed: " 'The boon we ask is founded upon RIGHT alone,' the women averred, and vowed 'to take upon themselves the task of asserting their rights against the unjust and mercenary conduct of their employers' " (Stansell 1986: 146). Here was a protofeminist claim, but one quite distinct from that voiced by the Female Moral Reform Society a decade earlier. Some middle- and upper-class women reformers did support the association's demands, but their desire to link the workers' cause to the "universal plight of womanhood" obscured rather than illuminated working women's plight which eventually undercut the value of the alliance (1986: 148).

Christine Stansell, like Dorothy Sterling, demonstrated the distance between working-class and African American women activists, on the one hand, and their more affluent white counterparts, on the other. At the same time, a number of scholars have continued to unravel the distinctions among middle-class white activists. In Rochester, New York, I distinguished three competing circles – well-to-do benevolent women from Rochester's oldest, nonevangelical Protestant churches; upwardly mobile moral reformers who embraced evangelicalism; and the more economically marginal radical Quakers noted above. Ann Boylan traced differences among "Timid Girls, Venerable Widows, and Dignified Matrons" in New York and Boston, tracing how life-cycle differences shaped women's activism. Lori Ginzberg analyzed changes in women's organizations across time, showing that those established in the flush of religious and moral fervor in the 1830s contained both conservative and progressive possibilities. Like Ryan, she suggested that benevolent work was an important vehicle for claiming a bourgeois gender identity. Ginzberg argued as well, however, that by the Civil War era, class rather than gender came to define benevolent ideology. In this period, business methods and legal frameworks, such as incorporation, replaced moral suasion as the governing principle of women's voluntary efforts.

By the 1990s, studies of antebellum women's activism that compared individuals, networks, and organizations across time or in the context of a single community gave way to more detailed investigations of specific movements and issues. The antislavery movement still garnered the greatest attention, but female benevolence, women's work for peace, dress reform, labor organizing, and woman's rights also received closer examination. Biographies of individual activists added a critical personal dimension to this literature, and documentary collections enriched our resources by providing scholars and students with ready access to a wide range of primary materials.

Among the burgeoning studies on abolitionism, women's historians explored black and white women's efforts in greater depth; illuminated the intricate and varied relations among religion, reform, and radicalism; and complicated any easy generalizations about what inspired women to act and what nurtured particular forms of activism. In "*Doers of the Word*," Carla Peterson located African American women abolitionists in the context of black speakers, writers, and preachers throughout the mid-nineteenth century. Jean Fagan Yellin and John Van Horne edited a collection on women's antebellum political culture that brought together a range of essays on black, white, and interracial antislavery societies. Julie Roy Jeffrey provided the first comprehensive survey of ordinary black and white women's abolitionist efforts, while Anna Speicher explored the religious world of five prominent lecturers in the cause. Biographies of Lucy Stone, Abby Kelley, Sojourner Truth, and Mary Ann Shadd Cary traced the distinct paths that these powerful women followed among the thicket of organizations, ideologies, and strategies that emerged between the 1820s and the 1850s. Finally, Mary Hershberger's pathbreaking 1999 article on women's petition campaigns against Indian removal in the late 1820s and early 1830s unveiled an important precursor to the wave of antislavery petitions that circulated a few years later.

Taken together, this body of scholarship made three major contributions to our understanding of antebellum women's activism. Much of the earlier literature had focused on those individuals and organizations that linked the battle against slavery to the campaign for woman's rights. The newer work highlighted a broader spectrum of activists, including both more conservative white women who rejected woman's rights and racial equality, and free black women, many (but not all) of whom viewed woman's rights as a distraction from the more critical campaign against slavery. Although any woman advocating abolition in the early to mid-nineteenth century was stepping beyond the bounds idealized in the cult of true womanhood, there were important distinctions in how severely those boundaries were tested. Many, mostly white, women sought to work within dominant gender conventions – accepting male leadership, forming whites-only ladies' auxiliaries, staying within evangelical churches, and denying any intent to promote their own rights. Others, including most blacks and smaller circles of whites, defied the racial and gender status quo. They joined interracial and/or mixed-sex associations; came out of mainstream churches and religious meetings; demanded equal rights within antislavery organizations and the larger society; and fought against racial discrimination in schools, public accommodations, and social welfare institutions. Between these two extremes, many women struggled to sustain their antislavery activism while walking the tightrope between racial accommodationism and egalitarianism, female activism and feminism. Although more evangelicals embraced a moderate or conservative mode of abolitionism and more Quakers the radical mode, the lines were never sharply drawn, especially when black evangelicals are incorporated into the analysis.

The second major contribution of studies completed in the last decade is the rich evocation of African American women's community work. Recovering the dense networks of literary, charitable, missionary, and reform societies among northern free blacks, historians recognize abolitionism as one strand in this wider activist tapestry. It is clear now that in dozens of cities and towns, the pioneers of women's antislavery work were African American. In more than one case, their efforts inspired, or shamed, white women into embracing the cause. In addition, African American women almost uniformly linked the eradication of slavery to the advancement of rights among free blacks. They also dedicated themselves to the support of fugitives from bondage, several of whom became leading spokespersons for the cause, including Ellen Craft and Harriet Jacobs. Sojourner Truth, too, though born into slavery in New York State, had to flee her master in order to gain freedom and pursue an activist life. It was this broader agenda of empowerment that marked the work of interracial abolitionist societies as well, suggesting the critical role of black women in defining the radical wing of the movement. At the same time, free black women seemed far more likely than their white counterparts to maintain their traditional religious affiliations and to view the church as a resource rather than a barrier.

The third contribution involves the scope of women's antislavery activism. As Gerda Lerner and Judith Wellman noted in the 1970s in their studies of antislavery petition campaigns, the abolitionist movement attracted the support of women in farming communities, small villages, boom towns, and large cities. These more recent studies confirm and expand upon this portrait by tracing the diverse array of women's antislavery sewing societies, fundraising fairs, participation in conventions, contributions to the abolitionist press, embrace of the free produce movement, protests against discrimination in churches, schools, and public transportation, work on the underground railroad, and aid to fugitive slaves. In addition, scholars have traced the ways that antislavery images, such as the shackled female slave, circulated through the wider culture along with women lecturers, women's antislavery writings, and women's petitions. Still, however, we need to make clearer the links between the everyday resistance of African American women in bondage and the development of antislavery efforts and discourse among free women, black and white.

Although it is clear now that not all abolitionists became woman's rights advocates, it is still acknowledged that nearly all pioneer woman's rights advocates embraced abolitionism. Those connections have now been more closely scrutinized, with greater attention to the roles played by African Americans and by men. Building on Benjamin Quarles's 1939 lecture, "Frederick Douglass and the Woman's Rights Movement," Rosalyn Terborg-Penn has recently explored the place of African American women in the struggle for the vote, beginning with their participation in antebellum woman's rights conventions. At the same time, Stacey Robertson has offered the first full-length analysis of an abolitionist man's commitment to feminism in her moving biography of Parker Pillsbury. Works such as these laid the groundwork for Bruce Dorsey's *Gender in the City*, the first fully gendered account of antebellum activism. Dorsey uses a case study of Philadelphia to address white and black women's and men's struggles against an array of social and political ills in the urban North, illuminating the distinct experiences of each group as well as the common concerns and practices that mark their efforts. Attentive to class and generational as well as race and gender relations, this book offers a pathbreaking model for future studies.

The work that has appeared over the past decade demands that we recast histories of antebellum activism on a broader historical plain. Studies of philanthropy by Kathleen D. McCarthy, utopian communities and peace movements by Wendy Chmielewski, and antebellum reform more generally by Lori Ginzberg suggest the benefits of a wider lens. New approaches to the history of woman's rights have proven especially fruitful. By analyzing more fully the racial, class, and gender dynamics of a far-flung movement rather than focusing only on the single path from Seneca Falls to suffrage, scholars are remapping as well as reimagining feminism's first wave. Historians have excavated evidence of woman's rights efforts in a variety of arenas both before and after Seneca Falls. Jacob Katz Cogan and Lori Ginzberg uncovered an 1846 petition to the New York State legislature by six women in Jefferson County, seeking the right to vote. Nancy Isenberg has traced debates over woman's rights in churches, state legislatures, and the family throughout the antebellum era. Focusing on claims for rights and citizenship rather than suffrage alone, she explores women's place in controversies over Sabbath laws, capital punishment, prostitution, temperance, property rights, and labor reform. Combined with evidence on working women's demands for rights culled from Dublin and Stansell, and the claims made by early utopian communalists such as Frances Wright, African American lecturers like Maria Stewart, and advocates of nonresistance, including Henry Wright, it seems clear that the Seneca Falls Woman's Rights Convention occurred in the midst of broad and contentious debates over the rights, roles, and relations of women and men.

Scholars have also focused greater attention on the revolutionary atmosphere in which the 1848 woman's rights conventions in Seneca Falls and Rochester unfolded. Bonnie Anderson's pathbreaking study, *Joyous Greetings*, locates the formation of a formal woman's rights movement in the United States in the history of European radical movements during the 1830s and 1840s. Isenberg extends this international perspective by documenting feminist-abolitionists' participation in protests against the US war with Mexico. My own current work – "Origin Stories: Remapping the Feminist First Wave" – explores, in addition, woman's rights advocates' concern with the abolition of slavery in the English and French Caribbean and immigrant, Indian, and Mexican/Mexican American women's involvement in struggles over rights during the antebellum era. At the same time, Judith Wellman is completing the most in-depth study to date of the Seneca Falls Woman's Rights Convention and the various women and men who participated in it. Taken together, this work reframes the emergence of woman's rights in the United States as a process that developed over several decades and in diverse arenas in the context of the international flow of people, movements, and ideas.

This new vision of the woman's rights movement owes much to recent reconsiderations of the concept of politics. Transformed by feminist activists and scholars in the 1960s and 1970s to include contests over power and resources within and beyond the state, several historians have offered compelling analyses of the particular meaning of politics in the mid- to late nineteenth century. Among these are Evelyn Brooks Higginbotham's persuasive interpretation of the struggles over authority in the Black Baptist Convention; Elizabeth Varon's recovery of southern women's extensive participation in the Whig Party; and, most notably, Elsa Barkley Brown's brilliant explorations of black women's critical roles in church, community, and electoral politics during the transition from slavery to freedom. As part of a cohort of scholars who have broadened the definition of politics to include individual and collective acts of resistance as well as more formal and institutional efforts at mobilization, Brown has reclaimed freed blacks' understanding of the vote as a communal rather than personal right and struggles for power as combining battles for economic, social, cultural, legal, and electoral resources and autonomy. Moreover, she, like Bruce Dorsey, urges us to be more attentive to gender, distinguishing between women's and men's activism where appropriate but also recognizing, as some early women's historians had suggested, the deeply intertwined character of their efforts.

As we move into a new century of activism and scholarship, we still have much to learn from those who launched religious, reform, and radical movements in the early to mid-nineteenth century. New work in the field must wield new understandings of politics and its intricate relations to religion, family, and community; draw connections among the activist agendas and visions of diverse groups of women and men; recognize the global dynamics that shaped US movements; and integrate more fully the detailed explorations of individual communities with more sweeping analyses of national and regional organizations, campaigns, and leaders. In doing so, we both capture the complex realities of antebellum women's activism and make their experiences speak more clearly to our own.

BIBLIOGRAPHY

Altschuler, Glenn C. and Saltzgaber, Jan M. (1983) *Revivalism, Social Conscience and Community in the Burned-over District: The Trial of Rhoda Bement.* Ithaca, NY: Cornell University Press.

Anderson, Bonnie (2000) *Joyous Greetings: The First International Women's Movement, 1830–1860.* New York: Oxford University Press.

Boylan, Anne (1986) "Timid Girls, Venerable Widows, and Dignified Matrons: Life Cycle Patterns among Organized Women in New York and Boston, 1787–1840," *American Quarterly* 38, pp. 779–98.

Braude, Ann (1989) *Radical Spirits: Spiritualism and Women's Rights in Nineteenth-century America.* Boston: Beacon Press.

Brown, Elsa Barkley (1994) "Negotiating and Transforming the Public Sphere: African American Political Life in the Transition from Slavery to Freedom," *Public Culture* 7, pp. 107–46.

Chmielewski, Wendy E. (1995) "'Binding Themselves the Closer to Their Own Peculiar Duties': Gender and Women's Work for Peace, 1818–1860," *Peace and Change* 20, pp. 466–90.

Chmielewski, Wendy E., Kern, Louis J., and Klee-Hartzell, Marlyn (eds.) (1993) *Women in Spiritual and Communitarian Societies in the United States.* Syracuse, NY: Syracuse University Press.

Cogan, Jacob Katz and Ginzberg, Lori D. (1997) "Archives: 1846 Petition for Woman's Suffrage, New York State Constitutional Convention," *Signs* 22, pp. 427–39.

Coleman, Willi (1990) "Travelling Black Women: Spreading the Anti-slavery Message Beyond Hearth and Home," in Frances Richardson Keller (ed.), *Views of Women's Lives in Western Traditions.* New York: Edwin Mellin Press, pp. 547–68.

Cott, Nancy F. (1977) *The Bonds of Womanhood: "Woman's Sphere" in New England, 1780–1835.* New Haven, CT: Yale University Press. Rpt. (1997), with new preface.

Davis, Angela Y. (1981) *Women, Race, and Class.* New York: Random House.

Dorsey, Bruce (2002) *Reforming Men and Women: Gender in the Antebellum City.* Ithaca, NY: Cornell University Press.

Dublin, Thomas (1979) *Women at Work: The Transformation of Work and Community in Lowell, Massachusetts, 1826–1860.* New York: Columbia University Press.

Dublin, Thomas (ed.) (1993) *Farm to Factory: Women's Letters, 1830–1860*, 2nd ed. New York: Columbia University Press.

DuBois, Ellen (1978) *Feminism and Suffrage: The Emergence of an Independent Women's Movement in America, 1848–1869.* Ithaca, NY: Cornell University Press.

Ginzberg, Lori D. (1990) *Women and the Work of Benevolence: Morality, Politics, and Class in the Nineteenth-century United States.* New Haven, CT: Yale University Press.

Ginzberg, Lori D. (2000) *Women in Antebellum Reform.* Wheeling, IL: Harlan Davidson.

Gordon, Linda (1976) *Woman's Body, Woman's Rights: A Social History of Birth Control in America.* New York: Grossman. Revised and updated ed. (1990), New York: Penguin.

Hersh, Blanche Glassman (1978) *The Slavery of Sex: Feminist-Abolitionism in America.* Urbana: University of Illinois Press.

Hershberger, Mary (1999) "Mobilizing Women, Anticipating Abolition: The Struggle against Indian Removal in the 1830s," *Journal of American History* 86, pp. 15–40.

Hewitt, Nancy A. (1984) *Women's Activism and Social Change: Rochester, New York, 1822–1872.* Ithaca, NY: Cornell University Press.

Higginbotham, Evelyn Brooks (1993) *Righteous Discontent: The Women's Movement in the Black Baptist Church, 1880–1920.* Cambridge, MA: Harvard University Press.

Isenberg, Nancy (1998) *Sex and Citizenship in Antebellum America.* Chapel Hill: University of North Carolina Press.

Jeffrey, Julie Roy (1998) *The Great Silent Army of Abolitionism: Ordinary Women in the Antislavery Movement.* Chapel Hill: University of North Carolina Press.

Kerr, Andrea Moore (1992) *Lucy Stone: Speaking Out for Equality.* New Brunswick, NJ: Rutgers University Press.

Lebsock, Suzanne (1984) *The Free Women of Petersburg: Status and Culture in a Southern Town, 1784–1860.* New York: W. W. Norton.

Lerner, Gerda (1977) *The Grimké Sisters from South Carolina: Pioneers for Woman's Rights and Abolition.* New York: Schocken Books.

Lerner, Gerda (1979) *The Majority Finds its Past: Placing Women in History.* New York: Oxford University Press.

McCarthy, Kathleen D. (1998) *Women and Philanthropy in the United States, 1790–1990.* New York: Center for the Study of Philanthropy, City University of New York.

Painter, Nell Irvin (1996) *Sojourner Truth: A Life, A Symbol.* New York: W. W. Norton.

Perdue, Theda (1985) "Southern Indians and the Cult of True Womanhood," in Walter J. Fraser, Jr., R. Frank Saunders, Jr., and Jon L. Wakelyn (eds.), *The Web of Southern Social Relations: Women, Family and Education.* Athens: University of Georgia Press, pp. 35–51.

Peterson, Carla L. (1995) "*Doers of the Word*": *African-American Women Speakers and Writers in the North, 1830–1880.* New York: Oxford University Press.

Quarles, Benjamin (1993) "Frederick Douglass and the Woman's Rights Movement," Occasional Paper Series, No. 1–1993. Baltimore: Morgan State University Foundation.

Rhodes, Jane (1998) *Mary Ann Shadd Cary: The Black Press and Protest in the Nineteenth Century.* Bloomington: Indiana University Press.

Robertson, Stacey M. (2000) *Parker Pillsbury: Radical Abolitionist, Male Feminist.* Ithaca, NY: Cornell University Press.

Ryan, Mary P. (1981) *The Cradle of the Middle Class: The Family in Oneida County, New York, 1780–1865.* New York: Cambridge University Press.

Scott, Anne Firor (1970) *The Southern Lady: From Pedestal to Politics, 1830–1930.* Chicago: University of Chicago Press.

Sklar, Kathryn Kish (1973) *Catharine Beecher: A Study in American Domesticity.* New Haven, CT: Yale University Press.

Smith-Rosenberg, Carroll (1971) "Beauty, the Beast, and the Militant Woman: A Case Study of Sex Roles and Social Stress in Jacksonian America," *American Quarterly* 23, pp. 562–84.

Speicher, Anna M. (2000) *The Religious World of Antislavery Women: Spirituality in the Lives of Five Abolitionist Lecturers.* Syracuse, NY: Syracuse University Press.

Stansell, Christine (1986) *City of Women: Sex and Class in New York City, 1789–1860.* New York: Alfred A. Knopf.

Sterling, Dorothy (ed.) (1984) *We Are Your Sisters: Black Women in the Nineteenth Century.* New York: W. W. Norton.

Sterling, Dorothy (1991) *Ahead of Her Time: Abby Kelly and the Politics of Antislavery.* New York: W. W. Norton.

Terborg-Penn, Rosalyn (1998) *African American Women and the Struggle for the Vote, 1850–1920.* Bloomington: Indiana University Press.

Varon, Elizabeth R. (1998) *We Mean to be Counted: White Women and Politics in Antebellum Virginia.* Chapel Hill: University of North Carolina Press.

Wellman, Judith (1980) "Women and Radical Reform in Antebellum Upstate New York: A Profile of Grassroots Female Abolitionists," in Mabel E. Deutrich and Virginia C. Purdy (eds.), *Studies in the History of American Women.* Washington, DC: Howard University Press, pp. 113–27.

Wellman, Judith (1991) "The Seneca Falls Woman's Rights Convention: A Study of Social Networks," *Journal of Women's History* 3, pp. 9–37.

Welter, Barbara (1966) "The Cult of True Womanhood, 1820–1860," *American Quarterly* 18, pp. 151–74.

Welter, Barbara (1976) *Dimity Convictions: The American Woman in the Nineteenth Century.* Athens: Ohio State University Press.

Yee, Shirley J. (1992) *Black Women Abolitionists: A Study in Activism, 1828–1860.* Knoxville: University of Tennessee Press.

Yellin, Jean Fagan (1989) *Women and Sisters: The Antislavery Feminists in American Culture.* New Haven, CT: Yale University Press.

Yellin, Jean Fagan and Van Horne, John C. (eds.) (1994) *The Abolitionist Sisterhood: Women's Political Culture in Antebellum America.* Ithaca, NY: Cornell University Press.

Chapter Nine

Conflicts and Cultures in the West

Lisbeth Haas

THE history of the West defies the conceptual and temporal boundaries set by historians who work from within the framework of the nation-state. By the start of the early national period, the histories of Southwestern and Plains Indian societies had long been influenced, to varying degrees, by the European colonial presence, especially the Spanish settlement of New Mexico (1598) and Texas (1690) and the transformations produced by French and English trade. The timing and nature of change in the region varied greatly. The Spanish conquest of California, for example, only began in 1769 and proceeded apace as the political structure of the United States, and new gender relations therein, took shape. The 1803 Louisiana Purchase moved the borders of the United States up against those of Spain. Fur traders and explorers established overland routes to the Pacific Northwest shortly thereafter. In 1821, Mexico won independence from Spain. Settlers from the United States, including slaveowners and enslaved persons, quickly began moving into Texas. Numerically overwhelming the Mexican and Indian populations, the settlers initiated a war for independence and Texas became a republic in 1836. Soon after the US Congress voted to annex Texas in 1845, Mexico and the United States went to war. In 1848, the United States acquired most of the Far West in the Treaty of Guadalupe Hidalgo that ended the war.

Indigenous women and Spanish colonial settlers who inhabited the various regions of the West bore distinctive histories that continued to influence the nature of society after the United States conquered successive areas and peoples. In addition, the US government forced the migration of nearly every eastern tribe to the area west of the Mississippi by 1848. Most African American women initially moved west as slaves when their owners claimed lands in Texas from the 1820s on. These settlements remained concentrated in Texas and along the eastern edge of the trans-Mississippi frontier until the early 1840s, when the first sustained migration of white women and children from the United States began on the overland trail.

Between 1840 and 1870, 250,000 to 500,000 people traveled overland to California, Oregon, and elsewhere. The gold rush in California that began in 1848 and waned after 1853 stimulated chains of family migration from all over the United States. It also initiated substantial migration from Asia, Europe, and Latin America.

Many Chinese women first arrived under coercive conditions during the gold rush. They faced an onslaught of racial hostility, and virtual exclusion after 1882. During these same years, Indian wars engulfed large areas of the Southwest and Plains. Only the Navajo received a substantial portion of reservation land in the Southwest. Elsewhere in the former Mexican territories, American migration ultimately created tremendous land loss, dramatic change, and substantial poverty, affecting the entire Mexican-descent and Native American population by 1880.

The West remained by far the most ethnically diverse area of the United States, a trend reinforced by migrations from around the world. Yet miscegenation laws, formulated as early as 1835 in the Texas republic, developed in the Far West to prohibit intermarriage between nonwhite and white persons. Although states in the South, East, and Midwest passed miscegenation legislation, none embraced the same range of purported racial groups as that written in the West. These regulations formed part of the legal and extralegal system of race inequality that shaped the West by 1880.

Until scholars of women began writing the history of the West in the late 1970s, the image of the area created by academic and popular media never embraced the multiple stories of the region's peoples and places. Instead, historians created a West "consistently identified with maleness – particularly white maleness" and a literature that "naturalizes and universalizes white manhood" more thoroughly than any other regional history (Johnson 1996: 255). The recovery of the "woman's West" changed the tale from one focused on gun-toting frontiersmen, miners, and ranchers to one focused on the creation of communities within a multi-ethnic frontier. However, the initial work on western women tended to frame the history from the perspective of white women migrants, despite scholars' intention to write a "multicultural" history.

This trend shifted as more historians began to write about nonwhite women from within the framework of indigenous, Spanish, Mexican, and Asian histories, thereby more accurately interpreting women's actions, communities, and politics. The growing body of scholarship on nonwhite residents, who formed a clear majority of women during these years, enables Anglo-American women's experiences to be interpreted more precisely as well. In this region, interethnic interactions and gender policies of conquest shaped all women's experiences, though they affected nonwhite women far more adversely than white women.

The Gendered Politics of Conquest

One of the major conflicts in the West involved the deployment of a highly gendered politics of conquest that proceeded simultaneously on the eastern and western seaboards. These policies, directed toward "civilizing" and culturally assimilating Indian peoples, attempted to impose new gender norms. Both Anglo-American and Spanish culture and practice demanded a shift away from the arrangements common in indigenous societies whereby men and women assumed complementary but differentiated roles that offered women power and autonomy from men in general, and from their husbands in particular. Though native societies differed greatly, men tended to assume primary responsibility for hunting, warfare, and interacting with the outside world. Even when men made most decisions about war and negotiations for peace, a number of societies assigned women some authority in this domain, especially over the fate of captives. At the same time, women tended to manage and "own" the place of family residence, household goods, the fields they cultivated, and the places where they gathered specific goods. Women derived multiple kinds of authority from their control over the production and distribution of food and from their role as mothers.

In the East, the government and missionaries adopted a cultural program of assimilation that encouraged men to farm and assume the position of head of household. This policy subverted the position of women, especially in indigenous societies organized around matrilineal and matrilocal practices. In these societies, kin relations passed through the female line and the female-centered household favored the mother–child relationship. Assimilation policies encouraged women to limit their work to the confines of the home and to those positions in the family, economy, and government that corresponded to gender norms then developing among Anglo-Americans. The US government also encouraged the adoption of constitutions, male suffrage, and patrilineal kinship systems for naming and land distribution.

Much of the debate among historians over Indian–white relations during these years has focused on whether native women lost power and status within their own societies through contact, trade, and the gender policies promoting assimilation and Christianity. Since the mid-1990s, scholars have favored the idea of women as "negotiators of change," the title of a set of essays edited by Nancy Shoemaker. Those essays describe the way women from particular tribal groups "sought alternatives and created a new understanding of their roles by merging traditional beliefs with cultural innovation" (Shoemaker 1995: 20). Among the Cherokee, for example, many women assumed new gender tasks around animal husbandry, spinning, weaving, and sewing cloth garments. Here, as elsewhere, they added this work to their former responsibilities without giving up their positions of power and autonomy. Yet these changes undermined the legal recognition of their power. The Cherokee established a national police force in 1808 to give protection to children as heirs to the father's property and to assure the widow her share, thus fostering a system of male proprietorship of the home and land. In 1827 the Cherokee nation adopted a constitution that extended the vote to free male citizens, building on men's traditional role in politics, but potentially freeing them from the need to represent the interests of the seven matrilineal clans. Women kept the clans and local governing councils alive, however, "as origination points for grassroots resistance, thereby diminishing the central control of the National Council over the majority of families" (Dunaway 1997: 179).

The Cherokee and other "civilized" tribes of the South were forcibly removed to Indian territory west of the Mississippi in the years following the Indian Removal Bill of 1830. The tensions between various factions over removal and after settlement in the West continued to involve struggles over proper gender roles and the rights of women and matrilineal clans. Whatever the descriptions of customary rights, almost all the tribal governments that formed in the West acknowledged Indian women's rights to land and property. Yet, they also placed ever greater amounts of political power in the hands of tribal men.

Historians have also traced women's negotiation of change through the fur trade, which covered a vast region extending from the Great Lakes to the Pacific Northwest and California. The most recent studies argue that both men and women participated in the trade, replacing the idea that the trade subordinated native women because it rested on men's hunting practices. Instead, the situation offered different opportunities to women, who played gender-specific but central roles, supplying particular goods to the Europeans and seeking items distinct from those men acquired. Women also created vital links between their communities and European traders through marriage.

Women across the fur-trading region commonly took up new kinds of work that integrated them into the emerging economies, often adding that work to their patterns of seasonal labor. But European men, who wrote most of the records about contact, were often unable to see women or dismissed their presence as insignificant. For example, when a delegation of women appeared before a military commander to protest the forced removal of Sauk Indians of the Fox-Wisconsin River area to west of the Mississippi in 1831, their protest went virtually unrecorded. An official transcript of the meeting merely noted, "One of the women then rose and said that the land was theirs and had never been sold and so forth." The autobiography of Black Hawk, in contrast, elaborated upon the demands the women made and recorded the major general's dismissal of them. The general, Black Hawk wrote, told the women "that the president did not send him here to make treaties with the women, nor to hold council with them!" (Murphy 1995: 73). Black Hawk's record demonstrates one of the ways native women's power continued to be acknowledged within indigenous societies while being dismissed by representatives of the US government.

Gender politics similarly pervaded the Spanish conquest of the Native American population in California that began in 1769. The Spanish intended to conquer and settle California by converting and "Hispanicizing" a majority of the Indian population through the work of Catholic missions. Missionaries employed strict guidelines concerning gender roles and values, emulating those in Spanish society. The priests taught shame toward the body, but their vigilance of bodily practices focused on women. While they took Christian boys and girls from their parents at around the age of eight and placed them in dormitories until marriage, they kept a far tighter surveillance over the girls, who often had to work within the confines of the dormitory patios. The missionaries took careful note, as well, of married women's pregnancies. Women caught practicing traditional modes of reproductive control were punished, and missionaries commonly reported their suspicions that women confined to the missions practiced abortion and infanticide.

Indigenous boys and men could assume positions that held particular kinds of authority within the missions, but few such positions were opened to girls or women. The native population voted men into positions as *alcaldes* or leaders who mediated between their communities and the missionaries. Boys and men interpreted and taught catechism, were among the few taught to read and write, and worked in jobs that brought greater liberty and authority, such as *vaquero* (cowboy) and sheepshearer. Men also assumed positions as master craftsmen in the manufacturing establishments of the missions. Women worked as artisans and completed common labor with other women, especially concerning food procurement and processing. They took care of the material needs of their families and communities under major constraints, and they worked on jobs with men that related to building, planting, and harvesting. Men, in contrast, very rarely assumed women's jobs. While women's modes of negotiating power within the missions have yet to be studied, scholars have traced their significant roles in resistance and rebellion. Only when this story has been fully told will we gain a better sense of women's myriad roles in, and responses to, the gendered politics of conquest.

Captivity, Conquest, and Status in the Borderlands

Analyses of conquest generally focus on the collective experiences of native women, but during expeditions of exploration and settlement, the role of cultural negotiator fell heavily on individual indigenous women who acted as translators and interpreters. Historians commonly portray their stories heroically, as they have done for Sacajawea, a Shoshone Indian woman who accompanied the Lewis and Clark expedition from the Missouri River to the Pacific coast in 1805. Yet Sacajawea, like most women who translated and interpreted in the early years of exploration and conquest, acted from within a context of pervasive violence and rape that accompanied exploration, contact, and Indian–white hostility. These women used their intelligence to ensure individual survival under extremely adverse conditions.

In New Mexico, people traded as slaves constituted one of the largest groups to negotiate culture under conditions of severe loss and inequality. Traded through a captive-exchange network that created one of the "vital, and violent, webs of interdependence" that knit together diverse communities from the Plains to the Rocky mountains, the system took thousands of indigenous women and men, and hundreds of Spanish women and children, into societies other than their own (Brooks 1996: 280). Settlers favored women, and purchased women captives for twice the price they paid for men. In New Mexico by 1800, these captive slaves and their descendents, called *genizaros*, numbered 7,000 persons out of a total population of 19,275. "Detribalized," renamed, and baptized to Catholicism, they could assume freedom, by law, upon the age of twenty-one or when assimilated into Spanish customs and practice. But in a society in which family honor and status intertwined closely with the degree to which women of the family remained protected from sexual aggression, *genizaro* women were particularly vulnerable as subject persons within Spanish households. Moreover, they retained a low status in a setting where social worth derived from a combination of factors, including legitimacy, ancestry, religion and the religious standing of one's family, race, occupation, and ownership of land.

Women settlers of Spanish, mestizo, and mulatto descent who inhabited New Mexico and other areas of the Spanish borderlands played a crucial role in colonization prior to US conquest. Their presence guaranteed the reproduction of family respectability, lineage, and status. Though they faced the harsh conditions of a frontier, they were granted a higher social standing than Indian women who, as a conquered people, retained the lowest place in Spanish and Mexican society. Yet intermarriage among settlers and the indigenous population and the assimilation of some native people meant these boundaries were never absolutely fixed. *Vecinos* or town residents who shared collective rights and responsibilities over land, water, irrigation systems, and the general welfare of the community, derived from indigenous, mixed, and Spanish descent, though most settlers emphasized their Spanish heritage. In their villages and towns, women of all backgrounds assumed a central role in agricultural production, the feeding of their families, and the trade in subsistence goods. They derived respect from their role in feeding and caring for the well-being of their families and dependent members of their communities.

Spanish and Mexican law gave all women access to ecclesiastical, civil, and military courts out of a tradition meant to protect family property and lineage rather than foster the independence of women. This contrasted sharply to English law, which folded the legal existence of women into that of their husbands. In the borderlands, women exercised their rights to sue (and be sued) and to retain control over their property and possessions after marriage. They also inherited property equally with their brothers and maintained joint rights with their husbands to any property accumulated during the marriage.

The Spanish (and, after 1821, Mexican) legal system enabled some women to become landowners and important members of their communities even if they remained single or engaged in unconventional behavior. It offered those who lived in patriarchal marriages the ability to contest treatment they considered abusive and unjust. In court records women voiced complaints against heads of household, including physical abuse by spouses and the failure of husbands to support them and their children. They also spoke out against bad examples the patriarch might set for his children, including infidelity (a charge men also made against women). Though the courts did not always hear or believe the women who brought suit, "access to the courts enabled women to demand that men fulfill their obligations as husbands and fathers, and held them responsible for exceeding their power and authority as heads of households" (Chavez 1999: 275).

The Overland Diaries and the Woman's Sphere

These histories of Indian and Spanish Mexican women defined the region prior to its incorporation into the United States and form a necessary background to understanding the significance of Anglo-American migration into the region. But to make them part of the study of the women's West, historians have had to expand beyond their initial focus on the westward migration. Some of the earliest women's histories of the West analyzed diaries and letters that Anglo-American women kept during their journey on the Overland trail. The first emigrant company to the Pacific mostly carried men on wagons in 1840. By the spring of 1842, over a hundred people, mostly families, left for California and Oregon. This massive movement by wagon train, which continued until the 1870s, when the railroad replaced wagons, captured the attention of both historians and the broader public. Here the diaries and letters written by women offer the only documents comparable in quantity to those left by men.

The first sustained analyses of these materials – by John Mack Faragher – contrasted men's and women's writing. He found that two-thirds of the content reflected similar, everyday concerns involving practical matters such as the economics of the trip, the health and safety of the travelers, and endless reflections on the landscape. Yet one-third of the diary entries spoke to the separate concerns of men and women. Women wrote about family and relational values, the happiness and health of their children, and family affection. They spoke to their longing for home and hearth, and expressed the importance that getting along with the traveling group held for them, as well as their need and desire for friendship, especially with other women. Men, in contrast, concerned themselves with violence and aggression and, most of all, with hunting. The commonality of their concerns emerged out of the shared understandings they forged through marriage, while the separate concerns replicated the world of the farming communities they left behind.

Most scholars who subsequently worked with the diaries found dramatic differences between men's and women's writing. Lillian Schlissel, for example, suggests that through their writing "women bring us a new vision of the overland experience" and articulate a sensibility vastly distinct from that of men toward the peoples and places they encountered on the trail (1982: 15). One of women's major refrains involved their fear over separation from family. While newlyweds and younger women spoke more favorably, women of childbearing age expressed their reluctance to leave home. The harsh conditions of childbirth, death, and widowhood were far more frightening and dangerous to women without the aid of their nearest kin.

While accepting differences between women and men, historians have also examined the differences among women involved in the westward movement. They have been concerned especially with how attitudes changed in the move from East to West and on continuities and discontinuities in the kinds of sentiments expressed prior to and during migration. A few argue that women who moved West held particular qualities and attributes not shared by those who remained in the East. Sandra Myres, for example, stresses women's spirit of adventure in moving West, their nonconformity to established gender roles, and successful adaptation to a new environment. Most recently, the diaries have been placed within the framework of narratives of travel and displacement. Since travel can call into question and transform the identity of the traveler, travel literature provides a space in which the writer charts and negotiates that displacement. In diaries of the western journey, "writing about the terrain, and autobiography, writing about the self, merge" (Roberson 1998: 213). The diarists' focus on topography and the natural environment becomes something more than describing what they saw. It reflects, as well, the conflicts, tensions, and fears they projected onto the physical world.

Judging from these interpretations of women's words, the West offered adventure and the possibility of nonconformity to some, while the four or more months of travel created anxieties about displacement for others. Whatever their overall assessment, many, perhaps most, Anglo women continued to embrace the ideologies and social roles governing womanhood that they brought from their place of origin. A substantial body of scholarship working in this vein describes how women utilized the tenets of domesticity in an attempt to place limits on men's behavior. Women sought especially to curb the multiple abuses men committed against women. They fought matrimonial cruelty, sexual abuse, desertion, prolonged absence, adultery, prostitution, and alcoholism. As it did back East, the ideology of separate spheres offered a means by which women could empower themselves in the domestic and public realm. The moral reform efforts of women in the West, however, produced "a prolonged battle over what the west was to become, a battle that often brought women into conflict with entrenched male interests" (Griswold 1988: 26).

The impulse to establish "female moral authority" developed out of a sustained history of middle-class women's reform efforts. One important aspect of this work focused on Native American communities and government policy toward native societies. During the 1820s, before the westward migration began, many women's groups, charitable and church organizations, focused on missions and mission schools for American Indian children as their priority for philanthropy. The women corresponded regularly with missionaries and Indian students, while their associations commonly provided clergymen with financial support, sent goods to Indian communities through the missions, and sponsored events to raise money. They organized opposition to the Indian Removal Bill in 1830 across the Northeast and Midwest, sponsoring a huge campaign that deluged Congress with petitions against its passage. They lost that battle, but women's groups continued to focus on missionary efforts among native people and on reforming US Indian policy through the remainder of the nineteenth century.

The elevated place moral reform held among the middle class made it an excellent vehicle for nonwhite women to negotiate greater legal freedoms and social rights for their communities. The LaFlesche sisters of the Omaha tribe, for example, lectured about conditions among the Omaha and other native people, raised money, built schools, encouraged education, and fought alcoholism and other social ills. They lectured before and worked with white women's groups on behalf of the Omaha and other tribes, yet remained identified with native culture and practices that continued to undergo change in response to new conditions.

Reform efforts by women, especially white women, were enhanced in the West as they secured greater rights over property, divorce, and voting than their sisters back East. Legislation in western states and territories bore the traces of Spanish and Mexican law. Many adopted the common property laws of Mexico that offered women half of the wealth gained through marriage and enabled women to retain control over their wages and over the property they brought into their marriage. Western states also developed the most expansive statutes for divorce and far more liberal judicial interpretations of matrimonial cruelty than elsewhere in the nation. The region soon experienced the highest divorce rate in the nation, with women bringing 70 percent of the suits in the late nineteenth century.

Gold Rush, Immigration, and Racial Conflict, 1848–1880

Yet despite the legal advantages of western settlement for women, many parts of the West remained largely male preserves. The gold rush of 1848 offers one prime example since men formed the vast majority of miners. In the initial rush, Indian men and women worked the mines alongside others, on land they had claimed for centuries. By late 1849, however, the white miners violently displaced Indians from gold mining and during the 1850s removed or killed the majority of California's native people who resided in those areas settled by miners.

Comparatively few non-Indian women joined the miners. By 1850 in the southern fields, the non-Indian population included only 800 women out of a total of 29,000 miners. By virtue of their very scarcity, all of these women stood to make significant money. Some actually panned for gold, but most sustained themselves by offering services and goods that remained ever scarce in the region. White and black women from the United States were scattered very sparsely through the mining camps. Many Sonoran women came with Mexican miners, and women from Peru, Chile, France, and a scattering of other places also migrated to the gold fields. Setting up businesses or working for others, they ran boarding houses, cooked and served food, washed clothing and other articles, dealt cards, sold goods, danced and offered sexual services for pay. Most of the life in the gold fields, however, revolved around the creation of male communities. Functioning in this multi-ethnic world, white men came to understand their masculinity differently or in particularly acute ways, based on "new hierarchies of gender, race, and ethnicity" (Johnson 2000: 166).

White miners directed strong anti-foreign sentiment against the Californios, Mexicans, and Latin Americans in their midst, passing a "foreign" mines tax in 1851, nearly two years after they began vigilante action to chase "aliens" out of the northern fields. Opposition from powerful merchants who depended on the business of Mexican and other "foreign" miners eventually persuaded the state to repeal the law. Yet it reimposed the tax against Chinese miners in 1853.

Most Chinese women who entered California during the two decades between 1850 and 1870 came as prostitutes, merchants' wives, or family servants. In 1860, as many as 85 to 97 percent of Chinese women worked as prostitutes. By 1870, that segment declined to around 71 percent, while women still only accounted for 7.2 percent of the total Chinese population. Unlike other women working in prostitution, the vast majority of Chinese women had been imported initially as unfree labor. Kidnapped, indentured, or enslaved against their will, these women were also purchased by procurers from poor parents. Commonly promising that good employment and marriage awaited the girls in America, they generally resold them once they arrived in the United States. The women worked under a wide range of conditions, but experienced an absence of political rights and limited access to legal recourse.

California legislation confined Chinese prostitutes to particular neighborhoods by 1866, echoing similar laws passed earlier elsewhere, when middle-class women's efforts to "reform" prostitution made it less visible. But restrictions against Chinese prostitutes also responded to the much larger anti-Chinese sentiment articulated by white men and women workers. By 1875, their combined forces resulted in the Page law that prohibited the entry of Chinese, Japanese, and Mongolian contract laborers, women for the purpose of prostitution, and felons. This law marked the first exclusion of a racially defined group of workers in the United States. It also produced local crackdowns against Chinese prostitution, so that by 1880, only 444 of the 2,052

Chinese women in San Francisco, and fewer than 1,000 of 3,834 Chinese women statewide, worked as prostitutes according to official counts.

By 1880 married women made up almost half the women in Chinatown due to the arrival of wives, the rescue of prostitutes from brothels, and/or their marriage to other Chinese immigrants. These women helped to build a community in the context of vile anti-Chinese sentiment and within a "bachelor society" that developed after the Chinese Exclusion law of 1882 denied entry to Chinese immigrants except for merchants, students, diplomats, and those born in the United States. During the six decades of legal exclusion (1882–1943), women's ability to enter the United States often rested on prolonged legal battles.

White women played two roles in the Chinese exclusion movement and its related politics. Missionary women set up a system of rescue, raiding brothels with police assistance when a woman made known her interest in being removed. The system rescued 1,500 girls and women between 1871 and 1901. Some returned to China, others to their former status, and a significant number married Chinese Christians and forged a new life in the United States. In these cases, Christian women sought to extend the benefits of civil society to women who otherwise had no legal recourse. At the same time, they placed restraints on the women's behavior, at least for the period they lived in the missions, by imposing middle-class Protestant ideals.

White working women, in contrast, fought alongside white working men to wage a systematic, relentless, and sometimes violent battle for Chinese exclusion. Native-born workers argued that Chinese labor, which they considered inherently degraded, caused the low wages and unemployment men and women faced in manufacturing industries such as cigars, shoes, and boots. They claimed that Chinese labor destroyed the wages a white family needed to live and the right to a decent wage for white working girls. Working women employing anti-Chinese rhetoric found wide support for their rights to unionize and gain a living wage among the ranks of white working men. By 1880, white women workers in California, especially in San Francisco, held union jobs in far greater numbers and in far more industries than elsewhere in the United States. Even after the passage of the Exclusion Act, white workers continued to define their interests against Chinese workers. Moreover, white women forged gender and race alliances with middle-class and wealthy white women, and established institutions designed to protect the condition of the white working girl.

Few African American women resided in the Far West. Most lived just west of the Mississippi River where slavery and its aftermath fostered southern institutions in Missouri, Texas, Arkansas, Louisiana, and Oklahoma. By 1850, only 392 black women lived in the Far West, most of whom arrived in California at the time of the gold rush. Some arrived enslaved, working for their owners and finding additional work as a means of purchasing their freedom and that of family members left behind. Free blacks similarly found employment as domestic laborers, selling goods, washing, cooking, and boarding gold seekers.

Free blacks also migrated to California and other western states seeking the riches other Americans aspired to find, but they encountered, instead, multiple legal restrictions. Though California's constitution prohibited slavery, partly in the interest of gaining quick admission to the Union, state law enabled slaveholders to bring their chattel through California, generating an effective movement to overturn the law from within the black community. The majority of western territories debated whether or not to enter the Union as slave states. Some tried to ban African Americans altogether from their territories. Most did not extend suffrage to African American men, nor allow blacks to testify against white persons in the courts. They attempted to compel blacks to ride on the back of streetcar lines, or tried to prohibit blacks from riding public transport altogether. In addition, most communities imposed, or attempted to impose, segregated and unequal schooling.

Black women worked primarily in domestic service, but some taught school where segregated educational systems existed, and others managed hotels and boarding houses, all of which constituted more prestigious and lucrative work. In both western states where southern institutions retained a hold and in those farther north like Montana, African American women held uncertain freedom and found little justice. Black women imprisoned in Kansas, for example, reflected the patterns prevalent in Louisiana and Texas. "Most were young, poor women charged with crimes connected to the domestic services they performed" (Butler 1989: 31). Those most frequently arrested were uneducated women who possessed few resources and whose crimes appeared to have been minor or nonexistent. Their sentences frequently exceeded the seriousness of the accusation.

As Peggy Pascoe has demonstrated, miscegenation laws that underpinned the system of white supremacy in the South after the Civil War found their counterpart in the West. Texas passed the first western miscegenation law as early as 1837 and Utah passed the last in 1939. These laws forbade marriages between whites and other racial groups, including African Americans and American Indians, persons of Chinese and Japanese descent (often termed Mongolians), and Filipinos (often called Malays). South Dakota added Koreans to the list, and Arizona included Hindus in its statutes. Persons of Mexican descent acquired the full rights of citizens in the Treaty of Guadalupe Hidalgo that ended the Mexican–American War and ceded the Southwest to the United States in 1848. Based on the Treaty, regional Mexicans elected to early state and territorial legislative bodies were able to negotiate a white racial status for all Mexicans. Yet most Anglo-Americans perceived Mexicans as distinctly nonwhite, and race discrimination developed through extralegal means.

Interracial marriages occurred in the West despite laws to the contrary, but their effects on women of color proved devastating nonetheless. Because these unions remained illicit, the women involved had no recourse to the property or wealth accumulated during the marriage upon separation or death. Scholars are only now beginning to study other aspects of interracial unions, asking how people interpreted each other from distinct cultural frameworks, the manner in which communities welcomed or excluded such couples and their children, and racial/cultural identities selected and/or inherited by the children.

Contested Terrain

Although Mexican-descent politicians managed to minimize the passing of legislation that legally discriminated against people of Mexican descent, no such protection existed for Native American people, who formed the majority of the population throughout the West in 1848 and whose land remained contested terrain between that date and 1880. Mexican and Native American inhabitants confronted the land hunger of American migrants who established, upon their migration to the region, a new economy and legal system. Despite the guarantee of property rights set forth in the Treaty of Guadalupe Hidalgo, Americans introduced laws that challenged the validity of Spanish and Mexican land grants made to individuals and the communal land rights of towns, thus affecting the land rights of the poor and rich alike. The battles over Spanish and Mexican land titles involved long years of litigation, spanning a period when the economy underwent vast and rapid change with the introduction of substantial amounts of capital invested in agriculture, mines, and livestock production.

Women, who held property rights under Spanish and Mexican law, increasingly contested this tremendous loss of land. In California, where the federal government set up a court to confirm Spanish and Mexican land titles, women appeared before the tribunal and in civil courts to fight for their property. They not only defended their land, but the very existence of their communities. In the cash-poor, pre-industrial economy that predominated in the former Mexican territories, land offered a means for individual and communal subsistence. The produce from women's gardens and the foods women produced from cows, chickens, and other animals bolstered their family economies. Land ownership and the commons enabled men and women to continue to engage in trade, which could be supplemented by migration for wage labor.

Women assumed an even more central role in their communities as men left to earn a wage in migratory or seasonal labor in the new mining, agricultural, and herding industries. Mexicans took advantage of the homestead laws and, like Anglo-Americans and Native Americans, homesteaded land near their original communities when possible, and farther away when necessary. But their lack of capital often kept them from prospering in the new market economy, where they found unequal prospects for success. The low wages paid to Mexican men, and even lower wages paid to Mexican women, often translated into poverty, a condition that loomed far larger for those without land. These conditions forced many families to find work in the new regional economy.

Native American women faced even more extreme conditions of loss. The United States did not recognize the land rights of native people who lived in the Southwest, and the Treaty of Guadalupe Hidalgo denied those rights to all "savages." Only a few groups, most prominently Pueblo Indians, successfully claimed rights of Mexican citizenship. Indian wars raged across the Southwest, engulfing parts of California during the 1850s and early 1860s, and erupted elsewhere in the Southwest and Plains region through the 1880s, lasting longest among the Apaches. The Apaches lived in kin-based bands. As with the Navajo, peace agreements made between one band and the government did not extend to other bands, and those who attempted to maintain the peace remained subject to white reprisal for the actions of others, perpetuating cycles of violence.

An incredible loss of life and of place shaped native histories during this era. The military rounded up whole villages, bands, and nations, taking survivors from warring groups and negotiating the removal of groups who did not or could not fight. By 1880, most native people had ceded their land in return for peace, resettlement, and annuities. The conditions for negotiation varied widely, favoring some groups far more than others. Tribal sovereignty enabled each group to govern itself, but the degrees of autonomy from the US government varied, and every tribe remained subject to government land policy, as it held all property acknowledged through treaty in trust. At the same time, the government intervened in tribal affairs and began to force native children to attend government boarding schools shortly after the Civil War ended.

Gender relations depended to a large extent on the roles, rights, and responsibilities Indian women traditionally held within their communities. Among the Navajo, for example, women continued to be the center of the family. Families resided in domestic groups called camps, organized along the female line of descent. The social organization of the camps emphasized the mother–child bond. Men married into the woman's household, and women's economic activity, performed in cooperation with female kin, remained at the heart of the Navajo economy. They controlled the land, raised livestock, especially sheep, farmed, gathered wild foods, and produced crafts. Men decided tribal policy, yet they remained accountable to the female head of their household when making decisions.

The Navajo's cultural life reflected these historical arrangements, but they experienced severe punishment and confinement before signing the treaty that assigned them reservation land. In 1859 different bands began to systematically raid New Mexican towns where Navajo slaves resided as a result of the captive-exchange system. They set free livestock and horses and raided agricultural supplies in an attempt to get rid of the Americans and punish their New Mexican allies. In response, 700 men volunteered from New Mexican villages to wage a campaign against the Navajo and their livelihood, killing sheep and destroying fields. In the winter Navajo bands began entering US forts and in 1864, the government forced 8,000 captive Navajo to march 300 miles to a fort far from their country. After four years they returned home, having lost well over 2,000 people to smallpox, and many others to the exertion of the trip and poor conditions under captivity. The reservation land they agreed to, and upon which they reestablished women-headed households, accounted for less than one-fourth of the land Navajo bands previously claimed.

New Directions

The story of the women's West initially developed within the confines of the national story. Most work focused on white women's movement to a West that was conceived of from the perspective of the East. It embraced questions about the family, women's separate spheres, work, reform movements, politics, and white women's relationship to nonwhite women. While many historians focused initially on the pioneer era, a large body of work now covers the period after 1880, when persistent and continuous Anglo-American migration brought far more women West than during the period 1840 to 1880.

This tendency to define the West from the perspective of the East gave way, in this essay as in the literature, to studies that emphasized the region's own history and that approached change during the period of US conquest from the perspective of that regional past. The literature on women is far slimmer when approached in this way. Nonetheless, scholarship on Chicanas – women of Mexican descent – has blossomed in recent years, addressing a series of well-defined problems concerning the histories of conquest and of women's rights, obligations, and experiences before and after the region became part of the United States. To varying degrees, historians working on the history of the former Mexican territories incorporate a concern for both indigenous and Spanish Mexican settler women simultaneously. Historians of Chinese women, who constituted the majority of female émigrés from Asia prior to 1880 except in Hawaii, also offer a growing literature and address a well-formulated narrative and set of problems concerning legal status, prostitution, immigration, and ethnicity.

Native women's history remains the most underdeveloped part of western women's nineteenth-century history. Work on indigenous histories has gained momentum as scholars move beyond the narrowness of national paradigms to embrace stories that fall outside of them. The influence of southern institutions – on Native Americans, African Americans, and white women – also needs to be better incorporated into the western narrative.

New work also pays more attention to language and its meaning when interpreting sources and problems. These new strategies for approaching the text have proved especially valuable for reading diaries and letters, court records and newspapers. In addition, scholars are taking gender far more seriously. Rather than writing analyses of women alone, those interested in gender examine the construction of womanhood and manhood. Male and female power, masculinity and femininity proved to be crucial elements at play in forging the West. The ways in which that occurred have only recently begun to be explored. These developments – a concern for analyzing both language and gender – are richly illustrated, for example, in Susan Johnson's recent book on the gold rush.

The major conflict that predominates in the current view of women in the nineteenth-century West focuses on European and American trade and expansion. Long before 1800, both factors created migration and warfare among Indian people themselves. They also fueled the emergence of a far-flung captive-exchange system that transferred captives among tribal groups and offered a ready supply to New Mexican settlers, who purchased detribalized people as slaves with the specification that once made Catholic and Hispanic they would regain their freedom. This prolonged warfare kept Spanish and Mexican society confined to a fairly narrow geographic terrain until after the Mexican–American War (1846–8) ended and the American military moved into the region to protect Anglo-American settlers as they claimed land. By 1880, most native women in the West lived on reservations, and the amount of land held by the regional Mexican population had declined dramatically, despite the efforts of women to defend their land and their communities from disintegration.

A major set of conflicts that stemmed from this expansion involved establishing and contesting American race relations as they took form out West. Women's rights were limited by their perceived racial standing. While some white women reformers engaged in movements to address the conditions suffered by native and Chinese women, more frequently their politics built on the rights they perceived as inherent to the white family and working girl. The struggles of white women for laws and social norms that better reflected their interests, although not necessarily the interests of all women, constituted a third struggle out West.

The vast number of cultures in the West meant women held many and widely different positions within their households and communities, depending on the kind of property rights and authority vested in them. Yet, the cultural politics of gender that assigned women separate spheres from men and that devalued married women's right to own and control property and to hold a central place in the economy became the dominant gender arrangement in the West, as in the East. Despite the normative roles assigned to them, women from all backgrounds who migrated into the region continued to infuse its richly textured communities with distinctive ideas about gender, culture, and community. Their migration and immigration contributed to the already diverse histories of regional populations. The structure of inequalities that had developed by 1880 would grow worse in subsequent years. In response, women continued to negotiate against adverse change from varying positions within their communities.

BIBLIOGRAPHY

Armitage, Susan and Jameson, Elizabeth (eds.) (1987) *The Women's West.* Norman: University of Oklahoma Press.

Brooks, James F. (1996) " 'This Evil Extends Especially... To the Feminine Sex': Negotiating Captivity in the New Mexico Borderlands," *Feminist Studies* 22, pp. 279–309.

Brown, Kathleen M. (1993) "Brave New Worlds: Women's and Gender History," *William and Mary Quarterly*, 3rd ser., 50, pp. 310–28.

Butler, Anne (1989) "Still in Chains: Black Women in Western Prisons, 1865–1910," *Western Historical Quarterly* 20, pp. 19–35.

Castañeda, Antonia (1992) "Women of Color and the Rewriting of Western History: The Discourse, Politics, and Decolonization of History," *Pacific Historical Review* 61, pp. 501–35.

Castañeda, Antonia (1998) "Engendering the History of Alta California, 1769–1848," in Ramón Gutiérrez and Richard J. Orsi (eds.), *Contested Eden: California Before the Gold Rush.* Berkeley: University of California Press, pp. 230–59.

Castillo, Edward (1994) "Gender Status Decline, Resistance and Accommodation among Female Neophytes in the Missions of California: A San Gabriel Case Study," *American Indian Culture and Research Journal* 18, pp. 67–93.

Chan, Sucheng (1991) "The Exclusion of Chinese Women, 1860–1943," in Sucheng Chan (ed.), *Entry Denied: Exclusion and the Chinese Community in America, 1882–1943.* Philadelphia: Temple University Press.

Chato, Genevieve and Conte, Christine (1988) "The Legal Rights of American Indian Women," in Vicki Ruíz, Janice Monk, and Lillian Schlissel (eds.), *Western Women: Their Lands, Their Lives.* Albuquerque: University of New Mexico Press, pp. 229–46.

Chavez, Miroslava (1999) "'Pongo mi demanda': Challenging Patriarchy in Mexican Los Angeles, 1830–1850," in Valerie J. Matsumoto and Blake Allmendinger (eds.), *Over the Edge: Remapping the American West.* Berkeley: University of California Press, pp. 272–90.

de Graaf, Lawrence B. (1980) "Race, Sex, and Region: Black Women in the American West, 1850–1920," *Pacific Historical Review* 49, pp. 285–313.

Deutsch, Sarah (1987) *No Separate Refuge: Culture, Class, and Gender on an Anglo-Hispanic Frontier in the American Southwest, 1880–1940.* New York: Oxford University Press.

Devens, Carol (1992) *Countering Colonization: Native American Women and Great Lakes Missions, 1630–1900.* Berkeley: University of California Press.

Diffendal, Anne P. (1994) "The LaFlesche Sisters: Victorian Reformers in the Omaha Tribe," *Journal of the West* 33, pp. 37–44.

Dunaway, Wilma (1997) "Rethinking Cherokee Acculturation: Agrarian Capitalism and Women's Resistance to the Cult of Domesticity, 1800–1838," *American Indian Culture and Research Journal* 21, pp. 155–92.

Faragher, John Mack (1979) *Women and Men on the Overland Trail.* New Haven, CT: Yale University Press.

Foster, Martha Harroun (1993) "Of Baggage and Bondage: Gender and Status among Hidatsa and Crow Women," *American Indian Culture and Research Journal* 17, pp. 121–52.

Foster, Martha Harroun (1995) "Lost Women of the Matriarchy: Iroquois Women in the Historical Literature," *American Indian Culture and Research Journal* 19, pp. 121–40.

Gardiner, Martha Mabie (1999) "Working on White Womanhood: White Working Women in the San Francisco Anti-Chinese Movement, 1877–1890," *Journal of Social History* 33, pp. 73–95.

González, Deena (1999) *Refusing the Favor: The Spanish-Mexican Women of Santa Fe, 1820–1880.* New York: Oxford University Press.

Griswold del Castillo, Richard (1988) "Anglo Women and Domestic Ideology in the American West in the Nineteenth and Early Twentieth Centuries," in Vicki Ruíz, Janice Monk, and Lillian Schlissel (eds.), *Western Women: Their Land, Their Lives.* Albuquerque: University of New Mexico Press, pp. 13–46.

Gutiérrez, Ramón A. (1991) *When Jesus Came, the Corn Mothers Went Away: Marriage, Sexuality, and Power in New Mexico, 1500–1846.* Stanford, CA: Stanford University Press.

Gutiérrez, Ramón A. (2000) "Crucifixion, Slavery, and Death: The Hermanos Penitentes of the Southwest," in Valerie J. Matsumoto and Blake Allmendinger (eds.), *Over the Edge: Remapping the American West.* Berkeley: University of California Press, pp. 253–71.

Haas, Lisbeth (1995) *Conquests and Historical Identities in California, 1769–1936.* Berkeley: University of California Press.

Harkin, Michael and Kan, Sergei (eds.) (1996) "Native Women's Responses to Christianity," Special Issue, *Ethnohistory* 43.

Hershberger, Mary (1999) "Mobilizing Women, Anticipating Abolition: The Struggle against Indian Removal in the 1830s," *Journal of American History* 86, pp. 15–40.

Holmes, Kenneth (ed.) (1989) *Covered Wagon Women: Diaries and Letters from the Western Trails, 1862–1865.* Lincoln: University of Nebraska Press.

Hurtado, Alberto L. (1999) *Intimate Frontiers: Sex, Gender, and Culture in Old California.* Albuquerque: University of New Mexico Press.

Jensen, Joan M. (1991) *Promise to the Land: Essays on Rural Women.* Albuquerque: University of New Mexico Press.

Jensen, Joan M. and Miller, Darlis A. (1980) "The Gentle Tamers Revisited: New Approaches to the History of Women in the American West," *Pacific Historical Review* 49, pp. 173–213.

Johnson, Susan Lee (1996) " 'A Memory Sweet to Soldiers': The Significance of Gender," in Clyde A. Milner (ed.), *A New Significance: Re-envisioning the History of the American West.* New York: Oxford University Press, pp. 255–88.

Johnson, Susan Lee (2000) *Roaring Camp: The Social World of the California Gold Rush.* New York: W. W. Norton.

Karttunen, Frances (1994) *Between Worlds: Interpreters, Guides, and Survivors.* New Brunswick, NJ: Rutgers University Press.

Kidwell, Clara Sue (1995) "Choctow Women and Cultural Persistence in Mississippi," in Nancy Shoemaker (ed.), *Negotiators of Change: Historical Perspectives on Native American Women.* New York: Routledge, pp. 115–34.

Koester, Susan (ed.) (1993) "Gender in the West," Special Issue, *Journal of the West* 32.

Levy, Jo Ann (1990) *They Saw the Elephant: Women in the California Gold Rush.* Norman: University of Oklahoma Press.

Matsumoto, Valerie J. and Allmendinger, Blake (eds.) (1999) *Over the Edge: Remapping the American West.* Berkeley: University of California Press.

Mihesuah, Devon Abbott (1993) *Cultivating the Rosebuds: The Education of Women at the Cherokee Female Seminary, 1851–1909.* Urbana: University of Illinois Press.

Montoya, María (2000) "Dividing the Land: The Taylor Ranch and the Case for Preserving the Limited Access Commons," in William G. Robbins and James C. Foster (eds.), *Land in the American West: Private Claims and the Common Good.* Seattle: University of Washington Press, pp. 121–44.

Moynihan, Ruth, Armitage, Susan, and Dichamp, Christiane Fischer (eds.) (1990) *So Much to be Done: Women Settlers on the Mining and Ranching Frontier.* Lincoln: University of Nebraska Press.

Murphy, Lucy E. (1995) "Autonomy and the Economic Roles of Indian Women of the Fox-Wisconsin River Region, 1763–1832," in Nancy Shoemaker (ed.), *Negotiators of Change: Historical Perspectives on Native American Women.* New York. Routledge.

Myres, Sandra L. (1982) *Westering Women and the Frontier Experience, 1800–1915.* Albuquerque: University of New Mexico Press.

Namias, June (1993) *White Captives: Gender and Ethnicity on the American Frontier.* Chapel Hill: University of North Carolina Press.

Pascoe, Peggy (1990) *Relations of Rescue: The Search for Female Moral Authority in the American West, 1874–1939.* New York: Oxford University Press.

Pascoe, Peggy (1999) "Race, Gender, and the Privileges of Property: On the Significance of Miscegenation Law in the U.S. West," in Valerie J. Matsumoto and Blake Allmendinger (eds.), *Over the Edge: Remapping the American West.* Berkeley: University of California Press, pp. 215–30.

Perdue, Theda (1989) "Cherokee Women on the Trail of Tears," *Journal of Women's History* 1, pp. 14–30.

Perdue, Theda (1998) *Cherokee Women: Gender and Culture Change, 1700–1835.* Lincoln: University of Nebraska Press.

Riley, Glenda (1998) "The Myth of Female Fear of Western Landscapes," *Journal of the West* 37, pp. 33–41.

Roberson, Susan A. (1998) " 'With the Wind Rocking the Wagon': Women's Narratives of the Way West," in Susan Roberson (ed.), *Women, America, and Movement: Narratives of Relocation*. Columbia: University of Missouri Press, pp. 213–34.

Ruíz, Vicki, Monk, Janice, and Schlissel, Lillian (eds.) (1988) *Western Women: Their Lands, Their Lives*. Albuquerque: University of New Mexico Press.

Schlissel, Lillian (1982) *Women's Diaries of the Westward Journey*. New York: Schocken Books.

Shoemaker, Nancy (1991) "The Rise or Fall of Iroquois Women," *Journal of Women's History* 2, pp. 39–57.

Shoemaker, Nancy (ed.) (1995) *Negotiators of Change: Historical Perspectives on Native American Women*. New York: Routledge.

Sleeper-Smith, Susan (2000) "Women, Kin, and Catholicism: New Perspectives on the Fur Trade," *Ethnohistory* 47, pp. 423–52.

Tong, Benson (1994) *Unsubmissive Women: Chinese Prostitutes in Nineteenth-century San Francisco*. Norman: University of Oklahoma Press.

White, Bruce (1999) "The Woman Who Married a Beaver: Trade Patterns and Gender Roles in the Ojibwa Fur Trade," *Ethnohistory* 46, pp. 109–47.

Winegarten, Ruth (ed.) (1995) *Black Texas Women*. Austin: University of Texas Press.

Yung, Judy (1995) *Unbound Feet: A Social History of Chinese Women in San Francisco*. Berkeley: University of California Press.

Chapter Ten

Rural Women

Marli F. Weiner

WHEN Thomas Jefferson envisioned an ideal United States inhabited by yeomen farmers, he offered few insights into the roles he thought farm women should fill in the new republic. Farm women were, in essence, invisible to the founding fathers and their ideological descendents: expected to perform domestic tasks and whatever else needed to be done, but not offered – or allowed to claim – a place in the nation. Their only legitimate way to participate was as Republican mothers, whose task it was to raise virtuous and patriotic sons, and not as women accorded equal or even complementary status with men.

Historians have likewise traditionally accorded farm women little attention. While in recent decades women have been the subjects of extensive historical investigation, rural men and women for the most part have not been at the center of study, in spite of their numerical preponderance in the population. Interested in change, historians have assumed that cities, not the countryside, should be the focus of their inquiry. While few viewed rural areas as frozen in time, historians of the nineteenth century have tended to characterize rural areas as traditional, more like the colonial past than the emerging urban, industrial, heterogeneous, conflict-laden, reform-minded future. Even those influenced by Frederick Jackson Turner have focused on the closing of the frontier as the symbolic center of American history, rather than on the vitality of the rural experience itself. Likewise, many historians of women have focused on reformers' efforts to open the public sphere to women as well as their activities in it, which they have understood as centered in the city.

Yet studying rural women offers the possibility of new ways of understanding American women's history. Not only were rural women the majority for much of the nation's history, they helped to shape many of its changes. Studying rural women's lives holds real potential for understanding women's work, family life, reform activities, access to power, and race relations. As rural women moved from one part of the continent to another and from countryside to city, they brought with them ideas and values that influenced every aspect of society, in the process helping to create not just regional cultures, but shaping the nation's ways of thinking as well. Of course, not all rural women shared the same ways of thinking; thus rural society is also an important location for historians seeking to come to terms with the consequences of similarity and difference in women's lives.

Studying rural women is particularly useful for evaluating the importance of region in women's lives. Region has been the central organizing principle for nineteenth-century historians who see the Civil War as a watershed in American history; they divide the nation into the key categories of North and South. Rural historians have sought to complicate that dichotomy, focusing much of their scholarship on the Midwest to the exclusion of other areas, in an effort to carve out yet another set of regional distinctions. Yet rural history offers greater potential than simply complicating traditional regional categories; it offers the potential to illuminate what women have in common across regions as well as to consider the relationship between what can best be considered local and what national characteristics.

The best rural historians have explored similarities and differences within the North, South, and West. As a result, the history of rural women has overlapped and merged with the history of northern women, southern women, and western women. Yet the questions asked focus on the specific character of rural life. For example, many historians of nineteenth-century southern women have focused on relations between wealthy white women and the slaves or freedwomen who worked in their fields, kitchens, and laundries. Rural southern historians, such as Brenda Stevenson and Laura Edwards, who have focused on particular counties, have been more interested in comparing the experiences of those same black women and the poor white women who labored in the fields and kitchens next door. Similarly, historians of northern white women have focused on factory work and reform efforts while Joan Jensen, Sally McMurry, and other rural historians have been more interested in butter making and similar forms of household production for the market. Such distinctions are somewhat arbitrary, yet they point to some of the complexities of exploring rural women's lives.

The big picture has come into play mainly when historians have examined the history of rural peoples in their own terms, rather than simply as a foil to the more dynamic developments associated with the city. They have understood the countryside as itself dynamic and changing: as the locus of population moved westward; as Native Americans, native-born whites, immigrants, and racial and ethnic minorities encountered one another and filled the landscape; as mechanization, railroads, and commercial agriculture changed what farmers did and how they did it; and as shifting patterns of production and consumption altered gender roles, family relationships, and domestic life. Through all of this, rural historians have sought to explore the ways in which women's experiences were both similar to and different from men's as well as the ways women's experiences varied from one another. Yet historians have not engaged in many explicit efforts to compare rural women's lives from place to place, arguing instead for the importance of local specificity. In the process, scholars have neglected the possibility of learning from the larger picture, not by ignoring differences but by balancing them with a more complex vision of what rural people shared with one another.

Historians do not, however, always agree on the meaning of the term rural. It has variously encompassed long-settled and frontier areas; areas of low population density, with or without villages and towns; areas devoted exclusively to farming or ranching as well as those with rural extractive industries like mining, lumbering, even fishing; areas with primarily subsistence economies and those engaged in large-scale commercial enterprises. Rather than seeking consensus on a single definition of rural, historians have tended to use the term in tension, as demanding qualification, although most often it is assumed to be more or less synonymous with areas devoted to farming. Such complexities have made rural history both a grab bag encompassing everything outside the nation's cities and a rich new way to understand American history.

Beyond the difficulties of drawing boundaries around what is rural, historians have had to grapple with the ways in which changes in rural areas in the nineteenth century influenced and were influenced by other areas of the nation. Were cities always the source of transformations that then flowed outward to the countryside, or did change move in both directions? Since individuals and families left country for city and, less often, city for country, what aspects of identity and culture can be said to have been grounded in place as opposed to class, race, ethnicity, religion, and all of the other factors that shape people's lives? Perhaps the key question has been how best to understand the interactions between people and their physical environment. Such questions have made rural history compelling and contentious.

Rural historians have also sought to explain women's complex relationship with nature. While no one argues for a crude determinism based on geography, all recognize that climate and topography have had a profound influence on women's daily lives. Nineteenth-century women themselves were acutely aware of their physical surroundings whenever they moved from one place to another. Their letters and diaries are filled with descriptions of scenery and plants, climate and insects, although with the exception of routine notations on the day's weather, few commented unless there was something unusual on which to report. Still, much more than in cities, rural women's lives were shaped by their natural environment; it helped determine how they would spend their days as well as the outcome of many of their labors.

For many historians inquiry begins with questions about how nineteenth-century rural women spent their days. Surprisingly, they have usually only asked whether and how much time women spent in the fields when studying black women, who worked extensively in the fields as slaves, and after emancipation, as sharecroppers. Historians disagree about the extent to which they did so voluntarily. Building on the work of Jacqueline Jones, most argue that black women would have preferred to devote themselves to childcare and other aspects of domestic life but were compelled to labor in the fields by white landowners who defined the terms of labor contracts. They claim that freedwomen understood field labor as a contribution to their families and so accepted it as a means of improving their children's educational and economic prospects, a decision that hardened into tradition even when those possibilities disappeared. Whatever the explanation, both during and after slavery there is little doubt that black women performed extensive amounts of field labor in addition to their domestic responsibilities.

Historians know less about the extent to which other women worked in the fields. Some Native American women did so according to their traditional gendered division of labor, a pattern that missionaries and government officials tried hard to break. The same is true for Mexican women living in the Southwest. However, we know very little about the extent to which white women worked in the fields anywhere in the United States. In many instances, time-consuming domestic responsibilities combined with assumptions about white women's physical limitations probably kept them out of the fields except during the most demanding moments in the agricultural cycle. In the South, ideas about race defined agricultural labor as the province of black men and women, providing an incentive to white men to keep their wives and daughters out of the fields even when they did not own slaves. Yet we do know that some white women routinely worked in the fields, particularly those whose husbands were absent or unable to do the work themselves, or too poor to hire a man to help them when necessary. This was probably most often the case in areas where endemic poverty and scarce options led many to try to eke out livings on smallholdings or marginal lands, and on the frontier, where the demands of breaking new ground could lead to a degree of role flexibility. Similarly, we know relatively little about the extent to which daughters in white families were expected to labor in the fields alongside their fathers and brothers, rather than helping their mothers. There is little doubt, however, that field labor was never considered white women's primary work.

Historians concerned about white women's daily lives have instead focused their attention on what was considered women's domain on the farm. Drawing on insights provided by historians of labor and of material culture, they have sought to recreate the physical realities of women's worlds by examining the spaces and objects with which they accomplished their daily tasks of cooking and cleaning, laundry and childcare. The most significant findings concern the extent to which women engaged in household commodity production for market. While the items produced and the circumstances varied over time and place, historians agree that rural women engaged in significant commodity production. Thomas Dublin, Jeanne Boydston, Christopher Clark, and others have argued that in the Northeast early in the century, that production typically took the form of selling surplus thread or cloth. Gradually, selling those products not needed for family use developed into the putting-out system, in which merchants provided raw materials to be processed by women (and children) in their homes. The putting-out system drew rural women from throughout the Northeast into home manufacturing of thread, hats, brooms, and numerous other items; eventually, manufacturers' dissatisfaction with the system's lack of reliability and their own lack of control over women's work led them to mechanize and consolidate operations within factories, but not before large numbers of women turned their homes into centers of production.

Women outside New England also earned significant amounts of money by engaging in household commodity production. In the mid-Atlantic states, as Jensen and McMurry show, they produced vast amounts of butter and cheese, at first selling the surplus from domestic needs and then turning their hands to direct production for market. Eventually, families purchased additional cows and redesigned work spaces in order to further this endeavor, sometimes shifting primary responsibility for dairying from women to men in the process. In many instances, women's efforts provided the most significant source of cash for the household, allowing them to pay mortgages and taxes and enhancing their standard of living. In the South, white women's opportunities for household production were more limited, but even there, women supplemented the family's income by sending surplus garden produce, dairy products, eggs, and soap to market and by producing mattresses and other items to sell. Those living on plantations were responsible for ensuring that slaves produced large quantities of clothing, preserved food, and other goods for domestic use by slaves and whites alike; sometimes they worked alongside the slaves to accomplish these tasks. Western women had perhaps the fewest opportunities to produce commodities for the market, but like women elsewhere, they engaged in extensive bartering transactions that allowed them to improve their quality of life.

Household commodity production for the market marks one of the significant ways in which rural women's lives differed from those in the city. Historians agree that over the course of the nineteenth century, urban women's lives were characterized by a shift from production to consumption; their homes no longer contained the tools needed to produce cloth, preserve food, and make soap as these items were increasingly produced in factories and available for purchase in the marketplace, thus freeing their time considerably. Instead, women were expected to devote themselves to purchasing the ever-widening array of consumer goods and were evaluated on their ability to do so with thrift, good sense, and good taste. Rural women, on the other hand, continued to produce goods for domestic use during much of the century and they may well have increased their production of things to sell, at least in the northeastern and mid-Atlantic regions. As farming in those regions became less able to compete with the products of larger-scale operations in the Midwest, families may well have increased their dependence on the income women were able to provide from dairying and other efforts. Rural women certainly did not enjoy the respite from productive work that industrial development made possible for middle-class urban women.

Historians do not agree, however, on the meaning of rural white women's household production for market. Some, such as Nancy Grey Osterud, suggest that women's contributions to the family economy gave them greater voice within the family as men recognized the importance of the cash their work made available. They argue that rural men and women interacted with "mutuality" and that marriages were relatively egalitarian. Others, including Glenda Riley and John Mack Faragher, suggest that patriarchal family traditions meant that women had little control over the money they earned and that their contributions did not allow them greater autonomy or authority. Sometimes, these matters revolved around whether surplus cash would be used for improvements to the farm or to the kitchen: the choice between a new plow and a new cookstove, for example. Most likely the answers to such questions vary according to the ethnic and religious traditions of individual families as well as the personalities involved; there is not likely to be a single pattern of family dynamics.

Similar questions arise in discussions of women's ownership of land. The Homestead Act of 1862 allowed unmarried women, widows, and female heads of household to claim land in the West under the same terms as men. While the numbers of women claiming land of their own varied from place to place, some women did take advantage of this opportunity. Still, many did so in order to enhance their family's claim or as a form of dowry before marriage; relatively few claimed land intending to live independently and permanently on it. Other than through the Homestead Act, few women had access to land ownership; for the most part women's earnings were too low to permit them to purchase land for themselves, and most states denied married women access to or control over property anyway. Here, too, patriarchal traditions encoded in custom and law suggest that while western women may well have had greater than usual access to property, like their counterparts in other regions of the country that property may not have granted them greater voice within their families.

In fact, historians debate the extent to which rural white women were able to influence the decision to move westward in the first place. Joan Cashin argues persuasively that not only were antebellum southern women excluded from the decision itself, they often regretted their husbands' insistence on geographic mobility and yearned for the familiar comforts and people of home. On the other hand, Nell Irvin Painter notes that black women fleeing the racism and poverty of the postwar South for Kansas were eager to take advantage of new opportunities. White women from other parts of the country may well have been only somewhat less reluctant than Cashin's southerners. Since the wealthy were unlikely to want to move to the frontier and the poor did not have the means to do so, most of the migrants left reasonably comfortable homes and farms to undertake the journey westward. Some of the women were undoubtedly eager for adventure and opportunity even as they were apprehensive about the hardships of the journey and getting started in new homes. Others perhaps focused more intently on the losses associated with moving westward, including families, churches, communities. Those who migrated into the West from Europe faced even more complex decisions and more permanent losses, although these were partially offset by the prevalence of family and community chain migration. The writings pioneering women left behind suggest that most felt a range of conflicting emotions, whether or not they endorsed the move.

All of these factors suggest that rural women's power within their families was ambiguous. While for some access to land or a cash income from household production meant the possibility of autonomy and influence within the family, for others autonomy and influence were limited at best. Women's power within communities was similarly ambiguous. In spite of the isolation about which they sometimes complained, rural women usually lived under the close watch of one another. Neighbors knew one another's business; gossip traveled quickly. Living under public scrutiny allowed women to provide help to those in need, or at least those considered deserving. Community could reinforce social ties, offering women opportunities for pleasant interactions even as they provided care and protection for one another. It also offered women the power to censure those whose behavior they found problematic, serving as a potent means of social control.

Most rural women were likely to be far too busy with the chores of daily life to worry much about their power in their families or communities. In fact, historians agree that rural women's days were filled with an unrelenting round of toil, lightened by occasional socializing. While urban women were able to take advantage of an array of consumer goods that included significant labor-saving devices, rural women for the most part performed long hours of difficult labor every day. Not only did they engage in commodity production for market, they also did everyday chores of cooking, washing, cleaning, and childrearing. These tasks could be especially daunting for women accustomed to easier circumstances who then moved westward, but even in long-settled rural areas, the work required was enormous. Simply hauling water and wood demanded time and energy; the house plans devised by the progressive farmers that Sally McMurry studied nearly all include a good-sized room for wood. Rural women continued to spin thread and produce cloth long after their urban counterparts purchased them. They continued to cook in open fireplaces long after wood or, later, coal-burning stoves became common in more urban areas. They cared for large numbers of animals, collecting eggs, plucking poultry for feathers, milking cows to make butter and cheese, slaughtering stock and salting the meat. They gathered wild food and preserved what they grew in extensive gardens. Most of the tasks rural women accomplished every day were either not required of most urban women or so attenuated by conveniences and the marketplace as to be relatively insignificant.

In addition to often-daunting domestic tasks, rural women were charged with responsibility for tending to their families. In cities, a growing range of institutions assumed some of the family's traditional functions, from schools to educate children to hospitals and asylums to care for the most seriously ill to charitable organizations to provide a cushion for the "worthy" poor, including children whose parents were dead or otherwise unable to care for them. Such institutions did not exist in rural areas, which meant that families had to provide for themselves, with perhaps occasional help from neighbors. In the best of circumstances, this might mean families enjoyed close ties, but it could also cause serious strain. In their roles as wives, mothers, and daughters, women often ended up providing many different kinds of care in addition to their other work responsibilities, leaving some to feel burdened and inadequate.

Caring for children was perhaps the most demanding of women's familial responsibilities. In less densely populated areas outside of the Northeast, where public schools were a high priority, this could often mean educating them at home; in most places schools were often expensive, sometimes nonexistent, and rarely easily accessible. Women who taught their children themselves did so knowing that the time was borrowed from other domestic tasks, lengthening what were already considerable hours of work for themselves and their children. Children's labor was often an economic necessity on the farm, marking the margin of survival. Rural women's fertility remained higher, longer than that of urban women because the labor of children was so necessary and perhaps also because their access to birth control information remained more limited. Women who were not literate, of course, could not educate their children, which may have been a source of anxiety.

Caring for children also meant nursing them through illnesses; like schooling, professional medical assistance could be expensive, nonexistent, or inaccessible. Many rural women became skilled at diagnosing and treating common ailments and learned to tend one another during and after childbirth. The nineteenth century may have marked the advent of professionalization in medicine, but its penetration into many rural areas remained limited, leaving women to cope with illness and accidents themselves.

Churches and the ministers to staff them were likewise not always available, especially in newly settled areas. By the nineteenth century women enjoyed unprecedented influence in religious institutions and in many places churches became important centers of socializing and support for them; in the Northeast churches could be centers of organizational and reform efforts as well. However, women were not always able to observe denominational loyalties in rural areas, as the cost of supporting a minister could be prohibitive. Circuit-riding ministers or lay leaders, usually male, sometimes became effective substitutes, but too often rural women found themselves forced to create informal arrangements or do without the solace organized religion could provide. Whether or not ministers were available, women usually claimed responsibility for providing religious training for their children; often they led family prayers as well.

Limited access to schools, doctors, and churches points to one of the chief complaints of rural women throughout the nineteenth century: their isolation. While historians tend to discuss isolation primarily in terms of those moving westward, it was a common complaint of rural women in other parts of the nation as well. Inadequate transportation and impassable roads, the burdens of domestic work, frequent pregnancy, and assumptions that women belonged at home and should not travel alone all conspired to prevent women from visiting family and friends or attending church as often as they might have wished. While these concerns eased as the spread of railroads made visiting cities and families easier and less expensive, isolation remained a complaint of rural women throughout the century and beyond.

Complaints about isolation suggest that rural women were well aware of other women's richer lives. While such observations remain subjective, there can be little doubt that rural women perceived some distance between their experiences and those of women in the cities. In fact, one of the key concerns of historians of rural women has been the extent to which they were aware of the ideology of domesticity and felt inspired or compelled to put its tenets into practice in their own lives. Predicated on the separation of spheres, the ideology of domesticity could not fit the reality of farm women whose husbands did not leave home to work and whose kitchens and dairies were the site of commodity production. It could not fit the reality of women whose children remained economic assets and whose own labor was vital to family well-being. Women who spent their days in ceaseless toil did not have time or money for the domestic niceties; those who did not have access to consumer goods could not be expected to cultivate the refinement they supposedly inspired. Conforming to fashionable expectations in dress, diet, and decor was impossible; so was devoting oneself exclusively to husband and children to make them happy and productive citizens. These were expectations geared to the urban middle class, which historians have assumed was the target audience for domesticity's proponents.

Yet rural women could not help but be aware of cultural expectations, and many struggled to comply with demands even though their location and, often, class circumstances made doing so difficult. Rising rates of literacy and lowering costs of printing and postage made magazines touting domestic ideals widely available even by mid-century. Ministers and schoolteachers echoed the message; so did politicians and doctors. While women in longer-settled areas were particularly likely to be exposed to these messages, those who migrated westward brought them along to the frontier, where they were most difficult to apply. Historians may never know the extent to which women were frustrated by their inability to practice domesticity as opposed to rejecting it as an urban idea misplaced in their rural environment.

Historians may also never know the extent to which that same rural environment allowed women to enjoy greater flexibility in their roles and behaviors than their urban counterparts. If rural life precluded the possibility of domesticity, it may well also have opened the way to freer relationships with men. Some historians, most notably Jensen and Osterud, have argued that rural women explicitly rejected domesticity, opening the way for more egalitarian marriages and more room for autonomy than in cities. Others, such as Julie Roy Jeffrey and Riley, suggest that whether or not they were able to practice domesticity, rural women's lives were so bound by conventional notions of gender that the possibilities inherent in their work for family survival and contributions to the family economy remained moot.

Much of this debate has hinged on the extent to which men and women did one another's work when necessary. While controversies remain, the emerging consensus is that women were far more likely to do traditionally male tasks, including field labor, than men were to do traditionally female tasks. Women, in other words, took on men's work in the face of emergencies like bad weather, accidents, or even a shortage of laborers, but men rarely helped with cooking or cleaning or childcare. Some historians view this as potentially liberating for women, others as an early version of what is now called the double day. Rural women themselves both resented the extra work and took pride in their accomplishments; unfortunately, we know little of what they – or their husbands – thought about their marriages. Whatever position individual historians take on these matters, there can be little doubt that rural women understood what the ideology of domesticity expected of them, whether or not they were willing or able to put it into practice.

Rural women's ability and desire to implement the ideology of domesticity into their daily lives, like so many other aspects of their experience, depended in large measure on the circumstances in which they lived. While in some respects the outlines of rural women's experiences transcended differences, the meanings they attached to those experiences as well as their details could vary considerably according to place, ethnicity, class, and ways of earning a living; they also changed over time. For example, women nearly universally were responsible for cooking, but what they cooked, where they obtained the food itself, its cultural significance, and who ate it could differ dramatically. Similarly, women were responsible for childcare, but what this meant in practice and how it was understood depended in part on race, the availability of birth control, kin, doctors, schools, hired or owned laborers, and opportunities for the future.

Perhaps the most significant difference influencing rural women's lives was where they lived. Region of the country, which in practice also defined roughly how long an area had been opened to European American settlement, shaped many aspects of rural women's lives. Climate, access to markets, and the price of land determined what crops farm families grew and what other sources of income might be available. Both population density and transportation influenced the availability of consumer goods, including magazines, newspapers, and other sources of news and ideas. Different regions were also home to different mixes of population; along the eastern seaboard, for example, there were relatively few Native Americans, while in the Southwest whites, Native Americans, and Mexicans mingled in complex ways. Before the Civil War, the presence or absence of slaves also shaped white women's rural lives. Even as a common rural home shaped women's experiences, then, their lives were also determined by where in the country they lived.

By the nineteenth century, most rural women in the northeastern and mid-Atlantic states lived in areas that had been settled for some time. Land for new settlements was scarce and expensive, and farming competed with other ways of making a living as regional specialization and improved transportation made purchasing food grown in what is now the Midwest ever less expensive. Rural women adapted to these circumstances by participating with their husbands in an economic strategy in which families engaged in a wide variety of activities in order to make ends meet. In addition to growing crops, families could engage in household commodity production or the putting-out system, both of which added significantly to women's labor but also the family budget. In addition, women in this part of the country worked with their families to harvest a range of commodities drawn from their environment, from ice to timber to berries to fish. Native American women made and sold baskets; others sold their skills as knitters or midwives or seamstresses. In all of these ways, northeastern rural women contributed to the family economy in an area increasingly marginal for farming; sometimes their work made the difference between family failure and survival.

Perhaps the most dramatic way in which northeastern rural women contributed to the family economy was by leaving the farm entirely, to move to one of the factory towns that flourished in the region beginning early in the century. Farmers' daughters were deliberately recruited as the first source of labor in the industrial production of textiles, work that had largely been theirs when done by hand at home. Their eagerness to take factory jobs reflected the lack of economic opportunity and limited prospects of home; as young men moved westward or to the city to seek their fortunes, so did young women become factory operatives. These young women earned a qualified independence; they could save money for their eventual marriages but were expected to send money home and to come home themselves when their families needed them. This early cohort of native-born farm daughters was later replaced in factories by immigrants, many of whom came from rural areas themselves. Yet these women's experiences defined the outlines of aspirations for subsequent generations of young women who left the countryside for the city in order to find work and opportunity. The result was, in many areas, sizable depopulation, especially of young people; gender imbalance because more men than women left; and a growing concern on the part of parents for developing strategies to keep at least a few of their children at home.

Despite the forces that pulled families apart, northeastern rural women were the most likely to be influenced by the ideology of domesticity. Enjoying higher rates of literacy than rural women elsewhere, they also had easy access to printed matter and other forms of popular culture. While the strength of ideas about women's proper role often meant limited access to education and jobs, it also encouraged women to see themselves as sharing experiences and outlooks based on a common biology. In turn, according to Nancy Cott and others, this could lead to an interest in reform, as women turned public assumptions about their morality, piety, and benevolence to efforts to improve their communities.

Although most work on antebellum activism focuses on urban areas or towns, rural women throughout the Northeast formed the backbone of numerous reform societies, from temperance to abolition to woman's rights; some even joined utopian communities. The first woman's rights convention was held in small-town Seneca Falls, New York, not Boston or Philadelphia, and drew a largely rural audience. Throughout the Northeast, rural women met in temperance and moral reform societies, gathered signatures on antislavery petitions, and held fundraising fairs for a host of causes. Historians have offered a range of explanations for northeastern women's commitment to reform, from the new-found leisure made possible by their access to factory-made cloth and other commodities to their anxiety about status displacement as all of the forces associated with modernization challenged their assumptions about their society. Whatever the explanation, there can be little doubt that northeastern rural women were active participants in and often leaders of the reform politics of their day, before and after the Civil War.

Southern white women were far less likely to engage in, or even sympathize with, reform, which was associated with abolitionism and woman's rights. Shaped by the consequences of slavery, rural women in the South understood race as well as gender to be central in defining their experience. For white southern women, rural experiences were also deeply stratified by class, with those at the top controlling the labor of slaves and those at the bottom struggling to survive in the context of a labor system that neither valued their contributions nor offered them many options.

White plantation women, by convention those whose husbands owned twenty or more slaves before the Civil War and by extension those who remained elite landowners once it was over, experienced life rather differently from their less wealthy counterparts. The wealthiest among them benefited from the labor of slaves and the income that labor generated in myriad ways. They divided their time between rural plantations and homes in cities or spent their summers traveling in order to avoid what were widely perceived as the dangers of summer miasmas to their health. Less wealthy slaveholding women did not necessarily enjoy either city homes or summers away, but they also benefited from the labors of slaves. Once a family's wealth allowed it sufficient numbers of slaves, white women could count on having at least a few permanently or temporarily assigned to domestic work under their direction.

Historians disagree about the extent and nature of white plantation women's work. Some claim that the presence of slaves exempted them from nearly all forms of labor, sometimes even including rearing their own children. Catherine Clinton and others argue that the presence of slaves added to the responsibilities white women faced even as it offered them respite from the most burdensome of domestic tasks. In this view, white women's productive labor was diminished, but their supervisory and managerial responsibilities were increased by the need to ensure adequate supplies of food, clothing, and medical care for what could sometimes be large numbers of slaves. There can be little doubt, however, that white plantation women enjoyed far more leisure than most rural women, which translated into improved opportunities for education and sociability, and occasionally into work for benevolent causes.

Historians know far less about the lives of white southern women whose husbands owned smaller numbers of slaves or none at all – which means the vast majority of rural southern women. Smaller slaveholders generally could not spare slave labor from the fields to assist their wives in the kitchen and laundry, although there is evidence that some sought to do so as much as possible. The wives of nonslaveholders, of course, did all of their own domestic work. Because the South was overwhelmingly rural and opportunities off the farm rare, white women had few choices other than marriage and the domestic responsibilities associated with it. Their options were limited even more by the patriarchal characteristics of their society, which depended on enforcing rigid race and gender hierarchies to keep order. As a result, many white southern rural women experienced life primarily as an unrelenting round of drudgery composed of hard domestic work, limited pleasure, frequent pregnancy and illness, poverty, and brutality. Of course, there were countervailing forces, particularly religion and family life. Evangelical religion was a strong presence in many such women's lives, offering both emotional solace for the hardships of life and a supportive community that was sometimes willing to intervene and offer protection from the worst of male abuses. Similarly, many southern women enjoyed extensive networks of relatives with whom they shared the pleasures and pains of life; family was valued for the emotional support its members could provide for one another.

Those rural women in the Northeast and the South who lived in longer-settled areas shared the advantages associated with such regions. They rarely had to endure the hardships of breaking new ground or living in temporary housing. They were likely to have neighbors to provide assistance and social opportunities. Those who could afford schools, medical care, and consumer goods usually had access to them. However, women living on the frontiers of settlement or in the West – wherever that happened to be at any given moment in time – could not necessarily count on such amenities. For women who migrated from longer-settled areas, the absence of such comforts could mean a sense of deprivation and real hardship. However, as frontiers gave way to greater population densities, churches, schools, stores, and other familiar comforts began to appear.

Rural women's experiences in the West were shaped in large measure by how recently the area had been opened to settlement by whites. As whites moved in, many Native Americans and Hispanics were squeezed out, but they did not disappear. The West was in fact marked by frequent cross-cultural interaction; for women, this could as often mean sharing food, services, and knowledge on an individual basis with women of another race as it meant fear, hostility, and violence. Still, the early stages of frontier contact were often difficult. Long-time occupants of the land found that their access to it was denied and their homes and ways of life threatened. Groups that had traditions of communal farming, with divisions of labor different from those practiced by whites, found their practices challenged and their patterns of land ownership and control ignored by whites eager to press their own claims to the land. In the process, Native American and Hispanic women found their authority challenged not just by whites, but sometimes also by their own men, who were eager to enjoy the advantages of male supremacy promised by adopting white practices. Sometimes, these women lost control of land and the social authority it conveyed; in other cases, men and women worked together to reject the encroachment of white traditions, with varying measures of success. The loss of communal farming traditions and the imposition of individual household arrangements, particularly in the Southwest, made these rural women's lives especially painful.

White settlers on the frontier faced their own difficulties. Incoming white families had to raise cash for necessities, transportation, and to buy what they needed to sustain themselves until they could harvest their first crops. Just getting to the West could mean months of weary travel. Once a white family arrived, it had to build shelter, clear land, and learn to farm on it, which often meant growing unfamiliar crops in difficult soil with little rainfall. It was in this stage of immediate necessity that women were likely to find themselves doing what was generally considered men's work, including plowing fields and raising buildings.

After the pioneer stage of hard work and improvisation was over, rural women in the West worked to create lives as similar as possible to those they remembered from home. Catharine Beecher had urged women to become "civilizers" of the West, in their roles as teachers, wives, and mothers, and many took her advice to heart, whether or not they heard it directly. Certainly western rural white women had a somewhat different political experience from those of their northeastern and southern peers. In the West, such women had far more political access than in other parts of the country; similarly, their reform efforts were often undertaken alongside men rather than in sex-segregated groups.

Historians disagree on why white western women were granted suffrage long before women in other parts of the country. Sandra Myres is among those who claim that the importance of women's contributions and the more flexible sex roles made necessary by the demands of opening new land to settlement encouraged men to grant them political access, suggesting a kind of frontier democracy at work. Others emphasize the propaganda value: when Wyoming enfranchised women there were few men and even fewer women in the territory; suffrage was offered by some as a means of advertising to attract more women settlers. Utah women were enfranchised partly as a means of deflecting criticism of the Mormon practice of polygamy and of adding to the electorate. Others emphasize the importance of outsiders in agitating for western suffrage. Still others argue that western suffrage was the result of political expediency, suggesting that local politics, often concerning temperance, and not a region-wide commitment to women's equality determined where women would be allowed to vote.

Still other historians suggest that western women's access to suffrage was the result of their greater political involvement with men, especially in the Granger movement. While this argument is not necessarily convincing, since women had cooperated extensively with men in reform causes in other parts of the country for decades, the Grange and later the Farmers' Alliance and populism did offer western women unprecedented opportunities to make their voices heard. The Grange, founded to improve rural social and family life, admitted women from the beginning, although they were assumed to be primarily concerned with domestic matters and their opportunities for leadership in the early years were limited to the three offices created specifically for them. Women also claimed political voices in the populist movement, but in neither organization did they do so specifically as women.

Region of the country was not the only factor shaping rural women's experiences. Race and ethnicity also determined their lives, in a variety of ways already discussed. There were ethnic divisions even among whites, particularly among those who migrated from Europe. In rural areas all over the continent, pockets of ethnic homogeneity developed as people sought to settle near others who spoke the same language and observed the same religion. Rural areas of what is now the upper Midwest, for example, were filled with migrants from northern Europe, perhaps attracted by its familiar climate and landscape. Boosters for some areas deliberately recruited immigrants from abroad, offering them the promise of cheap land and opportunity while simultaneously claiming they could replicate the social arrangements they preferred. However, in practice, many rural areas became quite ethnically diverse; while not as complex as urban areas, rural diversity nevertheless made life far different from the stereotype of homogeneity that has sometimes been associated with it.

Historians have only delved into rural race and ethnic relations in scattered ways. We know a good deal about relations between black and white women in the South. We know something about the interactions of Native Americans and whites in some areas, about Mexicans and whites in others, but relatively little about Native Americans and Mexicans. We know that popular prejudices and stereotypes of race and ethnic differences were not confined to cities, although sometimes the relative isolation of rural areas could lead to cross-group interactions, especially on the frontier. To some extent, these gaps in historians' knowledge are the result of gaps in our sources, but this remains an area that requires additional attention.

Ethnic and racial diversity in rural areas was perhaps more visible, but no more significant than divisions according to class. While differences between elite slaveholding women and their poor white neighbors in the South point to the most obvious class difference, in fact the economic differences between rich and poor could be nearly as wide in other regions. However, in most rural areas, even those longer-settled, the gap between rich and poor whites seemed narrow relative to what urban dwellers experienced. To some extent, the narrow range between the top and bottom of the social scale was more apparent than real; everyone in a given rural community was likely to know what everyone else was worth. However, strong traditions of mutual interdependence and neighborliness meant that economic distinctions could easily flatten out in the course of daily life. Women helped one another in times of childbirth, illness, or other emergencies, regardless of class and, sometimes, race and ethnicity. They sewed for one another and quilted together. They developed a widespread network of friends and neighbors with whom they bartered and borrowed time, household goods, and favors of all sorts in a complex pattern of mutual obligation that ignored all but the most extreme class differences.

Class differences were more visible for those women whose husbands prided themselves on being "progressive" farmers. These successful men generally earned more money than their neighbors, some of which they were likely to turn over to their wives to purchase labor-saving devices and other amenities. By late in the century, such families might well choose to send their sons to an agricultural or land-grant college to learn practical agriculture; their daughters might go to the same institutions to study domestic science or home economics. Such study was touted as a means of improving the quality of farm life by reducing the drudgery of women's work, although it may well have simply substituted one form of drudgery for another without substantively altering the nature of women's labors.

Rural women did not just live on farms. Some lived in mining camps, others in lumber camps, still others in military forts in areas the army was trying to protect for white settlement. Some even lived in the small towns that developed to serve rural peoples as centers of buying and selling, civic and associational life. There is some debate among rural historians whether these experiences "count" as rural, because the concentration of settlement was higher than that usually associated with farming. Yet in some respects, life in such communities more nearly resembled rural farm life than it did urban life. Women were still expected to take responsibility for domestic and family life, often in difficult conditions. Although there might be fewer opportunities for them to earn an income, they were still expected to contribute to family survival by participating in the family economy however they could. However, because men in these communities were often employed by a company or the government, their daily experiences were far more regimented than those on the farm; men deep in the mines or away on patrol may have seemed qualitatively more distant than those plowing in the next field, giving their wives an experience perhaps closer to that of the urban woman whose husband labored in a factory or shop all day.

The field of rural women's history is remarkable for the diversity of the experiences it encompasses. No less than in cities, rural women were shaped by differences of race, class, and ethnicity; by differing opportunities and varied efforts to enhance them; by conflict and cooperation with men. Historians who have chosen to see the city as the source of conflict in American society as well as of solutions to that conflict would do well to recognize the importance of what was, for most of the nineteenth century, the experience of the majority of American women.

BIBLIOGRAPHY

Barron, Hal S. (1984) *Those Who Stayed Behind: Rural Society in Nineteenth-century New England*. New York: Cambridge University Press.

Boydston, Jeanne (1990) *Home and Work: Housework, Wages, and the Ideology of Labor in the Early Republic*. New York: Oxford University Press.

Cashin, Joan E. (1991) *A Family Venture: Men and Women on the Southern Frontier*. Baltimore: Johns Hopkins University Press.

Censer, Jane Turner (1984) *North Carolina Planters and their Children, 1800–1860*. Baton Rouge: Louisiana State University Press.

Clark, Christopher (1990) *The Roots of Rural Capitalism: Western Massachusetts, 1780–1860*. Ithaca, NY: Cornell University Press.

Clinton, Catherine (1982) *The Plantation Mistress: Woman's World in the Old South*. New York: Pantheon.

Cott, Nancy F. (1977) *The Bonds of Womanhood: "Woman's Sphere" in New England, 1780–1835*. New Haven, CT: Yale University Press.

Danbom, David B. (1995) *Born in the Country: A History of Rural America*. Baltimore: Johns Hopkins University Press.

Deutsch, Sarah (1987) *No Separate Refuge: Culture, Class, and Gender on an Anglo-Hispanic Frontier in the American Southwest, 1880–1940*. New York: Oxford University Press.

Dublin, Thomas (1979) *Women at Work: The Transformation of Work and Community in Lowell, Massachusetts, 1826–1860*. New York: Columbia University Press.

Dublin, Thomas (ed.) (1981) *Farm to Factory: Women's Letters, 1830–1860*. New York: Columbia University Press; 2nd ed., 1993.

Edwards, Laura F. (1997) *Gendered Strife and Confusion: The Political Culture of Reconstruction*. Urbana: University of Illinois Press.

Faragher, John Mack (1979) *Women and Men on the Overland Trail*. New Haven, CT: Yale University Press.

Faragher, John Mack (1986) *Sugar Creek: Life on the Illinois Prairie*. New Haven, CT: Yale University Press.

Foote, Cheryl J. (1990) *Women of the New Mexico Frontier, 1846–1912*. Niwot: University Press of Colorado.

Fox-Genovese, Elizabeth (1988) *Within the Plantation Household: Black and White Women of the Old South*. Chapel Hill: University of North Carolina Press.

Friedman, Jean E. (1985) *The Enclosed Garden: Women and Community in the Evangelical South, 1830–1900*. Chapel Hill: University of North Carolina Press.

Hahn, Steven and Prude, Jonathan (eds.) (1985) *The Countryside in the Age of Capitalist Transformation: Essays in the Social History of Rural America*. Chapel Hill: University of North Carolina Press.

Harris, Katherine (1993) *Long Vistas: Women and Families on Colorado Homesteads*. Niwot: University Press of Colorado.

Jeffrey, Julie Roy (1979) *Frontier Women: The Trans-Mississippi West, 1840–1880*. New York: Hill and Wang.

Jensen, Joan M. (1981) *With These Hands: Women Working on the Land*. Old Westbury, NY: Feminist Press.

Jensen, Joan M. (1986) *Loosening the Bonds: Mid-Atlantic Farm Women, 1750–1850*. New Haven, CT: Yale University Press.

Jensen, Joan M. (1991) *Promise to the Land: Essays on Rural Women*. Albuquerque: University of New Mexico Press.

Jones, Jacqueline (1985) *Labor of Love, Labor of Sorrow: Black Women, Work and the Family from Slavery to the Present*. New York: Basic Books.

Kolodny, Annette (1984) *The Land Before Her: Fantasy and Experience of the American Frontiers, 1630–1860*. Chapel Hill: University of North Carolina Press.

McCurry, Stephanie (1995) *Masters of Small Worlds: Yeoman Households, Gender Relations, and the Political Culture of the Antebellum South Carolina Low Country.* New York: Oxford University Press.

McMillen, Sally G. (1990) *Motherhood in the Old South: Pregnancy, Childbirth, and Infant Rearing.* Baton Rouge: Louisiana State University Press.

McMurry, Sally Ann (1995) *Transforming Rural Life: Dairying Families and Agricultural Change, 1820–1885.* Baltimore: Johns Hopkins University Press.

McMurry, Sally Ann (1997) *Families and Farmhouses in Nineteenth-century America: Vernacular Design and Social Change.* Knoxville: University of Tennessee Press.

Marti, Donald B. (1991) *Women of the Grange: Mutuality and Sisterhood in Rural America, 1866–1920.* New York: Greenwood Press.

Myres, Sandra L. (1982) *Westering Women and the Frontier Experience, 1800–1915.* Albuquerque: University of New Mexico Press.

Osterud, Nancy Grey (1991) *Bonds of Community: The Lives of Farm Women in Nineteenth-century New York.* Ithaca, NY: Cornell University Press.

Painter, Nell Irvin (1976) *Exodusters: Black Migration to Kansas After Reconstruction.* New York: Alfred A. Knopf.

Pascoe, Peggy (1990) *Relations of Rescue: The Search for Female Moral Authority in the American West, 1874–1939.* New York: Oxford University Press.

Petrik, Paula (1987) *No Step Backward: Women and Family on the Rocky Mountain Mining Frontier, 1865–1900.* Helena: Montana Historical Society Press.

Riley, Glenda (1984) *Women and Indians on the Frontier, 1825–1915.* Albuquerque: University of New Mexico Press.

Riley, Glenda (1988) *The Female Frontier: A Comparative View of Women on the Prairie and the Plains.* Lawrence: University Press of Kansas.

Ryan, Mary P. (1981) *The Cradle of the Middle Class: The Family in Oneida County, New York, 1780–1865.* New York: Cambridge University Press.

Sachs, Carolyn E. (1983) *The Invisible Farmers: Women in Agricultural Production.* Totowa, NJ: Rowman and Allenheld.

Schlissel, Lillian (1982) *Women's Diaries of the Westward Journey.* New York: Schocken Books.

Schlissel, Lillian (1989) *Far from Home: Families of the Westward Journey.* New York: Schocken Books.

Scott, Anne Firor (1970) *The Southern Lady: From Pedestal to Politics, 1830–1930.* Chicago: University of Chicago Press.

Stevenson, Brenda E. (1996) *Life in Black and White: Family and Community in the Slave South.* New York: Oxford University Press.

Stratton, Joanna L. (1981) *Pioneer Women: Voices from the Kansas Frontier.* New York: Simon and Schuster.

Ulrich, Laurel Thatcher (1990) *A Midwife's Tale: The Life of Martha Ballard, Based on Her Diary, 1785–1812.* New York: Alfred A. Knopf.

Weiner, Marli F. (1998) *Mistresses and Slaves: Plantation Women in South Carolina, 1830–1880.* Urbana: University of Illinois Press.

Chapter Eleven

The Civil War Era

Thavolia Glymph

IN 1864 Hannah Johnson penned a letter now familiar to scholars of the Civil War to President Lincoln. In it, Johnson voiced her support for the Union cause and her pride in a son who had enlisted in the US Army. In deciding to enlist, she stressed, he had done no more than was his duty and his right. Like countless other women, northern and southern, Johnson was concerned for her soldier-son. By 1864 the Civil War had lasted far longer and cost far more in every way than anyone had foreseen in 1861. It had produced a staggering brutality that most could not have imagined. Letters from the front brought the reality of war to those who remained at home. "I fought almost ankle deep in the blood & brains of our killed & wounded," one soldier informed his mother after the bloodbath at Spotsylvania in the spring of 1864 (quoted in Edgar 1998: 370). Johnson's letter was different though from most letters from the home front. The source of the radically different ground upon which she spoke lay in her racial and political identities and the way in which the two fused: she was African American and the daughter of a runaway slave. This distinguished her understanding of the meaning of the war and her commitment to it. Hannah Johnson had backed her son's desire to enlist in the 54th Massachusetts Infantry Regiment: the "horrible Outrage"of slavery, she wrote, must be destroyed even if it meant her son might die in the process (Berlin et al. 1982: 582–3).

Yet somehow Johnson's son had neither anticipated nor expected that his race more than his politics would put him at such extraordinary risk, that the military code of conduct for the treatment of enemy soldiers who were black would be held in abeyance by the Confederate government. So she pleaded with the president to work harder on behalf of black soldiers, to demand equal treatment for those captured by Confederate forces, and if necessary, to prove the Union's commitment with retribution against captured Confederate soldiers. By doing so, she instructed the president, he might give concrete witness to his publicly stated moral convictions and leave a profound legacy.

Hannah Johnson's race also distinguishes the historiographical silence that came to envelop her articulation of the meaning of the war, its origins and transformation into a war for Union *and* freedom, and its legacy. In the written history of the war and in the nation's *collective memory* – that hybrid of public and cultural memory, part fact and part fiction, and so often so stunningly unreliable – African American women are an anomaly, visible but invisible. The nation's *collective memory*, unreliable but potent, takes hardly any notice at all of black women in the war, not as the mothers, wives, or daughters of black soldiers, not as Union patriots, not as active participants in the struggle to secure their freedom. Poor white working-class and small-farm women have not fared much better in Civil War and Reconstruction historiography or popular memory.

Rewriting the history of the Civil War and Reconstruction to include and account for the disparate experiences of American women in war and reconstruction remains the signal challenge of scholarship in the field. Some years ago, Maris Vinovskis asked famously whether social historians had lost the Civil War. The field has broadened significantly over the past decade but that, it turns out, is not to say much. Vinovskis's question, which had been raised earlier by several historians of the South, still resonates. Yet other questions, informed at least in part by social history, also beg our attention. "We are all Soldier's Wives or Mothers," one woman proclaimed during the war (quoted in Simkins 1963: 234). Did she and others who wrote similarly intend their pronouncements to be taken as statements of patriotism or lamentation, or both? Did such statements reflect the essence of women's participation and vision during the war? Did women share the same vision as men of the war's purpose or its conduct; did they share the same vision for peace and reconstruction? And what were the issues that divided women?

The record of the printed history of women in the Civil War and Reconstruction is a mixed and complicated one. Unlike the case in many fields in American history, women were never totally excluded from histories of the Civil War and source materials exist in abundance. Monographs and articles on women in the war predated the women's movement and the establishment of the discipline of women's studies by decades. Even works that focused on the military or political history of the war generally also included material on women. The story of Confederate women has never gone begging for an author; although the results, especially those sponsored by divisions of the United Daughters of the Confederacy, were not always useful. In addition, women's diaries and memoirs circulated widely as commercial publications and as privately printed manuscripts. Despite repeated calls for greater scholarly detachment and objectivity, however, writers continued to turn to the romantic and mythical. Portraits of sacrifice and subjection predominated, reinforced over time by popular culture, most famously *Gone With the Wind* (1939) and less famously but no less potent, *The Birth of a Nation* (1915). *The southern lady in wartime* became arguably an even more popular trope of southern white identity than the plantation mistress. Legends grew up around her stoic defiance in distress. Children exposed to R. G. Horton's *A Youth's History of the Great Civil War*, published immediately following the war, learned that southern women, like their menfolk, "were savagely torn from their families and sent to dungeons for such things as laughing at Federal soldiers, and other harmless acts" (1925: 138). The images of southern women in wartime to which most Americans were introduced or exposed were thus largely stock types: the vulnerable plantation mistress or the stoic farm wife defending family and nation. Like the purveyors of popular culture, historians generally paid little attention to what the vast majority of American women did and thought or to how they lived and survived the war, though there were telling exceptions, as discussed below.

From 1865 into the first decades of the twentieth century, American readers seemed not to tire of war stories and memoirs of the war and postwar period. Few histories of the war were deemed complete without a tribute to women's participation, whether a paragraph, page, or chapter. The memoirs of generals and regimental histories vied for attention and readership with memoirs authored by women recounting their experiences in field hospitals and on plantations. Yet only one such narrative, and that a fictionalized account – Louisa Alcott's *Little Women* (1868) – ever matched the popularity of such postwar bestsellers as Lewis Carroll's *Alice's Adventures in Wonderland* (1866). Still, women were as keen as men to leave a record of how the war had interested and affected them, some urged on by poverty and the need to earn a living.

Plans to publish women's narratives developed during the war. L. P. Brockett and Mary C. Vaughan, for example, began working on *Woman's Work in the Civil War: A Record of Heroism, Patriotism, and Patience* while battles still raged and published it in 1867. At some 800 pages, *Woman's Work* paid homage to the contributions of more than 500 Union women (none African American). In 1866, Frank Moore published *Women of the War: Their Heroism and Self-sacrifice.* Other important edited collections included *The Women of the Confederacy* (1906), edited by J. L. Underwood, and Matthew Page Andrews's *Women of the South in War Times* (1920). Andrews advertised his book as a "simple narrative" of southern women's "record of achievement, endurance, and self-sacrificing devotion" (1920: 3). Underwood dedicated his volume to his mother-in-law, who "cheerfully gave every available member of her family to the Confederate cause." Books chronicling the woman's war and women's sacrifices in particular enjoyed widespread appeal, North and South. Many writers hoped, like Andrews, that their work would also play a part in "instilling respect for and sympathy with the sufferings of the South" (1920: 5–6).

Mostly, the "woman's war" as traditionally written and understood was the history of white women, and more particularly, the history of middle- and upper-class white women. The complicity or silence of scholars of African American and women's history for most of the twentieth century helped to give this interpretation undue sanction, despite W. E. B. DuBois's early intervention cogently arguing for a different understanding. Benjamin Quarles's 1953 study, *The Negro in the Civil War*, was an early and important exception. He was responding, perhaps, to Charles H. Wesley in *The Collapse of the Confederacy*, who found in "the story of the Southern women in the war" one of the war's "heroic narratives" (1937: 103). It is clear that Wesley's reference is solely to white women. The problem did not disappear with the advent of women's or African American history. Papers presented at a 1983 conference sponsored by the American Historical Association to assess the state of the field of African American history delineated and focused on three major research themes; the Civil War was not among them. Darlene Clark Hine's seminal 1986 essay on African American women devoted a paragraph to the subject of black women and the Civil War; and a major historiographical essay on southern women by Jacquelyn Hall and Anne Firor Scott published a year later was silent on the subject. Marilyn Mayer

Culpepper's more recent history of women in the war is a study of northern and southern women but not black women. This is neither, Culpepper explains, "an oversight nor a deliberate exclusion." Rather, the decision is based on the paucity of black women's diaries and too few other primary sources. Culpepper writes that black women contributed "significantly" to the war effort; she does not seem to believe this, though. "Their real story ... unfolded during the Reconstruction years" (1991: 3).

Although the last twenty-five years of the twentieth century witnessed the emergence, spectacular growth, and maturation of the field of women's history, only a tiny fraction of this work has concerned women in the Civil War and Reconstruction. Not surprisingly, women's history scholars in the 1960s and 1970s first trained their sights on the study of northern women, which seemed historically richer – even more relevant – at the time. There scholars found a more visibly radical and activist women's movement and abundant and accessible archival sources to support research agendas. The first fruits of this new direction in the study of history focused most notably on those incipient women's reform movements that, over the course of the nineteenth century, would give form and direction to the campaign for woman's suffrage.

Northern women's lives thus came to be portrayed with increased narrative and theoretical sophistication. The impact that the spread of capitalist social relations in the countryside had on northern women and gender relations came into sharper focus. As a result, even as scholars turned their attention to the ways in which gender as an analytic category facilitated the methodological work of "seeing" women's work and their social lives more distinctly and forced a reinterrogation of men's lives, comparatively little attention was paid to working women, southern women, or the Civil War and Reconstruction. Although the methodological and theoretical insights pioneered in this period would ultimately shape a broader field of research, initially most energy went into studies of northern middle-class white women, women's reform organizations, and to a lesser extent farm women. One might surmise by the inattention to it that the Civil War was viewed as not very fertile, perhaps even inhospitable, ground for exploring questions of gender. Given this framework, the story of southern women during and after the war still attracted little attention beyond the South itself – mythic depictions of elite southern women excluded – where it continued to be authored largely by white southerners.

In recent years, scholars have given interpretive and methodological primacy to the analytic categories of race, class, and gender and have begun to challenge the terms and terrain of longstanding historiographical traditions. The challenge remains in its infancy, having not yet transformed the writing of Civil War or Reconstruction history. But a reinvigorated discussion is now possible and is taking place. Theoretical and methodological tools and insights gained from work over the past three decades in such diverse fields as African American history, African American studies, women's studies, labor and economic history, and slavery and emancipation are central to important new work that is published and underway. A growing body of work on women and war in the twentieth and early twenty-first centuries will also, I think, have a tremendous impact on the history of women in the Civil War. Thus, while a recent spate of new works on gender and race in the war and Reconstruction have established the basis for fuller treatments of poor women and non-European Americans, the period of the Civil War and Reconstruction remains the most racially gendered and regionally segregated historiographical space in US history. This essay traces the path that has led to this point and the ways in which new and emerging scholarship is transforming the field.

From any perspective, women's history remains the least studied and least analytically sophisticated aspect of the Civil War and Reconstruction. For a period that witnessed the most voluminous outpouring of writing by and about women of any in American history prior to the twentieth century, this seems on the surface an odd result. In letters, diaries, and memoirs, white women wrote incessantly, chronicling the political and social changes that were uprooting, rearranging, and transforming their lives. Middle-class and poor women wrote to Federal, Confederate, state, and local officials requesting information and support and voicing their views on military and political matters. Privately run commissions and agencies employed women and solicited their support and labor. Commission and agency records document women's concerns, their work, and the impact of the war on their lives. Military records and the records of the Freedmen's Bureau record the announcements of freedom from plantations, farms, and southern white homes as slaves walked or ran away or stayed put but gave their weight to slavery's disintegration.

Throughout the prolonged conflict, women, North and South, slave and free, were active participants in national and local debates over the meaning of the war, freedom, work, citizenship, and gender. After 1865 they continued to engage the political and social questions of the day. In the North, questions of what place black Americans would occupy in the new nation, what rights and freedoms they would enjoy, suffused and energized an increasingly less tentative debate about white female gender roles, suffrage, and citizenship. In the South, these same questions imbued a much more boisterous and violent struggle that energized both the African American struggle for full citizenship and the white supremacist movement of the postwar era.

Toward the end of the twentieth century, historians began to mount a challenge to the canonical and popularly understood notion of the "woman's war" as the story of middle- and upper-class white women. This shift owed a debt to the tremendous outpouring of new literature on slavery, emancipation, and Reconstruction beginning in the 1950s and 1960s. Pushed by the black freedom struggle and subsequently the women's movement, scholars confronted questions of imbalance, omissions, and racism in the historical literature. A renewed emphasis on social history also helped fuel this trend. Over the past three decades our understanding of Reconstruction has been dramatically reshaped, the Civil War less so. Scholarship of the last quarter of the twentieth century reveals a contested political landscape of tremendous complexity where relations of power are never as impervious to assault as they seem, where gender ideals are in flux. Rather than whispering timidly from the sidelines, women's political discourse plays a central role. The work of Elsa Barkley Brown, for example, challenged historians to rethink hidebound conceptualizations of the face of political activism and the definition of political work even as it advanced new methodological approaches to understanding women's political voices.

The destruction of slavery and the enlargement of the meaning and possibilities of the war, it is now clear, owed much to the efforts of slaves and free black people together with white abolitionists whose numbers were enhanced with each year of the war by the addition of northern white soldiers. Pioneering scholarship has reshaped our understanding of freedpeople's struggles to obtain land, to define and control familial relations and obligations, and to win and secure the vote for black men. More complex portraits of black women's political engagement in the struggle to define freedom and citizenship and of slaveholding women's involvement in the Civil War are being drawn. Yet much work remains to be done. Middle- and upper-class women remain the focus of the vast majority of new work published over the last ten years, just as they did over the last thirty. The field still lacks a monographic study of urban and industrial women workers during the Civil War or Reconstruction, or of farm women, nonslaveholding and small-slaveholding women in the South. To date, there is but one published monograph on black women in the Civil War – Ella Forbes's 1998 study, *African American Women During the Civil War.*

Historians of the "woman's war" have been largely concerned with four questions. What were the nature and extent of white women's wartime participation? What impact did the war have on white women and on gender relations? How did women's presence influence the war or its outcome? What was the legacy of women's wartime participation for white women's rights and white gender relations in the postwar period? From 1865 to the present, these questions have been batted back and forth and the answers have changed little over time, though they are now more detailed. How the war might have impacted African Americans, and vice versa, were questions conspicuous by their absence. For the most part, it has been argued, white women would stay within traditional boundaries, but by the war's end these so-called traditional boundaries were themselves fuzzy. Indeed, the war left no boundaries as it found them, despite the pre- and postwar effort to contain the claims of black and white working women that they were conscious of their rights as working women and as citizens, and white women's narratives of the war, within the rubric of womanly sacrifice.

Northern and southern accounts of the woman's war, from stories of their labors on the home front – managing slaves, running farms and households – to their work as nurses and occasionally their heroic exploits as spies or cross-dressed female soldiers, were crafted within a *language of sacrifice* that gendered women's contributions within the coterminously limiting framework of *feminine war heroism.* The linking of female heroism to sacrifice and male heroism to death was of course not unique to the Civil War. Here as elsewhere it had the effect of distorting and diminishing women's contributions to war and their political voices.

The *language of sacrifice* is deployed in specific ways to specific ends. Women's *sacrifices* are juxtaposed to men's work as soldiers and statesmen. Sacrifice is feminine, apolitical, and passive; it is class and race specific. Fighting and dying (and arranging the fighting and dying, the work of politicians and generals) is masculine, political, and active. No man is excluded because he is poor and, by the 1980s and 1990s, none would be because he was African American. Women suffer through men and for the loss of men. "My greatest grief," wrote one southern woman to her fiancé in the Confederate army, "is that we hear you were wounded and in the hospital, and I cannot be with you to nurse you" (Watkins 1994 [1882]: 185). Men suffer directly, tangibly in the loss of lives or limbs. Recruitment slogans urge men to join the fight for "home" and "country" – often conflating the two – and women line the streets to gaily *send men off to war.* In the South, as McCurry writes, "secessionists' gendered call to arms authorized a very local notion of defense – literally home protection – thus rendering the task of nation-making the more difficult" (2000: 109). It is the nation, however, that ultimately takes precedence in the minds of military and political leaders. By 1864 at least, Confederate strategy may have appeared to many white southerners more interested in country than home. War sloganeering no longer confidently conflated "home" and "country." The survival of "country" might require sacrificing "home," an idea that over the course of the Civil War more and more fueled debate, disaffection, and desertion. It might also require sacrificing the "self," as Drew Faust explains in *Mothers of Invention* (1996).

The American Civil War was in these ways like other modern wars that have employed a language of sacrifice. Such language is commonplace, and it inevitably exposes contradictions inherent in paternalistic and racist discourses and ideologies. During the Civil War, soldiers enlisted to defend home and liberty as their countries called them to do. On the ground this often left the practical everyday defense and care of the home to women. In their letters to male kin at the war front, women reported on the status of the corn crops, the hogs, and their efforts to raise cash by selling butter and eggs, while telling men to stick to *their* "post of duty." And when the home became clearly defenseless and its inhabitants hungry, as in the case of the Civil War South by 1864, home could just as easily become a rallying cry to take unauthorized leave of the army. The needs of the state then collided with those of the home. In the North, as Lyde Sizer finds, the writings of northern middle- and upper-class women also shifted dramatically as the war wore on. Images of "sorrowing women who cared little for national glory and much for the individual man" dominated writing in the last two years of the war. By the end of the war, northern women are depicted not only as having suffered – believing often to no good end – but as among the disfranchised, the war's "unconsulted" (Sizer 2000: 185, 264–5).

In declaring themselves "all Soldiers' Wives or Mothers," women invoked the privileges the governing gender system awarded them even as they claimed through such discourse a separate identity and nontraditional privileges. As the female kin of soldiers, they staked a claim to the interests of soldiers, of men, a claim to act and to be heard. War, as one group of scholars writes, is "a *gendering* activity, one that ritually marks the gender of all members of a society, whether or not they are combatants" (Higonnet et al. 1987: 4). War does not do this passively, however. That is, war does not automatically mark gender. At first glance, it seems that most of women's war work, which took the form of sewing, cooking, nursing, and nurturing soldiers' morale with homilies from home, hardly broke the gendered ground that had defined prewar society. But just as war marks gender, it also re-marks it. (Postwar societies of course expend a great deal of energy trying to erase the re-markings.)

During wars, women are often called upon to perform men's work, but they are not expected to continue to do so once the guns fall silent. As well, traditionally defined women's work is re-marked to meet the circumstances of wartime. In times of war, women are called upon to place their "womanly" talents in the service of the home/ state. It is not assumed that they will do so automatically, despite the contrary suggestion that emanates from accounts of women enthusiastically, even gaily, taking up the cause of war. Thus, Drew Gilpin Faust writes: "The appearance of celebratory accounts of women's wartime contributions even before the silencing of the guns at Appomattox suggests that these early paeans were as much prescriptive as descriptive; they were rhetorical weapons in an ongoing war" (1998: 228). Excellent studies by Elizabeth Leonard and Lyde Sizer also make this point.

What does it mean for national and gender ideologies when war makes women into the principal defenders of the home front at the same time that it requires them to speak softly about its disintegration lest they undermine the morale of men at the battle front? Studies of women in the Civil War wrestle with the very definition of home front. In its most common usage, the concept is narrowly defined and most frequently connotes the plantation home front despite the fact that it meant something quite different for yeomen women or, more pointedly, for slave women who often superficially occupied the same ground as planter women. The urban home front appears as a mere extrusion of the plantation – the site of planters' second homes or of safety for refugee planter families – rather than as a site with its own peculiar needs, labor demands, and other social issues.

One positive outgrowth of the shift in Civil War scholarship back to a concern with women has been a greater focus on the home front. The center of military and national political action might lie variously at Cold Harbor, Antietam, or Vicksburg, or in Richmond or Washington, DC; but it was the home front that was the marrow, the connective tissue, the lifeblood of the war. It was the home front that was the constant in people's lives, perceived as such even when it had itself become totally divorced from any sense of constancy.

This increased attention to the home front is in some ways a return to a traditional theme and focus. From the first, histories of the Civil War, though focused primarily on battles and leaders, routinely credited women with the ability to affect soldiers' morale and praised them for the sacrifices they had no choice but to endure. Some also noted the prejudice women encountered when they sacrificed womanly ideals to serve in army hospitals. The authors of these early histories were deeply ambivalent about how the war had affected women, and vice versa. Their ambivalence reflected the fears of many men that the work the war required of women might make them forever unfit to return to their traditional roles. Historians of the South stressed that women's sacrifices, though central to the ability of the Confederacy to remain afloat for four years, were yet inferior to men's.

Although they devoted their entire book to the subject of women, the authors of *The Women of the Confederacy* (1936), one of the first scholarly studies of the topic, wrote with no seeming embarrassment that studies with women as their focus must necessarily pale in comparison to those of men. Thus Francis Butler Simkins and James Welch Patton believed they had no choice but to subordinate "personalities [of women] to general movements, on the theory that eminence in the Confederacy was chiefly confined to political and military leaders, all of whom were naturally men." "Except in a very few instances," they maintained, "there were no women in the South who might be compared even remotely with Florence Nightingale, and there is something of the tawdry and the unreal about those who bid for the title of the Southern Joan of Arc." Further, they wrote that their project was ultimately constrained because they had had to rely in part on "notoriously romantic" memoirs of southern women, so different from the "ponderous and sophisticated writings of Confederate men" (1936: vi–vii). More recently, the principal writer for the film *The Civil War*, produced by Ken Burns, while expressing regret that they were unable to effectively cover women, nonetheless defended their decision this way: "we'd done more with women and the home front, but we could never find a way to make their appearances seem more than interruptions in the midst of the complicated, headlong, largely military story we found ourselves trying to tell" (Ward 1996: 144).

In traditional narratives of the war, women are always present but, whether given the space of a page or a book, their appearances seem like those in the film to be nothing "more than interruptions." In reality their appearance was measured, debated, and ranked. It is an irony of the war that this was true across class and race lines. Women, whether black or white, rich or poor, who ventured out into the public arena of war found some of the taint of tawdriness attached to them. Contemporary discourse and the first histories of the war went to great lengths to contain women's entrance and participation in it. White women are described and often describe themselves as being led to war work – and into the public sphere – out of a particularly gendered sense of duty and patriotism. In traditional texts as in contemporary iconography and narratives, the acceptance of even limited roles for white women (as nurses, clerks, or plantation managers) was inextricably tied to particular ideological representations.

Seen on the one hand as an extension of woman's natural domestic self, white women's wartime work was simultaneously cast as virginal. Women already marked by their historic presence in the public arena – as hucksters in the marketplace, domestic servants, and/or slaves – were old hands at working the always less well-tended margins of established gender relations and have rarely been considered a part of the "woman's war." In war the notion of margins and boundaries is risky at best. In the case of the Civil War, those margins that had been the least well tended in the antebellum period had a tendency to become dangerous flashpoints. Formerly wealthy women who were forced to work for wages at the treasury department or to bargain with slave women to have their handkerchiefs washed *and* ironed were in danger themselves of becoming marketplace hucksters. In the midst of war, women were called to take on virginal warrior status. Those who entered the domain of men should and would, if true women, experience a strong sense of displacement. Only virginal women would be shocked, for instance, by the male nakedness they might encounter in a hospital or by touching men who were strangers to them when mopping a sweated brow or bathing a wounded leg. Over time they would naturally get over the initial shock, but that shock must register. The cultural representation of virginal nurses thus worked in a literal and figurative sense.

Women's traditional domestic roles as healers and caretakers supposedly eased their entry into military hospitals and civilian commissions established to support the war effort. Yet there remained the inhospitable reception by military officers, a stigma attached to their presence, and an abiding concern among many nineteenth-century Americans that such work not only took women out of their proper sphere but that it might be hard to rein them back in. In her perceptive analysis of the historiographical treatment of women in the Civil War, Drew Faust traces this concern in wartime accounts and published histories of women in the war dating from the 1860s to the present. The earliest studies, as she points out, framed the analysis of women's place in the war for nearly a century following the surrender at Appomattox, leaving a crippling legacy for further research. Even with the perspective of time and after scholars had "shifted their focus from what women did for the war to what the war did for women" (Faust 1998: 230), African American women's part in the war was largely ignored. Studies by Jacqueline Jones, Clarence Mohr, and Leslie Schwalm, among others, have begun the work of revising this paradigm by addressing the experiences of African American women, but middle- and upper-class white women, including slaveholding women, continue to dominate the literature.

Moreover, despite the outpouring of new work, the questions at the heart of studies of white women remain little changed from 1882 when Elizabeth Cady Stanton, Susan B. Anthony, and Matilda J. Gage published Volume 2 of *The History of Woman Suffrage*. To the question of what long-term impact the war had on women's lives and gender ideology, Stanton, Anthony, and Gage answered that it was singularly transforming. Women had developed a new sense of self and as a result of their wartime experiences were ready to reach beyond traditional gender roles. Elizabeth Massey, the first historian of Civil War women in the modern period, agreed. The war, she wrote in 1966, "compelled women to become more active, self-reliant and resourceful, and this ultimately contributed to their economic, social, and intellectual advancement." Massey was convinced that "the Civil War was in part a social revolution" (1966: x). That had also been the conclusion of Agatha Young's study of northern women. This question yet comprises the central question of the most recent studies by Leonard, Culpepper, Sizer, Judith Ann Giesberg, and Jeannie Attie. There has been some tugging at it, some confrontation with the most frayed edges of the argument, but it has neither been overturned nor systematically revised.

Elizabeth Leonard, in her textual analysis of writings on white women's contributions to the war, contends that male writers and compilers immediately after the war were as much interested in chronicling women's achievements as in sending them back to the home. The new sense of self was not to be encouraged, however. The existence of a struggle to reverse it would support the general interpretation mounted by Stanton, Anthony, and Gage. Still, Leonard's study helps to position the study of Civil War women in the rapidly expanding body of work on war and women in the twentieth and twenty-first centuries and thus represents an important departure. At the same time, two recent studies of the long-neglected US Sanitary Commission have immeasurably enlarged our knowledge of women and gender in the Civil War. In *Civil War Sisterhood* (2000), Judith Ann Giesberg effectively shows that women provided key supply and logistical support for the Union army, gaining in the process experience in political work that would prove crucial to women's organizing efforts after the war. The story of the Commission, she writes, "is the story of how women of privilege ... and women of more modest means" came to form an effective network "that provided critical support to the U.S. Army throughout the war" (2000: 7). Despite the reference to women of "modest means," Giesberg's work retains the familiar focus on "women of privilege," as does the other recent study of the Commission by Jeannie Attie.

The renewed interest in northern women as evidenced by the work of Leonard, Giesberg, Attie, and Sizer represents an important development, but we still await studies of women of modest means, including not only less affluent white women, but also immigrant and African American women. Until this work is undertaken, it is impossible to know whether indeed the Civil War "created a revolution in woman herself," as Stanton, Anthony, and Gage claimed and Leonard, Giesberg, Attie, and Wendy Venet seem to reiterate. It is also impossible to gauge the significance of postwar calls for women's retreat from the public sphere. Giesberg sees the commission's branch leaders as rather powerful political actors in the Civil War who "created a new political culture for women" and "a model organizational structure for women's organizations in the postwar era" (2000: 7). The argument by Giesberg and Leonard that the Civil War provided the opportunity for northern middle- and upper-class women to wield institutional power complicates and extends the earlier work of Lori Ginzberg. All agree that the war transformed the scope and modes of women's activism. Attie, however, while presenting evidence that women adopted new political strategies, finds little to support the notion that wartime work had significant impact on their lives after the war in any direct or compelling way.

Despite the early hopes of Stanton, Anthony, and Gage, then, the Civil War does not appear to have been a watershed for either gender equality or "sisterhood." Sizer notes that northern women writers were interested primarily in the ways the war "opened up new space for them," not in the creation of some larger sisterhood (2000: 165). Even Giesberg admits that women's work "underwent no dramatic redefinition" (2000: 175). The war did, however, change perceptions of women and their capabilities. It inscribed even traditionally understood women's work with new meaning. Perceptions of the nature and value of their wartime work – even when such work seemed grounded in traditionally defined women's roles – had perforce to change. Clara Barton, *the nurse*, was also Clara Barton, *the soldier.* "I am," Barton wrote in 1863 to a friend who had urged her to put her efforts behind the peace movement, "a U.S. *soldier.*" As a soldier and not a politician or a man, she wrote, she was in no position to discuss the political merits of the peace movement, though she proceeded to give him a tongue-in-cheek and decidedly political argument.

> My business is staunching [*sic*] blood and the feeding [of] fainting men; my post the open field between the bullet and the hospital. I sometimes discuss the application of a compress or a wisp of hay under a broken limb, but not the bearing and merits of a political movement. I make gruel – not speeches; I write *letters home* for wounded soldiers, not political addresses – and again I ask you to pardon, not so much *what* I

> have said, as the fact of my having said anything in relation to a subject of which, upon the very nature of things, I am supposed to be profoundly ignorant. (Quoted in Oates 1994: 157–8)

Despite the gendered tasks to which she put her shoulders, Barton saw herself as a soldier. Like her, thousands of northern women cast their lot with the Union army, defying their society's notions of proper female conduct by leaving the home front. Yet as recent work demonstrates, and as Clara Barton herself suggests, the break was never a clean one. Women leaders in the US Sanitary Commission, Giesberg writes, saw their work as engaging "the political system directly," particularly through the deployment of political rhetoric and tactics. Yet, they believed they could do so without compromising their claims to a feminine morality. This stance, according to Giesberg, "allowed middle-class women to go to such 'promiscuous' places as the army camp and the working-class tenement" and to transform women's benevolent work from a local into a national movement without sacrificing the autonomy that antebellum women's local relief and reform organizations had enjoyed. "Claiming authority as professionals and political actors, branch leaders asserted the collective economic and political power of an extended cross-class female community, engaged in the decision-making process of a distinctly political organization, and proved themselves capable of sustaining the work over an extended period of time" (2000: 172).

Northern white women, torn over what use to put their wartime work to after victory, find few counterparts among middle- and upper-class women of the South. The war work of southern women was less organized, less publicly politicized, less conscious of itself as precedent-setting – at least it appears so on the surface. Compared to northern women, elite southern white women engaged the war differently. They were enjoined to defend the home front in the most literal sense; it is the story of that engagement that has so captivated students of the Civil War. In the modern imagination, the preeminent association of southern women with planter women continues to be prompted both by historical and popular literature. Historical attention to Confederate women owes much no doubt to the sense of drama that came to be associated with the wartime experience of southerners: Ben Butler's encounter with the women of New Orleans, the destruction of plantation homes by Sherman's troops, the desertion of slaves, the refusal of some white southerners to pledge their allegiance to the Confederacy or to disclaim such allegiance when the demands of country seemed too oppressive, all came in a sense to stand for women's experience of suffering and sacrifice. By contrast northern women had not lived in a war zone bedeviled by enemy soldiers or runaway and recalcitrant slaves. This came to be a central theme in white southerners' interpretation of the war and was repeated over and again in the following decades in literature and the various forms of popular culture. The Civil War chapter in Simkins's early history of the South was not so intriguingly titled "The Beleaguered Land." Forced to endure Union generals and troops and slaves who challenged their accustomed privileges, elite white women were left no choice, one wrote, but to "memorialize" the period as an era of immense suffering. That effort received an immeasurable boost decades later with the publication and subsequent filming of Margaret Mitchell's *Gone With the Wind.* Nurtured by Lost Cause movement slogans and propaganda, the fictional Scarlett O'Hara attained iconic stature as a symbol of white female beauty and, as important, white female grit. It is important to recall as well that her allures were not limited in their attractions to white people only. A black writer who recalls seeing the film as a child during its revival acknowledges this paradox. "In the middle of the movie," he writes, "Vivien Leigh as Scarlett suffers, and says she will never suffer again, and I loved her so much I didn't want her to suffer.... God didn't make people of her class and wealth and race to suffer" (Als 2000: 44). For most Americans, Leigh's "beautiful" face and her struggle *was* the face and struggle of women in the Civil War.

Although today, studies of northern and southern women in the Civil War seem to belong to separate and divergent fields, and the study of nonelite and African American women in either region has barely begun, one early work provided another model. In 1966, Mary Elizabeth Massey published *Bonnet Brigades,* which represented the first significant break in the field and attempted to treat the experiences of a wide range of women across the regional divide. Allan Nevins, in his introduction to the volume, sweepingly described it as "a thorough, comprehensive, and impartial history of the enormous work women did while the guns sounded, and the steps they meanwhile took toward the sweeping transformations that followed Appomattox" (Massey 1966: xiii). While Nevins was overly generous, Massey's study did represent an important milestone. It was the first scholarly account to attempt an inclusive, integrated synthesis of the war's impact on women.

Ultimately, Massey's work was constrained, in part by the magnitude of what she set out to do and the state of the field. She set out to tell the story of northern and southern women, slave and free, rich and poor. Secondary literature on the subject at the time was sparse and her self-imposed narrative structure, to give "an account of the impact of the war on women, not of women on the war," imposed its own restrictions. Her effort to remain above the quarrels of different schools of history – she would not attempt, she wrote, "to prove or disprove the theses of any school of history" – makes for an impoverished analytical perspective. While pledging that her work would be distinguished from past studies of women in that she would not "romanticize, idealize, or debunk the history of the women of either North or South," Massey was unable to overcome her own racial and class biases (1966: x). Many standard and stereotypical tropes of Confederate and neo-Confederate writing appear in her work: from "bloodthirsty" northern female rioters and uncomplaining and always patriotic plantation mistresses to the ever-loyal domestic servants who stood by their mistresses.

Still, Massey was in many ways ahead of her time. At a time when Civil War historiography still adamantly clung to the idea that war was the business of men and the history of war therefore primarily that of the part men played on the battlefield and in the halls of government, Massey was almost alone in addressing women and the social problems attendant on war: the rise in prostitution, abortion, drunkenness, theft, opium use, and general brutality. In devoting a separate chapter to black women, she stood alone. In including black women and writing about their philanthropic and volunteer work during the war, their lives as refugees and as contrabands, and the discrimination in pay and employment opportunities they suffered, *Bonnet Brigades* represented an important departure in the historiography. The intellectual breakthrough, however, was partial. The chapter titled "Women and Negroes" played to the standard racially gendered tropes: "Negroes" in the title alludes to black women and "Women," to white women. More intellectually indefensible, Massey portrays black women as, at best, indifferent mothers and lazy and dirty human beings.

Bonnet Brigades was published at a time when the historical profession was being challenged anew by the burgeoning fields of black studies and women's studies that called into question traditional methodologies and analyses while simultaneously working to structure new analytical and methodological tools. Massey's work was soon followed by a groundbreaking narrative of southern women's history, Anne Scott's *The Southern Lady*, published in 1970. This work and four more studies that appeared in the 1980s – Suzanne Lebsock's *The Free Women of Petersburg* (1984), Deborah Gray White's *Ar'n't I a Woman?* (1985), Jean Friedman's *The Enclosed Garden* (1985), and Elizabeth Fox-Genovese's *Within the Plantation Household* (1988) – provided much of the theoretical foundation and impetus for current work on the experiences of southern women during and after the war. Each of these books focused on the antebellum period, those by Lebsock, White, and Fox-Genovese exclusively, and each broke new ground.

The notion of the "southern belle" as commonly ascribed to, writes Scott, is fiction. In reality, she argues, elite white women's lives bore little resemblance to the popular image which held their primary indulgences to be leisure and luxury. Rather, their lives were consumed by work. Management of the domestic affairs of their homes (from the household production of slaves to the oversight of the domestic affairs of the slave quarters) entailed obligations that made it impossible, she claimed, for white female slaveholders to seriously cultivate an idyllic life of study, travel, and leisure. In *Ar'n't I a Woman?*, White deftly moved the discussion to a consideration of the world of female slaves, expertly showing the ways in which the white construction of a black femaleness made women particularly vulnerable members of the slave community, the objects of a racialized gender discourse that removed them from the protections of bourgeois gender sentiments. At the same time, she recreated the social networks and communal support systems that enslaved women constructed despite the brutal system in which they lived.

Building on these and other studies, Elizabeth Fox-Genovese's pioneering work offers both a compelling theoretical perspective and a fresh narrative approach to the study of the lives of black and white women in the antebellum South. Southern women's lives, she argues, were lived in black and white. The construction of gender roles in the South drew powerfully from the nature of the racially based slave society at its core. Fox-Genovese found little to no evidence for the notion that enslaved women and white women slaveholders were able to transcend their class positions to embrace their identity as women. Instead, she concluded, black and white women in the South were powerfully antagonistic enemies. The work of White, Fox-Genovese, Darlene Clark Hine, Gerda Lerner, Brenda Stevenson, and others on female slaves and slave resistance, along with that of Scott, Lebsock, and Friedman on white, mainly affluent, women's lives, illuminated the ways that class, race, and gender determined the experiences of southern women. As noted above, the effort to understand how these factors played out in the context of the Civil War and its aftermath has begun, but its emergence has been slow and uneven.

The starting point for the renewed attention to southern women and war can be traced to George C. Rable's *Civil Wars* in 1989, followed in the 1990s by Catherine Clinton's *Tara Revisited* (1995), LeeAnn Whites's *The Civil War as a Crisis in Gender* (1995), and Faust's *Mothers of Invention* (1996). These studies ended a near quarter-century drought in the study of Confederate women's experiences during the war. Taken together, they document the ways in which the war affected white women's relationships with slaves and their menfolk and their ideas about politics and war. Finding themselves on constantly shifting ground – their authority challenged by slaves, their homes turned to battlefields, their wealth evaporating, their status as white women increasingly of little value – elite women found the demands of war galling. They succumbed, Clinton argues, to stoic endurance. But neither stoic endurance nor active engagement, as critics of southern military policy or the Confederate government, led in the end to a significant shift in their values. Their class and race prejudices persisted, and at the end of the war they returned to traditional gender roles. In contrast to both early writings on northern women and to Anne Firor Scott's pioneering rendition of southern women's lives, there was, Rable argued, no "revolution" (1989: 227).

Faust's *Mothers of Invention* offers a formidable challenge to this conclusion and other longstanding assumptions about women in the war. White women's growing disaffection with the drawn-out military engagement and the Confederate men who led it, Faust argues, breached the dams of stoic endurance. In his 1906 study, Underwood had claimed that "never was there found a letter from a Confederate soldier's wife to her husband ... in which she exerted any of her woman's power or used any of woman's arts to decoy him from the army" (1906: 62). Faust, however, argues persuasively that many wives and mothers strayed from this official party line, encouraging their sons and husbands to leave the Confederate ranks and thereby contributing to sagging morale on the battle front. In and of itself, the argument that the internal disintegration of the Confederacy, the disintegration of its home front, was a major contributing cause of its ultimate defeat is, of course, not new. In the preface to *The Women of the Confederacy*, for example, Simkins and Patton had argued that the courage of southern white women as well as the valor of white men made it possible for the Confederacy to keep going for four years and that the collapse of the Confederacy "was due to the collapse of the morale of its women as well as to the defeat of its armies" (1936: vii). One of Faust's most significant contributions is in showing the precise ways in which this collapse occurred as the war challenged and disrupted assumptions about gender.

The extent to which similar disruptions occurred among nonslaveholding families, particularly the poorest of white southerners, remains unclear. Faust and Rable agree that shortages on the home front – the staple of traditional accounts – fed white women's growing disaffection. But because the study of women in the war has focused primarily on plantation mistresses, we know relatively little about how these shortages affected women across class and race lines. To what extent were certain gender assumptions which held across class lines in the antebellum era – as outlined, for example, by Stephanie McCurry – maintained during the war? Did they disintegrate, and if so, how quickly for which women? What was the pattern of the disintegration among poorer white southerners? Disaffection on the home front was not everywhere nurtured in the same soil. Did disaffection resonate differently when rooted in a Confederate policy that allowed army officers to impress a poor family's oxen as opposed to one that permitted impressment of slaves belonging to wealthy planters?

The absence of a son or father surely had greater material and social consequences for poor families. Poor farmers often relied upon oxen rather than mules for plowing. Oxen had the advantage of being cheaper but were thought too difficult for women to handle. So even though poor women in the South were accustomed to field labor, they had generally been able to avoid plowing. With men away in the army, many now had no choice but to get in behind oxen. An even bigger blow was Confederate confiscation or impressment of oxen for food. The absence of just one male or just one oxen was often devastating to poor families, leaving them unable to produce the surplus required to make market purchases of shoes, clothing, or salt.

State legislation designed to relieve the distress of indigent families was never sufficient to the task. "[P]oor men," wrote a private in the Confederate army to the governor of his state in December 1862, "have been compelled to leave the army to come home to provide for their families ... to stay in the army at eleven dollars per month and if we live to get home [and] pay sixty dollars for a sack of salt if we can get it at that ... we are poor men and are willing to defend our country but our families first and then our count[r]y." The wives and children of Confederate soldiers constituted, wrote another concerned Volunteer, "*the army at home*" whose "preservation and ... comfort are as essential to our success as that of our Soldiers in the field" (Ramsdell 1944: 28, 30). The larger part of "*the army at home*," North and South, consisted of working men and women whose sense of the war we know so little about.

Wars have a tendency to disorder socially constructed boundaries of all sorts and are particularly disruptive of the social constructions of gender precisely because they require, *always*, the mobilization of women. And in certain instances, such as the Civil War, the War of 1898, or the World Wars of the twentieth century, war can also irretrievably muddle racial constructions. Ultimately, however, women constitute the most essential component of civilian mobilization. The recent wars in Chechnya between Chechens and Russian forces are instructive. Chechen women are the most visible activists pushing for Russian accountability for their disappeared sons, and Russian women find that their part is not only to send their sons off to Chechnya as soldiers but to go there themselves to reclaim them, bargain for their lives, or bring their body parts back. If their sons are to live, says a Russian police investigator just returned from Chechnya, "You mothers must go there. Only you can save your sons" (Rubin 2001: 24). The Soldiers' Mothers' Committee of Russia collects data that authorities will not.

In recent years historians like Faust and Rable have returned to questions of civilian morale on the southern home front, questions put bluntly before the profession decades ago by scholars such as Charles W. Ramsdell, Bell Irvin Wiley, and William B. Hesseltine. Writing in the midst of the Great Depression, Hesseltine argued that class conflict wrenched the Confederacy. And, he wrote, inflation and other economic problems hurt southern women most. Poor women, he acknowledged, suffered the greatest hardships: "To the daughter of the aristocracy, deprived of her accustomed luxuries, the war was indeed severe. To the wife of the poor farmer, working in the fields and an object of neighborhood charity, or fleeing at night from the ravages of war, the cause for which she suffered frequently did not seem to be worth the candle" (1936: 546). The rage of the poor took aim at their wealthier neighbors and against speculators: "We are devouring each other," Bishop George F. Pierce stated in an appearance before the Georgia legislature in 1863 (quoted in Simkins 1963: 234). Much of the new scholarship on the home front remains, James Roark points out, "deeply invested in the question of responsibility for Confederate defeat" (1998: 203).

Just as the increased academic attention to women in the war helped to turn historians' attention back to the home front, home front studies in turn offer much of benefit to the study of women and the Civil War. The rage of upcountry white persons, for example, was surely the rage of women as much as men. In the face of the threat of losing the entire basis of their world, it is to be expected that wealthy southern women would embrace stoicism; poor white persons had much less to lose should the Confederacy fail. The defeat of the South, South Carolinian Emma LeConte wrote, left in its wake, in addition to "murdered fathers, brothers, and husbands," a population of "outraged women." Local and state studies of southern agriculture during the war are carefully documenting intraregional and interstate differences in wartime production of cash and food crops, differences sometimes determined by the path of Union invasion or occupation, sometimes by Confederate military strategy, and other times by the flight of slaves. These studies promise big rewards for scholars of women's history. Victoria Bynum anticipated the questions raised by such studies. In *Unruly Women* (1992), her provocative work on women in western North Carolina before and during the Civil War, she documents deep suspicion of and hostility to the Confederate leadership, illuminating the ways that different material conditions could shape responses to military and political developments.

Having to make do with the less brilliant glare of tallow candles when stearine ones could no longer be purchased could hardly have gained the sympathy of women for whom even tallow candles were a prewar luxury. For white women who had historically worked the fields beside their husbands and assisted with other farm chores, the complaints of elite women could and did easily appear frivolous. Catherine Edmondston had a slave "Dolly's spinning work *to arrange & superintend*" (Edmondston 1979, emphasis mine). Her slave Fanny, meanwhile, was responsible for making the candles "but 'Missus' must see her & arrange the wicks in the moulds." Even that much work on her part, Edmondston prophesied, would soon end, for "I am fully of the old opinion that there is no use in having a dog & barking for one's self." With the Confederacy disintegrating all around her in 1864, Edmondston kept up a pretense to southern antebellum norms of gentility: "Arranged the waiters for tea with the girls assistance, lit the candles, & superintended the tea table. Ordered breakfast, finished the inevitable pr of socks, darned two pr for myself, went to my room & closed the door with a warm bath & the evening lessons" (Edmondston 1979: 300, 606). Whatever images of the Old South women of Edmondston's class may have held on to, the defeat of the South forced revisions in their understanding of the war and the meaning of defeat. The desertion of slaves occasioned bitter cries of exasperation at the "nature" of black people alongside predictions of black people's imminent demise, a fate that their "laziness" or disinclination to work any longer for white people, planters declared, would ensure.

Still, even planter women did not necessarily share the same views by war's end. Grace Elmore, a South Carolina planter, was seemingly unshaken by the threat of defeat. "We are in God's hands, surely we will not be forsaken," she wrote. Louisa Dutton, a Virginia small slaveholder, must surely have believed differently when in the spring of 1862 her only slave Mary, thirty-five years of age, ran away and sought refuge on a Union gunboat lying in the mouth of the Rappahannock River. Poor white women would likely have not been surprised to hear women who rioted in protest of high prices and food shortages described as "mobs ... of low foreigners, Irish, Dutch, & Yankee," "hucksters in the market" fueled by greed for plunder, not the threat of starvation (Edmondston 1979: 378, 380). Local studies of women's lives grounded in the particularities of the movement of armies and the nature of local and household economies are needed to fully understand the war's impact on women and women's impact on the war across class, race, and location. Only then can we answer the question of whether the suffering engendered by the war led to the estrangement of white women (and which white women), as Faust argues, or whether, as Gary Gallagher submits, it made Confederate women (or just some of them) more ardent in their patriotism, which in turn bolstered morale on the war front, or whether, as Stephanie McCurry suggests, such questions are premised in the first place on false ground.

Over the past decade, as Faust notes, a growing body of scholarship has "complicated not only our understanding of the war but also of women themselves. Battlefront, home front, and the process of emancipation have all become gendered. At the same time, we are much more aware of the diversities within the category *women*, of females whose Civil War experiences differed in accordance with differences of race and class and age and region." Still, as she concludes, "we remain only at the beginning" (1998: 240). As the field moves forward, scholars will pioneer new interpretive and analytical frameworks, such as those being developed by Stephanie McCurry and Thavolia Glymph in their ongoing projects on women, war, and citizenship.

Yet important dilemmas remain. The path laid out by studies of northern women has not inspired emulation on the southern front. Despite its methodological and analytical sophistication, it was in many ways a region-specific model. While the historical experience of many American women in the nineteenth century could be explained in large measure by charting the impact of emergent capitalism, the model was problematic for understanding the experience of women in slave and post-emancipation societies. Notions of nineteenth-century domesticity might have looked theoretically the same North and South, but they played out quite differently on the ground, as any transplanted northern woman who found herself the mistress of a plantation or a tutor to the children of the planter class readily understood. It seems critical, then, that rather than simply drawing comparisons between North and South, scholars need to pursue local, regional, interregional, and interdisciplinary studies guided by gender, race, and class analyses as well as attend to cross-national perspectives based on other post-emancipation and colonial societies.

Just one glance at poor women's actions under specific local circumstances, North and South, suggests the promise of studies that cut across traditional historiographical boundaries. In her important analysis of labor and class strife in the Pennsylvania coal mines during the Civil War, Grace Palladino offers a too brief but intriguing glimpse into the politics of the wives, mothers, and daughters of the coal miners who often joined their menfolk or pushed ahead of them in resisting growing business consolidation and concentration and worsening wages and working conditions. Their strategies of resistance and modes of political expression were strikingly similar to those adopted by former slave women in the low country of South Carolina.

At the same time as we search for similarities across regions, we must keep in mind the often vast differences within regions. How comparable, for instance, were the politics of Hannah Johnson and the Hunt sisters of Illinois, who believed that the South must be defeated even "if it takes all we have got, our property and our lives"? If necessary, they believed, the North should be prepared to accept great losses, to "wallow in blood up to our horses bridle bits before we give it up" and "let the cannons roar till evry rebel shall lay down his arms and beg for mercy." Yet, even here we must be cautious. Recent studies of black and white women abolitionists in the North suggest the complex dynamics of ideologically compatible but racially distinct communities, reminding us that common ground can sometimes, if only temporarily, be carved out of uncommon experiences. The Hunt sisters' letters do not reveal the source of their conviction that the nation's resources should be so wholeheartedly committed to the defeat of the South. The interpretive and analytical grounding that informs Stephanie McCurry's new work might also shed much-needed light on the politics of northern white women. Understanding the "power of gender in public discourse and ... the complicated relationship between public rhetoric and private consciousness," McCurry argues, is central to understanding how the case for political obligation was made in the South (2000: 98). While studies of northern white middle- and upper-class women suggest the ways in which the threat to the nation posed by the slaveholding South pulled women into the war and allowed them to see their labor as nurses and ladies' aid society workers as valuable and self-sacrificing, they do not make explicit that in this way women were also called to fulfill their political obligations.

Scholars of women in postbellum America, it would seem, also have much to gain from studies of post-emancipation societies elsewhere in the western world and from studies of postcolonial worlds. In these studies, formerly enslaved and colonized people are often in the forefront of analysis, offering a model for histories of Civil War and Reconstruction, where African American women remain for the most part tangential despite their ubiquitous presence and the quite consequential roles they played. Slave women like slave men, more than one Union commander noted, drew the conclusion that the war was to destroy slavery. What Union commanders considered an uninformed belief led thousands of slave women to quit slavery and to walk hundreds of miles, often alone, to get to Union lines. Some left in the company of male relatives and other family members. The war's disruptive effects pushed others on the road involuntarily, some forced to join slaveholders fleeing approaching Union armies, becoming in the process refugees on the wrong side of the lines. Removal to interior plantations further disrupted black family and community life. Male slaves were often the first to be transported upcountry or leased out. Faced with resistance to forced removal, slaveholders forced slave men to the bargaining table by locking down corn and meat rations for their families.

If white women were seen as central to victory by the Union and Confederate governments, black women were generally viewed as just the opposite: "a curse to the soldier as to themselves," wrote one Union officer. Still, in an important sense slave women had a far greater impact on the war than any other group. Notwithstanding their lack of official status, black women were arguably the most politicized of the war's participants. As women, their actions, their thoughts, their politics were the least constrained by notions of nineteenth-century gender propriety. Interviewed in the 1930s, black women recalled their wartime activities as secret service agents, as spies in planters' homes, and runners for the Loyalty League, as in effect grassroots organizers in slave communities across the South. They recalled the thirst for newspapers and knowledge of the progress of the war, the special requests they made to Union soldiers to burn down their masters' homes. The Civil War saw the complete disintegration of the relationship between enslaved and slaveholding women, one of the most referenced but least analyzed aspects of the social revolution that was a legacy of the Civil War. At the same time, the receipts of black women's labor as plantation workers in Union-held territory flowed into the US Treasury and helped to keep the Union afloat. As cooks and nurses they contributed, even as they endured disparaging comments from white women nurses, Sanitary Commission officers, and Union soldiers.

In the end, African American women, unlike white women North and South, were not permitted an official standing in the Civil War or traditionally, as noted above, in the canonical literature of US history or new fields of women's and African American history. The story of black men's participation in the Civil War became a better-known one largely due to the success of the film *Glory* (1989). The story of black women's role in the fight for freedom and citizenship, their struggle to place before the nation a different understanding of the rights of women, has yet to be fully explored but there are encouraging signs. Recent work by Ella Forbes and Noralee Frankel are welcome additions to the literature. Though more limited in geographical focus and in its overall attention to the Civil War, Frankel's *Freedom's Women* (1999), on Mississippi, is in many ways the sturdier of the two. Forbes's more general text will be of less use to scholars of history, though its probing of heretofore underutilized resources invites greater attention to them. The greater weakness may reside in Forbes's premise that African American women experienced the war through African American men and "achieved a certain nobility by playing a secondary role to their husbands, fathers, sons and brothers" (1998: vii). This premise seems seriously flawed. Black women, slave and free, served in the war in the traditional roles allowed women – as nurses, cooks, seamstresses – but they also ventured the furthest of any American women beyond them. Rosa, mother and slave, was hanged for her role in leading a black unit that was authorized by neither the Confederate nor Federal governments. Thousands of other black women acted on their own counsel to flee, often with their children, whose fathers might be in Union uniform.

Other important new work includes that by Darlene Clark Hine and Kathleen Thompson, Leslie A. Schwalm, Marli F. Weiner, Laura Edwards, and Michelle Krowl. In *A Shining Thread of Hope* (1998), Hine and Thompson devote a chapter to the wartime participation of black women, which they note "is seldom mentioned even in African American histories." Schwalm's study of slavery and freedom in the rice country of South Carolina aims to show the critical role black women played in the destruction of slavery and the ways in which "gender and race informed the articulation of power" and policy development (1997: 3). While the heart of Schwalm's book concerns the postwar era, she provides a provocative and illuminating portrait of the intersection of race, gender, and federal policy in the low country. Marli F. Weiner also devotes a section in her book on southern women to African American experiences in the Civil War, and a recent dissertation by Michelle A. Krowl on black women in Civil War Virginia further adds to our understanding of race, gender, class, and politics during the war. All of these studies and others underway provide a richer context for postbellum analyses like that of Laura F. Edwards, whose study of Granville County, North Carolina, suggests the power of studying Reconstruction from a local perspective that highlights gender, race, and class dynamics. And Elsa Barkley Brown's intensive studies of black women's and men's emancipatory efforts in postwar Richmond, Virginia, offer provocative insights into a distinctive world of black politics and society.

At the end of the Civil War, Faust writes, the "women of the South's master class faced the war's legacy: A rising sense of personal desperation, an eroding confidence in those on whom they had relied for protection, and an emerging doubt about their own ability to endure prompted women to reconsider the most fundamental assumptions about their world" (1996: 234). Among the most important of these were the comfort and leisure that had come with membership in the master class along with a sense of superiority to all other women, especially slave women. Emancipation, as Faust claims and as I argue in my own work, unleashed a social revolution in the plantation household whose significance and meaning for the South's race and gender relations for decades to come have only begun to be explored. In the 1890s, a white woman tells a Vanderbilt social scientist that the war's most significant impact on women of her class was that they went "From being queens in social life" to "mere social drudges" (Faust 1996: 250). We know of course that white women of the former master class were not drudges for long, but the memory of that short intervening period had powerful repercussions for a much longer time.

The struggle of black women in Reconstruction, then, to assert their freedom and to claim a political voice had repercussions not only for the political and economic history of the period but for the social as well. While women of the master class experienced loss and a sense of desperation, black women experienced exhilaration and a sense of control over their lives for the first time. They seemed to have no doubt initially that they would contribute to the public and civic lives of their communities. The resulting struggle is a history that can now be told. In 1861 American women reckoned the price of liberty and its definition differently and took their places in the struggle as they reckoned those as well. In 1865 they reckoned the price they had paid and that some would yet have to pay to lead more public and political lives. Following the war, they faced "an almost reactionary reassertion of the private and domestic and a rejection of the more public and political burdens women had been urged to assume," and some withdrew (Faust 1996: 242). At the start of the twenty-first century, we know far too little about those who stayed in the fight, about those for whom the fight was the struggle to earn a daily if not a living wage in northern industries or southern mills or to make a sharecropper's crop. Schwalm's most incisive arguments, for instance, involve what she calls "the gendered imperatives of free labor ideology and the social order envisioned by it" (1997: 351). We also know too little of the psychological toll that the rape of black women during the war must have taken on its victims. These questions are at the heart of recent work on women in the postbellum period (see, for example, Julie Saville as well as Edwards and Schwalm) and will define future scholarship in the field.

We have assumed for far too long that the Civil War *really* involved only men. We have written and taught as though women's concerns were nonpolitical, as though the calls to war were ideologically neutral in matters of race and gender and class. Redefining categories of analysis and conceptual frameworks will permit us to "see" more and to better understand the complicated role that women played in the war, the effects the war had on women, and how gender and race were used as weapons of the war. It then becomes clear that the Ladies' Refugee Aid Society of Kansas, organized by black women in Kansas to aid fugitive slaves who fled to Lawrence during the war, was by the very nature of its work a political organization. Women, black and white, Union and Confederate, understood the politics of war and its legacy. In 1897 at the national convention of Women's Relief Corps (WRC), an organization of patriotic Union women, a dispute arose over a proposal from the Department of Kentucky to effectively segregate the department. Julia Layton, a black member and the wife of a Union veteran, protested, reminding the convention that her husband's four-year naval service had helped to make "his country free." In response to the proposal another black delegate stated: "It was my brother and sister who aided your brother, your son, to fight. . . . How can you forget what my people did for yours – your boys, your husbands and your sons?" (O'Leary 1999: 85–6). Black women, like white women, were determined not to forget. So Layton, a member of the Potomac Corps, went south to aid black women who had formed a corps in the deep South. And despite threats to burn their meeting hall, the black women's corps of Marche, Arkansas, kept up their political work: organizing to remember the Civil War and emancipation.

BIBLIOGRAPHY

Als, Hilton (2000) "GWTW," in James Allen et al. (eds.), *Without Sanctuary: Lynching Photographs in America*. Santa Fe, NM: Twin Palms Publishing, pp. 38–44.

Andrews, Matthew Page (comp.) (1920) *The Women of the South in War Times*, 2nd printing. Baltimore: Norman, Remington Co.

Ash, Stephen V. (1995) *When the Yankees Came: Conflict and Chaos in the Occupied South, 1861–1865*. Chapel Hill: University of North Carolina Press.

Attie, Jeannie (1998) *Patriotic Toil: Northern Women and the American Civil War*. Ithaca, NY: Cornell University Press.

Berlin, Ira et al. (eds.) (1982) *Freedom: A Documentary History of Emancipation, 1861–1867*. Ser. II: *The Black Military Experience*. New York: Cambridge University Press.

Brockett, L. P. and Vaughan, Mary C. (1867) *Woman's Work in the Civil War: A Record of Heroism, Patriotism, and Patience*. Philadelphia: Zeigler, McCurdy.

Brown, Elsa Barkley (1994) "Negotiating and Transforming the Public Sphere: African American Political Life in the Transition from Slavery to Freedom," *Public Culture* 7, pp. 107–46.

Bynum, Victoria E. (1987) " 'War Within a War': Women's Participation in the Revolt of the North Carolina Piedmont," *Frontiers* 9, pp. 43–9.

Bynum, Victoria E. (1992) *Unruly Women: The Politics of Social and Sexual Control in the Old South*. Chapel Hill: University of North Carolina Press.

Campbell, Edward D. C. and Rice, Kym (eds.) (1996) *A Woman's War: Southern Women, Civil War, and the Confederate Legacy*. Richmond and Charlottesville: Museum of the Confederacy and University of Virginia Press.

Clinton, Catherine (1982) *The Plantation Mistress: Woman's World in the Old South*. New York: Pantheon.

Clinton, Catherine (1995) *Tara Revisited: Women, War, and the Plantation Legend*. New York: Abbeville Press.

Clinton, Catherine and Silber, Nina (eds.) (1992) *Divided Houses: Gender and the Civil War*. New York: Oxford University Press.

Culpepper, Marilyn Mayer (1991) *Trials and Triumphs: Women of the American Civil War*. East Lansing: Michigan State University Press.

Dannett, Sylvia (1959) *Noble Women of the South*. New York: Thomas Yoseloff.

Diffley, Kathleen (1992) *Where My Heart is Turning Ever: Civil War Stories and Constitutional Reform, 1861–1876*. Athens: University of Georgia Press.

Dublin, Thomas (1994) *Transforming Women's Work: New England in the Industrial Revolution*. Ithaca, NY: Cornell University Press.

DuBois, W. E. B. (1935) *Black Reconstruction*. New York: Russell and Russell.

Edgar, Walter (1998) *South Carolina: A History*. Columbia: University of South Carolina Press.

Edmondston, Catherine Ann Devereaux (1979) *Journal of a Secesh Lady: The Diary of Catherine Ann Devereaux Edmondston*, ed. Beth G. Crabtree and James W. Patton. Raleigh: North Carolina Division of Archives and History.

Edwards, Laura F. (1997) *Gendered Strife and Confusion: The Political Culture of Reconstruction*. Urbana: University of Illinois Press.

Fahs, Alice (2001) *The Imagined Civil War: Popular Literature of the North and South, 1861–1865*. Chapel Hill: University of North Carolina Press.

Faust, Drew Gilpin (1996) *Mothers of Invention: Women of the Slaveholding South in the American Civil War*. Chapel Hill: University of North Carolina Press.

Faust, Drew Gilpin (1998) "'Ours As Well As That of the Men': Women and Gender in the Civil War," in James M. McPherson and William J. Cooper, Jr. (eds.), *Writing the Civil War: The Quest to Understand.* Columbia: University of South Carolina Press, pp. 228–40.

Fields, Barbara Jeanne (1985) *Slavery and Freedom on the Middle Ground: Maryland During the Nineteenth Century.* New Haven, CT: Yale University Press.

Forbes, Ella (1998) *African American Women During the Civil War.* New York: Garland Publishing.

Forten, Charlotte L. (1981) *The Journal of Charlotte Forten*, ed. Ray Allen Billington. New York: W. W. Norton.

Fox-Genovese, Elizabeth (1988) *Within the Plantation Household: Black and White Women of the Old South.* Chapel Hill: University of North Carolina Press.

Frankel, Noralee (1999) *Freedom's Women: Black Women and Families in Civil War Era Mississippi.* Bloomington: Indiana University Press.

Friedman, Jean E. (1985) *The Enclosed Garden: Women and Community in the Evangelical South, 1830–1900.* Chapel Hill: University of North Carolina Press.

Gallagher, Gary (1997) *The Confederate War.* Cambridge, MA: Harvard University Press.

Gallman, J. Matthew (1990) *Mastering Wartime: A Social History of Philadelphia During the Civil War.* New York: Cambridge University Press.

Giesberg, Judith Ann (2000) *Civil War Sisterhood: The U.S. Sanitary Commission and Women's Politics in Transition.* Boston: Northeastern University Press.

Ginzberg, Lori D. (1990) *Women and the Work of Benevolence: Morality, Politics, and Class in the Nineteenth-century United States.* New Haven, CT: Yale University Press.

Glatthaar, Joseph T. (1985) *The March to the Sea and Beyond: Sherman's Troops on the Savannah and Carolinas Campaigns.* Baton Rouge: Louisiana University Press.

Glymph, Thavolia (1996) "This Species of Property: Female Slave Contrabandists in the Civil War," in Edward D. C. Campbell and Kym Rice (eds.), *A Woman's War: Southern Women, Civil War, and the Confederate Legacy.* Charlottesville: University Press of Virginia, pp. 55–71.

Glymph, Thavolia (2000) "African American Women in the Literary Imagination of Mary Boykin Chestnut," in Robert Louis Paquette and Louis A. Ferleger (eds.), *Slavery, Secession and Southern History.* Charlottesville: University Press of Virginia, pp. 140–59.

Hall, Jacquelyn and Scott, Anne Firor (1987) "Women in the South," in John Boles and Evelyn Thomas Nolen (eds.), *Interpreting Southern History: Historiographical Essays in Honor of Sanford W. Higginbotham.* Baton Rouge: Louisiana State University Press, pp. 454–509.

Hesseltine, William B. (1936) *A History of the South, 1607–1936.* New York: Prentice-Hall.

Higonnet, Margaret Randolph et al. (eds.) (1987) *Behind the Lines: Gender and the Two World Wars.* New Haven, CT: Yale University Press.

Hine, Darlene Clark (ed.) (1986) *The State of Afro-American History: Past, Present, and Future.* Baton Rouge: Louisiana State University Press.

Hine, Darlene Clark and Thompson, Kathleen (1998) *A Shining Thread of Hope: The History of Black Women in America.* New York: Broadway Books.

Hodes, Martha (1992) "Wartime Dialogues on Illicit Sex: White Women and Black Men," in Catherine Clinton and Nina Silber (eds.), *Divided Houses: Gender and the Civil War.* New York: Oxford University Press, pp. 230–45.

Horton, R. G. (1866–8) *A Youth's History of the Great Civil War in the United States [War Between the States] from 1861 to 1865.* New York. Rpt. (1925), ed. Mary D. Carter and Lloyd T. Everett, Dallas, TX: Southern Publishing.

Jones, Jacqueline (1985) *Labor of Love, Labor of Sorrow: Black Women, Work and the Family from Slavery to the Present.* New York: Basic Books.

Kolchin, Peter (1998) "Slavery and Freedom in the Civil War South," in James M. McPherson and William J. Cooper, Jr. (eds.), *Writing the Civil War: The Quest to Understand*. Columbia: University of South Carolina Press, pp. 241–60.

Krowl, Michelle A. (1998) "Dixie's Other Daughters: African American Women in Virginia, 1861–1868," Ph.D. dissertation, University of California, Berkeley.

Lebsock, Suzanne (1984) *The Free Women of Petersburg: Status and Culture in a Southern Town, 1784–1860*. New York: W. W. Norton.

Leonard, Elizabeth D. (1994) *Yankee Women: Gender Battles in the Civil War*. New York: W. W. Norton.

Leonard, Elizabeth D. (1999) *All the Daring of the Soldier: Women of the Civil War Armies*. New York: W. W. Norton.

Lerner, Gerda (1969) "The Lady and the Mill Girl: Changes in the Status of Women in the Age of Jackson," *Midcontinent American Studies Journal* 10, pp. 5–15.

McCurry, Stephanie (1995) *Masters of Small Worlds: Yeoman Households, Gender Relations, and the Political Culture of the Antebellum South Carolina Low Country*. New York: Oxford University Press.

McCurry, Stephanie (2000) "Citizens, Soldiers' Wives and 'Hiley Hope Up' Slaves: The Problem of Political Obligation in the Civil War South," in Nancy Bercaw (ed.), *Gender and the Southern Body Politic*. Jackson: University Press of Mississippi, pp. 95–124.

Massey, Mary Elizabeth (1964) *Refugee Life in the Confederacy*. Baton Rouge: Louisiana State University Press.

Massey, Mary Elizabeth (1966) *Bonnet Brigades: American Women in the Civil War*. New York: Alfred A. Knopf.

Mitchell, Reid (1993) *The Vacant Chair: The Northern Soldier Leaves Home*. New York: Oxford University Press.

Mohr, Clarence L. (1986) *On the Threshold of Freedom: Master and Slaves in Civil War Georgia*. Athens: University of Georgia Press.

Moore, Frank (1866) *Women of the War: Their Heroism and Self-sacrifice*. Hartford, CT: S. S. Scranton.

O'Leary, Cecelia Elizabeth (1999) *To Die For: The Paradox of American Patriotism*. Princeton, NJ: Princeton University Press.

Oates, Stephen B. (1994) *A Woman of Valor: Clara Barton and the Civil War*. New York: Free Press.

Palladino, Grace (1990) *Another Civil War: Labor, Capital, and the State in the Anthracite Regions of Pennsylvania, 1840–68*. Urbana: University of Illinois Press.

Paludan, Phillip Shaw (1988) *"A People's Contest": The Union and the Civil War*. Lawrence: University Press of Kansas.

Quarles, Benjamin (1953) *The Negro in the Civil War*. Boston: Little, Brown.

Rable, George C. (1989) *Civil Wars: Women and the Crisis of Southern Nationalism*. Urbana: University of Illinois Press.

Ramsdell, Charles W. (1944) *Behind the Lines in the Southern Confederacy*. Baton Rouge: Louisiana State University Press.

Ransom, Roger (1989) *Conflict and Compromise: The Political Economy of Slavery, Emancipation and the American Civil War*. New York: Cambridge University Press.

Roark, James L. (1998) "Behind the Lines: Confederate Economy and Society," in James M. McPherson and William J. Cooper, Jr. (eds.), *Writing the Civil War: The Quest to Understand*. Columbia: University of South Carolina Press, pp. 201–27.

Rubin, Elizabeth (2001) "Only You Can Save Your Sons," *New York Times Magazine*, July 8, pp. 22–9 *passim*.

Saville, Julie (1994) *The Work of Reconstruction: From Slave to Wage Laborer in South Carolina, 1860–1870*. New York: Cambridge University Press.

Schwalm, Leslie A. (1997) *A Hard Fight for We: Women's Transition from Slavery to Freedom in South Carolina*. Urbana: University of Illinois Press.

Scott, Anne Firor (1970) *The Southern Lady: From Pedestal to Politics, 1830–1930*. Chicago: University of Chicago Press.

Silber, Nina (1993) *The Romance of Reunion: Northerners and Southerners, 1865–1900*. Chapel Hill: University of North Carolina Press.

Simkins, Francis Butler (1963) *A History of the South*. New York: Alfred A. Knopf.

Simkins, Francis Butler and Patton, James Welch (1936) *The Women of the Confederacy*. Richmond: Garrett and Massie.

Sizer, Lyde Cullen (2000) *The Political Work of Northern Women Writers and the Civil War, 1850–1872*. Chapel Hill: University of North Carolina Press.

Stanton, Elizabeth Cady, Anthony, Susan B., and Gage, Matilda Joslyn (eds.) (1882) *The History of Woman Suffrage*, Vol. 2. Salem, NH: Ayer.

Sterkx, H. E. (1970) *Partners in Rebellion: Alabama Women in the Civil War*. Rutherford, NJ: Farleigh Dickinson University Press.

Sterling, Dorothy (ed.) (1984) *We Are Your Sisters: Black Women in the Nineteenth Century*. New York: W. W. Norton.

Stevenson, Brenda E. (1996) *Life in Black and White: Family and Community in the Slave South*. New York: Oxford University Press.

Thomas, David Y. (1926) *Arkansas in War and Reconstruction, 1861–1874*. Little Rock: Central Printing Co.

Underwood, Rev. J. L. (1906) *The Women of the Confederacy*. New York: Neale Publishing.

Venet, Wendy Hamand (1991) *Neither Ballots nor Bullets: Women Abolitionists and the Civil War*. Charlottesville: University Press of Virginia.

Vinovskis, Maris A. (1990) "Have Social Historians Lost the Civil War?," in *Toward a Social History of the American Civil War*. New York: Cambridge University Press.

Ward, Geoffrey C. (1996) "Refighting the Civil War," in Robert Brent Toplin (ed.), *Ken Burns's The Civil War: Historians Respond*. New York: Oxford University Press, pp. 141–51.

Watkins, Sam (1994 [1882]) "*Co. Aytch.*" Wilmington, NC: Broadfoot Publishing.

Weiner, Marli F. (1998) *Mistresses and Slaves: Plantation Women in South Carolina, 1830–1880*. Urbana: University of Illinois Press.

Welter, Barbara (1966) "The Cult of True Womanhood, 1820–1860," *American Quarterly* 18, pp. 151–74.

Wesley, Charles H. (1937) *The Collapse of the Confederacy*. Washington, DC: Associated Publishers.

White, Deborah Gray (1985) *Ar'n't I a Woman?: Female Slaves in the Plantation South*. New York: W. W. Norton.

Whites, LeeAnn (1995) *The Civil War as a Crisis in Gender: Augusta, Georgia, 1860–1890*. Athens: University of Georgia Press.

Wiley, Bell Irvin (1943) *The Plain People of the Confederacy*. Baton Rouge: Louisiana State University Press.

Wiley, Bell Irvin (1975) *Confederate Women*. Westport, CT: Greenwood Press.

Young, Agatha B. (1959) *The Women and the Crisis: Women of the North in the Civil War*. New York: McDowell, Obolensky.

Chapter Twelve

Marriage, Property, and Class

Amy Dru Stanley

"I CONSIDER her my property." So a freedman declared of his wife soon after slave emancipation in the United States (quoted in Bynum 1992a: 331). His notion of marriage was by no means a peculiar legacy of the institution of chattel slavery. It was found in the law of the nineteenth century. It was affirmed by spokesmen of both the genteel and the laboring classes – in the North as well as the South. It was protested by feminists, who objected to the dependency relations of marriage. Only recently, however, have historians come systematically to link questions of marriage with questions of labor and relations of class.

A generation ago the scholarly debate over class centered on issues of structure, culture, and consciousness. "Class," the British historian E. P. Thompson famously wrote in 1963, is "not a thing." His *Making of the English Working Class* – the seminal study of class formation during the industrial revolution – sought to rescue laboring people and their aspirations and experience from obscurity: "the poor stockinger, the Luddite cropper, the . . . hand-loom weaver, the 'utopian' artisan." Criticizing crudely deterministic economic models of social relations, Thompson argued that class is not a fixed structure or category. He claimed that class experience is largely shaped by productive relations, but that class consciousness represents the understanding of experience in cultural terms. He stated that class is "made" – not given; that it is a relationship. But he said very little about marriage. He noted that wife-sale was one of the old English customs undermined by the new industrial discipline, and that the factory bell tore apart laboring families, calling both men and women to work, disrupting "customary relations between man and wife." Thompson's study thus offered a crucial insight, but one that he did not pursue: as the working class was in the making during the rise of industrial capitalism, old ways of marriage were being unmade. According to Thompson, the problem was the nature of the evidence, which revealed "so little about essential relations . . . between men and women" (Thompson 1963: 11, 12, 416, 413).

My purpose is not to use *The Making of the English Working Class* as a foil for illustrating either the flaws of scholarship on class formation or the virtues of scholarship on gender. That has been done ably already. Rather, my intent is to trace how historians have come to analyze the connections between marriage and class, taking

Thompson's work as a point of departure. This entails examining both the conceptual frameworks of historians and the evidence left by contemporaries, for it turns out that the sources say much more about the relationship between husband and wife than Thompson thought. It also involves some further excursions across the Atlantic, for studies of the American scene have been decisively influenced by classic works in British and European history. And as the words of the ex-slave who asserted title to his wife begin to suggest, issues of property lie at the heart of the connection now understood by historians between the rights and obligations of marriage and the ideals and relations of class. Almost a half-century after Thompson wrote, the conclusion advanced by feminist historians is that marriage helped to forge distinctions of class.

American jurisprudence of the nineteenth century was nothing if not explicit about the centrality of property rights in marriage. It also enunciated an analogy between the relations of authority and submission at stake between husbands and wives and those at stake between employers and workers. The husband held property in the "person of his wife" and all she acquired by "labor, service or act," law books declared. Like a hireling to a master, she owed service and obedience to her husband in exchange for his material support. "Whatever she earns she earns as his servant, and for him; for, in law, her time and her labor, as well as her money are his property.... He is the stronger, she is the weaker; all that she has is his" (quoted in Stanley 1998: 16, 182). According to the law, both marriage and wage labor were "domestic relations" of dominion and dependency rooted in the property rights of the master of the household.

It was precisely the significance of the husband's property in his wife's person and labor that was missing from the analysis fashioned by Thompson and his followers on both sides of the Atlantic. No historian criticized this tradition of class analysis from the standpoint of gender more forcefully than did Joan Scott in her 1988 book, *Gender and the Politics of History.* She recognized *The Making of the English Working Class* as an exemplary text, but she maintained that although Thompson claimed to explore class as a cultural phenomenon contingent on particular historical circumstances, he ended up adhering to a narrow and rigid definition of class as an expression of men's experience of work relations. Class should be understood not as a "masculine construction," she wrote, but rather in light of "representations of sexual difference." In feminist history, "[c]lass and gender become inextricably linked ... as representation, as identity, as social and political practice." Scott focused attention not on material relations in the workplace, but instead on the power of language – and especially on the creation of meaning through difference – in constructing class identity. This was the conceptual basis of her dispute not simply with Thompson but also with the British historian Gareth Stedman Jones, who was waging his own debate with Thompson about the "linguistic" as opposed to the empirical "reality" of class in nineteenth- and twentieth-century England. Like Scott, Stedman Jones acknowledged his debt to Thompson's cultural approach; but, also like Scott, he insisted that class was constructed through language – a perspective that, again like Scott's, reflected the influence of French poststructuralist theory. In Scott's view, the problem with Stedman Jones's *Languages of Class* (1983) was that it did not take the analysis of language far enough, for it was blind to the play of gender difference in constituting class. Language, wrote Scott, is a "system of meaning" that is "constructed through differentiation.... Positive definitions depend on negatives." In other words, male workers defined themselves in contrast to women – and the workplace in opposition to the household sphere. What both Thompson and Stedman Jones overlooked is how male working-class identity rested on sets of "differentiation... inclusions and exclusions... that relied on sexual difference for their meaning." At the core of such distinctions lay property rights, according to Scott. "The masculine representation of class" rested on the fact that men were considered to "have property in labor" but women were not. But Scott did not extend this line of argument far enough. While linking differences of class and sex, she nonetheless overlooked the husband's property in his wife as well as in himself. Marriage was not yet central to the scholarly debate over class (Scott 1988a/b: 64, 88, 59, 60, 72, 64).

But it became so as feminist historians probed more deeply into the lives and values of those who confronted capitalist transformation during the nineteenth century. The tolling of the factory bell was symbolic of these profound changes: the accumulation of capital that fueled the industrial revolution, the ideological separation of home and work into distinct sexual spheres, the traffic in free labor as a market commodity, the emergence of new social relationships of authority and submission – the making of the working class and the middle class. It has now become clear that marriage was central to all of these changes – as both a property relation and a set of ideals through which the experiences of class were represented.

For men to make their fortunes through marriage was not new to the era of industrial capitalism, as common-law doctrines of coverture had long granted men title to their wives' assets as well as to their labor. What was new to the industrial era was the funneling of marriage settlements into enterprises such as mills, mines, and manufactories. By marrying women of property, husbands secured the wealth necessary to become entrepreneurs, a point highlighted by the British historians Leonore Davidoff and Catherine Hall in their study of middle-class formation and gender relations in England. Wifely sources of wealth were especially important where institutions of credit were uncertain, as was the case not simply in England but also in antebellum America. Thus the property relations of marriage – the dependency of wives and the dominion of husbands – proved vital to both capital accumulation and the emergence of the bourgeoisie. Notably, the legal reforms of coverture, the married women's property acts of the nineteenth century, were intended by state legislatures less to abridge husbands' rights than to protect family assets from the husband's creditors by entitling his wife to possess property in her own name.

So, too, did marriage underwrite the cultural identity of the new middle class. The prevailing wisdom is that the class consciousness of the emergent bourgeoisie was rooted in the ideal of separate gender spheres, which in turn rested on the codes of sex difference that were dictated by marriage. Here historians have inquired into class by exploring evidence dealing not with productive relations but rather with household relations, by studying diaries and advice literature and sermons and tracts on domestic economy. Such evidence yields insights into realms of belief and desire not expressed in more conventional sources on politics, economy, and state. Men and women of the middle classes joined in affirming the dualities of work and home, market and family, public and private to make sense of the changes in their world wrought by the expansion of market relations. As a New England minister declared in 1827,

> It is at home, where man . . . seeks a refuge from the vexations and embarrassments of business, an enchanting repose from exertion, a relaxation from care by the interchange of affection: where some of his finest sympathies, tastes, and moral and religious feelings are formed and nourished; – where is the treasury of pure disinterested love, such as is seldom found in the busy walks of a selfish and calculating world. (Quoted in Cott 1977: 64)

According to landmark studies by Nancy Cott and Mary Ryan, the ideal of separate spheres that associated men with the workplace and women with the home helped to shore up the cultural authority of the class that stood most to benefit from the ways of the "selfish and calculating world."

But the extent to which the divide between home and work represented a reality or a myth remains a topic of scholarly debate. In *The Cradle of the Middle Class*, Ryan finds that the doctrine of separate sexual spheres bore "some resemblance to social reality" reflecting capitalist development and the consolidation of the northern middle class (1981: 191). Cott stresses the symbolic dimensions of the doctrine, though also noting that it was grounded in actual "material change" that separated the domains of husband and wife (1977: 66). Likewise Eugene Genovese and Elizabeth Fox-Genovese, historians of the American South, argue that the rule of separate spheres distinguished Yankee homes from southern households which were still places of both production and consumption. But other historians view the idea of separate spheres principally as a fiction that expressed bourgeois longing for a realm of experience unscathed by the market, a fiction that legitimated commodity relations by idealizing the home as a realm of sentiment and the dependent wife as the embodiment of virtue. There is agreement, however, that separate spheres doctrine expressed the proprietary character of marriage while providing the middle class a language of self-definition and mediating the disruptions of industrial capitalism. It represented "a middle-class ideal, a cultural preference for domestic retirement and conjugal-family intimacy over both the 'vain' and fashionable sociability of the rich and the promiscuous sociability of the poor," writes Cott. Instead of challenging "the modern organization of work and pursuit of wealth . . . it accommodated and promised to temper them" (Cott 1977: 92, 69).

If in the North the property relations of marriage figured in the making of the middle class, in the Old South they served to ally white men of different classes – planters who owned scores of slaves and yeomen who worked the land themselves, either with or without a few slaves. For Stephanie McCurry, in *Masters of Small Worlds* (1995), the central question is the "meanings and values" that held non-slaveholders and small slaveholders to planters. She finds the answer in the dependency relations of southern households – in the social relations of "power and privilege" that were based on the master's property not simply in his chattel slaves but also in his wife. In a region where social inequality was blatant, marriage bore "a great deal of the ideological weight" of the defense of slavery. In drawing an analogy between slavery and marriage as domestic relations of sovereignty and subordination, proslavery theorists sought to obscure differences of class, to forge a bond between elite slave masters and masters of humble homes, to equate title to a slave with title to a wife. "The legitimacy of male authority over women within the household was the cornerstone of the slavery edifice," McCurry writes. "In reaching beyond masters and slaves to all relations of southern households, proslavery publicists bid for the loyalties of all white male adults. They repeatedly reminded white southerners of every class that slavery... represented simply the most extreme and absolute form of the legal and customary dependencies that characterized the Old South" (McCurry 1995: 213, 214, 216, 213). Finding common ground as masters at home, yeomen and planters joined in defense of the Confederacy.

Marriage, therefore, marked the line between conditions of freedom and of slavery. Utterly lacking in self-ownership, chattel slaves might marry informally but could not claim the property rights of marriage – for, as Brenda Stevenson notes in her study of southern family life, however much they might aim to carry out the exchange of female service and male protection, they could neither fulfill the legal obligations nor exercise the legal rights of husband and wife. Just as slavery allowed white men to call themselves equals by reason of their race, so the very fact that slaves had no legal right of marriage made the institution that much more essential to the identity of free people of different classes. Defenders and critics of slavery could agree that the marriage rights defined men as free. Sounding oddly like a slaveholder, the abolitionist leader William Lloyd Garrison declared that a free man was "master of his own person, of his wife" – a status mitigating the plight of even the poorest working man with nothing but his labor for sale, making him unlike a slave (quoted in Stanley 1998: 29). Conversely, abolitionists deplored the destruction of marriage as the single most awful feature of chattel slavery. Intimately knowing southern households, former slaves made marriage a dominant theme of their antislavery narratives. Frederick Douglass bitterly mocked the defense of slavery as a "domestic institution" in a society where marriages were sundered on the auction block and planters commanded the "bodies and souls" of black men and women alike (quoted in Stanley 1996: 87, 88). In other words, denying men the right to be master of a wife defined them as slaves.

Only very recently has marriage become the centerpiece of studies of slavery and abolition. It no longer appears peripheral to accounts of unfree plantation labor or the transition to the wage system or sectional conflict and Reconstruction – thanks to the pathbreaking scholarship of Herbert Gutman, and more particularly to that of Fox-Genovese, McCurry, Stevenson, and Victoria Bynum on the antebellum era and of Elsa Barkley Brown, Laura Edwards, and Julie Saville on the postbellum era. Plantation and church records, legal cases, proslavery tracts, the testimony of slaves and ex-slaves, the records of the Freedmen's Bureau – such evidence has allowed the rewriting of southern history. As Edwards explains, her study of Reconstruction "adds gender to the mix" of "race and class," and begins by examining marriage as "the cornerstone for all other social relations... positioning people... as either dependents or independent household heads" (1997: 6, 18). The insights offered by this scholarship are considerable, insights to which my own work on the post-bellum wage contract and marriage contract has sought to contribute. Marriage now appears deeply significant not only to class and race relations in the Old South but also to the fundamental social changes following from slave emancipation – the transformation of chattel property into sellers of their own free labor and of slave masters into buyers. For at the same time as a hireling class was being made of ex-slaves, bondsmen were transformed into masters at home, masters not simply of their own persons but of their wives as well. In the words of a black corporal, who was teaching his troops that the entitlements of marriage constituted the bedrock of their collective identity as a freedpeople: "The Marriage Covenant is at the foundation of all our rights. In slavery we could not have *legalised* marriage: *now* we have it . . . and we shall be established as a people" (quoted in Edwards 1997: 47). Seemingly, freedmen adhered to antislavery arguments about the connection between marriage and emancipation.

But there was substantial division among former slaves, former masters, and Yankee liberators over exactly what rights were afforded by lawful marriage – and the conflict encompassed matters of property and class formation. According to a rich literature on emancipation, freedpeople aspired to be an independent yeomenry, a class of landed proprietors cultivating their own farms rather than a wage-laboring class. And, according to the newest findings, such aspirations in no small measure reflected freedmen's aim to prevent former slave masters from retaining property rights in the labor and bodies of freedwomen. "Political overtones," writes Julie Saville, "attended the reconstitution of families in the wake of emancipation" (1994: 105). In the eyes of many former bondsmen, the right to be sole owners of their wives' labor was a foundation of freedom, a right that turned on ownership of productive property and their wives' withdrawal from wage labor. Thus did freedmen declare both their wives and housework their own "property," while opposing the wage system as antithetical to mastery at home. "The people here would rather have the land than work for wages," explained one South Carolina freedman. "I think it would be better to sort out the men and give land to those who have the faculty of supporting their families" (quoted in Stanley 1999: 203). This vision did not bar a wife's productive labor as her husband's dependent, but it did run counter to her hiring by white employers. As a Tennessee freedman averred, "When I married my wife, I married her to wait on me" (quoted in Stanley 1998: 49). To this way of thinking, the right to marry and claim property in a wife's labor was a bequest of emancipation; freedom promised that a wife should not have to serve two masters.

That was not a promise accepted by former slaveholders, however. As tenaciously as freedmen they asserted title to the labor of freedwomen, who in turn registered their own views by resisting agricultural wage work. In outrage, planters demanded that the Freedmen's Bureau force both husbands and wives into the fields, arguing that their interests as an employing class in assuring cultivation of staple crops prevailed over the property rights of husbands. "Most of the Freedwomen who have husbands are not at work," expostulated a planter. "Now these women have always been used to work out & it would be far better for them to go to work for reasonable wages . . . . [T]heir labor is a very important percent of the entire labor of the South" (quoted in Stanley

1999: 201). The clashing arguments of ex-slaves and ex-slaveholders, as both asserted title to freedwomen's labor, distilled the material and cultural opposition between the property relations of marriage and the commodity relations of wage labor.

More ambivalent were the views of Yankee liberators, for they simultaneously pledged freedmen the property rights of husbands as an incentive to wage labor and required wives to perform wage labor alongside their husbands. Presiding over the transformation of chattel property into a free working class, they contradictorily affirmed both the moral virtue of freed wives' housework and the economic value of their wage employment. They delivered paeans both to separate gender spheres and to the sway of the free market economy. As a Republican statesman explained to a gathering of ex-slaves just days after Appomattox, "Freedom does not mean that you are not to work. It means that when you do work you shall have pay for it, to carry home to your wives." Yankee missionaries in the South taught that tidy homes were an emblem of racial uplift and passed out spelling books that contained rules such as the following: "The Bi-ble con-tains ma-ny di-rec-tions.... Wives, sub-mit your-selves un-to your own hus-bands." Agents of the Freedmen's Bureau institutionalized the rules of coverture along with those of the wage system. On the one hand, they declared that freedwomen must learn to keep house – to sew, mend, bake – and that freedmen must keep their wives "in subjection" and that the national government provided "you a right to yourselves, your wives, and children" in return for allegiance to the union and hard work (quoted in Stanley 1998: 48, 49, 142). But on the other hand, when land distribution was not forthcoming, they enjoined freedmen to ensure that their wives did wage work in the fields and authorized husbands to sign labor contracts for their wives, receive their wages, and bring suits in court on their behalf. According to one Bureau agent, husbands must compel their wives to work for wages on account of sheer economic necessity: "Unless something is done by the Bureau to induce the freedmen to make the female members of their families work in the crops next year there will be destitution among them" (quoted in Stanley 1999: 200). For the Bureau, freedom meant that wives of ex-slaves must inevitably serve two masters – husbands and planters.

It is therefore well established that marriage was integral to the remaking of class and race relations in the New South. So, too, has it been brought to light that marriage was deeply bound up with the rise of the wage system and capitalist social relations in the North. Evidence ranging from labor newspapers and reformers' tracts to texts on political economy, legal cases, and government reports illuminates the connection. In the now classic study, *City of Women* (1986), Christine Stansell was the first to uncover the dynamic interaction of working-class formation and relations between the sexes in the antebellum era. Focusing on New York City, she shows how capitalist development and, in particular, the increasing wage dependency of men disrupted the material basis of the traditional dependency relations of marriage: the exchange of a husband's support for a wife's service. The incapacity of working men to provide family subsistence obliged both wives and daughters to put their labor up for sale in the market and thereby undermined husbands' entitlements at home. "The structures of household life that supported beliefs in masculine authority and female moral weakness eroded under economic and social pressures," Stansell writes. "As industrial capitalism modified gender relations . . . so it threw into question relationships of male authority and female subservience long taken for granted, based on the power husbands and fathers derived from supervising work under their own roofs or on their own farms.'' She demonstrates that women's industrial wage work in the home mediated between the demands of employers and families, thereby lessening ''cultural disruptions.'' She offers no simplistic argument that industrial capitalism emancipated wives, for she underscores the fragility of any form of independence bought through wage labor; but she does find that the decline of the traditional household economy based on male ownership of productive property evoked new tensions between the sexes – ''a great renegotiation of what, exactly, men and women owed each other'' (Stansell 1986: 30, 77, 106, 81).

By the time, then, that Yankees in the South were teaching ex-slaves that the wage system would uphold a husband's property in his wife, proletarianization in the North had already come to trench on such rights. Agents of the Freedmen's Bureau and others clung to a notion of marriage that was being undermined by capitalist wage relations. Yet this is not Stansell's principal concern. Ultimately, she is less interested in the problem of marriage than in the condition of single young women who worked for wages and whose sexuality was neither controlled by fathers nor possessed by husbands, a form of autonomy that troubled both working men and middle-class reformers. Not the plebeian wife but the ''Bowery girl'' – with her independent air, bold stride, and flashy clothing – takes center stage in *City of Women*. By contrast, wives make their appearance scrimping to make ends meet, coming to the aid of neighbors in the tenements, and suffering from domestic violence. Stansell opens up the inquiry into class, capitalism, property, and marriage, but her own study dwells more on exchange between the sexes outside the bonds of marriage.

Subsequent studies of Yankee proletarianization and marriage begin where Stansell leaves off. And, in a major analytical shift, the question of housework – along with the rise of factories and the transformation of craft workshops – dominates the discussion. A subject once buried in outmoded Home Economics books, the wife's dependent labor in the home has come to be seen as essential to the rise of industrial capitalism. Jeanne Boydston's *Home and Work* (1990) explores the significance – literally the value – of women's unpaid housework in the wage economy of the antebellum North. For Boydston, the question is not simply the disruptive effects of burgeoning capitalism on home life. Rather, she inverts the question, by examining how gender figured in structuring change, by asking how the relations of labor and property between husband and wife shaped capitalist development. She criticizes scholarship that treats industrialization as ''exterior to family life'' and that looks just at ''the *effect* of industrialization on the presumably distinct systems of the family. . . . According to this model, households were altered by industrialization, but the purposes, structures, and labor patterns of family life were not themselves instrumental in the transition.'' She asks, ''What was the material relation between unpaid housework and the emergence of an industrial economy?'' (Boydston 1990: 121, 122).

The point is that capitalist transformation and the making of new class relations must be analyzed from the vantage points of both housework, which seemingly had no cash value, and wage work, which had an obvious cash value – that is, from the vantage points of both the marriage contract and the wage contract. Housework was the quid pro quo that the wife owed her husband in return for his protection and support, the object of his property in her labor. As the market dependency of northern households deepened in the early nineteenth century, housework became increasingly joined to the cash nexus, involving spending and saving money and searching for credit instead of producing goods necessary for subsistence such as clothing, candles, and soap. Though unpaid and considered to have no economic value, housework nonetheless remained productive labor, for it reproduced the laboring population and its product was "the household itself." It was also essential to the accumulation of capital, Boydston argues. For "uncounted labor in the home" allowed employers to pay wages below the level of family subsistence and garner greater profits, "a difference... critical to the development of industrialization." Thus housework – enshrined as the heart of domesticity – played a "constitutive economic role" in the forging of capitalism and wage relations (Boydston 1990: 125, 137, 122).

By the late nineteenth century the circumstances of marriage had emerged as a focal point of class identity and class antagonism. A remarkably wide range of Americans assessed the legitimacy of class differences in terms of the marriage bargain. The rights and obligations of husband and wife were understood to be inextricable from the rights and obligations of those who owned productive property and of those who did not. Ministers and other moralists joined with political economists, sociologists, statesmen, and statisticians in asserting both that a man's claim to his wife would induce him to work hard and that his wages ought to support the dependency relations of marriage. It was an article of faith for the sociologist William Graham Sumner, who did anything but question existing class inequalities, that "In a free state... every man is held and expected to take care of himself and family" (quoted in Stanley 1998: 147). Congressional inquiry into the nature of the wage system and the condition of laboring people took legislators on tours of tenement homes, to take stock of the food, the furnishings, the tidiness of the rooms, and led them to seek testimony on whether a man's wages were enough to allow him to marry and support a wife. Meanwhile, northern working men joined former slaves in measuring their freedom and unfreedom according to whether or not they possessed property not simply in themselves but also in their wives. So, for example, in a piece entitled "Slaves of the Tobacco Industry," the labor leader Samuel Gompers fulminated about the home life of cigar makers in New York City: "The housewife would lose too much valuable time cooking a meal; she has other work to do: making wrappers and rolling cigars" (quoted in Stanley 1999: 207). In the postbellum North as well as in the South, the question of whether a wife must serve two masters lay at the nub of the conflict over class.

What is striking, therefore, is the meaning imputed to housework. For decades working men had defended their claim to a wage sufficient to support a family as a birthright of free men. What was new in the postbellum agitation over home life was the ideological weight that housework – or, more precisely, its absence – bore in laborers' critiques of their condition as a class. In the words of the machinist, Ira Steward, "The dirt of the poor man's hovel is the miasma of the rich man's parlor" (quoted in Stanley 1998: 161). For laboring men, the disordered home offered a vivid way of symbolizing their loss of property in their wives' labor, a loss that they viewed as a betrayal of freedom rooted in the traffic in labor as a market commodity and their position of wage dependency. The salience of housework is demonstrated in studies by Mary Blewett on textile operatives in Fall River, Massachusetts, and by Eileen Boris on cigar makers in New York City. Blewett writes of housework being "negotiable" among husbands and wives who were both employed in the mills, Boris of working men's descriptions of wretched homes robbed of the wife's labor, descriptions that were rooted in "sentimentality" about women's traditional place in the household and that suggested the "respectability" of men who were able to support their families on their own. Just as abolitionists had deplored the rupture of husband and wife under slavery, so working men in the Gilded Age denounced the destruction of marriage and the sacrifice of home life to "the Moloch of wage slavery." It is more than likely that such discontents contributed to the patterns of violence, desertion, and separation that studies by Timothy Gilfoyle, Pamela Haag, and Hendrik Hartog show were common in nineteenth-century marriages. Gompers described the tenement rooms where entire families manufactured cigars at home: "tobacco, filth, and human beings, thrown together... husbands, wives, and children sit unceasingly at their work." Mothers rocked cradles and nursed infants while they rolled cigars; meals were eaten in haste among the tobacco scraps at the work table; the meager food was uncooked – "smoked sausage or something similar which does not need to be prepared first" (quoted in Stanley 1998: 158, 159). Deprivation of housework stood as testimony to the deprivations of class.

Implicitly, such negative portraits of proletarian home life – of the property rights of marriage gone utterly awry – idealized the conventional relationship of wifely dependence and husbandly dominion. In so doing, they laid bare the contradiction between the old rules of the marriage contract and the new realities of wage labor. So I have argued in my own book, *From Bondage to Contract* (1998). In an era and a nation where industrial capitalism developed in concurrence with the contest over slavery and emancipation, Americans who voiced the convictions of the ascendant bourgeoisie taught no doctrine more steadfastly than that the bonds of marriage transcended the inequalities of class. By their lights, the husband's title to his wife was an ideal to which men of differing classes and differing races might aspire. And, indeed, propertied and propertyless men, white men and black men, did embrace that doctrine. However, by their lights, it was precisely the cooking, scrubbing, and mending undone in their own homes that illustrated that their situation as hireling laborers subverted their claim to property in their wives.

The question of how class is made has receded from the prominent place in history writing that it occupied a quarter of a century ago. To be sure, the moment of class analysis has hardly passed, but the intensity of the debate has lessened considerably. E. P. Thompson and his American school have been so influential that most historians do not doubt that class is not a deus ex machina – the byproduct alone of relations of production. They do not question that class is created and recreated not simply in the factory and workshop but just as centrally in the spheres of culture and politics. It now appears virtually beyond dispute that class is a question of consciousness just as much as it is a question of economic structures. Most would agree that class is made through language as well as constructed through material relations.

Today, the more provocative claim is that the experience of class and the understanding of class are as much about differences of sex as about differences between owners and workers. That is the claim of the scholarship that has been under review here – scholarship that addresses both the middle class and the working class and the households of both white and black people, free and slave, and that ranges from the industrializing North to the agrarian South. The new historical literature on marriage and class argues that capitalist transformation did not simply disrupt the traditional relationship of husband and wife but also was furthered by the persistence of long-standing domestic customs. It argues as well that marriage lay at the very center of the debate over the legitimacy of class in nineteenth-century America, indeed that it was in terms of the bond between husband and wife that differences of class were at once validated and challenged. Such arguments have been grounded in evidence registering both empirical matters and the play of language.

It should not be surprising that, historically, marriage and class have borne so directly upon one another. The linchpin of the connection is property. It is the husband's property in his wife that underlies marriage as a relation of authority and subordination, and it is property in the labor of free persons that underlies capitalist class relations. But the linkage is more than one of equivalences, analogies, or parallels. For the buying and selling of labor irrespective of sex has unsettled the claims of husbands to their wives. At the same time, Americans otherwise very different have joined in reckoning the justice of class on the basis of the property relations of marriage.

BIBLIOGRAPHY

Basch, Norma (1982) *In the Eyes of the Law: Women, Marriage, and Property in Nineteenth-century New York.* Ithaca, NY: Cornell University Press.

Blackmar, Elizabeth (1989) *Manhattan for Rent, 1785–1850.* Ithaca, NY: Cornell University Press.

Blewett, Mary H. (1991) "Manhood and the Market: The Politics of Gender and Class among the Textile Workers of Fall River, Massachusetts, 1870–1880," in Ava Baron (ed.), *Work Engendered: Toward a New History of American Labor.* Ithaca, NY: Cornell University Press, pp. 92–113.

Boris, Eileen (1991) " 'A Man's Dwelling House is His Castle': Tenement House Cigarmaking and the Judicial Imperative," in Ava Baron (ed.), *Work Engendered: Toward a New History of American Labor.* Ithaca, NY: Cornell University Press, pp. 114–41.

Boydston, Jeanne (1990) *Home and Work: Housework, Wages, and the Ideology of Labor in the Early Republic.* New York: Oxford University Press.

Bynum, Victoria E. (1992a) *Unruly Women: The Politics of Social and Sexual Control in the Old South.* Chapel Hill: University of North Carolina Press.

Bynum, Victoria E. (1992b) "Reshaping the Bonds of Womanhood: Divorce in Reconstruction North Carolina," in Catherine Clinton and Nina Silber (eds.), *Divided Houses: Gender and the Civil War.* New York: Oxford University Press, pp. 320–33.

Clark, Elizabeth B. (1990) "Matrimonial Bonds: Slavery and Divorce in Nineteenth-century America," *Law and History Review* 8, pp. 25–54.

Cott, Nancy F. (1977) *The Bonds of Womanhood: "Woman's Sphere" in New England, 1780–1835.* New Haven, CT: Yale University Press.

Cott, Nancy F. (2000) *Public Vows: A History of Marriage and the Nation.* Cambridge, MA: Harvard University Press.

Davidoff, Leonore and Hall, Catherine (1987) *Family Fortunes: Men and Women of the English Middle Class, 1780–1850.* London: Hutchinson.

Edwards, Laura F. (1997) *Gendered Strife and Confusion: The Political Culture of Reconstruction.* Urbana: University of Illinois Press.

Fox-Genovese, Elizabeth (1988) *Within the Plantation Household: Black and White Women of the Old South.* Chapel Hill: University of North Carolina Press.

Genovese, Eugene (1991) "'Our Family, White and Black': Family and Household in the Southern Slaveholders' World View," in Carol Bleser (ed.), *In Joy and Sorrow: Women, Family, and Marriage in the Victorian South, 1830–1900.* New York: Oxford University Press, pp. 69–87.

Gilfoyle, Timothy J. (1994) "The Hearts of Nineteenth-century Men: Bigamy and Working-class Marriage in New York City, 1800–1890." *Prospects* 19, pp. 135–60.

Grossberg, Michael (1985) *Governing the Hearth: Law and the Family in Nineteenth-century America.* Chapel Hill: University of North Carolina Press.

Gutman, Herbert (1976) *The Black Family in Slavery and Freedom, 1750–1925*, 1st ed. New York: Pantheon Books.

Haag, Pamela (1992) "The 'Ill-use' of a Wife: Patterns of Working-class Violence in Domestic and Public New York City, 1860–1880," *Journal of Social History* 25, pp. 447–77.

Hall, Catherine (1992a) "The Early Formation of Victorian Domestic Ideology," in *White, Male, and Middle-class: Explorations in Feminism and History.* New York: Routledge, pp. 75–93.

Hall, Catherine (1992b) "The History of the Housewife," in *White, Male, and Middle-class: Explorations in Feminism and History.* New York: Routledge, pp. 43–71.

Hall, Catherine (1992c) "Gender Divisions and Class Formation in the Birmingham Middle Class, 1780–1950," in *White, Male, and Middle-class: Explorations in Feminism and History.* New York: Routledge, pp. 94–107.

Hartog, Hendrik (1997) "Lawyering, Husbands' Rights, and the Unwritten Law in Nineteenth-century America," *Journal of American History* 84, pp. 67–96.

Hartog, Hendrik (2000) *Man and Wife in America: A History.* Cambridge, MA: Harvard University Press.

Jones, Gareth Stedman (1983) *Languages of Class: Studies in English Working-class History, 1832–1982.* New York: Cambridge University Press.

Kerber, Linda K. (1988) "Separate Spheres, Female Worlds, Woman's Place: The Rhetoric of Women's History," *Journal of American History* 75, pp. 9–39.

Kerber, Linda K. (1998) *No Constitutional Right to Be Ladies: Women and the Obligations of Citizenship.* New York: Hill and Wang.

Lindsay, Matthew J. (1988) "Reproducing a Fit Citizenry: Dependency, Eugenics, and the Law of Marriage in the United States, 1860–1920," *Law and Social Inquiry* 23, pp. 541–85.

McCurry, Stephanie (1995) *Masters of Small Worlds: Yeoman Households, Gender Relations, and the Political Culture of the Antebellum South Carolina Low Country.* New York: Oxford University Press.

Ryan, Mary P. (1981) *The Cradle of the Middle Class: The Family in Oneida County, New York, 1780–1865.* New York: Cambridge University Press.

Saville, Julie (1994) *The Work of Reconstruction: From Slave to Wage Laborer in South Carolina, 1860–1870.* New York: Cambridge University Press.

Scott, Joan C. (1988a) "On Language, Gender, and Working-class History," in *Gender and the Politics of History.* New York: Columbia University Press, pp. 53–67.

Scott, Joan C. (1988b) "Women in *The Making of the English Working Class,*" in *Gender and the Politics of History.* New York: Columbia University Press, pp. 68–90.

Siegel, Reva (1994) "Home as Work: The First Woman's Rights Claims Concerning Wives' Household Labor, 1850–1880," *Yale Law Journal* 103, pp. 1073–1217.

Smith-Rosenberg, Carroll (1985) *Disorderly Conduct: Visions of Gender in Victorian America.* New York: Alfred A. Knopf.

Stanley, Amy Dru (1996) "Home Life and the Morality of the Market," in Melvyn Stokes and Stephen Conway (eds.), *The Market Revolution in America.* Charlottesville: University of Virginia Press, pp. 74–96.

Stanley, Amy Dru (1998) *From Bondage to Contract: Wage Labor, Marriage, and the Market in the Age of Slave Emancipation.* New York: Cambridge University Press.

Stanley, Amy Dru (1999) "'We Did Not Separate Man and Wife, But All Had to Work': Freedom and Dependence in the Aftermath of Slave Emancipation," in Stanley L. Engerman (ed.), *Terms of Labor: Slavery, Serfdom, and Free Labor.* Stanford, CA: Stanford University Press, pp. 188–212.

Stansell, Christine (1986) *City of Women: Sex and Class in New York City, 1789–1860.* New York: Alfred A. Knopf.

Stevenson, Brenda E. (1996) *Life in Black and White: Family and Community in the Slave South.* New York: Oxford University Press.

Thompson, E. P. (1963) *The Making of the English Working Class.* New York: Pantheon.

White, Deborah Gray (1985) *Ar'n't I a Woman?: Female Slaves in the Plantation South.* New York: W. W. Norton.

Ziegler, Sara L. (1996) "Wifely Duties: Marriage, Labor, and the Common Law in Nineteenth-century America," *Social Science History* 20, pp. 63–96.

Chapter Thirteen

Health, Sciences, and Sexualities in Victorian America

Louise Michele Newman

WHEN we think of female sexuality in Victorian America, what images most often come to mind? White schoolgirls, giggling and flirting, with their arms wrapped around each other? Middle-class newlyweds, fully clothed in petticoats and corsets, impassively enduring sexual intercourse with their husbands for the sake of having children? Working-class and rural women stealing kisses from their beaux in parks and fields? Immigrant streetwalkers propositioning clients in urban slums? Female slaves and domestic servants fighting off, or tearfully submitting to, the advances of their owners and bosses? Hovering around these images are fundamental questions that have troubled historians for the last thirty years – questions concerning the extent to which sexuality is a biological or physiological entity inhering in bodies (essentialism) and/or derives from culture and ideology (constructionism). But we may also wonder whether these images represent fundamental differences in the ways that women of different races and classes experienced sex, or whether they are stereotypes that continue to shape our thinking about the Victorian era because the discourses that produced them are still operating today.

Historiography of the 1970s concentrated on the difficult task of trying to reconstruct female sexual experiences from empirical sources that were largely prescriptive (of norms and ideals) rather than descriptive (of actual experience). What constituted "sex" in the nineteenth century? What types of sexual activities gave Victorian women pleasure? Did women who professed to love one another have sex together? How often did heterosexual couples have sexual intercourse? Historians continue to ponder these questions in an attempt to ascertain whether Victorians were as sexually repressed as sexologists of the late nineteenth and early twentieth centuries – Havelock Ellis and Sigmund Freud prominent among them – maintained.

Historiography of the 1980s shifted the terrain to exploring how sexual ideologies helped determine social status and reinforced racial boundaries. White elites and

I would like to thank Gina Morantz Sanchez, Sheryl Kroen, and Andrew Gordon for their helpful criticisms and warm encouragement.

many immigrant groups required female chastity to maintain a sense of familial honor. A double sexual standard generally operated whereby the sexual fidelity of wives was insisted upon while husbands were allowed sexual transgressions, particularly if these involved prostitutes, domestic servants, or women of "lower" classes or "inferior" races. Whereas privacy and reticence characterized white middle-class romance, the courtships of many other groups, notably Native Americans, Mexicans, and blacks, were public events, often interpreted by whites as licentious and immoral. Some minority groups, unlike their white counterparts, did not stigmatize the children born to consensual unions, even if the parents were not legally married. As in pre-industrial societies elsewhere, romantic love, sexual eroticism, and reproduction could coexist simultaneously within nonmarital unions, and fertility rates for these groups remained much higher than for the white middle classes.

Despite very different methodological and theoretical approaches, however, historians often agree on a number of points: first, that the Victorian era was characterized by incomplete, conflicting, or erroneous information about female health and reproduction. For example, nineteenth-century physicians were often misinformed about the female reproductive cycle and advised women to limit the size of their families by restricting sexual intercourse to the days when in fact they were the most fertile. Most scientists, doctors, and healers assumed that health was achieved when the body's finite amount of "vital force" was in balance and so believed that women's health was much more precarious than men's because menstruation, pregnancy, lactation, and menopause were all potentially dangerous, destabilizing moments when the body had to achieve a new balance. Education or mental work might overtax women's brains, draining necessary energy away from the reproductive organs and thereby interfering with women's ability to have children. Moreover, the educated elite, adhering to Lamarckian understandings of biological inheritance, believed that any physical or mental developments acquired during a woman's lifetime – whether assets or debilities – would be transmittable to her offspring.

Second, historians agree that many nineteenth-century authorities on women's health and morality (primarily ministers and some physicians) believed that "good" Christian women felt little or no sexual desire but instructed women that they were obligated to engage in sexual intercourse with their husbands to fulfill their marital duties. In the United States between 1790 and 1830, Nancy Cott argued, a new discourse of sexual morality accompanied the rise of evangelical Protestantism, in which (the white middle-class) woman was held to be passionless. Earlier, colonists had adhered to a Renaissance belief that "woman" like "man" (the categories were given no explicit racial or class attributes) experienced natural sexual desires and that woman's sexual appetites were at least as great as man's. These understandings were reflected in colonial laws, which permitted men of European descent to sue their unfaithful wives' lovers in order to recover damages, encapsulating the view not only that such men held property in their wives but also that the value of this property was diminished when wives had sex with men other than their husbands. Furthermore, many states believed that women pursued adulterous relationships in order to satisfy their (excessively) lustful desires and so mandated harsh punishments for adultery, especially when these extramarital relationships crossed the color line. Colonial legislators in Maryland and other southern states outlawed marriages of English women who "to the disgrace of our Nation doe intermarry with Negro slaves," insisting that such marriages were "*always* to the Satisfaction of their Lascivious & Lustful desires" (quoted in Bardaglio 1999: 114, emphasis in original).

Why did the idea of female passionlessness appear in the Victorian era? Cott proposed that a developing middle class needed to differentiate itself both from a British American aristocracy as well as from lower orders of working classes and immigrants. As US society became increasingly class conscious and class stratified in the early nineteenth century, Cott argues, the newly emerging professional and commercial middle classes began to consider sexual promiscuity an aristocratic excess that threatened middle-class virtue and domestic security. Protestant ministers redefined virtue primarily in sexual terms, designating sexual self-control for men as one of the highest human virtues, and upholding female chastity before, and fidelity within, marriage as the archetype for female moral character.

More recently, however, in response to Michel Foucault's challenge to explore how sex was "put into discourse" (Rabinow 1984: 299), historians in the 1980s and 1990s have moved away from analyzing how ideology shaped individual experience. They have focused instead on articulating the manifold ways in which sexualities functioned as a mode of power in Victorian culture and exploring how white elites in the nineteenth century constructed sexual norms to maintain their social authority and political dominance. From contact, European settlers asserted their right to subjugate and rule native peoples in terms of the need to civilize sexual savages. After the American Revolution, whites argued that virtuous Christian women had transcended their inherently primitive sexual natures to become chaste, civilized citizens of the Republic, while most other groups of women, black women as well as immigrant, working-class, and ethnic women, were presumed to be stuck in savagery. Throughout the Victorian period, both during and after slavery, whites used the sexuality of minority peoples as a foil against which they constructed themselves as racially superior in order to legitimize their political and economic dominance.

Although historians agree that profound changes in sexual practices were taking place during the nineteenth century, as evidenced by dramatically declining birthrates and precipitously increasing abortion rates, they disagree over whether these phenomena meant that white middle-class women were taking unprecedented control over their own sexuality. Historians have come up with very different ways to characterize female sexuality in the Victorian era. For example, Rachel Maines has argued that medicine pathologized female sexuality in this period, conceptualizing the female orgasm as a crisis point of a disease. Other historians have focused on a seemingly opposite phenomenon, arguing that "an emergent middle-class emphasized sexuality as a means to personal intimacy" with the result that a fundamental shift in the dominant understanding of sexuality occurred "from a primary association of sex with reproduction within families to a primary association [of sex] with emotional intimacy and physical pleasure for individuals" (D'Emilio and Freedman 1988: xv).

If, in the end, we find it impossible to choose between these views, it may because they are not as incompatible as they first appear. Not just the female orgasm, but female sexual pleasure more generally, was made suspect by ministers and physicians, psychologists, and educators. At the same time, many groups of women increasingly asserted their right to sexual autonomy and physical pleasure. We may not know as much about how sex was experienced by different groups of women as we may have supposed we did, but recent historiography has given us a much better understanding of how sexuality operated as a powerful discourse to define and maintain social, religious, ethnic, and racial boundaries, solidifying white elites' social authority and political power, while helping to intimidate, disfranchise, and exploit nonwhites, immigrants, and the working classes.

Demographic and Empirical Evidence

What do declining fertility rates, rising abortion rates, and love letters tell us about the sexual experiences of middle-class Victorian women? Because empirical data concerning sex in the nineteenth century are rare and fragmentary, historians have attempted to extrapolate women's experiences from mainly three types of primary sources: first, demographic statistics taken from the US census, which show that birthrates dramatically declined over the course of the nineteenth century; second, prescriptive sources – that is, popular advice books, medical texts, religious tracts, and political speeches, which advocated a sexual morality that upheld female chastity before marriage, condemned adultery, and framed sex solely in terms of procreation; and third, women's passionate love letters, which provided evidence of women's close emotional bonds and intimate relationships with other women and with men. Daniel Scott Smith was perhaps the first historian to use the demographic data to document a decline in married women's fertility over the nineteenth century, finding that the average number of children born to white women decreased from 7.04 in 1800 to 6.14 in 1840, 4.24 in 1880, and 3.56 in 1900. Taking into account such factors as a later marriage age and an increase in women remaining single, Smith concluded nonetheless that at least half to three-quarters of this decline was due to a reduction of fertility within marriage. For Smith, the data suggested that women were purposefully restricting the size of their families, but how? Were these women having less sex than women of earlier generations? Smith's work could not address these questions because he was not concerned with distinguishing whether the reduction in fertility occurred because of reduced frequency of sexual intercourse (abstention) or increased use of contraception (withdrawal).

To complicate matters further, as historians D'Emilio and Freedman point out, the decrease in the aggregate fertility rate obscures enormous regional, racial, and ethnic differences and underestimates the truly remarkable declines in fertility that were occurring in the native-born middle class. One study has found that for women born between 1846 and 1850, whose childbearing years ended in the 1890s, almost half of those with husbands in the professions or in business had two or fewer children. This astonishing figure is all the more remarkable given that, in the 1870s, lawmakers had outlawed the use of the mails to disseminate birth control information and had succeeded in criminalizing abortion. Much higher birthrates persisted in frontier communities, in southern states where white women married at a younger age, and among immigrant families, such as the Irish and Germans. Enslaved blacks also had higher fertility rates than whites, although their birthrates were declining overall as well.

James Mohr and other historians have also documented that as fertility rates fell precipitously, abortion rates increased dramatically, from approximately one abortion for every twenty-five to thirty live births in 1800 to 1830 to as high as one in every five or six live births by the 1850s and 1860s. Given these statistics, it is possible that the frequency of sexual intercourse within marriage remained steady (or even increased) over the century, while fertility rates declined, as couples developed more confidence in available forms of birth control and knew they could resort to effective abortifacients if the "menses were delayed." What seems clear, as James Mohr has argued, is that through the middle of the 1820s, the vast majority of white women who had abortions were single women who feared the social consequences of an illegitimate pregnancy. But this trend changed sometime in the second or third decade of the nineteenth century. By the mid-1840s, married women began aborting fetuses in significant numbers, either to postpone the birth of a first child or to space out subsequent pregnancies.

Historians continue to be puzzled by these trends and are unable to specify why and how middle-class white Americans decided to limit their fertility so dramatically. The best account to date, Janet Farrell Brodie's *Contraception and Abortion in Nineteenth-century America* (1994), argues that in the decades after 1830, reproductive control became a commercial enterprise in an expanding market economy, permitting white middle-class Americans increased access to new information about old and new methods – douching, condoms, spermicides, abortion-inducing drugs, withdrawal and rhythm methods, as well as early varieties of the diaphragm. For Brodie, the decline in marital fertility occurring between 1800 and 1870 speaks to a complex interplay between the supply and demand for birth control: better birth control methods, including more effective abortifacients, were more widely disseminated at the same time that many middle-class couples were coming to desire fewer children.

So what was going on in white middle-class married women's practice of sex over the course of the century? Did the frequency of sexual intercourse for married couples drop off? Did the declining birthrates in any way reflect the women's movement's encouragement to married women to assert their right to "voluntary motherhood" and say no to sexual intercourse? Historians continue to debate the answers to these questions. D'Emilio and Freedman argue that the decrease in birthrates suggests that the social purity movement succeeded in reshaping middle-class conjugal relations, and that the call for voluntary motherhood in fact did give middle-class women more control over childbearing. Smith concurs that "women asserted themselves in the family" but he also notes that while certain birth control measures, notably douching and the sponge, may have permitted women greater control over their fertility, the "major practices" continued to be withdrawal and abstinence, methods which indicated that men continued to be actively involved in decisions about fertility (Smith 1974: 132, 123).

What was the relationship between falling birthrates and the newly emerging ideal of female passionlessness? Did fewer women have orgasms – or did women have fewer orgasms – as it came to be understood that conception could take place without women experiencing sexual pleasure? It may be logical to suppose so; after all, if women were brought up to believe that sexual pleasure was immaterial to having a family and that experiencing sexual pleasure would place their moral character in doubt, then any physical sensations bordering on pleasure might well be repressed, ignored, or reinterpreted. The problem is a puzzling one, and the empirical record does not offer any conclusive answers. The legions of hysterical women who went to physicians seeking genital massages to relieve their neurotic symptoms speak to the dissatisfying sexual lives of many married women. But the extraordinary diaries and letters of Mary Pierce Poor offer another perspective entirely, suggesting that the ideal of passionlessness did not play a role in the sexual life of at least one middle-class New England couple.

Despite Mary Poor's exceptionalism (she had many more children than was the norm for someone of her race, class, and region), Mary Poor illustrates the dilemmas sexual intercourse and motherhood posed for white middle-class Victorian women in general. Motherhood provided Mary with a legitimate social role and means of self-definition, but it also limited what she could do in the public sphere and represented a threat to her health and life. Her attempts to limit and space her many pregnancies, which were not always successful, derived from her concern that more children would interfere with her ability to care for those already born and her deep fear that she would die in childbirth. For Mary, it appears that sexual intercourse was both intensely desired and equally dreaded, especially as fears of becoming pregnant mounted with each subsequent pregnancy. Nonetheless, Mary did not question the importance of maternity, although she chafed at the demands of the role and did not find the domestic sphere adequate for her ambitions. With three young children, she created other roles for herself, taking up reform activities and pursuing her own education.

What is most remarkable about this source, however, is the way it demonstrates that sexual intimacy was a key component of the Poors' life together. In 1868 after twenty-seven years of marriage, Mary began her diary with a lament: "Of 365 nights, Henry spent at home 123." Mary's diary also indicates that she did not want to use abstinence to limit her fertility, although it seems the couple tried physical separation during one summer. As Mary wrote to her husband, "I do not like to be long separated from you. We are happiest together, do not let us try absence again. I want to be with you, wherever you are, the rest of the summer and the rest of my life" (quoted in Brodie 1994: 26). Although few (if any) sources like Mary's diaries are currently known, Mary's way of keeping careful records of both her periods (with small pluses) and sexual intercourse with her husband (small x's) may not have been that unusual. In Mary's case, the extant records begin in 1845, four years after her marriage, and continue until 1877, when she was fifty-seven and her husband sixty-five, long past her menopause in 1868 at age forty-eight. Mary continued her record keeping long after there was any procreative or contraceptive reason to do so, suggesting that she kept a record for personal reasons and that sexual intimacy with her husband played an important role in her life.

One third of all of Mary's sexual notations occurred in mid-menstrual cycle, which was considered the safe period by many Victorian medical experts, when by today's calculations she would have been most fertile. Over a period of twenty-one years, from 1842 to 1863, the Poors had seven children, with two additional pregnancies ending in miscarriages. Early in the marriage and near the end of Mary's childbearing years, the births of their children were close together, suggesting that the couple was not as careful about using contraception at these times, or if they were, that the measures they took failed. Yet, Mary was able to space her middle pregnancies up to forty-three months at a time, so she was probably using other methods as well. Following the births of their third, fourth, fifth, and sixth children, the couple reduced the number of times they had sex in the four months after Mary's period returned, most likely as a deliberate strategy to prevent a quick consecutive pregnancy. The evidence also makes it clear that Mary relied on extended breastfeeding to help lower the probability of conception (although this method did not always bring about the desired result) and delayed weaning past the point considered healthy by her family and medical advisers. Brodie surmises that Mary used douching after sexual intercourse as well, a procedure to which she was introduced as a health measure when she took a water cure in 1851. Whether she also used other methods – condoms and abortifacients – is more difficult to determine.

How did this couple determine when and how often they would have sexual intercourse? The diaries do not say, but Brodie has calculated that the frequency of intercourse was consistent over the many years of the Poors' marriage, with no weekly or seasonal patterns. In 1849, when the Poors had been married eight years and had had three children, the x's appear on average once every five days. In 1868, when they had been married for twenty-seven years and had had seven children, the x's appear once every 7.2 days. In the twenty-two years between 1849 and 1871, the Poors had sexual intercourse on average 4.8 times a month, an average that Brodie observes is remarkably similar to the frequencies reported by white middle-class couples in family-planning studies of the 1970s. The data do not address the question of whether the Poors had additional sexual encounters that went unrecorded in Mary's diaries because they did not involve sexual intercourse.

Multiple, not Alternative, Sexualities for Middle-class White Women: Homosociality as a Complement to Heterosexuality

In the late 1970s and early 1980s, historians also began to explore the history of homosexuality, finding that sexual norms in the Victorian era did not stigmatize female intimacies as abnormal or perverse in the way that twentieth-century psychoanalytic discourses would. As Carroll Smith-Rosenberg, Lillian Faderman, and others have argued, white middle-class women's feelings of romantic love were often directed at and fulfilled by other women in the nineteenth century, when most moved within a world bounded by home, church, and the institution of visiting – a world in which entire days, even weeks, might be spent almost exclusively with other women. Female friendships and intimacies followed the biological ebb and flow of women's lives: marriage, pregnancy, childbirth, weaning, sickness, and death. The female bonds that formed during these times were often physical as well as emotional. This was especially true in rural areas and small towns, where the vast majority of white women lived during the Victorian era. When their husbands traveled, women commonly moved in with other women, sharing the marital bed.

Significantly, these intense, long-lasting emotional and intimate relationships among women did not preclude or threaten heterosexual marriages. Many of these relationships formed in childhood and continued through adolescence may have been briefly suspended during heterosexual courtships, but were then resumed once women were settled in their adult lives. For most of the nineteenth century, many women who expressed romantic feelings for other women were also married to men. Historians continue to debate whether to characterize women's "homosocial" relationships as erotic or sexual and disagree over whether same-sex romances developed as compensation for an emotional distance that resulted from men and women's relegation to separate spheres. The historiography looks to extant primary sources, such as love letters, to help settle the question, but epistolary evidence cuts both ways. On the one hand, women often addressed their female friends as they would a male lover, with effusive declarations of love and longing. On the other hand, contemporaries did not represent their love for other women as sexual and believed that their female relationships were more spiritual than their heterosexual relationships because they were not characterized by carnality.

The question also remains how these middle-class white women of the nineteenth century experienced their marriages. Again epistolary evidence is indeterminate: some women expressed great desire for their female lovers while lamenting the lack of connection they felt to their husbands. Others imagined bringing their woman lover and their husband together in one union. Smith-Rosenberg argues that the intense passion of women's relationships with one another contrasted greatly with the formality and stiffness of heterosexual relationships that derived in part from the "rigid gender-role differentiation within the family and within society as a whole" (1985: 60). But Karen Lystra contends that a too-rigid notion of separate spheres has led historians to assert a false idea of male–female emotional distance. Although there is no doubt that many middle-class Victorian women had intense relationships with other women, Lystra argues, these relationships did not preclude many of them from also attaining deeply satisfying heterosexual relationships. "Whatever the depth and intensity of Victorian women's relationships with their own sex," Lystra writes, "they had profoundly intimate emotional relationships with men" as well (1989: 11).

In the second half of the century, however, a visible and culturally significant group of single women eschewed heterosexual marriage altogether to form what was popularly referred to at the time as "Boston marriages." Faderman points out that these women were generally financially independent of men, often considered themselves "New Women" (the late nineteenth-century precursor to the twentieth-century feminist), and/or were pioneers in male-dominated professions. Sometimes these women had been previously married to men. For example, in 1854 Annie Fields married the publisher James Fields when she was nineteen, but after his death in 1881 she shared a Boston marriage with the novelist Sarah Orne Jewett that lasted almost three decades. Sometimes women tried to bridge their homosocial and heterosocial worlds. Alice Fletcher lived for sixteen years simultaneously with a much younger man, Francis La Flesche, whom she referred to as her adopted son, and with Jane Gay, a close female companion, until she was forced to make a choice between them. (Fletcher chose La Flesche.) For Faderman, the question is an open one whether these relationships among women were experienced as "erotic" or "sexual" by the women involved. "It is probable," Faderman writes, "that in an era when [white middle-class] women were not supposed to be sexual, the sexual possibilities of their relationships [with one another] were seldom entertained" (1981: 414).

The Passionless Lady and the Sexual Slave: Racialized Constructions of Female Sexuality

Historiography from the mid-1980s to the present has called attention to how sexual ideologies affected women of different races in different ways. If white women could be said to be gaining increasing sexual autonomy over the course of the nineteenth century (and I am not sure that such was the case), certainly the same could not be said of enslaved black women, who experienced the humiliations of bondage in explicitly sexual ways, and who were continually sexually harassed and assaulted by white men under slavery, during Reconstruction, and afterwards. Laura Edwards finds that emancipation heightened the vulnerability of African American women to sexual violence, as white men continued to use rape and other ritualized forms of sexual abuse to limit black women's freedom and reinscribe antebellum racial hierarchies. During slavery, economic incentives condoned white men's rape of female slaves as a way to increase slaveholdings at a time when the importation of additional slaves from Africa had become illegal.

On the one hand, then, the sexual behavior of white women was carefully monitored throughout the nineteenth century – even while it was asserted that a chaste Christian woman did not desire sex. On the other hand, whites continued to assert that black women were inherently promiscuous, justifying white men's sexual assaults of black women, enslaved or free, with the explanation that black women had seduced their attackers. Summarizing these phenomena, Jacquelyn Dowd Hall captures the way in which these two images, the passionless Lady and the sexual Slave, were historically connected – or, to put the point theoretically, the way in which sexuality was racialized in order to reinforce existing social hierarchies and maintain white political domination: "the [idea of the] passionless lady," writes Hall, "arose in symbiosis with the [idea of the] primitively sexual slave" (1983: 333). More recently, Sharon Block has shown that rape was a crime whose definition was (and remains) structured by race: because enslaved women could not serve as witnesses in cases concerning white defendants, they could not testify against white men who sexually assaulted them. Accordingly, no historian has yet recorded a conviction of a white man for the rape of a slave. Thus while early republican statutes did not explicitly exclude enslaved women from being considered victims of rape, most whites believed that black women could not be raped because they were purportedly always desirous of sex. By contrast, many mid-Atlantic and southern legislatures passed statutes that set harsh punishments for black men's sexual assaults on white women.

Historian Deborah Gray White has explained how the view that black women were exceptionally libidinous was nourished by the conditions under which slave women lived and worked in the late eighteenth and early nineteenth centuries. In fields and in masters' homes, slave women labored bent over, with their skirts up around their hips to keep their clothing clean and dry. On the auction block, slave women's bodies were disrobed for close inspection, and slave buyers fondled women's breasts and kneaded their stomachs to determine their capacity for childbearing. During whippings, female slaves were stripped naked, "tied up and exposed to the public gaze of all." Some masters took pleasure in beating slave girls, placing them in sexually suggestive poses – on all fours, with breasts and buttocks in full view (1985: 32–3).

If during slavery white men took their access to black women as an unquestioned prerogative (while declaring taboo any sexual activity between black men and white women), during Reconstruction white men continued to exert sexual control over black women and feared that black men would retaliate by sexually assaulting and harassing their former mistresses. Within the framework of the passionless Lady, sexual alliances between white women and black men could only be fathomed in terms of black men's assault upon white women's purity. In *Southern Horrors* (1892), Ida B. Wells-Barnett, a black journalist and political activist of the late nineteenth century, exposed the racist constructions embedded in these ideas, finding in many instances that rape was the pretext used to justify the lynching of black men when in fact the miscegenation was voluntary or, alternatively, the victim had had no relationship with a white woman but had challenged the economic or political domination of local white power. For her suggestion that white women voluntarily slept with black men, Ida B. Wells-Barnett's press was burned, her life was threatened, and she was run out of the South. Even Frances Willard, president of the Women's Christian Temperance Union, found Wells-Barnett's suggestion that miscegenation between white women and black men was often voluntary both untenable and offensive, indicating the extent to which the idea that a white woman could want to have sex with a black man had become unthinkable to white liberals.

Sharp social divisions existed between public (white male) and private (white female) domains, and the state was not supposed to interfere in (white) people's personal (sexual) lives. Yet, state legislatures increasingly regulated sexual behavior, notably in cases concerning interracial sex between white women and black men. The sexual alliances of white women and black men were deemed to be much more problematic than those of white men and black women, not the least because mixed-race offspring in the antebellum period took the legal status of the mother. In the case of mixed-race children of free white mothers, the children were considered to be both black and free, thus violating the biracial caste system by blurring the distinction between slave and black on the one hand, and free and white on the other. By contrast, the mixed-race offspring of white men and black women did not threaten the boundary between slavery and freedom because the mixed-race offspring assumed the legal status of their black mothers, who were generally enslaved.

Racialized Constructions of Sexual Health and Sexual Disease

A common goal of many health reformers in the nineteenth century was to increase the physical size and strength of white middle-class women, whether through dress reform, diet, or purposeful exercise, in response to the perception that the health of middle-class white women had deteriorated to the point that it constituted a national crisis. "[There is] a terrible decay of female health all over the land," Catharine Beecher wrote in 1855, "bringing with it an incredible extent of individual, domestic and social suffering" (quoted in Todd 1998: 149). Whether this generation of middle-class white women was in fact sicker than their grandmothers (or just perceived themselves to be so), however, is open to question. Regina Markell Morantz argues that women at the time may have indeed suffered more illnesses and poorer health than women of earlier generations due to a variety of factors: the damage that corsets and tight lacing did to female bodies; the unsanitary living conditions common in crowded urban neighborhoods; and the tendency for urban middle-class women to get much less fresh air and exercise than rural housewives got out of necessity in earlier times. To improve "woman's health," several different exercise regimes developed over the century: gymnastic programs were imported from Europe in the 1820s; light calisthenics were introduced in the 1830s and 1840s; heavy lifting was advocated in the 1850s and 1860s; and new gymnastics routines appeared in the 1870s and 1880s.

In the 1830s and 1840s, the movement to strengthen middle-class women through physical exercise received support from American phrenologists, whose radical influence in the mid-nineteenth century was somewhat akin to Freud's in the early twentieth century. Orson Fowler, one of the most renowned American phrenologists, found the "muscular feebleness of most American women . . . disgraceful" and argued that muscle-building exercise would make women healthier, both by increasing their brain size and enhancing their maternal capacities (quoted in Todd 1998: 178). Health reformers and woman's rights activists like Harriet Austin, Eliza Farnham, and Sarah Hale expounded similar views. These ideas represented a radical departure from conventional vitalist notions about the mind and body, which held that the body had finite resources that were used up during a person's lifetime. Vitalists cautioned against physical exercise because it purportedly placed too great a demand on the body's vital reserves. Women especially were advised to avoid exercise because of the danger posed to reproduction. By contrast, Fowler and his followers believed that demanding physical exercise (weightlifting in particular) would enlarge the body's vital reserves, increase the size of women's brains (thereby enlarging their intelligence), and improve women's chances of giving birth to healthy children. As a Lamarckian, Fowler also believed that improvements in the brain and muscles that resulted from exercise could be passed on to future generations via the inheritance of acquired traits. In 1842 Fowler adopted the phrase "natural waists or no wives" as a eugenic campaign slogan, urging men "who wish healthy wives and offspring to shun small waists and patronize full chests" (quoted in Todd 1998: 179).

For centuries hysteria, or womb disease, was considered a common and chronic ailment in women, and as late as the first half of the nineteenth century physicians continued to believe that hysteria resulted from insufficient and/or unsatisfying sex. As fertility of white Americans fell precipitously, US physicians became increasingly concerned that contraceptive practices were interfering with women's health, and began to argue that the "orgasmic" (that is, turgescent or congestive) condition in women was supposedly relieved by the soothing effect of semen released into the vagina. In this model, both withdrawal and abstention could lead to uterine disease, since the female genitalia did not receive the health benefits of male emission, and some physicians were suspicious of all contraceptive practices for this reason.

By the second half of the nineteenth century, however, physicians disagreed over the etiology and causes of hysteria. Some physicians still held to the traditional view that hysterical women suffered from a lack of fulfilling sex and prescribed the conventional cure of marriage. Others began to suspect that a major cause of the disease was masturbation (a practice one might expect not to be prevalent in an era that upheld passionlessness for women as an ideal, yet it seemed to be on the rise). The physician C. Bigelow, writing in 1875, was one of many who warned against masturbation on the grounds that "many [women] experience the nervous orgasm or spasm, which acts as harmfully on them, when much indulged in, as on males." Ironically but characteristically, Bigelow considered orgasm brought about by intercourse "healthful and medically desirable" (quoted in Maines 1999: 54).

While masturbation was denigrated as a possible cure to hysteria, professional masturbation might do the trick (pun intended). As Maines has argued, genital massage to orgasm was frequently performed by physicians and midwives as an office procedure in an attempt to cure or arrest hysteria. It seems that this was a very lucrative business for some physicians. By mid-century, the previously accepted (and acceptable) notion that the lack of pleasurable sexual intercourse was the cause of hysteria came under increasing pressure, as many physicians now believed that hysteria resulted from overindulgence in sexual intercourse or from self-stimulation, rather than from sexual deprivation or repression of sexual feelings. If masturbation was becoming common among middle-class white women, then the ideal of passionlessness may have functioned as a check on a sexuality that white men found increasingly threatening – an ideal respected more in the breach than in actual practice (not unlike the ideal of female chastity before marriage in the 1950s). Given today's belief that upwards of 70 percent of women cannot reach orgasm by penetration alone during sexual intercourse, those nineteenth-century physicians who discouraged women's self-masturbation as leading to disease appear grossly ignorant of female sexual functioning.

Historians like Maines have offered evidence of this sort to support arguments about the harmfulness of patriarchal control over female sexuality, which denied women the right to stimulate themselves for their own pleasure, while transferring these rights to husbands and physicians. However, the same evidence can also be interpreted to suggest that there were experts in the nineteenth century who knew, however inchoately, the ideal of female passionlessness to be a lie and a dangerous one at that. For example, as R. J. Culverwell wrote in *Porneiopathology* (1844), "continence in females," although thought "to be the brightest ornament a woman possesses," had pathological effects, as "is truly attested by the miseries of hysteria and other nervous derangements" (quoted in Maines 1999: 36). Culverwell clearly was reiterating the conventional wisdom that insufficient or inadequate sexual intercourse could lead to hysteria. But contained in this statement was also an implicit critique of a society that denied white middle-class women's sexual pleasure by setting forth an ideal that was grossly insensitive to female sexual needs. The empirical record contains dozens of physicians who knew from their medical practices that white women could have pleasurable orgasms and who recommended that these women seek this pleasure with their husbands.

Not surprisingly, given racialized understandings of female health and sexuality, physicians did not believe that black or lower-class women suffered from the same nervous and sexual diseases as middle-class white women. In contrast to white women, black women supposedly experienced childbearing as easy and unpainful. Such observations emanated from a racist discourse that assumed black biological and cultural inferiority and grounded these assumptions in physical, emotional, and moral differences from white women. Birthing was assumed to be easier for "primitive" and "savage" women because whites believed that these women had "underdeveloped" nervous systems, stemming from their smaller brains (evidenced by their smaller heads), rendering them impervious to physical pain, and because they believed that their fetuses could pass through the birth canal with less difficulty (presumably because black women had wide hips). Such beliefs facilitated and justified physicians' use of black women as medical subjects for experimental procedures that they considered too painful and brutal to try out on white women. Given their belief in separate and distinct races, it is particularly ironic that nineteenth-century physicians were willing to engage in an experimental medicine that was trying to understand the structure and functioning of white bodies through a reliance on black subjects.

In the second half of the nineteenth century, physicians identified neurasthenia as a "cultural" as well as physiological disease of the upper middle classes. Although it was known that both men and women succumbed to this disease, in the late nineteenth century neurasthenia was categorized with hysteria and chlorosis as part of the "hysteroneurasthenic disorders." George Beard's diagnosis, popularized in 1884, included many symptoms whose elements were consistent with the normal functioning of female sexuality under social conditions that interpreted normal sexual functioning as pathological. John and Robin Haller have argued simply that neurasthenia "was part of a much larger self-evaluation of America's concept of civilization" (1974: 42). Neurasthenia helped to mark the race/gender/class differences of white women as more dainty, more frail, and more sensitive to pain than nonwhite or working-class women – hence culturally superior, although biologically inferior, to these other groups of women. As the Hallers write, "neurasthenia [was] a reservoir of class prejudices, status desires, urban arrogance, repressed sexuality and indulgent self-centeredness" (1974: 42).

Although from the perspective of social status it was much better for a woman to be diagnosed as suffering from neurasthenia than from hysteria, it is not clear what etiologically distinguished the two diseases. Medical explanations of neurasthenia at the time were confused: was abstinence, overindulgence, or some reproductive difficulty in conception or birthing the cause (or effect?) of neurasthenia? Was neurasthenia a biological condition inherent in female physiology, or a social disease of the white upper-middle classes caused by overcivilization? Was it brought on by idleness and dissipation or by too much physical labor? Or was it too little physical labor and too much brain labor? Physicians put forth all of these possibilities, sometimes even acknowledging the contradictions and inconsistencies, as they tried to make sense of the indisputable statistical evidence that there was an inverse relationship between culture/class and reproduction/fertility. What bothered physician and commentator alike was that the more cultured and civilized the woman, the fewer children she was likely to have.

The precipitous decline in "civilized" (white) women's birthrates, a well-known fact from the 1870s on, brought up an ironic paradox that greatly troubled white middle-class Victorians: the supposed moral superiority of elite white women would be of no social-evolutionary value whatsoever if the white race failed to reproduce itself in sufficient numbers to maintain its racial superiority and political dominance. The very basis of these white women's evolutionary superiority – their refinement, daintiness, and heightened femininity, their sexual disinterest; their emotional instability and physical weakness, etc. – were, for the first time in US history, understood by scientists and physicians, educators, and even the general public, as impeding future racial progress. How was society to eliminate the conditions that caused white women to suffer hysteroneurasthenic disorders *without* endangering the class and social structures that led to these conditions? Within the logic of this discourse, neurasthenia threatened not just the health and well-being of a woman and her family, but also her race (through her inability to reproduce) and her country (her inability to raise model citizens) – in short, white civilization as a whole. In other words, if neurasthenia was a problem of "(over)civilization," how could the civilized white race continue to progress without this disease interfering with the births of future healthy offspring?

Clearly then, sex, seemingly the most private and personal of acts, had much larger cultural meanings and functions, helping to construct and maintain social hierarchies and racial and gender inequalities. The backdrop to these public discussions about women's health and sexuality was the declining fertility rate among the white middle classes and a concern that, were this trend to continue unabated, white elites would soon be overrun by lower classes of peoples. White elites thought of themselves as racially superior to other races in part because of the supposed sexual purity of white women. Herein lay a dilemma indeed – how to get white women to have more children when they were not supposed to like sex? Just as some physicians criticized white women for insufficient reproduction, they criticized black, immigrant, and working-class women for excessive reproduction, often attributing these groups' higher birthrates to their women's hypersexuality. Underlying all of these criticisms were whites' eugenic concerns about the "progress" or "future of the race" and their own racial/political domination.

Conclusion: The Two-sex Model of Sexuality and the Spirit of Capitalism

Since the wide dissemination of Foucault's work in the mid-1980s, historians of sexuality have understood, to quote Thomas Laqueur, "that sexuality is not an inherent quality of the flesh that various societies extol or repress.... It is instead a way of fashioning the self 'in the experience of the flesh,'...[which] exist[s] in relation to historically specifiable systems of knowledge" (1990: 13). From the Renaissance through the eighteenth century, scientific and medical treatises, as well as great works of literature, asserted that women experienced sexual desire at least to the same extent as men, if not more. Yet, sometime during the late eighteenth century, women's sexual nature changed, or rather, scientific and popular discourses about women's sexuality changed. As Laqueur has explained, the assumption that female physical pleasure, or orgasm, was necessary for reproduction was rejected completely by the late eighteenth century as medical science discovered that conception could take place "with no tell-tale shivers or signs of arousal" (1986: 1). Earlier representations of the clitoris as that organ " 'which makes women lustful and take delight in copulation,' without which they 'would have no desire...nor would they ever conceive,' " as one Renaissance midwifery text put it, "came to be regarded as controversial, if not manifestly stupid" (quoted in Laqueur 1986: 1).

If Cott's explanation for the emergence of the idea of female passionlessness relied on developments in religion and commerce, Laqueur's analysis looks to science and politics to explain how an undifferentiated human sexuality was bifurcated into two distinct and different modalities: one male, the other female. For both Laqueur and Londa Schiebinger, science's "discovery" – that the two sexes were distinct from one another, with fundamentally differing anatomies, physiologies, and sexualities – developed during the Enlightenment in response to new political demands that the rights of man be extended to woman. Schiebinger begins her analysis by posing the question narrowly: why, in the late eighteenth century, did the medical community develop the new field of comparative anatomy, when previously scientists had not found it necessary to focus on skeletal differences between the sexes? The answer, for Schiebinger, is that European societies, needing to defend existing gender inequalities, attributed them to so-called "natural" physiological, anatomical, and biological differences between the sexes.

Enlightenment demands for women's equality, therefore, brought about unexpected and paradoxical results: in calling for universal rights (undifferentiated by sex), Enlightenment radicals helped foster an ideology and science of sexual difference. In the process of this discursive construction, the scientific community, Schiebinger argues, in the absence of women, but also in opposition to women, devalued and excluded from scientific practice a specific set of moral and intellectual qualities, feeling and instinct primary among them, that scientists viewed as feminine. At the same time, the presumed masculine qualities of reason and rationality were deemed critical to scientific methodology. As Schiebinger writes, "the feminization of feeling and the masculinization of reason [were] produced and reproduced by a specific division of labor and power in European society" (1986: 72).

Laqueur articulates the same problem more broadly: why, in the late eighteenth century, he asks, do scientific discourses (biology, anatomy, medicine) alter the conception of gendered sexuality from a one-sex model, in which the two sexes were understood to be arranged on a single scale, with the female appearing as an inferior version of the male, to a two-sex model, characterized by two distinct sexes, incommensurable in their differences? The "discovery" that women need not have an orgasm to become pregnant, Laqueur argues, should not be understood simply as a matter of "progress" in scientific knowledge. Rather, "the political, economic and cultural transformations of the eighteenth century created the context in which the articulation of radical differences between the sexes became culturally imperative" (1986: 35).

It is critical to note that although a two-sex model of sexual difference was used to justify existing gender inequalities and in the end helped to bolster patriarchal institutions, there was nothing inherently discriminatory in the ideology of sexual difference. Incommensurability of the sexes did not have to be interpreted to mean women were inferior to men. Indeed, in the aftermath of the American and French Revolutions, a two-sex model held forth liberatory potential for (and thus appealed to) women seeking equality, because it replaced a discourse in which woman was represented as similar, but also vastly inferior, to man. In the United States at least, white middle-class women used the ideology of incommensurability to strengthen their authority within the family, to increase their social status as a group, and to organize a political movement to bring about their equality with white men. As Cott points out, the ideology of passionlessness functioned to protect middle-class women, who whether by censure under the double sexual standard, unwanted pregnancy and health problems, or bad marriages upon which they were financially dependent, had so much more to lose in heterosexual relationships than did men. It is not difficult to understand why, then, white middle-class women in the United States argued for distinctly feminine forms of citizenship throughout the nineteenth century.

New discourses for understanding female sexuality and the sexed body were wielded to demand political change. Equally significant, these new discourses affected the ways in which women approached physical intimacy with men, thought about marriage and reproduction, and experienced sex. The challenge facing scholars today is to describe the impact these new discourses had on the ways different racial and social groups of women (and men) understood and experienced female sexuality. Was the discourse of passionlessness powerful enough to actually diminish white women's sexual pleasure? What about other groups of women, for whom it was assumed that the discourse did not apply? Did this discourse affect what people did in bed? Were other erotic behaviors, practiced in earlier times, relinquished and "sex" limited to the procreative act? After all, what would be the point of extended lovemaking if the woman involved was believed to be incapable of sexual pleasure? How was the relationship between husband and wife for different groups affected by an ideology that specified that a good woman did not enjoy sex but only submitted to intercourse out of an obligation to please her husband and a desire to have children? Did thoughtful, caring husbands, out of consideration for their wives' feelings, reduce their frequency of marital intercourse and find other sexual partners? (Historians have documented that prostitution rose dramatically during this period but generally attribute this phenomenon to economic and demographic factors, such as the increasing numbers of working-class women needing to support themselves and increasing numbers of single men residing in urban areas.)

In the future, scholars will have to look for answers to these questions in the empirical record, but a remarkable 1992 article by Henry Abelove may offer some theoretical guidance and inspiration. Abelove deduces from demographic data showing large population increases in late eighteenth-century England that the incidence of cross-sex genital intercourse must have increased dramatically. Abelove points out that this rise in sexual intercourse correlates with a dramatic rise in virtually all indices of production – this is the time of the English Industrial Revolution. But Abelove rejects the usual explanation that economic factors were encouraging people to have larger families and speculates instead that as production became discursively and phenomenologically central to society in ways that it had never been before, other types of behaviors and customs judged to be nonproductive came under ever-intensifying negative pressure. Abelove hypothesizes that the same thing may have happened in the realm of sex: "productive" sexual behavior – i.e., cross-sex genital intercourse – became discursively and phenomenologically central to sexuality in ways that it had never been before, and nonproductive, i.e., nonreproductive, sexual behaviors diminished in frequency and duration and were redefined as foreplay.

Future accounts of Victorian sexuality may want to explore the interrelationships of these phenomena, which have currently been studied in isolation from one another: the privileging of sexual intercourse as "sex"; science's articulation of a two-sex model of sexuality; the cultural ideal of female passionlessness; the pathologization of the female orgasm; the social acceptability of homosociality; and the racialization of female sexuality that produced the symbiosis of the passionless Lady and the primitively sexual Slave. All were integral to the development of capitalism as it took place under the specific historical conditions that made up antebellum and postbellum society in the United States.

BIBLIOGRAPHY

Abelove, Henry (1992) "Some Speculations on the History of 'Sexual Intercourse' during the 'Long Eighteenth Century' in England," in Alexander Parker, Mary Russo, Doris Sommer, and Patricia Yaeger (eds.), *Nationalisms and Sexualities.* New York: Routledge, pp. 335–42.

Bardaglio, Peter W. (1999) " 'Shamefull Matches': The Regulation of Interracial Sex and Marriage in the South before 1900," in Martha M. Hodes (ed.), *Sex, Love, Race: Crossing Boundaries in North American History.* New York: New York University Press, pp. 112–40.

Bederman, Gail (1995) *Manliness and Civilization: A Cultural History of Gender and Race in the United States, 1880–1917.* Chicago: University of Chicago Press.

Block, Sharon (1999) "Lines of Color, Sex and Service: Comparative Sexual Coercion in Early America," in Martha M. Hodes (ed.), *Sex, Love, Race: Crossing Boundaries in North American History.* New York: New York University Press, pp. 141–63.

Brodie, Janet Farrell (1994) *Contraception and Abortion in Nineteenth-century America.* Ithaca, NY: Cornell University Press.

Brown, Kathleen M. (1996) *Good Wives, Nasty Wenches, and Anxious Patriarchs: Gender, Race, and Power in Colonial Virginia.* Chapel Hill: University of North Carolina Press.

Cayleff, Susan E. (1987) *Wash and Be Healed: The Water-cure Movement and Women's Health.* Philadelphia: Temple University Press.

Cott, Nancy F. (1978) "Passionlessness: An Interpretation of Victorian Sexual Ideology, 1790–1850," *Signs* 4, pp. 219–36. Rpt. (1984) in Judith W. Leavitt (ed.), *Women and Health in America: Historical Readings.* Madison: University of Wisconsin Press, pp. 57–69.

Davis, Angela Y. (1981) *Women, Race and Class.* New York: Random House.

Edwards, Laura F. (1997) *Gendered Strife and Confusion: The Political Culture of Reconstruction.* Urbana: University of Illinois Press.

Faderman, Lillian (1981) *Surpassing the Love of Men: Romantic Friendship and Love between Women from the Renaissance to the Present.* New York: William Morrow.

D'Emilio, John and Freedman, Estelle B. (1988) *Intimate Matters: A Social History of Sexuality in America.* New York: Harper and Row.

Hall, Jacquelyn Dowd (1983) " 'The Mind That Burns in Each Body': Women, Rape and Racial Violence," in Ann Snitow, Christine Stansell, and Sharon Thompson (eds.), *Powers of Desire: The Politics of Sexuality.* New York: Monthly Review Press, pp. 328–49.

Haller, Jr., J. S. and Haller, R. M. (1974) *The Physician and Sexuality in Victorian America.* Urbana: University of Illinois Press.

Hill, Marilynn Wood (1993) *Their Sisters' Keepers: Prostitution in New York City, 1830–1870.* Berkeley: University of California Press.

Hodes, Martha M. (1993) "The Sexualization of Reconstruction Politics: White Women and Black Men in the South after the Civil War," *Journal of the History of Sexuality* 3, pp. 402–17. Rpt. (1993) in John C. Fout and Maura Shaw Tantillo (eds.), *American Sexual Politics: Sex, Gender and Race since the Civil War.* Chicago: University of Chicago Press, pp. 59–74.

Hodes, Martha M. (1997) *White Women, Black Men: Illicit Sex in the Nineteenth-century South.* New Haven, CT: Yale University Press.

Hodes, Martha M. (ed.) (1999) *Sex, Love, Race: Crossing Boundaries in North American History.* New York: New York University Press.

Jones, Jacqueline (1985) *Labor of Love, Labor of Sorrow: Black Women, Work and the Family from Slavery to the Present.* New York: Basic Books.

Laqueur, Thomas (1986) "Orgasm, Generation and the Politics of Reproductive Biology," *Representations* 14, pp. 1–41.

Laqueur, Thomas (1990) *Making Sex: Body and Gender from the Greeks to Freud.* Cambridge, MA: Harvard University Press.

Lystra, Karen (1989) *Searching the Heart: Women, Men, and Romantic Love in Nineteenth-century America.* New York: Oxford University Press.

McGregor, Deborah K. (1998) *From Midwives to Medicine: The Birth of American Gynecology.* New Brunswick, NJ: Rutgers University Press.

Maines, Rachel P. (1999) *The Technology of Orgasm: "Hysteria," The Vibrator and Women's Sexual Satisfaction.* Baltimore: Johns Hopkins University Press.

Mark, Joan (1988) *A Stranger in Her Native Land: Alice Fletcher and the American Indians.* Lincoln: University of Nebraska Press.

Mason, Michael (1994) *The Making of Victorian Sexuality.* New York: Oxford University Press.

Mohr, James C. (1978) *Abortion in America: The Origins and Evolution of National Policy, 1800–1900.* New York: Oxford University Press.

Morantz, Regina M. (1977) "Making Women Modern: Middle-class Women and Health Reform in 19th-century America," *Journal of Social History* 10, pp. 490–507. Rpt. (1999)

in Judith Walzer Leavitt (ed.), *Women and Health in America: Historical Readings*, 2nd ed. Madison: University of Wisconsin Press, pp. 346–58.

Newman, Louise M. (1999) *White Women's Rights: The Racial Origins of Feminism in the United States.* New York: Oxford University Press.

Pascoe, Peggy (1990) *Relations of Rescue: The Search for Female Moral Authority in the American West, 1874–1939.* New York: Oxford University Press.

Rabinow, Paul (ed.) (1984) *The Foucault Reader.* New York: Pantheon Books.

Russett, Cynthia E. (1989) *Sexual Science: The Victorian Construction of Womanhood.* Cambridge, MA: Harvard University Press.

Schiebinger, Londa (1986) "Skeletons in the Closet: The First Illustrations of the Female Skeleton in Nineteenth-century Anatomy," *Representations* 14, pp. 42–82.

Schiebinger, Londa (1993) *Nature's Body: Gender in the Making of Modern Science.* Boston: Beacon Press.

Smith, Daniel Scott (1974) "Family Limitation, Sexual Control and Domestic Feminism in Victorian America," in Mary S. Hartmann and Lois Banner (eds.), *Clio's Consciousness Raised.* New York: Harper and Row, pp. 119–36.

Smith-Rosenberg, Carroll (1975) "The Female World of Love and Ritual: Relations between Women in Nineteenth-century America," *Signs* 1. Rpt. (1985) in Carroll Smith-Rosenberg, *Disorderly Conduct: Visions of Gender in Victorian America.* New York: Oxford University Press, pp. 53–76.

Stansell, Christine (1986) *City of Women: Sex and Class in New York City, 1789–1860.* New York: Alfred A. Knopf.

Sterling, Dorothy (ed.) (1984) *We Are Your Sisters: Black Women in the Nineteenth Century.* New York: W. W. Norton.

Todd, Jan (1998) *Physical Culture and the Body Beautiful: Purposive Exercise in the Lives of American Women, 1800–1870.* Macon, GA: Mercer University Press.

Ulrich, Laurel Thatcher (1982) *Goodwives: Image and Reality in the Lives of Women in Northern New England, 1650–1750.* New York: Alfred A. Knopf.

Vrettos, Athena (1995) *Somatic Fictions: Imagining Illness in Victorian Culture.* Stanford, CA: Stanford University Press.

Walters, Ronald G. (ed.) (1974) *Primers for Prudery: Sexual Advice to Victorian America.* Englewood Cliffs, NJ: Prentice-Hall.

Wells-Barnett, Ida B. (1969) *On Lynchings: Southern Horrors* (1892), *A Red Record* (1895), and *Mob Rule in New Orleans* (1900). Rpt., New York: Arno Press.

White, Deborah Gray (1985) *Ar'n't I a Woman?: Female Slaves in the Plantation South.* New York: W. W. Norton.

Yellin, Jean Fagan (1989) *Women and Sisters: The Antislavery Feminists in American Culture.* New Haven, CT: Yale University Press.

Part III

Modern America, 1880–1990

CHAPTER FOURTEEN

Education and the Professions

LYNN D. GORDON

IN 1859, following a one hundred-year period of remarkable expansion in American women's access to schooling, and in the midst of a national controversy over women's higher education, abolitionist and woman's rights advocate Thomas Wentworth Higginson sarcastically inquired, "Ought women to learn the alphabet? There the whole question lies. Concede this little fulcrum, and Archimedea will move the world before she has done with it." Higginson correctly identified the widespread fears that educated women would no longer be content within their homes, leaving the professions and politics to men. Indeed, supporters of women's education were most successful when they separated themselves and their cause from woman's rights, insisting that the well-educated woman longed only to enhance her sphere, not abandon it.

Over one hundred years after Higginson's essay appeared in the *Atlantic Monthly*, modern feminists maintained that the conservative aims of educators had succeeded all too well. Since the late nineteenth century, most female college graduates had either never worked for wages outside the home, or worked intermittently in the least prestigious and lucrative middle-class occupations. As late as 1963, Betty Friedan excoriated "sex-directed educators" who prepared women only for domesticity.

As these debates indicate, American women's access to and use of education has been inseparably linked to and limited by concerns about the power of schooling to effect changes in women's sociocultural roles. However, recent scholarship has provided a more balanced assessment of women's educational and professional history, finding that even within the constraints of restrictive gender ideologies, many women utilized their educations to follow bold and innovative paths.

Elementary and secondary schools, and a few colleges, opened to girls and women in the early and mid-nineteenth century, and their graduates entered new professional fields, especially teaching. The Civil War and its after-effects accelerated women's entry into higher education, the workforce, and public life. The Morrill Land Grant Act (1862) mandated the sale of public lands to support state universities, opening higher education to students who could not afford the tuition at private colleges.

Parents and state teachers' associations argued that these state-funded schools should be available to young women, particularly for teacher education. By the

1870s, women could attend state universities in the Midwest and West. In the East, however, private men's institutions persuaded state legislatures to assign land-grant funds to them instead of founding new, potentially competitive, universities that might have been coeducational. And in the South, as late as 1912, only seven state universities admitted white women. In 1885, the Mississippi State College for Women opened its doors, initiating a pattern of separate schools for white women in southern public higher education that persisted well into the twentieth century. The University of Virginia did not admit women until 1970.

At the same time, private women's colleges flourished, particularly in the East and the South, regions with the most resistance to coeducation. The founding of the Seven Sisters Colleges (although they did not officially receive that collective designation until 1926) inaugurated a new era in women's higher education. Established between 1865 (Vassar) and 1894 (Radcliffe), they determinedly created curricula that matched or exceeded those at the best contemporary men's colleges, and expected their students to complete a four-year course for the BA degree. Indeed, their standards were so high that some had preparatory departments until the 1890s, because few applicants could pass college-level entrance examinations.

Southern philanthropists and community leaders also established white women's colleges in the 1880s and 1890s. Of these the most prominent were the Woman's College of Baltimore (now Goucher College), Agnes Scott College, H. Sophie Newcomb Memorial College of Tulane University, and Randolph-Macon Women's College. Achieving collegiate standards took more time in the South, due to the collapse of white women's secondary education during the Civil War. Not until the 1920s, for example, was Newcomb College able to disband its preparatory department. Graduates of southern women's colleges sometimes entered northern women's colleges as sophomores, taking second bachelors' degrees to prepare adequately for graduate work. In 1903, Elizabeth Avery Colton, who earned one bachelor's degree at Statesville Female College in North Carolina, and a second at Mount Holyoke, founded the Southern Association of College Women to raise standards for white women's college work. In 1921 the organization merged into the American Association of University Women.

In the late nineteenth century, educational opportunities also expanded for African American women. After the Civil War, over six thousand northern teachers, most of them women, dedicated themselves to the education of the freedpeople. In the 1870s, local and state governments in the South gradually assumed responsibility for providing public primary education for both white and black children, although the latter were relegated to segregated, poorly equipped, underfunded, overcrowded schools. By 1900, southern black illiteracy, estimated at around 90 percent in 1865, had been cut in half. Congressional passage of a second Morrill Act (1890) put pressure on southern states to establish public higher education for African Americans. However, these new segregated public colleges were mostly agricultural, technical, and teacher-training institutes. Faced with the limitations of these institutions, missionaries and African American communities supported liberal arts education in private secondary schools and colleges with the aim of creating a black professional and leadership class.

Whether by choice or due to financial necessity, African American schools were coeducational. The Atlanta Baptist Female Seminary, established in 1881 by the Woman's American Baptist Home Missionary Society in conjunction with leaders of Atlanta's African American community, was the exception. The founders argued successfully to both white and black audiences that the creation of a black middle class required cultivated, pious, and thrifty wives and mothers. They persuaded John D. Rockefeller to fund the creation of a campus; the school was renamed for his wife's family, the Spelmans. Spelman became a college in 1923 and is the only historically black school to have remained a women's institution throughout its history.

At most private institutions educating African Americans, the curriculum combined liberal arts courses with vocational studies. At Spelman, for example, students could specialize in teacher education, missionary work, nursing, and even, for a short time, agriculture. Thus when professional positions were unavailable, black college women had other means of making a living. As with institutions for southern whites, high academic standards and baccalaureate status were not achieved until the 1920s or later. In 1900, W. E. B. DuBois reported that 2,272 African American men and 252 African American women held baccalaureate degrees; of these, only 156 African Americans, including twenty-two women, had graduated from black colleges. That situation, however, slowly reversed itself. In the late nineteenth and early twentieth centuries, exclusionary admissions policies and a hostile social atmosphere discouraged black attendance at white colleges and universities outside the South. Raymond Wolters has estimated that of approximately 13,000 black college students in the United States in 1927, only 1,500 did not attend black institutions.

The historiography of African American education often overemphasizes the role of white missionary teachers and the debates over liberal vs. vocational education between W. E. B. DuBois and Booker T. Washington, slighting the educational leadership of black women, particularly in creating opportunities for high-quality secondary education and teacher training. Lucy Laney, Charlotte Hawkins Brown, Fanny Jackson Coppin, Anna Julia Cooper, and Nannie Helen Burroughs, along with the institutions they established and directed, deserve greater scholarly attention. Perhaps the most prominent female African American educator of her generation was Mary McLeod Bethune, who founded the Daytona Educational and Industrial Institute (1904) in a rented house in Florida; in 1918, it became a high school, the Daytona Normal and Industrial Institute, and in 1923, Bethune-Cookman College.

New educational opportunities also opened for other women and girls of color in the late nineteenth and early twentieth centuries, although some, like those for Native Americans, came with a high price tag. Boarding schools, established by the Bureau of Indian Affairs, were intended, said their advocates, to rescue the remaining Indian population, now concentrated on western reservations, from oblivion. White reformers insisted that only by abandoning tribal languages, dress, customs, and ways of making a living would the next generation of Indians survive. Although the Bureau established both day and boarding schools on the reservations, most educators preferred boarding schools farther away, to remove students from parental and tribal influences. For Indian girls, boarding school education meant training in Victorian gender ideology and "woman's sphere." Girls who remained on the reservations sometimes received a similar education from "field matrons," sponsored by the Bureau of Indian Affairs between the 1890s and 1938. Over four hundred white missionary women served as field matrons; perhaps an additional thirty-five were Native American women, graduates of boarding schools.

White women missionaries were also active in New Mexico and Colorado, seeking to bring Protestantism and domesticity to Catholic families of Mexican descent. They were influential as well in educating Chinese immigrant women, whom they regarded as especially in need of westernization and salvation through Christianity. Among the small population of female Chinese immigrants on the West Coast, a significant number were prostitutes, sold by their families or kidnapped into sexual slavery. Missionaries sometimes rescued these women, literally caged by their "owners," and educated them, with the expectation that they would marry Christian Chinese men.

Children in Asian and Mexican communities of the West were often forced to attend segregated schools. Educated Mexican women sometimes opened small private schools in their own homes. And Asian parents established Chinese and Japanese schools, to educate their children in the language, religion, and culture of their home countries.

Catholics also established their own school systems, to protect their children from Protestant and secular influences. By the late nineteenth century, between one third and one half of American Catholic families sent their children to parochial elementary schools; and many also patronized academies for Catholic girls. As more Catholic women moved into professional and semi-professional occupations, parents sought higher education for their daughters. The church, however, became alarmed at the numbers of young Catholic women attending secular colleges. Opposing coeducation, church officials were persuaded to allow religious women to establish Catholic women's colleges. Among the first such institutions were the College of Notre Dame (Maryland, 1896) and Trinity College (Washington, DC, 1897). In 1915 there were fourteen new colleges, many evolving from Catholic girls' seminaries and academies; by 1925, thirty-seven Catholic women's colleges had been founded in the United States.

Jewish families worried more about the Irish Catholic teachers than the Protestant and/or secular values expressed through the public school curriculum. Yet the vast majority of Jewish parents embraced public education for both their sons and their daughters. Gender controversies in Jewish communities centered around the nature of religious education. Boys attended after-school or weekend programs to study Hebrew and religious rituals, but traditional families rarely provided girls with such training. A Jewish boy routinely celebrated his bar mitzvah, or religious coming of age, when he turned thirteen; not until 1922 did the first Jewish girl become a "bat" mitzvah. However, Reform Jews "confirmed" both boys and girls at age fifteen, and Socialist families supported a cultural, Yiddish-based Jewish education for their children, through programs organized by such progressive associations as the Workmen's Circle. Like members of other ethnic groups, Jewish families more often sent sons to college than daughters, but by the early twentieth century small numbers of Jewish women had gained college degrees.

As Higginson's essay indicates, women's educational advances in the late nineteenth and early twentieth centuries were not uniformly well received. Opponents of the "New Woman," such as Dr. Edward Clarke, author of *Sex in Education, Or A Fair Chance for the Girls* (1873), claimed that studying put too much strain on girls' nervous and reproductive systems. During menstruation the flow of blood, he argued, should be directly to the ovaries; schoolwork directed it to the brain. The result was illness, fatigue, shriveled ovaries, and women who could not give birth to healthy children. Clarke's book was enormously popular, going through seventeen editions by the end of the century. Other critics worried that the association on campuses of adult men and women would lead to immorality; that rhetoric about education enhancing traditional womanly roles masked desires for careers and public influence; that women students could not meet colleges' academic demands and would prevent men from developing an appropriate campus social life.

Educators, women physicians, and woman's rights advocates rushed to the defense of women's higher education, denouncing Clarke's citation of cases as inaccurate and his reasoning as flawed. In 1885 the newly formed Association of Collegiate Alumnae conducted a study concerning the health of college women. Their committee's survey of 1,300 women college graduates found that slightly over 20 percent reported improvement in their health while attending college, and few suffered serious illnesses. Others pointed out that the presence of women students might actually improve the rough manners and morals of campus social life.

Despite the controversies, American women moved quickly into higher education – by 1870 they made up one third of the undergraduate population, and more girls than boys attended the country's 1,000 public high schools. Still, the debates particularly affected the intellectually egalitarian women's colleges, which defensively proclaimed their social and political conservatism. Women's colleges instituted strict rules regarding their students' conduct, dress, food, and exercise, including rigorous physical education requirements. And all colleges and universities officially discouraged women students from considering careers other than motherhood or teaching (before marriage), and took a dim view of institutional connections to the woman's rights movement.

Most white women who attended college between the 1860s and the 1890s, the "first generation of college women," came from Protestant families of some means. Yet daughters of the most elite families did not attend college in the late nineteenth century; higher education was a dangerous experiment and might make women unmarriageable. This first generation was well aware of its pioneer status and unfavorable public image. At coeducational schools, women students struggled against the hostility and ridicule of male students and faculty, but they lacked both the numbers and the resources to develop a meaningful campus life. In contrast, at women's colleges, students formed organizations and, often in defiance of the rules and regulations, created strong campus cultures. Still, evidence from the letters and essays of early students demonstrates that they considered coeducational universities academically superior, and cherished the freedom found at such schools.

Women students puzzled over the question of "after college, what?" As critics had predicted, many educated women were not content to live like their mothers and grandmothers. The most famous member of this generation was Jane Addams, a graduate of Rockford College in Illinois. She found medical school not to her liking and foundered for several years, enduring health problems, depression, and feelings of uselessness before founding Hull House, the emblematic social settlement of the Progressive era, in 1889.

Settlement work spread quickly among college women; perhaps, as John Rousmaniere has pointed out, because residents lived communally, continuing the intellectual and emotional fellowship of their student days. Although the movement began as a means of bringing middle-class culture to the poor, residents soon turned to attacking the evils of industrial society. Using skills learned in college, such as survey research, they investigated the social conditions of the immigrant poor, lobbied for legislation to address specific problems, and established coalitions among people of different social classes. Settlement residents and charity organization workers founded the National Conference on Charities and Corrections in the early twentieth century, and published a journal, the *Survey.* Between 1898 and 1919, seventeen schools of social work were established, mostly for graduate work. As director of the Charity Organization Department of the Russell Sage Foundation, social work educator Mary Richmond organized summer institutes across the country to teach principles of "scientific charity," and her *Social Diagnosis* (1917) became the basic text for social work practice.

Rooted in older traditions of female benevolence, social work faced difficulties in claiming professional status. In 1915, educational reformer Abraham Flexner argued that the field had no distinctive body of "scientific" knowledge. Social workers responded by raising educational standards through the attachment of social work schools to colleges and universities. The Chicago School of Civics and Philanthropy was the model for such efforts, affiliating with the University of Chicago in 1920 as the Graduate School of Social Service Administration. However, the professionalization of social work proceeded slowly. In the early 1920s, only around 40 percent of social workers held undergraduate degrees.

In the late nineteenth century, an aspiring female physician could enter either a homeopathic or a "regular" medical school, including seven women's medical colleges, for example, the New England Medical College, the Woman's Medical College of Pennsylvania, and the New England Hospital for Women and Children. Yet the numbers of women physicians began to decrease early in the twentieth century. As medicine became more scientific and laboratory-based, the women's medical colleges could not afford to maintain the new educational standards. Some universities accepted women into their medical schools (in 1893, Johns Hopkins University admitted women after receiving a $500,000 "incentive" from feminists and women philanthropists), but imposed a 5 to 6 percent quota on women students for much of the twentieth century.

During the Civil War, nursing had become a respectable profession for women. By 1900, over four hundred nurses' training schools had been founded; in 1926, two thousand such schools were attached to American hospitals and had graduated over seventeen thousand nurses. Hospital training schools offered student nurses minimal classroom time and extensive work on the wards. Nursing meant hard labor and subordination, both to female superintendents and to doctors. Most nurses were young, unmarried women from working-class homes, who left the profession after a few years for marriage or less strenuous employment. Efforts to recruit middle-class high school- or college-educated women into nursing were not greatly successful. Still, some women gained influence and opportunities in the profession by branching out into visiting and school nursing, nurse-midwifery, and military nursing. In 1901 the Army created the Nursing Corps, followed by the Navy in 1908. Almost nine thousand white nurses served with the American Expeditionary Force in Europe during World War I.

The few educated middle-class women in nursing led the fight to professionalize their field. They formed the American Nursing Association (ANA) in 1897, published the *American Journal of Nursing*, and sought to raise educational standards in nursing through state examinations and licensing. In 1922, directors of the ANA called for high school graduation as an entry requirement for nursing. When various states proposed laws restricting the hours of women's labor, hospitals and nursing associations opposed the inclusion of student nurses in their provisions. Nursing, they argued, was not a trade, to be classified and regulated with other trades. Rank-and-file nurses reacted angrily against such attitudes, and against professionalization generally, believing it threatened their status and livelihood. The long-term trend, however, was with the reformers. In 1923, the Goldmark Report took the hospital training schools to task for providing so little real education to student nurses. This and other studies led to a long-term trend toward baccalaureate programs for nurses.

Doctoral programs in the arts and sciences lagged far behind teaching, medicine, and nursing in opening their doors to women. Indeed, the Association of Collegiate Alumnae established fellowships for graduate work in Europe to meet the needs of American women who could not study in their own country. In 1877, Helen Magill became the first woman to receive a Ph.D. from an American school: Boston University, in the field of Greek drama. In the 1890s, American graduate schools more often opened their doors to female students, including some, like Yale, that would not admit undergraduate women. The new University of Chicago was particularly well known for offering opportunities to women, although the bulk of scholarship money went to men. However, women with Ph.D.s rarely found faculty positions at coeducational universities, and never at men's colleges. Some became faculty and administrators at women's colleges, and others were appointed Deans of Women at coeducational schools to watch over female undergraduates. Still others, discouraged by the lack of opportunities in their profession, entered settlement or reform work.

Similarly, the legal profession, with its ties to politics and the public image of aggressive courtroom warriors, opened slowly and reluctantly to female practitioners; in 1890, only 208 American women were practicing lawyers. Early women lawyers did not attend law school but apprenticed themselves, in time-honored fashion, to practicing lawyers – usually fathers, husbands, or brothers. Although apprenticeships did not disappear until the 1920s, law school attendance became increasingly important as a means of professional success, but, as with medical schools, women had difficulty gaining admission. Midwestern coeducational state universities had the most women law students. Yale University admitted women to its law school in

1918; Columbia in 1926; but Harvard not until 1950. Strict quotas on female admissions, women's difficulty in gaining access to the informal study groups so important to success in law school, and "Ladies' Days," when women students were singled out for intense and humiliating questioning, kept the number of women lawyers small until well into the twentieth century. As late as 1968, only 5 percent of law students were women.

Journalism provided greater professional opportunities for women in this period. Mindful of pleasing women readers, editors willingly hired at least one female reporter to cover "women's news." A few such reporters moved on to political or city news "beats." In the 1890s, sensationalist newspapers like Joseph Pulitzer's *New York World* hired "stunt girls," young women who donned disguises, insinuated themselves into unusual situations, and reported the ensuing stories. Foremost among the stunt girls was Nellie Bly (Elizabeth Cochran Seaman), who made her reputation through exposés of the horrendous conditions in women's prisons and asylums. In the early twentieth century, many papers also hired women as "sob sisters," who wrote sentimental feature stories oriented toward women readers. In the 1910s, however, and thereafter, a few women became "front page girls" or "women newspapermen," with jobs comparable to those of the best male reporters.

The establishment of journalism schools, beginning in the 1910s, was controversial. Editors complained that the emphasis on hiring college-educated journalists deprived them of the talents of the off-the-streets hardboiled working-class reporters who, they claimed, were the backbone of the newspaper industry. For women, however, journalism schools, mostly located at large state universities, proved a great boon. In addition to courses in newspaper reporting and editing, they could be trained for jobs in advertising, public relations, magazine work, and business management, especially at magazines such as the *Ladies' Home Journal*, the *Woman's Home Companion*, *McCall's*, and *Good Housekeeping*.

It was in the field of education, however, that women gained the greatest access to professional careers. Women teachers and female educational reformers had a major impact on elementary and secondary schools during the Progressive era. In the late nineteenth and early twentieth centuries, most states passed compulsory education legislation and laws requiring the certification or licensing of teachers. Normal schools, public and private, gradually "upgraded" into teachers' colleges to meet demands for better teacher education and to remain competitive with the normal departments of state universities. Graduate work in education and in the new field of child study also became available.

In 1916, Radcliffe graduate Lucy Sprague Mitchell founded the Bureau of Educational Experiments, later known as the Bank Street College of Education. At Bank Street, Mitchell brought together an array of teachers, social workers, psychologists, and physicians to discuss bringing the latest educational research into the public schools. She was also influential in the creation of more realistic children's literature, as exemplified in her own *Here and Now Storybook* (1921) and the popular children's books of her colleague Margaret Wise Brown, author of *Goodnight Moon* (1947).

Teachers in the public schools, particularly in the cities, experienced the difficulties of bureaucratization and paternalistic, authoritarian supervision by male principals and superintendents alongside the demands of growing numbers of immigrant schoolchildren. New teachers' unions, however, sought improvements in pay, salary equity with men, the right for women teachers to marry, and educational reforms. In 1897, the Chicago Teachers' Federation (CTF) was founded, affiliated with the Chicago Federation of Labor (1902), and in 1916 became the first local in the American Federation of Teachers; a controversial move, because many teachers preferred a middle-class professional association to a trade union. However, the CTF's best-known leader, Margaret Haley, wanted both the labor affiliation and professional status. She fought for women's right to speak and to vote within the mostly female but male-dominated National Education Association (NEA), and in 1910 was instrumental in arranging the first election of a woman to the NEA presidency.

During the Progressive era, too, women administrators were not as uncommon as they became in the mid-twentieth century. City school superintendents Ella Flagg Young of Chicago, Susan Miller Dorsey of Los Angeles, Julia Richman of New York City, and Annie Webb Blanton, state superintendent of public instruction in Texas, were among the best known, but women also served as county superintendents and elementary school principals in many communities.

In the early twentieth century, women educators helped to design gender-oriented vocational curricula for high school girls. Federal funds, provided through the Smith-Lever Act (1914) and the Smith-Hughes Act (1917), helped schools establish such programs. For girls, vocational education meant courses in home economics or "domestic science." By the end of the nineteenth century, scientists and social scientists, including members of the first generation of college women, established "sanitary [domestic] science" as a scholarly field. Ellen Richards at the Massachusetts Institute of Technology and her student Marion Talbot, who became Dean of Women at the University of Chicago, argued that women needed to study their homes and communities through the prisms of chemistry, biology, sociology, and psychology. Armed with such knowledge, college women could become a potent force for social and communal reform. Thousands of young women studied sanitary science, and many became food chemists, nutritionists, and teachers of home economics. Below the college level, domestic science courses tended to be far more instrumental – cooking and sewing in preparation for family life. And some women's organizations, including the influential National Women's Trade Union League and the Women's Educational and Industrial Union, argued unsuccessfully against gender-differentiated vocational education, maintaining that girls should have the same access to skilled trades as boys.

Yet the most popular aspect of girls' vocational education was not home economics but the commercial curriculum, designed to train middle-class girls for clerical and secretarial positions. In 1930, half of Americans in the fourteen-to-eighteen age bracket were in high school, and one out of six students enrolled in commercial education courses. Scholars of vocational education argue that it created de facto sex-segregated schools and that, as clerical work "feminized," it became a dead-end occupation with little status, low pay, and few opportunities for advancement.

During the late nineteenth century, with the growth of public libraries, librarianship also became an acceptable career for an educated woman. The field professionalized quickly, through the founding of the American Library Association and its *Library Journal* (1876) and the establishment of schools of librarianship (the first at Columbia University, 1886, founded by Melvil Dewey). Like teaching, however, library work quickly became a feminized profession, marked by low pay and dominated by male directors and supervisors.

By the early twentieth century, education stretched far beyond the library and the classroom. Study circles, reading clubs, and ladies' clubs of all kinds were common features of life in middle-class America. Women between the ages of twenty and forty represented the largest group of "students" in the extensive adult education system developed by the Chautauqua Movement. The Woman's Christian Temperance Union, the General Federation of Women's Clubs, the Women's Educational and Industrial Union, the Young Women's Christian Association (YWCA), the National Congress of Mothers (later the Parent–Teacher Association), the National Council of Jewish Women, and other local, state, and national women's groups actively promoted educational as well as civic, religious, cultural, and political causes. Women also fought, successfully in many cases, for "school suffrage," i.e., the right to vote in school board elections.

For African American women, club work and reform offered especially important opportunities for social and civic education. In the late nineteenth century, and for most of the twentieth, the vast majority of African American women, single or married, worked as domestic servants, laundresses, or in agriculture. A black middle class had emerged, defined, in part, by the occupations of its members. Yet only 3 percent of black female workers were employed in the professions. Middle-class black women most often worked as elementary and high school teachers. In black schools, as in white, the teaching profession quickly feminized. Following the appointment of Sarah Woodson Early to the faculty of Wilberforce University in 1866, black women also taught in the black colleges and teacher-training institutes of the South. Such jobs, however, were in short supply, as African American faculty only gradually replaced white instructors. Moreover, black women academics suffered gender as well as racial discrimination. Not until 1987, with the appointment of Johnnetta Cole, did Spelman College have an African American woman president.

Black nurses struggled to gain a foothold in their profession. Few hospital training schools admitted African American nursing students. In 1886, a donation from John D. Rockefeller established the first black nurses' training school at Spelman Seminary. Concerned about the lack of adequate nursing care in black hospitals and communities, black club women and physicians founded additional nursing schools in the 1890s. Black nurses faced difficulties obtaining both private duty positions (few black families could pay them, and white families would not hire them) and hospital staff jobs. They received less pay than white nurses for the same kind of work, and could not serve in the military during World War I.

In 1908, black women founded the National Association of Colored Graduate Nurses (NACGN), with headquarters in New York City, to work for equal pay and status. Its most prominent and successful director, Mabel K. Staupers, with Eleanor Roosevelt's backing, persuaded Congress to allow black nurses to serve during World War II. In 1943, the Cadet Nurse Corps was created, and over five hundred black women became army nurses. Staupers also led the effort to integrate the ANA. In the 1940s, the ANA created biracial organizational committees and granted individual memberships to southern black nurses, who could not gain access to state-level associations. In 1950, Staupers proudly presided over the dissolution of the NACGN and the incorporation of its members into the ANA. In the 1970s, however, black nurses grew frustrated over the failure of the ANA to address racism. Although maintaining their presence in the ANA, they formed the National Black Nurses' Association.

Beginning in the 1860s, a handful of black women graduated from women's medical colleges; in 1900, 115 African American women were practicing physicians. The demise of the women's medical colleges in the early twentieth century created great difficulties for black women, who found it even harder than whites to gain entrance to traditional medical schools. By 1914, only Howard University Medical School in Washington, DC, and Meharry Medical College in Nashville, Tennessee, routinely admitted black women as medical students. In 1920, the number of black female physicians had declined to sixty-five (compared to 3,885 black male doctors). Excluded from the professional societies and networks of their male classmates and colleagues, and from white women's medical organizations, black women were hard pressed to obtain internships or start private practices. Many were forced to take badly paying jobs in social welfare organizations.

Similarly, black women could operate as journalists only within the confines of the black press; fortunately, the latter offered opportunities beyond the chance to be a sob sister or a stunt girl. Black women edited and wrote for an array of organizational and educational journals, as well as daily newspapers. Ida B. Wells-Barnett began her career as the editor of a weekly newspaper in Memphis, Tennessee. She continued to write articles and pamphlets in her lifelong international crusade against lynching. Charlotta Bass was probably the first African American woman to own and operate her own newspaper in the United States; she published the *California Eagle* from 1912 until 1952, when she ran for vice-president on the Progressive Party ticket. Alice Allison Dunnigan struggled for recognition and better pay while covering national politics for the Associated Negro Press (ANP) during the 1940s and 1950s in Washington, DC, and Ethel Payne became the one-person Washington Bureau for the *Chicago Defender*.

Many historians consider the Progressive era an age of professionalization. Armed with college and graduate degrees, middle-class men embarked on prestigious and lucrative careers in fields with rapidly expanding bodies of specialized knowledge. The significance and prestige of both the professions and professionals grew exponentially. For women, however, links between education and the professions were more complex than for men. Women who entered the professions stressed their commitment to public service. They supported what William L. O'Neill called "social feminism," i.e., the belief that women needed education, the authority of professional status, and suffrage to meet their special, gendered obligations to make the world a more just and moral place. Excluded from the professional societies and structures for advancement and rewards so important to men's careers, they formed their own clubs and organizations and awarded their own fellowships and prizes.

In *Unequal Colleagues* (1987), Penina M. Glazer and Miriam Slater identified strategies employed by successful women professionals, including superperformance, separatism, subordination, and innovation. More commonly, however, women professionals entered what sociologist Amitai Etzioni called the "semi-professions," for example, the feminized fields of elementary schoolteaching, nursing, librarianship, and social work. Etzioni's terminology reflects the low pay, bureaucratization, and limited autonomy in these fields.

Moreover, as noted above, the professionalization of any occupation, though raising its status and often the salaries of its practitioners, was not an unmixed blessing. Higher educational standards and restricted entry provided new obstacles for women, who were less likely than men to have the financial means for additional years of schooling. Most new or more elite professional schools either would not admit women at all, or only a very few. Within teaching, nursing, and social work, professionalization created divisions between middle-class, more highly educated leaders, working-class practitioners, and women of color. And with professionalization, women distanced themselves from their patients/clients/students. The increase of knowledge and technique in virtually every field in the early twentieth century, and the emphasis on advanced degrees and licenses, meant that women professionals served people ever-less knowledgeable than they were, often people of lower social classes and different races. Widespread beliefs concerning racial hierarchy, Anglo-Saxon superiority, and the need for Americanization influenced interactions with clients, and affected professionals' judgments about appropriate social policies and professional practices.

How successfully women professionals, in particular, bridged those gaps has been hotly debated. Did middle-class white professional women, with the stated aim of making the world a better place, especially for other women and their children, meet the needs of working-class and immigrant families? Did they feel closer to their clients because of the common bonds of womanhood? Or did they, mired in ethnocentric, middle-class morality, simply impose their knowledge on others, give inappropriate orders and advice, and in doing so, advance their own needs for status and power?

Most historians have found white middle-class women professionals culture-bound and lacking empathy. As evidence, they point to the Americanizing efforts of female teachers, social workers, and missionaries in settlement houses, public schools, and Indian boarding schools, and the insistence among women doctors and nurses that immigrant women learn new methods of childrearing. Susan Smith, however, argues that black women professionals – doctors, teachers, nurses, and social workers – cooperated with African American communities to achieve important local and national health reforms. Yet the work of nurse Eunice Rivers Laurie with the federal government's notorious Tuskegee Syphilis Study in the 1930s and 1940s speaks to the possible deleterious effects of professionalization within African American communities. East European Jewish immigrant women frequently complained that middle-class German Jewish educators and social workers disapproved of and interfered with their family culture and religious practices. Recently, scholars such as Kathryn Kish Sklar and Kathleen Weiler have offered a more balanced portrayal of such interactions, arguing that, despite their cultural and class-based blindness and occasional arrogance, female professionals provided otherwise unavailable services and information to women and families badly in need of both.

The Allied victory in World War I and passage of both the prohibition and woman suffrage amendments to the Constitution led educated women to anticipate not only a better and more just world, but also one in which they would play expanded roles. Yet succeeding generations of college women did not continue to make inroads into higher education and the more prestigious professions. The percentage of women students in colleges, graduate and professional schools and women practitioners in medicine, law, and academia declined or increased very modestly between 1920 and 1970. The numbers rose again only with the advent of the modern feminist movement. Much of the historiography on American women in the twentieth century has thus focused on the issue of women's unfulfilled expectations.

Scholarship on women's education and the professions is not nearly so rich for the mid-twentieth century as for the previous hundred years, and historians who study this period disagree as to the timing and rationale for women's "retreat" from higher education and professional life. Can we locate the decline in the well-documented resurgent conservatism of the 1920s, the Great Depression of the 1930s, wartime fears about gender-role dislocation in the 1940s, or the "feminine mystique" years of the late 1940s and 1950s? Did women's choices and lifestyles create the decline? Did college women's growing interest in matrimony, for instance, and the advent of compulsory heterosexuality and homophobia in the 1910s and thereafter, effect declines in women's professional and political participation? Did college graduates' intermittent labor force participation make it impossible for most women to make significant professional contributions? Did the few prominent women professionals ("queen bees") not do enough to help other women? What impact did the collapse of political feminism in the mid-1920s have on women's education and the professions? How did all these factors affect minority women and women of color? Some of these questions have been addressed; most have not, and it is difficult to weave existing studies into a clear narrative.

The campus lives of the second generation of women college students, those graduating between the 1890s and 1920, provide some indication of the difficulties ahead. For white women, the successes and achievements of the first generation of college women proved a mixed blessing. Throughout the Progressive era, critics of women's higher education argued that the dire prophecies concerning the impact of New Women on American family life had come to pass. Around 10 percent of American women born between 1860 and 1880 never married; in 1800 the birthrate for American women was 7.0; by 1900, it was 3.56. The divorce rate, though still quite modest, had risen to 5 percent by the turn of the century. Clearly, educated women had more options than ever before and did not always make traditional choices.

Among teachers, academics, nurses, and settlement reformers, marriage was uncommon and professional women in these fields sometimes lived together as couples. Patricia Palmieri found such arrangements to be so common at Wellesley College, with its all-female faculty, that they were called "Wellesley marriages." Historians disagree about the sexual nature of these relationships, but the letters and diaries of the partners provide ample proof of their love for each other and its physical expression in hugging, kissing, and sharing beds. Such marriages were often lifelong partnerships, considered, in the pre-World War I era, socially respectable. That would soon change.

Americans' social and cultural anxieties regarding immigration, racial issues, the closing of the frontier, imperial expansion following the Spanish American War, and women's new prominence in political and public life led to fears of what President Theodore Roosevelt called "race suicide." New Women were simply not having enough children, and thus "old-stock" Americans of Anglo-Saxon Protestant descent would soon lose political and cultural control of the nation to the children of foreigners. Articles on the marriage rate of college women filled the pages of popular periodicals. In vain did the Association of Collegiate Alumnae and women social scientists argue that college women married, but at a later age than other women in their generation, and that therefore it was too early to evaluate the impact of higher education on marriage and family life. And despite inconsistent statistical evidence on the marriage rates of the first generation of college women, we can tentatively conclude that as many as half remained single.

Apart from the race suicide scare, historians have noted widespread cultural concern at the turn of the century about "effeminization," particularly in religion and education. Psychologist G. Stanley Hall attacked the relationship between women teachers and adolescent boys, whom, he thought, suffered from too much feminine coddling. Through organizations such as the Boy Scouts, the publication of western novels, enthusiasm for the "strenuous life," the new prominence of male evangelicals such as Billy Sunday and "muscular Christianity," middle-class white men sought to reassert their cultural dominance.

Arguing that the growing female presence on coeducational campuses had already driven men from liberal arts courses and would soon cause male students to abandon higher education, administrators and faculty tried to limit the numbers of women students. State university presidents in the Midwest and West frequently lamented their inability to create separate women's colleges, due to inadequate funds. Private universities such as Rochester, Western Reserve, and Tufts established coordinate single-sex schools, while the University of Chicago decided on "segregation," i.e., the separation of classes for freshmen and sophomore men and women. Other private schools, like Stanford, and even some state schools, such as Michigan, imposed admissions quotas on women.

Despite this growing and ominous backlash, the campus experiences of the second generation of American college women were far more positive than those for the first generation. Their increased numbers caused universities to hire Deans of Women and additional female support staff to help women students organize housing and extracurricular activities. Alumnae returned to campus frequently to talk with students, provide career guidance, and urge involvement in the social reform movements of the day. Women students developed a rich organizational and cultural life on coeducational campuses, albeit one separate from the male students.

They formed basketball teams, debate societies, drama clubs, musical organizations, philanthropic groups (e.g., social settlement societies), and civic and political clubs. On many campuses, women had their own student government, honor societies, and even their own newspaper. Sororities, or women's fraternities, became a significant factor at coeducational schools around the turn of the century, particularly because so few universities had dormitories for women students. Although sororities created activities and social events for some women students, they excluded women from lower socioeconomic backgrounds, Jews, and African Americans. In the early 1900s African American women founded their own sororities, as did Jewish women.

Women at single-sex colleges developed an even richer campus life than their cohorts at coeducational schools. Sororities were less often found at women's colleges, which prided themselves on the inclusivity of their student life. Since their student bodies were more homogeneous in terms of social class and religion than those at coeducational universities, divisions seemed clearly injurious to community life. Indeed, both Wellesley and Barnard students banned secret societies during the 1910s. Moreover, despite the official administrative conservatism of the Seven Sisters, branches of the Intercollegiate Socialist Society and the College Equal Suffrage League (founded 1906) flourished there. Even in the South, where religious and political conservatism placed more restrictions on women students, campus life expanded greatly during this era, with students organizing to pressure faculty and administrators into granting concessions about speakers, meetings, organizations, and holidays.

Still, white women students of this generation were deeply conflicted about the career vs. marriage dilemma – most firmly believed they would have to choose one or the other. Increasingly, they decided to marry. As economist Mary Cookingham has demonstrated, the marriage rate of white college women rose steadily after 1905 and gradually became indistinguishable from that of noncollege women. Although many worked intermittently during the course of their lives, most did not undertake sustained commitments to demanding careers.

Historians have explained this phenomenon in different ways. Some attribute it wholly to the backlash against educated and professional women, and the race suicide scare. Others argue that wealthier and more fun-loving women, less purposeful than the pioneers of the first generation, started enrolling in colleges and universities in the early twentieth century, resulting in greater sociability on and off campus and higher marriage rates. Yet what little evidence we have regarding women college students' socioeconomic backgrounds suggests no changes during this era; most still came from the ranks of the upper middle classes. A modified version of that argument might be an increased acceptance among upper-middle-class men of college-educated women as acceptable wives.

Changing sexual mores in the early twentieth century also afforded college women more opportunities for unchaperoned interaction with young men. Even women's colleges started to allow male guests at proms and on other occasions. The advent of motion pictures, automobiles, cabarets, and telephones gave couples more privacy, encouraging premarital sexual contact. Nancy Cott has argued that sexual liberation was a key component of an egalitarian feminism emerging among young women in the 1910s. Questioning the ideology of separate spheres and women's special moral role, and taking advantage of improved contraceptive devices, young people foresaw possibilities for new kinds of marriages – sexually fulfilling to both partners. The more daring among them believed that women should be able to engage in nonmarital, premarital, or extramarital sex.

Marriage rates among educated women might, then, have risen because heterosexuality seemed less confining and more interesting; or alternatively, because same-sex relationships became suspect as "deviant." In the 1910s, readers of Havelock Ellis, Sigmund Freud, and their American interpreters cast a jaundiced eye on the personal partnerships among the first generation of college and professional women. "Smashes" (women students' crushes on each other) were viewed as problematic, and a plethora of advice literature, including short stories, novels, and articles in women's magazines, enjoined students to be cautious about such relationships.

The lack of research on both African American women's sexual relations and their experiences in higher education makes it difficult to compare their experiences across generations and with those of white students. The campus life of black women almost certainly became more variegated and more liberal in the early twentieth century. Spelman students, for example, worked together with male students from Morehouse College to produce a yearbook and literary magazine. At Howard University, students founded three sororities: Alpha Kappa Alpha, Delta Sigma Theta, and Zeta Phi Beta. Black students at Butler University in Indianapolis established a fourth, Sigma Gamma Rho. Alumnae of these organizations performed significant service and educational work in African American communities. Yet social regulations continued to be quite strict at the historically black colleges, a fact that some scholars attribute to concern about black women's "respectability." It is, however, worth noting that Catholic and southern white women's colleges, with similarly religious atmospheres, also maintained such regulations until well into the twentieth century.

Whatever their expectations and proclivities, the second generation of college women encountered a cultural and political postgraduation climate markedly different from that of the Progressive era. Many scholars have emphasized a break with the reform-oriented political culture of the Progressive era in favor of a more individualistic ethos in the 1920s. The virtual demise of organized feminism in the mid-twentieth century has been attributed to internal struggles over the Equal Rights Amendment in that same decade. Apart from that issue, however, many young women of the period considered feminism outmoded, irrelevant, and an unattractive manifestation of "manhating." Believing themselves the equals of men, they welcomed the freedom to combine marriage with demanding professional careers. Yet lacking or disdaining a political language to analyze and address their difficulties, many women struggled and faltered in the pursuit of equality.

And despite egalitarian hopes, women continued to encounter resistance within the professions. In the 1920s, women doctors and women lawyers abandoned single-sex professional associations in favor of integration within the American Medical Association and the American Bar Association. To their dismay, they were quickly marginalized within those organizations. And as the first generation of college women retired from faculty positions at women's colleges, administrators responded to the growing homophobia directed at Wellesley-type marriages and women's institutions by hiring married male faculty to provide a more "normal" image for their students.

Nor did the situation on college campuses during the 1920s hold much promise for the future. Paula Fass has demonstrated the overwhelmingly social concerns of both men and women students, and the dominance of campus life by fraternities and sororities. Although college women agitated for increased personal freedom, including the right to smoke, their interest in larger cultural and political matters or in their own professional futures seemed far more muted than before the war. Conscious of their social standing, and wishing to perpetuate the Protestant elite, many colleges, including women's colleges, established quotas to limit the numbers of Jewish and Catholic students, and most private institutions continued to exclude African Americans completely.

Some scholars, however, view the 1920s as more promising for professional women. Joyce Antler maintains that the creation of new lifestyles constituted a form of personalized feminism in the post-suffrage years. And Frank Stricker has urged historians not to focus on the "I traded my lawbooks for cookbooks" features in popular magazines of the 1920s, arguing that these impressionistic pieces were more than balanced by women's favorable assessments of combining marriage and career in other publications. The passage of the Sheppard-Towner Act in 1921, with its funding for women physicians, nurses, and social workers in public and maternal health; the development of psychiatric social work; and the increasing numbers of students in primary and secondary schools created additional opportunities for women professionals. In addition, some women's reform groups continued to function throughout the 1920s and 1930s, creating, for example, labor colleges for working-class women, of which the most notable was the Bryn Mawr Summer School for Women Workers. In 1926, Smith alumna and Harvard Ph.D. Ethel Puffer Howes founded the Institute for the Coordination of Women's Interests at Smith to help married women learn to balance their intellectual and professional interests with their family lives. Lois Scharf argues that feminism remained on the national agenda in the 1920s, through an intense nationwide debate over women combining careers with childrearing.

The Great Depression, however, ended that debate. Concerned about joblessness, over 80 percent of Americans told pollsters they opposed employment for married women. Federal, state, and local governments passed laws limiting married women's right to work in various professions and occupations; teachers, in particular, suffered from this legislation. The impact of the Depression on teaching was especially unfortunate for the children of immigrants, especially Jewish women, who by the 1930s were sufficiently well educated to seek teaching positions. African American women, too, were harmed by the economic crisis, with black schools and hospitals unable to maintain the level of services developed over the previous decades.

Some white women professionals did well during the 1930s. Social workers became the backbone of many New Deal relief programs. The extraordinary women's network in the Democratic Party led to positions for some of its members in the alphabet agencies of the New Deal. Nursing was also positively affected by the economic downturn. Few people could afford private duty nurses in the 1930s; and graduate nurses sought positions on hospital staffs, supplementing or replacing inexperienced student nurses, who received more classes and increased supervision. Although their pay remained low throughout the decade, graduate nurses in hospital positions were steadily employed, raising both the quality of care for patients and professional standards. An oversupply of journalists and straitened budgets caused most newspapers to adhere to a policy of hiring only one female reporter. Yet Eleanor Roosevelt did much to enhance the position of women journalists by holding her own press conferences and insisting that only female reporters attend.

We know little about the educational experiences of female high school and college students of the 1930s, or how they viewed their professional prospects. With the exception of Ruth Markowitz's work on activist Jewish women at the city colleges of New York, studies of college students' politics during the 1930s focus on men. It would be interesting to know how young women thought of prominent women of their day. Did they aspire to careers in aviation, like Amelia Earhart? Did the example of Eleanor Roosevelt inspire them to go into politics? What did they think of the glamorous career women portrayed on screen by actresses such as Katharine Hepburn and Rosalind Russell? Did they hope for positions as female editors and writers for women's magazines, or as famous columnists like Dorothy Thompson and Anne O'Hare McCormick? What did they think of the women faculty, teachers, nurses, doctors, and lawyers whom they might have known personally?

During World War II, girls continued to be the majority of high school graduates; and by the end of the 1940s, 61 percent of teenage girls were graduating from high school. Women, however, still constituted less than half of all undergraduates, largely because the military sent so many men to colleges and universities for specialized training. However, the absence of traditional male undergraduates afforded women students unprecedented opportunities for campus leadership, opened wider the doors of medical and law schools and newsrooms to white women and nursing schools to black women; and school districts relaxed limitations on teachers' right to marry. Facing a shortage of engineers, the federal government established intensive training programs for women. As with the 1930s, however, we know little about the "campus experience," the aspirations of educated women, or the activities of women professionals during the war.

Most scholars now agree that the "feminine mystique" began not in the 1950s but immediately following the war. To make room for returning veterans, entitled to educational benefits under the provisions of the 1944 GI Bill, colleges and universities cut back on the admission of women students. Female veterans also received educational benefits, but represented only 3 percent of the military during the war. As a result, only 65,000 women were educated under the GI Bill, compared to 2.25 million men. Women made up 40 percent of all college graduates in 1940, but in 1950 only 25 percent. Their share of masters' and doctoral degrees also declined in the postwar years, as professional schools and internship/clerkship programs reinstated sex-based quotas.

In the late 1940s and 1950s, psychologists, sociologists, doctors, psychiatrists, and other social commentators resurrected the debate over the appropriateness of liberal arts education for women. Women educated like men, they argued, would want to live like men, and would therefore make unhappy, neurotic wives and mothers. During the baby-boom years, when Americans married younger, had larger families, divorced less frequently, and regarded the nuclear family as a hedge against the evils of Communism, such criticisms took their toll. Educators hastened to supply ideas for female-friendly curricula, recommending, in particular, courses on marriage and family life, childrearing, and cooking. Lynn White, president of all-female Mills College in California, authored *Educating Our Daughters* in 1950, arguing for new "feminine" values in higher education to improve women's service to their families and communities.

Most women's college presidents took issue with White. Presidents of the Seven Sisters Colleges and Harold Taylor of Sarah Lawrence College, among others, fought for women's intellectual equality, although they did not attack assumptions that college women would lead primarily domestic lives. Some supporters of women's liberal arts education used the argument that the Cold War made it imperative for the United States to cultivate the scientific and linguistic skills of girls as well as boys. The Radcliffe Institute, founded by Radcliffe College President Mary Bunting in 1950, was designed to help older women regain their standing in various professional fields, including science and the arts.

In the 1940s and 1950s, black college women continued to face segregation and limited professional opportunities, mostly imposed by whites, but sometimes by black men as well. Although more black women than black men graduated from college, a trend that began in the 1920s, women held far fewer advanced and professional degrees. Pauli Murray, lawyer, civil rights activist, and Episcopal minister, criticized her fellow students at Howard University Law School for attacking Jim Crow while ignoring their own creation of "Jane Crow." In her 1956 study of four hundred members of black sororities, Jeanne Noble discussed at length the "double burden" of her subjects, as African Americans and as women. The women in Noble's study wanted education to offer them opportunities for self-fulfillment and for success as wage earners, while also preparing them for family life. Unlike white college women, they found no contradictions in those objectives. Noble also argued strongly for relaxation of the strict discipline still in effect at the historically black colleges and expressed concern about the "oversupply" of black college women compared to black college men.

During the 1960s and 1970s, the educational atmosphere changed dramatically. Endorsing Betty Friedan's analysis of the "sex-directed educators," feminists sought equity, both for women students and women faculty, in schools and colleges. New federal laws and executive orders, derived from the civil rights movement, paved the way to achieving feminists' educational goals. Between 1961 and 1965, Presidents John F. Kennedy and Lyndon B. Johnson issued a series of executive orders requiring federal contractors to "take affirmative action" to hire minorities and women, and to set goals and timetables to achieve proportional representation. In 1972, the Higher Education Amendments, and Title IX in particular, extended the protection of the Civil Rights Act of 1964 to employees of educational institutions. Although challenged on occasion, Congress has defended the provisions of Title IX when necessary. In 1988, for instance, Congress passed the Civil Rights Restoration Act, directing that the provisions of Title IX apply to entire institutions, not just federally funded programs, over President Ronald Reagan's veto.

These laws and the efforts of feminist groups to see them enforced significantly changed the face of American education. Admissions quotas against women and minorities in colleges and graduate and professional schools were gradually eliminated. Today's schools cannot have different rules governing the social conduct of students based on sex, race, or religion; they must not restrict women or minority students' participation in work study projects or federally funded internships to clerical duties; they may not discriminate against pregnant teachers; they may not attach teaching positions to coaching duties in a way that discriminates against women applicants; they must provide athletic facilities and scholarships for women as well as men. The hiring and tenuring of women and minority faculty has come under greater scrutiny; colleges are now required to advertise positions, rather than simply utilizing the "old boy" network to locate candidates. Discriminatory practices did not cease, but it became more difficult to deny jobs and promotions to women academics. Admissions quotas against women and racial and ethnic minorities in colleges, graduate, and professional schools were gradually dropped.

Spurred by government policies and their own need to attract the best students, the country's prestigious all-male colleges, including the Ivy League schools, the Little Ivy League (Amherst, Bowdoin, Williams), the University of Virginia, Catholic men's colleges and universities, and the service academies had all coeducated by the early 1970s. Similarly, many women's colleges, including Vassar, and all the Catholic schools, opened their doors to men. Top-ranked graduate and professional schools began recruiting African American, Latina/Chicana, and Asian American students.

The curriculum as well as the demographics of higher education have been transformed. Most notably, the first women's studies program, founded at San Diego State University in 1970, became both a scholarly enterprise and a forum for community activism. By 2000, over six hundred such programs existed in colleges and universities across the country. Women's studies not only revolutionized scholarship, particularly in the humanities and social sciences, but also led to research on women's education and professional roles, which addressed persistent remaining inequities. Scholars investigated such issues as the low numbers of girls and women taking mathematics and science courses, and entering technical and scientific fields; the "chilly classroom climate" in higher education; and sexual assaults/harassment at colleges and universities.

Moreover, unlike earlier advocates for women's education, modern feminists sought equality of outcomes and urged women to use their training for careers outside the home. More women entered medicine, academia, and law; fewer became schoolteachers and nurses. Many Protestant denominations appointed women clergy; Reform and Conservative Jewry opened their rabbinical seminaries to women. Some Catholics, especially political organizations of religious women, argued, though unsuccessfully, for the ordination of women as priests. And although women sometimes formed separate societies within their professions, these were explicitly feminist groups designed to bring about gender equity, not carve out a distinctive and limited "woman's sphere."

In the past twenty years, the quest for gender equality in education and the professions has taken some unpredictable twists and turns. Currently, American women constitute over half of all undergraduates. Not all these women are teenagers or young adults; returning students, some with grown children and grandchildren, have become familiar faces in college classrooms. In the early twenty-first century, as in the early twentieth, some find these demographics problematic and worry that higher education will attract ever-fewer male students.

As in the 1920s, modern feminism seems outmoded to many students, who believe gender inequities have been resolved. Yet research demonstrates the persistence of inequality, although its manifestations are often more subtle and thus harder to address. One such study found that neither male nor female teachers in elementary and high schools viewed their behavior as gender discriminatory until investigators presented them with videotapes of their classes for analysis. Research on the social attitudes of male and female college students, the next generation of professionals, shows a lack of commitment to or interest in gender equity. A recent anthropological study of both white and black women students concluded that women's professional ambitions are diverted, while in college, by peer-group pressures to find a husband.

Indeed, some educators have argued for a revival of separatism, based in part on research demonstrating that graduates of women's colleges throughout the twentieth century were two to three times as likely as women graduates of coeducational schools to be cited for career achievement. These data hold up whether the college is predominantly white or historically black; whether a Seven Sisters college or a less elite institution. The percentage of women attending single-sex colleges has been declining since the late nineteenth century; and few women's schools remain. So researchers are beginning to identify specific factors at women's colleges leading to their graduates' successes; perhaps coeducational institutions could incorporate some of those features.

The connection between women's education and their participation in public life no longer troubles most Americans; the vast majority of women, married or single, mothers or childless, work for wages outside the home. Yet professional women argue that having a feminist perspective or agenda works against their socialization into a community of colleagues. Like their sisters one hundred years ago, they have discovered that male colleagues resent discussions or charges of gender inequities, and, feeling personally attacked, sometimes retaliate. Affirmative action policies are particularly unpopular within formerly male-dominated professions, especially in those such as academia where jobs are scarce for both sexes.

American women's educational history is not a tale of unbroken progress; and today the benefits of education remain inequitably distributed. The educational attainments of white middle-class women closely match those of white middle-class men; but women with lower socioeconomic standing and in some ethnic and racial groups remain disadvantaged. The continued greater educational attainment of women can create tensions within communities of color. Gender equality within schools at all levels of the educational system remains elusive, particularly since inequities may result from students' interactions with each other as much as from institutional constraints or teachers' behavior.

Yet despite the persistent social and political conservatism of educators, schools, and sometimes classmates, American women have found education liberating.

Whether undertaken for self-fulfillment, or for religious, cultural, or professional purposes, schooling has allowed girls and women to imagine, and sometimes realize, possibilities beyond their appointed sphere. Education is an inefficient and insufficient means of achieving equality, but it surely is a necessary condition for doing so.

BIBLIOGRAPHY

Antler, Joyce (1986) *Lucy Sprague Mitchell: The Making of a Modern Woman*. New Haven, CT: Yale University Press.

Cookingham, Mary E. (1984) "Bluestockings, Spinsters, and Pedagogues: Women College Graduates, 1865–1910," *Population Studies* 38, pp. 349–64.

Drachman, Virginia G. (1998) *Sisters in Law: Women Lawyers in Modern American History*. Cambridge, MA: Harvard University Press.

Eisenmann, Linda (ed.) (1998) *Historical Dictionary of Women's Education in the United States*. Westport, CT: Greenwood Press.

Fass, Paula S. (1977) *The Damned and the Beautiful: American Youth in the 1920s*. New York: Oxford University Press.

Fitzpatrick, Ellen (1990) *Endless Crusade: Women Social Scientists and Progressive Reform*. New York: Oxford University Press.

Garrison, Dee (1979) *Apostles of Culture: the Public Librarian and American Society, 1876–1920*. New York: Free Press.

Glazer, Penina Migdal and Slater, Miriam (1987) *Unequal Colleagues: The Entrance of Women into the Professions, 1890–1940*. New Brunswick, NJ: Rutgers University Press.

Gordon, Lynn D. (1989) "Race, Class, and the Bonds of Womanhood at Spelman Seminary, 1881–1923," *History of Higher Education Annual* 9, pp. 7–32.

Gordon, Lynn D. (1990) *Gender and Higher Education in the Progressive Era*. New Haven, CT: Yale University Press.

Herbst, Jurgen (1989) *And Sadly Teach: Teacher Education and Professionalization in American Culture*. Madison: University of Wisconsin Press.

Higginbotham, Evelyn Brooks (1993) *Righteous Discontent: The Women's Movement in the Black Baptist Church, 1880–1920*. Cambridge, MA: Harvard University Press.

Higginson, Thomas Wentworth (1859) "Ought Women to Learn the Alphabet?" *Atlantic Monthly* 3, pp. 137ff.

Hine, Darlene Clark (1989) *Black Women in White: Racial Conflict and Cooperation in the Nursing Profession, 1890–1950*. Bloomington: Indiana University Press.

Holland, Dorothy C. and Eisenhart, Margaret A. (1990) *Educated in Romance: Women, Achievement, and College Culture*. Chicago: University of Chicago Press.

Horowitz, Helen Lefkowitz (1984) *Alma Mater: Design and Experience in the Women's Colleges from their Nineteenth-century Beginnings to the 1930s*. New York: Alfred A. Knopf.

Hummer, Patricia M. (1979) *The Decade of Elusive Promise: Professional Women in the United States, 1920–1930*. Ann Arbor, MI: University Microfilms Research Press.

McCandless, Amy Thompson (1999) *The Past in the Present: Women's Higher Education in the Twentieth-century American South*. Tuscaloosa: University of Alabama Press.

Markowitz, Ruth Jacknow (1993) *My Daughter the Teacher: Jewish Teachers in the New York City Schools*. New Brunswick, NJ: Rutgers University Press.

Mihesuah, Devon Abbott (1993) *Cultivating the Rosebuds: The Education of Women at the Cherokee Female Seminary, 1851–1909*. Urbana: University of Illinois Press.

Morantz-Sanchez, Regina (1985) *Sympathy and Science: Women Physicians in American Medicine*. New York: Oxford University Press.

Muncy, Robyn (1991) *Creating a Female Dominion in American Reform, 1890–1935*. New York: Oxford University Press.

Murphy, Marjorie (1990) *Blackboard Unions: The AFT and the NEA, 1900–1980*. Ithaca, NY: Cornell University Press.

Noble, Jeanne (1956) *The Negro Woman's College Education*. New York: Teacher's College Press.

Palmieri, Patricia A. (1995) *In Adamless Eden: The Community of Women Faculty at Wellesley*. New Haven, CT: Yale University Press.

Pascoe, Peggy (1990) *Relations of Rescue: The Search for Female Moral Authority in the American West, 1874–1939*. New York: Oxford University Press.

Reverby, Susan (1987) *Ordered to Care: The Dilemma of American Nursing, 1850–1945*. New York: Cambridge University Press.

Rosenberg, Rosalind (1982) *Beyond Separate Spheres: Intellectual Roots of Modern Feminism*. New Haven, CT: Yale University Press.

Rossiter, Margaret (1982) *Women Scientists in America: Struggles and Strategies to 1940*. Baltimore: Johns Hopkins University Press.

Rossiter, Margaret (1995) *Women Scientists in America: Before Affirmative Action, 1940–1972*. Baltimore: Johns Hopkins University Press.

Rousmaniere, John (1970) "Cultural Hybrid in the Slums: The College Woman and the Settlement House, 1889–1894," *American Quarterly* 22, pp. 45–66.

Rury, John L. (1991) *Education and Women's Work: Female Schooling and the Division of Labor in Urban America, 1870–1930*. Albany: State University of New York Press.

Sadker, Myra and Sadker, David (1995) *Failing at Fairness: How Our Schools Cheat Girls*. New York: C. Scribner's Sons.

Sanday, Peggy Reeves (1990) *Fraternity Gang Rape: Sex, Brotherhood, and Privilege on Campus*. New York: New York University Press.

Scharf, Lois (1980) *To Work and to Wed: Female Employment, Feminism, and the Great Depression*. Westport, CT: Greenwood Press.

Shaw, Stephanie J. (1996) *What a Woman Ought to Be and to Do: Black Professional Women Workers During the Jim Crow Era*. Chicago: University of Chicago Press.

Solomon, Barbara Miller (1985) *In the Company of Educated Women: A History of Women and Higher Education in America*. New Haven, CT: Yale University Press.

Stricker, Frank (1976) "Cookbooks and Law Books: The Hidden History of Career Women in 20th-century America," *Journal of Social History* 10, pp. 1–19.

Tidball, M. Elizabeth et al. (1999) *Taking Women Seriously: Lessons and Legacies for Educating the Majority*. Phoenix, AZ: Oryx Press.

Tyack, David and Hansot, Elisabeth (1990) *Learning Together: A History of Coeducation in American Public Schools*. New Haven, CT: Yale University Press.

Warren, Donald (ed.) (1989) *American Teachers: Histories of a Profession at Work*. New York: Macmillan.

Weiler, Kathleen (1999) *Country Schoolwomen*. Berkeley: University of California Press.

CHAPTER FIFTEEN

Wage-earning Women

ANNELISE ORLECK

AMERICAN popular culture has, at different times, ignored and idealized wage-earning women. Historical scholarship has been shaped both by these long periods of invisibility and by the dominance of a few vivid icons. Early in the twentieth century, progressive journalists introduced to the American reading public the "farbrente maydlakh" (fiery girls) who labored in sweatshops sewing the vogue fashions of the day. These young immigrant workers made dramatic cameo appearances as the firebrands igniting spontaneous walkouts and massive garment strikes in the years before World War I. Then just as suddenly they disappeared from public view, retreating to Brooklyn and Queens neighborhoods to raise nice Jewish and Italian children. Or so the popular story goes. Mid-century Rosie the Riveter appeared: sweaty, muscled, and tough but ultimately womanly because she was doing her feminine duty in supporting her man. The woman behind the man behind the gun, she kept our World War II soldiers in planes, ships, and armaments. If she had to leave her children in daycare centers or with extended family it was okay, for a while. Then she too allegedly returned to hearth and home.

In the wake of 1960s feminist activism, images of both young working women and working mothers again generated popular discussion. Self-help books by the score, surveys, television news, and women's magazines all introduced the newest icon, "supermom," representing the millions of women who, now with some measure of public support, twisted themselves into knots juggling wage work and children. Even Hollywood lauded the working mother, harboring a particular affection for tough, loving waitresses played by Michelle Pfeiffer and Helen Hunt among others. After years of representation as loyal sidekicks, simmering sexpots, or sexless Jane Hathaways, rebellious secretaries finally found some popular vindication. In the offbeat 1980 film, *9 to 5*, so titled for the pioneering clerical workers' union of the same name, Lily Tomlin, Jane Fonda, and Dolly Parton ended sexual harassment in typical Hollywood fashion, not by organizing or picketing but by hog-tying their sleazy boss. There was talk of a sequel in the wake of the Hill–Thomas hearings, the Paula Jones suit, and the impeachment of Bill Clinton, which gave fresh currency to the issue of sexual harassment in the workplace.

Precisely because these evocative icons have shaped popular conceptions of the lives and history of wage-earning women in the United States, they have also influenced scholars of working women. The immigrant women who filled early twentieth-century industrial shops have captured the attention of numerous historians who have evoked them in a variety of seemingly contradictory but all partially accurate incarnations: as hot-headed momentary militants, politically sophisticated career activists, and enthusiastic modern consumers enraged by the lack of a clean, safe place at work where they could hang their fashionable hats. Heated interpretive battles have also engaged historians examining the complicated realities underlying the promise of temporary independence that "Rosie" sold to millions of American women in the 1940s. Historians differ over whether the wartime mobilization of defense workers opened any lasting opportunities for wage-earning women. They disagree about the impact of unionization on working women's class and gender consciousness. Indeed, historical studies have raised doubts about the relevance of making any general claims about the effect of World War II on American women, given the ways that race, class, and national origin so dramatically affected prewar, wartime, and postwar work opportunities. (For example, while wartime defense jobs doubled the percentage of Chinese women laboring in professional, managerial, or clerical jobs – the so-called primary sector – to nearly 60 percent, the increases for black women were far more limited, with fewer than 18 percent moving out of the service sector jobs where they had long been concentrated.)

Analysts of American women's work during the second half of the twentieth century have followed the boom in "pink-collar" and service sector employment, with many of them choosing to focus on clerical, retail, and service workers. Though much of the literature on recent trends in wage-earning women's organizing has come from anthropologists and sociologists, the nationwide upsurge of rebellious activity among clerical, hospital, hotel, and communications workers since the 1970s has energized historical debates about women's motivations for unionizing, about the influence of gender on contemporary modes of organizing, and about what impact these new majority-female unions will have on the form and politics of the twenty-first century labor movement.

The fiery girls, Rosie, the rebellious secretaries, and smart-talking waitresses, and the historians who have examined them, illuminate important dynamics in working women's history. But they also obscure the tremendous range of experiences, kinds of work, temporal and regional variations that have distinguished working women in this country one from another. Historians of working women have tended to pay closer attention to some workers and forms of work than to others. The icons have all been white; most have been industrial or clerical workers. There are fewer histories of women of color in the workforce, though regional economies and public policy in many parts of the country have been based on unexamined assumptions about these women's "natural" capacities for both productive and reproductive labor. The centrality of African American, Chicana, and Asian American women to agricultural and service sector work makes such histories vital to any larger understanding of the evolution of women and wage work in the United States.

The small but growing number of historians who have written about women of color in the workforce have illustrated key commonalities in the experiences of America's laboring women, perhaps most importantly the inseparable and interactive relationship between family work and wage labor. But they have also made clear that there have been some fundamental differences in the experience, treatment, and representation of wage-earning women of color. These scholars have opened up important theoretical questions about the intersections of gender, class, and race, the colonization of women's bodies, and the ways that working women of color – particularly domestic and agricultural workers – have been used as foils against which white women measured their own superior status. The literature on working women of color has also helped to break the hold of the icons. Just as popular representations of working women have rarely included imagery of domestic workers, tenant farm wives, or immigrant prostitutes on the waterfront in old San Francisco, so too have we had fewer analyses of this kind of woman worker than we have of others. But, increasingly, historians are uncovering fascinating details about the lives of these less well-known women workers. As their histories come to be integrated with the better-known stories, we are beginning finally to shake up popular as well as scholarly notions of women's relationship to waged labor in the twentieth century.

With all its peaks and valleys, it must be said that the history of wage-earning women is one of the richest and best-developed subfields in US women's history. The quality, range, and creativity of the vast outpouring of scholarship on wage-earning women since the early 1970s make this thirty-year period one of the most fertile in the historiography of American women. The task of writing this essay has been both the more daunting and the more exciting for it. What follows is in no way intended to be a thoroughgoing historiography of wage-earning women in the United States. Instead, it is an attempt at sketching the history and topography of the field in such a way as to emphasize some of its most important contributions and also to suggest areas where more work might be done.

An Historical Perspective: The Long, Slow Emergence of a Field

Writing on wage-earning women in this country has long been moved and shaped by historians and social scientists who supported the labor movement, regulatory legislation, and grassroots activism by women workers. Feeling themselves faced by complex and sometimes conflicting challenges, scholars of working women have often tried to address several audiences simultaneously – other scholars, government policy makers, activists, and sometimes working women themselves. Speaking in multiple voices, seeking interaction with as well as inspiration from organized working women, scholarship on wage-earning women has both chronicled and been part of the history of working women and the evolution of laws affecting them.

The most fertile periods in the historiography of US working women have, not surprisingly, coincided with bursts of feminist activity nationally. The first major outpouring of scholarship on the subject arose out of feminist social reform in the Progressive era. Women journalists and social scientists anxious to provide evidence of the need for governmental regulation of the industrial workplace published a series of exposés and workplace studies early in the century documenting working conditions, wages, hours, clothing, and leisure preferences of "the working girl." These studies by activist researchers, most importantly social investigator Mary Van Kleeck, became a part of the rationale for a developing social welfare state with a particular interest in what policy historian Mimi Abramovitz has called "regulating the lives of women."

Van Kleeck and other scholars testified at public hearings, served on government committees, and worked with public and private agencies to shape legislation affecting poor and working women. Their political vision and their scholarship were shaped by the maternalist social welfare vision of the settlement house movement, out of which some of them came, as well as the environmentalist can-do spirit of Progressive-era social science. And so they spoke in the language of uplift and protection. From regulation of hours and safety conditions to minimum wage and maternity leave, this body of legislation was founded on notions of women workers' differences from male workers. Fiercely defended by most women labor leaders and their middle-class allies against assaults by conservative courts, manufacturers' associations, and feminists focused on abstract notions of equality, these laws almost certainly improved the lives of millions of working women. Indeed, despite lackluster enforcement and diluted goals, the body of safety laws may well be said to have saved untold numbers of lives. Still, regulatory legislation aimed specifically at women workers also reinforced and institutionalized notions of gender difference in the twentieth-century welfare state. While these laws unquestionably protected many women workers, they limited opportunities for many others into the 1990s. In the century's final decade a suit by women workers for a Vermont plumbing systems manufacturer finally overturned most of the remaining legal regulations mandating what kinds of work women can and cannot do.

The detailed literature left by early twentieth-century activist women scholars also laid an important part of the foundation for a later history of wage-earning women. Among the best-known early products of this scholarship were two general studies of women's relation to trade union activism written by sympathetic observers: Alice Henry's *Women and the Labor Movement* (1923) and Theresa Wolfson's *The Woman Worker and the Trade Unions* (1926). Henry, an Australian-born labor journalist, created a vivid record of working women's organizing campaigns, strikes, and union activism in the first two decades of the century. An activist in the Chicago Women's Trade Union League, Henry derived much of her material from the pages of the National Women's Trade Union League publication, *Life and Labour*, which she edited from 1911 to 1915. Henry's study was a product of the gender politics of the League, a woman-centered narrative emphasizing the liberatory potential of cross-class sisterhood. Arguing that working-class women could function as something of a bridge between the labor and feminist movements, Henry foreshadowed a later generation of studies of women and trade union activism that would come out of the 1970s feminist movement.

Wolfson, a Brooklyn College professor of labor economics, set the stage for another strain in later histories. Focusing on relations between men and women in labor unions, she set out to explain the absence of women in the higher levels of union leadership. In the process of researching that question Wolfson came to believe that an antagonistic climate toward women in labor unions depressed the levels of women's involvement and limited the effectiveness of even devoted women activists. While writing the book, Wolfson conducted an extensive correspondence with the sensitive and volatile International Ladies' Garment Workers' Union (ILGWU) education secretary, Fannia Cohn, whose stories of disrespect and verbal abuse by male union officials provided a strong emotional undercurrent for the well-documented scholarly narrative. Because few historians attempted to publish analyses of women's trade union activism over the next fifty years, these texts remained unusually influential, framing and shaping the questions of feminist historians writing half a century later.

Henry and Wolfson strongly believed in the possibility of a bread-and-roses, as opposed to a bread-and-butter, labor movement. Their faith was reinforced by the garment and textile strikes that had swept up hundreds of thousands of young women workers from Brooklyn, New York, to Kalamazoo, Michigan. These "uprisings" had brought 40 percent of women garment workers into unions by 1919. They also revealed deep tensions within "the women's trades" between a bureaucratic leadership and a militant grassroots. Tens of thousands of women left the garment unions during the 1920s as increasingly conservative male leaders stamped out shop-floor protests demanding a more democratic labor movement. A decade earlier, militant strikes involving hundreds of thousands of women as well as men had fueled the hopes of "allies" like Wolfson and Henry that an egalitarian gender-integrated labor movement was the wave of the future. By the 1920s, destructive battles for the "soul" of the garment unions left them pessimistic about whether there was any future at all for women in the trade unions.

By the mid-1920s many women unionists and allied scholars had hung their hopes on a labor education movement that had its roots in the aspirations of the militant young garment strikers of the previous decade. Labor education would be the means to build egalitarian and socially conscious unions that, as Fannia Cohn put it, appealed to a worker's head as well as her stomach. The idea that unions should provide their members with a progressive education as well as the means to earn a living drew together union activists (many of them women) and sympathetic academics, Wolfson among them. From the 1910s through the 1940s, worker education programs attracted economists, historians, social workers, and literary critics who saw in the labor movement the promise of social transformation. Volunteering their time, they came to teach in Fannia Cohn's ILGWU education department courses, or at experimental institutions like Bryn Mawr Summer School for Women Workers, or Brookwood Labor College, and these teaching experiences affected their writing. They determined to create readable, accessible scholarship that was relevant and useful to men and women in the trade union movement, at the same time as they worked to make the study of labor unions and of women and work respectable.

In the pre- and post-World War II years the explicit political mission of labor education made its practitioners vulnerable to a powerful conservative backlash both within the labor movement and culture-wide. Radicals were purged from trade unions and university faculties. Voices for greater gender equity in the labor movement came to be associated with Communism and the dreaded charge of "dual unionism." Brookwood College and the Bryn Mawr Summer School both came under attack by conservative forces within the labor movement and faded away. By the late 1940s few scholars addressed labor questions at all, and those who did saw themselves as studying a largely, if not exclusively, male world.

As a result the early scholars of working women had almost no effect on the field of labor history as it developed during the 1940s, 1950s, and early 1960s. "Institutionalist" historians displayed little interest in women, shop-floor workers, or the lives of working-class people beyond the workplace and the union hall. Accounts by former union officials, for example, garment union leaders Benjamin Stolberg and Abraham Bisno, were dismissive or denigrating in their references to women in the labor movement. Women appeared rarely in these accounts either as grassroots activists or as leaders. And when they did, the references tended to replicate prevailing gender ideologies. Women as a group were portrayed not as workers but as transients walking across the public field of vision only briefly before turning to their "natural" roles as wives and mothers. Individual women who devoted themselves to labor activism were too often described with deep ambivalence as beloved but pitied misfits, courageous but somehow "off." Professional labor historians were less sarcastic but displayed little more interest in women.

The 1960s wrought all sorts of transformations in historical writing, as activist scholars once again sought to forge links between academic research and social protest movements. Calls for a rewriting of American history "from the bottom up" gave rise to a "new labor history," as well as new political, social, and women's histories with the focus shifted from a small leadership elite to the mass of ordinary men and women. Taking inspiration from E. P. Thompson's classic, *The Making of the English Working Class* (1963), and from numerous works by the equally influential American historian Herbert Gutman, the "new labor historians" moved beyond the shop floor to examine associational culture, rituals, and community life across working-class America. The new labor history, Mari Jo Buhle wrote in a 1989 chronicle of the relationship between labor and women's history, "strove to envision class as a culturally as well as materially constructed phenomenon" and it illustrated in vivid detail that "conscious or collective expressions [of class] take many forms beyond trade unions and political parties" (1989: 57). Class and class consciousness were neither uniform nor static, radical historians argued. They were grounded in local and regional cultures, in generational identities, in workplace skills, and in ethnic and immigrant community life.

In their attempt to capture and explain the wide range of forms and expressions that working-class consciousness and culture took, the practitioners of the new working-class history incorporated sociological and anthropological methodologies and insights as well as techniques of quantitative data analysis. Three decades of fascinating working-class community studies flowed from the ferment of the late 1960s, creating a richly textured history of everyday working-class life in the United States. Among other contributions, some of these studies offered important insights into the ways that race and ethnicity have structured and fractured class formation and identity. Still, this literature remained almost completely male-centered. Gender, when it was discussed, did not modify or revise concepts of class in any substantive way; and women tended to appear in short, bracketed sections or described in relationship to male workers as wives, sisters, mothers, or daughters even if they worked for wages and protested alongside male neighbors and relations.

Renewed scholarly attention to wage-earning women came instead out of the larger women's history movement that flowered in the 1970s. Influenced by classical as well as 1960s Marxism, by the theoretical dynamism and methodological creativity of many of the new working-class histories, and perhaps most importantly by the rich variety of feminist politics sweeping the country, a new generation of women's historians began to make the history of wage-earning women in the United States a field in its own right. Not unlike earlier scholars of women and labor, 1970s pioneers of working-class women's history were driven by practical political questions as much as they were by a desire to research and theorize the relationship between class and gender. "Where are the Organized Women Workers?" economist Wolfson had asked in 1925. Fifty years later, historian Alice Kessler-Harris asked exactly the same question in a *Feminist Studies* article that blazed the path for a new explosion of women's labor history.

The first historical studies of women and labor grew directly out of Wolfson's question and Kessler-Harris's reframing of it. Very much in the tradition of earlier labor educators, the authors of these early studies hoped to increase respect for working women in and outside the labor movement. Barbara Wertheimer's *We Were There: The Story of Working Women in America* (1977) traced working women's protest from the colonial era to the Lawrence textile strike of 1912. The narrative, like the title, aimed to restore women to their rightful place in the history of American labor activism. Wertheimer was a labor educator and an important early figure in the Coalition of Labor Union Women, a working-class feminist federation that grew out of the struggles for race and gender equity that rocked the labor movement during the 1960s. She wrote in clear prose for a general readership, hoping that the example of earlier women activists would inspire working women in the 1970s and 1980s. Two years later, Philip Foner – a venerable old-Left labor historian, released a 1,500-page, two-volume study entitled *Women and the American Labor Movement: From the First Trade Unions to the Present.* Foner, former education director for the International Fur and Leather Workers' Union, had already written multi-volume histories of the general labor movement and of the ambivalent relationship between black workers and organized labor. Like Wertheimer, he was writing for a labor movement audience as much as he was for fellow historians. Paying homage to those who had begun to examine life outside of the workplace and the union hall, he rightly insisted that women's involvement in organized labor activism had yet to be chronicled. Foner's and Wertheimer's lucid narratives became sourcebooks both for labor education programs and for academic historians.

From the late 1970s through the mid-1980s there was an astonishing burst of creativity among historians of women and work. New studies in the field ranged across time from the colonial era to World War II, and across occupations from textile mills to office work, from retail sales and domestic labor to nursing and librarianship. Historians linked gender segregation of labor to the development of capitalism and the construction of class and gender relations. They documented the increase in wage labor force participation by married women during the Depression of the 1930s and the contradictory ways that the double-edged sword of economic necessity cut and reshaped expectations of women's proper role. They disagreed about the relative weight of domestic ideologies and work experience in shaping wage-earning women's consciousness. And they examined the history of coalition building between working women, working-class men, and middle- and upper-class feminists.

Meredith Tax, Mari Jo Buhle, and Nancy Schrom Dye all published studies in 1980–1 that examined early twentieth-century attempts at cross-class and cross-gender coalition building among Progressive and Socialist activists. Tax looked at a variety of Socialist, Progressive, feminist, and trade union alliances, Buhle at women in the Socialist movement, and Dye focused on the New York Women's Trade Union League. All three dramatically evoked the fragility of relations between women across class lines and between women and men within the labor and Socialist movements. Each unearthed histories of coalitions that were, sooner or later, eroded or exploded by internal tensions. These texts were both shaped by and, in part, aimed at 1970s activists who had their own experiences with the difficult art of coalition politics.

These attempts to make sense of the forces driving and destroying historical alliances laid important theoretical groundwork for later historians of working women by concretizing what Joan Kelly had called in 1976 "the methodological implications of women's history." Kelly credited women's historians with broadening "our conception of historical change itself... to include the relation of the sexes." But that was not enough. "What now needs to be worked out," she insisted, "are the connections between changes in class and sex relations" (1976: 817). Tax, among others, accepted the challenge. "Much Marxist history," she wrote, "contains an accurate picture of what has happened to working class men as they have been affected by changes in their economic and social life. Once we know as much about what has happened to working class women as their very different lives become caught up in the same developments, we will be able to write the history of the whole class" (1980: 15). Some historians of working-class women were even more ambitious, Mari Jo Buhle would later argue, looking back from the more sober vantage point of 1989. Their goal in attempting to theorize and historicize the ever-changing links between gender and class was nothing less, wrote Buhle, than "to recast the entire narrative structure of American history" (1989: 61).

Alice Kessler-Harris took a good stab at doing exactly that in her sweeping study, *Out to Work: A History of Wage-earning Women in the United States* (1982). Kessler-Harris traced women's increasing integration into the paid labor force from the colonial era through the 1970s, linking trends in women's paid labor with evolving domestic gender ideologies, technological and economic transformations, internal migrations, and mass immigration. She factored in ethnic differences and cross-class relations, and measured the impact of the battle between women over "protective labor legislation" on the developing welfare state. Well before the emergence of whiteness studies, she offered the beginnings of an analysis of the ways that constructions of white womanhood segregated the labor force, dividing black from white native-born working women in the American South, and white immigrants from Chinese immigrant women in the West.

One of the signal achievements of the book was the way it wove together women's unpaid domestic work with wage labor, illuminating the ways that both interacted with changes in cultural expectations of women. As far back as the late 1930s, maverick Communist Party theorist Mary Inman had argued that women's reproductive and unpaid domestic labor in the home had economic value and was as essential to sustaining industrial capitalism as was factory production. Several feminist political and economic theorists picked up and elaborated on that theme during the 1970s. In the 1980s historians began to concretize that assertion and to factor it into their analyses of social and economic change. Researching and tracing those connections over time, Kessler-Harris argued, also would help historians with the thorny task of illuminating working-class women's consciousness.

"Women's work," Kessler-Harris wrote in the conclusion to *Out to Work*,

> has to be seen not as divided between family work and wage work, but as all of a piece . . . Women may perform one kind of task or another at a given moment of the day or cycle in their lives. They may choose to reject one or the other role entirely, their behavior and their opportunities indelibly influenced by ideology, culture, and socialization. Thus, shifts in technology and labor force needs, the changing structure and function of the family, and changing ideas about women and their roles are intertwined – as dependent on each other as the separate strands of a braid. Like a braid, these strands may be parted for purposes of analysis, but to look at one without the others is to compound illusion. (1982: 322)

In a similarly ambitious and groundbreaking book published in 1985, Jacqueline Jones traced the linkage between family and waged work among African American women from slavery through the 1970s. In *Labor of Love, Labor of Sorrow*, Jones warned against adopting a "consensus view of American working women's history" that obscures black women's experiences by incorrectly subsuming them under those of white workers (1985: 6). The singularly exploitive slave labor system fundamentally distinguished perceptions of, and historical realities for, black women workers. Since slavery, Jones showed, black women's work experiences have continued to be shaped by race as well as sex segregation of the labor force. In part due to the low wages earned by black men, black married women have had a far higher rate of workforce participation than white married women. Though black women workers shared with their white counterparts "the problems of low pay, pink collar 'ghettoization,' sexual harassment, political assaults on reproductive rights, and the lack of quality and affordable child care," they have historically made and currently continue to earn less than white women, white men, and black men (1985: 325–6).

Jones made painfully clear the ways that images of black women and work constructed under slavery continued to have resonance in twentieth-century public policy formulation. From post-Reconstruction state laws tying African Americans to the land to the 1965 Moynihan Report, with its powerful effect on social welfare policy makers, black women have been alternately condemned as emasculating "matriarchs" whose participation in waged labor made them overbearing at home, and as parasites when they accept public assistance that might allow them to stay home with young children. Jones wrote:

> The general lack of understanding about black women's work and family roles is particularly significant because it has had such disastrous consequences for federal social policy. It is a cruel historical irony that scholars and policymakers alike have taken the manifestations of black women's oppression and twisted them into the argument that a powerful black matriarchy exists. The persistent belief that any woman who fulfills a traditional male role, either as breadwinner or household head, wields some sort of all-encompassing power over her spouse and children is belied by the experiences of black working women . . . Though perhaps "freed" or "liberated" from narrow sex role conventions, they remained tied to overwhelming wage-earning and child-rearing responsibilities. (1985: 7)

A decade after the first publication of *Labor of Love*, Jones updated her book to show the persistence of race, sex, and class discrimination against African American working women, who continued to be "disproportionately represented in jobs with obvious and dramatic health hazards," while being concentrated in sectors of the workforce least likely to carry health insurance. In a particularly frightening illustration of the links between home and workplace, Jones reminded readers that "at the same time these women were more likely to live in areas plagued by hazardous waste sites – places like the Mississippi Delta's 'Cancer Alley' or the toxic dumping grounds of Warren County, North Carolina" (1995: 329–30).

Jones's allusions to the emerging "environmental justice" movement were picked up by other scholars and journalists who, in the 1990s, began to document the role played by African American women and other women of color in recasting American environmentalism through community-based protests against toxic dumping that brought together their roles as workers and mothers. One particularly dynamic environmental justice leader, Texan Patsy Ruth Oliver, explained in a 1993 interview the way that toxics had illustrated the links between home and work. She was the recipient, she explained, of a dubious honor. She both lived and worked on Environmental Protection Agency (EPA) Super Fund sites. (Super Fund was created by Congress in 1980 to clean up the nation's worst toxic waste dumps.) As she investigated her own situation, she came to understand that this was a reality shared predominantly by working-class people of color.

From the community organizations created by women like Oliver, to the national black women's groups whose trajectory and activism were traced by Deborah Gray White in her sweeping study, *Too Heavy a Load: Black Women in Defense of Themselves, 1894–1994* (1999), working-class black women have grappled with and developed activist ideologies that challenged intersecting oppressions based on race, class, and gender. Historians chronicling their experience have had to theorize and give narrative expression to those social and political complexities. That task has been taken up by a growing number of women's historians since the 1970s, following the lead of

Jones and White, Vicki Ruíz, Elizabeth Clark-Lewis, Darlene Clark Hine, and others – all of whom laid foundations for a historiography of working-class women of color in the United States that both intersected with and diverged from the larger historiography of wage-earning women.

Organizing, Consuming, and Recreating: Historians and Working Women since the 1970s

Both Jacqueline Jones's warning against creating a consensus history of American working women and Alice Kessler-Harris's caveat about misleading attempts to separate the history of family labor from that of wage work apply as well to those who write historiographic essays. Historians have set forth a staggering range of narratives and analyses of women and work over the past thirty years. In the interests of brevity and for the purposes of analysis I have been obliged here both to lump together and to separate historians of wage-earning women into neat categories. These categories are to some extent misleading. The authors noted below both differ from one another and interact with one another far more than is reflected in the following summaries of their work. Many of these historians confer with one another, build on one another's work, refine one another's analyses, and address overlapping concerns. Still, their emphases and the routes they have taken to assessing both consciousness and action have been different.

One important strand of the post-1970s scholarship flows from Theresa Wolfson's search for organized women workers, or more directly from Kessler-Harris's reframing of Wolfson. Politically oriented historians beginning with James Kenneally and Sharon Hartman Strom in the early 1980s and later including Stephen Norwood, Elizabeth Faue, Vicki Ruíz, and myself, among others, have lavished much attention on women's labor activism. Seeking to make sense of working-class women's politics, these historians have built their analyses around questions of relationship: between women workers, male union leaders, middle-class feminists, and the expanding state apparatus. This literature is rooted in an abundance of documentary evidence left by middle-class progressive women and union men, a much smaller body of written sources left by working-class women leaders, and important oral history interviews with women labor organizers. For a variety of reasons, including the richness of the source base for that period, a large percentage of these women's labor historians have focused on the first half of the twentieth century.

This literature has transformed historical understandings of the early twentieth-century labor and woman's suffrage movements and of the progressive and New Deal-era government regulation of workplace and living conditions for the working poor. It has become clear that working-class women played instrumental roles in each of these movements, contributing organizing strategies, political and social goals that reflected an integrated and shifting gender–class consciousness – a political vision that some have called industrial feminism. Robin Miller Jacoby and Susan Stone Wong traced the expression of that vision in labor education programs. Others explored links between the personal and political networks that industrial feminists established. Personally and politically, women labor activists walked a fine line in alternately supportive and frustrating relationships with working-class men in the labor movement and with middle-class women in progressive reform associations and later in the Roosevelt-era Democratic Party.

Framed by an analysis that sees gender, class, and ethnicity as continually constructing one another, as dynamic forces shaping social relations rather than as static identities, this scholarship has moved wage-earning women from the periphery to the center of American historical inquiry. We now find several generations of activist wage-earning women operating in a complex nexus of shifting alliances and power relationships with the male union leaders who dominated the old labor history and with the affluent women reformers whose contributions to suffrage and progressive reform were all that most high school and college students knew of American women's history just a few years ago. Positioning working-class women as political actors has opened up the borders and recast the stage of American political history.

Key to the reconceptualization of American political history was the work of historians who argued that politics happened on women's turf as well as men's, on neighborhood streetcorners, in food markets, in kitchens and living rooms and bedrooms as often as it did in union halls, on capital steps, and in voting booths. Political activities in the so-called "domestic sphere" often took different forms and expressed different goals than did conventional male politics. Still, historians of working-class women's politics have clearly shown that these women's activities influenced public sector politics as strongly as unions and political parties shaped women's consciousness and politics at home and in their neighborhoods. Studies of housewives' protests against the high cost of food and housing during the first half of the twentieth century strongly suggest a cross-fertilization between labor and Socialist politics and a tradition of housewife actions around subsistence issues that can be traced back to the eighteenth-century American colonies as well as to Europe. The influence of union ideology on women strikers was clear even to contemporaries. On June 1, 1908, one *New York Times* reporter began his discussion of a meat boycott this way: "When East Siders don't like something they strike." The work of historians Paula Hyman and Dana Frank has shown that such cost-of-living strikes also influenced the politics of the labor movement, which began to organize "at the point of consumption" as well as at points of production. By the Depression, housewife protesters demanded and received a hearing from their elected representatives locally and in Washington. As consumer consciousness grew in the 1930s, these militant working-class housewives allied themselves with a labor-based social consumer movement, critiquing individualist consumer strategies. Their legacy can be found in rent control legislation, price supports, public housing bills, and community control of schools.

Ardis Cameron, in a groundbreaking article entitled "Bread and Roses Revisited" (1985), and in her book *Radicals of the Worst Sort* (1993), has shown that we cannot fully understand even conventional political activities like workplace strikes without examining the way that women organizing in working-class neighborhoods infused union battles with concerns rooted in home and community as well as the workplace. Re-envisioning the political contours of the Lawrence mill strike of 1912, Cameron wrote:

> housewives and operatives blended and mixed to form a great human chain of marching strikers, merging issues of the home with those of the workplace. Who could tell where the outrage of low wages ended and the "lash of youthful hunger" began? By what alchemy were poor health, child mortality, and filthy streets separated from shop floor issues of overwork, poor conditions and declining wages? Linking arms and pressing their claims shoulder to shoulder, women gave a totality to worker militancy, which they themselves defined as a "fight for bread and roses." (1993: 3)

This politics of integration, linking women's and men's spheres, workplace and community, Cameron argues, "struck a deep and responsive chord in an America undergoing rapid and dramatic change" (1993: 3). Writing about African American and a handful of white washerwomen in Atlanta thirty years earlier, Tera Hunter found the same "totality to worker militancy" as striking washerwomen made use of existing social and worksite networks, went door to door and used peer pressure on strikebreakers to win a city-wide increase in the rates that washerwomen could charge for their work and a simultaneous enhancement of their status both within the black community and the city at large. "The washerwomen . . . exercised remarkable leverage in the face of class, gender and racial hostility," Hunter concludes. "White employers certainly had the power to confine black women to domestic work, but not the unilateral power to determine how and under what conditions that labor would be performed. African-American women's pragmatic adaptations to the former did not constitute consent to their own oppression. They openly and clandestinely contested the conditions of domestic labor in multiple ways" (1997: 97).

Through ever more sophisticated use of gender analysis, historians have also stretched the old labor history into completely new shapes. In her wide-ranging introduction to the important collection, *Work Engendered* (1991), Ava Baron argued that gender analysis provides telling insights into the processes by which men as well as women constructed their notions of workplace and class solidarity. In articles for that collection and in their larger works, Patricia Cooper, Nancy Hewitt, and Elizabeth Faue documented the romance with masculine militancy embedded in the culture of various nineteenth- and twentieth-century unions. Recruiting campaigns that sought to attract men to union activism by selling it as a chance to reclaim "virility" and patriarchal authority had great allure for male workers at times when rapid mechanization and deskilling were diminishing individual workers' dignity. Constructing the unions as preserves for worker masculinity would seem to have left little room for women workers to take visible leadership roles. Still Cooper, Hewitt, and Faue argue that unions built around what Faue calls "the demands of sentimental patriarchy" opened as well as limited opportunities for women's political participation. Faue and Hewitt note that much women's participation had to take place in periods when labor unions were built on community- and family-based organizing. Nevertheless, gender segregation of the labor force, and the masculine orientation of many unions, left women workers to organize themselves in ways that were linked to but different from masculinist unions.

Patricia Cooper has shown that, particularly in exclusively or mostly female shops, shared workplace experience generated in women workers a strong sense of group identity. Her findings were reinforced by my own research on garment workers and by Vicki Ruíz's studies of cannery workers. Women garment workers, cigar makers, and cannery workers countered the fraternity of male workers with their own gendered labor vision and forms of organizing. As unions became more centralized and bureaucratized from the 1920s through the 1940s, Faue has shown, shop-floor and community-based organizers had increasingly less say in union politics. Though grudgingly accepted by male union officials as necessary for organizing on the local level, women's militance came to be seen as disruptive by the 1930s when the National Labor Relations Act and the mass organizing drives of the Congress of Industrial Organizations (CIO) gave unions a strong presence in national policy making. ILGWU president David Dubinsky referred to labor education pioneer Fannia Cohn in long-suffering tones as his "cross to bear." ILGWU executives described lone female vice-president Rose Pesotta in the early 1940s as restless, unstable, and abrasive. After years of being a "voice lost in the wilderness," Pesotta resigned from the ILGWU Executive Board in 1944, hoping to dramatize the hostility of male union leadership to the demands of women activists.

Like historians of women's activism more generally in the United States, scholars of women's labor activism seemed to accept the idea that women became ever more marginalized and less powerful in the unions until the ferment of the late 1960s. However, studies of union women's political activism after World War II in some of the newer industrial and service unions strongly suggest otherwise. Nancy Gabin and Dorothy Sue Cobble have changed our sense of the 1950s as a "doldrum" period for feminism, out of which the 1960s and 1970s women's movements somehow exploded full-blown. These historians document 1940s and 1950s campaigns for hiring, pay, and promotion equity, maternity leave and benefits that clearly laid the groundwork for feminist activism in later decades. "Far from being an era of retreat for women's activism," Cobble persuasively argues, "working-class feminism flowered in the post-war decades, due in part to the steady increase of wage-earning women and the rise of union power" (1994: 58).

Using a different analytic frame, some historians of working-class women have looked beyond activism to cultural forces to explain the dynamics through which gender, class, and ethnicity interacted. Elizabeth Ewen, Kathy Peiss, Susan Glenn, Miriam Cohen, and Nan Enstad have all posed questions of identity, consumption, acculturation, and modernity to better understand the processes by which working women of different ethnic groups have forged both personal and group consciousness. As Enstad argues in chapter 17 in this volume, most of those who have examined working women's enthusiastic embrace of consumption and mass culture have found that consumerism was both liberatory and constraining. Liz Lunbeck, for example, has shown how dance halls, amusement parks, and other working-class gathering places nurtured the development of a freer sexuality among young working women. But she also vividly evoked the condemnation that followed such flouting of "respectable" norms for female behavior as reformers and psychologists identified a new deviant and a new social problem: "the hypersexual girl." Jacquelyn Dowd Hall and Vicki Ruíz have both argued that engagement with popular culture images of modern femininity – for example, flappers and film stars – allowed young Appalachian women in the

1920s and Mexican American women in the 1930s to create new modes of rebellion against gender and generational norms. Sometimes these "disorderly women" channeled their rebelliousness into strikes and spontaneous workplace uprisings. But rebellion could also be expressed through flamboyant dress, sexually expressive dances, and blues lyrics among other modern pastimes. Shared workplace experiences, paeans to individual freedom in films, advertisements, and popular music, and a burgeoning youth culture created a generation gap that divided young working women from their mothers – immigrant or native-born, black, white, Latino, or Asian – and that changed their political as well as personal forms of expression.

While it is tempting to see in mass culture the basis for generational solidarity across lines of difference, historians who have focused on race and ethnicity, citizenship status, and regional context illustrate deep and often unbridgeable divisions among working women. One essential difference in the experience of working women of color has been the colonization of their bodies. Judy Yung and Huping Ling have shown how stereotypes about the anatomy and exoticism of Chinese and Japanese immigrant women fueled a legal trade in women's bodies in nineteenth-century California and Hawaii. Evelyn Nakano Glenn, Susan Tucker, Tera Hunter, and other historians of domestic workers have illustrated numerous ways that objectification of the bodies of women of color paved the way for a range of twentieth-century oppressions not experienced in the same way by white working women. Stereotypes of black women as strong bodies and/or sexual predators allowed white women employers to see domestic workers as being without families of their own, literally nothing more than labor-saving devices to aid in the fulfillment of their wifely and motherly duties. Federal and state governments reinforced this idea of domestic workers as extensions of white housewives by denying federal labor protections and social security to domestic workers until after World War II, and after that time failing to enforce those protections for fear of intruding on the sacred private space of the home. Taboos on regulating private space also gave cover to male employers who raped or sexually harassed domestic laborers.

Despite their political marginalization and physical vulnerability, and in the face of race and sex segregation of the labor force that has historically forced large percentages of women workers of color into this kind of labor, domestic workers have demonstrated both personal resilience and creativity in organizing themselves. Tera Hunter's work on African American washerman in late nineteenth-century Atlanta has already been mentioned. Elizabeth Clark-Lewis and Bonnie Thornton Dill conducted extensive oral histories with African American women who did domestic labor in twentieth-century Washington, DC, and more northern cities. They found that both through networking with one another and through negotiation with employers, these working women were able to exert control over wages, hours, working conditions, and the manner in which they were treated. Their work echoes findings by the National Association for the Advancement of Colored People (NAACP) activist Ella Baker and African American journalist Marvel Cooke during the 1930s when they investigated conditions among black migrant women who had moved from the South to northern cities seeking work. Even those reduced to bargaining for day work on city streetcorners learned quickly how to band together to increase wages for all of them. In addition, as Sharon Harley's work illustrates, African American domestic workers developed a class identity that recognized and reflected race and sex segregation of labor. She quotes domestic worker May Anna Madison on the distinction between black and white work identity. She said: "One very important difference between white people and black people is that white people think that you *are* your work . . . Now, a black person has more sense than that because he knows that what I am doing doesn't have anything to do with what I want to do or what I do when I am doing for myself. Now, black people think that my work is just what I do to get what I want" (1995: 25).

In some parts of the country, especially during the first half of the century, work was what women of color did simply to survive under a white supremacist system that exploited their bodies in systematic ways. What they wanted was less important than what large planters expected in terms of a family labor force and the number of hands needed to eke out a subsistence living for themselves and their children. Rosalinda González documents landlord expectations that Mexican tenant women in 1930s Texas bear "at least eight children." Mexican women renters and sharecroppers, like their black and white counterparts in the Southeast, were forced into a continual cycle of childbearing to expand the cheap farm labor force. Pregnant women and small children worked in the fields alongside men and older children. González and others have done important work on Mexican women farm workers. There should be comparable study of the experience of women sharecroppers in the Southeast. Jacqueline Jones, Kimberly Phillips, and Elizabeth Clark-Lewis have given us some sense of the daily lives of African American women in the early twentieth-century plantation world. But the cotton kingdom survived through the end of the 1940s, with continued economic exploitation of the bodies of black women both as "breeders" of the labor force and as domestic laborers. This is a rich field for further study.

The work of González, Ruíz, Neil Foley, and others also illustrates another key dimension of the experience of Mexican women farm workers. They illustrate the ways that Mexican women's reproductive capacities became bargaining chips used by growers seeking to pit "cheap" Mexican labor against the wage demands of white and African American farm workers. Foley's study of Texas also makes it clear that claims and privileges of whiteness separated farm women one from the other, even when all were economically marginal. For example, hiring women of color as domestic laborers and eschewing field work reinforced a gender identity in white farm women that was heavily based in notions of the superiority of whiteness.

Foley's work points to the importance of developing whiteness as a component of the identity of white working women not only in the South, as Dolores Janiewski and Beverly Jones have done in their explorations of the relations between black and white women tobacco workers, but also in the North. From the garment shops of the Lower East Side in the 1910s to the defense plants of the East Bay during World War II to the medical centers where hospital workers organized in the 1970s, "whiteness" played an increasingly explicit role in dividing wage-earning women one from the other. These distinctions were made clear in the kinds of jobs they were hired for and in their perceptions of why they organized, how they organized, and what they expected from employers. European immigrant women have largely been treated as if they were colorblind because they operated in almost all-white worlds – living in white-ethnic enclaves, working in shops among other European immigrants. The issues of racial consciousness and race relations among northern and western working women have yet to be fully explored, though it has become increasingly clear to historians of immigration that part of the process of acculturation for most immigrant groups, as well as for native white working-class populations, has involved distancing themselves from people of color.

The important role played by whiteness in forging white working-class identities helps us to understand why, as Vicki Ruíz and Margaret Rose have pointed out, ethnic cohesion remained primary for many Mexican women workers. Ruíz and other historians who have written about working women of color remind us that local cultures – though they have often been interpreted as conservative forces constraining women's activism – have been seen as essential resources by women workers organizing in a racist environment. In the prewar California climate of violent racism and mass deportations of Mexican workers, for example, building class solidarity that transcended ethnic divisions was always difficult and often impossible. In the San Joaquin Valley agricultural workers' strike of 1933, the responses of both police and elected officials were clearly racialized. They threatened strikers with deportation and expressed little concern about either the murders of Mexican workers or the malnutrition-related deaths of four strikers' children: "Those damn Mexicans," Ruíz quotes one county supervisor as saying, "can lay out in the street and die for all I care." And a deputy sheriff, later questioned by investigators about the conduct of police during the strike, defined his police responsibilities along racial lines: "We protect our farmers here... But the Mexicans are trash... We herd them like pigs" (1998: 75). While disregard for the physical safety of workers was never limited to people of color, the particular violence and viciousness they faced inevitably marked both the class and gender consciousness of women of color.

Building a sense of community and Mexican solidarity was essential to survival, Ruíz argues, for women organizing in such a context of institutionalized racism. The Mexican women Ruíz has studied saw everything they did – their wage labor, union activism, and work in voluntary associations – as community building. This remained true through the end of the twentieth century. On the penultimate page of her sweeping study Ruíz quotes a more recent Latina immigrant, Salvadoran-born packinghouse organizer Yanira Merino: "I'll always see whatever work I do as an extension of my family" (1998: 150). Beverly Jones's interviews with African American women tobacco workers similarly revealed that a majority "conceptualized the central meaning of their work in relation to their families" (1984: 446). Again, operating in a racist environment black women tobacco workers built overlapping networks, drawing strength from the respected positions they occupied in church and women's community groups to resist degradation at work.

As many historians have found, women workers also channeled workplace militance to reorder power relations in the home. Jones's workers began to display a "consciousness of female strength if not feminism" that transformed their relations with husbands and children. Xiaolan Bao has found that, after the 1960s, a resurgent New

York garment industry turned Chinese immigrant women into the primary breadwinners for working-class Chinese families in New York. Chinese women garment workers became both *nei zi* (guardian of domestic affairs) and *wei zi* (parent who deals with the outside world), giving them far more power and respect in their families than had been the tradition in China. What Bao calls "the depatriarchalizing process" in these families had a mixed impact on the lives of immigrant women. Shouldering dual responsibilities, many felt driven like "headless flies." Affordable day care became the galvanizing issue for Chinese ILGWU organizers, fueling the unionization of Chinatown garment shops in the early 1980s. In 1982, 20,000 Chinese immigrant women walked out of New York garment shops, creating the largest strike in the history of New York's Chinatown. When the union failed to bargain with manufacturers for affordable day care, the strikers marched to the office of union president Jay Mazur and threatened to leave their babies there. In 1984, they won their victory when the Garment Industry Day Care Center of Chinatown opened. Paid for by the union and by manufacturers, it is a visible manifestation of the reciprocal relation between familial concerns and women's union consciousness.

Studying a strike led by black women hospital workers in Durham, North Carolina, in the 1970s, Karen Sacks found that familial influences gave content and form to both modes of organizing and political demands. Workers' conceptions of workplace solidarity and entitlements to dignified treatment were based on notions of adulthood and shared responsibility that they had learned from their families. And once again, workplace organizing was rooted in communal patterns that had little to do with traditional union structures. Sacks argued that many analyses of labor militance and political activism have been limited by gender-biased notions of leadership. Studying the Duke University Medical Center strike, she identified what she called "centerpeople," almost all black women who derived respect among other workers from their skills at community building. These women were essential to the formation of strike networks and the formulation of goals and strategies. They served as mediators between women workers at the grassroots and the largely male union officials who fit more traditional definitions of leadership and whom Sacks calls "spokespeople." Without the work of centerpeople, Sacks argues, the strike could neither have been organized nor sustained.

Sacks's work, and that of other scholars examining service and pink-collar workers' organizing in the 1980s and 1990s, reinforces the gender analysis of those historians who have written about women industrial workers' organizing in earlier eras. Job segregation and the sexual division of labor in home and family settings have long distinguished the style and content of working women's organizing. By the 1990s, women's issues and women's models of organizing were having an impact on the labor movement as a whole because women workers of color in the service and pink-collar sectors had become the driving force behind a resurgent labor movement. The famed "maids' revolt" in Las Vegas in the early 1990s galvanized the largest union local in the country today. Its president, Hattie Canty, is an African American mother of ten who likes to boast that Las Vegas is the only city in the country where hotel maids are able to buy their own houses and send their children to college. The importance of women of color to the late twentieth-century labor movement, Peter Seybold argues, has transformed the kinds of goals that labor unions now work toward. Childcare, sexual harassment, job safety, healthcare, and affirmative action were all key issues in labor union negotiations during the mid-1990s. Still, as John Hoerr, Elly Leary, and others have pointed out in looking at some of the new women's unions, like the Harvard Union of Clerical and Technical Workers, the "feminist nonadversarial" approach to labor relations – problem solving through joint committees of labor – has often left unionized workers without autonomous means to enforce their demands.

And, despite the extraordinary energy displayed by women clerical and service workers at the end of the twentieth century, the situation for women in industry has hardly been positive. Sources at the amalgamated garment and textile union, UNITE, estimate that, by the mid-1990s, more than 200,000 workers, mostly Asian, Caribbean, and Central American immigrant women, labored under sweatshop conditions in New York City alone. Thousands of illegal Asian and Mexican immigrants were being held in slave conditions in New York and California garment shops and houses of prostitution by human smugglers who demanded payment in labor for the inflated prices they charged to bring people over the border. Sweatshop labor and globalization had destabilized established unions, especially in border towns like El Paso, Texas. In 1992–3, when Emily Honig revisited the Chicana Farah workers she had first interviewed during their 1970s strike, legacies of the successful strike were hard to find in the lives of the women who had sparked and sustained it.

Finally, the 1980s and 1990s saw a resurgence of unregulated home production in the United States with most of it being performed by women. As Eileen Boris explained it in the conclusion to her massive 1994 study of the history of industrial homework, three forces have coincided to drive down wages that women could command for working at home. The final two decades of the century saw mass immigration on a scale surpassing even that of the century's early decades, which created an abundance of undocumented workers willing to produce garments at home for far below union rates. The capacity of government agencies to enforce protective labor laws was nearly extinguished during the Reagan and Bush presidencies both because of ideological opposition to labor regulation and as a budget-cutting measure. Finally, steady growth in the numbers and percentage of women in the paid labor force created increased tension over the problem of how mothers could combine wage work with childcare. Without better options, millions of mothers of small children began once again to perform waged labor in their homes. In the late 1970s, garment union investigators found homework being done in all five boroughs of New York City as well as Boston, San Francisco, Los Angeles, Chicago, Miami, New Hampshire, and upstate New York (1994: 343). The locales and numbers have continued growing.

Homework, Boris has written, was touted by conservatives as a lifestyle choice made by mothers who did not believe in day care rather than an unregulated form of labor that drove down wages industry-wide and exposed women and children to hazardous modes of production. In the early 1980s Republicans in Congress championed the cause of the Vermont knitters, rural mothers who challenged a ban on homework in knitted outerwear because they had few other employment options that allowed them to be at home with their children. But by the 1980s it was not only garments being produced at home. In cities across the United States women tapped at computer keyboards in their basements or living rooms, data entry having replaced the types of outwork done by women in previous decades. In California, Mexican, Filipino, Korean, and Southeast Asian immigrant women handled dangerous chemicals as they made computer chips in their homes. In the depressed farm regions of upstate New York and the Midwest, native-born women made electrical as well as electronic components. Throughout American history, Boris makes clear, the persistence of a gender ideology that allots women primary responsibility for the care of children and ailing adult relatives has supported the system of underpaid, nearly impossible to unionize home production. Boris's research provides one final and powerful illustration of how impossible it is to understand the history of women's wage work in this country without closely exploring and remapping the relationship between home and shop floor, domestic and public spheres.

Even once we have rethought and revised long-held conceptions about relations between women's work at home and outside of the home, is it possible to draw any general conclusions about wage-earning American women during the last century? I would say not and that seems to me a positive rather than a negative statement: reflective of the depth, range, and quality of the work historians have already done in the field. During the mid-1980s a crisis mentality gripped some labor historians who despaired that synthetic statements about "the working class" were no longer possible now that class analysis had been complicated by concerns of gender, race, ethnicity, generation, and region, to name just the major categories of analysis that have modified notions of class. Since that time, feminist, poststructuralist, and queer theorists have helped most historians become more comfortable with the idea that human identities and motivations are and always have been complex, fluid, and ever-shifting. This is as true for wage-earning women as for everyone else. Large-scale economic, cultural, and technological changes have affected working women's consciousness, motivations, and action along with gender, race, class, age, region, and religion. And then there must be room for those inexplicable differences that grow out of the uniqueness of individual personalities and the workplace chemistry between those individuals. It is enough to make a historian's head spin. But, again, that is a good thing. Perhaps with some distance from the traumatic 1980s, we can finally say that definitive synthesis is neither possible nor desirable. What we have instead in the extensive literature on the history of American wage-earning women is a body of work sufficiently dynamic, contradictory, and fascinating that it will hopefully move a new generation of students and scholars to add their voices to the fray.

BIBLIOGRAPHY

Abramovitz, Mimi (1988) *Regulating the Lives of Women: Social Welfare Policy from Colonial Times to the Present*. Boston: South End Press.

Anderson, Karen (1981) *Wartime Women: Sex Roles, Family Relations and the Status of Women During World War II.* Westport, CT: Greenwood Press.

Bao, Xiaolan (1997) "Chinese Mothers in New York City's New Sweatshops," in Alexis Jetter, Annelise Orleck, and Diana Taylor (eds.), *The Politics of Motherhood: Activist Voices From Left to Right.* Hanover: University Press of New England, pp. 127–37.

Baron, Ava (ed.) (1991) *Work Engendered: Toward a New History of American Labor.* Ithaca, NY: Cornell University Press.

Benson, Susan Porter (1986) *Counter Cultures: Saleswomen, Managers, and Customers in American Department Stores, 1890–1940.* Urbana: University of Illinois Press.

Boris, Eileen (1994) *Home to Work: Motherhood and the Politics of Industrial Homework in the United States.* New York: Cambridge University Press.

Brody, David (1979) "The Old Labor History and the New: in Search of an American Working Class," *Labor History* 20, pp. 111–26.

Buhle, Mari Jo (1981) *Women and American Socialism, 1870–1920.* Urbana: University of Illinois Press.

Buhle, Mari Jo (1989) "Gender and Labor History," in J. Carroll Moody and Alice Kessler-Harris (eds.), *Perspectives on American Labor History: The Problems of Synthesis.* Dekalb: University of Northern Illinois Press, pp. 55–79.

Bullard, Robert (ed.) (1993) *Confronting Environmental Racism: Voices from the Grassroots.* Boston: South End Press.

Cameron, Ardis (1985) "Bread and Roses Revisited: Women's Culture and Working-class Activism in the Lawrence Strike of 1912," in Ruth Milkman (ed.), *Women, Work and Protest: A Century of Women's Labor History.* London: Routledge and Kegan Paul, pp. 42–61.

Cameron, Ardis (1993) *Radicals of the Worst Sort: Laboring Women in Lawrence, Massachusetts, 1860–1912.* Urbana: University of Illinois Press.

Cobble, Dorothy Sue (1991) *Dishing It Out: Waitresses and their Unions in the Twentieth Century.* Urbana: University of Illinois Press.

Cobble, Dorothy Sue (1994) "Recapturing Working-class Feminism: Union Women in the Postwar Era," in Joanne Meyerowitz (ed.), *Not June Cleaver: Women and Gender in Postwar America, 1945–1960.* Philadelphia: Temple University Press, pp. 57–83.

Cohen, Miriam (1992) *Workshop to Office: Two Generations of Italian Women in New York City, 1900–1950.* Ithaca, NY: Cornell University Press.

Cooper, Patricia (1987) *Once a Cigar Maker: Men, Women and Work Culture in American Cigar Factories, 1900–1919.* Urbana: University of Illinois Press.

Cooper, Patricia (1991) "The Faces of Gender: Sex Segregation and Work Relations at Philco, 1928–1938," in Ava Baron (ed.), *Work Engendered: Toward a New History of American Labor.* Ithaca, NY: Cornell University Press, pp. 320–50.

Crain, Marion (1994) "Gender and Union Organizing," *Industrial and Labor Relations Review* 47, pp. 227–48.

Dill, Bonnie Thornton (1988) " 'Making Your Job Good Yourself': Domestic Service and the Construction of Personal Dignity," in Ann Bookman and Sandra Morgen (eds.), *Women and the Politics of Empowerment.* Philadelphia: Temple University Press, pp. 33–52.

Dye, Nancy Schrom (1980) *As Equals and Sisters: Feminism, Unionism and the Women's Trade Union League of New York.* Columbia: University of Missouri Press.

Enstad, Nan (1999) *Ladies of Labor, Girls of Adventure: Working Women, Popular Culture and Labor Politics at the Turn of the Twentieth Century.* New York: Columbia University Press.

Ewen, Elizabeth (1985) *Immigrant Women in the Land of Dollars: Life and Culture on the Lower East Side, 1890–1925.* New York: Monthly Review Press.

Faue, Elizabeth (1991a) *Community of Suffering and Struggle: Women, Men, and the Labor Movement in Minneapolis, 1915–1945.* Chapel Hill: University of North Carolina Press.

Faue, Elizabeth (1991b) "Paths of Unionization: Community, Bureaucracy, and Gender in the Minneapolis Labor Movement of the 1930s," in Ava Baron (ed.), *Work Engendered: Toward a New History of American Labor.* Ithaca, NY: Cornell University Press, pp. 296–319.

Foley, Neil (1997) *The White Scourge: Mexicans, Blacks and Poor Whites in Texas Cotton Culture.* Berkeley: University of California Press.

Foner, Philip (1979) *Women and the American Labor Movement: From the First Trade Unions to the Present.* New York: Free Press.

Frank, Dana (1985) "Housewives, Socialists and the Politics of Food: The 1917 Cost of Living Protests," *Feminist Studies* 11, pp. 255–85.

Frank, Dana (1994) *Purchasing Power: Consumer Organizing, Gender, and the Seattle Labor Movement, 1919–1929.* Cambridge, MA: Harvard University Press.

Gabin, Nancy F. (1990) *Feminism in the Labor Movement: Women and the United Auto Workers, 1935–1975.* Ithaca, NY: Cornell University Press.

Glenn, Evelyn Nakano (1986) *Issei, Nissei, War Bride: Three Generations of Japanese American Women in Domestic Service.* Philadelphia: Temple University Press.

Glenn, Susan A. (1990) *Daughters of the Shtetl: Life and Labor in the Immigrant Generation.* Ithaca, NY: Cornell University Press.

González, Rosalinda (1987) "Chicanas and Mexican Immigrant Families, 1920–1940: Women's Subordination and Family Exploitation," in Lois Scharf and Joan M. Jensen (eds.), *Decades of Discontent: The Women's Movement, 1920–1940.* Boston: Northeastern University Press, pp. 59–83.

Gutman, Herbert (1977) *Work, Culture and Society in Industrializing America.* New York: Alfred A. Knopf.

Hall, Jacquelyn Dowd (1986) "Disorderly Women: Gender and Labor Militancy in the Appalachian South," *Journal of American History* 73, pp. 354–82.

Harley, Sharon (1995) "When Your Work is Not Who You Are: The Development of Working-class Consciousness among Afro-American Women," in Darlene Clark Hine, Wilma King, and Linda Reed (eds.), *"We Specialize in the Wholly Impossible": A Reader in Black Women's History.* Brooklyn: Carlson Publishing, pp. 25–37.

Henry, Alice (1923) *Women and the Labor Movement.* New York: G. H. Doran and Co.

Hewitt, Nancy A. (1991) " 'The Voice of Virile Labor': Labor Militancy, Community Solidarity and Gender Identity among Tampa's Latin Workers, 1880–1921," in Ava Baron (ed.), *Work Engendered: Toward a New History of American Labor.* Ithaca, NY: Cornell University Press, pp. 142–67.

Honig, Emily (1996) "Women at Farah Revisited: Political Mobilization and its Aftermath among Chicano Workers in El Paso, Texas, 1972–1992," *Feminist Studies* 22, pp. 425–52.

Hunter, Tera W. (1997) *To 'Joy My Freedom: Southern Black Women's Lives and Labors After the Civil War.* Cambridge, MA: Harvard University Press.

Hyman, Paula (1980) "Immigrant Women and Consumer Protest: The New York City Kosher Meat Boycott of 1902," *American Jewish History* 70, pp. 126–40.

Jacoby, Robin Miller (1984) "The Women's Trade Union League School for Women Organizers," in Joyce Kornbluh and Mary Frederickson (eds.), *Sisterhood and Solidarity: Worker's Education for Women, 1914–1984.* Philadelphia: Temple University Press, pp. 5–35.

Janiewski, Dolores (1985) *Sisterhood Denied: Race, Gender, and Class in a New South Community.* Philadelphia: Temple University Press.

Jetter, Alexis (1997) "A Mother's Battle for Environmental Justice," in Alexis Jetter, Annelise Orleck, and Diana Taylor (eds.), *The Politics of Motherhood: Activist Voices From Left to Right.* Hanover: University Press of New England, pp. 44–52.

Jones, Beverly W. (1984) "Race, Sex and Class: Black Female Tobacco Workers in Durham, North Carolina, 1920–1940 and the Development of Female Consciousness," *Feminist Studies* 10, pp. 441–51.

Jones, Jacqueline (1985) *Labor of Love, Labor of Sorrow: Black Women, Work and the Family from Slavery to the Present.* New York: Basic Books; 2nd ed., 1995.

Kelly, Joan (1976) "The Social Relations of the Sexes: Methodological Implications of Women's History," *Signs* 1, pp. 809–23.

Kenneally, James J. (1981) *Women and American Trade Unionism.* Montreal: Eden Press.

Kessler-Harris, Alice (1975) "Where are the Organized Women Workers?" *Feminist Studies* 3, pp. 92–111.

Kessler-Harris, Alice (1982) *Out to Work: A History of Wage-earning Women in the United States.* New York: Oxford University Press.

Kessler-Harris, Alice (1989) "A New Agenda for American Labor History: A Gendered Analysis and the Question of Class," in J. Carroll Moody and Alice Kessler-Harris (eds.), *Perspectives on American Labor History: The Problems of Synthesis.* Dekalb: University of Northern Illinois Press, pp. 217–36.

Kessler-Harris, Alice (1990a) *A Woman's Wage: Historical Meanings and Social Consequences.* Lexington: University of Kentucky Press.

Kessler-Harris, Alice (1990b) "Gender Ideology in Historical Reconstruction: A Case Study from the 1930s," *Gender and History* 2, pp. 31–9.

Leary, Elly (1997) "The Women Who Organized Harvard: A Model of Feminist Labor Organization?" *Monthly Review* 49, pp. 1–9.

Leeder, Elaine (1993) *The Gentle General: Rose Pesotta, Anarchist and Labor Organizer.* Albany: State University of New York Press.

Ling, Huping (1998) *Surviving on the Gold Mountain: A History of Chinese American Women and their Lives.* Albany: State University of New York Press.

Lunbeck, Elizabeth (1987) "A New Generation of Women: Progressive Psychiatrists and the Hypersexual Female," *Feminist Studies* 13, pp. 513–43.

Matthei, Julie A. (1982) *An Economic History of Women in America: Women's Work, the Sexual Division of Labor and the Development of Capitalism.* New York: Schocken.

Norwood, Stephen (1990) *Labor's Flaming Youth: Telephone Operators and Worker Militancy, 1878–1923.* Urbana: University of Illinois Press.

Orleck, Annelise (1993) "We Are That Mythical Thing Called the Public: Militant Housewives in the Great Depression," *Feminist Studies* 19, pp. 147–72.

Orleck, Annelise (1995) *Common Sense and a Little Fire: Women and Working-class Politics in the United States, 1900–1965.* Chapel Hill: University of North Carolina Press.

Orleck, Annelise (1997) " 'If It Wasn't for You, I'd Have Shoes for My Children': The Political Education of Las Vegas Welfare Mothers," in Alexis Jetter, Annelise Orleck, and Diana Taylor (eds.), *The Politics of Motherhood: Activist Voices From Left to Right.* Hanover: University Press of New England, pp. 102–18.

Peiss, Kathy (1986) *Cheap Amusements: Working Women and Leisure in Turn-of-the-century New York.* Philadelphia: Temple University Press.

Phillips, Kimberly L. (1999) *Alabama North: African-American Migrants, Community and Working-class Activism in Cleveland, 1915–1945.* Urbana: University of Illinois Press.

Rose, Margaret (1994) "Gender and Civic Activism in Mexican-American Barrios in California: The Community Service Organization, 1947–1962," in Joanne Meyerowitz (ed.), *Not June Cleaver: Women and Gender in Postwar America, 1945–1960.* Philadelphia: Temple University Press, pp. 177–200.

Ruíz, Vicki (1987) *Cannery Women, Cannery Lives: Mexican Women, Unionization, and the California Food Processing Industry, 1930–1950.* Albuquerque: University of New Mexico Press.

Ruíz, Vicki (1998) *From Out of the Shadows: Mexican Women in Twentieth-century America.* New York: Oxford University Press.

Sacks, Karen B. (1988a) *Caring by the Hour: Women, Work and Organizing at Duke Medical Center.* Urbana: University of Illinois Press.

Sacks, Karen B. (1988b) "Gender and Grassroots Leadership," in Ann Bookman and Sandra Morgen (eds.), *Women and the Politics of Empowerment.* Philadelphia: Temple University Press, pp. 77–96.

Scharf, Lois (1980) *To Work and to Wed: Female Employment, Feminism, and the Great Depression.* Westport, CT: Greenwood Press.

Seybold, Peter (1996) "Trends in U.S. Labor Movement," *The Futurist* 30, p. 44.

Stolberg, Benjamin (1944) *Tailor's Progress: The Story of a Famous Union and the Men Who Made It.* New York: Doubleday.

Strom, Sharon Hartman (1983) "Challenging Women's Place: Feminism, the Left and the Industrial Unionism of the 1930s," *Feminist Studies* 9, pp. 359–86.

Tax, Meredith (1980) *The Rising of the Women: Feminist Solidarity and Class Conflict, 1880–1917.* New York: Monthly Review Press.

Van Kleeck, Mary (1914) *Working Girls in Evening Schools.* New York: Russell Sage.

Van Kleeck, Mary (1917) *A Seasonal Industry.* New York: Russell Sage.

Wandersee, Winifred (1980) *Women's Work and Family Values, 1920–1940.* Cambridge, MA: Harvard University Press.

Weiner, Lynn (1985) *From Working Girl to Working Mother: The Female Labor Force in the United States, 1820–1980.* Chapel Hill: University of North Carolina Press.

Wertheimer, Barbara (1977) *We Were There: The Story of Working Women in America.* New York: Pantheon.

White, Deborah Gray (1999) *Too Heavy a Load: Black Women in Defense of Themselves, 1894–1994.* New York: W. W. Norton.

Wolfson, Theresa (1926) *The Woman Worker and the Trade Unions.* New York: International Press.

Wong, Susan Stone (1984) "From Soul to Strawberries: The International Ladies Garment Workers' Union and Worker's Education, 1914–1950," in Joyce Kornbluh and Mary Frederickson (eds.), *Sisterhood and Solidarity: Worker's Education for Women, 1914–1984.* Philadelphia: Temple University Press, pp. 39–57.

Yung, Judy (1995) *Unbound Feet: A Social History of Chinese Women in San Francisco.* Berkeley: University of California Press.

Chapter Sixteen

Consumer Cultures

Susan Porter Benson

PIECING together an overview of the history of gender, women, and consumption recalls that other women's piecework activity, quilting, and particularly the polyrhythmic design of African American women's quilts as described by Elsa Barkley Brown (1989a). First, a connected discussion of women and consumption has not emerged, so that there is not a uniform pattern in work that touches on the topic; this fabric is emphatically not all of a piece. Second, some aspects of the connections between gender and consumption have gotten far more attention than others, and so the field has a few sizable pieces but they do not necessarily contribute the most to the overall design. Third, much of the most intriguing work about gender and consumption has been embedded in studies in which it is but an ancillary theme, so that our quilt also has a great many small but vividly colored pieces that do not always fit together with geometric symmetry.

The substance of the history of women, gender, and consumption reflects the visual metaphor. Quilts, combining factory-made fabrics with considerable home labor, embody women's relation to the marketplace: while deeply drawn into that world, they have continued to engage in nonmarket production of goods and services. Mirroring the multiple patterns in our quilt and its roots in and out of commercial production, women's experience of the market has been mixed and uneven. Consumption has offered the potential for self-expression and satisfaction even as it tied women to the subordination of traditional gender roles. Even more important, for the majority of women quilting and consumption have had more to do with utility – with family provisioning – than with the purely ornamental or aesthetic. If any single theme underlines the complicated design of our historiographical quilt, it has been the effort to assay the changing nature of consumption's doubleness and to explore the shifting balance between the poles of market and nonmarket behavior, liberation and limitation, and subsistence and discretionary spending.

This gendered view of the marketplace does not fit neatly with the reigning paradigms in the history of consumption. Although scholars have traced the origins of consumer culture well back into previous centuries, there is broad agreement that the late nineteenth century saw a sea change both in consumption as it was experienced and in commentary on it. Early work argued that mass consumption swept like a tsunami through older social and cultural patterns. Jackson Lears saw a shift from prudential virtues to therapeutic values:

> In the United States as elsewhere, the bourgeois ethos had enjoined perpetual work, compulsive saving, civic responsibility, and a rigid morality of self-denial. By the early twentieth century that outlook had begun to give way to a new set of values sanctioning periodic leisure, compulsive spending, apolitical passivity, and an apparently permissive (but subtly coercive) morality of individual fulfillment. The older culture was suited to a production-oriented society of small entrepreneurs; the newer culture epitomized a consumption-oriented society dominated by bureaucratic corporations. (Lears 1983: 3)

Jean-Christophe Agnew emphasized a related aspect of the change: "It is at the point where consumption converts its meaning from a disease into a cure that we may begin to speak of a consumer culture in the sense that we experience it" (1983: 74).

The new culture grew in the soil of industrialization, which produced dramatic changes in material life. Throughout the nineteenth century, but especially in the years after the Civil War, mass production vastly increased the quantity and variety of goods available in the marketplace. From a macroeconomic point of view, abundance eclipsed scarcity as the key material dynamic of American life. Some historians argued that industrialization not only fostered the supply side of the therapeutic ethic by increasing what was on offer in the marketplace, but that it also produced new types of demand by making work increasingly alienating and driving workers to turn to consumption for satisfactions they could no longer find in work. Further, cultural historians pointed to new notions about human psychology. The conjunction of middle-class formation and consumer culture, they argued, produced a shift from an emphasis on character to a stress on personality, in Warren Susman's formulation, or "the movement of objects from expressions of status to guarantors of identity," as Neil Harris put it (1990: 197).

More recent work in the history of consumption has qualified these large generalizations, sometimes by shifting the early cultural focus to one more informed by social history and sometimes by moving toward a more dialectical view of the effects of mass consumption. Jackson Lears, for example, writing the history of advertising in the United States, argued that consumer culture "was less a riot of hedonism than a new way of ordering the existing balance of tensions between control and release" (Lears 1994: 10–11). This measured view fits more comfortably with what historians of women have had to say about consumption. The therapeutic ethic had in any event a dubious applicability to women, to working-class people, to farming families, and to communities of color. Women's predominantly dependent and subordinate economic position inevitably undermined the pleasures of consuming, as did their responsibilities for family provisioning. Far from riding a tide of abundance, a majority in the United States lived on insufficient incomes before World War II. During the 1920s and 1930s, as Roland Marchand noted, advertisers' definition of a "mass audience . . . referred primarily to those Americans with higher-than-average incomes" and assumed that as much as two-thirds of the nation's population was disfranchised in the marketplace (1985: 64). Urban working-class families and farm families faced perennial shortages of cash. Race and ethnicity further disadvantaged people of color and immigrants: job discrimination led to lower wages and patterns of exclusion either curtailed their consumption or made them pay a social price for it. In addition, the notion of the therapeutic ethic assumes that people consume as individuals, whereas the evidence suggests that they approach the marketplace at least as often as members of families or of larger collectivities. There is no doubt that mass consumption made broad inroads on American lives, but it did so less like a tidal wave than like a slowly rising river, seeping into some corners, taking over whole chunks of terrain but passing others by.

Far from simply sweeping all before it in a great homogenizing wave, consumption is protean, susceptible to being harnessed by a variety of social and cultural forces and infused with as many different meanings as there are contexts. This argument is similar to those made by historians of technology and can be illustrated with an example from that field: the diffusion of the wood-fired cookstove. Ruth Schwartz Cowan argues that stoves did not save but increased women's labor, bringing with them the obligation to cook more elaborate and time-consuming meals and the onerous labor of rust-preventing cleaning and polishing. What she does not recognize, however, is that these circumstances were linked to a particular culture – that of the Anglo middle class – and to a humid climate. The women in southwestern Hispanic villages who, Sarah Deutsch tells us, eagerly purchased similar stoves probably had a very different experience with them: stoves made the cooking of traditional foods more convenient and were not prone to rust in the arid climate. This example suggests that the meanings of consumption, however variable, are not random but patterned, shaped by class, race, ethnicity, gender, age, region, and many other factors.

Linked to the protean quality of consumption is the difficulty of defining just what activities should be included in this category. One definition might be that consumption includes all activity in the marketplace that involves money. By this standard, consumption is everywhere: virtually all living in the United States after 1880 relied on money in one respect or another, and few aspects of life have been untouched by the money economy. Even African American sharecropping women and Native American women, sharing the dubious distinction of being the groups most excluded from the cash economy, gained limited access to cash, in the first case raising chickens for sale and in the second selling products to Anglo tourists and collectors. The gap between an African American mother who spent her chicken money on school shoes for her children and a wealthy white suburban woman shopping for a matched ensemble in a department store yawns so wide, however, as to make the connection trivial. A useful distinction can be made between maintenance consumption that involves meeting basic needs for food, clothing, shelter, and health and that which involves the use of discretionary income to make choices beyond the basics. The majority of Americans before World War II lived in a world dominated by the first and punctuated by occasional ventures into the second. This generalization, of course, must be qualified by rising expectations for material comfort and consumer goods during the period under discussion.

The gendering of consumption is as mixed as its experience along other axes. By our starting point of 1880, a broad consensus had emerged that consumption was gendered female, but this notion, like much of what is written on the subject, rested largely in the experience of the white middle class. Mary Ryan's argument for the emergence, by the middle of the nineteenth century, of a rough "definition of the male as breadwinner, the woman as wise and frugal consumer" was based on her study of the emerging European American middle class (1981: 199). This definition signals a twofold change: both men and women abandon household production, and women take over consumption from men. The experience of these changes, however, was more subtle, varied, and complex. Writing of the same antebellum era as Ryan, Jeanne Boydston argued that family economies were "mixed economies" in which consumption and production complemented rather than diverged from each other.

Persisting assumptions that consumption was female focused on its most obvious aspect: purchasing. Taking place outside the home, in public or in places open to the public, purchasing at first appears to be the easiest dimension of consumption to study. Clifford Trafzer, for example, offers one of our few direct glimpses of Native American women's consumption in his 1995 article detailing Yakima women's domination of purchases from Indian agents in the early twentieth century, but he acknowledges that his sources tell him nothing about the power relationships underlying these purchases. As he recognizes, the person who does the purchasing does not always make the decisions about the allocation of income and the choices of goods and services, and purchasers frequently act on behalf of others. Because decision making and, to some degree, use tend to be more private acts than purchasing, they have been more difficult for historians to investigate and the lion's share of historical attention has gone to purchasing. Similarly, when decision making has been studied, it has been easier to explore the messages of advertisers than their reception by consumers. The result is that historians of consumption have disproportionately focused on the production of culture through business and advertising and much less on ordinary people's experiences of consumption.

Early on, historians followed the received wisdom and assumed that the consumer was a woman. They studied urban, white, middle-class women who were unlikely to be in the paid labor force and in whose social-reproduction work shopping was central. These women were purchasers of goods, but not necessarily the only or even the principal users of them, and we know very little about their role as decision makers. Were they simply executing choices made by other family members, or were they the decision makers themselves? Largely dependent upon others for the money they spent, these women lacked autonomy in the marketplace. Historians also characterized working-class consumption as female, for reasons structurally similar but differently inflected. Working-class women, too, tended to be in charge of spending the family fund, but in their lives the problem was not one of executing choices but of managing inadequate resources to meet family needs. Deciding which bills to pay and which to put off is a task that involves more anxiety than autonomy.

Recent work, however, has pointed to the persisting and even expanding role of men as consumers. In the rural South, men continued to be the primary consumers through at least the mid-nineteenth century; Ted Ownby argues that white women – and then only town women, not farm women – did not come into their own as shoppers until the 1880s and 1890s in Mississippi. African Americans' family shopping, at least as reported by white home economists, was still handled predominantly by men well into the 1930s; this pattern probably owed less to male dominance than to a desire to shield women from the insults of white storekeepers and clerks.

Consumption, always adaptable, had a range of meanings for urban white men. The ideology of organized labor, Lawrence Glickman argues, took a "consumerist turn" in the late nineteenth century, leading male workers to "think about themselves as consumers and to ponder the power of consumer organizing" (1997: 5). Working-class husbands and sons typically had more "spending money" at their disposal than did wives and daughters, and devoted it to therapeutic consumption – commercial entertainment, fraternal activities, sports, and drink – while wives managed the family fund. George Chauncey has pointed to the importance of commercial venues for the development of a gay men's culture in New York, and David Nasaw's work on public amusements discusses the myriad male-oriented forms of commercial leisure that persisted even as entertainment entrepreneurs sought the air of respectability that would attract women as well. Mark Swiencicki argues that "the present-day male love of style, recreation, and consumer goods goes back more than a century," but that it has been obscured by the categories used by the census and by historians (1998: 777). Male-oriented magazines featured gendered advertising campaigns; from the late 1930s until at least the 1950s, as Kenon Breazeale and Barbara Ehrenreich have shown, these messages were consciously misogynistic and hedonistically critical of the male-breadwinner ethic.

The power of the notion of female-gendered consumption derived in large part from work on advertising and other institutions of consumption, which took US women's history's now much-criticized line of least resistance and focused on white middle-class urban women. For these women, at least until World War II, department stores were the key venue of middle-class consumption and advertising was the key medium. Historians' arguments about department stores set the tone for much that would follow, emphasizing the contradictory ways in which these flagship institutions of the culture of consumption simultaneously manipulated, dominated, catered to, and offered women opportunities to exercise agency. Studies of department stores, further, illustrated the moralism that Daniel Horowitz placed at the center of his pathbreaking *The Morality of Spending: Attitudes toward the Consumer Society in America, 1875–1940* (1985). Observers have been especially judgmental of women's consumption.

Department stores barraged women with intense, sexualized appeals and promises to satisfy their every whim, assaulting the self-control that Victorian culture had nurtured. The picture that historians paint of women customers' behavior in these commercial palaces is not an attractive one. Their inhibitions lowered, women engaged in actions that were illegal (as Elaine Abelson showed in her study of shoplifting), unethical (returning dresses after wearing them), or childish (making unreasonable demands for service and attention), and evoked a moralistic scorn in the minds of store managers and the general public. At the same time, we can see in these actions some assertion of women's agency: subordinated by gender in their families and in society at large, customers took advantage of stores' eagerness for their patronage and asserted their race and class prerogatives to get what they wanted.

Women who worked in these stores found opportunities to use gender-based skills, to find relatively clean, safe, and well-paid employment, and to pursue not just agency but ambition by moving up the ranks of a hierarchy that was more receptive to women than most businesses, although still dominated at policy levels by men. Like other aspects of consumption, department stores drew distinctions based on race, ethnicity, and class. Frankly unwelcoming to women of color either as customers or as any but the most servile or behind-the-scenes workers, conscious apostles of Anglo standards of taste, department stores incarnated whiteness. Price-segregated departments further sorted customers by class, keying amenities to the price of a department's merchandise and offering goods affordable to working-class customers only in symbolically placed bargain basements.

Historians' studies of advertising follow along many of the same lines as department stores. At least until World War II, they agree, most advertisers primarily targeted the white middle class and discounted working-class consumers, especially recent immigrants and African Americans. Not surprisingly, then, advertisers' appeals played on constructions of race, class, and gender. Roland Marchand argued that advertisements exploited women's fears, insecurities, and guilt, seeing consumers primarily as "an emotional, feminized mass, characterized by mental lethargy, bad taste, and ignorance" (1985: 69). Both he and Jennifer Scanlon also found, however, more positive gendered messages that connected "consumption to improved marriages, lighter household responsibilities, and . . . greater political freedom" (Scanlon 1995: 134). Advertising messages were powerfully shaped by the demographics of those who wrote them: elite white men and women who defined their female audience as "white, middle-class, stay-at-home women" (Scanlon 1995: 195). Scanlon and Simone Weil Davis, however, argued that advertising women had a more complicated perspective than men in the industry. Scanlon pointed out that they shared with social workers and progressive reformers a belief in the "social and educational importance of their work" (1995: 185) even as they condescendingly sought to transform stay-at-home women's lives through consumption. Davis argued that women's multivalent subjectivity led them to write ads "intermingling . . . shame and pleasure, irony and conviction" (2000: 18). These writers reinforce Nancy Cott's argument that white feminists' messages about choice and self-realization were increasingly reduced to choices within the world of consumption and the patriarchal family and to limited occupational opportunities. Even worse, the notion that consumption offered liberation could become dangerous: during the 1930s, as Andrea Tone has shown, advertisers used "hucksterism, fraud, and misinformation" to flog unsafe and ineffective contraceptive devices to a female public newly conscious of birth control (1996: 500).

Advertising courted the dollars of white women and offered an elite among them a chance for well-paid if not policy-making employment, but it did the opposite for women of color. Ellen Garvey argued that trade cards figured prominently in girls' play during the last quarter of the nineteenth century and gave collectors "the pleasure of being like every other girl" (1996: 49), but they in fact gave precious little such pleasure to African American and Native American girls. Marilyn Maness Mehaffy showed that these brightly colored cards constructed the white female consumer in opposition to figures of African American women who represented the primitive, the natural, and the dirty. Jeffrey Steele found in these same cards the reduction of Native American women to icons of fecundity on the one hand and eroticized imperial objects on the other. Women of color seem simply to have disappeared from the Anglo-oriented store, newspaper, and magazine ads that supplanted trade cards after the 1890s; according to Marchand, these ads virtually excluded Asian and Hispanic women, portrayed Native Americans only through historical stereotypes, and even effaced the mostly African American women who toiled in domestic service by portraying maids as stylish young white women. Vicki Ruíz and Judy Yung, by contrast, found that by the 1920s in the Spanish-language press and the 1930s in the Chinese-language press, both ads and editorial content encouraged new ways of consumption with the same promises of happiness and self-fulfillment that were made in English-language papers.

If historians have emphasized abundance as the primary shaper of white middle-class urban women's encounters with the marketplace, they have seen scarcity as a continuing brake on the marketplace experience of working-class and farm women. If the glass is half-full for the former, it is half-empty for the latter. Those who study working-class consumption benefit from a vast body of work by women reformers and settlement house workers extending from the late nineteenth century through the 1920s and tapering off during the 1930s. These writers and observers, although hardly devoid of race or ethnic bias, at least listened attentively to working-class people and often preserved their voices for historians. At the same time, they still saw women's consumption through moralistic lenses, albeit ones differently focused than those through which critics viewed white middle-class women's market encounters.

Numerous studies of women immigrants considered consumption as part of women's encounter with a new country. Most authors saw it as part of what Vicki Ruíz, writing about Mexican women immigrants during the twentieth century, referred to as cultural coalescence. She argued that "Immigrants and their children pick, borrow, retain, and create distinctive cultural forms.... People navigate across cultural boundaries and consciously make decisions with regard to the production of culture, [but]... people of color have not had unlimited choice [because of] race and gender prejudice and discrimination" (1998: xvi). Age to some degree distinguished the consumption world of older married immigrant women from that of their younger, unmarried counterparts. Historians of women migrants from Mexico, Italy, and Eastern Europe have emphasized women householders' rootedness in traditional cultures and patterns of mutual aid and their role as "good managers" of an almost-always insufficient family fund. Working-class women householders developed shopping as a powerful family survival strategy. With inadequate income to supply their families with basics and only rarely enjoying discretionary income, they mostly balanced competing claims on their inadequate resources. Shopping – knowing how to assess value, building relationships with merchants, sniffing out good bargains, and haggling for the best deal – was not a therapeutic exercise but a deadly serious effort to make every penny count. Immigrant women developed this skill in varying measures; and beginning in the 1930s, they were increasingly likely to exercise it in chain stores than in small shops run by merchants of their own ethnicity. Since they relied primarily on access to others' wages, working-class women's power in family interactions could be as important to their consumer success as their skills at haggling. Most working-class men, whether husbands or sons, kept a portion of their wages for their own use; how much they turned over to their wives and mothers was a frequent bone of contention.

Immigrant wives and mothers, however, accepted certain aspects of market life in the United States. They earned wages despite cultural resistance to married women's paid labor; their irregular wages, whether earned outside or inside the home, made crucial contributions to the family fund. They also encountered commercialized popular culture, primarily through films during the 1920s. Scattered through working-class neighborhoods, early movie houses offered cheap and accessible entertainment that was compatible with childcare; no one minded a crying baby during a silent film. Andrew Heinze goes somewhat farther than other scholars in characterizing the Jewish woman householder – known as the *baleboste* – as an eager and accomplished figure in embracing mass consumption.

Immigrant daughters, especially during their first years in the labor force, were more likely than their fathers and brothers to turn over their entire pay envelopes to their parents. Nonetheless, historians agree that young single working-class women were more immersed than their mothers in the culture of consumption because of their increasingly universal employment outside the home between the time they left school and marriage or childbearing. Although immigrant daughters in general saw their wages as contributions to the family fund, almost all had some spending money of their own, even if it was only lunch-and-carfare money from which they could save a few cents, and struggles over the "allowance" that young women workers would receive out of their wage were a continuing source of discord in working-class families. The workplace peer group paid a great deal of attention to consumption, whether in the form of clothing or commercialized leisure. Because their wages were low and their families made heavy demands on those wages, these women faced the marketplace from a position of great disadvantage. They resorted to a variety of ways to expand their participation in the culture of consumption: allowing men to treat them to entertainment, sometimes in exchange for varying levels of sexual favors; occasional prostitution; installment credit, usually on ruinous terms; relentless bargain hunting; and using their own skills to make clothing and decorate hats. As Susan Glenn has noted of Jewish immigrants, "the lines between mothers and daughters over issues of leisure and consumption cannot be rigidly drawn" (1990: 162). The generations had something to teach each other: although the younger women had the edge on knowledge about styles and fashion, they often turned to older women to learn the key skills of bargain hunting to make their funds go farther.

The lives of farm women, white and black, also reflect the power of cultural coalescence. In part because of the interest of reformers in bringing farm life into technological parity with urban life, we know more about the ideas and experience of farm women as consumers than we do about any other group. Farm women were in a particularly intriguing position in regard to the world of consumption because they continued to be deeply and visibly embedded in production. In fact, they were a special case of the tendency of women in general to continue to do some household production or cash-replacement activity. Histories of farm women emphasize the significance of their production work well into the late twentieth century, whether assisting in the family's principal agricultural activity, producing or preserving food for the family, or manufacturing household items such as clothing or bed linens. This productive work, however, changed its nature because of changes in the marketplace. By the late nineteenth century, few farm women still made cloth at home, instead using store-bought cloth and – in the 1920s – turning to printed feed and flour sacks for their raw material. Sarah Deutsch found that southwestern Hispanic women turned traditional domestic skills such as house plastering, sewing, weaving, and mattress-making into paying occupations, and Rebecca Sharpless found that women on Texas cotton farms did the same with their sewing. Small luxuries such as matched sets of decorated dishes began to appear in farm houses, even those of the relatively poor Texas cotton growers. Sharpless and Mary Neth, like those who studied urban working-class women, point to generational differences over consumption; older and younger women differed, for instance, over the need for such household amenities as curtains.

Historians generally agree that, in spite of the double-barreled encouragement to consume that bombarded them from advertisers in farm journals and mail-order catalogs and from Progressive and agricultural reformers, farm women and their families tended to consume in line with their traditions and economic situations. Farmowners across the board had more elaborately furnished and equipped houses than did the more mobile group of tenants and sharecroppers. As a general rule, investment went first into the cash-producing activity of the farm, so that a wife might scrub clothes on a washboard while her husband ran the latest model of tractor or milking machine. For those who rented their farms, investment in electricity made little sense when they might move on; a truck or car in which to cart the family's possessions or an easily movable machine like a treadle-powered sewing machine was a wiser choice. Not surprisingly, both on Texas cotton farms and in southwestern Hispanic farm villages, sewing machines were ubiquitous: without requiring the investment in electricity, the sewing machine dramatically increased a woman's efficiency in producing clothing and household linens – as well as such farming tools as cotton sacks – in much the same fashion as farm machinery increased her husband's. Labor-saving seems, however, not to have dominated farm women's consumption decisions: explaining one woman's scorn for washing machines, Mary Neth argued that "for farm people, raised in hard times, accustomed to hard work, proud of their work skills and their ability to make do, the new conveniences were both extravagant and disruptive" (1995: 196). Census surveys showed that midwestern farm families adopted telephones and automobiles before tractors, radios, electricity, and running water, reflecting a desire to foster community connections and sociability.

Farm women and urban working-class women both had limited access to the consumption infrastructure because of their concentration in rural areas and in the poorer sectors of cities. Farm women's access to stores was limited, although they were connected to the developing institutions of mass consumption by mail-order catalogs. They found electricity much more elusive. Despite the Rural Electrification Administration, electricity remained a convenience restricted to a minority of midwestern farms: only in Wisconsin and Indiana did electricity reach as many as a third of farms in 1940, and by 1950 fewer than three-quarters of the farms in four out of ten midwestern states had electricity. Class and race mattered as much here as elsewhere, with farm tenants being less likely than owners, and African American tenants less likely than European American tenants, to have electricity. Perhaps more to the point, electricity did not necessarily ease a woman's life. Dairying states, for example, had a higher rate of electrification than other agricultural areas because electricity was far more useful in milking and dairy processing than in the production of staple grains. Using an electric iron or stove might seem wasteful while using electric milking machines would have an obvious payoff. Urban working-class women encountered similar problems. Within urban areas, chain stores with their lower prices and larger stocks tended to shun working-class neighborhoods, and, as Susan J. Kleinberg has shown in the case of Pittsburgh, public utilities gave far better service to wealthier areas.

Just as middle-class women's consumption came to be seen as a problem when women too eagerly accepted the messages of the marketplace, so too was the consumption of working-class and farm women targeted when it grated on the sensibilities of the native-born white bourgeoisie. Kathy Peiss (1986) has pointed to late nineteenth-and early twentieth-century reformers' worries about the moral effect of commercial leisure and the desire for stylish clothing on young working-class women, even as they urged the adoption of more "American" ways of thinking and behaving. Beginning in the 1910s and extending through the 1930s, proponents of Americanization sought, among other things, to imbue immigrant women householders with "American" consumption habits, using settlement house programs and schools to convey their message. These programs primarily targeted women; George Sanchez found that Americanization programs in Los Angeles focused on Mexican housewives during the mid-1910s and the late 1920s, urging them to retain patriarchal family structures while learning English and adopting Anglo foodways and methods of housekeeping. Other immigrant groups faced similar pressures, either on adult women householders or on their daughters through home economics programs in schools. Ted Ownby, tracing nearly two centuries of the culture of consumption in Mississippi, found that white racism made it very difficult for freedpeople to gain the means and the opportunity to consume very much, but that white moralists nonetheless condemned freedpeople for being irresponsible spendthrifts – yet another instance of whites' projecting onto blacks aspects of white culture and conduct that they found disquieting. Government agencies and agricultural reformers encouraged farm women to continue their efforts in domestic manufacture, but at the same time urged patterns of middle-class urban consumption on them. Those whose lives reformers hoped to change picked and chose from their messages in another example of cultural coalescence: Katherine Jellison found, for example, that farm women shunned extension programs that urged them to modernize their household equipment but embraced those that enhanced the domestic production of sewing and food preservation.

If historians have seen European American women as the most individualistic consumers, and immigrant and farm women as consuming with family or community collectivity in mind, they have seen African Americans as the most self-consciously group-oriented in their behavior and attitudes toward consumption. As in many aspects of African American life, gender was often eclipsed by race in shaping experiences of consumption. Evelyn Brooks Higginbotham has pointed to a politics of respectability that infused the Women's Convention of the National Baptist Convention, a politics that rested in part on a conviction that consumption threatened to undermine race unity by dividing wealthy from poor African Americans as well as being "detrimental to individual character and race progress" (1993: 209–10). Stephanie Shaw points to the lessons in "moderation, especially in personal consumption" taught to young women by African American families across the class spectrum (1996: 20). These lessons in thrift fostered cross-class solidarity but they also sought to present young women as sexually virtuous in defense against white men's sexual attacks and white ideas about black women's sexual immorality. Elaborate levels of consumption were not, however, incompatible with race uplift. Glenda Gilmore points to the post-emancipation generation of educated and prosperous African Americans like Sarah Dudley and Charles Pettey, who melded consumption with prominent roles in politics, churches, education, and business, building a bulwark of late Victorian respectability that included carriages and comfortable homes as well as impeccable conduct.

By necessity as well as by inclination, the poorest of southern African Americans after emancipation embraced these lessons. Drawn deeply into debt by sharecropping, they had little access to cash. The shopping they did, whether at the plantation stores that were less venues "for selling goods than for maintaining power relations" or in general stores, was anything but a liberatory experience: they were more likely than whites to buy only subsistence goods, to fall more deeply into and to take longer to get out of debt, and to be treated as second-class citizens when they came to shop (Ownby 1999: 68). Looking for signs of a therapeutic culture of consumption, Ownby finds that for freedpeople, "the search for independence had come to outweigh the taste and desire for most goods" (1999: 77). For most, pleasurable consumption was limited to inexpensive treats at Christmas time and was embedded in family or community rather than individual contexts. Consumption, for the most part, only underlined southern African Americans' subordination to white racism and involved patronizing unsympathetic white merchants. Post-emancipation entrepreneurial opportunities were most accessible in services such as barbering, hairdressing, and undertaking, while businesses that sold goods such as clothing and furniture (and required the investment of scarce white-controlled capital) tended to be monopolized by whites. African Americans' money was more welcome in southern stores than they were: before the changes wrought by the civil rights movement, they were commonly required to use back entrances, denied the right to try on clothing, shoes, or hats, and addressed by their first names rather than by polite forms of address.

As in other communities, generational and class differences over consumption emerged within the African American community by the turn of the twentieth century. Tera Hunter found a complicated geography of commercialized leisure within the

Atlanta African American community. The more restrained Auburn Avenue looked down on the rougher and less inhibited amusements of Decatur Street, and private clubs sorted black Atlantans by class and skin tone. Higginbotham told of early twentieth-century Baptist women's condemnation of the consumption excesses of African Americans, and by the 1930s southern African Americans who remembered a more collective ethic of consumption condemned the more individualistic ways of the younger generation.

In addition to looking at the experience of specific groups with consumption, historians have explored different categories and items of consumption and, in general, have argued that consumption has increasingly pervaded almost all aspects of life. Perhaps most notably, consumption infiltrated the world of youthful peer culture and courtship for young people of virtually every group in the early decades of the twentieth century. Historians, following the lead of Kathy Peiss (1986), first looked at the large industrial cities of the Northeast and Midwest, but soon found that the reach of cultures of consumption went far beyond this industrial heartland. Women in all settings seemed to share a common experience of danger and pleasure in the expanding realms of commercial leisure. As courtship moved from family settings to commercial settings, schools, the streets, and – as Beth Bailey, writing of white middle-class courtship customs, put it – "from front porch to back seat," it increasingly involved spending money. It was a powerful cross-group fact that young men commanded more cash than young women, and so women became dependent upon men for their participation in courtship and leisure. The negotiation of the consequences of that dependence became a staple of youthful lives during the twentieth century.

The courtship and peer cultures of immigrant and African American women provide another example of cultural coalescence and of the limits of mass culture, at least before World War II. On the one hand, Italian, Jewish, and Mexican American families tried to resist the new patterns by continuing the tradition of chaperonage, and Chinese and Japanese families did so through arranged marriage, although by the 1920s both practices were on the way out. On the other hand, historians have found that even as young women of European, Asian, Mexican, and African origin eagerly embraced the new commercialized leisure, they continued to frequent neighborhood institutions such as churches, YWCAs, mutual aid and benevolent institutions, and ethnic/fraternal events. Courtship stood on the overlapping boundaries of traditional and commercial cultures, and young women had a foot in each camp. Men, as well as women, sought to partake of both worlds, as Randy McBee shows in his discussion of young men's social clubs and their determination to remain respectable in the eyes of the community.

Consumption increasingly permeated white middle-class leisure as well. Ellen Garvey explores various aspects of this shift at the turn of the century. She points to the ways in which children, especially girls, collected trade cards from advertisers and constructed elaborate scrapbooks of them, took part in magazine contests, and played games with advertising. More active leisure patterns emerging in the late nineteenth-century United States required new equipment such as tennis rackets and bicycles. Garvey traces the gendering of bicycles in advertising campaigns that linked women's mobility to their sexuality, autonomy, and gender roles. Magazines, which became a more important leisure-time staple for women (magazines for men were spun as adjuncts to business life) in the late nineteenth and early twentieth centuries, went hand in glove with advertising; the boundaries between editorial content, fiction, and advertising became ever blurrier. Students of the 1920s have pointed to the ways in which chocolate consumption was linked to heterosexual courtship, with the woman as dependent receiver of chocolate gifts, and radios began to be marketed to women as aesthetically pleasing additions to a cozy domestic circle.

The last century has also seen dramatic changes in women's appearance, linked to the increased consumption of cosmetics and clothing. Kathy Peiss, tracing women's use of cosmetics from the mid-nineteenth through the mid-twentieth centuries, found their growing acceptance as part of "a dramatic performance of the self in a culture increasingly oriented to display, spectatorship, and consumption" (1998: 39). Women's use of cosmetics, however, was not always what advertisements wanted them to be; Peiss argues that women tended to adopt cosmetics piecemeal rather than as part of "beauty systems" pushed by manufacturers, to take the counsel of their friends more seriously than that of professionals or ads, and to embed their use of cosmetics in the whole of their daily lives rather than root them in romantic fantasies. Similarly, Julie Willett saw women's beauty shops as woven into the fabric of daily life, providing sociability for both black and white women, and for the former also "a means to carve out some space free from white oppression and [a reflection of]... African American desires for economic independence" (2000: 19).

Clothing, like cosmetics, was linked to one's sense of self. Factory-made clothing for women lagged behind that for men; in 1880, ready-made women's clothing was limited to cloaks, underwear, and corsets, items which could be made in relatively standardized ways. Ready-made dresses, suits, skirts, and waists (blouses) were widely available by the turn of the century, although mostly at the low end of fashion and quality. By the eve of World War I, however, manufacturers offered women a combination of fashion and quality in off-the-rack garments, and the trend toward simpler unconstructed styles in the 1920s further democratized fashion. Fashion magazines and mail-order catalogs brought the latest styles to the attention of all, even to cash-poor African American sharecroppers. Clothing for African Americans became a mark of their status as free people and of their independence from the conditions of their wage labor. Students of immigrant and migrant life such as Elizabeth Clark-Lewis have emphasized the importance of "American" dress to newcomers and urban dress to those from rural backgrounds. Sharon Strom has argued that dressing the part also became increasingly important as women moved into white-collar and professional positions.

Expenditures for women's ready-made clothing surpassed those for men's in 1919, although the trend was unevenly distributed. Through the 1920s and 1930s rural home demonstration agents earnestly urged women to sew as much as they could; in 1942, Mississippi white women in farmowning families still spent only two-thirds what their menfolk did for clothing. Once again, a race difference emerges: at the same time that demonstration agents were urging white women to wear attractive and stylish clothing, they exhorted African American women to stick to sewing household goods and clothing made out of flour, sugar, and feed sacks and proudly enumerated the over 50,000 garments thus constructed in 1930. For a broad range of women, sewing remained a way to meld domestic production and consumption and to use their skills to close the gap between what was available or affordable in stores and their desire for self-adornment. The sewing machine and the availability of paper patterns in the late nineteenth century enabled women to sew larger quantities of more stylish clothing. Scholars are only beginning to explore the meanings of women's home sewing, but young women were a prime target of pro-sewing campaigns. By the 1930s, they almost universally received instruction in sewing either in schools or in 4-H Clubs; and in the post-World War II era, they were the objects of ads encouraging them to attract men with fashionable home-sewn clothes. A 1997 survey showed that a third of adult American women sew at home, but we know very little about the meaning of this activity or how it is related to women's attitudes about consumption.

Women's work, both paid and unpaid, underwent changes as the reach of consumption expanded. Although women had a long history of employment in the manufacture of consumer goods such as cloth, clothing, and shoes, the long-term shift of employment from agriculture to manufacturing to service drew women into a central role as workers in establishments serving others' consumption. White women dominated the sales forces of department stores by the late nineteenth century, and women of all groups were involved in family and ethnic businesses. Historians have also pointed to the involvement of women in the entertainment and tourist industries: Chinese women in San Francisco and African American women in New York worked in bars and night clubs that attracted tourists to their communities, and Seminole women sold their patchwork clothing and dolls in commercial tourist villages.

Female consumption also offered entrepreneurial possibilities for women, and historians generally agree that the 1920s was a pivotal decade: after that, women tended to be edged out or marginalized by corporations or male entrepreneurs. A "female economy" of dressmakers and milliners, studied by Wendy Gamber, catered to women's taste for custom-made apparel from the mid-nineteenth century through the 1920s, offering opportunity for entrepreneurship to both black and white, but it declined as fashionable clothing became simpler, cheaper, and more widely available. Women took advantage of the elaboration of the consumer culture of toys to become dollmakers in the late nineteenth and early twentieth centuries, but, argues Miriam Formanek-Brunell, they were pushed aside during the 1920s by corporations and by more traditional gender roles that limited their autonomy. Beauty culture offered women opportunities in manufacturing and selling cosmetics; Kathy Peiss describes the rise of black and white female cosmetics entrepreneurs beginning in the late nineteenth century, but found both increasingly supplanted by mass-market firms beginning in the 1920s. Beauty shops, the majority of them owned and run by women, grew dramatically in number beginning in the first decades of the twentieth century. Increasing segregation during the "nadir" of race relations, changing styles, and the low capital requirements for establishing a salon opened opportunities for African American and Mexican American as well as Anglo women. Women held their own more effectively in beauty shops than in the cosmetics industry, Julie Willett argued, but racial segregation produced a different trajectory for African American and European American beauty operators. During the 1930s, white – but not black – women hairdressers were undermined by professional associations dominated by white men. Corporate domination, according to Willett, decisively transformed the industry only in the mid-1970s, when chains undercut independent shops owned by black and white women alike.

Women's work within the home has been transformed by mass consumption. Over the course of the twentieth century, household equipment such as hot and cold running water, bathrooms, and a host of electric appliances has become the rule. Susan Strasser and Ruth Schwartz Cowan agreed that this transformation has dramatically curtailed the hard physical labor once involved in keeping house, but they saw this as a trade-off rather than a net gain. Strasser emphasized the loss of many of the satisfactions of old-fashioned housekeeping. Cowan, writing as a historian of technology, argued that this shift relieved men and children of work in the home but actually increased women's burden – hence her title, *More Work for Mother* – by "creat[ing] new chores and new standards" (1983: 89). The former include the provision of transportation which is no longer dependably provided by the private sector, and the latter include the elaboration of simple household tasks into more complicated and time-consuming efforts. Other scholars have noted that more elaborate household technology has been accompanied by the concentration of women of color in domestic service – yet another form of consumption primarily engaged in by prosperous European Americans.

Finally, far from depoliticizing women consumers, mass consumption has had varied political implications. Commodities could be used to cement social connections rather than to provide individual gratification or draw invidious distinctions. Historians have noted that farm and working-class families used their radios in social settings rather than just in the privacy of the nuclear family. Mary Murphy is one of a number of scholars who have noted that working-class people did not try to outdo one another in consumption but instead observed "unspoken yet collectively acknowledged norms" (1997: 15).

Consumption could also be a part of a politics of everyday life that enhanced women's sense of dignity, independence, and power. Susan Levine has pointed to the ways in which skilled workers' wives articulated a class-based consumer culture and worked with their husbands' unions to make consumption a part of working-class identity. Workers used consumer goods as organizing tools: cameras, for example, in the 1912 Lawrence strike and automobiles in the 1934 southern textile strike. Clothing, however, was probably the most politically weighted commodity of all. Jacquelyn Dowd Hall, Nan Enstad, Mary Blewett, and Stephen Norwood have linked the wearing of fashionable clothing to European American women's struggles for workplace dignity. Ted Ownby pointed out that the simple act of buying clothing rather than receiving it from the landowner (as freedpeople had earlier done from their enslavers) was a mark of freedom for African American sharecroppers. African American woman wage earners, Tera Hunter and Elizabeth Clark-Lewis have argued, used clothing to "demarcat[e] the line between work and play" and distance themselves from the humiliating conditions of their jobs (Hunter 1997: 182).

African Americans, more than others, have made their consumption explicitly political. Elsa Barkley Brown and Gregg Kimball have pointed out that, in turn-of-the-century Richmond, "Jane and Jim Crow were not only 'city slickers,' they were also natty dressers, appearing in a variety of sophisticated attire" (1996: 105). Civil rights activists such as Anne Moody recalled how the differences between the consumption levels and experiences of blacks and whites shaped their understanding of racial inequality. African American communities persistently tried to establish and foster black businesses. Elsa Barkley Brown showed how this effort could serve women's race and gender needs in her discussion of a black-owned and run Richmond department store, which operated from 1905 to 1912 under the leadership of Maggie Lena Walker and the Independent Order of St. Luke. The St. Luke Emporium provided rare white-collar employment to African American women and sold reasonably priced goods to the community. Walker urged a politics of consumption upon Richmond African Americans: "The only way to kill the Lion [of prejudice] is to stop feeding it" (quoted in Brown 1989b: 626–7). African Americans actively used the consumer boycott: against the spread of segregation laws in the turn-of-the-century South, during the 1930s in "Don't Buy Where You Can't Work" struggles and in Housewives' Leagues campaigns urging African American consumers to spend their money within the black community, and during the 1960s and 1970s as part of the civil rights movement. In less organized fashion, Lizabeth Cohen (1990) argues, black consumers in Chicago turned away from white-owned family businesses in favor of chain stores that offered jobs and fair treatment. The use of consumer activity on both sides of the civil rights movement, by black activists as well as by their white opponents, once again demonstrated the protean quality of consumption.

White middle-class and working-class women also linked consumption to activism. Jewish and Italian women in New York and Providence, studied by Judith Smith and Paula Hyman, boycotted merchants of ethnic foods to protest high prices. Women reformers incorporated consumer culture into their efforts. Kathleen Waters Sander and Margaret Finnegan noted the ways in which women organized to alleviate female poverty and to gain the vote appropriated the forms and techniques of mass consumption. Kathryn Kish Sklar pointed to the origins of the National Consumer's Leagues in abolitionists' boycotts of slave-made goods and organized labor's union label campaigns. The realities of consumption, however, made exertion of women's consumer power difficult. When movements such as the National Consumer's League or the union label crusades urged women to buy only goods produced under decent or unionized working conditions, women faced a difficult choice between ethical purchasing and the demands of their budgets, since retail prices reflected better wages and working conditions. Examining this tension in 1920s Seattle, Dana Frank found "an inherent contradiction between the . . . concerns of working-class housewives and the concerns of trade-union members" (1994: 6). Most women, particularly those recently and precariously arrived in the middle class or those still in the working class, provisioned their households on slender budgets and had no choice but to purchase bargain-priced goods. Almost certainly, women's organized consumer actions did more good by investigating and publicizing the conditions of wage-earning women's lives than by the direct exercise of women's consumer power. State action, such as rationing of food during World War II, was probably more effective in actually changing women's consumption habits.

Most of what has been written about women, gender, and consumption has focused on the period before World War II. Much remains to be learned about how women coped with the new forces shaping their consumption in the last half of the twentieth century: changes in family structure; increased participation in wage earning; urbanization and suburbanization; a new wave of immigration and a revival of ethnic/racial consciousness; and the increased domination of the marketplace by giant corporations. A few scholars have opened the way to a fuller understanding. Lizabeth Cohen (1996) argues that suburban shopping centers empowered women in the family and in public space but constrained them as consumers and workers. Elizabeth Pleck points to the emergence of a post-sentimental pattern in family celebrations, a key feature of which is an increased reliance on the marketplace by wage-earning women who lack the time to make elaborate home-made holiday foods, decorations, and gifts. Pleck and Micaela di Leonardo have explored the ways in which white immigrant women and women of color have used consumption to preserve ethnic traditions. Emerging work suggests that women's worlds of consumption will continue to partake of the complexity of the quilting metaphor with which this essay began: mixing market and nonmarket behavior; shaped by race, ethnicity, class, and age; and reflecting women's agency in crafting a multitude of worlds of consumption instead of bowing under to the power of the market.

BIBLIOGRAPHY

Abelson, Elaine (1989) *When Ladies Go A-Thieving: Middle-class Shoplifters in the Victorian Department Store.* New York: Oxford University Press.

Agnew, Jean-Christophe (1983) "The Consuming Vision of Henry James," in Richard Wightman Fox and T. J. Jackson Lears (eds.), *The Culture of Consumption: Critical Essays in American History, 1880–1980.* New York: Pantheon, pp. 65–100.

Benson, Susan Porter (1986) *Counter Cultures: Saleswomen, Managers, and Customers in American Department Stores, 1890–1940.* Urbana: University of Illinois Press.

Benson, Susan Porter (1996) "Living on the Margin: Working-class Marriage and Family Survival Strategies in the U.S., 1919–1941," in Victoria de Grazia and Ellen Furlough (eds.), *The Sex of Things: Essays on Gender and Consumption.* Berkeley: University of California Press, pp. 212–43.

Benson, Susan Porter (1998) "Gender, Generation, and Consumption in the United States: Working-class Families in the Interwar Period," in Susan Strasser, Charles McGovern, and Matthias Judt (eds.), *Getting and Spending: European and American Consumer Societies in the Twentieth Century.* Cambridge: Cambridge University Press, pp. 223–40.

Bentley, Amy (1998) *Eating for Victory: Food Rationing and the Politics of Domesticity.* Urbana: University of Illinois Press.

Blewett, Mary H. (1998) *Men, Women, and Work: A Study of Class, Gender, and Protest in the Nineteenth-century New England Shoe Industry, 1780–1910.* Urbana: University of Illinois Press.

Boydston, Jeanne (1990) *Home and Work: Housework, Wages, and the Ideology of Labor in the Early Republic.* New York: Oxford University Press.

Breazeale, Kenon (1994) "In Spite of Women: *Esquire* Magazine and the Construction of the Male Consumer," *Signs* 20, pp. 1–22.

Brown, Elsa Barkley (1989a) "African-American Women's Quilting: A Framework for Conceptualizing and Teaching African-American Women's History," *Signs* 14, pp. 921–9.

Brown, Elsa Barkley (1989b) "Womanist Consciousness: Maggie Lena Walker and the Independent Order of Saint Luke," *Signs* 14, pp. 610–33.

Brown, Elsa Barkley and Kimball, Gregg D. (1996) "Mapping the Terrain of Black Richmond," in Kenneth W. Goings and Raymond A. Mohl (eds.), *The New African American Urban History.* Thousand Oaks, CA: Sage, pp. 66–115.

Cameron, Ardis (1993) *Radicals of the Worst Sort: Laboring Women in Lawrence, Massachusetts, 1860–1912.* Urbana: University of Illinois Press.

Carlat, Louis (1998) "'A Cleanser for the Mind': Marketing Radio Receivers for the American Home, 1922–1932," in Roger Horowitz and Arwen Mohun (eds.), *His and Hers: Gender, Consumption, and Technology.* Charlottesville: University of Virginia Press, pp. 115–38.

Chauncey, George (1994) *Gay New York: Gender, Urban Culture, and the Making of the Gay Male World, 1890–1940.* New York: Basic Books.

Clark-Lewis, Elizabeth (1996) *Living In, Living Out: African American Domestics and the Great Migration.* New York: Kodansha International.

Cohen, Lizabeth (1990) *Making a New Deal: Industrial Workers in Chicago, 1919–1939.* New York: Cambridge University Press.

Cohen, Lizabeth (1996) "From Town Center to Shopping Center: The Reconfiguration of Community Marketplaces in Postwar America," *American Historical Review* 101, pp. 1050–81.

Cohen, Miriam (1992) *Workshop to Office: Two Generations of Italian Women in New York City, 1900–1950.* Ithaca, NY: Cornell University Press.

Cooper, Gail (1998) "Love, War, and Chocolate," in Roger Horowitz and Arwen Mohun (eds.), *His and Hers: Gender, Consumption, and Technology.* Charlottesville: University of Virginia Press, pp. 67–94.

Cott, Nancy (1987) *The Grounding of Modern Feminism.* New Haven, CT: Yale University Press.

Cowan, Ruth Schwartz (1983) *More Work for Mother: The Ironies of Household Technology from the Open Hearth to the Microwave.* New York: Basic Books.

Davis, Simone Weil (2000) *Living Up to the Ads: Gender Fictions of the 1920s.* Durham, NC: Duke University Press.

Deutsch, Sarah (1987) *No Separate Refuge: Culture, Class, and Gender on an Anglo-Hispanic Frontier in the American Southwest, 1880–1940.* New York: Oxford University Press.

Deutsch, Sarah (2000) *Women and the City: Gender, Space, and Power in Boston, 1870–1940.* New York: Oxford University Press.

Di Leonardo, Micaela (1987) "The Female World of Cards and Holidays: Women, Families, and the Work of Kinship," *Signs* 12, pp. 440–54.

Ehrenreich, Barbara (1983) *The Hearts of Men: American Dreams and the Flight from Commitment.* New York: Doubleday.

Enstad, Nan (1999) *Ladies of Labor, Girls of Adventure: Working Women, Popular Culture and Labor Politics at the Turn of the Twentieth Century.* New York: Columbia University Press.

Ewen, Elizabeth (1985) *Immigrant Women in the Land of Dollars: Life and Culture on the Lower East Side, 1890–1925.* New York: Monthly Review Press.

Finnegan, Margaret (1999) *Selling Suffrage: Consumer Culture and Votes for Women.* New York: Columbia University Press.

Formanek-Brunell, Miriam (1993) *Made to Play House: Dolls and the Commercialization of American Girlhood, 1830–1930.* New Haven, CT: Yale University Press.

Frank, Dana (1994) *Purchasing Power: Consumer Organizing, Gender, and the Seattle Labor Movement, 1919–1929.* Cambridge, MA: Harvard University Press.

Gamber, Wendy (1997) *The Female Economy: The Millinery and Dressmaking Trades, 1860–1930.* Urbana: University of Illinois Press.

Garvey, Ellen Gruber (1996) *The Adman in the Parlor: Magazines and the Gendering of Consumer Culture, 1880s to 1910s.* New York: Oxford University Press.

Gilmore, Glenda (1996) *Gender and Jim Crow: Women and the Politics of White Supremacy in North Carolina, 1896–1920.* Chapel Hill: University of North Carolina Press.

Glenn, Susan A. (1990) *Daughters of the Shtetl: Life and Labor in the Immigrant Generation.* Ithaca, NY: Cornell University Press.

Glickman, Lawrence (1997) *A Living Wage: American Workers and the Making of Consumer Society.* Ithaca, NY: Cornell University Press.

Greenberg, Cheryl (1997) *Or Does It Explode? Black Harlem in the Great Depression.* New York: Oxford University Press.

Hall, Jacquelyn Dowd (1986) "Disorderly Women: Gender and Labor Militancy in the Appalachian South," *Journal of American History* 73, pp. 354–82.

Harris, Neil (1990) *Cultural Exclusions: Marketing Appetites and Cultural Tastes in Modern America.* Chicago: University of Chicago Press.

Heinze, Andrew R. (1990) *Adapting to Abundance: Jewish Immigrants, Mass Consumption, and the Search for American Identity.* New York: Columbia University Press.

Helvenston, Sally I. and Bubolz, Margaret M. (1999) "Home Economics and Home Sewing in the United States, 1870–1910," in Barbara Burman (ed.), *The Culture of Sewing: Gender, Consumption and Home Dressmaking.* Oxford and New York: Berg, pp. 303–25.

Higginbotham, Evelyn Brooks (1993) *Righteous Discontent: The Women's Movement in the Black Baptist Church, 1880–1920.* Cambridge, MA: Harvard University Press.

Hine, Darlene Clark (1993) "The Housewives' League of Detroit: Black Women and Economic Nationalism," in Nancy A. Hewitt and Suzanne Lebsock (eds.), *Visible Women: New Essays on American Activism.* Urbana: University of Illinois Press, pp. 223–41.

Horowitz, Daniel (1985) *The Morality of Spending: Attitudes toward the Consumer Society in America, 1875–1940.* Baltimore: Johns Hopkins University Press.

Hunter, Tera W. (1997) *To 'Joy My Freedom: Southern Black Women's Lives and Labors After the Civil War.* Cambridge, MA: Harvard University Press.

Hyman, Paula (1980) "Immigrant Women and Consumer Protest: The New York City Kosher Meat Boycott of 1902," *American Jewish History* 70, pp. 91–105.

Jellison, Katherine (1993) *Entitled to Power: Farm Women and Technology, 1913–1963.* Chapel Hill: University of North Carolina Press.

Kersey, Harry A., Jr., and Bannan, Helen M. (1995) "Patchwork and Politics: The Evolving Roles of Florida Seminole Women in the Twentieth Century," in Nancy Shoemaker (ed.), *Negotiators of Change: Historical Perspectives on Native American Women.* New York: Routledge, pp. 193–212.

Kidwell, Claudia B. and Christman, Margaret C. (1974) *Suiting Everyone: The Democratization of Dress in America.* Washington, DC: Smithsonian Institution Press.

Kleinberg, Susan J. (1989) *The Shadow of the Mills: Working-class Families in Pittsburgh, 1870–1917.* Pittsburgh: University of Pittsburgh Press.

Leach, William (1993) *Land of Desire: Merchants, Power, and the Rise of a New American Culture.* New York: Pantheon.

Lears, T. J. Jackson (1983) "From Salvation to Self-realization: Advertising and the Therapeutic Roots of the Consumer Culture, 1880–1930," in Richard Wightman Fox and T. J. Jackson Lears (eds.), *The Culture of Consumption: Critical Essays in American History, 1880–1980.* New York: Pantheon, pp. 1–38.

Lears, T. J. Jackson (1994) *Fables of Abundance: A Cultural History of Advertising in America.* New York: Basic Books.

Levine, Susan (1991) "Workers' Wives: Gender, Class, and Consumerism in the 1920s United States," *Gender and History* 3, pp. 45–64.

McBee, Randy D. (2000) *Dance Hall Days: Intimacy and Leisure among Working-class Immigrants in the United States.* New York: New York University Press.

Marchand, Roland (1985) *Advertising the American Dream: Making Way for Modernity.* Berkeley: University of California Press.

Margerum, Eileen (1999) "The Sewing Needle as Magic Wand: Selling Sewing Lessons to American Girls after the Second World War," in Barbara Burman (ed.), *The Culture of Sewing: Gender, Consumption and Home Dressmaking.* Oxford and New York: Berg, pp. 193–205.

Matsumoto, Valerie (1993) *Farming the Home Place: A Japanese American Community in California, 1919–1982.* Ithaca, NY: Cornell University Press.

Mehaffy, Marilyn Maness (1997) "Advertising Race/Raceing Advertising: The Feminine Consumer(-Nation), 1876–1900," *Signs* 23, pp. 131–74.

Meyerowitz, Joanne J. (1988) *Women Adrift: Independent Wage-earners in Chicago, 1880–1930.* Chicago: University of Chicago Press.

Mink, Gwendolyn (1995) *The Wages of Motherhood: Inequality in the Welfare State, 1917–1942.* Ithaca, NY: Cornell University Press.

Mumford, Kevin (1977) *Interzones: Black/White Sex Districts in Chicago and New York in the Early Twentieth Century.* New York: Columbia University Press.

Murphy, Mary (1997) *Mining Cultures: Men, Women, and Leisure in Butte, 1914–1941.* Urbana: University of Illinois Press.

Nasaw, David (1993) *Going Out: The Rise and Fall of Public Amusements.* New York: Basic Books.

Neth, Mary (1995) *Preserving the Family Farm: Women, Community, and the Foundations of Agribusiness in the Midwest, 1900–1940.* Baltimore: Johns Hopkins University Press.

Norwood, Stephen (1990) *Labor's Flaming Youth: Telephone Operators and Worker Militancy, 1878–1923.* Urbana: University of Illinois Press.

Ownby, Ted (1999) *American Dreams in Mississippi: Consumers, Poverty, and Culture, 1830–1998.* Chapel Hill: University of North Carolina Press.

Peiss, Kathy (1986) *Cheap Amusements: Working Women and Leisure in Turn-of-the-century New York.* Philadelphia: Temple University Press.

Peiss, Kathy (1998) *Hope in a Jar: The Making of America's Beauty Culture.* New York: Metropolitan Books.

Pleck, Elizabeth H. (2000) *Celebrating the Family: Ethnicity, Consumer Culture, and Family Rituals.* Cambridge, MA: Harvard University Press.

Ruíz, Vicki (1998) *From Out of the Shadows: Mexican Women in 20th-century America.* New York: Oxford University Press.

Ryan, Mary P. (1981) *The Cradle of the Middle Class: The Family in Oneida County, New York, 1780–1865.* New York: Cambridge University Press.

Sanchez, George (1993) *Becoming Mexican American: Ethnicity, Culture, and Identity in Chicano Los Angeles.* New York: Oxford University Press.

Sander, Kathleen Waters (1998) *The Business of Charity: The Woman's Exchange Movement, 1832–1900.* Urbana: University of Illinois Press.

Scanlon, Jennifer (1995) *Inarticulate Longings: The Ladies' Home Journal, Gender, and the Promises of Consumer Culture.* New York: Routledge.

Sharpless, Rebecca (1999) *Fertile Ground, Narrow Choices: Women on Texas Cotton Farms, 1900–1940.* Chapel Hill: University of North Carolina Press.

Shaw, Stephanie J. (1996) *What a Woman Ought to Be and to Do: Black Professional Women Workers During the Jim Crow Era.* Chicago: University of Chicago Press.

Sklar, Kathryn Kish (1995) *Florence Kelley and the Nation's Work: The Rise of Women's Political Culture, 1830–1900.* New Haven, CT: Yale University Press.

Smith, Judith E. (1985) *Family Connections: A History of Italian and Jewish Immigrant Lives in Providence, Rhode Island, 1900–1940.* Albany: State University of New York Press.

Steele, Jeffrey (2000) "Reduced to Images: American Indians in Nineteenth-century Advertising," in Jennifer Scanlon (ed.), *The Gender and Consumer Culture Reader.* New York: New York University Press, pp. 109–28.

Strasser, Susan (1982) *Never Done: A History of American Housework.* New York: Pantheon.

Strom, Sharon Hartman (1992) *Beyond the Typewriter: Gender, Class, and the Origins of Modern American Office Work, 1900–1930.* Urbana: University of Illinois Press.

Swiencicki, Mark A. (1998) "Consuming Brotherhood: Men's Culture, Style, and Recreation as Consumer Culture, 1880–1930," *Journal of Social History* 31, pp. 773–808.

Tone, Andrea (1996) "Contraceptive Consumers: Gender and the Political Economy of Birth Control in the 1930s," *Journal of Social History* 29, pp. 485–506.

Trafzer, Clifford E. (1995) "Horses and Cattle, Buggies and Hacks: Purchases by Yakima Women, 1909–1912," in Nancy Shoemaker (ed.), *Negotiators of Change: Historical Perspectives on Native American Women.* New York: Routledge, pp. 176–92.

Walsh, Margaret (1979) "The Democratization of Fashion: The Emergence of the Women's Dress Pattern Industry," *Journal of American History* 66, pp. 299–313.

Willett, Julie A. (2000) *Permanent Waves: The Making of the American Beauty Shop.* New York: New York University Press.

Yung, Judy (1995) *Unbound Feet: A Social History of Chinese Women in San Francisco.* Berkeley: University of California Press.

Chapter Seventeen

Urban Spaces and Popular Cultures, 1890–1930

Nan Enstad

A JOOK joint, Atlanta, 1910. Big Sue has shed the overalls she wears at her job in the steel mill for a stylin' dress that makes heads turn on Decatur Street, and is bumping and grinding out the new dance, the Funky Butt, to the sweet, low bluesy sounds of the live band. The mostly African American crowd knows an expert when it sees one, and they shout out their approval. The music, the clothes, the dance, the club itself, the neighborhood, all constitute a culture, a space in which Sue and her compatriots make meaning out of the intolerable conditions of their exploited labor and the race and gender politics of the city of Atlanta. Here, as the proprietor takes their hard-earned cash, they purchase a space – not one free of the hierarchies which shape their world, but one in which they engage those hierarchies on different terms than in their workplaces and other public places.

The live radio show, "National Barn Dance," Station WLS, Chicago, 1929. Myrtle Eleanor Cooper, born in Boone, North Carolina, and recently relocated to Chicago from Elizabethton, Tennessee, where she worked in a hosiery mill, walks up to the big radio studio microphone. Myrtle introduces herself as "Lulu Belle," shaping herself into the model of southern hick that audiences love to love, and sings songs that are an amalgam of traditional ballads, blues, and Tin Pan Alley recently dubbed "country music." Ironically, these songs allow Lulu to make money as a "southern country girl" in a northern city after struggling to make a living in the South. Before her publicity photograph, Lulu sheds the fashionable clothes she wears on the street for a plain, gingham dress that matches the fiction of the southern country girl. Lulu Belle goes on to become one of the most popular country singers of her day.

Both Sue and Lulu took part in commercialized popular culture, that is, both made meaning in their lives through an interaction with the economic markets which traded in cultural spaces and products. While American "consumer" culture can be traced to the colonial era, the expansion of the industrial economy by the 1870s meant that manufacturers specifically targeted young working women as a market, distinct from their roles as consumers for their families. Their inclusion as individual buyers, first for clothing and cheap fiction, marked the beginning of a new era in which the proliferation of personal products crossed class and race lines. In addition, the burgeoning entertainment economy brought vaudeville, motion pictures, dance halls, and jook joints to urban and often small-town environments. The owners of these spaces welcomed and indeed solicited women's attendance; these public spaces in turn provided the possibilities for the development of new subcultures based in pleasure and self-display.

The increasingly national distribution of popular culture products blurred the differences between local cultures, but did not eradicate them. Though Sue was a participant in Atlanta leisure life and Lulu was a performer on a nationally syndicated radio show, we should not be fooled into seeing their experiences as completely juxtaposed or belonging to different moments of an evolutionary change. Sue danced within a local culture, but she danced to a music that was increasingly national, as musicians traveled through the vaudeville circuits and as "race records" took the music into individual homes. Likewise, though Lulu performed for a national audience, the new popularity of country music spawned a vitalization of *local* music cultures across the South, and musicians saw new-found hope of making a living through the possibilities offered by radio. Lulu's songs and her status as a star thus held distinctive and powerful meanings for audiences back home in North Carolina and Tennessee.

Although the commercialism of leisure concerns all historical actors, it holds particular salience for historians of women for two reasons: first, the female presence in public space was part of what was new about consumer culture for everyone. It was what made these spaces and activities particularly "modern." Second, goods and entertainment were often sold to women as part of a new freedom available in the modern city, juxtaposed to their constricted mobility within the traditional, patriarchal family.

Herein lies one of the key problems that women's historians have faced. The public spaces of leisure and the cultures which take root in relation to consumer products are just as imbued with social hierarchy as any other in US society. Though capitalists often tried to sell goods to women through *promises* of freedom, they clearly could not and did not fully wish to deliver on these promises. The cultural opportunities Sue and Lulu experienced emerged not from a new freedom but from what the market would bear: Decatur Street in Atlanta was a red-light district that supported a number of for-profit music venues that would not have been tolerated on the high-tone, white-dominated Peachtree Street. Sears-owned radio station WLS (the letters stood for "World's Largest Store") was less interested in music than in filling programming space designed to sell products. People like Sue and Lulu who cared about music, dance, and culture had to work within the constraints of these contexts. Nevertheless, women imbued public spaces and consumer products with their own meanings as they fashioned subcultures and subjectivities. The resultant meanings were diverse, and sometimes exceeded or opposed existing hierarchical structures and ideologies. Despite the fact that producers could not free women from gender, class, or race hierarchies, women themselves made that promise salient, albeit not fully realized, when they creatively embraced and utilized popular culture as a resource with which to construct new identities in the city. Both Sue and Lulu utilized this resource to make themselves valuable despite the low wages paid them as industrial or domestic workers. Urban spaces, then, became vibrant arenas of cultural production despite painful constraints. Historians have dealt with these paradoxes in different ways over time, driving a creative and dynamic field of inquiry with great relevance for women's history, and US history as a whole.

This essay examines some of the major historical scholarship on women, urban spaces, and commercialized popular culture. It is based primarily on the era of 1890–1930, in part because this is when commercialized leisure proliferated and enabled women to create new social practices within popular culture, and in part because this time period has been the focus of most women's history scholarship on this topic to date. It examines work that takes women as subject matter and explores their socially situated experiences with popular culture; studies which exclusively explore *representations* of women or gender in popular culture texts are not included. My goal is to provide a frame for understanding the past twenty years of dynamic and diverse scholarship in this field and a window for viewing the promises and possibilities for its future.

Let me begin by pointing out that the study of women and popular culture is by no means a unitary subject. It includes Sue, a participant who may be expert, but makes no money from her skills, and Lulu, who as a migrant woman worker hit it big as a performer and made far more money than others of her class could through factory or domestic work. It encompasses, also, the female radio listeners of Lulu's broadcasts scattered across the country, and the purchasers of race records, who heard in their own homes the sounds that Big Sue danced to in public. Also part of this subject matter are the proprietors at various levels of cultural production and reception, and the reformers who worked to influence the relationship between industries and consumers that was transforming urban and small-town landscapes. At all levels, these diverse historical actors participated in a tectonic movement, a slow but steady development in which people translated new technologies and economies into community configurations, possibilities, and hierarchies. Thus, when women's historians questioned the meanings of commercialized popular culture, they engaged an inquiry about a major change in US society and women's relationship to it. They have asked what happened to women as well as what parts women played in this drama. They have asked, too, who women could become in this new context; that is, they have engaged the central question of the nature of the formation of the female self and female agency in relationship to consumer society.

I would like to suggest that we can fruitfully analyze critical work on women and popular culture by examining four conceptions of the self which critics have used to understand women's relationship to consumerism in the past one hundred years: they have seen the self in terms of "character," "consciousness," "identity," and "subjectivity." These concepts have been somewhat sequential: black and white Progressive reformers at the turn of the twentieth century utilized the notion of "character," which had its roots in nineteenth-century Victorian thought; the idea of "consciousness" also has roots in the nineteenth century but became prevalent in cultural criticism in the 1940s with the work of the Frankfurt School; "identity" became a guiding principle in the 1980s social history; and poststructuralists from the late 1980s to the present introduced the idea of "subjectivity." (More about the definitions of these terms shortly.) However, newer approaches did not fully displace the old and most historical works carry the influences of more than one of these conceptual approaches. My purpose in utilizing these concepts is not to pigeonhole scholars into camps but rather to illuminate central theoretical concerns in the scholarship that often remain implicit, and thus to reveal past and present trends in critical thought.

Women's historians are best seen as part of a tradition of cultural criticism that began in the Progressive era, when female reformers questioned the effects of women's participation in consumer culture. First and foremost, they were interested in whether popular culture would be likely to affect the ways women acted in the world, or to use the language of social history, how it affected women's agency. Reformers did not hold identical opinions about the value or detriment of popular culture on young women, but most operated within a notion of the self based in "character." Lillian Wald, settlement house worker on the Lower East Side of New York City, saw the self as something crafted by the individual through discipline, education, and the refining influence of high culture. It was only through harnessing one's instincts and desires for the purposes of rational, willed action that one achieved "character" and agency. Wald saw the young women in the ghetto as victims of an economic system that prevented such development of the self. She blamed industrial capitalism for causing this problem and did what she could to ameliorate it by bringing education and refinement to the ghetto through the Henry Street Settlement. For Wald, because young women could not pursue the development of self, they were dissipated, irrational, and more instinctive than cultured. She believed that Lower East Side women's irrational desire for consumer items signaled the degree of damage that the industrial order created. This undermined young women's agency and made them unable to act truly in their own self interest.

Leslie Woodcock Tentler was the first among women's historians to engage rigorously the question of what working women's participation in the growing consumer culture meant. In her book, *Wage-earning Women*, Tentler argued that commercialized leisure, including dance halls, amusement parks, and movie theaters, provided women "space and privacy" within which they created "more daring standards of sexual conduct" (1979: 111). Like Wald, she linked self and agency in her assessment: "Certainly," she argued, "the greater freedom in dress, manners and morals that came about in the early twentieth century altered the self image of many women, altering too their sense of what was possible in the lives they led" (1979: 113). With this, Tentler inaugurated a line of inquiry that continues to engage women's historians. But Tentler quickly concluded that the continued economic dependence of working women meant that their greater social freedoms "did not fundamentally change the life possibilities of young women" (1979: 114).

Tentler was influenced by Marxist views which conceptualized the self in terms of "consciousness." One's consciousness emanated directly from material conditions and one's experience and position in social hierarchies. A working-class position – especially wage labor – would provide instances of oppression that could reveal the nature of the power structure and prompt radicalism. However, various forces might intervene and produce a "false consciousness," causing a person to identify with the ruling class rather than with workers. Class and gender "consciousness," for Tentler, was an awareness of one's true place in power relations. Tentler was also arguing *against* a predominant view, held by both orthodox Marxists and liberal historians, that women gained "liberation" when they became wage workers because paid labor disrupted family and ethnic controls and brought women into a relationship to the market that could prompt class consciousness. Tentler argued that women did not achieve class consciousness in this period, not because of their lack of refinement, as Wald believed, but because they still did not think of themselves as workers. Drawing next on the Frankfurt School notion that popular culture typically functioned to deceive people about their true place in power structures, Tentler proposed that ideas about marriage and romance disseminated through novels, songs, and other media taught women to look to marriage, not class-based collective action, as their salvation from workplace drudgery. Romantic notions served at once to chain women's class consciousness and their gender consciousness: "Little in the experience of... most working-class women prepared them to adopt assertive, class-conscious attitudes toward their employment.... Among their peers, young working women were encouraged to seek future security and mobility through marriage rather than employment. They learned to accept a work world that defined women as dependent and marginal employees" (1979: 80).

The notion of consciousness, unlike that of character, allowed Tentler to take popular culture seriously and assess its effects. While Wald saw popular culture as an *impediment* to the development of the self, Tentler saw it as *constitutive* of the self and thus as crucial to understanding women's lives. But neither Tentler nor Wald saw women as agents in this drama. Rather, women were simply effects, products of their experiences, for Tentler, or their lack of experiences, for Wald. Neither learned very much about women's actual subcultural activities. Though Tentler noted that women's popular culture changed their "self image," she did not explore the implications of this beyond the world of dating, because she asserted that only economic independence could produce noteworthy change in gender dynamics. She thus reduced women's diverse experiences in leisure and consumption to a means of gaining "greater social freedom."

In the mid-1980s, Kathy Peiss, Elizabeth Ewen, and Joanne Meyerowitz profoundly revised this interpretation by shifting their attention to working-class women's identities, rather than their consciousness, and by documenting closely the social history of women's daily experiences. Peiss, Ewen, and Meyerowitz focused their studies quite differently though all examined working-class women at the turn of the twentieth century. Peiss's *Cheap Amusements* (1986) looked explicitly at working women and the rise of commercial amusements in New York City; Ewen's *Immigrant Women in the Land of Dollars* (1985) focused on the immigration of Jewish and Italian women to New York's Lower East Side and discussed work, family, and commercial leisure within an examination of the process of "Americanization"; Meyerowitz's *Women Adrift* (1988) explored single female migrants to Chicago and the subcultures they created. All three rejected earlier "liberation" models of wage earning as well as Tentler's thesis. Peiss criticized Tentler's model, saying, "it would be misleading to view the consciousness of most young women solely in terms of a desire for marriage and to argue that their leisure activities simply affirmed... a traditional patriarchal order" (1986: 62).

Meyerowitz explicitly advocated a "subcultural approach" which "emphasizes both the possibilities of change created by wage work and the constraints that limited women wage earners' freedom of action" (1988: xxii). All three documented ways in which commercial culture offered women a public space in which to push against existing constraints. In particular, the authors showed that women claimed a new sexual expressiveness in the dance halls, amusement parks, and motion picture theaters, even as they also experienced renewed sexual and gender inequities.

Peiss, Meyerowitz, and Ewen also validated the study of popular culture in new ways. They participated in broad changes in women's and labor history by shifting attention from an exclusive focus on the workplace as the source of "consciousness" to the myriad experiences that constituted daily life and shaped working-class, ethnic, and gender identities. In their books, popular culture was situated neither as impediment to the formation of character or self, nor as a deflection from true class consciousness, but as a crucial location in which gender, class, race, and ethnic identities developed. As such, cultural spaces and activities required careful research to reconstruct the particular social relations that women experienced. Peiss set out to "explore the trivia of social experience for clues to the ways working women constructed and gave meaning to their lives" (1986: 3). Meyerowitz examined how migrant women "formed social and economic relationships in the city to substitute for the support and companionship of family" (1988: xviii). Ewen showed how Americanization meant both exchanging one nationality for another *and* entering an industrial and consumer society. She asserted that in order to understand how these two aspects worked together one must reconstruct how women were "initiated into the culture of daily life," including "community activities, shopping, leisure, and recreation" (1985: 15). For all three, the self is constructed within culture, and particular identities will thus be revealed in part through a study of its spaces and products.

But Peiss, Ewen, and Meyerowitz did not argue only that popular culture offered women opportunity for new identities and agency. Indeed, all three found that women were reinscribed into social hierarchies through activities that felt liberating. Peiss argued that, "unaccompanied by substantive changes in the allocation of power, work and resources by gender, [commercial culture] served to foreclose women's options" (1986: 188). Meyerowitz, likewise, argued that women's subculture "failed to remedy low wages, promoted female economic dependence and encouraged women to value themselves as sexual objects" (1988: 141). Ewen showed that the new commercial culture could be the source of painful rifts in the family and the loss of community bonds. Peiss encapsulated the new historiographic stance when she called for "a doubled vision, to see that women's embrace of style, fashion, romance and mixed-sex fun could be a source of autonomy and pleasure as well as a cause of their continuing oppression" (1986: 6).

What Peiss succinctly stated in a sentence has proved to be the impetus for over a decade of scholarship. In what ways can popular culture experiences be a source of autonomy or agency? How exactly did women in different contexts shape this space and their activities within it? In what particular ways was popular culture a cause of continuing oppression? Since the mid-1980s, articles and books in women's history have taken up these questions, focusing on several key themes, most of which were inaugurated by Peiss, Ewen, and Meyerowitz: changes in the uses of public spaces, reformers' responses to women's popular culture activities (including new notions of female delinquency), the impact of popular culture on formal political action, women's experiences as performers and consumers, and the formation of race and ethnic identities. In the process of pursuing these questions, historians have taken the study of popular culture in new and exciting directions. My comments now turn to these developments; I will return to notions of the "self" and subjectivity at the close of the essay.

One of the most influential of Peiss, Ewen, and Meyerowitz's innovations was the attention to how women occupied a new kind of public space when they engaged in leisure activities. They showed how dance halls, amusement parks, and motion picture theaters constituted new arenas uniquely open to women, while historians Robert W. Snyder and William Leach, also writing in the 1980s, showed the particular relationship of vaudeville and department stores to female consumers. Snyder, in *The Voice of the City* (1989), argued that as vaudeville opened its doors to women in the late nineteenth century, it adopted a more "respectable" image and promised audiences edifying and morally uplifting entertainment. Producers knew that they needed to attract middle-class women as audience members in order to realize vaudeville's profit potential. Thus, women's participation as audience shifted the marketing and the content of vaudeville considerably. However, it did not turn it into refined, Victorian entertainment. Rather, Snyder argued that the participation of women helped break down class divisions in entertainment consumption and exposed the middle class to cultural forms – music, dance, and comedy – that emerged first within working-class urban cultures. Likewise, department stores wooed a female clientele. William Leach, in "Transformations in a Culture of Consumption" (1984), argued that department stores created a female-oriented space in which the gaze was solicited and directed toward sumptuous displays of products. Leach found department stores to be "emancipatory" for women precisely because they provided a new urban space that made middle-class women's lives more secular, more public, and more invested in individualism. Collectively, these historians mapped a profoundly altered public urban landscape that was transforming daily life and social relations.

In 1991, film scholar Miriam Hansen suggested that these transformations in public life had great political as well as social implications. She argued in *Babel and Babylon* that motion pictures created the possibility for an "alternative public sphere," one with particular importance for women (1991: 15). Hansen drew explicitly on the work of three women's historians: Peiss and Ewen's findings on working women as audience for motion pictures and Joan Landes's theoretical argument in *Women and the Public Sphere in the Age of the French Revolution* (1988). Landes showed that the nineteenth-century ideal of the public sphere, originating in the Enlightenment, was inherently gendered: the citizen was a man who gained his capability for rational citizenship through property ownership and participation in the public world of business, which was ideologically juxtaposed to and obscured the domestic sphere's economic functions and origins. Women, by definition, could not occupy public space respectably without escort; if they did so, they risked being considered "public women" or prostitutes. Hansen argued that the emerging "industrial-commercial public spheres" such as motion picture theaters could challenge the Enlightenment ideal of "public" and "private" by inserting into its binary equation a third public space. This third space affected older forms of cultural practice, "creating an unstable mixture" (1991: 92). By providing women a public place to congregate, motion picture theaters and similar arenas could destabilize the definition of public identities and thereby create an alternative public sphere. Because politics and full citizenship were dependent on a definition of public visibility and participation, this shift promised to have myriad effects on women, men, and US society. Hansen showed that the significance of women's participation in popular culture thus extends to the very shaping of public life and gender definitions themselves.

Lauren Rabinovitz's book, *For the Love of Pleasure* (1998), built directly on Hansen's work and pointed out that because the patriarchal gaze was one of the primary means of regulating public life, "looking relations" were particularly charged in the new public spaces of leisure at the turn of the century. As both spectator and spectacle in these new public domains, women found their own gaze solicited and directed, even as they became the object of the male gaze and part of the spectacular landscape of amusements. Thus they were both consumer and product in the new arena. Moving beyond Leach's optimism about women's emancipation as consumer spectators, Rabinovitz studied looking relations across social spaces in early twentieth-century Chicago, including department stores, amusement parks, the 1893 World's Fair, and motion pictures in order to explore the "relationship between women's leisure and the construction of a modern female subject" (1998: 11).

Historians have also extended Peiss's and Meyerowitz's work on reformers' efforts to control women's popular culture activities and have demonstrated that the regulation of women's bodies and behaviors shifted at this time from the family to social institutions and the state. Women's increased public presence transgressed Victorian codes of behavior, which prompted reformers' increased surveillance of them. Reformers sought to label and control the expanded range of behaviors and social transgressions that women could try out in the new, public sphere away from family supervision. A number of historians have focused on the construction of female "delinquency," rooted in part in commercial leisure activities. Some historians focus on reformers' attempts to regulate the spaces and cultural forms of commercial leisure: the hours and lighting of dance halls and motion picture theaters, and the content of vaudeville shows and movies. Others look at the efforts to regulate women themselves. Here I discuss only the latter.

Historians who focus on delinquency have demonstrated that women's participation in commercial popular culture prompted changes in private and state efforts to control women's sexuality and in understandings of "normal" adolescent female behavior. Historians chart whether reformers saw women as victims or as agents of their moral demise and find change over time as well as differences according to the race of the women in question. Mary Odem, in her book *Delinquent Daughters* (1995), argued that reformers in late nineteenth-century Los Angeles saw young white women as victims of untrustworthy men, most of whom they met at places of amusement; such a view prompted them to push for age-of-consent legislation in order to involve the judicial system in controlling male behavior. However, during the first two decades of the twentieth century, Odem argued, reformers "replaced the model of victimization with one of female delinquency that acknowledged the sexual agency of young women" (1995: 4). Hazel Carby and Tera Hunter found different patterns in their studies of African American women. Carby, in "Policing the Black Woman's Body in an Urban Context," found that white and black middle-class reformers regarded working-class black women and men as "easily victimized subjects who quickly succumbed to the forces of vice and degradation" (1992: 739). Tera Hunter, in *To 'Joy My Freedom*, found that middle-class reformers described white women as "vulnerable, innocent victims exploited by entertainment companies, saloon keepers and unscrupulous men. Black women of the same class, however, were usually described as agents of moral decline and decay" (1997: 154).

Reformers' understanding of women's agency directed their efforts at regulation. Odem argued that when reformers shifted from a victimization model to seeing women as sexual agents, they shifted their regulatory efforts from men to women. This prompted a change in the relationship of women to the state, as reformers pushed for an increase in legislation, state reform programs and institutions. Once they achieved these goals, however, reformers found that they could not control the new programs and institutions, which often were sexist and more punitive than reformers intended. This increase in state involvement also had an impact on working-class family life, as distraught parents could now call upon a state agency to help them control undutiful daughters. Thus, the shift in women's mobility through the public spaces of amusements had profound implications for the role of the state and for the governance of family life. Here is an example of the ways popular culture as a third space created what Hansen termed an "unstable mixture." Both the most classically "public" and "private" realms – the state and the family – shifted regulatory functions in an attempt to control women in this third space, further blurring idealized distinctions between the two spheres.

Regulation served not only to control women but to construct meanings of race, class, and age. Carby argued that reformers associated blackness with vice. This was exacerbated by the fact that many black women frequented places of amusement not only as consumers, but as paid workers in entertainment and service. In addition, because of housing discrimination, blacks found themselves relegated to the neighborhoods surrounding red-light districts. Thus, Carby found that reformers engaged in a series of "moral panics" that focused on controlling the agency of young, black women and simultaneously constructed race ideologies. In addition, black reformers secured their own class positions "in the process of claiming the rights to circumscribe the rights of young black working-class women and to transform their behavior on the grounds of nurturing the progress of the race as a whole" (1992: 746). Of course, what constituted delinquent behavior was not fixed. Ruth Alexander, in *The "Girl Problem"* (1995), argued that by the 1920s, psychologists developed notions of middle-class "adolescence" which defined behaviors seen as deviant or dangerous ten years earlier among working-class young women as normative for a particular stage of life. Thus, young women, reformers, state agents, psychologists, and entertainment industry marketers laid the groundwork for the emerging distinction between a normative, white, middle-class youth culture and working-class leisure cultures still associated with vice and deviant sexuality.

The ways that commercialized leisure transformed public space also has proved significant for women's political actions and identities. Hansen's notion of an "alternative public sphere" is important here because it offers us an opportunity to see how changes in public life, while not originating in politics, could have ramifications for how politics and political identities were conceived. Women increasingly gained public identities through their participation in consumer culture; since many other forms of public identities were closed to women, these held particular importance for them. Historians have begun to explore the impact of changes in public space and public identities on how politics were defined and pursued at various levels, by all historical actors but particularly by women. At root, this effort challenges presumptions prevalent in Tentler's and earlier scholarship that popular culture diverted people from class consciousness and could only be studied in juxtaposition to politics.

Historians have argued that popular culture and the transformation of public space are significant for politics in a number of ways. One of the first arguments was that an increased desire for fashionable clothing and tickets to entertainment venues could prompt greater dissatisfaction with low wages and, consequently, political action. Historians have also argued that the styles created in consumer culture became key to the formation of a politicized culture and identity. Stephen Norwood, in *Labor's Flaming Youth* (1990), argued that the "solidarity of youth" in general facilitated organizing among young telephone operators in Boston. Furthermore, he argued that the workers and strikers built a political culture through the use of shared references, display, and values rooted in popular culture. Similarly, historians have argued that women fashioned political identities wielding resources initially used to form public identities in popular culture, and that they marshaled these new identities in occupying political spaces heretofore reserved for men. Jacquelyn Hall argued in "Disorderly Women" that "through dress, language, and gesture, female strikers [in Elizabethton, Tennessee] expressed a complex cultural identity and turned it to their own rebellious purposes" (1986: 308). My own work, *Ladies of Labor, Girls of Adventure* (1999), showed that New York strikers in 1909 utilized identities formed in popular culture to claim political agency. Finally, Margaret Finnegan, in *Selling Suffrage* (1999), demonstrated that suffrage activists employed the techniques of the department store and advertising in constructing their political styles and strategies. Suffragists made use of the shopping spaces uniquely created for them as middle-class women: they often rented store windows for political displays and cooperated with department stores to promote suffrage paraphernalia, such as special hats, banners, and pins. Finnegan found both negative and positive effects of "blurring the boundaries between the commercial and the civic environments" and argued that women's "concern with managing impressions, appearances, and self-presentation" made them more conservative (1999: 75, 109).

Historians have begun looking at how women performers participated in shaping consumer culture and its possibilities, despite severe limits on their autonomy. The burgeoning entertainment industry drew women to the public spaces of leisure not only as audience, but also as workers and performers. Women found jobs in vaudeville as actors, musicians, comedians, dancers, and chorus girls; they worked in motion pictures as actors, extras, and screenwriters; they worked in radio as actors, announcers, and musicians. Indeed, the female form in public view was a key component of the appeal of the new commercial culture, and women capitalized upon and influenced the meanings of this phenomenon. Of course, despite the expansion of opportunities, women's enhanced role as performers was not all positive: the terms of labor were often highly exploitive, the narratives of skits and films were typically sexist, racist, and nativist, and the patriarchal gaze governed most female displays.

Hazel Carby, in "It Jus' Be's Dat Way Sometime" (1986), argued that blues singers of the 1920s, popular on the vaudeville circuit and on race records, created a space for voicing African American women's concerns. Comparing the blues songs to African American women's literature, Carby noted that the music of women's blues singers engaged themes of migration, work, and sexuality which "embodied the social relations and contradictions of Black displacement: of rural migration and the urban flux" (1986: 242). The Blues Queens, with their glamorous gowns and regal styles, celebrated black women's beauty and "asserted a woman's sexual independence" in the face of a society which denied both (1986: 245). Angela Davis, in *Blues Legacies and Black Feminism* (1998), traced a black feminist working-class tradition in the Blues Queens. Susan Glenn, in *Female Spectacle* (2000), argues that female theater performers in the late nineteenth century fostered greater sexual freedom for women and emphasized individualism, personality, and female self-development through their stage performances and in their self-representations, anticipating key aspects of the feminist movement of the early twentieth century. Glenn explains that popular performers were more than reflections of historical changes: they were proto-feminists and self-conscious innovators who participated in broad-based shifts in modern thought that displaced earlier notions of "character" with a new notion of self.

M. Alison Kibler, in *Rank Ladies* (1999), also explored women vaudeville performers and argued that comedy teams like the Elinore sisters exploited ethnic, class, and gender hierarchies in creating their humor. Like blacks who had to wear blackface to gain entrance to vaudeville and musical theater in the late nineteenth century, Kate Elinore faced sexist exclusions in vaudeville where men were comedians, so Kate based her comedic character on female impersonators, many of whom utilized sexist representations to create their humor. Nevertheless, her transgressions challenged the gendered construction of humor in male/female comedy teams and mocked traditional definitions of femininity. Other white women employed the racist tradition of blackface to claim clown status and escape the position of stylized, erotic objects. Thus, new possibilities for white female behaviors came through the endorsement and extension of gender, race, and ethnic hierarchies. These scholars have not looked only at textual readings of performances and representations of gender. Rather, they have asked how female performers as historical actors and as cultural workers negotiated the constraints of the industry, participated in the construction of themselves as products or "stars," and had a broad social impact through their stage personas.

Historians have encountered quite different challenges when studying the thousands of ordinary women who took part in popular culture by purchasing stylish clothing, attending vaudeville, motion pictures, and amusement parks, and reading popular, mass-distributed fiction. One challenge is that critics who see the self in terms of "character" and "consciousness" have typically declared that these experiences exemplify the dangerous effects of corporate capitalism. Critics associated fashion, popular narratives, and scripted dances with passivity and manipulation; indeed, with femininity itself. Juxtaposed with leisure such as a parade or an athletic event that is active, creative, participatory, and productive (all traits coded as masculine in the nineteenth century), consumer-based popular culture has often been targeted as destructive of agency, meaning, and community spirit. All the worse that women seem to be such important markets for these industries. Arguing for women's agency in spite of these still-lingering associations is challenging. A second challenge is that sources into these most common and daily experiences with popular culture are elusive. Even highly mediated sources into the responses of audiences are difficult to find. As a result, historians have focused on reconstructing elements of daily practices from diverse sources and some have been especially attuned to issues of theory and method.

One way scholars have justified the importance of women's popular culture is to maintain a dichotomy between active and passive popular culture but to shift the line between them so that women's popular culture is revealed as active and meaningful. Tera Hunter employed this strategy in her analysis of women dancing in Atlanta jook joints. Hunter argued that for women like Sue, cited at the beginning of this chapter, dance was *productive*. Indeed, Hunter likened it to "hard work," in which mastery of technique, style and sheer endurance combined to confer status on the dancer. This work, unlike the poorly paid labor that most black women performed during the day, was satisfying and provided a sense of worth and beauty. Hunter contrasted the activity of dance to the passivity of other amusements: "Unlike other commercialized recreation, such as the new amusement parks, where one encountered replicas of industrial life in the mechanized, standardized forms of play, dance halls still allowed for a great deal of creativity, imagination, improvisation, and, thereby, change" (1997: 185). (In contrast, other historians, such as Michael Kammen, have celebrated amusement parks as particularly productive and participatory.) Hunter's analytic strategy allowed her to trace meanings in African American dance that were roundly denigrated at the time as trivial and that might currently be dismissed as scripted, or merely "fun" and sexual, but not socially significant.

Other historians argue that women *actively* utilized even mass-produced goods to create their own popular culture practices. Film historian Kathryn Fuller, in *At the Motion Picture Show*, demonstrated that audience members wove publicity materials, fan publications, film gossip, and the experience of going to the movies, along with the films themselves, into a "truly popular culture of film" (1996: 115). Kathy Peiss, in *Hope in a Jar* (1998), looked at women's use of make-up in the context of industry attempts to market the products. By comparing industry rhetoric with women's self-descriptions, Peiss found that while producers linked appearance and female personality in advertisements, ignoring the impact of "time, hard work, and illness on the body," women themselves "incorporated cosmetics into the 'true story' of their lives, adopting the confessional techniques of advertisers but changing the subject" to include exactly those unspeakable topics (1998: 184). My own work demonstrated that the meanings of working women's consumption of fashion, dime novels, and motion pictures can be explored by reconstructing the series of shared activities that surrounded these products. I found that when working-class women purchased products in working-class neighborhoods and shared and discussed them at the workplace, they imbued the products with their own meanings and used them to construct themselves as "ladies," in opposition to their devalued status in the labor market and the society as a whole. Regina Kunzel, in "Pulp Fictions and Problem Girls" (1995), analyzed a story about an unwed mother published in *True Confessions* in cooperation with the Children's Bureau, which ran a column adjacent to the story offering assistance to real-life unwed mothers. Kunzel placed the story in the context of Children's Bureau sources, including letters in response to the story from unwed mothers, and argued that women strategically used popular narrative conventions to appeal to Children's Bureau authorities. Letter writers resisted punitive constructions of unwed pregnancy and were discursively active in creating their own stories of themselves.

Historians have also looked at consumer culture as a site of the formation of race and ethnic identities. Though consumer culture was fundamentally imbued with the effects of race and ethnic hierarchies, popular culture spaces sometimes allowed people to create distinctive race and ethnic identities that served as the basis for creativity and solidarity. Popular culture at once offered spaces of cultural exchange between groups, particularly in red-light districts or through mass-distributed records or radio shows, and spaces apart where a particular group might coalesce, form cultural ties, or create a new cultural identity. Elizabeth Ewen argued that popular culture had particular meaning for young, female Jewish and Italian immigrants because women's mobility and commodity purchase in the new country were key aspects of "Americanization." Ewen attempted to side-step the binary opposition between "traditional" and "Americanized" that has plagued immigration history. She argued that young women used popular culture to create new Italian and Jewish American cultures but that creation was a source of generational conflict. Susan Glenn, in *Daughters of the Shtetl*, even more rigorously resisted the concepts "traditional" and "Americanized." She substituted the word "modernity" for "Americanization" in order to evade a notion of "wholesale acceptance of American values and institutions" and to convey the fact that industrialization, the rise of commercial leisure, and resulting cultural changes were happening among Jewish women on both sides of the Atlantic (1990: 3). Vicki Ruíz, in *From Out of the Shadows*, also rejected the "two worlds" model: "Mexican American women... navigated across multiple terrains at home, at work, and at play. They engaged in cultural coalescence. The Mexican American generation selected, retained, borrowed and created their own cultural forms" (1998: 67). Ruíz showed how Mexican American women challenged the chaperone system as part of their creation of a collective identity based in consumer culture. Tera Hunter explored how segregation in Atlanta ironically meant that blacks would have their own places of entertainment within which to nurture a distinctive culture. This culture – the music, styles, and dances – became national because entertainers traveled on set circuits and because blacks migrated in massive numbers from rural to urban areas and from South to North.

The collective accomplishments of scholars in this dynamic field of study epitomize how women's history has profoundly challenged and revised established ways of viewing history and historical inquiry. Since the auspicious first flowering in the 1980s, works in this field have been on the leading edge of scholarly innovation. Peiss, Ewen, and Meyerowitz asked the question, could women find greater freedom in popular culture, and if so, in what way? All three argued that women found the greatest increase in autonomy sexually. That is, women were able to shift sexual mores and expand their sexual options. Of course, all also argued that women were not able to entirely escape sexual oppressions, but they did say that in the realm of leisure women could push successfully against the conventions of family and reformers and create new practices of dating. The increase in sexual mobility did not make for true freedom because, they argued, women remained economically dependent, both in relationship to male peers and in labor and family economies. In the 1990s, historians demonstrated that the impact of women's popular culture participation was even more profound than this implies. While no historian argued that women achieved more "freedom" than Peiss, Ewen, and Meyerowitz found, they did show how the changes in women's lives were central to transformations in public life in general. This had myriad ramifications, including the recreation of gender, race, ethnic, and class hierarchies within the new consumerism; shifts in understandings of the "self"; and changes in the ways politics would be defined and pursued in the twentieth century. Collectively, historians since the early 1990s have shown that exploring the history of women and popular culture sheds light on central transformations in US society.

As this field continues to develop, historians will likely pay new attention to the questions of oppression and agency. While all historians cited here note the oppressive nature of popular culture, more attention has been given to delineating and explicating the opportunities for agency. Historians are now well prepared to bring sophistication to the question of how popular culture reinforced painful social hierarchies, without returning to a "false consciousness" model or losing a sense of women's agency. Women's lack of economic independence was part of the oppression, as it made them susceptible to exploitation by men, employers, and family members. However, the problems with consumer culture were even more pervasive than this daily vulnerability. Historians have only begun to consider rigorously how the shaping of information and representations by advertisers and popular culture producers affected women's daily lives and possibilities for being. Precisely because commercialized popular culture is part of a story of the colonization of public life by market interests, struggles over popular culture are important sites of battle, battles that are not always won. What we have lost, and what we never had, will also become part of this story.

In an effort to reconceptualize agency and oppression, women's historians have shifted gradually from using a notion of identity to connote the self, that is, by looking to women's identifications (as working-class, as women, etc.) and how those were historically constructed, to a notion of "subjectivity." "Subjectivity" connotes a self always in process, always becoming, in relationship to the discursive resources available. This has particular relevance for how agency is construed. Agency has typically been defined as the binary opposite of oppression, as the force of opposition within the self that rises up against power. One's identifications, in this view, bear central relevance because it is through one's identifications as Chicana, working-class, woman, etc., that one can see and understand the race, class, and gender oppression experienced and find the resources to act collectively. However, the notion of subjectivity considers agency as a product of the imperfect and limited set of cultural and material resources available. Agency is not juxtaposed to oppression, it arises imperfectly from it. How one can imagine oneself and come to speak is already limited by the oppressions of the day. Understanding identity formation is crucial to analyzing social change but identities cannot in themselves explain agency. Women's historians are perfectly situated to look at agency and social change through attention not *only* to discourse and representations, but to how these became imbricated in women's daily lives. That is, because women's historians look at women in a particular time, place, and social context, they can provide the sort of grounded study that will best put new perspectives and methods to work.

The opportunities for exciting new work are many. Future scholarship will fruitfully explore the experiences of women in small-town, non-East Coast areas. Scholarship to date has focused overwhelmingly on major urban areas, mostly in the Northeast. Though much of the US population remained in small towns or rural areas, migration and immigration along with the spread of mass-produced popular culture through motion picture distribution, mail-order catalogs, newspapers, pulp fiction, and traveling vaudeville meant that people all over the country were affected, albeit differently, by these changes. New work on rural and small towns will certainly transform current understandings. Likewise, there is a compelling opportunity for studies of the popular culture practices of women of color, including immigrants. Such studies have a particular potential to analyze the subjective level of historical experience and the daily formation of social hierarchies. In addition, very little scholarship has been done on women over the age of twenty-five, or married women. Consumer culture celebrates the ideal of the young woman; certainly older women were affected by popular culture in different ways. Sexual subcultures, particularly the development of lesbian, bisexual, and queer subcultures, could also be fruitfully explored, as George Chauncey's *Gay New York* (1994) demonstrates, through attention to popular culture and urban spaces. Studies of gender and men's popular culture promise to reveal more clearly the larger implications of the work already done on women, by showing the ways in which these changes not only shifted definitions of femininity but of masculinity, citizenship, and personhood. Finally, new work will surely provide as compelling and transformative insights about the post-World War II era as has scholarship on the turn of the century and the interwar years. Both in subject matter and in approach, the field of gender and popular culture promises to continue to be dynamic, interdisciplinary, and engaged with central social and political concerns about US society.

BIBLIOGRAPHY

Alexander, Ruth M. (1995) *The "Girl Problem": Female Sexual Delinquency in New York, 1900–1930.* Ithaca, NY: Cornell University Press.

Butler, Judith (1997) *Excitable Speech: A Politics of the Performative.* New York: Routledge.

Carby, Hazel V. (1986) "'It Jus' Be's Dat Way Sometime': The Sexual Politics of Women's Blues," *Radical America* 20, pp. 9–24.

Carby, Hazel V. (1992) "Policing the Black Woman's Body in an Urban Context," *Critical Inquiry* 18, pp. 738–55.

Chauncey, George (1994) *Gay New York: Gender, Urban Culture, and the Making of the Gay Male World, 1890–1940.* New York: Basic Books.

Davis, Angela Y. (1998) *Blues Legacies and Black Feminism: Gertrude "Ma" Rainey, Bessie Smith and Billie Holiday.* New York: Pantheon Books.

Enstad, Nan (1999) *Ladies of Labor, Girls of Adventure: Working Women, Popular Culture and Labor Politics at the Turn of the Twentieth Century.* New York: Columbia University Press.

Ewen, Elizabeth (1985) *Immigrant Women in the Land of Dollars: Life and Culture on the Lower East Side, 1890–1925.* New York: Monthly Review Press.

Finnegan, Margaret (1999) *Selling Suffrage: Consumer Culture and Votes for Women.* New York: Columbia University Press.

Fuller, Kathryn H. (1996) *At the Motion Picture Show: Small-town Audiences and the Creation of Movie-fan Culture.* Washington, DC: Smithsonian Institution Press.

Glenn, Susan A. (1990) *Daughters of the Shtetl: Life and Labor in the Immigrant Generation.* Ithaca, NY: Cornell University Press.

Glenn, Susan (2000) *Female Spectacle: The Theatrical Roots of Modern Feminism.* Cambridge, MA: Harvard University Press.

Hall, Jacquelyn Dowd (1986) "Disorderly Women: Gender and Labor Militancy in the Appalachian South," *Journal of American History* 73, pp. 354–82.

Hansen, Miriam (1991) *Babel and Babylon: Spectatorship in American Silent Film.* Cambridge, MA: Harvard University Press.

Hunter, Tera W. (1997) *To 'Joy My Freedom: Southern Black Women's Lives and Labors After the Civil War.* Cambridge, MA: Harvard University Press.

Kammen, Michael (1999) *American Culture, American Tastes: Social Change in the Twentieth Century.* New York: Alfred A. Knopf.

Kibler, M. Alison (1999) *Rank Ladies: Gender and Cultural Hierarchy in American Vaudeville.* Chapel Hill: University of North Carolina Press.

Kunzel, Regina G. (1995) "Pulp Fictions and Problem Girls: Reading and Rewriting Single Pregnancy in the Postwar United States," *American Historical Review* 100, pp. 1465–87.

Landes, Joan (1988) *Women and the Public Sphere in the Age of the French Revolution.* Ithaca, NY: Cornell University Press.

Leach, William (1984) "Transformations in a Culture of Consumption: Women and Department Stores, 1890–1925," *Journal of American History* 71, pp. 311–42.

Meyerowitz, Joanne J. (1988) *Women Adrift: Independent Wage-earners in Chicago, 1880–1930.* Chicago: University of Chicago Press.

Norwood, Stephen (1990) *Labor's Flaming Youth: Telephone Operators and Worker Militancy, 1878–1923.* Urbana: University of Illinois Press.

Odem, Mary E. (1995) *Delinquent Daughters: Protecting and Policing Adolescent Female Sexuality in the United States, 1885–1920.* Chapel Hill: University of North Carolina Press.

Peiss, Kathy (1986) *Cheap Amusements: Working Women and Leisure in Turn-of-the-century New York*. Philadelphia: Temple University Press.

Peiss, Kathy (1998) *Hope in a Jar: The Making of America's Beauty Culture*. New York: Metropolitan Books.

Rabinovitz, Lauren (1998) *For the Love of Pleasure: Women, Movies, and Culture in Turn-of-the-century Chicago*. New Brunswick, NJ: Rutgers University Press.

Ruíz, Vicki (1998) *From Out of the Shadows: Mexican Women in Twentieth-century America*. New York: Oxford University Press.

Snyder, Robert W. (1989) *The Voice of the City: Vaudeville and Popular Culture in New York*. New York: Oxford University Press.

Tentler, Leslie Woodcock (1979) *Wage-earning Women: Industrial Work and Family Life in the United States, 1900–1930*. New York: Oxford University Press.

Wald, Lillian (1915) *The House on Henry Street*. New York: Henry Holt.

Chapter Eighteen

Women on the Move: Migration and Immigration

Ardis Cameron

We are all Caribbeans now in our urban Archipelagoes . . . Perhaps there's no return for anyone to a native land – only field notes for its reinvention.

James Clifford

Continent, city, country, society:
The choice is never wide and never free.
And here, or there . . . No. Should we have stayed at home,
wherever that may be?

Elizabeth Bishop

According to recent reports from the United Nations, there are more than 23 million refugees in the world today. Another 24 million men and women live in nations not their own under conditions of "internal displacement." In the Americas, genealogists and local storytellers routinely redraw the borders of family history forcing millions to look across the oceans for ancestral origins, ethnic identities, home lands. In the United States alone, fully 46 million immigrants entered the country between 1820 and 1975. During the peak decades of the late nineteenth and early twentieth centuries, US immigration officials recorded annual arrivals in the millions: during several years, twice that number crossed into America. In the late fall of each year, millions would reverse course, returning to Italy, Greece, Bohemia, Mexico, and Canada for the winter or whenever the mines shut down, the construction stopped, or the harvest ended. During the height of immigration into the United States from southern and eastern Europe, over a million Italians alone crossed the border to leave and more than half the Hungarian, Croatian, and Slovene immigrant population joined them as "birds of passage." By any measure, the history of the nineteenth and twentieth centuries is a history of motion: of men and women, boys and girls on the move.

Mobility of this magnitude has brought questions of travel to the surface of recent scholarship. For the emigrant, the immigrant, the displaced, the exile, the migrant, the itinerant, and the evicted, what does it mean to travel? What too are we to make of these assertions of difference among "travelers" who share modern experiences of displacement but whose ability to represent that experience has differed dramatically? What kinds of cultural capital accrue to the exile but at the expense of the migrant, the immigrant, the evicted? And can we even use such a term as "travel" given the cultural baggage it carries as a product of historically privileged groups and practices? How too can we locate amidst such extraordinary comings and goings, border crossings and diasporas, displacements and migrations, a "field" of study capable of mapping the complexities of such mobility? And what about home, place, and native land? Are there no "roots" in this history of routes? Finally, what of the relationship between immigration and formations of nation, race, and gender? To what extent, in other words, is the history of migration and immigration simultaneously a story of geographic crossings *and* constitutive displacements: a complex tale that questions the logics of rootedness, "native," and the assumptions of the "local."

Questions of Travel and Displacement

Questions like these emerge not only through the magnitude and history of modern displacements, but through a common recognition among a growing number of scholars that stories of migration and immigration cannot be separated from narratives of power. Articulated most forcefully in the recent works of Mary Louise Pratt, Lisa Lowe, James Clifford, Caren Kaplan, and Inderpal Grewal, literary and cultural critics, geographers, anthropologists, and historians have begun to recognize that modern narratives of exploration and discovery, of exile and ex-patriotism, of occidental ethnography and travel accounts, and of "integration" fiction, especially novels written in English by non-English-speaking immigrants, both produce hegemonic forms of knowledge and authority and generate through "eyewitness observation" and the "fiction of reconciliation" representational regimes that visualize dominant modes of Self and "Other." In the process, they generate aesthetic categories and ahistorical values. In *Immigrant Acts*, for example, Lowe builds upon the work of Frantz Fanon to explore the power of the Anglo-American novel as a cultural institution that "regulates formations of citizenship and the nation, genders the domains of 'public' and 'private' activities, prescribes the specialization of race relations, and, most of all, determines possible contours and terrains for the narration of history" (1996: 98). Rather than a supplement to "a people and place," human mobility and the kinds of cultural representations it acquires more accurately *locates* and *organizes* the geographies through which definitions of self, nation, race, and gender take on meaning and shape.

Asking questions about travel has thus revealed the place of migration and immigration in constructions of "Home," "Nation," and "Empire," of race and gender, and of the exoticizations and mystified fantasies that make up western hierarchies of difference and modernist erasures of power and inequality. Questioning travel has also shaken up the romanticized nomadology embedded in European American discourses of exile and exploration, of leisure and tourism, of home and away, of dwelling and homelessness, of borders and frontiers. To what extent has the "new" cosmopolitan figure, asks Tim Brennan, in tandem with high-profile third world authors who have elevated exile into first world careers, both valorized "a rhetoric of wandering" and uncoupled the material conditions of an internationalized pool of labor, the regionalization of capitalist labor markets, and cultural inequalities, from western attempts to accommodate to destabilized identities? Caren Kaplan's work is especially instructive here. Deliberately linking discourses of "travel" and "displacement," Kaplan pries open the western fascination with experiences of movement, distance, and estrangement to reveal the connections between European American critical practices, human displacements, and the legacy of colonialism. By focusing on the production of specific historical constructs of modern displacements, Kaplan brings into postmodernist critical practice both the material conditions of modern "travel" and the kinds of political work cultural representations and metaphors of travel and displacement perform, especially in articulations of "theory." Like Lowe, Kaplan poses questions of travel in such a way as "to render it historically and politically viable" (Kaplan 1996: 26). Histories of movement thus become histories of formation and meaning-making as new subjects emerge in tandem with vast social and economic changes and take on meaning amidst and in relation to the imagined places they transit, occupy, and leave behind.

Despite the feminist possibilities of such an approach to immigration and migration, "travel" contains its own historical baggage. Uncomplicated by migration, immigration, and displacement, there is more than just a whiff of colonialism and class privilege that surrounds the term. For historians of women in particular, "travel" has too often been a vehicle of erasure; a word made meaningful through its very distance from things female: home and harem, domesticity and dependence, immobility and passivity. As literary critic Gillian Brown points out in her work on the implications of gender and domesticity for individualism, the preeminent figure of immobility for the nineteenth century was the female hysteric whose strange postures freeze normal bodily motion and activity. To be a traveler was in many ways to be a particular kind of man or an unusual type of woman.

Still more difficult is to conceive of poor women as travelers. Social historians have been more likely to think of laboring female travelers as migrants, immigrants, servants, deportees, refugees, displaced persons, transients, even as wayward, homeless, runaways, adrift, or simply as "women in motion," terms that mark both the material realities of wage-earning women and the destabilizing nature of female mobility. For these scholars, hotels conjure up modern systems of tourism where privileged clientele shuttle about the globe as men and women of color and those who are poor relocate to clean rooms, iron clothes, carry bags, serve food. To think of travel is thus to imagine not boats, but steerage, calloused feet, boxcars, backstairs, the endless lines and humiliations of Ellis island. As bell hooks has argued in *Black Looks*, "Travel is not a word that can be easily evoked to talk about the middle passage, the Trail of Tears, the landing of Chinese immigrants, the forced relocation of Japanese-Americans, or the plight of the homeless" (1992: 173).

Still, travel has its uses. For historians who have come to view with a practiced skepticism the ahistorical glosses and abstract aestheticisms that can at times substitute for cultural criticism, it is this troubled legacy that procures temporality and specificity. It mitigates against the power of erasure: "I hang onto 'travel' as a term of cultural comparison," writes Clifford in his influential article, "Traveling Cultures," "precisely because of its historical taintedness, its associations with gendered, racial bodies, class privilege, specific means of conveyance, beaten paths, agents, frontiers, documents, and the like. I prefer it to the more neutral, and 'theoretical,' terms such as 'displacement,' which can make the drawing of equivalences across historical experiences too easy" (1997: 39). Coupled, as Kaplan would have it, with discourses of "displacement," travel becomes a strategic term; a tool encumbered by history so that it can never be anything but a site of contestation, of disruptions, of fierce comings and goings, of places traversed, secured, policed, subverted, vacated, left behind, entered into, remade.

Far from peripheral to the historical understanding of immigration and migration, questions of travel remind us that human mobility must not be severed from the legacies of domination and the kinds of asymmetric power relations "travelers" accrue through cultural representation. Gender and race move to the center of analysis as shaped by and producers of nationality, sexuality, and regional identity. To map the field of migration and immigration history today is thus to begin by rejecting any one model or paradigm as explanatory and universal and to reject the sharp dichotomies – between industrial and pre-industrial, home and away, primitive and modern, stability and rootless – that traditionally shaped the historical study of migration and immigration. Nor should we leave unexplored the value and meaning of terms employed to describe modern experiences of displacement. What is won and what is lost when historians separate out as culturally distinct experiences, acts of migration from those of nomadism, of immigration from diaspora, or of exile from emigrant? Who gains and who loses? And if, as Clifford suggests, "we are all Caribbeans now" – cultural hybrids and cosmopolitan subjects – is the history of American immigration simply a forward march across cultural borders and into an inventive hybridity (Clifford 1988: 73)? Is there anything inherently progressive in the "deterritorialization" of culture? As feminist historians, where do we locate ourselves as we map the itineraries of women in motion – the borders of dislocation/location? Do we presume a white or Anglo culture as we deconstruct and destabilize "others"? Are there roots or just routes? Rootlessness or a new sense of place? "Here, or there . . . the choice is never wide and never free . . . Should we have stayed at home, wherever that may be?" (Bishop 1983: 93).

Stories of Assimilation

Beginning in the 1920s, questions of human mobility, if not travel, emerged in tandem with a new generation of historians whose own roots in America were frequently less than a generation old. The questions they asked were informed not by a skepticism toward the West's fascination with displacement, but rather by its understated place in American history. As Oscar Handlin so famously put it in his classic study, *The Uprooted: The Epic Story of the Great Migrations that Made the American People*, "Once I thought to write a history of the immigrants in America. Then I discovered that the immigrants were American history" (1951: 3). Handlin's

Uprooted along with his earlier portrait of Irish heroism, *Boston's Immigrants, 1790–1865: A Study in Acculturation* (1941), marked both the ascension of immigration history in the academy and the triumphalist framework of the liberal assimilationist model that would posit sharp and exacting lines between the backward peasant world of tradition and the American world of urban modernity and individual opportunity. Most fully articulated by Handlin, English scholars like Philip Taylor, and the Chicago School of sociology, this immigration history offered a story of heroic struggles among an uprooted and disoriented population who found in America's industrializing society a means to shake off the shackles of collective ignorance and oppression and embrace the future as modern individuals in a "free" and competitive society. Not without its critics (most notably Rudolph Vecoli and Frank Thistlewaite), it was a narrative that could easily absorb older tales of frontier triumphs and national progress. Scripted as both a story of America and as a uniquely American story, US immigration history provided explanatory power to narratives of American exceptionalism even as it was structured by them. America was the magnet for "men on the move" – to use Handlin's phrase – and their struggles to "make it" demonstrated the special role of American institutions and the unique place of the United States in processes of modernization.

In works like *Old World Traits Transplanted* (1969) by Robert E. Park and Herbert A. Miller, *The Polish Peasant in Europe and America* (1958) by William I. Thomas and Florian Znaniecki, and *The Atlantic Migration, 1607–1860* (1961) by Marcus Lee Hansen, immigration thus took on new legitimacy as a distinct chapter in a familiar narrative of American destiny and destination. But in shaping a new subject for research, scholars scripted as well a new historical actor: the generic "immigrant" who emerged as an undifferentiated huddled mass of men and, occasionally, women transplanted to new shores. It was not simply that women were left out of this story, but rather that differences of all kinds were conflated under the highly generalized term "immigrant," what became for Handlin a synonym for "peasant." Bound together by a legacy of a primitive past, they implicitly shared a desire to adopt new worlds and visions, adapt to industrial society, embrace capitalism, and assimilate into urban modernity. In this context, differences are reduced to those who have the right skills to do so and those who do not. It becomes a story of opposites – of old and new, of assimilation and tradition, of backward and forward – and, as such, allows for subject formation and identity only as positions of opposition and difference. Women, like men, made appearances in this story, but neither class, gender, nor ethnic difference altered their roles as humble toilers after the American dream. Differences within racial and ethnic cultures were eclipsed by stories of commonality and heroic struggle. The image of immigrant women, while somewhat vague, was split between a shrewd and calculating opponent of local officials and a well-meaning but ignorant drudge – "the oxen without horns." Head covered in the traditional babushka, her arms filled with babies and baggage, such portraits circulated not only in the epic stories of historians but as staged photographs that uncritically illustrated dozens of textbooks throughout the twentieth century.

It is here, then, in the narratives that structured immigrant and migration history, where we can best sort out women's entrance into and disruptive place in the field.

Equally affected by global displacements, women variously comprised between 30 and 50 percent of the immigrants who entered the United States in the years between 1850 and 1920 from Europe, Asia, and South America. By 1920, 48 percent of southern Italian arrivals were female; and according to Alan Kraut, Slavic women during the same time period outnumbered men 65 percent to 35 percent. Millions more were never counted by immigration officials. Mexican men and women entered with or without visas crossing the southern border of the United States to reach the "American West," *el Norte* to millions of *braceros*, some of whose relatives had never actually left Mexico but who nevertheless found themselves north of home as US borders moved south. Others traveled south as undocumented Canadians criss-crossing the borders of New England to find work in job-hungry textile mills or to visit family and friends. Transient as a group, French Canadian women were more likely than either their male counterparts or any other group of immigrant workers to find a job in a textile mill and to stay there, a trait that made their recruitment increasingly attractive to New England's "lords of the loom."

In modern discourses of human mobility, however, women moved in and out of rhetorical circulation primarily as powerful tropes for "home," stability, rootedness, and custodians of tradition. Women on the move entered the imaginary landscape of immigration narratives as a problematic subtext. Whereas in tales of assimilation this often rendered female subjects (as well as ethnic, class, and gender differences) invisible, it also made female immigrants and migrants, especially mothers, responsible for group failures, both at the homeplace as "unmeltable" ethnics, and at the workplace as reluctant participants in working-class organization.

This story was especially brought home and made explicit in the scholarship of the 1970s as historians and sociologists began to reject the "melting pot" assumptions of their predecessors. In works like *Beyond the Melting Pot: The Negroes, Puerto Ricans, Jews, Italians, and Irish of New York City* (1970) by Nathan Glazer and Daniel Patrick Moynihan, Michael Novak's *The Rise of the Unmeltable Ethnics: Politics and Culture in the Seventies* (1972), Irving Howe's *World of Our Fathers* (1976), as well as in progressive studies of immigrant labor and working-class history, women seemingly shared, in ways that cut across categories of race, class, and ethnic difference, an unflinching allegiance to home, family, and tradition that implicitly and, at times, explicitly undermined collective attempts among people on the move to enter the American mainstream or to remake it. Claiming that movement into the city alienated newcomers and led to social disorganization, neo-assimilationists like Glazer and Moynihan describe family life and a woman's place in it using terms like "pathology" and "cultural deficiency." Culture became for male and female migrants alike an arsenal of assimilation, but it was women's position in the household that often became the measure for success or failure. Frequently portrayed as clinging to the old, as dominating the family, and as unwilling or unable to learn English, to vote, to throw away their olive oil and buy American, women no longer on the move took on visibility primarily in relation to their role as accelerators or deterrents to assimilation and upward mobility. In turn, female immigrants and "unmeltable ethnics" were scripted in opposition to the values of individualism, the nuclear family, patriarchy, consumption, and electoral politics.

Because immigrants provided a needed fillip to working-class political organization and worker militancy in the decades that bridged the nineteenth and twentieth centuries, labor historians also turned a keen eye on greenhorns from Europe, Asia, and the American South. Rejecting the notion that migration was either a sharp break from the past or a source of disorientation and disunion, labor historians followed the lead of Herbert Gutman to explore the adaptive strategies of urban newcomers, including black migrants from the South as well as Europeans. While these studies emphasized cultural adaptation and the importance of grafting shop-floor traditions of reciprocity and mutuality onto "indigenous" forms of American radicalism, they tended to ignore the political possibilities of female "habits of visiting" and the kinds of networks they formed. If old-world traditions among male arrivals worked to solidify class consciousness and renew radicalism in American workplaces, female ties to the past retarded assimilation at best and deterred labor militancy at worst. Trapped in a narrative of liberal assimilation, albeit "from the bottom up," women remained vaguely "old world" even as their male counterparts took on new specificity as participants in their own making in a vibrant "world of our fathers."

Questions of Gender

Second-wave feminism worked in tandem with a record number of women entering Ph.D. programs in American history to mount a gradual assault on the liberal-assimilationist model. While the thrust of many of these works in the late 1970s and early 1980s was to question the degree to which immigrants Americanized, they differed from earlier models by emphasizing the complex terrain of community, family, and female collaborative activity. Challenging the contention that modernization and migration severed immigrants from traditions of mutuality, reciprocity, and the bonds of kin, Virginia Yans-McLaughlin, Tamara Hareven, Donna Gabaccia, and Maxine Seller emphasized continuity over disruption by focusing on particular populations and by bringing into focus the differences between male and female experiences of migration and immigration. With the publication of Yans-McLaughlin's *Family and Community: Italian Immigrants in Buffalo, 1880–1930* (1977), Hareven's *Family Time and Industrial Time* (1982), and Seller's collection, *Immigrant Women* (1981), immigration history moved not just beyond the melting pot but away from the generic "oxen without horns." By putting women at the center of analysis, dozens of monographs chronicled women's participation in the family economy, noting the many ways in which wives and mothers continued rural traditions by piecing together bits of this and that and the extent to which they differed both from men and, at times, from daughters as well. Far from disoriented or "uprooted," female immigrants utilized traditional values and skills to provide for their families and to recreate in new places familiar patterns of life, work, and neighborhood.

Rich in detail, studies like these also raised questions about the effects of immigration and industrial urban life on relations between husbands and wives. Did participation in the wage labor force loosen traditions of patriarchy? To what extent did migration itself disrupt traditional female responsibilities and obligations? How did family time and industrial time work together? While Yans-McLaughlin found Italians reluctant to send wives into the workplace, an increasing number of married women in French Canadian families took jobs outside the home. By 1900, 15 percent of married French Canadians in Rhode Island drew paychecks and by 1908 wives would make up 35 per cent of the total French Canadian female workforce in New England's textile mills. Clearly experiences of immigration differed among ethnic groups, but premigration traditions that viewed the family as a work unit continued as women found new ways to make ends meet.

For Asian communities, however, the racialized politics of immigration and naturalization law altered the family in profound ways. Barred from immigration by the Page Act of 1875 and later by bans that prevented the spouses of Chinese male laborers from joining their husbands, Chinese women were effectively eliminated from both Chinese community life and the family economy. "Bachelor" communities replaced traditional divisions of labor so that men took up "feminized" occupations in laundries, restaurants, and other tertiary sector occupations, a situation that scholars would return to as questions of gender, race, and the construction of American citizenship emerged in the 1990s. The subsequent exclusion and disfranchisement of the Chinese in 1882, Asian Indians in 1917, the Japanese in 1924, and Filipinos in 1934 delayed for generations the formation of the kinds of family and community networks so essential to European immigrant survival and political organization. Far from a shared immigrant experience, studies of Asian and Mexican women revealed the uncommon histories of female migrants and the importance of understanding their differing positions in race, class, and gender hierarchies.

For the most part, however, historians of immigrant women turned their gaze toward Europe, challenging the dichotomy between pre-industrial and industrial societies, which they viewed as too static to describe either the migrants left behind or the America they embraced. Building on the work of the "new" social history and historical demography, immigration history let slip its focus on incoming populations to embrace a more reciprocal view between places left behind and places of arrival. Increasingly, the economic transformations and uneven patterns of industrialization at "home" brought into focus the gendered processes of migration and settlement. Studies like Elizabeth Pleck's *Black Migration and Poverty* (1979), Donna Gabaccia's *From Sicily to Elizabeth Street: Housing and Social Change among Italian Immigrants, 1880–1930* (1984), Judith Smith's *Family Connections* (1985), Elizabeth Ewen's *Immigrant Women in the Land of Dollars* (1985), and Louise Lamphere's *From Working Daughters to Working Mothers: Immigrant Women in a New England Industrial Community* (1987) emphasized worlds in flux and the thick web of friends, kin, and community in transitions from here to there. Joining studies on "The Raza" and black migration, these works used oral histories, census records, letters, and ethnography to argue for the importance of women's role in maintaining family cohesion, but in a context of shifting economic and social changes that often challenged assumptions about the family economy. No longer under the supervision of household workshops, Smith found that sons and daughters of Italian and Jewish immigrants were more likely to find employment outside the neighborhood, creating a new set of possibilities for children and new tensions for their parents.

By focusing on specific immigrant groups as well as on specific occupations, historians increasingly unpacked the complex experience of immigrant women, further complicating cherished images and unexamined assumptions. In *Erin's Daughters in America* (1983), Hasia Diner laid to rest the stereotype of a male pioneer migration by showing both the predominance of women among Irish immigrants and the importance of sisters in establishing chain migrations for family members to follow. The mothers of both Elizabeth Gurley Flynn and James Michael Curley, the flamboyant mayor of Boston, journeyed to America with the assistance of their sisters, while numerous others turned to aunts, widows, or grandmothers as travelers' aids. In rigorous detail Diner shows this to be the pattern, not the exception. Both Smith and Miriam Cohen show as well the ways in which generational differences altered experiences of migration and immigration between mothers and daughters. In *Workshop to Office* (1992), Cohen challenges the view that patriarchal values kept Italian wives and daughters out of the paid labor force either in southern Italy or in urban America. Italian daughters eagerly entered the workplaces of New York City, where job opportunities for unskilled females were plentiful if not lucrative. Most continued to understand their work in terms of family need, but changing patterns of work necessitated alterations in household authority. Furthermore, the opportunities for generating income in American cities seldom overlapped with traditional female responsibilities such as childbearing and childrearing. In rural Italy and Russia, spatial divisions between home and work were never as sharp as in urban environments of America, so that wives and mothers typically found their options constrained less by patriarchal values than by the industrial conditions they faced upon arrival.

Cash in a girl's pocket could also lessen parental controls in ways unimagined before migration. As contributors to the family economy, immigrant daughters challenged fathers, mothers, and at times brothers over control of their wages. In larger cities this meant taking advantage of newly created "cheap amusements," while at other times it meant joining, even organizing labor unions so as to increase wages and provide more opportunities to participate in the emerging consumer culture. In smaller towns like Providence, Rhode Island, Lawrence, Massachusetts, Paterson, New Jersey, and Barre, Vermont, entertainment and leisure remained more family and neighborhood centered, revolving around activities organized by ethnic associations, mutual aid societies, labor unions, and political clubs. But these too would feel the undertow of commercialized leisure as movies, dance halls, and amusement parks grew more popular and came within the reach of small-town residents. Cash wages jostled gender relations and hierarchical patterns in immigrant families; but by "putting on style," working daughters came to challenge as well a wage system that oppressed immigrant households regardless of gender, race, or age.

By bringing women into the immigrant story, these studies brought much-needed specificity to the experience of displacement and migration. They showed in great detail the importance of immigrant women in establishing "toeholds" for newcomers and in building ethnic communities. Both Irish and Syrian women were the traditional "pioneers," while in textile manufacturing centers like Lawrence, Massachusetts, Jewish daughters and sisters were often brought over by fathers or brothers before sending for sons. In these cases, gender segmentation at the workplace, as well as skills learned by daughters and wives working in rural factories, rather than traditions of patriarchy became the crucial factor in deciding the pecking order of chain migrations. In addition to contributing to the family economy, both wage and non-wage-earning wives often became the primary negotiators with landlords, shopkeepers, and neighbors to find the best prices and manage childcare, food preparation, boarders, and housekeeping. In the process they cemented friendships across ethnic divides even as factory management sought to segregate their husbands and children by nationality on the shop floor. Female networks among immigrant women proved crucial not only to the formation of neighborhood ethnic church groups, charitable societies, and mutual aid clubs, but to the creation of solidarity in times of crisis, such as during the kosher meat riots on the Lower East Side of New York City, the "pasta wars" in Providence, Rhode Island, the "bread and roses" strike of 1912 in Lawrence, Massachusetts, the agricultural "wars" in Wheatland, California, and the struggles to organize cannery workers up and down the West Coast. In unskilled and semi-skilled occupations that maintained fewer divisions between female and male workers of the same ethnicity, such as in cigar making, tobacco processing, and field labor, women immigrants and migrants more easily overcame gender differences and pay inequalities to give, as Nancy Hewitt put it, "the edge to cooperation over conflict in both workplace and union" (1991: 146). If the responsibilities and desires of immigrant women and their daughters differed from those of men, women nevertheless demonstrated a similar willingness to engage in collective struggles and contribute to the vitality of community life.

Studies like these did not simply emphasize the continuity of old-world traits and women's position in the family, community, and workplace. They illustrated as well the ways in which the performance of traditional female obligations and responsibilities literally, if not conceptually, dissolved the borders between home and work, kin and kith, public and private. Building on the work of feminist anthropologists, cultural theorists, and historians of women, culture became something constructed rather than fixed, a set of values, beliefs, and traditions more "in use" than "in place." Gender itself became less a synonym for women and more an unstable aspect of subjectivity, even a signifying practice. Studies of immigrant women thus helped open up new spaces for exploring female experience at the ground level, where subjectivity and identity take on shape and meaning. In Tampa, Florida, changing gender identities and expectations among Cuban, Italian, and Spanish cigar workers could at times generate visions of solidarity between virile men *and* women on the shop floor while at other times, notions of true manhood and virility bound together German, Anglo, and Spanish factory owners with older immigrant union members to undermine worker protest. In Lawrence, Massachusetts, Irish women operatives in the 1880s found themselves increasingly isolated from union leadership by newly shaped narratives of male-centered craft "traditions" and emerging demands for a "family" wage. In both cities immigrant men turned to more conservative constructions of gender in response to women's growing prominence in local factories. Subject to shifting conditions and economic circumstances, gender emerged fraught with contradiction and contestation.

In her study of Jewish daughters of the shtetl, Susan Glenn noted as well the role of peer-group sociability in the garment industry in crafting for women new-world fantasies as well as shaping multiple identities as workers, women, and immigrants. While Glenn positioned protest and activism in opposition to commodity culture, she more recently demonstrated the power of popular culture to unfix subjectivity and open up conceptual bridges between leisure time activity, commodity culture, and identity formation. In the "imitation craze" that swept the theatrical world of vaudeville in the early twentieth century, Glenn found an audience of native and foreign-born alike who reveled in opportunities to mimic others, try on new personalities, and, in general, to "be somebody else." Part of a larger cultural remapping of selfhood, the art of mimicry, a specialty of the vaudeville comedienne, articulated new conceptual possibilities for becoming an "American" woman and for understanding what that new self might look like. "Putting on style" can thus be seen as an act of self-invention and personal recreation rather than as a simple attempt to imitate an already established "American" identity or immutable type.

For women new to America as well as for southern migrants new to northern and southern cities, consumer culture thus provided more than escape from daily toil and struggle. As Nan Enstad points out in *Ladies of Labor, Girls of Adventure* (1999), working-class fantasy and immigrant dreams could under certain circumstances forge political visions and turn consuming subjects into agents of protest. Engaging in a new landscape of commodities and pleasures, immigrant women and their daughters succeeded in fashioning an assortment of identities including those that were decidedly political.

Traveling Disciplines

One of the ironies of immigration history is that it becomes a "field" through narrations of mobility: of displacement, migration, unrootedness, interaction, diaspora, and resettlement. It takes on disciplinary specificity to the degree that borders are crossed, cultures deterritorialized, and frontiers traversed. Yet like all attempts to define the disciplinary boundaries of a "field," locating immigration history demonstrates as well what recent "border studies" and their critics have shown, that "a border is always and only secured by a border patrol" (Michaelsen and Johnson 1997: 1). What I have been describing above is a "field" that has always been traversed and resistant to disciplinary policing. Yet despite the influx of trespassing feminists, labor historians, "new" social historians, African American critics, and cultural anthropologists, the story of American immigration has been primarily a tale of inclusion: of how ethnic men and women struggled to make new lives and new selves in a democratic and modernized "nation of immigrants." In the United States, such a story has taken on mythic status, and it might be argued that much of American public policy has been organized and formulated upon the structure of Americanization narratives despite a generation of second-wave feminist scholarship. For all the rich detail and new knowledges about immigrant women that these studies have produced, we still find borders of immigrant history patrolled by the theoretical imagination of Americanization. Albeit, as James Barrett argued, the process is now viewed "from the bottom up" rather than, as Handlin contended, by the grand odyssey through the meritorious boot strap of democracy and individual opportunity. As Clifford

Rosenberg has argued, "It is time to . . . move beyond Handlin's perspective instead of dwelling on all that it ignored" (1998: 425).

Two trends suggest that immigration history is moving well beyond visions of the American melting pot. The first emerges out of gains made in ethnic studies and African American history, while the second calls attention to the power of global market forces to determine the immigrant experience. Explicitly challenging the notion that racism in America was an historical aberration in the immigrant story, Matthew Jacobson draws upon the recent work of Karen Brodkin and David Roediger to move race "to the foreground of historiography on European immigration and assimilation" (1998: 12). Like Brodkin and Roediger, Jacobson makes good use of a generation of feminist scholarship that has deessentialized cultural identity and demonstrated the inherent instability of categories of race, gender, and sexuality. In these accounts of American immigration, the historical meanings of whiteness and its power to confer or deny both legal citizenship and social inclusion in the national imaginary become the central organizers of American political life and national identity. By unpacking "whiteness," these studies destabilize "America" as well so that national subjectivity and national belonging are themselves repositioned as historically constructed, the result of contest and negotiation through which both race and nation take on meaning as "a language and logic" (Jacobson 1998: 274).

From this perspective, immigrants move into historical view as central to the formation of, and contestation over, white racial identity and the kinds of cultural politics they spawned. Migrants entering the country found themselves in a shifting terrain of identities, simultaneously inhabiting gradations of whiteness and "other." Newcomers from Naples became "Italians" along with their northern enemies from Turin, although differences in pigmentation could turn the dark-skinned southerners into "in-between" peoples and occasionally into "Turks" or "Africans." The alchemy of race and the privileges of whiteness thus shaped national citizenry as concept, image, and story which placed, displaced, and relocated individuals along a hierarchical axis of whiteness. The volatility and maintenance of racial ascription and national identity, rather than "assimilation" or cultural difference, brings conflict and struggle to the center of immigrant narratives and provides a periodization shaped not by progressive moves toward "inclusion" but by the turbulence involved in becoming, denying, and defining "whiteness."

Like men, immigrant women moved within the parameters and hierarchies of shifting racial classifications, but because scientific discourses posed women as the biological reproducers of "whiteness" and "other," their ability to procreate came under new scrutiny and attack in the decades between 1880 and 1930. Restrictive new immigration laws as well as a cadre of new "visual inspectors" at US ports of entry turned their gaze on so-called feeble-minded women who, along with unmarried and unescorted female immigrants, were suspected of loose morals and high rates of reproductivity. Even among the native-born, the privilege of "whiteness" occurred in proportion to the distance women and girls traveled beyond the borders of female respectability. Guided by the eugenicist notion that "mothers are more responsible than fathers in generating bad offspring," anti-immigration laws fueled racist sentiments by ascribing to female persons the weak link in the social evolution of the "great white race" (Rafter 1988: 66). Concerns over "race suicide" also put demands on "Anglo-Saxon" women who, by laying claim to the more scientific label "Caucasian," further distanced themselves from "uncivilized" types, creating, as Gail Bederman has argued, a sharp wedge between white women reformers and their African American allies. Tracing "bloodlines" and collecting genealogies back to revolutionary ancestors, patriotic societies of Anglo-Saxon women set down the borders of national purity so that by 1900, a racial aristocracy of northern and southern "Daughters" stood ready to forget disunion for the fantasy of white racial purity. Joining their male counterparts in the Immigration Restriction League, they "policed both the racialized boundaries of the national body and the geographic borders of the nation" (Smith 1999: 143).

For Asian women, the racialization of citizenship ascribed "gender" to the Asian American subject through a series of legal acts. Both the Page Law of 1875 and later restrictions on the wives of Chinese laborers drastically reduced the immigration of Chinese women into the United States, but restrictions that made it illegal for Chinese men to obtain citizenship meant that female citizens who married a Chinese man would also lose citizenship. "Masculinity" and "whiteness" moved in tandem with the meanings of citizenship so that "as the state extended citizenship to non-white male persons, it formally designated these subjects as 'male' as well" (Lowe 1996: 11). As late as 1943 with the enfranchisement of Chinese immigrants, the Chinese subject remained male and was presumed masculine even as the laws were modified to allow for the naturalization of Chinese women. Immigration not only altered the visual landscape of the United States, it racialized and gendered the meaning of American citizenship as well.

If categories of "whiteness" played crucial roles in the making and remaking of American citizenship laws and national identity, market forces proved equally critical in determining the successes and failures of Chinese, Japanese, Korean, Asian Indian, Filipino, Mexican, and southern European immigrants. "Cheap labor," argues Nancy Green, was as important a category as gender or ethnicity in understanding the immigrant experience, and because women comprised one of the "cheapest" labor pools in the world, their history cannot be severed from the needs and transformations of global capital (Green 1997: 16). While historians have long noted the complicated patterns of migration in the decades that bridged the nineteenth and twentieth centuries, the "birds of passage" they studied tended to be male artisans or field hands who, like the Italian *golondrina*, left "home" in November to harvest flax or wheat in Santa Fe or northern Cordoba, then moved in December and April to cut corn in Buenos Aires, and returned in May to Piedmont to plant spring crops. Disrupting normative accounts that assumed a one-way movement from Europe to America, scholars described a system of "proletariat globe-trotting" (Foerster 1919: 37). But men were not the only workers drawn into local and international systems of migration and the kinds of reciprocal movement they involved. By the nineteenth century, every member of a working family needed to be prepared to move.

In the decades that followed 1930, women from Mexico, the Philippines, and South America began to outnumber men in this pattern of migration, work, settlement, and return. Taking up low-level jobs in the high-tech industries or "unskilled" female jobs in garments, domestic labor, and the needle trades, they also entered "export-processing zones," tightly controlled squalid factory towns specifically designed by US corporations to keep foreign-born women workers within the national pool of cheap labor but physically beyond its national borders. Like their female counterparts in the first decades of the twentieth century, women turned to these industries not because of "old-world" experience or intrinsic female ability, but because of "industry's eternal search for cheaper, more docile labor and workers' search for greater earning potential" (Rosenberg 1998: 425). And like a generation before them, "the timing of arrival and the relative condition of the labour market" were as much a factor in their survival as the kinds of ethnic networks they were able to establish and sustain (Green 1997: 105).

The decades between 1880 and 1930 were not the first to witness massive waves of immigrants into the United States, nor were these the only years to experience the fits, starts, and reversals of white racial formation and national identity. But in these decades, scholars located what would become the central narratives of immigration history, and they have been disproportionately influential in shaping the field. Hoping to shake things up a bit, questions of travel have begun to reimagine the borders of human mobility and cultural identity, and to move American immigration history away from static models of assimilation and "inclusion" toward more complicated understandings of human mobility in relationship to the internationalization of cheap labor and constructions of "nation," "citizenship," "race," "home," and "away." Spurred by a new generation of scholars, what Aihwa Ong has called "diasporic feminists," immigration history is rapidly remapping the terrains of human mobility and its complex history, calling attention to the simultaneity of racial identities and processes of "whiteness" and challenging any one model or paradigm as explanatory and universal, or any one "history" as shared and totalizing. From this perspective the migrant, the immigrant, the displaced, and the detoured women of the world take on new visibility as both historical subjects "on the move" and as multiple discourses always in formation. To question travel is thus to both uproot immigration history and historicize the shifting routes and itineraries of cultural theory and identity politics.

BIBLIOGRAPHY

Barrett, James (1992) "Americanization from the Bottom Up: Immigration and the Remaking of the Working Class in the United States, 1880–1930," *Journal of American History* 79, pp. 996–1020.

Bederman, Gail (1995) *Manliness and Civilization: A Cultural History of Gender and Race in the United States, 1880–1917.* Chicago: University of Chicago Press.

Bishop, Elizabeth (1983) *The Complete Poems, 1927–1979.* New York: Farrar, Straus, and Giroux.

Brennan, Timothy (1989) "Cosmopolitans and Celebrities," *Race and Class* 31, pp. 1–20.

Brennan, Timothy (1997) *At Home in the World: Cosmopolitanism Now.* Cambridge, MA: Harvard University Press.

Brodkin, Karen (1998) *How Jews Became White Folks and What That Says about Race in America*. New Brunswick, NJ: Rutgers University Press.

Brown, Gillian (1990) *Domestic Individualism: Imagining Self in Nineteenth-century America*. Berkeley: University of California Press.

Cameron, Ardis (1993) *Radicals of the Worst Sort: Laboring Women in Lawrence, Massachusetts, 1860–1912*. Urbana: University of Illinois Press.

Clifford, James (1988) "Tell About Your Trip: Michel Leiris," in *The Predicament of Culture: Twentieth-century Ethnography, Literature, and Art*. Cambridge, MA: Harvard University Press, pp. 165–75.

Clifford, James (1997) *Routes: Travel and Translation in the Late Twentieth Century*. Cambridge, MA: Harvard University Press.

Cohen, Miriam (1992) *Workshop to Office: Two Generations of Italian Women in New York City, 1900–1950*. Ithaca, NY: Cornell University Press.

Diner, Hasia R. (1983) *Erin's Daughters in America: Irish Immigrant Women in the Nineteenth Century*. Baltimore: Johns Hopkins University Press.

Enstad, Nan (1999) *Ladies of Labor, Girls of Adventure: Working Women, Popular Culture and Labor Politics at the Turn of the Twentieth Century*. New York: Columbia University Press.

Ewen, Elizabeth (1985) *Immigrant Women in the Land of Dollars: Life and Culture on the Lower East Side, 1890–1925*. New York: Monthly Review Press.

Foerster, Robert F. (1919) *The Italian Emigration of Our Times*. Cambridge, MA: Harvard University Press.

Gabaccia, Donna R. (1984) *From Sicily to Elizabeth Street: Housing and Social Change among Italian Immigrants, 1880–1930*. Albany: State University of New York Press.

Glazer, Nathan and Moynihan, Daniel Patrick (1970) *Beyond the Melting Pot: The Negroes, Puerto Ricans, Jews, Italians, and Irish of New York City*. Cambridge, MA: MIT Press.

Glenn, Susan A. (1990) *Daughters of the Shtetl: Life and Labor in the Immigrant Generation*. Ithaca, NY: Cornell University Press.

Glenn, Susan A. (1998) " 'Give an Imitation of Me': Vaudeville Mimics and the Play of the Self," *American Quarterly* 50, pp. 47–76.

Green, Nancy L. (1997) *Ready-to-Wear and Ready-to-Work: A Century of Industry and Immigrants in Paris and New York*. Durham, NC: Duke University Press.

Grewal, Inderpal (1996) *Home and Harem: Nation, Gender, Empire, and the Cultures of Travel*. Durham, NC: Duke University Press.

Handlin, Oscar (1941) *Boston's Immigrants, 1790–1865: A Study in Acculturation*. Cambridge, MA: Harvard University Press.

Handlin, Oscar (1951) *The Uprooted: The Epic Story of the Great Migrations that Made the American People*. Boston: Little, Brown.

Hansen, Marcus Lee (1961) *The Atlantic Migration, 1607–1860: History of the Continuing Settlement of the United States*. New York: Harper.

Hareven, Tamara K. (1982) *Family Time and Industrial Time: The Relationship between the Family and Work in a New England Industrial Community*. New York: Cambridge University Press.

Hewitt, Nancy A. (1991) " 'The Voice of Virile Labor': Labor Militancy, Community Solidarity and Gender Identity among Tampa's Latin Workers, 1880–1921," in Ava Baron (ed.), *Work Engendered: Toward a New History of American Labor*. Ithaca, NY: Cornell University Press, pp. 142–67.

hooks, bell (1992) *Black Looks: Race and Representation*. Boston: South End Press.

Howe, Irving (1976) *World of Our Fathers*. New York: Harcourt Brace Jovanovich.

Jacobson, Matthew Frye (1998) *Whiteness of a Different Color: European Immigrants and the Alchemy of Race.* Cambridge, MA: Harvard University Press.

Kaplan, Caren (1996) *Questions of Travel: Postmodern Discourses of Displacement.* Durham, NC: Duke University Press.

Kraut, Alan M. (1982) *The Huddled Masses: The Immigrant in American Society, 1880–1921.* Arlington Heights, IL: Harlan Davidson.

Lamphere, Louise (1987) *From Working Daughters to Working Mothers: Immigrant Women in a New England Industrial Community.* Ithaca, NY: Cornell University Press.

Lowe, Lisa (1996) *Immigrant Acts: On Asian American Cultural Politics.* Durham, NC: Duke University Press.

Michaelsen, Scott and Johnson, David E. (1997) *Border Theory: The Limits of Cultural Politics.* Minneapolis: University of Minnesota Press.

Nee, Victor and Nee, Brett de Bary (1973) *Longtime Californ': A Documentary Study of an American Chinatown.* New York: Pantheon Books.

Novak, Michael (1972) *The Rise of the Unmeltable Ethnics: Politics and Culture in the Seventies.* New York: Macmillan.

Park, Robert E. and Miller, Herbert A. (1969) *Old World Traits Transplanted.* New York: Arno Press.

Peiss, Kathy (1986) *Cheap Amusements: Working Women and Leisure in Turn-of-the-century New York.* Philadelphia: Temple University Press.

Pleck, Elizabeth H. (1979) *Black Migration and Poverty, Boston, 1865–1900.* New York: Academic Press.

Pratt, Mary Louise (1992) *Imperial Eyes: Travel Writing and Transculturation.* New York: Routledge.

Rafter, Nicole Hahn (1988) *White Trash: The Eugenic Family Studies, 1877–1919.* Boston: Northeastern University Press.

Roediger, David R. (1991) *The Wages of Whiteness: Race and the Making of the American Working Class.* New York: Verso.

Rosenberg, Clifford (1998) "Beyond the Melting Pot?" *Contemporary European History* 7, pp. 421–9.

Ruíz, Vicki (1987) *Cannery Women, Cannery Lives: Mexican Women, Unionization, and the California Food Processing Industry, 1930–1950.* Albuquerque: University of New Mexico Press.

Salyer, Lucy E. (1995) *Law Harsh as Tigers: Chinese Immigrants and the Shaping of Modern Immigration Law.* Chapel Hill: University of North Carolina Press.

Seller, Maxine S. (1981) *Immigrant Women.* Philadelphia: Temple University Press.

Smith, Judith E. (1985) *Family Connections: A History of Italian and Jewish Immigrant Lives in Providence, Rhode Island, 1900–1940.* Albany: State University of New York Press.

Smith, Shawn Michelle (1999) *American Archives: Gender, Race, and Class in Visual Culture.* Princeton, NJ: Princeton University Press.

Thistlewaite, Frank (1969) "Migration from Europe Overseas in the Nineteenth and Twentieth Centuries," in Stanley N. Katz and Stanley Kutler (eds.), *New Perspectives on the American Past*, Vol. 2. Boston: Little, Brown.

Thomas, William I. and Znaniecki, Florian (1958) *The Polish Peasant in Europe and America.* New York: Dover.

Yans-McLaughlin, Virginia (1977) *Family and Community: Italian Immigrants in Buffalo, 1880–1930.* Ithaca, NY: Cornell University Press.

Chapter Nineteen

Women's Movements, 1880s–1920s

Kirsten Delegard

TURN-OF-THE-CENTURY women's organizations won renown long before there were formally trained historians interested in writing about women. Keenly aware of how easily their work could be forgotten, ridiculed, or misconstrued, veteran activists like Elizabeth Cady Stanton, Annie Wittenmeyer, Carrie Chapman Catt, and Jane Addams made sure to leave their own record of events, penning histories of their movements. As a result, the first histories of settlement houses, temperance groups, the campaign for the vote, and women's clubs predated any scholarly interest in the organizing work of women. These accounts helped to anchor women's activism of this period in the historical record and in popular imagination. Saloon-smashing temperance crusaders, marching suffragettes, and idealistic settlement house workers spring easily to mind for most Americans when asked to conjure figures from women's past.

These rich records drew some of the first women's historians, including Eleanor Flexner and Anne Firor Scott, to the study of women's activism in the decades from the 1880s to the 1920s. As these pioneering scholars dug past the well-known autobiographies and authorized histories, they uncovered a dynamic world of local, state, and national women's associations and organizations. Their analysis of this world established a scholarly literature that is still growing forty years later. Women's historians now consider this period a veritable golden age of women's organizations, which multiplied rapidly in both number and membership and among every class, race, ethnicity, and region. This period continues to fascinate scholars, who view it as setting the stage for women's modern involvement in the American society and polity. Yet their conclusions speak not just to those interested in the history of women; they have forged a new understanding of the forces driving American reform and a redefinition of politics. Historians can no longer write about modern reform without acknowledging women's work in both the halls of power and at the grassroots; they can no longer see political history as limited to the study of elections, elected officials, and party operatives.

Women moved en masse into activism of all sorts during these years. Their organizations and associations provided the institutional foundation for widespread political engagement related to an extraordinary array of issues and problems. The campaign for suffrage was only the most well-known manifestation of this mass mobilization. Middle-class white women across the country worked for the prohibition of liquor, legal protections for women workers, government programs aimed at improving maternal and child health, laws to raise the age of sexual consent, municipal reforms like adequate sanitation and the establishment of playgrounds and parks, pure food and milk, and the peaceful settlement of international conflicts. Women from the same backgrounds fought female enfranchisement, blocked the expansion of the welfare state, championed white supremacy, and demanded the expansion of the American military after World War I. Rural women focused on progressive farming and populism in the late nineteenth century; some then developed variations on urban reform issues such as public and maternal health and temperance. A smaller number advocated radical agendas and supported the efforts of Socialist and anarchist organizers who traveled throughout the West and Midwest; other rural residents embraced conservative agendas and by the early twentieth century demonstrated against "radicals" who sought to speak in farming communities. Working-class women in company towns and in cities across the country marched, struck, and built unions that represented their interests, sometimes allying with and sometimes defying their male counterparts to demand fairer pay and improved working conditions. In immigrant communities, mothers and wives organized boycotts to force down the price of milk, bread, pasta, and kosher meat and formed cooperatives and union label leagues to improve their buying power and consumer leverage. African American women mobilized in the workplace and the community, seeking better job opportunities, pay, and working conditions and helping to establish and sustain schools, churches, kindergartens, day nurseries, hospitals, and mutual aid societies. Even as they strove to meet the economic needs of their families and neighbors, they also fought racism, promoted "racial uplift," campaigned for temperance, exposed the horrors of lynching and other forms of racial violence, and demanded suffrage for blacks and for women.

Many activists in this period sought to bridge social cleavages, believing that women from all backgrounds shared an interest in protecting home, families, and children. Yet women from different races, classes, and ethnic backgrounds found it difficult to agree on the most pressing problems of the day. Even as they sought to achieve social harmony, for instance, few white middle-class women were able to shed the blinders of race and class privilege in order to make common cause with African American, working-class, or immigrant women. As a result, activists frequently worked at cross-purposes and sometimes descended into open conflict. Class, race, and ethnicity determined what problems seemed most urgent. For instance, while African American women campaigned to end disfranchisement, white women fought for enfranchisement. Middle-class and native-born women denounced child labor and demanded children attend school; working-class women organized to raise their own wages so that children would not have to work. Working-class and immigrant women remained preoccupied with finding well-paid and safe work that they could combine with household and childcare responsibilities; at the same time, native-born white women worked to school them in vocational and domestic skills that prepared them only for low-paid and low-skilled positions. Indeed, the educational programs offered by middle-class reformers to the masses of immigrants and African Americans were focused far more on demonstrating the superiority of white, native-born standards of living than with improving the material realities of the "students" themselves.

Scholars have explored this rich maze of women's activism from three main angles. Each approach builds on earlier histories, neither eclipsing nor closing off still vibrant areas of inquiry. A first wave of scholars considered the campaigns, goals, and organizations dominated by white, mainly urban, middle-class women. Their first goal was to establish that women were independent activists whose motives were distinct from those of their husbands, fathers, and male allies. Their second goal was to bring women's history into the heart of mainstream American political history by demonstrating that it was impossible to understand the ebb and flow of progressive reform in the United States without taking the work of women into account.

A second group of scholars focused on working-class, immigrant, African American, and rural activists, asserting that class, race, ethnicity, and residence shaped women's activism in critical ways. These scholars uncovered a wider spectrum of women's activism and illuminated the diversity of women's political cultures and agendas. They were attentive to spontaneous and short-lived movements for change as well as more established organizations and campaigns. As they added new groups, modes of activism, and agendas to the history of the period, they also cast fresh light on middle-class white women, highlighting race and class biases that had been hidden when these women were studied in isolation. Moreover, as this work developed, it revealed that fault lines ran through, rather than just along the borders of, immigrant communities and communities of color. Class and ethnic prejudices were not the sole province of middle-class white women. Black clubwomen who advocated respectability as one means of challenging racist assumptions among whites often demanded that the black masses adopt lifestyles and behaviors at odds with their material conditions and cultural beliefs. A similar dynamic developed within immigrant communities in which long-settled members of an ethnic group, such as German Jews, looked down upon more recent arrivals, in this case Russian and other East European Jews, who they feared would revitalize anti-immigrant attitudes and movements. Over time, studies of specific communities of women activists vied with those focused on the interactions between (mainly white, middle-class) reformers and their (mainly working-class, immigrant, and African American) "clients" or on the coalitions and conflicts among diverse groups of activists.

The first set of historians established the breadth of white middle-class women's commitment to social change; the second revealed the limits of their vision. Yet even as they critiqued earlier histories, scholars of working-class, immigrant, African American, and rural women shared their broader mission: to uncover the range of women's involvement with progressive causes and demonstrate how women have been a driving force behind progressive social change in the United States. So while the "heroines" changed, the overarching narrative stayed the same. But the clashes chronicled by historians attentive to racial, class, ethnic, and regional diversity have inspired a search for another kind of conflict among women.

Most recently, a relatively small group of scholars – including myself – has set out to document women's devotion to an entirely different set of causes associated with conservatism and the far right. We have found that women on the right came into their own as an independent political force in the years following World War I. Years of public engagement by radical and moderate women paved the way for conservatives to embrace political and social mobilization. Some were closely linked early in their careers to their counterparts in prohibition campaigns and women's clubwork; others gained their first experiences in anti-suffrage campaigns, or were moved to action by post-World War I fears that Bolshevism and other forms of radicalism were subverting American political and military might. No matter what their issue or their personal political history, these activists set themselves on a collision course with other women. One of their main purposes was to counter the claim that women left of center spoke for the entire female sex. (Fifty years later, this pattern would be repeated in response to second-wave feminism.)

This recent work expands the boundaries of the scholarship on women's movements, demonstrating an even greater diversity of causes and priorities. It cannot be considered in isolation from earlier scholarship. As they worked to thwart their liberal and radical foes, conservative women demonstrated a significant power to shape the political possibilities of progressives. For years, scholars dismissed conservative women as pawns of powerful men and thus as irrelevant to the larger political culture of women's voluntary associations and the broader dynamics of social change. Now it is clear that many women activists on the right claimed agency on their own and had tremendous power to derail the efforts of their liberal and radical sisters.

"Domesticating" Politics

As soon as scholars discovered the rich world of white middle-class voluntary associations, they were determined to prevent the reform campaigns they led from being consigned to the margins of American history. Forced to be ambitious by skeptical colleagues who doubted that studying women was legitimate or important, historians such as Eleanor Flexner, Anne Scott, and Ruth Bordin were driven to make sweeping claims. Winning more than a tenuous toehold for women's history, they forced the reframing of the grand narrative of the "Progressive era." Pioneers of the field started by examining women's demands for political equality, especially the campaign for the vote; but they quickly recognized that vast numbers of women were politically mobilized before passage of the Nineteenth Amendment to the US Constitution granting women's suffrage. Ultimately, women's historians transformed the definition of politics by including struggles for power and efforts at social change that occurred outside the electoral arena. In this way, they rejuvenated political history, once the province of presidents and elected officials, and blurred the line between public and private issues and concerns. Thus women's history, once marginalized by established scholars as relevant only for understanding the evolution of the domestic realm, moved center stage in explorations of public activism and social policy at the turn of the twentieth century.

Women's suffrage had gained considerable attention even before the emergence of women's history as a field. Eleanor Flexner's classic study, *Century of Struggle*, published in 1959, examined the campaign for women's enfranchisement in a sweeping narrative that embraced African American and working-class as well as white middle-class activists and addressed issues in the South and West as well as the Northeast. It remains the best single-volume synthesis of the US suffrage movement. Much of the work that Flexner's study spawned, however, was less focused on the vote itself than on the larger context of women's reform organizations, which surged during the last two decades of the nineteenth century and the first two of the twentieth. Anne Firor Scott, for example, recognized early on that women's efforts at community improvement, their participation in educational reform, temperance, and municipal housekeeping campaigns, as well as their suffrage work, made them central players in the definition and implementation of the panoply of reforms known as progressivism.

The pioneering work of Flexner and Scott introduced a generation of historians to the gendered visions of progressive reform articulated by early twentieth-century activists. In 1910, for example, feminist and journalist Rheta Childe Dorr had proclaimed, "Woman's place is Home . . . But Home is not contained within the four walls of an individual house. Home is the community. The city full of people is the Family. The public school is the real Nursery. And badly do the Home and the Family need their mother" (quoted in Baker 1984: 632). The same year, Jane Addams asserted that "if the street is not cleaned by the city authorities, no amount of private sweeping will keep the tenement free from grime; if the garbage is not properly collected and destroyed a tenement house mother may see her children sicken and die of diseases from which she alone is powerless to shield them. . . . In short, if women would keep on with her old business of caring for her house and rearing her children, she will have to have some conscience in regard to public affairs lying quite outside her immediate household" (quoted in Rosenberg 1992: 38–9). Throughout the 1980s and early 1990s, historians wielded these claims to show the way that middle-class reformers employed the rhetoric of domesticity to justify their activism and explored as well how women exploited this involvement to break free of the domestic claim. Largely focused on questions of emancipation, scholars demonstrated that women's organizations served as vehicles for female autonomy, fostering supportive personal and professional networks and providing institutional homes that allowed them to live outside the structure of the traditional family and offered them careers and some degree of financial independence.

For some the internal workings of this women's world of reform served as an important focus of research. Allen Davis's *Spearheads for Reform* (1967), Estelle Freedman's "Separatism as Strategy" (1979), and Kathryn Kish Sklar's "Hull House in the 1890s" (1985) all explored the significance of single-sex associations and institutions for women's personal growth as well as political influence. The very strength that came from such association, Sklar argued, made it possible for these communities of women to develop effective alliances with like-minded men in pursuit of municipal and state reform legislation. Other historians, such as Ruth Bordin in her study of the temperance crusade and Karen Blair in her exploration of women's clubs, highlighted the vast array of work undertaken by women's associations and their substantial impact on social reform, especially at local and state levels. Yet here, too, it was assumed that women activists gained personal satisfaction and some degree of independence through their collective efforts at community improvement.

By the late 1980s and 1990s, however, interest waned somewhat in questions of personal emancipation and community improvement. Building on the work of Freedman, Sklar, Bordin, and others, scholars examined how women wielded power and what effects they had, not only on the women and children they sought to serve, but also on public policy and the state. Synthesizing a large body of literature on the mass mobilization of middle-class women in settlement houses, in the local branches of organizations like the Woman's Christian Temperance Union and the General Federation of Women's Clubs, and in umbrella groups like the National Consumer's League, historians advanced a structural argument. Middle-class women's reform efforts at the turn of the twentieth century were significant for the mark they left on the American state, especially the evolving welfare state. These historians have illuminated first how women realized the limits of voluntary efforts, many of which were not comprehensive enough to address the problems they confronted. Assistance to poor women and children, for instance, could not eradicate the roots of poverty. That required engagement with municipal, and ultimately with state and federal, governments. They did not abandon interest in the private entirely, however. Robyn Muncy, for instance, tied the attraction of settlement work for some women to the paucity of personal and professional opportunities that could meet their need for both intimate bonds with other women and productive careers for themselves. And Linda Gordon made clear the ways that reformers' public actions often intruded on the private lives of working-class women. Still, Muncy and Gordon along with Sklar, Molly Ladd-Taylor, Seth Koven, Sonya Michel, and Estelle Freedman were primarily interested in analyzing the development of a "female dominion" in American reform, the creation of a "maternalist" agenda for social change, and the implementation of this agenda through voluntary and then state-supported welfare programs.

Through protective labor legislation, mothers' pensions, public health campaigns, juvenile courts, maternal and child welfare programs, and dozens of other initiatives, women reformers expanded the role of government agencies and forced the state to provide minimum standards, safeguards, and emergency funds for large numbers of Americans who were vulnerable and exploited. Once women's roles in the formation of the American welfare state are taken into account, it becomes impossible to understand changes in government and society without attention to women's reform organizations. Indeed, as William Chafe has argued, not only did women form the backbone of "small p" progressive social change at the turn of the twentieth century, but they also forged the critical links between Progressive-era programs and the expansion of the welfare state during the New Deal.

Yet the federal government's embrace of women's social welfare initiatives was not a triumphal tale. First, as Muncy has forcefully argued, the absorption or co-optation of women's reform programs by state agencies ultimately destroyed many of the organizations that had driven these changes in the first place. Moreover, the alliances forged between women activists, women professionals and academics, and those who needed or demanded their services broke down when small numbers of the first two groups were pulled into government agencies to serve as administrators and experts. At the same time, as Gordon, Ladd-Taylor, and others have so effectively demonstrated, women who gained government posts rarely wielded sufficient power to implement their programs as originally envisioned. Rather, the political give-and-take demanded in electoral and legislative arenas and the limits imposed by judicial review assured that well-placed Congressional leaders and powerful bureaucrats, rather than newly appointed women reformers, would shape the implementation of social welfare programs. Combined with the racial and class prejudices that had influenced much of white middle-class women's activist agenda, the constraints reformers faced working within state and federal structures ensured that the programs implemented would be far narrower than those initially planned.

Many studies of the welfare state, focused on contests for authority within the federal government, necessarily highlighted the activities of those women – largely middle-class and elite white women – with the greatest access to political power. Yet by the 1980s and 1990s, the history of women's activism had moved well beyond the confines of middle-class white women's voluntary organizations. The increased attention to issues of race, class, and ethnicity influenced arguments about women, reform, and the state. As Patrick Wilkinson shows in his provocative 1999 review of literature on women and the welfare state, "The Selfless and the Helpless," concerns about the class and race limits of social welfare policies required scholars to engage critical questions about female agency. If women were the movers and shakers behind such policies, then they must be held at least partly accountable for the ways that this legislation etched racial, class, and gender discrimination more deeply into the law. If they were not to be held accountable, this was evidence that those women who gained access to government positions had, in fact, wielded little power.

As Wilkinson notes, some scholars of the welfare state had long been grappling with these issues. Linda Gordon and Mary Odem, for instance, in their respective studies of domestic violence and female delinquency in the late nineteenth and early twentieth centuries, probed the complex dynamics that shaped interactions among individuals, families, low-level female professionals, and state agencies, including the courts. Some mothers, for instance, invited social workers into their homes or asked juvenile courts to help control their delinquent daughters; but few realized how quickly they could lose all claims to authority over their children once the state intervened. At the same time, Molly Ladd-Taylor demonstrated the ways that ordinary, often poor, women demanded assistance from federal agencies such as the Children's Bureau after passage of the Sheppard-Towner Maternity and Infancy Protection Act in 1921. Indeed, Ladd-Taylor argues, "the Sheppard-Towner Act was the product of an unusual alliance between grass-roots mothers, clubwomen, and Children's Bureau officials." Julia Lathrop, first head of the Bureau, had corresponded with poor mothers about their ill health and the suffering they and their children endured, and designed a bill to provide education and medical resources for pregnant women and new mothers. "Grass-roots mothers thus played an important if indirect role in the creation of one of the earliest United States social welfare measures" (1994: 168).

Recasting Women's Activism

The examination of poor, working-class, immigrant, and African American women's influence on and interactions with white middle-class women reformers was just one reflection of a burgeoning interest in a wider range of women's activism. From the first explorations of women's associations, some scholars had focused on those outside the white middle class. Studies of African American women's activism had a long and distinguished history. In 1972, Gerda Lerner published a pathbreaking collection, *Black Women in White America*, that provided abundant evidence of African American women's engagement with a variety of issues and movements. Sharon Harley and Rosalyn Terborg-Penn's 1978 anthology, *The Afro-American Woman: Struggles and Images*, revealed the breadth of women's activism in the nineteenth and twentieth centuries, documenting as well the discrimination they faced in education, politics, the workforce, and white women's political movements. Over the next decade a spate of articles moved the discussion forward, followed by a series of seminal monographs, including Cynthia Neverdon-Morton's *Afro-American Women of the South and the Advancement of the Race, 1895–1925* (1989), Jacqueline Rouse's *Lugenia Burns Hope* (1989), and Dorothy Salem's *To Better Our World* (1990). Studies of working women's organizing efforts, especially in immigrant communities, also appeared in these years. In 1977, Barbara Wertheimer's *We Were There: The Story of Working Women in America* chronicled laboring women's issues and activities; Paula Hyman explored the New York City kosher meat boycotts in a 1980 article; and Ruth Milkman's 1985 anthology, *Women, Work and Protest*, brought together a dozen provocative essays on women's labor organizing.

By the late 1980s and 1990s, studies of activism among African American and other women of color, immigrant women, and working-class women not only expanded historians' understanding of the scope of women's public efforts but also, once again, transformed the conceptualization of progressivism and politics. By highlighting these campaigns to achieve personal autonomy, communal advancement, and social justice, despite the barriers created by government officials, economic leaders, and white middle-class reformers, scholars offered important challenges to existing interpretations. They also revealed significant connections between so-called progressive reforms and efforts at class and racial exclusion.

A collection of essays published in 1991, Noralee Frankel and Nancy Shrom Dye's *Gender, Class, Race, and Reform in the Progressive Era*, effectively showcased the work that was recasting understandings of women's movements. Highlighting studies of working-class and middle-class African American women as well as those of laboring women, the volume illustrated key themes and debates among those challenging conventional wisdom. Some authors who examined immigrant women, such as Ardis Cameron and Nancy Hewitt, emphasized the ways that interethnic and gender solidarity sustained working-class communities in the face of exploitation by employers and discrimination by the native-born white community. Others, including Eileen Boris and Alice Kessler-Harris, focused on how supposedly progressive legislation constrained laboring women's agency by imposing middle-class constructions of the family and gendered notions of free labor on working-class communities. In the same volume, Sharon Harley argued that African American women did not necessarily view the workplace as the most important source of their identity or the most likely arena for collective struggle. Often consigned to ill-paid and isolated domestic labor, they focused instead on community-based efforts to advance the race. As Rosalyn Terborg-Penn then demonstrated, community tragedies, such as lynchings, drove some women into national and international campaigns to stop the brutal violence against African American men and women.

Studies of activism among working-class women and women of color multiplied rapidly. Evelyn Brooks Higginbotham explored issues of class, respectability, and the politics of uplift in the Black Baptist church; Sarah Deutsch and Vicki Ruíz analyzed the efforts of Mexican and Mexican American women to sustain their families and communities in the Southwest; Dorothy Sue Cobble recovered the long history of labor organizing among waitresses; Elizabeth Faue and Dana Frank offered detailed studies of women's labor and consumer politics in Minneapolis and Seattle; Tera Hunter and Elsa Barkley Brown traced the emancipatory politics of newly freed black women in Atlanta and Richmond; Glenda Gilmore examined the ways that Jim Crow shaped middle-class African American women's activism in late nineteenth-century North Carolina; and Jacquelyn Dowd Hall addressed diverse forms of resistance among white working-class women in mill towns across the South. Others focused renewed attention on the interactions between middle-class white women reformers and the poorer women of color whom they saw as the beneficiaries of their efforts. Peggy Pascoe was especially effective in capturing the critical work performed by white women reformers on behalf of Chinese immigrant women and others caught in horrible circumstances, on the one hand, and the race and class blinders that often distorted those reformers' vision and implementation of social change, on the other.

In the past decade, the voluminous literature on women's activism has dramatically recast a number of arguments based on middle-class white women's movements. Certainly the racist, nativist, and elitist views of many native-born white women reformers have been revealed in this work, and the consequences of such views for the strategies adopted by reform campaigns and the construction of the welfare state analyzed. Indeed, the very definition of certain kinds of institutions based on white women's experience had blinded us to the existence of alternate possibilities. Elizabeth Lasch Quinn makes this point persuasively in *Black Neighbors* (1993), which reveals not only the limited vision of settlement work embraced by white women reformers, but also the way that their vision led historians to ignore institutions, often religiously based, that provided similar services in African American communities.

In addition, work on working-class women and women of color has made clear the significance of locally based and spontaneous movements – such as food boycotts and wildcat strikes – whether or not they resulted in more permanent institutional changes. Attention to these and other forms of grassroots struggles over power that do not take traditional electoral or legislative forms have forced scholars, including many women's historians, to rethink the very definition of politics. Was the newly emancipated domestic servant who uses her mistress's make-up in Tera Hunter's *To 'Joy My Freedom* (1997) making a political statement? Were the Klan women who organized a "poison squad of whispering women" less politically engaged than men who participated in other types of grassroots organizing? Were the Cuban and Italian immigrant women in Tampa, Florida, who turned out for a mass meeting of strikers in 1920, but ignored the advent of women's suffrage, political activists? What about the women who watched their children when they walked the picket line? The meaning of public activities could vary considerably even for those engaged in more conventional political behavior. What did the vote itself represent when cast by middle-class white women protesting passage of the Fifteenth Amendment in 1872; by working-class women in western cities in the 1890s; by African American men in the same period; by immigrant women in New York State in 1918; and by African American women across the South in 1920, before the loopholes created by the Nineteenth Amendment could be closed?

Like politics, the rubric of maternalism holds a different significance when viewed in the light of scholarship on working-class women and women of color. Jacquelyn Dowd Hall has noted that the maternal imagery used by reformers like Jane Addams "casts [them] as the asexual, motherly saviors of the poor, eliding the issue of sexuality in the reformers' lives" (1993: 168). Jane Addams, who shared her life with Mary Rozet Starr, another female reformer and philanthropist, may have been particularly aware of the power this rhetoric evoked. Addams and Starr were relatively open about their relationship, not too shy to inform unfamiliar hotelkeepers of their desire for a room with one double bed. Maternalist rhetoric was not necessary to mask their relationship, since romantic friendships between women, or Boston marriages as more committed relationships were called, had not yet been tarred with the brush of perversion. Still Addams, like many settlement house workers and other white middle-class women reformers of the period, was an unmarried, childless woman pursuing a pathbreaking public career in an era when concerns about race suicide made potential subversives of any woman of this class who did not reproduce. Thus maternalist claims were often invoked by reformers who did not lead the domestic lives they so heartily applauded, yet who held up poor, immigrant, and African American women to precisely the standards they chose to ignore.

As Hall and Deborah Gray White have shown, neither working-class nor African American women could so easily jettison social norms. Given the lurid sexualization of African Americans in late nineteenth-century society, most middle-class black women reformers embraced the traditional forms of marriage and motherhood even if they did not, in fact, abide by domestic strictures for long. Widowhood allowed a woman to live a relatively independent life while carrying the title of Mrs. as a marker of community respect and public credibility, but even divorce was acceptable as long as it was secured without scandal or fanfare. For working-class white women activists, many of whom were young and single, threats of both sexual exploitation and sexual scandal were rife. Ola Delight Smith, a militant labor organizer in early twentieth-century Atlanta, had married young, perhaps in hopes of averting sexual intimidation. Instead, she was accused of adultery by factory owners and civic leaders in a smear campaign intended to diminish her influence with the city's striking workers. For Smith, being a "bad" wife and mother was as damaging as being single. Certainly maternal rhetoric could not shield her from attack; indeed, middle-class maternalists in Atlanta were as likely to condemn her as were their male counterparts.

Finally, studies of working-class and women of color activists challenge any attempt to view single-sex organizations and institutions as the sine qua non of women's movements. Although African American, immigrant, and laboring women often organized on their own, either in independent associations or as auxiliaries to men's unions, clubs, and societies, they also joined male relatives, neighbors, and co-workers in campaigns for social, economic, and political change. Indeed, studies by Hall, White, Hewitt, Deutsch, Barkley Brown, and others demonstrate time and again the importance of women's participation in both mixed-sex and single-sex movements. For many African American, immigrant, and working-class women, these are not alternate paths to public action but deeply intertwined aspects of ongoing struggles for emancipation and justice.

The explosion of work on women activists in working-class, immigrant, and African American communities has dramatically transformed interpretations of politics, progressivism, and activism. We still have significant groups of women whose activism has not been studied in depth for this period, such as Native American, Asian and Asian American, and Scandinavian women. And we have too little work that analyzes diverse groups of activists in the context of the same issue or location. Comparing the anti-lynching campaigns of black and white women as they are portrayed by Jacquelyn Dowd Hall, Rosalyn Terborg-Penn, Gail Bederman, and Linda McMurry suggests the power of such an approach. Similarly, Nancy Hewitt's *Southern Discomfort* (2001), which examines native-born white, Cuban and Italian immigrant, and African American women activists in Tampa at the turn of the twentieth century, reveals the potential of comparative work to illuminate important similarities and differences among activists across race, class, and ethnicity. Such work provides a particularly important counterpoint to the more numerous studies that bring white middle-class activists into conversation only with those women of color and working-class women who require assistance or uplift.

Women on the Right

The emphasis in studies of women's movements has shifted from recovering middle-class white women's reform activities to dissecting the ways that gender shaped campaigns for social justice and social change to analyzing the interplay of race, class, and gender in diverse forms of women's activism. Despite the rich, varied, and detailed studies produced by scholars to date, most have focused only on what they considered progressive social movements and have explained differences in agendas, strategies, priorities, and modes of activism largely as products of socio-economic location. Movements once considered conservative, such as temperance and prohibition, have been recast as forerunners of campaigns against domestic violence and sexual abuse and as attentive to the needs of working-class as well as middle-class women. Until very recently, those that could not be rescued by such redefinitions, including the anti-suffrage movement, the Women of the Ku Klux Klan, and more mainstream conservative efforts to combat Bolshevism and the welfare state, have been largely ignored. Yet by the 1920s, tens of thousands of women were active in these causes. In these years, women's voluntary associations in Indiana, politicized by the Klan, agitated for local and state intervention in the name of racist causes. At the same time, right-of-center activists centered in Massachusetts fought to curb the expansion of the federal welfare state. Boston Brahmin Elizabeth Lowell Putnam worked with the Woman Patriot Publishing Company, the Sentinels of the Republic, and an ad hoc group opposed to banning child labor to convince lawmakers that federal restrictions on child labor and programs promoting maternal health would ultimately harm more women and children than they would help. My own work on female anti-radicals during the 1920s and 1930s demonstrates the mass appeal among women of mainstream conservative activism, including efforts to expand the military and internal surveillance of suspected political dissenters.

The studies on right-wing and conservative women that have appeared in the last decade suggest that many traditional assumptions about their motives, ideologies, and significance are misguided. Perhaps most importantly, Kathleen Blee, Nancy MacLean, Sonya Michel, and Ruth Rosen, researching Klanswomen and conservative maternalists, respectively, have demonstrated that many women combined agendas in ways that confound current interpretations. Women in the Klan saw no contradiction in participating in the Klan while advocating women's suffrage, temperance, and moral reform. Blee argues that the Klan seemed merely to be the best way for women to protect themselves and their children. In fact, MacLean explains that white women invoked the racist ideology of the Klan to extract protection from white male violence. More mainstream conservatives like Elizabeth Lowell Putnam saw no inconsistency in working for years with progressive maternalists to develop locally based maternal health programs, only to fight those same activists when they proposed federal sponsorship of similar programs. Some conservative and right-wing activists are easier to pigeonhole, confining themselves to racist causes or moving directly from anti-suffrage efforts in the pre-World War I period into postwar campaigns against Bolshevism. Yet many women embraced a form of maternalism while rejecting progressivism, radicalism, or liberalism. Like their progressive foes, women who fought for white supremacy or to restrict the growth of the federal government believed they were working on behalf of women and children.

Studying women on the right also illuminates the limits of using sociological terms to explain activism. Throughout this period, profound ideological differences arose among women of the same social, educational, and class backgrounds. Kathleen Blee was one of the first scholars to argue that class was no predictor of activism. My work on mainstream conservatism reinforces her research on the midwestern Ku Klux Klan. Female anti-radicalism was a movement of white middle- and upper-class women and played on the fears of those classes. Yet similar types of women promoted and fought anti-radicalism. In fact, many had shared organizational loyalties in the decades before World War I. The critical factor in determining whether an affluent woman pursued the unfinished business of the Progressive era or turned her attention to countersubversion seems to have been her reaction to warnings about the Russian Revolution and its threat to domestic stability. Those who believed in the Bolshevik threat viewed many of their former co-workers, particularly those engaged in expanding the welfare state and combating militarism, as Communist sympathizers or dupes or as dangerous radicals. The common ground they had once shared with their new foes rendered many progressive women, especially those holding government appointments, vulnerable to attack. Their campaign against less conservative women created a devastating division in the ranks of women activists during the 1920s. Conservatives forced some centrist women's groups to purge more radical members from their ranks and others to retreat from overtly political activities altogether.

In the years after the passage of the Nineteenth Amendment, conservative women made it impossible for broad-based centrist groups to continue as advocates for progressive causes. The early advocacy of groups like the General Federation of Women's Clubs has been too often forgotten. If remembered it has been understood as the victim of racial and class prejudice. It was just as much a casualty of a conservative campaign to shrink the welfare state, expand the military, and strengthen the internal security state. Conservative activists were most successful in making progressive maternalism controversial, too closely tarred with the brush of Bolshevism for the respectable matrons of the middle-of-the-road groups like the General Federation of Women's Clubs. Women did not turn their backs on activism once they were enfranchised; they remained active in the single-sex groups conceived during the Progressive era. But it was not until the economic crisis of the Great Depression opened new possibilities for government intervention that ideas originally conceived by women activists in the 1890s gained sufficient support to be implemented. Even then, the echoes of anti-radicalism would restrict the scope and influence the gender and racial biases written into expanded welfare policies. Until we recognize the power of conservative women's movements to influence the larger political landscape, we cannot adequately assess the gains and losses of their progressive counterparts.

Conservative women activists proved far more than a thorn in the side of progressive activists. In addition to stalling and even overturning progressive measures, they established the ideological and institutional roots of American anti-Communism. They fanned fears of the radical menace to argue for larger military budgets, intensified domestic surveillance of political dissenters, and the designation of the *Star Spangled Banner* as the national anthem, an act freighted with symbolic importance by military supporters and anti-militarists alike. They pressured state legislators, generally with great success, to require the pledge of allegiance in every classroom, adopt loyalty oaths for teachers, mandate the use of "patriotic" textbooks, and institute universal military training for public school students.

Even as they challenge the model of women's activism grounded in case studies of diverse women working for social justice, historians of the right share the longstanding desire of feminist scholars to win recognition for the vital role that women activists played in bringing about social change. Yet these scholars do not conflate social change with progressive change. They demonstrate that women's work was more broad-ranging, their political sympathies more polarized than previously illustrated. Women were critical in winning influence and legitimacy for white supremacy, conservative attacks on the welfare state, and ultimately the anti-Communism that would come to dominate the post-World War II political landscape.

New Beginnings

The history of the suffrage movement, one of the most well-studied of women's campaigns, suggests how the three approaches outlined here have interacted to form richer but also competing historical interpretations. As noted above, Eleanor Flexner's *Century of Struggle* offered a superb starting point for scholarship on the topic. Sensitive to the racial, class, and regional dynamics of the movement, Flexner sketched out a broad terrain as the basis for future scholarship. Yet until the 1980s, most scholars continued to focus largely on the efforts of white middle-class women, particularly those who followed the lead of Elizabeth Cady Stanton and Susan B. Anthony in campaigns for state and then federal suffrage. Critiques of these heroes of the suffrage movement erupted in the late 1970s, led by scholars studying African American women, who pointed out that despite the abolitionist roots of most early woman's rights advocates, many suffrage leaders had adopted racist and nativist positions by the late nineteenth century.

Historians of the southern suffrage movement have been especially attentive to the dynamics of race. Elsa Barkley Brown, Suzanne Lebsock, Glenda Gilmore, Marjorie Spruill Wheeler, and Elna Green offered diverse readings of women's engagement with voting rights in the former Confederacy. Taken together they chart the wide array of positions championed by white and black women in the region: ardent anti-suffragists; virulently racist advocates of state's rights suffrage; moderate white suffragists who neither contributed nor responded to racist critiques of women's enfranchisement; and African American women who fought black men's disfranchisement, quietly advocated their own political rights, and quickly mobilized to vote when the opportunity arrived in 1920. In Tampa and other multiracial southern cities, the picture was complicated by the presence of female immigrants who were often quite militant in defense of workplace or community rights, but rarely interested in electoral politics. Native American women provide yet another perspective on voting rights as they sought to maintain their place within tribal structures, which were under assault from federal officials, and demand racial and gender equity in the larger society. Still, the driving force in conflicts over women's suffrage in the South remained the tensions between rights for white women and those for blacks.

In recent years, the study of black women and suffrage has moved beyond the southern context. *African American Women and the Vote*, published in 1997, brings together articles by a number of scholars that address the efforts of northern and southern activists from 1837 to 1965. Building on extensive research regarding the ties between abolition and woman's rights, on reconceptualizations of the vote as a familial or communal possession in the post-Civil War era, and on the literature on women in the civil rights movement, this volume portrays African American women as active agents in the ongoing battles for enfranchisement. In *African American Women and the Struggle for the Vote* (1998), Rosalyn Terborg-Penn hones in on the period from 1850 to 1920, recovering black women's and men's individual and collective efforts on behalf of suffrage and analyzing white suffragists' varied reactions to the initiatives taken by activists of color. These studies suggest the value of additional research on the independent suffrage activities of other groups, including white working-class and immigrant women and Native Americans.

The studies of southern and African American suffrage campaigns form the foundation upon which Louise Newman built her argument in *White Women's Rights* (1999). Here, however, rather than critiquing individual leaders of the white suffrage movement as racists, Newman argues that feminism as an ideology was forged in the crucible of race and racism. Feminism and its political counterpart, the campaign for suffrage, emerged at a moment when imperialist projects abroad and civilizing missions at home accentuated racial hierarchies. According to Newman, progressive white women in the United States absorbed these attitudes and values and incorporated them into their vision of rights. Although based mainly on intellectual portraits of a dozen women, not all of whom would have accepted the label of feminist, or even suffragist, *White Women's Rights* directs our attention to the ways that dominant racial and imperial assumptions shaped white women's activism in the late nineteenth and early twentieth centuries.

Studies of the West offer an important terrain for such work. Certainly, the western suffrage movement has attracted significant attention. Since the late nineteenth century, suffrage advocates and their historians have told the story of women who first gained the right to vote in frontier territories and states. Only recently, however, have scholars attempted to complicate these celebratory tales. In *An Army of Women* (1997), Michael Goldberg offers us a long view of women's political struggles in Kansas. Famous for its bloody battles over abolition in the 1850s and 1860s, Kansas was declared "the great experimental ground of the nation" by the *New York Times* in 1887 (quoted in Goldberg 1997: 4). Here the suffrage movement was grounded not in urban reform efforts, but in a mix of agrarian radicalism and temperance militancy. Yet despite some early victories in municipal suffrage, temperance, and moral purity campaigns, the statewide movement for enfranchisement became mired in the shifting sands of Populist, Republican, and Democratic politics and proved unable to replicate victories for women's votes in Wyoming, Utah, Colorado, and other western states. Gayle Gullett's history of the California women's suffrage movement also demonstrates the ways that local and state campaigns for women's votes were caught up in the larger forces of reform politics. In this case, however, women progressives forged an alliance with their male counterparts that led to victory in the statewide referendum on women's suffrage and helped to legitimize women's public and political work more broadly.

In the cases of both Kansas and California, the middle-class respectability of suffrage advocates was ultimately considered crucial to success, yet we have little sense of how bourgeois ideals combined with territorial conquest and capitalist development to shape the class, racial, and ethnic dynamics of these movements. We need, for instance, more detailed studies of how the leaders' decision to adopt a moderate guise affected the fate of less affluent, immigrant, and African American women in these states and throughout the West as a whole. Unlike studies of suffrage in the South, those on the West have rarely noted, much less analyzed, the racial exclusions built into territorial and state enfranchisement laws. Yet no western state adopted truly universal suffrage, with Asian, Mexican, and Native American women among those most often denied the vote. Martha Mabie Gardiner's work on white working women's involvement in the anti-Chinese movement in late nineteenth-century San Francisco suggests the need to explore racial alliances on behalf of women's suffrage more closely. At the same time, Sarah Barringer Gordon's analysis of the interplay of debates over polygamy and suffrage that surrounded women's enfranchisement in Utah reminds us that in certain circumstances religion could be conceived in racial terms, complicating further efforts to construct any simple narrative of the West as the vanguard of women's suffrage.

In the North, the suffrage story has been the least transformed by questions of race. Ellen DuBois's biography of Harriet Stanton Blatch, however, has illuminated critical alliances between middle-class and working-class white advocates of suffrage, native-born and immigrant, in the Northeast. Her work reminds us as well of the critical importance of both mainstream efforts to lobby federal and state legislators and the more radical activities favored by militants who chained themselves to the White House fence and endured prison and hunger strikes to publicize the cause. This need to "sell" suffrage serves as the centerpiece of Margaret Finnegan's 1999 study. By linking women's activism to changing modes of consumption and advertising, Finnegan reminds us of the ways that women's movements were transformed by cultural and economic as well as political circumstances. Nancy Cott's *The Grounding of Modern Feminism* (1987) had earlier linked the development of different strategies of political advocacy with changes in popular attitudes about women's roles. As older notions of woman's rights vied with newer visions of feminist emancipation in the early twentieth century, many younger women adopted modern political agendas along with modern fashions in dress, courtship, and behavior. Cott argues persuasively, however, that more traditional women's voluntary organizations, far from being diminished by enfranchisement, were infused with new vigor. Indeed, they multiplied rapidly after 1920. It was not simply, then, that innovative or alternative political and social practices, like suffrage, replaced those already in existence. Instead, many forms of activism and many visions of social change coexisted, competing for attention and advocates even as they combined to transform the landscape on which change occurred.

Most recently, interest in the international connections among suffragists has sparked a wave of comparative work. Rosalyn Terborg-Penn has explored ties between African American and Afro-Caribbean activists, while Leila Rupp has examined the links among suffragists and other, mainly white, women reformers in the United States and western Europe. This work promises to provide a whole new range of challenges regarding the ways that imperial ventures and racial hierarchies played out within and across nations, including the United States. Yet even as scholars adopt global perspectives on the suffrage campaign, we remain largely uninformed about those women who opposed female enfranchisement. Once again, that is, women's historians have relegated conservative women to the margins, or the footnotes, with little serious attention to their arguments, allies, and agendas.

The case of women's suffrage, then, illuminates the critical themes that have marked studies of women's movements as a whole. It also reminds us of the challenges that remain as we seek to integrate analyses of race, class, ethnicity, region, and gender; understand women's activism in the context of local, regional, national, and international developments; and attend to women's conservative as well as progressive agendas and practices. We might think of the three approaches to historicizing women's movements sketched here as conversations that need to be brought into dialogue with one another. Recognizing the possibility, indeed inevitability, of debate, argument, and conflict, it is nonetheless crucial to push the dialogues forward as a means of both understanding the past and grappling with the present.

BIBLIOGRAPHY

Baker, Paula (1984) "The Domestication of Politics: Women and American Political Society, 1780–1920," *American Historical Review* 89, pp. 620–47.

Blair, Karen (1980) *The Clubwoman as Feminist: True Womanhood Redefined, 1868–1914.* New York: Holmes and Meier.

Blee, Kathleen (1991) *Women of the Klan: Racism and Gender in the 1920s.* Berkeley: University of California Press.

Bordin, Ruth (1981) *Women and Temperance: The Quest for Power and Liberty, 1873–1900.* Philadelphia: Temple University Press.

Boris, Eileen (1993) "The Power of Motherhood: Black and White Activist Women Redefine the 'Political,'" in Seth Koven and Sonya Michel (eds.), *Mothers of the New World: Maternalist Politics and the Origins of Welfare States.* New York: Routledge, pp. 213–45.

Brown, Elsa Barkley (1997) "To Catch the Vision of Freedom: Reconstructing Black Women's Political History, 1865–1880," in Ann D. Gordon with Bettye Collier-Thomas et al. (eds.), *African American Women and the Vote, 1837–1965.* Amherst: University of Massachusetts Press, pp. 66–99.

Buhle, Mari Jo (1981) *Women and American Socialism, 1870–1920.* Urbana: University of Illinois Press.

Cameron, Ardis (1993) *Radicals of the Worst Sort: Laboring Women in Lawrence, Massachusetts, 1860–1912.* Urbana: University of Illinois Press.

Chafe, William (1993) "Women's History and Political History: Some Thoughts on Progressivism and the New Deal," in Nancy A. Hewitt and Suzanne Lebsock (eds.), *Visible Women: New Essays on American Activism.* Urbana: University of Illinois Press, pp. 101–18.

Cobble, Dorothy Sue (1991) *Dishing It Out: Waitresses and their Unions in the Twentieth Century.* Urbana: University of Illinois Press.

Cott, Nancy (1987) *The Grounding of Modern Feminism.* New Haven, CT: Yale University Press.

Davis, Allen F. (1967) *Spearheads for Reform: The Social Settlements and the Progressive Movement, 1890–1914.* New Brunswick, NJ: Rutgers University Press.

Delegard, Kirsten (1999) "Women Patriots: Female Activism and the Politics of American Anti-radicalism, 1919–1935," Ph.D. dissertation, Duke University.

Deutsch, Sarah (1987) *No Separate Refuge: Culture, Class, and Gender on an Anglo-Hispanic Frontier in the American Southwest, 1880–1940.* New York: Oxford University Press.

DuBois, Ellen (1997) *Harriet Stanton Blatch and the Winning of Woman Suffrage.* New Haven, CT: Yale University Press.

Faue, Elizabeth (1991) *Community of Suffering and Struggle: Women, Men and the Labor Movement in Minneapolis, 1915–1945.* Chapel Hill: University of North Carolina Press.

Finnegan, Margaret (1999) *Selling Suffrage: Consumer Culture and Votes for Women*. New York: Columbia University Press.

Flexner, Eleanor (1959) *Century of Struggle: The Woman's Rights Movement in the United States*. Cambridge, MA: Harvard University Press.

Frank, Dana (1985) "Housewives, Socialists and the Politics of Food: The 1917 Cost of Living Protests," *Feminist Studies* 11, pp. 255–85.

Frank, Dana (1994) *Purchasing Power: Consumer Organizing, Gender, and the Seattle Labor Movement, 1919–1929*. Cambridge, MA: Harvard University Press.

Frankel, Noralee and Dye, Nancy Shrom (eds.) (1991) *Gender, Class, Race, and Reform in the Progressive Era*. Lexington: University of Kentucky Press.

Freedman, Estelle B. (1979) "Separatism as Strategy: Female Institution Building and American Feminism, 1870–1930," *Feminist Studies* 5, pp. 512–29.

Freedman, Estelle B. (1996) *Maternal Justice: Miriam Van Waters and the Female Reform Tradition*. Chicago: University of Chicago Press.

Gardiner, Martha Mabie (1999) "Working on White Womanhood: White Working Women in the San Francisco Anti-Chinese Movement, 1877–1890," *Journal of Social History* 33, pp. 73–95.

Gilmore, Glenda (1996) *Gender and Jim Crow: Women and the Politics of White Supremacy in North Carolina, 1896–1920*. Chapel Hill: University of North Carolina Press.

Goldberg, Michael Lewis (1997) *An Army of Women: Gender and Politics in Gilded Age Kansas*. Baltimore: Johns Hopkins University Press.

Gordon, Ann, with Bettye Collier-Thomas et al. (eds.) (1997) *African American Women and the Vote, 1837–1965*. Amherst: University of Massachusetts Press.

Gordon, Linda (1988) *Heroes of their Own Lives: The Politics and History of Family Violence, Boston, 1880–1960*. New York: Viking Books.

Gordon, Linda (1991) "Black and White Visions of Welfare: Women's Welfare Activism, 1890–1945," *Journal of American History* 78, pp. 559–90.

Gordon, Sarah Barringer (1996) "The Liberty of Self-degradation: Polygamy, Women's Suffrage and Consent in Nineteenth-century America," *Journal of American History* 44, pp. 815–47.

Graham, Sarah Hunter (1996) *Woman Suffrage and the New Democracy*. New Haven, CT: Yale University Press.

Green, Elna (1997) *Southern Strategies: Southern Women and the Woman Suffrage Question*. Chapel Hill: University of North Carolina Press.

Gullett, Gayle (2000) *Becoming Citizens: The Emergence and Development of the California Women's Movement, 1880–1911*. Urbana: University of Illinois Press.

Hall, Jacquelyn Dowd (1979) *Revolt Against Chivalry: Jessie Daniel Ames and the Women's Campaign Against Lynching*. New York: Columbia University Press.

Hall, Jacquelyn Dowd (1986) "Disorderly Women: Gender and Labor Militancy in the Appalachian South," *Journal of American History* 73, pp. 354–82.

Hall, Jacquelyn Dowd (1993) "Ola Delight Smith's Progressive Era: Labor, Feminism and Reform in the Urban South," in Nancy A. Hewitt and Suzanne Lebsock (eds.), *Visible Women: New Essays on American Activism*. Urbana: University of Illinois Press, pp. 166–98.

Harley, Sharon and Terborg-Penn, Rosalyn (eds.) (1978) *The Afro-American Woman: Struggles and Images*. Port Washington, NY: Kennikat Press.

Hewitt, Nancy A. (2001) *Southern Discomfort: Women's Activism in Tampa, Florida, 1880s–1920s*. Urbana: University of Illinois Press.

Higginbotham, Evelyn Brooks (1993) *Righteous Discontent: The Women's Movement in the Black Baptist Church, 1880–1920*. Cambridge, MA: Harvard University Press.

Hunter, Tera W. (1997) *To 'Joy My Freedom: Southern Black Women's Lives and Labors After the Civil War.* Cambridge, MA: Harvard University Press.

Hyman, Paula (1980) "Immigrant Women and Consumer Protest: The New York City Kosher Meat Boycott of 1902," *American Jewish History* 70, pp. 126–40.

Koven, Seth and Michel, Sonya (1990) "Womanly Duties: Maternalist Politics and the Origins of Welfare States in France, Germany, Great Britain, and the United States, 1880–1920," *American Historical Review* 95, pp. 1076–1108.

Ladd-Taylor, Molly (1986) *Raising a Baby the Government Way: Mothers' Letters to the Children's Bureau, 1915–1932.* New Brunswick, NJ: Rutgers University Press.

Ladd-Taylor, Molly (1994) *Mother-work: Women, Child Welfare, and the State, 1890–1930.* Urbana: University of Illinois Press.

Lebsock, Suzanne (1993) "Women Suffrage and White Supremacy: A Virginia Case Study," in Nancy A. Hewitt and Suzanne Lebsock (eds.), *Visible Women: New Essays on American Activism.* Urbana: University of Illinois Press, pp. 62–100.

Lerner, Gerda (ed.) (1972) *Black Women in White America: A Documentary History.* New York: Vintage Books.

MacLean, Nancy (1991) "White Women, Klan Violence in the 1920s: Agency, Complicity, and the Politics of Women's History," *Gender and History* 3, pp. 285–303.

MacLean, Nancy (1994) *Behind the Mask of Chivalry: The Making of the Second Ku Klux Klan.* New York: Oxford University Press.

McMurry, Linda O. (1998) *To Keep the Waters Troubled: The Life of Ida B. Wells.* New York: Oxford University Press.

Michel, Sonya and Rosen, Ruth (1992) "The Paradox of Maternalism: Elizabeth Lowell Putnam and the American Welfare State," *Gender and History* 4, pp. 364–86.

Milkman, Ruth (ed.) (1985) *Women, Work and Protest: A Century of Women's Labor History.* London: Routledge and Kegan Paul.

Morgan, Francesca (1998) " 'Home and Country': Women, Nation and the Daughters of the American Revolution, 1890–1939," Ph.D. dissertation, Columbia University.

Muncy, Robyn (1991) *Creating a Female Dominion in American Reform, 1890–1935.* New York: Oxford University Press.

Neverdon-Morton, Cynthia (1989) *Afro-American Women of the South and the Advancement of the Race, 1895–1925.* Knoxville: University of Tennessee Press.

Newman, Louise M. (1999) *White Women's Rights: The Racial Origins of Feminism in the United States.* New York: Oxford University Press.

Nielsen, Kim (2001) *Un-American Womanhood: Antiradicalism, Antifeminism, and the First Red Scare.* Columbus: Ohio State University Press.

Odem, Mary E. (1995) *Delinquent Daughters: Protecting and Policing Adolescent Female Sexuality in the United States, 1885–1920.* Chapel Hill: University of North Carolina Press.

Pascoe, Peggy (1990) *Relations of Rescue: The Search for Female Moral Authority in the American West, 1874–1939.* New York: Oxford University Press.

Quinn, Elizabeth Lasch (1993) *Black Neighbors: Race and the Limits of Reform in the American Settlement House Movement, 1890–1945.* Chapel Hill: University of North Carolina Press.

Rosenberg, Rosalind (1992) *Divided Lives: American Women in the Twentieth Century.* New York: Hill and Wang.

Rouse, Jacqueline (1989) *Lugenia Burns Hope: Black Southern Reformer.* Athens: University of Georgia Press.

Ruíz, Vicki (1998) *From Out of the Shadows: Mexican Women in Twentieth-century America.* New York: Oxford University Press.

Rupp, Leila (1997) *Worlds of Women: The Making of an International Women's Movement.* Princeton, NJ: Princeton University Press.

Salem, Dorothy (1990) *To Better Our World: Black Women in Organized Reform, 1880–1920.* Brooklyn: Carlson Publishing.

Scott, Anne Firor (1970) *The Southern Lady: From Pedestal to Politics, 1830–1930.* Chicago: University of Chicago Press.

Scott, Anne Firor (1992) *Natural Allies: Women's Associations in American History.* Urbana: University of Illinois Press.

Shaw, Stephanie J. (1996) *What a Woman Ought to Be and to Do: Black Professional Women Workers During the Jim Crow Era.* Chicago: University of Chicago Press.

Sklar, Kathryn Kish (1985) "Hull House in the 1890s: A Community of Women Reformers," *Signs* 19, pp. 658–77.

Sklar, Kathryn Kish (1995) *Florence Kelley and the Nation's Work: The Rise of Women's Political Culture, 1830–1900.* New Haven, CT: Yale University Press.

Terborg-Penn, Rosalyn (1983) "Disaffected Black Feminists," in Lois Scharf and Joan Jensen (eds.), *Decades of Discontent: The Women's Movement, 1920–1940.* Westport, CT: Greenwood Press, pp. 261–78.

Terborg-Penn, Rosalyn (1998) *African American Women and the Struggle for the Vote, 1850–1920.* Bloomington: University of Indiana Press.

Thurner, Manuela (1993) "'Better Citizens Without the Ballot': American Antisuffrage Women and their Rationale during the Progressive Era," *Journal of Women's History* 5, pp. 33–60.

Tilly, Louise and Gurin, Patricia (eds.) (1990) *Women, Politics, and Change.* New York: Russell Sage Foundation.

Wertheimer, Barbara (1977) *We Were There: The Story of Working Women in America.* New York: Pantheon.

Wheeler, Marjorie Spruill (1993) *New Women of the New South: The Leaders of the Woman's Suffrage Movement in the Southern States.* New York: Oxford University Press.

White, Deborah Gray (1996) "Private Lives, Public Personae: A Look at Early Twentieth-century African-American Clubwomen," in Nancy A. Hewitt, Jean O'Barr, and Nancy Rosebaugh (eds.), *Talking Gender: Public Images, Personal Journeys, and Political Critiques.* Chapel Hill: University of North Carolina Press, pp. 106–23.

White, Deborah Gray (1999) *Too Heavy a Load: Black Women in Defense of Themselves, 1894–1994.* New York: W. W. Norton.

Wilkinson, Patrick (1999) "The Selfless and the Helpless: Maternalist Origins of the U.S. Welfare State," *Feminist Studies* 25, pp. 571–97.

CHAPTER TWENTY

Medicine, Law, and the State: The History of Reproduction

LESLIE J. REAGAN

HUMAN reproduction has long been a focal point of feminist analysis, activism, and research. At times, the feminist focus on reproduction has resulted in an overemphasis on the themes of heterosexuality and pregnancy to the neglect of other topics. Moreover, the focus on the female role in reproduction raises the danger of essentializing women: women are equated with reproduction; the only part of a woman's body that matters is her uterus; the only part of a woman's life that matters is her biological capacity to bear children and her social role to rear them. In focusing on women and reproduction, do we perpetuate the nineteenth-century idea that "the Almighty, in creating the female sex, had taken the uterus and built up a woman around it" (Smith-Rosenberg and Rosenberg 1999: 113), overlooking both women's myriad nonreproductive activities and the male role in reproduction? Understanding reproduction, broadly defined, in American life and politics is essential for understanding the history of women and gender and American history as well.

Reproduction is not only a personal and familial experience; it is a fundamental component of gender ideology and of individual as well as national identity. It is also a site of fear and fantasy at the individual, group, and national levels. Yet for generations reproduction received little attention from historians. Pregnancy and childbearing – with their inherent female-ness, their seemingly natural quality, their connotations of blood, sex, emotion, life, and death – were precisely the type of topics that the historical profession trivialized rather than made central. And yet, as Frederick Engels understood, reproduction is as much a basic organizing structure of society as the division of labor, the economic system, or the political order. Only as feminist scholars put women and their perspectives and experiences at the forefront of research did the political significance of reproduction become evident.

The history of reproduction, in fact, lends itself to investigation of the state, law, and public policy and, simultaneously, deepens our knowledge about the power of gender, sexuality, race, and family. Regulation of reproduction by religious and state authorities has been so commonplace that nineteenth-century scientific historians and postwar consensus historians traditionally overlooked analyses of family and reproduction. Yet the state's involvement in reproduction can be seen in measures designed to prevent or promote births, intervention in actual birthing and obstetrical practices, and the legal regulation and definition of marriage and the "legitimacy" of children, which in turn relate to citizenship, child custody, and childrearing. Foreign policies in the United States and elsewhere routinely take population – and its rise and fall – into account when surveying the nation's place and power in the world. Furthermore, the reproductive arena has been a site in which male supremacy and racial power have been enacted and enforced.

The historiography focused around issues of reproduction initially divided between histories of medical specialties and techniques and women's history. As feminist historians turned their attention to reproduction, scholarship moved in two directions: policy history and histories of the experience of, and cultural norms regarding, reproduction from the perspective(s) of women. In the latter case, historians have examined the variety of reproductive traditions along racial and class lines within the United States. Scholars are also increasingly demonstrating the ways in which the racial politics of the United States are both embedded within and carried out via reproductive policy. Most recently, historians have paid more attention to men and their social and biological roles in reproduction and, with the rise of the pro-life movement and the visibility of the fetus in American culture, to the fetus as well. A few scholars have drawn comparisons among reproductive policies in different nations, but the need for more international comparisons is plain.

The earliest histories of reproduction were written by medical practitioners who traced the rise of obstetrics – including its techniques and leaders – or who investigated the practice and legal status of birth control and abortion since antiquity. Among professional historians, early work in family history analyzed census and parish records to study and compare regional, national, and world fertility patterns and then hypothesized from quantitative data about the sources of change in fertility. These analyses tended to focus on the underlying economic system and an assessment of the economic value of children and to overlook whether women and men in the family might have had different interests in this area. France was famous for expressing its fears that a declining birthrate meant the country would be outnumbered by and vulnerable to its German neighbor. Interestingly, the relationship between national interests and reproduction faded from histories of reproduction as scholars of the 1970s and 1980s turned to social history and women's culture.

The first feminist literature of the 1970s, often produced by nonhistorians, blamed the medical profession for claiming control of women's bodies and reproduction, and by extension, for the subordination of women in the society as a whole. Since then, as historians have investigated the relationship between physicians and female patients and realized how little power most nineteenth-century physicians held, scholars have revised this picture and located the drive to control the female body in a more complex web of power, pointing in particular to the state's interest and investment in controlling family formation, the expression of sexuality, and reproduction of the population. Furthermore, scholars have uncovered the female demand for surgeries and treatments that later feminists condemned as abusive. The earlier studies were not devoid of insight, for it is certainly true that the majority of the (male) medical profession participated in and defended male supremacy as did most men, but historians are now asking how physicians gained the authority to make decisions *for* women and for patients in general, rather than in consultation with them.

One of the first tasks of scholars interested in treating reproduction historically was to tackle the assumption that reproduction was, on the one hand, an unchanging and merely biological process or, on the other hand, something which had changed only recently as a result of technological advances. Like studies of sexuality, which emerged with the history of women and reproduction, the new historians of women insisted that reproduction was a socially created and constructed process, subject to historical change. Becoming pregnant, childbearing, the rise or decline in fertility were neither natural events nor automatic results of "modernization," but related to the economic and political structure, the subordination and empowerment of women, and decisions made and actions taken by women and men.

To demonstrate that pregnancy had never in human history been a naturally occurring event free of human intervention and that the desire to control reproduction was not new, Linda Gordon, in *Woman's Body, Woman's Right* (1976), showed that women worldwide had created and used various means of birth control since antiquity. *Woman's Body, Woman's Right* remains the single most important book in the field for the breadth and depth of its research and analysis. It provides an overall outline of the history of reproduction from the eighteenth century through the twentieth and places American history within a larger context of European intellectual traditions and politics. Gordon's book, unlike many other social histories, never left the world of politics – including legislation, political parties, court cases, and grassroots organizing – behind, but brought together the experiences and agency of women with political and economic analyses. The development of capitalism, Gordon showed, underpinned changes in the expectations of women, in family size, and in the demand for contraceptives and abortion. One of Gordon's most important insights was her analysis of "voluntary motherhood." Nineteenth-century feminists' advocacy of abstinence within marriage as a method for choosing when a woman would become a mother "voluntarily," Gordon showed, was a forerunner to the modern movement's emphasis on maximizing sexual activity and happiness through the use of what we now call "birth control." Voluntary motherhood required that women be able to reject the sexual advances of their husbands. Women had to be able to say "no" before they could say "yes." The move toward accepting female sexuality owed a great deal, Gordon showed, to the work of the most radical and most frequently denounced organizers at the turn of the century, including anarchist Emma Goldman. This history was suppressed as the birth control movement professionalized. Margaret Sanger herself, one of the early radicals, participated in this rewriting of history in order to attract the support of physicians and other medical "experts."

Gordon argued that population control (the effort by government and international agencies to promote policies that encouraged or forced a lower birthrate among specific populations) had different roots than the feminist call for voluntary motherhood. The two became intertwined, however, as Planned Parenthood made common cause with the US government and corporate philanthropists who urged the promotion of contraceptives and sterilization among African Americans at home and third world people abroad. Such programs began quietly during the Great Depression of the 1930s when the US government began funding the provision of contraceptives in the hopes of reducing the number of children who would require state assistance.

James Reed and Ellen Chesler added depth to the story laid out by Gordon. In particular, they complicated our understanding of Margaret Sanger and her supporters – such as Dr. Clarence Gamble, who funded the establishment of birth control clinics, and Dr. John Rock, who developed the Pill – by highlighting the ambiguities in their personal and professional lives. Despite her own disapproval, Chesler showed that Sanger retained the ideals learned during her early associations with sex radicals, continuing to embrace affairs long after the free love movement had been abandoned and even after her own organization adopted a more socially acceptable image.

In his history of birth control, David Garrow focuses on the movement's development in the twentieth century, analyzing both progressive coalitions and the hostility of the Catholic church. Garrow's meticulous project traces the phone calls and connections among attorneys, doctors, intellectuals, philanthropists, and activists to show how, starting in the 1920s and 1930s, women and men in the Connecticut Birth Control League and the American Civil Liberties Union began advocating and creating a legal understanding of privacy, which would recognize the right of women and men to make decisions about sex and procreation without interference by the state. Their intellectual and organizational work helped produce two of the most important US Supreme Court decisions of the twentieth century, *Griswold v. Connecticut* (1965) (recognizing a "zone of privacy" within which the state could not interfere with a married couple's right to make decisions about family and the use of contraception) and *Roe v. Wade* (1973) (legalizing abortion).

Although early research by Linda Gordon and James Mohr historicized the criminalization of abortion and contraception in the 1860s and 1870s, scholars long continued to treat the era of illegal abortion as static. Indeed, memories of illegal abortion in the 1950s and 1960s and pictures of "back-alley butchers" tended to be projected back into the nineteenth century. Prior to the 1870s, abortions early in pregnancy were legal under common law. Only late abortions, induced after "quickening" when the woman felt movement, were called abortions and considered a violation of morality and law. After 1880, abortion from conception on was illegal in every state as a result of a physician-led campaign to control medical practice and stop abortions among middle-class Protestant women. My concern was what happened once abortion was criminalized. In *When Abortion Was a Crime* (1997), I argued that women continued to seek abortions and physicians and midwives continued to provide abortions openly.

Contrary to accepted interpretation, it was not unmarried women who most used abortion at the turn of the century, but married women. The press, however, gave most attention to abortion among the unmarried and highlighted stories of seduction. My analysis of criminal trial records, medical literature, and newspapers showed that it is a mistake for historians to read law, official medical policy, and discourse as "reality," or even as fairly accurate markers of the attitudes and practices of either the general public or the medical profession. The arenas within which public discussions occurred were very different from intimate conversations among women, between members of couples, and between women and midwives, doctors, or pharmacists. Public discourse on abortion consistently condemned abortion, yet deep social history provides strong evidence that abortion was widely practiced and understood. Indeed, the acceptance of abortion seems to be an American tradition. Furthermore, the moral distinction between contraception and abortion so central to much of American political thinking now was largely created by the birth control movement itself as it sought legitimacy. Although some specialists in obstetrics continued to promote an anti-abortion attitude within their profession, most of their colleagues ignored them and many reputable physicians provided abortions. Nonetheless, zealous anti-abortion physicians did forge an alliance with the state to enforce the criminal abortion laws.

The state, I found, was strongly committed to regulating abortion. Police and prosecutors enforced the law and, particularly in the early twentieth century, punished the women who had abortions by interrogating them on their deathbeds or by public shaming. The methods of enforcing the law changed over time and in the 1940s police began raiding and closing what had been longstanding, open, and safe abortion practices. The dramatic shift in the state's interest in abortion parallels George Chauncey's findings regarding the state's response to gay men and their social and sexual world. In both cases, the state moved from ignoring open abortion clinics and gay bars much of the time to vigorously observing, raiding, and repressing them. The repression of the 1950s and 1960s produced the most dangerous period in the history of abortion. At the precise moment that maternity was becoming safer, abortion became deadlier. Furthermore, danger and safety were inscribed by racial difference. The history of abortion in this period indicates the state's commitment to enforcing gender expectations, marriage, and maternity. Yet abortion was decriminalized in the early 1970s; how? The long history of private discussion about the need for and private practice of abortion moved into the public arena where it generated a new discourse about abortion, sexuality, and women's rights and, ultimately, changed the law. Historians often assume that power originates in the public realm and that public discourses and policies intrude into the private. I urge historians to rethink this assumption and to consider carefully the public power of conversations and activities that occur in spaces typically treated as "private."

In the 1900s, the state moved from wielding legal prohibitions on contraception and abortion to shape the ethnicity of the nation's population to using the "surgical solution" to prevent the reproduction of specific categories of people. The groups targeted and the rationalization for their sterilization changed over the twentieth century. As Philip Reilly and others have shown, eugenics grew out of nineteenth-century Malthusianism, which pointed to overpopulation as the cause of poverty, along with the ideas of Cesare Lombroso and Richard Dugdale, who attributed criminality and "degeneracy" to heredity. By the 1910s, some Americans advocated the segregation of degenerates in order to protect the health of the rest of the population. The first sterilization programs were directed at incarcerated men. Dr. Harry Sharp, chief surgeon of the Indiana Reformatory, for example, sterilized prisoners without legal grounds or consent and encouraged physicians in 1902 to press for state laws permitting institutions to "render every male sterile who passes its portals, whether it be almshouse, insane asylum, institute for the feeble-minded, reformatory or prison" (quoted in Reilly 1991: 32). Although the eugenicists won state legislation, they also faced numerous court cases, which they frequently lost.

Sterilization quickly moved from a program directed at incarcerated men and their capacity to impregnate and reproduce to one that focused directly on women, the sex that brought children into the world. At the turn of the century, states began building institutions to hold "degenerate" and wayward girls, usually defined by their sexual activity outside of marriage. Leaders of these institutions soon advocated sterilization to ensure that degeneracy and retardation were not passed on to the next generation. As the Great Depression hit, the reasons for justifying sterilization changed dramatically and the financial capacity of the potential parents became the primary concern. As concern shifted to the taxpayer, the number of sterilizations increased and were increasingly done on women – the source of poor children. The number of involuntary sterilizations declined some in the 1940s, but once the war ended and surgeons returned, sterilization continued apace into the 1960s. Furthermore, in numerous communities, physicians and welfare officials coerced poor women of color who needed welfare benefits as well as women who sought legal therapeutic abortions into "agreeing" to sterilization in exchange for social services or medical treatment.

Despite the state's interest in women of color, not until legal scholar Dorothy Roberts's 1997 study were black women and the entirety of their reproductive experiences placed at the forefront rather than the margins of analysis. "Because race was defined as an inheritable trait," Roberts argues, "preserving racial distinctions required policing reproduction. *Reproductive politics in America inevitably involves racial politics*" (1997: 9, emphasis in original). In *Killing the Black Body*, Roberts revisits the history of the birth control movement, documents the breadth of sterilization abuse of African American, Puerto Rican, and Native American women in the 1960s and 1970s, and analyzes the new reproductive technologies and the punitive policing of poor black mothers. Roberts reexamines the history of Margaret Sanger and the birth control movement's alliance with the eugenics movement. She is less interested, however, in the question of whether or not Sanger was herself a racist than in the ideas she promoted, which, Roberts argues, would in a racist society, inevitably, be read in a racist way. "Sanger . . . promoted two of the most perverse tenets of eugenic thinking: that social problems are caused by reproduction of the socially disadvantaged and that their childbearing should therefore be deterred. In a society marked by racial hierarchy, these principles inevitably produced policies designed to reduce black women's fertility" (Roberts 1997: 81). If scholars take Roberts's message to heart, they will be forced to rethink their presentation of pronatalism in the twentieth century and public health, maternal, and infant health policies in light of how they participated not only in class or gender domination, but also in white supremacy.

In 1989, Jessie Rodrique offered the first social history of the early twentieth-century black community's grassroots efforts on behalf of birth control. African American leaders encouraged the founding of clinics in their communities and encouraged blacks – through community newspapers, magazines, churches, and other forums – to plan their families and use birth control for the benefit of themselves, their children, and their race. At the same time, leaders resisted racist insistence on reducing family size among the black population. Building on Rodrique's work, Johanna Schoen found that African American women sought out various means of controlling their reproduction. Schoen's analysis moves away from the birth control movement to departments of public health. Her study analyzes efforts in North Carolina, where the first state-run birth control program was established in 1937; by the 1950s, the state managed one of the largest sterilization programs in the country. Schoen documents the evident interest of state officials in using sterilization as a permanent method of reducing both the black population and the number of African Americans receiving state welfare services. Yet, at the same time, because she investigates the intricacies of individual requests, approvals, and denials for sterilization, Schoen shows that, with dignity and drive, black women sought out sterilization procedures for themselves. Living in economic and medical poverty, black women used a state agency as a resource and worked the system to win a procedure that could end their fears of pregnancy and unwanted childbearing. Her findings confirm Gordon's important observation: when authorities offer birth control methods in order to manipulate the size of specific populations, their rationale should not be confused with why people accept the methods offered.

In the 1970s, historians of women and medicine also began to investigate pregnancy and childbirth. Recent scholars who derive questions from Foucault are likely to frame the issues in terms of "power"; earlier feminist scholars used the concept of "control." They asked who controlled the process of childbearing. First, scholars of the eighteenth and nineteenth centuries showed that childbirth was neither "natural" nor pathological, the latter perspective developed by specialists in obstetrics at the end of the nineteenth century. Second, historians found that early American women, and indeed the majority of women into the twentieth century, experienced childbirth as a social event in their own homes, surrounded and assisted by a community of female family and friends. Midwives presided over the birthing process and played central roles in their community, as Laurel Thatcher Ulrich showed in her distinguished study of colonial New England, *A Midwife's Tale* (1990).

Ulrich's study followed on Judith Walzer Leavitt's earlier analysis of the transition from midwife- to physician-attended childbirth. Leavitt's focus on childbearing women and her compelling analysis of the dynamics in the birthing room challenged the assumptions of both medical historians and feminist scholars. *Brought to Bed* (1985) demonstrated for historians of medicine that attention to the patient, rather than exclusive attention to the profession, would significantly revise – even reverse – our understanding of medical knowledge, practice, and physician–patient interactions. Contrary to some earlier feminist analyses, man-midwives, as they were initially called, did not barge in and take over. Instead, Leavitt showed, physicians entered the birthing room only as upper-class urban women invited them in. Physicians' scientific knowledge and access to instruments promised to save the lives of mothers and newborns who might otherwise die in dire circumstances. Even as physicians entered, however, women still made decisions and ruled in the birthing room. Furthermore, only the male physician with the capacity to cross gender lines and communicate and care within a female-dominated space could succeed.

As childbirth moved into the hospital in the twentieth century, however, Leavitt shows how control slipped away from birthing women and moved into the hands of physicians and nurses. Leavitt's analysis of the impact of the transition from home to hospital on patients, rather than treating the hospital from the perspective of medical education or institutions, is a major contribution. As hospitals standardized their practices, as new rules prohibited helpers from participating and turned them into "visitors," the laboring woman lost her advocates and her ability to control the birthing experience. In the hospital, the pregnant woman of the mid-twentieth century became an object and childbirth an event that happened to her. The pressure in the late twentieth century for "natural" childbirth, to allow husbands into the birthing room, and for nurse-midwives arose from these oppressive conditions. And while each of these movements to remake childbirth and to return power to the pregnant woman has had a measure of success, for the masses of American women today, childbirth is increasingly a technological event, their bodies tested and under medical control.

Many of the hospital rules and routines that generated isolation and resentment at mid-century had been instituted several decades earlier in response to high maternal mortality in the United States. Prior to the turn of the century, death at childbirth, though mourned, tended to be treated as inevitable. Childbirth was a leading cause of death for women (15,000 deaths per year into the mid-1930s), second only to tuberculosis, though it generated less panic and official attention than epidemics of infectious diseases. In an effort to make maternal and infant mortality visible, female reformers, public health activists, and some physicians along with the US Children's Bureau, investigated and advertised the problem. Together they produced a national mandate for reducing maternal and infant deaths. The fact that the United States, in comparison to other nations, consistently ranked low in maternal mortality was a national embarrassment. In response to the problem, specialists in obstetrics demanded improved medical training of physicians, urged greater control of midwives, and promised birthing women that science and hospitals ensured safety. Nonetheless, the truth well into the 1930s, as physicians themselves knew but obscured, was that deliveries done in the home were safer and midwives often had better records than doctors in terms of infant and maternal survival.

In 1910 midwives delivered half of the nation's babies in the home, but by 1930, midwives had virtually disappeared. The earliest studies on midwives by Frances Kobrin and Judy Barrett Litoff asked why male physicians replaced female midwives at deliveries. For answers, they pointed to the strenuous medical campaign of the 1890s to the 1920s to eliminate midwives and new legislation designed to tightly control their practices. The medical profession and state officials together wanted to eliminate "backward" practitioners whom they blamed for infant and maternal deaths; and, it seemed, they succeeded. Yet as historians moved away from analyzing medical publications and instead conducted community studies of midwives, their findings forced reconsideration. Midwives did not disappear. Indeed, in Massachusetts, the state that enacted the toughest midwife-control measures, Eugene Declerq found that midwifery flourished in the first decades of the twentieth century. In Wisconsin, Charlotte Borst found that physicians did slowly replace foreign-born midwives in the city as midwives failed to professionalize and as second-generation Americanized women chose doctors. These doctors, however, like the midwives before them, shared their patients' ethnic heritage.

Hundreds of midwives still practiced after 1930, but they were not white, urban, or northern. Black midwives still delivered virtually all African Americans born in the South and many white infants too. Oral histories and anthropological studies were the first to bring black "granny" midwives to scholarly attention. Susan L. Smith's pathbreaking book on the black women's public health movement, *Sick and Tired of Being Sick and Tired* (1995), found not only that African American midwives persisted in the face of a national campaign against them, but also that they were essential to public health efforts in the rural South. The willingness of midwives to gain new knowledge and to link poor black families with white health officials made early public health efforts in the region possible. Nonetheless, state officials monitored midwives, threatened their livelihoods if they failed to comply with new rules, and encouraged their retirement. As hospitals were desegregated and states stopped licensing midwives, their numbers fell. By the 1980s, only a handful of African American midwives survived.

Although gender, race, and class hostilities contributed to the marginalization of midwifery, the declining authority of public health combined with the exclusion of midwives from formal medical education and hospitals in the United States (in contrast to Britain) contributed to the near disappearance of midwifery. Nonetheless, we have recently seen a revival of midwifery – including both lay midwives practicing against the law and nurse-midwives practicing in and advertised by hospitals. The history of midwifery has been a rich area of research, yet questions remain. As traditional midwifery lost its place, what did the daughters of midwives, who might have followed in their mothers' footsteps, do instead? Nurse-midwives also deserve further historical attention. How did they interact with doctors, nurses, and (lay) midwives, and with whom did they ally, identify, or struggle?

Related to the history of biological reproduction and health is the history of the social reproduction of children, yet the histories of motherhood, fatherhood, childrearing, and child health tend to be treated separately from birth control and obstetrics. Not only has the social value of children changed dramatically as children have come to be seen as objects of emotional value rather than sources of labor, but the correct methods of feeding, disciplining, teaching, and interacting with children have all shifted over time and unevenly among different social groups. Ellen Ross's *Love and Toil: Motherhood in Outcast London, 1870–1918* (1993) offers a beautifully written model for the field. She brings together a rich study of working-class family life in turn-of-the-century London with maternal mortality data and hospital and obstetrical practices, and connects it back to the newly emerging web of visiting nurses and social workers who helped and advised mothers while simultaneously observing them. The new reform movements helped mothers by giving advice and promoting a welfare state that offered healthcare and income, but they also created new standards that required the obedience of mothers.

Childrearing practices have been subject to semi-official and official state intervention in the United States as well as in Britain. The American movement for maternal and infant health, which gained federal and state funding under the 1921 Sheppard-Towner Act, offered, as Molly Ladd-Taylor and others have shown, needed advice to mothers and health services. American business also promoted "scientific motherhood" in this period and, Rima Apple found, helped turn mothers away from breastfeeding to the more "modern" method of bottle feeding. As educational campaigns created new norms for childrearing, however, they divided mothers between the "good" and the "bad." Single mothers and poor, foreign-born women in early twentieth-century tenements were easily labeled bad, just as at the end of the century poor African American women personified the bad mother in the press, in politics, and in the minds of much of the white public. Social workers and other authorities observed mothers in practice, and those who failed to live up to current childrearing standards faced fines, deductions in social or welfare services, and possibly state removal of children. Today, any new mother – whether she has private health insurance and a private room or receives public aid and delivers in a ward – may find a doctor threatening to call in state agents to investigate a charge of child "abuse" if she refuses to permit tests of her newborn. It is a rare and brave woman who does not give in to the doctor's orders. Yet, as Linda Gordon demonstrated in her 1988 study of family violence, state intervention in the family was not always unwelcome. Indeed, turn-of-the-century mothers themselves often called in police and social workers to rein in abusive husbands and fathers or, as Mary Odem showed more recently, to discipline daughters and sons who stayed out late, failed to turn over their pay envelopes, or appeared to be sexually active.

If they did not wind up in juvenile hall, young women who explored their sexuality outside of marriage might find themselves in unwed mothers' homes instead. The fate of single mothers underlines the social, legal, and economic importance of marriage and makes visible the social consequences for women who failed to conform to virginity when unmarried, childbearing within marriage, and economic dependency on husbands. Institutions for unmarried mothers have received attention from several scholars. Early twentieth-century unwed mothers' homes offered a secret place away from the neighborhood where women could wait out the end of their pregnancies and deliver. The homes were intended to rehabilitate women, teaching them proper sexual mores and preparing them for futures as domestic workers. Yet as Regina Kunzel found, the middle-class religious women and, later, social workers who ran the institutions had created a space in which many young women discovered not that they were immoral, but rather that there were plenty of other women like them. Indeed, the "inmates" traded contraceptive and abortion information. And as Peggy Pascoe showed, immigrant women sometimes used the resources offered by such institutions to gain leverage against abusive husbands or as an escape from prostitution.

In the late 1930s and 1940s, thinking about unwed motherhood among social workers, psychologists, and psychiatrists shifted, becoming more racialized. As middle-class white women entered these homes in larger numbers, social workers no longer focused on sexual delinquency, the standard analysis of working-class women. Now experts highlighted neurosis. Social workers urged white unmarried mothers to accept the idea that their newborns would be better off placed with a married adoptive couple. In doing so, the unmarried mothers proved their newfound maturity and won praise. As Rickie Solinger argues, the pregnancy and motherhood of these unmarried white women was thus erased and silenced and each was remade into a nonmother ready for marriage. Black unmarried mothers, in contrast, were rarely encouraged to consider placing children for adoption and instead were pathologized, investigated by the state welfare system, and sterilized.

American culture and law favored the married, nuclear family with biological ties and stigmatized parent–child ties produced through other means, including adoption. In the 1850s, individual states first legally recognized adopted children and allowed them to inherit, but the state played no part in regulating adoption practices. Private charitable agencies as well as physicians, midwives, lawyers, friends, neighbors, and parents themselves could all be involved in negotiating adoption arrangements (which were usually not formalized in law). Turn-of-the-century professional associations of social workers and the Children's Bureau were the first to attempt to standardize adoption, to ensure that parental consents had been obtained prior to placement, and that potential adoptive parents were investigated. Yet by the 1940s, only half of all adoptions were arranged through licensed agencies.

Wayne Carp investigates the history of adoption in terms of the secrecy or openness regarding the identities of birth parents, adopted children, and adoptive parents. He finds that the secrecy imposed on the process for all involved was a mid-twentieth-century creation. Earlier in the century, agencies freely provided names and addresses of birth parents to adult adoptees. Confidential records and a policy of permanent secrecy regarding the identity of the birth mother developed in the 1940s and 1950s as a result of demands for secrecy from the growing number of white and affluent unmarried birth mothers who were deciding to place their newborns with adoptive families. The adoption system and its policies of secrecy were soon undermined as birth mothers and adoptive parents alike grew resentful of agency rules and scrutiny and chose to go around them by making their own arrangements through private attorneys.

The question "to whom does a child belong?" is not only individual or legal; it is also national and highly provocative. The social and political anxieties expressed about adoption make visible the belief that biological inheritance makes community and nation. Nations as well as religious and racial communities invest children with their identity, their beliefs, their future. At different moments, these groups express a sense of collective ownership of children. Today, the most tense debates center on transracial (domestic) adoptions, specifically the adoption of black and brown children by white adoptive parents. The interest in matching children and adoptive parents has a long history, but initially the concern centered on keeping children in the faith that they inherited by birth; loyalty to race came to the forefront later. Catholics and Jews established their own orphanages and social agencies in order to prevent the absorption of abandoned and orphaned children into Protestantism. In *The Great Arizona Orphan Abduction* (1999), Linda Gordon analyzes a 1904 orphan train bound West that went awry. New York City Irish "orphans" were periodically taken West by Catholic nuns who settled them into adoptive families selected by the church. In this case, local Anglos in Arizona protested the children's placement with Mexican Catholics and kidnapped the orphans. The resulting case, which ultimately reached the US Supreme Court, illuminates regional differences in racial understanding and the powerful role of women in creating and policing racial difference. After seeing the new Catholic families with whom the orphans were to be placed in their small Arizona community, it was Protestant Anglo women who objected to "white" children going to Mexicans and demanded that their men take action. The court, the press, and the public then validated the abductions and white supremacy in the name of the best interests of the child. The trip West promised the children "not only parents [and]...upward mobility," Gordon argues, but "transformed them from Irish to white" (1999: 19).

At the end of the twentieth century, the driving force behind adoptive parents and adoption agencies is usually presumed to be infertility. Yet the complexity and historical evolution of adoption practices deserve closer attention. At the turn of the century, it was not unusual for independent unmarried women – such as female physicians and reformers – to adopt children and social agencies routinely looked to farm families who needed help as potential placements for older boys and girls. Currently, it is estimated that half of all adoptions in the United States are by relatives. Furthermore, while affluent and infertile white American couples are extremely visible and catered to by the adoption industry, African Americans, low-income families, single men and women, lesbian women and gay men (who may or may not be "infertile"), and parents of biological children also adopt. Finally, the development of an almost universally condemned state-run foster-care system to protect children, which also advocates their permanent adoption, deserves critical, feminist attention.

Infertility also requires attention, however. Since the mid-nineteenth through the twentieth centuries, American women turned to doctors for help in becoming pregnant. Gynecological surgeons, as Regina Morantz-Sanchez, Margaret Marsh, and Wanda Ronner have shown, had crowds of female patients clamoring for surgeries, experiments in artificial insemination, and hormone therapy. The medical response to infertility was thoroughly gendered. Married couples and doctors alike assumed that the problem was to be found and solved in the body of the woman. By the 1930s doctors increasingly encouraged men to be examined as well, but female physicians were more insistent on requiring examination of both partners before operating on the woman, while their male colleagues tended to be more protective of male shame. In the 1950s, as in the 1980s and 1990s, infertility clinics were jammed even though medicine had little new to offer, and most treatments did not result in successful pregnancies. Their popularity was not an indicator of new medical knowledge, but of the pro-natalism of the period.

Although compared to others, the American state tends to take a fairly hands-off attitude toward the new reproductive technologies, leaving ethical and regulatory questions to be worked out in private practice and to the new specialty of reproductive medicine, the state and insurance policies both promote these ("assisted") methods of producing biological children over adoptive families. Parents-to-be via assisted reproductive technologies, like biological parents who conceived as a result of sexual intercourse, are not required to submit to state-mandated investigations of their health, home, income, attitudes about parenting, or possible criminal background. Instead, their ability to parent is assumed because of the biological tie to their children. This is not to say that all biological parents avoid scrutiny; as Roberts underlines, black women's motherhood is automatically questioned and easily terminated by the state. Nonetheless, the presumption of good parenting among whites and among affluent Americans of all races gives incentive to potential parents to pursue assisted reproduction even when many of these technologies are known to fail more often than they succeed. State-mandated insurance coverage of assisted reproduction gives financial incentive as well. In Illinois, and several other states where state law requires that insurance policies cover assisted reproduction (but not adoption, contraception, or abortion), the state encourages biological reproduction of those with the good fortune to have insurance, while masking the social price tag for promoting these procedures, and biological ties more generally, as the basis of family.

Rayna Rapp's *Testing Women, Testing the Fetus* (1999), a superb anthropological investigation of contemporary genetic science and new technologies in the United States, uncovers how genetic knowledge is produced, used, and interpreted by pregnant women as well as by health workers, counselors, and lab technicians. For historians, such studies can offer new questions and add textures to our own analyses. Rapp argues that the pregnant women who use or refuse amniocentesis are "moral pioneers" (1999: 306). They think carefully about the implications of genetic testing, the possibility of receiving a "positive" diagnosis indicating genetic problems in the fetus, which then necessitates deciding what to do with this information – whether to abort or carry the pregnancy to term. Knowing their total responsibility for a new child, Rapp shows, pregnant women take that responsibility extremely seriously as they make decisions about the future for their own private families and for humanity as a whole. As a historian, I want to add that while the specific technology and available information is new, women have long been at the center of moral decision making as they contemplated pregnancy and abortion and made the best possible decision in the circumstances within which they lived for the potential child, the existing family, and themselves.

In the 1980s, abortion moved center stage in the nation's public life. The pro-life movement showed its political and cultural muscle with the election of Ronald Reagan to the presidency, and with its success in transforming the abortion debate into one about the personhood of the fetus rather than the lives of women, sexuality, or civil liberties. Since then, feminist scholars have moved from debating the personhood of the fetus to analyzing how, precisely, the fetus has been made into a person. Much of this work has been done by anthropologists and other cultural scholars. Feminist historians too have investigated how medicine, law, science, and popular culture together have created a fetus whose health and well-being is separate from the pregnant woman who brings it to birth and life. Scientific drawing, beginning in the thirteenth century as well as photography in the twentieth, contributed to the creation of the fetus as a separate entity. The efforts of female reformers and public health activists to teach every childbearing woman about prenatal care and protecting the health of the child before birth also contributed to the idea that the developing embryo is an entity separate from the pregnant woman, yet one for whose health she is responsible from pre-birth through adulthood.

The personification of the fetus, some researchers find, helped to criminalize the mother by the end of the twentieth century. In her analysis of fetal alcohol syndrome (FAS), Janet Golden deconstructs how a problem discovered and framed in the early 1970s as medical, chronic alcoholism among pregnant women, was transformed into, first, a public health crisis, and then into a criminal problem identified with a specific racial group, namely Native Americans. According to Golden, anti-abortion and anti-alcohol politics, new representations by the media, fear of the disabled, as well as the racist fears attached to children born with FAS, all contributed to the rise of punitive state policies. By the mid-1980s, state public health agencies began requiring that new warnings about alcohol be directed at all women, a pattern that reversed the nineteenth-century assumption that alcoholism was a male problem and that alcoholic *fathers* produced children who were likely to be "feeble-minded," "criminal," or both. As Native American activists, and especially prize-winning author Michael Dorris, began speaking out about the problems of alcohol on the reservation, FAS was racialized and turned into a policy issue. Despite a long history of coercive state policy toward Native Americans, Dorris considered the jailing of pregnant women a possible solution to the problems of children with FAS. The new public policy response to these women was to punish them for producing children who were seen more as future criminals than as babies. The history of FAS at the end of the twentieth century, like the history of the woman who became known as "Typhoid Mary" at the start of the century, underscores how frighteningly easy it is for the American state, often with public support, to move from considerations of public health to coercion, particularly if the individual involved is already from a suspect social group. It is especially easy when the person failing to conform is a pregnant woman and the community harmed is the fetus within her.

Throughout history, the vast majority of women have devoted much of their physical and emotional lives to reproduction in all of its various aspects. The investigation of reproduction puts the lives of women – with the work, dilemmas, passions, and relationships of great significance to them – at the forefront of intellectual research and knowledge, thus radically changing the discipline of history. The proliferation of excellent scholarship and its deep personal and political importance to many women outside of the academy speaks to the significance of this work. As this essay indicates, many scholars are engaged with topics that are currently contested, and they hope to bring historical analysis into public policy debates. Similarly, the history of medicine, with its ties to contemporary medical education and its focus on life and death, may encourage connections to the present. Much of the best historical research on reproduction thus illuminates the historical nature of the contemporary world.

As scholars have historicized reproduction, they have also recognized that there is no single or typical experience. Race and class are as essential to the practice and theory of reproduction as gender. Reproduction, scholars have demonstrated, is not simply about the production of babies, but about power in all its manifestations. One notable feature of recent scholarship is its analysis of law and the state, which has not only revealed the importance of reproduction to the state but has also advanced our understanding of the state and its organization, contradictory impulses, power, and lack thereof. Here, more comparative analysis would be helpful. Comparative work may indicate the role of international influences and social movements as well as similarities among nations. The American state and its relationship to medicine is not identical to the French or British state, however, and applying theories derived from European histories may lead to mistaken assumptions and conclusions even as it inspires new questions.

A growing number of historians have analyzed the medical projects of European empires, but American historians have been slow to investigate the US colonial project and place it within this larger history. American medical imperialism is an area rich for research. Putting the stamp of the American medical system – with all of its gendered, racial, class, and sexual hierarchies – on countries worldwide, whether official colonies or not, appears to have been one of the first actions of Americans abroad. Several new and forthcoming studies underscore the centrality of medicine and state regulation of reproduction and sexuality to American power. Chia-Ling Wu's research on the implantation of American obstetrics in Taiwan, Susan Smith's study of Japanese midwives in the Pacific states and Hawaiian territory and Americans in Occupied Japan, and Michelle Moran's work on leprosy in Hawaii and on the application of colonial knowledge to the mainland all demonstrate the potential of such studies.

Furthermore, the ways in which reproduction has been used to produce and bolster national identity and patriotism deserve greater attention in the American context. The role of Catholics in creating new social movements that championed female sexuality and reproductive control, as well as the divisions within the membership of the Catholic church over these issues, also merits further analysis. Other fruitful areas for research include historical analyses of children themselves, of sex education, and of the women's health movement. Historians of medicine and reproduction can learn from cultural studies to give greater attention to representations, their production, multiple meanings, and circulation. Experimental work that brings together historical research and memoir offers another exciting possibility.

Finally, it seems imperative that scholars break through the boundary between public policy and personal experience, which has too long divided the field. Abortion and motherhood, obstetrics as a specialty and international population control programs, personal decisions and domestic social policy are too often treated separately. Treating these topics without reference to one another recreates the divisions of private/public that are otherwise under scrutiny from historians of gender. The history of reproduction should build on detailed, careful work into the nitty-gritty of reproductive experiences together with economic, political, cultural, and poststructural analyses. National politics, economic forces, and ideology all give structure to the events and emotions of reproduction; daily life, intimate interactions, hopes, dreams, and suffering change and give shape to practices and state policies. As the history of reproduction builds on and brings together all of these histories and creatively pursues new avenues, it will be a rich field indeed with much to tell us about American power and life at all levels, from the most intimate to the international.

BIBLIOGRAPHY

Apple, Rima D. (1987) *Mothers and Medicine: A Social History of Infant Feeding, 1890–1950.* Madison: University of Wisconsin Press.

Borst, Charlotte G. (1995) *Catching Babies: The Professionalization of Childbirth, 1870–1920.* Cambridge, MA: Harvard University Press.

Carp, E. Wayne (1998) *Family Matters: Secrecy and Disclosure in the History of Adoption.* Cambridge, MA: Harvard University Press.

Chauncey, George (1994) *Gay New York: Gender, Urban Culture, and the Making of the Gay Male World, 1890–1940.* New York: Basic Books.

Chesler, Ellen (1992) *Woman of Valor: Margaret Sanger and the Birth Control Movement in America.* New York: Simon and Schuster.

Declerq, Eugene R. (1985) "The Nature and Style of Practice of Immigrant Midwives in Early Twentieth-century Massachusetts," *Journal of Social History* 19, pp. 113–29.

Engels, Frederick (1942 [1884]) *The Origin of the Family, Private Property and the State in the Light of the Researches of Lewis H. Morgan.* New York: International Publishers.

Garrow, David J. (1994) *Liberty and Sexuality: The Right to Privacy and the Making of Roe v. Wade.* New York: Macmillan.

Golden, Janet (1999) " 'An Argument that Goes Back to the Womb': The Demedicalization of Fetal Alcohol Syndrome, 1973–1992," *Journal of Social History* 33, pp. 269–98.

Gordon, Linda (1976) *Woman's Body, Woman's Right: A Social History of Birth Control in America.* New York: Grossman. Revised and updated (1990), New York: Penguin.

Gordon, Linda (1988) *Heroes of their Own Lives: The Politics and History of Family Violence, Boston, 1880–1960.* New York: Viking Books.

Gordon, Linda (1999) *The Great Arizona Orphan Abduction.* Cambridge, MA: Harvard University Press.

Holz, Rosemarie (2002) "The Birth Control Clinic: Women, Planned Parenthood, and the Birth Control Manufacturing Industry, 1923–1973," dissertation, University of Illinois, Urbana-Champaign.

King, Charles R. (1991) "The New York Maternal Mortality Study: A Conflict of Professionalization," *Bulletin of the History of Medicine* 65, pp. 476–80.

Klaus, Alisa (1993) *Every Child a Lion: The Origins of Maternal and Infant Health Policy in the United States and France, 1890–1920.* Ithaca, NY: Cornell University Press.

Kobrin, Frances E. (1966) "The American Midwife Controversy: A Crisis of Professionalization," *Bulletin of the History of Medicine* 40. Rpt. (1984) in Judith W. Leavitt (ed.), *Women and Health in America: Historical Readings.* Madison: University of Wisconsin Press, pp. 318–26.

Kunzel, Regina G. (1993) *Fallen Women, Problem Girls: Unmarried Mothers and the Professionalization of Social Work, 1890–1945.* New Haven, CT: Yale University Press.

Ladd-Taylor, Molly (1994) *Mother-work: Women, Child Welfare, and the State, 1890–1930.* Urbana: University of Illinois Press.

Leavitt, Judith Walzer (1985) *Brought to Bed: Childbearing in America, 1750–1950.* New York: Oxford University Press.

Litoff, Judy Barrett (1978) *American Midwives: 1860 to the Present.* Westport, CT: Greenwood Press.

Loudon, Irvine (1992) *Death in Childbirth: An International Study of Maternal Care and Maternal Mortality, 1800–1950.* New York: Oxford University Press.

Marsh, Margaret and Ronner, Wanda (1996) *The Empty Cradle: Infertility in America from Colonial Times to the Present.* Baltimore: Johns Hopkins University Press.

Mohr, James C. (1978) *Abortion in America: The Origins and Evolution of National Policy, 1800–1900.* New York: Oxford University Press.

Moran, Michelle (2002) "Leprosy and American Imperialism: Patient Communities and the Politics of Public Health in Hawai'i and Louisiana, 1888–1959," dissertation, University of Illinois, Urbana-Champaign.

Morantz-Sanchez, Regina (1999) *Conduct Unbecoming a Woman: Medicine on Trial in Turn-of-the-century Brooklyn.* New York: Oxford University Press.

Morgan, Lynn M. and Michaels, Meredith W. (1999) *Fetal Subjects, Feminist Positions.* Philadelphia: University of Pennsylvania Press.

Odem, Mary E. (1995) *Delinquent Daughters: Protecting and Policing Adolescent Female Sexuality in the United States, 1885–1920.* Chapel Hill: University of North Carolina Press.

Pascoe, Peggy (1990) *Relations of Rescue: The Search for Female Moral Authority in the American West, 1874–1939.* New York: Oxford University Press.

Rapp, Rayna (1999) *Testing Women, Testing the Fetus: The Social Impact of Amniocentesis in America.* New York: Routledge.

Reagan, Leslie J. (1997) *When Abortion Was a Crime: Women, Medicine, and Law in the United States, 1867–1973.* Berkeley: University of California Press.

Reagan, Leslie J. (2000) "Crossing the Border for Abortions: California Activists, Mexican Clinics, and the Creation of a Feminist Public Health Agency in the 1960s," *Feminist Studies* 26, pp. 323–48.

Reed, James (1978) *From Private Vice to Public Virtue: The Birth Control Movement and American Society since 1830.* New York: Basic Books.

Reilly, Philip R. (1991) *The Surgical Solution: A History of Involuntary Sterilization in the United States.* Baltimore: Johns Hopkins University Press.

Roberts, Dorothy (1997) *Killing the Black Body: Race, Reproduction, and the Meaning of Liberty.* New York: Vintage Books.

Rodrique, Jessie M. (1989) "The Black Community and the Birth Control Movement," in Kathy Peiss and Christina Simmons (eds.), *Passion and Power: Sexuality in History.* Philadelphia: Temple University Press, pp. 138–54.

Ross, Ellen (1993) *Love and Toil: Motherhood in Outcast London, 1870–1918.* New York: Oxford University Press.

Rothman, Barbara Katz (1989) *Recreating Motherhood: Ideology and Technology in a Patriarchal Society.* New York: W. W. Norton.

Schoen, Johanna (1996) "A Great Thing for Poor Folks: Birth Control, Sterilization and Abortion in Public Health and Public Welfare," Ph.D. dissertation, University of North Carolina, Chapel Hill.

Smith, Susan L. (1995) *Sick and Tired of Being Sick and Tired: Black Women's Health Activism in America, 1890–1950.* Philadelphia: University of Pennsylvania Press.

Smith, Susan L. (2004) *Japanese American Midwives: Culture, Community and Health Politics, 1880–1950.* Urbana: University of Illinois Press.

Smith-Rosenberg, Carroll and Rosenberg, Charles E. (1999) "The Female Animal: Medical and Biological Views of Woman and Her Role in Nineteenth-century America" (1973). Rpt.

in Judith Walzer Leavitt (ed.), *Women and Health in America: Historical Readings*, 2nd ed. Madison: University of Wisconsin Press, pp. 111–30.

Solinger, Rickie (1992) *Wake Up Little Susie: Single Pregnancy and Race Before Roe v. Wade.* New York: Routledge.

Ulrich, Laurel Thatcher (1990) *A Midwife's Tale: The Life of Martha Ballard, Based on Her Diary, 1785–1812.* New York: Alfred A. Knopf.

Wu, Chia-Ling (1997) "Women, Medicine, and Power: The Social Transformation of Childbirth in Taiwan," Ph.D. dissertation, University of Illinois, Urbana-Champaign.

Chapter Twenty-One

The Great Depression and World War II

Karen Anderson

THE years of the Great Depression and World War II created enormous disruptions in the lives of Americans. During the 1930s, destitution and desperation haunted Americans as millions lost their jobs while others lost savings, homes, farms, and hopes. In the war years, prosperity returned but the mobilization of millions of men into the armed services and the movement of millions of other Americans, including many women anxious to take jobs in war industries, strained family lives, urban services, and gender relations. At the same time, high levels of demand in unionized, well-paid manufacturing jobs dramatically increased economic opportunities for white women and for people of color, although racial and gender barriers remained strong, especially in the South.

These crises caused many to alter family and gender relations, to move to new places, and to develop new expectations of governments at all levels. Because they changed customary economic roles and social relations, the Depression and the war fostered political mobilization by many workers and racial ethnic groups. Although much of the historical literature on these events focuses on the assumptions and actions of political elites, it is critical to analyze changes in everyday lives and in the relationship between citizens and the state in order to understand fully historical change in American society and culture. In recent years, scholars focusing on the lives and actions of women and cultural constructions of gender have contributed significant new insights into the politics and social relations of this period.

In an early and important article, Ruth Milkman analyzed the effects of the Great Depression on women's paid work and on women's unpaid domestic labor. She found that employed men were more likely to lose their jobs in the early years of the Depression than women workers because most of the cutbacks occurred in industries and occupations, like steel and construction, that were dominated by men. By the mid-1930s, however, women workers faced higher rates of job loss than men as employers cut positions in service, clerical, and other occupations held largely by women. At the same time, many African American women workers faced displacement from traditional jobs in domestic service as employers replaced them with others from a pool of increasingly desperate white women. While racial boundaries within female occupations thus shifted, men did not take over "women's work" in significant numbers. Employers and male workers alike held to traditional ideas about the "feminine" nature of work in certain clerical, sales, and service categories. Gender segregation in the labor force was buttressed by these strongly held assumptions about appropriate work for women and men. The retention of women's jobs during the Depression illustrates, as Susan Ware has cogently observed, that "women's work is crucial (not marginal) to the functioning of the American economic system" (1982: 37).

Moreover, women's work was crucial to the economic well-being of their families. Despite tremendous obstacles, including systematic workplace discrimination and popular hostility, the number of women workers increased during the 1930s. The percentage of women in the labor force increased from 24.3 percent in 1930 to 25.7 percent in 1940. Married women showed similar increases, with the proportion in the labor force going up from 11.7 percent to 15.2 percent during the Depression decade. This increase occurred because women entered the labor force to assist in the support of their families after other workers in their families lost jobs and suffered wage cuts. At the same time, as Elizabeth Faue observed, "women's persistence in the labor force . . . symbolically violated the social order" (1991a: 169).

As the case of San Antonio, Texas, demonstrates, however, pre-Depression patterns of race and gender segregation in the labor force often created different outcomes for different groups of women workers. African American women, who were confined almost exclusively to work in domestic service, and Mexican American women, most of whom worked in industrial homework, faced substantially higher levels of displacement than Anglo women. The latter worked primarily in sales and clerical, sectors of the economy that experienced lower levels of unemployment. Workers in all groups experienced wage and hours cuts, but their effects were most harmful for San Antonio's women of color, most of whom were already impoverished before the Depression. Employers forced Mexican American women, in particular, to accept extremely low wages. The low level of private charity, most of which was directed to Anglo families, and race and gender discrimination in public assistance meant that those who had the most also secured the most protection from the effects of the economic crisis.

Milkman examined the economic importance of women's domestic labor during the Depression, the significance of which crossed lines of race, ethnicity, and even class. As families experienced drastic declines in income, women used their domestic skills to provide goods and services that they had previously purchased. They made and repaired clothing, cultivated gardens, learned to make low-cost meals, canned food, and sold baked goods and other items to better-off neighbors. Moreover, they also called upon their interpersonal skills to manage the heightened tensions families experienced with declining incomes and economic insecurity.

Not surprisingly, the Depression had dramatic effects on family structures and dynamics. Many people deferred marriage out of the conviction that the male breadwinner had to have a steady income before he could start a family. Men's unemployment sometimes caused family frictions, particularly when their wives and children provided most or all of the family income and, implicitly or explicitly, challenged the authority of the father as head of the household. Families often had to double up as incomes declined, and some families were forced out of their homes. However noble extended family patterns may appear to be in theory, in practice many Americans found such arrangements to be stressful and difficult. Women faced an increased amount of emotional work as they tried to reduce the inevitable conflicts.

Family tensions sometimes resulted in family break-ups. Although divorce rates went down in the early years of the Depression, when some unhappy couples stayed married either to pool resources or because they could not afford the costs of a divorce, desertions and separations increased and by 1936, divorce rates had returned to 1920s levels. The result was an increase in female-headed households. Lois Helmbold, for example, found a 20–25 percent increase in households headed by women in the four cities she studied. Julia Kirk Blackwelder found a similar increase in San Antonio. As a result, many women in San Antonio, including large numbers of Mexican Americans, used a new state law to pursue husbands and ex-husbands for nonsupport.

Arguments over sexuality and reproduction also strained some marriages and, over the long years of economic hardship, altered public attitudes and policies regarding birth control and abortion. Some wives refused sex to their husbands because they could not afford another child or because they believed their husbands could not require sexual relations when they were not supporting the family. As Leslie Reagan's work demonstrates, women's need for reproductive services and the economic distress that had heightened it led to an increase in such services. The American Birth Control League opened hundreds of new clinics and doctors' willingness to perform illegal abortions grew as more women implored them to offer assistance. One physician-abortionist in Chicago, for example, performed over 18,000 abortions between 1932 and 1941. Over 200 other physicians in the area referred women patients to her for the illegal procedure. Although official medical societies and publications continued to condemn abortion, many physicians liberalized their views, concluding that doctors should consider social circumstances as well as medical ones when responding to patients' requests to terminate pregnancies.

As Helmbold's work has demonstrated, conflicts over the extent of relatives' obligations to kin also divided families during the Depression. In particular, unmarried women found that family members expected them to contribute income and unpaid labor to their households. During the 1930s, many unmarried women contributed substantially or wholly to the support of families. When they lost jobs or became ill and unable to help others, however, their relatives often felt no obligation to reciprocate. In fact, such women were much more likely to receive assistance from friends than from grown children, siblings, and parents. At the same time, conflicts with adult children or their spouses often meant that mothers were not welcome in the homes of their children and had to turn to welfare officials for help. Helmbold found evidence of such patterns in European American and African American households, although black women sometimes coped by sending their children to stay with women relatives while they worked elsewhere.

Normative ideas about gender relations affected federal policies as well as family dynamics. In *Dividing Citizens: Gender and Federalism in New Deal Public Policy* (1998), Suzanne Mettler has contributed a provocative and useful examination of the ways that assumptions about gender relations structured important welfare and regulatory legislation in the 1930s. According to Mettler, the Social Security Act of 1935 (SSA) and other New Deal measures created two forms of citizenship for their beneficiaries: a national citizenship for white male workers and state citizenship for women and people of color. They did so by giving the states great control over eligibility requirements, stipend levels, and the general administration of policies, like Aid to Dependent Children (ADC), that were designed to benefit women and came later to include more women of color. Policies designed to benefit male workers, including the unemployment compensation and pension provisions of the SSA, were administered nationally and excluded from coverage many occupations disproportionately held by men of color and women, including domestic service and agricultural work. According to Mettler, these differences meant that white women and people of color were "treated as dependent persons who required supervision and protection rather than as bearers of rights" (1998: 24). New Deal welfare policies thus helped to form a divided and unequal citizenship based on gender and race.

This same pattern occurred in some regulatory policies as well. Although it did not explicitly use racial or gender criteria, the Fair Labor Standards Act of 1938 had a disparate impact on women and nonwhite male workers. It exempted agricultural, retail, and domestic and other service workers – groups that were disproportionately women or people of color – from its wages and hours provisions, as well as many clerical workers. Moreover, the women workers in excluded occupations made lower wages than men who worked in them and were more likely than men to be working below the legal minimum provided in covered job categories. As a result of the absence of state support for their economic well-being, significant numbers of employed white women and people of color made sub-minimum wages over the next few decades.

These policies developed for a variety of reasons, some directly related to gender relations and some not. As Gwendolyn Mink has noted, public officials generally "treated working women collectively as an anomaly," and, therefore, could not take their workplace rights seriously (1995: 127). Democratic Party leadership was willing to make compromises in some programs in order to secure the support of advocates of states' rights, especially those from the South. Party leaders were unwilling to interfere in the racial caste system that characterized agriculture in the region and, to some extent, in the West. Some northerners, many of whom had been active in Progressive-era reform, believed that the states could be laboratories for experiments in liberal programs and did not want them limited by the federal government. Moreover, neither women nor racial ethnic groups benefited from strong social movements in the 1930s that could have exerted influence over New Deal laws. In particular, the disfranchisement of blacks in the South radically limited their ability to affect the content of New Deal policies.

The development of the Indian New Deal, under the leadership of Bureau of Indian Affairs (BIA) Commissioner John Collier, represented an important break from the policies of the era that preceded it. Committed to his vision of Indian self-determination, economic development, and cultural autonomy, Collier reversed critical policies pursued by his predecessors, most notably the land allotment system built on assumptions about the desirability of male-headed families in which men acted as primary breadwinners. Alison Bernstein has documented American Indian women's roles in influencing BIA policies in these years, but noted that Collier's main advisers were white men and that women's access to power was limited. In my own work, I found that the Indian New Deal gave women some autonomy from the white-dominated state in family matters, encouraged crafts production by women as a development strategy, required tribal governments to enfranchise women, and offered some resources that were critical to women's ability to support their families. At the same time, the BIA and some of the tribal governments formed under its auspices pursued policies detrimental to women's interests. These included the sheep herd reduction policy imposed on the Navajos, which impaired women's ability to earn a livelihood for themselves and their families.

The absence of a strong feminist movement may not have affected Depression policies significantly because many women reformers shared with other New Dealers a belief in a traditional family system in which men were expected to support dependent women and children through wage work. This family wage ideology justified programs for male workers designed to protect them from the vagaries of economic cycles through provisions for unemployment compensation and a federal pension system. Despite the increasing numbers of women in the labor force and working-class families' historic reliance on more than one wage earner, unemployed women could not receive unemployment compensation unless their work lives resembled those of men in terms of a generally long-term, full-time commitment to wage labor. As Linda Gordon has noted in *Pitied But Not Entitled: Single Mothers and the History of Welfare* (1994), Depression-era discussions of public assistance policies ignored women's low wages and economic dependence as causes for the poverty experienced by women and children.

As a remedy for these problems, the Social Security Act provided small levels of support for some women who were trying to raise minor children without economic support from men. For those families whose male breadwinner was absent or disabled, the government created ADC, ostensibly in order for mothers to stay home with their children. Unlike those who received unemployment compensation, its recipients were subjected to means and morals tests. Because eligibility requirements and assistance levels were established by the states, benefits tended to be low and many women who met the criteria of economic need were denied assistance. In fact, the monthly stipends were so low that most who received ADC had to combine it with wage work and other forms of support just to get by. In the South, black women could be declared "employable" and denied benefits irrespective of their success in getting jobs or the adequacy of their wages to family support. Women could be denied assistance for keeping houses that did not meet caseworker standards for neatness, for having social relationships with men, for failing to attend church, and for other "moral" offenses. This supervisory approach was conspicuously absent in policies designed for men, prompting Linda Gordon to conclude that those who created programs designed primarily for men "considered the supervision inherent in casework unneeded, demeaning, as an attack on a (largely unconscious) masculinity" (1994: 178).

Despite these significant shortcomings, New Deal policies provided more support to more single mothers than the various mothers' pensions and other forms of public assistance available to them before 1933. In the early years of the Roosevelt administration, the infusion of support from federal relief programs, such as the Works Progress Administration (WPA) and the Federal Emergency Relief Administration (FERA), enabled states to increase assistance to women and children. This resulted in lower levels of family break-up as public officials placed fewer children from families headed by women in foster care because their mothers could not support them. At the same time, as Linda Gordon has demonstrated, New Deal administrators were very reluctant to provide support for women because they feared that women receiving federal assistance would usurp men's roles as breadwinners and attempt to control family finances.

In 1939, women reformers and their allies secured amendments to the Social Security Act that provided benefits for widows of men covered under the provisions of the original law and for surviving minor children upon the death of a father eligible under the act. As Mink has noted, this change distinguished the legal treatment of widows of insured men, whose benefits would no longer be morals- or means-tested, from those still under the auspices of ADC – single mothers, divorcees, and deserted women. For widows whose husbands had worked in occupations excluded from Social Security coverage – disproportionately women of color – ADC provided the main source of federal support. The 1939 amendments, therefore, set the stage for the association of ADC with poor women of color.

Indeed, wage earning by women, especially those who were married, came under intense public attack during the Depression years. As in the past, critics charged that working wives neglected their domestic and maternal responsibilities and competed inappropriately with men for jobs. High rates of unemployment made the latter charge particularly powerful in the 1930s. As a result, employers, especially those in the public sector, discriminated against married women as they made decisions about layoffs and hiring. Lawmakers included a provision in the 1932 Economy Act (Section 213) that people whose spouses also worked for the federal government would be denied federal jobs and would be the first fired if an agency was cutting back. Predictably, the vast majority of those fired under Section 213 were women. Various local and state governments passed similar legislation. But, as Susan Ware has noted, these laws did little to ease unemployment. King County, Washington, for example, gained fifty jobs under such a law, but had 83,000 unemployed workers.

As these studies suggest, New Deal legislation had mixed implications for women's economic well-being. Constrained by the family wage ideology and by a tendency to scapegoat women workers for the problems men experienced in the labor market, reformers assumed that benefits for men would trickle down to women and children. Women of color experienced even more difficulties, primarily because reformers designed relief and regulatory policies to conform to the requirements of a racially discriminatory labor market. At the same time, some of the relief programs offered more to women and minorities than state and local charities and public assistance programs had provided in the past.

This occurred despite the fact that the administration of Franklin D. Roosevelt relied heavily on a network of women reformers and bureaucrats in the implementation of its policies. Linked by dense and strong personal and professional ties, these women secured federal appointments for women, worked together to improve their access to important decision makers, and deployed reform organizations on behalf of desired legislation. As Ware has documented, they shared similar perspectives on politics and policies largely because they came from similar backgrounds. They were generally white, well educated, and experienced in social welfare and political work. Many were related to men who had served in important political positions, from mayors to US Senators. Moreover, they were successful in securing more appointments and influence for women in the federal government than ever before and in creating a larger role for women in the Democratic Party.

Their integration into the state bureaucracy and the Democratic Party, however, came with limits and costs. None of the women bureaucrats, including Labor Secretary Frances Perkins, were insiders in the Roosevelt administration. Moreover, their exclusion from significant policy-making discussions, their growing distance from the independent political domain they had created during the Progressive era, and their reluctance to embrace programs for women limited their effectiveness. William Chafe has suggested that they sacrificed the autonomy they had secured earlier "to a sex-neutral government bureaucracy whose ultimate agenda was still controlled by men" (1991: 42).

Within the labor movement as well, women faced possibilities and difficulties during the 1930s. Chafe stresses that the formation of the Congress of Industrial Organizations (CIO) in 1935 enabled an increase in women's participation in organized labor. As an alternative to the crafts-based American Federation of Labor (AFL), the CIO organized industrial workers in all skill and occupational categories and promoted organizing campaigns in female-dominated industries like textiles. Moreover, according to Faue, its emphasis on grassroots mobilization and its incorporation of issues pertinent to working-class communities (like relief) facilitated women's identification with and support for the labor movement. At the same time, union leadership, particularly at the national level, remained in the hands of men, who associated leadership with masculinity and defined union policies largely in terms of the needs of men workers. In the long run, the bureaucratization of labor organizations, the centralization of authority in national unions, labor's alliance with the state, and men's monopoly on formal power marginalized women in the labor movement.

The Great Depression ended when wartime preparedness revitalized the American economy, shifting dramatically the economic and social context within which women made decisions about sexuality, family, work, and politics. The most important change involved the extreme labor shortage that opened unionized, well-paying jobs previously held only by men to large numbers of women workers. The availability of jobs for women in centers of defense industry, mostly located outside the South, promoted a large migration that had its own effects. Whether employed or not, women migrants faced massive housing shortages and shared with other women the challenge of managing scarcities in consumer products, pressures to increase their community service work in support of the war, and opportunities for new social freedoms. Not surprisingly, wartime trends affected women from different social groups – based on class, race, age, and marital status – in different ways. In addition, as work by Anderson and Milkman demonstrates, women's opportunities varied widely, depending on the region, city, industry, or plant in which they sought or secured employment.

The wartime changes in women's lives had implications far beyond the workplace. They threatened to undermine many of the stereotypes that provided the ideological support for a gender system that relegated women to domesticity and to low-paying, low-mobility jobs. Increasing access to well-paid jobs during the war challenged the economic basis of men's power within the family and the society. These changes were especially important for working-class women, who provided most of the female labor in America's factories, before and during the war. Their new roles meant that they could aspire to jobs which paid almost as much as their husbands'. Moreover, the skills that they demonstrated in those jobs undercut the sense of relative worth which working-class men gained from the assumption that physically arduous, mechanized, and skilled work was beyond the capacities of women.

Not surprisingly, historians have differed in their assessments of the short-term and long-term effects of World War II on women. William Chafe, for example, stresses the accelerated growth of the female labor force in the 1940s, a trend that was especially pronounced among married women and women over the age of thirty-five. Chafe saw these changes as especially significant because they endured after the war and indicated the beginning of an accommodation between women's domestic roles and their work lives. During the war years, the numbers of women in unions grew dramatically, women workers' wages increased, and public attitudes shifted to some extent in favor of married women's employment.

At the same time, as Chafe and others have noted, labor force discrimination persisted despite the labor shortage caused by the war. Employers routinely assigned women and men to different kinds of work, labeled women's jobs "light" or "unskilled," paid women less than men for the same or equivalent work, and denied women opportunities for advancement. Although the federal government remained formally committed to a policy of equal pay for equal work in defense industries, it gave companies many loopholes to justify inequitable pay for women, worried that increasing women's pay would be inflationary, and "permitted" but did not require raising women's wages when they were lower than men's for the same work. State policies, therefore, were critical to the retention of gender segregation in work and the maintenance of lower pay for women.

Both Karen Skold and Ruth Milkman have closely examined the persistence of job segregation based on gender and the rationales that accompanied it. Skold found that women working in the Kaiser shipyards in Portland were concentrated in jobs as welders, helpers, and laborers and underrepresented in various higher-paying crafts and supervisory jobs. According to Milkman, managers assigned workers to jobs based on gender, "guided by a hastily revised idiom of sex-typing that adapted prewar traditions to the special demands of the war emergency" (1987: 49). That often meant that employers and others ascribed women's success in previously male jobs to women's purported superiority in manual dexterity or their willingness to do monotonous work. Once the war was over, returning the jobs to men required an equally rapid shift to an ideology that described the work as too difficult for women. As Nancy Gabin observed, the wartime experiences "exposed the arbitrary character of occupational segregation by sex" (1990: 48).

Women industrial workers also faced difficulties from male co-workers and male-dominated unions. According to Milkman and Gabin, labor unions often maintained separate seniority lists by gender or job and pressured employers to limit the jobs to which women could be assigned, reserving the better-paying jobs for men. Although many unions gave support to the idea of equal pay for equal work, the fact that they did so to protect men's jobs and wage scales made their position contradictory and contributed to compromises that maintained unequal pay levels. Once on the job, male co-workers could also make adjustment difficult for women by harassing them or refusing to offer proper training or assistance to them.

For women of color, the situation was even more difficult. Previously confined primarily to work in domestic service and agriculture, they faced systematic barriers to employment that endured despite the magnitude of the labor shortage and the existence of the federal Committee on Fair Employment Practice (FEPC). As Eileen Boris has demonstrated, African Americans faced discrimination rooted in whites' fears about bodily contact and social intimacy as white co-workers and employers "based moral judgments on physical appearance" (1998: 94). These fears were widely shared, North and South, leading to more limited opportunities for men and women of color in the better-paying defense jobs. African American women, often stereotyped as sexually immoral, faced an especially virulent prejudice at work. White women, for example, protested the presence of black women workers, particularly when it involved using the same restroom facilities.

As a result, when labor-short employers decided to broaden their hiring practices, they often looked first to white women or men of color. In order to secure the employment opportunities ostensibly safeguarded by the federal government, African American women had to file complaints with the FEPC, protest at plant gates, and work with unions and civil rights organizations to put pressure on discriminatory employers. Employment opportunities for Mexican American women may have improved most in California, where expansion of the aircraft industry created new opportunities. Elsewhere in the Southwest, employer discrimination limited many Chicanas to work in service and traditional female-employing industries.

As I demonstrated in *Changing Woman: A History of Racial Ethnic Women in Modern America* (1996), Native American women's wartime experiences both resembled and differed from those of other women of color. They also faced the patterns of discrimination and expanded opportunities experienced by Latinas and African American women. In addition, many left the reservations for the first time to seek employment in defense centers, leading to more cross-cultural contact and to greater exposure to the mores and practices of the dominant society. On the reservations, the war created jobs in traditionally male crafts, like silversmithing, for a few women. It also intensified the economic pressure on Indian women to marry under white laws, because the program of allotments for servicemen's dependents required that local or tribal governments register the marriages if wives were to receive benefits.

Japanese American women shared with their families the traumatic and difficult experiences of removal to concentration camps mandated by government policies that defined all people of Japanese ancestry in specified areas of the West as security risks. For most, this meant the loss of freedom, privacy, and property. Within the camps, however, women experienced radical changes in the organization of labor. Because so much domestic labor – including especially cooking – was socialized and because families had to live in overcrowded compounds, women found their housework reduced. The government expected most camp inmates to work and paid all the same low wages, irrespective of sex. According to Valerie Matsumoto, these shifts tended to erode the authority of elders, including women, and to give young women somewhat enhanced autonomy from their families. When the government decided to allow some young women to go to school in the East, it created an opportunity for them to develop more independent lives. Most women, however, shared with the men in their families the loss of freedom, property, income, and community standing that resulted from the internment policies.

In addition to workplace transformations, all women experienced dramatic changes in their unpaid domestic labor. Overcrowded housing, shortages of consumer goods and services, the need to do volunteer work for the war effort, and inadequacies in public services made women's domestic and public unpaid labor more difficult and time-consuming. As Amy Bentley has observed, "wartime food rationing campaigns collapsed the boundaries between women's public and private lives" (1998: 5). At the same time, the necessity for women to use their domestic skills on behalf of the state did not "disturb gendered notions of democracy and citizenship" (1998: 31). In-migrant women faced special problems trying to support state interests and their families' well-being because established businesses gave priority to prewar customers and the housing in-migrant women got tended to be poor in quality and remote from commercial services.

Wartime especially complicated the domestic labor of women of color, who faced greater difficulties because rapid population growth and racial discrimination in housing created a particularly critical shortage in defense centers. Families had to pile into small rooms and apartments that were often substandard as well as severely overcrowded. This meant more labor for women, who had to do what they could to improve their homes and to harmonize family relations strained by poor conditions and a lack of privacy. The exception to this was publicly funded housing projects. According to Gretchen Lemke-Santangelo, African American women who had migrated from the South to the East Bay area in northern California – and were lucky enough to get into public housing – found the accommodations better than the others available to them and better than what they had left behind. Moreover, "government housing was woman-centered, spatially conducive to the formation of helping networks" (1996: 88). Public housing authorities, however, allocated a disproportionate number of the units built during the war to white defense workers and their families.

Wartime changes, especially the introduction of thousands of women workers into industrial jobs previously considered appropriate only for men, posed a serious ideological challenge to definitions of womanhood constructed around domesticity. As a result, policy makers and others devoted a great deal of energy to reconciling prewar definitions of femininity and women's diverse wartime roles. According to Leila Rupp, the US government, in its campaign to get women to take defense jobs, stressed a "personalized patriotism" that encouraged women to view war work in terms of providing materials that would protect their loved ones in military service and hasten the end of the war. American recruitment efforts downplayed high wages as a motivation for women seeking war work, thus reinforcing the view that women acted "as wives and mothers responding to the needs of the country or of their men rather than as workers" (1978: 170). Higher wages, however, drew women into defense work in larger numbers than in Germany, where wages were lower and allotments for servicemen's dependents were higher than in the United States. America's more successful mobilization of women for defense work increased its military capacity, contributing to victory.

Maureen Honey's *Creating Rosie the Riveter: Class, Gender, and Propaganda During World War II* (1984) examined the roles of government officials and magazine writers and publishers in shaping popular culture during the war years and in advancing interpretations of women's roles in wartime industries that reflected their anxieties about the loyalty and capacity of working-class people and about women's commitments to their conventional roles in American homes and families. By interpreting women's work in heavy industries during the war as an expression of their support for family members in the service and as a form of feminine sacrifice (after all, their emotions and desires were ostensibly invested only in the family), these propagandists sought to contain the emancipatory possibilities of wartime changes. By depicting working-class women in less "skilled" work than middle-class women and as less independent than their more privileged counterparts, they particularly emphasized the need of working-class women (who formed a substantial majority of the real "Rosies") for a romanticized return to domesticity.

In no other domain of the wartime experience was the disparity between traditional ideas of gender and women's new roles more pronounced than in the military. According to Susan Hartmann, the war years transformed women's status in the military by formally incorporating them into the Army, Navy, and Marines and by expanding the duties they performed. This occurred in part because the military's bureaucratization necessitated a larger support staff and the military wanted that staff to be subject to military control. At the same time, the military assigned most white servicewomen to traditional work in clerical and nursing jobs and black servicewomen to custodial and food service work. Leisa Meyer has observed that the military, which was intent on reducing the possibility that women's military participation would alter civilian gender roles, created less nontraditional work for women than did the civilian sector.

As Meyer demonstrates, women's military service raised fears regarding women's economic, social, and sexual independence. Because the public associated men's military service with sexual assertiveness, many assumed that women's military roles either involved sexual service to soldiers or made them vulnerable to sexual exploitation. Soon a vicious rumor campaign developed, initiated mainly by servicemen, that claimed that women serving in the Women's Army Corps (WAC) in particular were either lesbians or engaged in inappropriate heterosexual behaviors. To improve the public image of the WAC, female military leaders exercised special vigilance over the recruitment, appearance, and behaviors of military women. WAC director, Colonel Olveta Culp Hobby, set higher educational standards for WAC recruits, believing that white middle-class and educated women were more moral than women from other social groups. Military policies reinforced the sexual double standard by denying prophylactics and birth control to servicewomen while providing them for male soldiers, by disciplining women for sexual behaviors that were implicitly encouraged in men, and by failing to protect servicewomen from sexual harassment and assault. Women who were perceived to be "mannish" or rumored to be involved in lesbian relationships faced investigations and discharge. At the same time, lesbians also found spaces in military life to form relationships and supportive communities and to define lesbian identities.

Officials on the homefront also exercised a heightened vigilance over women's sexuality during the war years. Under the guise of a public health program designed to protect servicemen from venereal disease, the Social Protection Division of the Office of Community War Services urged local law enforcement officials to broaden their morals laws to criminalize behaviors like sex not for hire, to incarcerate women suspected of immoral behaviors until they were found to be free from venereal disease, and to provide or require rehabilitative services for women, even if they were healthy and had not broken a law. Communities varied in their response to this federal initiative, but many heightened their surveillance over women's conduct in public. They used morals and public health laws to imprison women without filing formal charges, to refer them for counseling if they were believed to be sexually active outside of marriage, and, in some cases, to inform their employers or families regarding their conduct. This program, of course, was directed solely at women.

Concern that wartime conditions might promote women's sexual autonomy and weaken their commitment to marriage and motherhood also fostered increased restrictions on abortion. During the 1940s, hospital abortion committees replaced individual physicians as the arbiters of women's access to legal therapeutic abortions. This reflected a growing caution on the part of some doctors and hospitals, who were wary of becoming known for performing abortions. It also derived, in the words of Susan Hartmann, from the "pervasive conviction that woman's destiny lay in childbearing" (1982: 173). Doctors' increasing use of psychological frameworks to interpret women's requests for abortions in the 1940s "reflected Freudian stereotypes about woman's purpose rather than women's actual experience" (1982: 174). As Leslie Reagan has noted, that actual experience included a vulnerability to dismissal when employers found out they were pregnant. Women's desire to retain wartime jobs, therefore, combined with employers' policies to increase their need for abortions.

Women workers entered the postwar period with significant liabilities. The most important was the almost universal assumption that men, and particularly military veterans, had the first claim on jobs. According to my own work, this was institutionalized in the veterans' preference provisions of the GI Bill, passed in 1944, and expressed in employer policies. Structural shifts in the economy – with a decline in the manufacturing sector and increases in demand for workers in clerical and sales work – facilitated the shift of women back into low-skill, low-paying "women's jobs." Discriminatory policies by the US Employment Service, which could deny unemployment compensation to women who were not seeking "suitable" work (meaning traditional women's work) and to married women, operated to force women out of manufacturing jobs. Finally, the lower seniority accrued by some women workers, discrimination by employers and labor unions, and the lack of any legal recourse against sex discrimination made it very difficult for women to retain their wartime gains at work. As Nancy Gabin has documented, "discriminatory practices in transfers, layoffs, and recalls violated and abrogated [women's] seniority rights" (1990: 112). Neither women's unemployment nor their right to equal opportunity at work were taken seriously by policy makers, unions, or employers.

Historians disagree on the degree and significance of women's protests against discrimination in the postwar period. Some conclude that women generally wanted to reestablish traditional family lives based on their domestic labor. Others note the institutional and ideological barriers to protest, concluding, as Nancy Gabin did, that given "the obstacles to both individual and collective action as well as the strength of opposition to the continued presence of women in the plants, it is perhaps surprising that any protest occurred" (1990: 138). Her study reveals that women with a strong union (such as the United Auto Workers), committed in the abstract to the principle of equal seniority rights, were offered a space to protest postwar discrimination. Those women – whose coalition included a significant number of African American women – filed grievances, picketed employers, and pressured the union at all levels to protect their seniority rights and to end various forms of discrimination in seniority arrangements. That space for protest, however, was narrowed by the active opposition of rank-and-file men and some union officers to women working in industrial jobs with decent wages. I found that some women workers also filed appeals protesting discriminatory practices by the US Employment Service during the reconversion period.

During and after the war, the absence of a large and unified feminist movement impeded women's ability to translate wartime changes into long-term gains. As Susan Hartmann and others have noted, differences in perspective and goals based on race and class continued to divide women activists. Women's organizations continued their disputes over an equal rights amendment, initiated before the Depression and war, as working-class women remained opposed while some business and professional women supported it. Similarly, white women reformers and the National Council of Negro Women disagreed over the kind of childcare system that should be created during the war and over the bureaucratic location that would best serve their goals. As a consequence, women's organizations were unable to develop a coherent focus for collective activities. Moreover, the largely middle-class constituency of most women's groups remained out of touch with the concerns of working-class women who flooded into defense jobs.

The historical scholarship on American women during the Great Depression and World War II stresses the tenacity of the belief that women should make marriage and family the main priority in their lives; the flexibility and durability of beliefs that called into question women's ability to perform certain kinds of industrial and managerial work, even in the face of contrary evidence; the persistence of gender segregation and the stereotypes that sustained it, despite rapid transformations in the economy; and the insistence of most government officials, employers, and union leaders that women's employment was aberrant while men rightly made claims to jobs and to government support when wage earning was interrupted. At the same time, it also demonstrates the centrality of women's waged employment and their unpaid domestic labor to the well-being of their families, to the economy, and to the state. The increasing labor force rates of women, whether married or not, during and after the 1930s attests to the inadequacy of family wage ideologies to the economic needs of women and their families.

Although historians differ on the meanings of the Depression and war for gender relations and women's status in the postwar period, virtually all find a legacy of contradictions. Wage work by women, especially married women with children, continued to increase even as American culture stressed the importance of women's family roles to national and familial well-being. Moreover, both elements of this paradox received reinforcement as Americans interpreted the meanings of the recent past in their lives. Desires for economic security and family stability played out over issues of women's proper place. In the meantime, men retained their control over the economic, political, and cultural institutions that defined the possibilities and policies within which gender relations would be defined.

BIBLIOGRAPHY

Anderson, Karen (1981) *Wartime Women: Sex Roles, Family Relations and the Status of Women During World War II.* Westport, CT: Greenwood Press.

Anderson, Karen (1982) "Last Hired, First Fired: Black Women Workers During World War II," *Journal of American History* 69, pp. 82–97.

Anderson, Karen (1996) *Changing Woman: A History of Racial Ethnic Women in Modern America.* New York: Oxford University Press.

Bailey, Beth and Farber, David (1992) *The First Strange Place: The Alchemy of Race and Sex in World War II Hawaii.* New York: Free Press.

Bentley, Amy (1998) *Eating for Victory: Food Rationing and the Politics of Domesticity.* Urbana: University of Illinois Press.

Bernstein, Alison (1984) "A Mixed Record: The Political Enfranchisement of American Indian Women During the Indian New Deal," *Journal of the West* 23, pp. 13–20.

Blackwelder, Julia Kirk (1984) *Women of the Depression: Caste and Culture in San Antonio, 1939–1949.* College Station: Texas A & M Press.

Boris, Eileen (1998) " 'You Wouldn't Want One of 'Em Dancing with Your Wife': Racialized Bodies on the Job in World War II," *American Quarterly* 50, pp. 77–108.

Chafe, William H. (1991) *The Paradox of Change: American Women in the 20th Century.* New York: Oxford University Press.

Cook, Blanche Weisen (1992) *Eleanor Roosevelt.* Vol. 2. New York: Penguin.

Faue, Elizabeth (1991a) *Community of Suffering and Struggle: Women, Men, and the Labor Movement in Minneapolis, 1915–1945.* Chapel Hill: University of North Carolina Press.

Faue, Elizabeth (1991b) "Paths of Unionization: Community, Bureaucracy, and Gender in the Minneapolis Labor Movement of the 1930s," in Ava Baron (ed.), *Work Engendered: Toward a New History of American Labor.* Ithaca, NY: Cornell University Press, pp. 296–319.

Gabin, Nancy F. (1990) *Feminism in the Labor Movement: Women and the United Auto Workers, 1935–1975.* Ithaca, NY: Cornell University Press.

Gordon, Linda (1994) *Pitied But Not Entitled: Single Mothers and the History of Welfare.* New York: Free Press.

Hartmann, Susan M. (1982) *The Home Front and Beyond: American Women in the 1940s.* Boston: Twayne.

Helmbold, Lois Rita (1987) "Beyond the Family Economy: Black and White Working-class Women During the Great Depression," *Feminist Studies* 13, pp. 629–55.

Hoff-Wilson, Joan and Lightman, Marjorie (eds.) (1984) *Without Precedent: The Life and Career of Eleanor Roosevelt.* Bloomington: Indiana University Press.

Honey, Maureen (1984) *Creating Rosie the Riveter: Class, Gender, and Propaganda During World War II.* Amherst: University of Massachusetts Press.

Kessler-Harris, Alice (1995) "Designing Women and Old Fools: The Construction of the Social Security Amendments of 1939," in Linda K. Kerber, Alice Kessler-Harris, and Kathryn Kish Sklar (eds.), *U.S. History as Women's History: New Feminist Essays.* Chapel Hill: University of North Carolina Press, pp. 87–106.

Lash, Joseph P. (1971) *Eleanor and Franklin: The Story of their Relationship.* New York: W. W. Norton.

Lemke-Santangelo, Gretchen (1996) *Abiding Courage: African American Migrant Women and the East Bay Community.* Chapel Hill: University of North Carolina Press.

Matsumoto, Valerie (1994) "Japanese American Women during World War II," in Vicki L. Ruíz and Ellen Carol Dubois (eds.), *Unequal Sisters: A Multicultural Reader in U.S. Women's History.* New York: Routledge, pp. 436–49.

Mettler, Suzanne (1998) *Dividing Citizens: Gender and Federalism in New Deal Public Policy.* Ithaca, NY: Cornell University Press.

Meyer, Leisa D. (1996) *Creating G. I. Jane: Sexuality and Power in the Women's Army Corps During World War II.* New York: Columbia University Press.

Milkman, Ruth (1979) "Women's Work and the Economic Crisis: Some Lessons from the Great Depression," in Nancy F. Cott and Elizabeth H. Pleck (eds.), *A Heritage of Her Own: Toward a New Social History of American Women.* New York: Simon and Schuster, pp. 507–41.

Milkman, Ruth (1987) *Gender at Work: The Dynamics of Job Segregation by Sex During World War II.* Urbana: University of Illinois Press.

Mink, Gwendolyn (1990) "The Lady and the Tramp: Gender, Race, and the Origins of the American Welfare State," in Linda Gordon (ed.) *Women, the State, and Welfare.* Madison: University of Wisconsin Press, pp. 92–122.

Mink, Gwendolyn (1995) *The Wages of Motherhood: Inequality in the Welfare State, 1917–1942.* Ithaca, NY: Cornell University Press.

Reagan, Leslie J. (1997) *When Abortion Was a Crime: Women, Medicine, and Law in the United States, 1867–1973.* Berkeley: University of California Press.

Ruíz, Vicki (1987) *Cannery Women, Cannery Lives: Mexican Women, Unionization, and the California Food Processing Industry, 1930–1950.* Albuquerque: University of New Mexico Press.

Rupp, Leila (1978) *Mobilizing Women for War: German and American Propaganda, 1939–1945.* Princeton, NJ: Princeton University Press.

Scharf, Lois (1980) *To Work and to Wed: Female Employment, Feminism, and the Great Depression.* Westport, CT: Greenwood Press.

Skold, Karen Beck (1989) "The Job He Left Behind: American Women in the Shipyards During World War II," in Carol R. Berkin and Clara M. Lovett (eds.), *Women, War and Revolution.* New York: Holmes and Meier, pp. 55–75.

Wandersee, Winifred D. (1980) *Women's Work and Family Values, 1920–1940.* Cambridge, MA: Harvard University Press.

Ware, Susan (1981) *Beyond Suffrage: Women in the New Deal.* Cambridge, MA: Harvard University Press.

Ware, Susan (1982) *Holding Their Own: American Women in the 1930s.* Boston: Twayne.

Chapter Twenty-Two

Rewriting Postwar Women's History, 1945–1960

Joanne Meyerowitz

THE history of women in the postwar United States has a readily recognizable popular incarnation. On television shows, in Hollywood movies, and also in feminist lore, a stereotype has reigned since the 1950s. Stated at its simplest, the stereotype invokes women's retreat to domesticity after World War II. In the mass media, it usually takes the form of *Happy Days*, when cheerful mothers graced the domestic scene and cared lovingly for their children. For conservatives, this postwar history appears as a tragic romance laced with nostalgia for the "family values" of the postwar years, values allegedly lost in the social turmoil of the 1960s. In the feminist rendition, the stereotype of domestic retreat takes on a different valence. There it refers to the "bad old days," when women succumbed to a "feminine mystique" that stunted their psychological growth and tethered them tightly to the confines of the home.

Until recently, historians have written a more scholarly version of the same story. In the most common account, reduced here to a thumbnail sketch, the postwar years stand out as markedly different from the years before and after. During World War II, women entered the labor force in unprecedented numbers, and some of them defied the norms of gender by taking jobs in heavy industry traditionally held by men. After World War II, they found themselves pushed from the better-paying industrial jobs. As the political and cultural climate took a conservative turn, women encountered a resurgence of gender ideals that limited them to home, marriage, and motherhood. As Elaine Tyler May describes it: "In the wake of World War II ... the short-lived affirmation of women's independence gave way to a pervasive endorsement of female subordination and domesticity" (1988: 89). In this account of postwar history, the domestic ideology prevailed until the feminist movement triumphed in the 1960s.

This older history is now under revision. In the past decade or so, US women's historians have begun to rewrite the history of the postwar era. In roughest outline, recent historians have taken two divergent approaches. Some historians take a closer look at the gender conservatism of the postwar era. They explore the ideological underpinnings of the postwar domestic ideal, its associations with Cold War politics, liberalism, and the anxieties of the atomic age, and its ramifications for various groups of women and various concepts of gender. Other historians question the pervasiveness of the postwar domestic ideal. They explore other ideals of the era – individual achievement, for example, or civic participation – and they investigate the ways in which diverse groups of postwar women challenged, transformed, and resisted the domestic stereotype. The first approach attempts to explain the conservatism of the era; the second looks to other elements of postwar history.[1]

These divergent approaches shape the debates among historians in three key areas: women's activism, women's sexuality, and representations of women in popular culture. But we should not overemphasize the depth of the divisions. Many historians combine the two approaches. They acknowledge the contradictory ideals, competing trends, and disparate behaviors of women in the postwar years. One can explain the conservatism of the postwar years and also look beyond it. In many instances, the two approaches represent differences in emphasis more than out-and-out disagreement. Most historians who study women and gender in the postwar years agree on a number of overarching themes.

In the postwar years, for instance, certain social indicators supported the domestic stereotype. After World War II, increasing numbers of Americans moved to the rapidly growing suburbs. From 1950 to 1968, people who lived in suburban areas jumped from 24 to 35 percent of the total population. During the 1950s the number of homeowners increased by more than 9 million. As more people bought homes and as industries shifted from war production to the production of consumer goods, more Americans purchased major home appliances, such as refrigerators, and new household items, such as televisions. And they had more babies. The baby boom began during World War II and peaked in 1957. In the 1950s, American women tended to marry young and gave birth to an average of 3.2 children, a significant leap from the average of 2.4 during the 1930s. The domestic stereotype of the era draws heavily on these trends. In the 1950s variant of the domestic ideal, the woman at home is repeatedly drawn as a white, middle-class, suburban mother, caring for kids in a well-equipped modern home.

Other indicators, historians agree, contradict that domestic image. In the postwar era, the number of women working for wages increased. The numbers dipped right after World War II, but from 1947 on, the proportion of women, especially married women, in the labor force rose steadily. The heightened demand for women workers in the expanding service sector accompanied the growing supply of women from a wide range of backgrounds who sought wage work, including part-time jobs. In 1950, only 21.6 percent of all married women worked for wages; by 1960 the figure had risen to 30.5 and continued to rise thereafter. The number of women attending college also increased, though not as rapidly as the number of men, many of whom had access as veterans to free tuition under the 1944 GI Bill. Furthermore, historians of US women now agree that we need to pay close attention to diversity among women. African American women in the rural South, Mexican American women in the urban West, women active in civic reform, and women nurses, teachers, and waitresses, to give just a few examples of sizable groups, rarely lived lives that wholly accorded with the domestic ideal. In short, not all women were suburban, white, married, and middle class, and even those who were did not necessarily stay at home.

Activists: Retreat and Advance

For years now, historians have studied women's activism in movements for social reform. In the nineteenth and early twentieth centuries, diverse groups of American women formed an array of voluntary associations to further political causes, to act as "social mothers" who cared for the "less fortunate," and to demand their own rights. As a number of recent histories make clear, women's reform activities continued in the post-World War II era. But some historians portray postwar activism as a moment of retreat in an age of conservatism, and others find in it forward motion in accord with a long-term trend toward greater public participation by women.

On one side, historians point to an ideological climate inhospitable to women's reform activities. In a search for postwar security, these scholars claim, middle-class Americans looked to masculine strength and the patriarchal home as protective forces in a dangerous world. Various postwar commentators worried about a "crisis in masculinity," about men who lacked the strength to protect family, community, or nation. When women competed with men in the public realm, they said, they undermined men's sense of masculine vitality. In this ideological climate, women who stayed at home as "good mothers" reassured the national psyche, and women who pursued public roles threatened to weaken the nation. "Women," Elaine Tyler May writes, "were the focus of concern. It was important to recognize their increasing sexual and economic emancipation, but to channel those energies into the family. Outside the home (or even inside the home without a strong male authority), they would become a dangerous, destructive force" (1988: 109).

Histories that emphasize the inhospitable climate often note the damaging impact of the postwar years on women's organizations. Take, for example, the National Woman's Party, a predominantly white feminist organization that first appeared in the suffrage movement of the 1910s and supported the Equal Rights Amendment from the 1920s on. It survived the postwar years, but as a small, weak, elitist organization, "not a broadly based, grass-roots, progressive movement" (Rupp and Taylor 1987: 7). It could not attract a younger generation of women, and in the postwar years, it had little direct impact on public policy. Or take the National Women's Trade Union League, a cross-class organization founded in 1903. It worked actively in the early twentieth century to promote women's participation in labor unions, but after years of financial hardship it closed its doors in 1950. Or the National Council of Negro Women, a federation of middle-class African American women's organizations founded in the 1930s. In the 1950s, it lost members and failed to bring in new ones. It "appeared to many young women as an archaic 'do-nothing' organization" (White 1999: 186). Women's reform activism, which had flourished earlier in the twentieth century, seemed to dwindle in the years after World War II.

Indeed, the Red Scare, a series of attacks on Communism within the United States, decimated the American left and damaged any women's organizations associated with or suspected of left-wing politics. In 1946, women on the political left founded the short-lived Congress of American Women, but in 1950, after the Justice Department ordered its board to register as "foreign agents," the organization disbanded. The Women's International League for Peace and Freedom, a pacifist group, flourished in the years between the two world wars, but after 1945 it suffered from bitter infighting as some members accused others of supporting Communist goals. The wide-ranging condemnations of left-of-center activists stifled political expression and promoted self-censorship among those who feared that their campaigns for social change might appear too radical. The Red Scare also led to direct attacks on particular women activists associated with the Communist Party USA or other left-wing groups. Luisa Moreno, for example, had built a career as a labor union organizer and activist for the civil rights of Latinos. She had also been a member of the Communist Party. In 1950, she returned to Guatemala, the country of her birth, in what was labeled "voluntary departure under warrant of deportation" (Ruíz 1998: 84).

On the other side, historians examine the ways in which some reform activities and even some forms of feminism thrived in the postwar years, despite the conservatism of the Cold War era. If we define feminism to include a variety of activism on behalf of justice for women, we find various advocates of women's rights working ardently during the postwar era. Mainstream women's organizations lobbied to have women appointed to federal office and to expand women's educational opportunities. In a number of trade unions, women pushed for what some historians now label "working-class feminism." In 1944, women in the United Auto Workers formed their own Women's Bureau within the union, and through the 1950s, they called for "sex-blind treatment" in the labor market (Gabin 1990: 158). They demanded equal access to the jobs traditionally reserved for men. In the female-dominated service occupations, union women called for equal pay, a higher minimum wage, and paid maternity leaves. In the postwar years, these women rarely called themselves "feminists." At the time, the term referred primarily to members of the National Woman's Party who wanted an Equal Rights Amendment to the US Constitution. Nonetheless, women union activists opposed women's economic subordination and acted to end it.

Some historians also note the contradictory impact of Cold War culture. While the anxieties of the era could foster a climate damaging to women's activism, they could also, as women reformers realized, promote women's public participation. If the nation needed stronger defense against Communism, then women could push to participate as equal partners in the nation's civil defense. In 1955, Alice Leopold, head of the Women's Bureau, a federal agency in the Department of Labor, made such a case in her opening remarks at the Conference on Effective Use of Womanpower. "In these days," she said, "when individual contributions can count so heavily for the national good, there is no room for the old clichés that women ought to go home and let the men do it; that women's place is in the home – and nowhere else" (quoted in Kessler-Harris 1982: 385). In a similar vein, the Assembly of Women's Organizations for National Security, a federation organized in 1951, called for "full utilization of the talents and capacities of women" and "maximum participation and use of womanpower in national security" (quoted in Meyerowitz 2001: 111). As Susan Hartmann writes, "conflicting elements" in Cold War thought not only helped "sustain cultural conservatism," they also "promoted gender role changes" (1994: 86).

Historians of the postwar era are just beginning to explore the range, forms, and consequences of women's activism in the postwar years. But several points now seem clear. First, too much focus on national activism cloaks the growth of women's political engagement at state and local levels. In the postwar years, women ran for local political office, lobbied for local and state legislation, and campaigned in their home communities – suburbs as well as cities and towns – for desegregation, voter registration, "decent literature," breastfeeding, better schools, traffic safety, and numerous other causes. In New York City, women organized major protests against the threat of nuclear war. In California, working-class mothers and middle-class educators organized massive successful campaigns for state legislation to provide funds for childcare centers. They had greater success at securing funds than their counterparts who organized at the national level. Second, women volunteers routinely used their status as mothers to enhance their political clout, while women professionals used their credentials and expertise to the same end. Third, in the postwar years women worked in mixed-sex organizations more often than they had earlier in the century. As a number of historians have noted, the mixed-sex organizations almost always had men in formal positions of authority. It was in the separate women's organizations that women held the top positions of leadership.

The rise of the civil rights movement placed race at the center of the reform agenda and demonstrated the power and limits of mixed-sex organizations in advancing women's interests. The flowering of civil rights activism engaged African American, Latina, Asian, and Native American women in revitalized campaigns for racial justice, often in organizations that included men and women. In the South, African American women played a central role in the civil rights movement of the era. In 1955, as history books have long noted, Rosa Parks, an officer in the Montgomery, Alabama, branch of the National Association for the Advancement of Colored People (NAACP), refused to give up her seat on a bus and agreed to serve as the test case in the courts to dismantle segregation in public transportation. Ruby Hurley coordinated 350 southern chapters of the NAACP, Ella Baker organized the first projects of the Southern Christian Leadership Conference, Septima Clark and Bernice Robinson developed Citizenship Schools in the Sea Islands of South Carolina, and Daisy Bates led the highly public move to integrate schools in Little Rock, Arkansas. And hundreds of lesser-known women, we now know, worked through grassroots women's and mixed-sex organizations in local civil rights campaigns. In Atlanta, Georgia, for example, women participated actively in the voting rights campaign of 1946, and in Montgomery, Alabama, Jo Ann Gibson Robinson and the Women's Political Council helped organize and sustain the bus boycott in 1955 and 1956. Women led as organizers and educators "because of their deep ties to community groups and institutions," but they rarely held the limelight as the most visible leaders (Nasstrom 1999: 114).

Elsewhere in the nation, women participated in other post-World War II civic movements on behalf of racial-ethnic minorities. In the late 1940s and 1950s, Mexican American women in California worked in the Community Service Organization

(CSO), a mixed-sex civic group. Once again, women rarely held the public positions of leadership, but they took a leading role in fundraising, citizenship classes, voter registration, and neighborhood improvements. Dolores Huerta, later vice-president of the United Farm Workers' Union, began her long activist career in the CSO. Likewise, Japanese American women participated in the movement to rebuild and relocate communities after incarceration during World War II, and Chinese American women worked with community groups designed to help new immigrants who arrived by the thousands under the War Brides Act of 1945 and the Alien Fiancées and Fiancés Act of 1946. In all of these cases, mixed-sex organizations nurtured public activism by women of color but limited their ability to rise to the highest leadership positions. Although civil rights organizations fought for racial advancement regardless of sex, few of them directly challenged women's subordination.

White women reformers, frequently working in single-sex organizations, also began to pay greater attention to issues of race than they had earlier. At the same time, however, they gave lesser attention to issues of class. In the postwar years, for example, the Young Women's Christian Association (YWCA), a multiracial organization, closed its programs for women who worked in industry and launched a concerted campaign to challenge racial segregation. As Susan Lynn writes, "racial discrimination began to replace class oppression as the major paradigm of social inequality in the Y's programs and in U.S. life" (1992: 6). By the mid-1950s, the women activists who focused their efforts on issues of class were found primarily in unions.

Historians of US women tend to focus on (and empathize with) left-of-center women activists, but right-wing women also engaged in political movements. Despite the wider support for conservative goals, the activism of far-right women seemed to decline in the postwar years. "The mass movement of profascist women who opposed World War II," Glen Jeansonne writes, "has no major counterpart in postwar politics" (1996: 178). But even conservative women did not necessarily listen to those commentators who called for women to stay at home. Phyllis Schlafly, the best-known anti-feminist activist of recent years, was a mainstream Republican in the 1950s. In Alton, Illinois, she held leadership positions in the local branches of the YWCA, Community Chest, League of Women Voters, and National Conference of Christians and Jews. In 1952, she ran for Congress (and lost), and later in the decade she served at the national level in the Daughters of the American Revolution and the National Federation of Republican Women. Like many other well-known activists of the 1960s and 1970s, she launched her career in the 1950s.

Sexuality: Contained and Liberalized

Historians' approaches to activism – those who emphasize retreat and those who emphasize ongoing activism – have their parallels in the area of sexuality. Historians disagree over whether postwar changes contributed more to "sexual containment," as Elaine Tyler May writes, or to "sexual liberalism," as Estelle B. Freedman and John D'Emilio suggest (May 1988: 114–34; D'Emilio and Freedman 1997: 242). In the postwar years, the word "containment" referred to George F. Kennan's formulation of Cold War foreign policy, in which the United States aimed to "contain" Communist government to the areas where it already existed. But social and cultural historians have begun to use the term more broadly to refer to a domestic corollary to foreign policy, a particularly restrictive regulation of sexuality that sought to contain sexual relations within heterosexual marriage. Police and judges enforced the laws against "deviant" sexual practices, and psychologists and psychiatrists portrayed women who strayed from the marital norm as immature, maladjusted, and mentally ill. "Sexual liberalism" refers to the twentieth-century sexual ethos that celebrated sexual pleasure as central to human happiness and incited proliferation of certain forms of sexuality. In the postwar years, for example, the eroticization of popular culture proceeded apace as the courts chipped away at obscenity laws. Representations of sex multiplied exponentially in a booming market for girlie magazines, risqué novels, and pornography, even as commentators decried the shift in mores.

On both sides of the debate, historians cite emblematic texts to support their interpretation of the postwar era. Those historians who emphasize "sexual containment" often turn to *Modern Woman: The Lost Sex* (1947), a popular anti-feminist diatribe that railed against "the severely distorted sexuality of our age" (297). Its authors, journalist Ferdinand Lundberg and psychiatrist Marynia Farnham, applauded domesticity, denounced women who had sexual relations outside of marriage, and claimed that women found positive sexual fulfillment only when they desired motherhood. Those historians who focus on "sexual liberalism" tend to pay closer attention to the Kinsey reports: *Sexual Behavior in the Human Male* (1948) and *Sexual Behavior in the Human Female* (1953). Written by Alfred C. Kinsey and his colleagues at the Institute for Sex Research at Indiana University, these bestselling volumes publicized the findings of interviews with thousands of white Americans asked about their sexual practices. The stunning results suggested that sexual behavior varied enormously. In their second volume, Kinsey and his colleagues showed that many women had sexual intercourse outside of marriage, engaged in homosexual behavior, and had the same capacity to experience sexual pleasure as did men. To a certain extent, Kinsey's dispassionate scientific tone hid his sexual liberal agenda: he hoped to dispel the moralistic views and the existing legislation that aimed to restrict the sexual behavior of consenting adults, women as well as men.

Virtually all historians who write about women's sexuality in the postwar years recognize both its regulation and its increasing public presence. In fact, some historians argue that the heightened visibility of sex outside of marriage, seen especially during World War II, led to heavy-handed attempts to stigmatize "deviant" sexual practice after the war ended, and conversely that postwar publicity about "sex crimes" enhanced the visibility of "deviant" options. But historians of women do differ in whether they emphasize the enforcement of restrictive sexual norms or the growing liberalization of sexual expression. Was the "containment" of sexuality a show of power, a flexing of muscle by a triumphant tradition, or was it a last gasp, a feeble attempt by the losers in a longstanding war over sex? In much of the literature, readers will find one emphasis or the other.

How, for example, should we characterize the public campaigns against abortionists and homosexuals that appeared repeatedly in the postwar era? In the 1940s and

1950s, police in a number of cities launched initiatives to suppress the underground practice of abortion. They raided the offices of abortionists, many of whom were women, and the press published sensational accounts of the arrests and subsequent trials. Likewise, trashy magazines printed lurid exposés of the allegedly strange "twilight world" of lesbians, and the police raided lesbian bars and arrested the customers. But the history of sexual containment tells only half the story. In the same years as the exposés and arrests, a small group of doctors, lawyers, and public health professionals began to campaign publicly for more liberal abortion laws, and mainstream magazines began to publish articles calling for legalization of abortion in cases in which pregnancy had resulted from rape or endangered the health of the woman. Similarly, despite the threat of arrest, urban working-class lesbians, as Elizabeth Lapovsky Kennedy and Madeleine Davis show, created their own thriving butch–femme subcultures in the social settings of bars and house parties. And a few middle-class women founded the Daughters of Bilitis, the first American organization calling for civil rights for lesbians. Were the campaigns against abortionists and homosexuals signs of the strength of "containment," or were they the signs of a conservative moral panic in a sexually liberal world?

On one side, historians who emphasize the strength of sexual containment have begun to delineate the particular ways in which the regulation of women's sexuality changed in the postwar years. Regina Kunzel and Rickie Solinger, for example, have examined the shifting attempts to explain and control unwed mothers. Here, too, it seems, the category of race began to supplant the category of class. In the postwar era, as before, unmarried pregnant women faced a disciplinary regimen imposed by the physicians, reformers, and social workers they encountered. In the early twentieth century, though, those who provided services for unwed pregnant women tended to cast their clients as working-class delinquents in need of rehabilitation. During and after World War II, as the rates of unwed motherhood rose, they increasingly envisioned their clients in terms of race. White women who got pregnant outside of marriage were more often seen as middle-class neurotics, mentally ill women who required psychological care. In contrast, black women were seen as the victims of an impoverished culture. This racialized construction of unwed motherhood informed social work and welfare policy. As part of their treatment, white women were pressured to put their babies up for adoption. Black women were expected to keep their babies, and they were often refused the social services – maternity homes, for example – accorded their white counterparts. Although more white women than black entered the welfare rolls under the Aid to Dependent Children (ADC) program, it was the unwed black mother who bore the brunt of public hostility over government expenditures for poor women who had sex outside of marriage.

On the other side, historians who emphasize the rise of sexual liberalism have started to examine the ways in which postwar women debated issues of sexuality. Women argued among themselves about whether girlie pictures and magazines degraded women through commercialized exposure or liberated them from a Victorian sense of shame that had kept them from a healthy appreciation of their own bodies. In the pages of *Ebony* and *Negro Digest* magazines, for example, African American women debated whether photos of semi-clad women imitated "the vices of the white man" or honored black women's beauty (quoted in Meyerowitz 1996: 20). Similarly, women disagreed over whether women should avoid or engage in premarital sexual intercourse. On college campuses, women administrators helped enforce the rules – curfews, sex-segregated dormitories – that aimed to prevent sexual intercourse among students. But as Beth Bailey concludes, "The overelaboration of rules, in itself, is evidence that the controls were beleaguered." Women students, along with men, "developed systems for skirting the rules and evading penalties" (Bailey 1999: 80). In the urban Beat subculture, the 1950s variant of a bohemian counterculture, young women were more openly rebellious in their sexual experimentation. They directly rejected the sexual mores that they associated with suburban, middle-class conformity and with their mothers' generation. The differences among women move us away from accounts in which women appear primarily as the victims of a repressive sexual regime and suggest instead that they also engaged actively in contemporary debates over competing visions of appropriate sexual behavior.

Popular Culture: Domestic and Other Ideals

For years, historians of US women followed the lead of Betty Friedan, who assessed the postwar popular culture as detrimental to women. In her bestselling book, *The Feminine Mystique* (1963), Friedan argued that journalists, magazine editors, advertisers, educators, and social scientists promoted a stifling domestic ideal that held that women could find fulfillment only from marriage, motherhood, and family. Friedan targeted women's magazines as the key popular source of this damaging "feminine mystique," which, she said, trapped women in the home and stifled their potential. With conscious hyperbole, Friedan labeled the home a "comfortable concentration camp" in which housewives lost their freedom and sense of identity. As a brilliant polemic, Friedan's book helped launch the 1960s feminist movement, but as a history text, it only scratched the surface of the postwar years. Friedan's discussion of American women dwelled on affluent, white housewives and implicitly excluded the many women who were not middle or upper class, married, white, and domestic. Her version of popular culture also collapsed complexity and diversity into a single theme. In more recent accounts of postwar culture, some historians have moved from describing "the feminine mystique" to exploring its roots and its political meanings. Other historians have questioned its hegemony. They point to the contradictions within the domestic ideal and to the competing ideals that sometimes undermined it.

Those historians who elaborate on the postwar domestic ideal have linked it to national politics. In Elaine Tyler May's innovative and influential assessment, postwar domestic ideals resulted from the anxieties of the Cold War era. In the wake of the Great Depression and World War II, and with the ongoing threat of atomic war, a pervasive fear of decline, destruction, and death made "a home filled with children" seem a source "of warmth and security" (1988: 23). Popular culture promoted a comforting form of familiar domesticity in which the father served as head of the family and the mother as fulltime housewife. If political concerns bolstered the domestic ideal, then the domestic ideal in turn shaped popular political images. In *Life* magazine, as Wendy Kozol shows, photographs of families suggested a particular vision of American national identity. *Life* represented the United States visually as a nation of white, middle-class families, an imagined community of suburban male breadwinners, female homemakers, and their children. The magazine also used maternal images to legitimate US foreign policy, to suggest that American men fought the Cold War to protect mothers and children. The domestic ideal thus served to justify the policies of the era. "Cold War 'patriotism,'" Emily Rosenberg concludes, was "expressed as the nation's international assertiveness" and "became metaphorically linked to traditional gender roles of male assertiveness and female subordination" (1994: 69).

The postwar domestic ideal took its intellectual cues from the increasingly influential field of psychology, especially psychoanalysis. In the years after World War II, psychologists and psychiatrists had growing cultural clout. As Mari Jo Buhle finds, "psychoanalysis reached the peak of its popularity and its professional prestige" in the 1940s and 1950s. At the same time, "an overt antifeminism emerged as a central theme" in psychoanalytic thought (1998: 171). The psychoanalyst experts routinely promoted traditional femininity while lambasting feminism. They urged women to pursue motherhood and avoid careers. And they also warned mothers not to assert too much authority within the home. Powerful mothers, they said, would damage their children and undermine fathers' authority. Postwar political liberals, Ruth Feldstein argues, relied heavily on such stereotypes of "bad mothers" – smothering white "moms" and domineering black "matriarchs" – who allegedly damaged their sons psychologically, thereby creating male citizens who were either too passive or too aggressive. In this line of psychological thought, "bad mothers" weakened American democracy. In the postwar years, these kinds of psychological arguments made their way into popular books, magazine articles, and Hollywood movies and gave an anti-feminist cast to the discourse on political liberalism as well as on domesticity.

Other scholars have begun to delineate the cultural limits of the domestic ideal. In the postwar years, mass-circulation magazines celebrated women's public achievements more often than they celebrated domesticity. A wide array of magazines featured positive stories on women politicians, entertainers, and authors who made a mark in the public realm. In the mass media, the so-called American Dream of individual success made women as well as men celebrities and subtly subverted the domestic ideal. Women's magazines also published articles that endorsed women's participation in the wage labor force and included frequent stories on the discontent of housewives. Instead of glorifying domesticity, *Ladies' Home Journal*, *Woman's Home Companion*, *McCall's*, and other magazines routinely presented housewives as unhappy, anxious, and depressed.

In other media, too, the domestic ideal was contradicted by conflicting messages. In the 1950s, Brandon French writes, Hollywood movies "recorded American women's dissatisfaction and tentative rebellion with a surprising degree of fidelity" (1978: xxi). The "double text" of the movies simultaneously promoted domesticity and critiqued it. On television, *Father Knows Best* and *Leave It to Beaver* offered the most conventional visions of domesticity. But other shows defied such easy categorization. *I Love Lucy* featured a zany housewife whose spirit and will could not be contained within the walls of the home, and *Our Miss Brooks* presented a smart, sharp-tongued schoolteacher who refused to suffer fools gladly. In general, the popular media reflected and shaped what media critic Susan J. Douglas labels "postwar schizophrenia about women's proper roles" (1994: 51), and they presented what film critic Jackie Byars calls "conflicting constructions of femininity" (1997: 217). The mother-and-housewife image was only one construction among many. At various points in various media, other pat constructions of femininity – the sex kitten, the glamorous sophisticate, the talented entertainer, the career woman, the working gal, the lady politician, the girl athlete, the creative artist, and the selfless public servant – all appeared in positive pose. These two-dimensional caricatures of women were surely not feminist icons, but they were not domestic icons either.

Competing intellectual trends also filtered into popular advice. While some psychoanalysts and their popularizers may have supported conservative gender ideals, other psychologists and their popularizers backed away from them. In the postwar years, pastoral counselors, who worked through Protestant churches, "moved away from . . . rigid conceptualizations of men's and women's roles" (Myers-Shirk 2000: 117). They rejected psychoanalysis and turned to the new human potential psychology, which emphasized women's (and men's) autonomy and the pursuit of "self-realization." In sum, for virtually every source that promoted domesticity in the culture, we can locate other sources that undermined it.

What did this cultural complexity mean for women? From a detailed longitudinal study of middle-class married couples in northern California, Jessica Weiss suggests that some women (and men) "made their own uses of prescriptions." More generally, she finds, popular advice literature advocated active fathering as well as mothering, greater communication between husbands and wives, and flexible as well as traditional gender roles within the home. Thus even when the popular culture dwelled on domesticity, it sometimes moved away from traditional gender roles and advocated more egalitarian patterns of marriage and the sharing of household tasks. In the face of contradictory advice and shifting life-cycle patterns, some women and men experimented, argued, negotiated, and debated "their way to compromise and change" (Weiss 2000: 226–7).

Conclusion

Today, when complexity is in vogue, we can acknowledge the contradictions and ambiguities – the ways that postwar activists both retreated and advanced, the heightened regulation of sexuality and the greater visibility of a range of sexual expressions, the power of a domestic ideal and the limits of its sway. We can point to the diversity among women and rethink the kinds of questions – were suburban housewives happy or trapped? – that train our vision on white middle- and upper-class married women. Perhaps soon we can also move away from assessments that evaluate the postwar years as either wholly conservative on issues of gender or surprisingly liberal.

In the meantime, though, the histories we write still tend to emphasize one approach or the other and still inform the ways we understand World War II and the 1960s. When we envision the postwar era primarily as a time of retreat, containment, and restrictive domestic ideals, we tend to see the changes of wartime as temporary and we tend to portray the 1960s as a reaction against the postwar years. When we depict the postwar era as a time of ongoing activism, increasingly liberal sexual norms, and contradictory cultural messages, we tend to give greater weight to the longlasting legacy of wartime social change, and we tend to explain the liberalism of the 1960s as an outgrowth of postwar developments, a time when the seeds of change planted in the postwar years sprouted and bloomed. In this view, as others have noted, the civil rights movement, feminist movement, gay liberation movement, anti-war movement, sexual revolution, and counterculture all had their roots in the postwar years. These not-so-new social movements, we might conclude, were both nurtured and stunted by the ground in which they grew.

NOTE

1 I should say at the outset that I am not an outside observer in these revisionist endeavors. My own research is closely associated with the second approach, and this essay, as readers will no doubt notice, tends to favor it as well.

BIBLIOGRAPHY

Alonso, Harriet Hyman (1994) "Mayhem and Moderation: Women Peace Activists during the McCarthy Era," in Joanne Meyerowitz (ed.), *Not June Cleaver: Women and Gender in Postwar America, 1945–1960.* Philadelphia: Temple University Press, pp. 128–50.

Bailey, Beth (1999) *Sex in the Heartland.* Cambridge, MA: Harvard University Press.

Bao, Xiaolan (1994) "When Women Arrived: The Transformation of New York's Chinatown," in Joanne Meyerowitz (ed.), *Not June Cleaver: Women and Gender in Postwar America, 1945–1960.* Philadelphia: Temple University Press, pp. 19–36.

Breines, Wini (1992) *Young, White, and Miserable: Growing Up Female in the Fifties.* Boston: Beacon Press.

Buhle, Mari Jo (1998) *Feminism and Its Discontents: A Century of Struggle with Psychoanalysis.* Cambridge, MA: Harvard University Press.

Byars, Jackie (1997) "The Prime of Miss Kim Novak: Struggling over the Feminine in the Star Image," in Joel Foreman (ed.), *The Other Fifties: Interrogating Midcentury American Icons.* Urbana: University of Illinois Press, pp. 197–223.

Chafe, William H. (1991) *The Paradox of Change: American Women in the 20th Century.* New York: Oxford University Press.

Cobble, Dorothy Sue (1994) "Recapturing Working-class Feminism: Union Women in the Postwar Era," in Joanne Meyerowitz (ed.), *Not June Cleaver: Women and Gender in Postwar America, 1945–1960.* Philadelphia: Temple University Press, pp. 57–83.

D'Emilio, John and Freedman, Estelle B. (1997) *Intimate Matters: A History of Sexuality in America*, 2nd ed. Chicago: University of Chicago Press.

Davidson, James West and Lytle, Mark Hamilton (1986) "From Rosie to Lucy: The Mass Media and Images of Women in the 1950s," in West and Hamilton (eds.), *After the Fact: The Art of Historical Detection*, 2nd ed. New York: Alfred A. Knopf, pp. 364–94.

Deslippe, Dennis A. (2000) *"Rights, Not Roses": Unions and the Rise of Working-class Feminism, 1945–80.* Urbana: University of Illinois Press.

Douglas, Susan J. (1994) *Where the Girls Are: Growing Up Female with the Mass Media.* New York: Times Books.

Feldstein, Ruth (2000) *Motherhood in Black and White: Race and Sex in American Liberalism, 1930–1965.* Ithaca, NY: Cornell University Press.

Felsenthal, Carol (1981) *The Sweetheart of the Silent Majority: The Biography of Phyllis Schlafly.* Garden City, NY: Doubleday.

Fousekis, Natalie Marie (2000) "Fighting for Our Children: Women's Activism and the Battle for Child Care in California, 1940–1965," Ph.D. dissertation, University of North Carolina, Chapel Hill.

French, Brandon (1978) *On the Verge of Revolt: Women in American Films of the Fifties.* New York: Frederick Ungar.

Gabin, Nancy F. (1990) *Feminism in the Labor Movement: Women and the United Auto Workers, 1935–1975.* Ithaca, NY: Cornell University Press.

Garrison, Dee (1994) " 'Our Skirts Gave Them Courage': The Civil Defense Protest Movement in New York City, 1955–1961," in Joanne Meyerowitz (ed.), *Not June Cleaver: Women and Gender in Postwar America, 1945–1960.* Philadelphia: Temple University Press, pp. 201–26.

Garrow, David (ed.) (1987) *The Montgomery Bus Boycott and the Women Who Started It: The Memoir of Jo Ann Gibson Robinson.* Knoxville: University of Tennessee Press.

Giddings, Paula (1984) *When and Where I Enter: The Impact of Black Women on Race and Sex in America.* New York: William Morrow.

Harrison, Cynthia (1988) *On Account of Sex: The Politics of Women's Issues, 1945–1968.* Berkeley: University of California Press.

Hartmann, Susan M. (1994) "Women's Employment and the Domestic Ideal," in Joanne Meyerowitz (ed.), *Not June Cleaver: Women and Gender in Postwar America, 1945–1960.* Philadelphia: Temple University Press, pp. 84–100.

Jeansonne, Glen (1996) *Women of the Far Right: The Mother's Movement and World War II.* Chicago: University of Chicago Press.

Kaledin, Eugenia (1984) *Mothers and More: American Women in the 1950s.* Boston: Twayne.

Kennedy, Elizabeth Lapovsky and Davis, Madeline D. (1993) *Boots of Leather, Slippers of Gold: The History of a Lesbian Community.* New York: Routledge.

Kessler-Harris, Alice (1982) *Out to Work: A History of Wage-earning Women in the United States.* New York: Oxford University Press.

Kozol, Wendy (1994) *Life's America: Family and Nation in Postwar Photojournalism.* Philadelphia: Temple University Press.

Kunzel, Regina G. (1993) *Fallen Women, Problem Girls: Unmarried Mothers and the Professionalization of Social Work, 1890–1945.* New Haven, CT: Yale University Press.

Kunzel, Regina G. (1995) "Pulp Fictions and Problem Girls: Reading and Rewriting Single Pregnancy in the Postwar United States," *American Historical Review* 100, pp. 1465–87.

Ling, Huping (1998) *Surviving on the Gold Mountain: A History of Chinese American Women and their Lives.* Albany: State University of New York Press.

Lynn, Susan (1992) *Progressive Women in Conservative Times: Racial Justice, Peace, and Feminism, 1945 to the 1960s.* New Brunswick, NJ: Rutgers University Press.

McEnaney, Laura (2000) *Civil Defense Begins at Home: Militarization Meets Everyday Life in the Fifties*. Princeton, NJ: Princeton University Press.

May, Elaine Tyler (1988) *Homeward Bound: American Families in the Cold War Era*. New York: Basic Books.

Meyerowitz, Joanne (1993) "Beyond the Feminine Mystique: A Reassessment of Postwar Mass Culture, 1946–1958," *Journal of American History* 79, pp. 1455–82.

Meyerowitz, Joanne (ed.) (1994) *Not June Cleaver: Women and Gender in Postwar America, 1945–1960*. Philadelphia: Temple University Press.

Meyerowitz, Joanne (1996) "Women, Cheesecake, and Borderline Material: Responses to Girlie Pictures in the Mid-twentieth-century United States," *Journal of Women's History* 8, pp. 9–35.

Meyerowitz, Joanne (2001) "Sex, Gender, and the Cold War Language of Reform," in James Gilbert and Peter Kuznick (eds.), *Rethinking Cold War Culture*. Washington, DC: Smithsonian Institution Press, pp. 106–23.

Michel, Sonya (1999) *Children's Interests/Mothers' Rights: The Shaping of America's Child Care Policy*. New Haven, CT: Yale University Press.

Moskowitz, Eva (1996) "'It's Good to Blow Your Top': Women's Magazines and a Discourse of Discontent, 1945–1965," *Journal of Women's History* 8, pp. 66–98.

Myers-Shirk, Susan E. (2000) "'To Be Fully Human': U.S. Protestant Psychotherapeutic Culture and the Subversion of the Domestic Ideal, 1945–1965," *Journal of Women's History* 12, pp. 112–36.

Nasstrom, Kathryn L. (1999) "Down to Now: Memory, Narrative, and Women's Leadership in the Civil Rights Movement in Atlanta, Georgia," *Gender and History* 11, pp. 113–44.

Reagan, Leslie J. (1997) *When Abortion Was a Crime: Women, Medicine, and Law in the United States, 1867–1973*. Berkeley: University of California Press.

Rose, Margaret (1994) "Gender and Civic Activism in Mexican American Barrios in California: The Community Service Organization, 1947–1962," in Joanne Meyerowitz (ed.), *Not June Cleaver: Women and Gender in Postwar America, 1945–1960*. Philadelphia: Temple University Press, pp. 177–200.

Rosenberg, Emily S. (1994) "'Foreign Affairs' after World War II: Connecting Sexual and International Politics," *Diplomatic History* 18, pp. 59–70.

Ruíz, Vicki (1998) *From Out of the Shadows: Mexican Women in Twentieth-century America*. New York: Oxford University Press.

Rupp, Leila J. and Taylor, Verta (1987) *Survival in the Doldrums: The American Women's Rights Movement, 1945 to the 1960s*. New York: Oxford University Press.

Solinger, Rickie (1992) *Wake Up Little Susie: Single Pregnancy and Race before Roe v. Wade*. New York: Routledge.

Solinger, Rickie (1994) "Extreme Danger: Women Abortionists and their Clients before Roe v. Wade," in Joanne Meyerowitz (ed.), *Not June Cleaver: Women and Gender in Postwar America, 1945–1960*. Philadelphia: Temple University Press, pp. 335–57.

Swerdlow, Amy (1995) "The Congress of American Women: Left-Feminist Peace Politics in the Cold War," in Linda K. Kerber, Alice Kessler-Harris, and Kathryn Kish Sklar (eds.), *U.S. History as Women's History: New Feminist Essays*. Chapel Hill: University of North Carolina Press, pp. 296–312.

Weigand, Kate (1992) "The Red Menace, the Feminine Mystique, and Ohio Un-American Activities Commission: Gender and Anti-Communism in Ohio, 1951–1954," *Journal of Women's History* 3, pp. 70–94.

Weiner, Lynn Y. (1994) "Reconstructing Motherhood: The La Leche League in Postwar America," *Journal of American History* 80, pp. 1357–81.
Weiss, Jessica (2000) *To Have and to Hold: Marriage, the Baby Boom, and Social Change.* Chicago: University of Chicago Press.
White, Deborah Gray (1999) *Too Heavy a Load: Black Women in Defense of Themselves, 1894–1994.* New York: W. W. Norton.

Chapter Twenty-Three

Civil Rights and Black Liberation

Steven F. Lawson

IT is impossible to write about the civil rights movement without recognizing the centrality of women. Two pioneering events associated with the launching of the movement, *Brown v. Board of Education* in 1954 and the Montgomery, Alabama, bus boycott in 1955, drew women to the forefront. Linda Brown, an elementary school student from Topeka, Kansas, lent her name to the landmark suit resulting in the Supreme Court's proclamation against racially segregated public schools. A year later, Rosa Parks, a middle-aged seamstress and respected community activist in Montgomery, refused to abide by the city's segregationist policy and give up her seat to a white man on a crowded bus, thereby precipitating a successful year-long boycott. Yet hardly had Brown and Parks appeared on the scene than the focus of the movement shifted to men. The Reverend Martin Luther King, Jr., a newcomer to Montgomery in 1955 and far less involved in civil rights activities than Mrs. Parks, quickly vaulted to the center of attention as the foremost leader of the civil rights struggle, a position he never relinquished. Whether they were ministers or secular leaders of civil rights organizations, men commanded the bulk of the publicity devoted to coverage of the freedom struggle. Occasionally, women such as Rosa Parks gained notice, but they were long the exceptions to the male-dominated portrayal of the civil rights movement.

The paradox of women's importance to the black freedom movement and their relative invisibility in discussions of it requires explanation. Traditionally, historical narratives have been driven by political events occurring on a grand, nationwide scale. Groups that lobbied Congress, brought cases before the Supreme Court, and met with presidents stood out as movers and shakers. The major organizations that fit this description – the National Association for the Advancement of Colored People (NAACP), the National Urban League, the Southern Christian Leadership Conference (SCLC), the Congress of Racial Equality (CORE), and the Student Nonviolent Coordinating Committee (SNCC) – were all led by men during the peak of the movement. The media, especially television, which developed as the main source of news during the 1950s and 1960s, focused the spotlight on men. This hardly comes as a surprise because during the postwar era affairs of state and matters of weighty public policy were seen as resting predominantly in male hands. Cameras recorded demonstrations in which women participated in significant numbers, but the male heads of the preeminent civil rights groups served as spokesmen for the protests and, in turn, attracted most of the limelight. Women such as Rosa Parks gained visibility when their actions sparked demonstrations that attracted national coverage, but then faded into the background as male leaders such as Dr. King presented black demands to a national audience.

Despite outward appearances, however, women played critical roles in securing first-class citizenship for African Americans. The key to understanding the contributions of black women rests in distinguishing between types of leadership. Males occupied formal leadership positions, as gendered divisions of labor common to mixed-sex organizations thrust men into the most visible roles in dealing with public officials. Because churches furnished the staging areas for mobilizing many black communities, ministers undertook primary responsibility for voicing their congregants' demands. Male pastors who participated actively in the movement exhibited the paternalistic, self-confident style of leadership that they were familiar with in running their ministries. The Reverend King's SCLC, an alliance of male ministers, operated in this fashion. The style proved unacceptable to Ella Baker, an experienced activist who served as its executive director. Baker, neither a minister nor a man, bristled from the male chauvinism she experienced in running the organization. One of the few women who held a senior position in a major civil rights group, Baker represented an alternative brand of leadership, one that reflected the experiences of women. She recognized that top-down leadership, whether in the form of ministerial-led associations or in hierarchical, secular groups like the NAACP, marginalized the efforts of women and relegated them mainly to secretarial and clerical positions. She advocated, instead, decision making that did not depend on either charismatic or bureaucratic authority; rather, Baker wanted people in local communities, women and men, to define their own goals and develop solutions to achieve them. In these day-to-day grassroots activities, women typically excelled. Black women formed the backbone of community life; their voluntary labor kept the churches functioning during the week and filled on Sundays, and their network of social clubs and interactions extended lines of communication throughout the community to bring black people of different classes and social standing together in times of crisis.

As Charles Payne observed with respect to the movement in the Mississippi Delta, "men led, but women organized" (1990: 1). Women not only sustained the community through religious and social activities, they also nurtured the civil rights struggle in their familial roles as wives and mothers. Without the sources of support they provided, the movement would never have gotten off the ground. Because the struggle relied on young people as plaintiffs in education cases and as marchers in demonstrations, women had enormous influence in shaping their children's decision to join the cause. It took great courage and faith to put their daughters' and sons' lives in jeopardy in the face of often brutal white resistance. Both inside and outside the home, women played an essential part in building the foundation for the movement to flourish. Depicting women as organizers, however, does not do justice to the leadership they exhibited. They did not usually hold official titles or follow formal job descriptions, but operating behind the scenes in routine, often gendered ways, women functioned as "bridge leaders." According to Belinda Robnett, who coined this term, women in the civil rights movement served as intermediaries between local communities, where their power was greatest, and regional and national civil rights agencies, where their access was much more limited.

In the last decade, scholarship on the civil rights movement has begun to explore the significance of women in the struggle against white supremacy. As historians moved away from studying macro-politics, they have highlighted how ordinary women and men gave meaning to their lives in the face of modernizing forces that undermine community: centralization, bureaucratization, and globalization. With respect to African Americans, this has meant detailed case studies of the various ways southern blacks reacted to racism. As scholars probed into local conditions, they increasingly discovered the importance of women as agents of change. Most of these women did not leave personal papers for historians to use in resurrecting their experiences, but oral histories have now opened to view the lives of people who were neglected. At the same time, a younger generation has reshaped the field of women's history, extending coverage beyond white women in the Northeast, the earlier focus of attention, to include women of color, especially in the South and Southwest. This trend has particularly stimulated interest in African American women and their participation in the civil rights struggle.

African American women's historians have shown that women's involvement in the civil rights era followed a much longer trajectory in anti-racist campaigns. Paula Giddings and Deborah Gray White separately have traced the intimate relationship between black women and racial advancement. With segregation, disfranchisement, and lynching in the ascendancy by 1900, black women seized opportunities to rise out of the nadir of oppression. Ida B. Wells, a brilliant newspaper editor and propagandist, spoke out vigorously against lynching and derided the supposed manliness of "civilized" whites for engaging in such beastly and cowardly behavior. Along with white women such as Mary White Ovington and black and white men, she helped organize the NAACP in 1909. The disfranchisement of black men in the South at the turn of the century placed them on a par with their black sisters who had yet to obtain suffrage. Turning this situation into something hopeful, African American women, North and South, sought to improve their communities by working together to raise standards of education, social service, and public health. The majority of women who were politically active did not join protest organizations such as the NAACP, but expressed their desire for progress through women's clubs. Mary Church Terrell's National Association of Colored Women (NACW), formed in 1896, adopted as its motto: "Lifting As We Climb." This racial uplift ideology depended on women as the guardians of moral purity to lead the way in improving the social and cultural conditions of all African Americans.

The passage of the Nineteenth Amendment in 1920 gave southern black women the right to vote in principle, but in practice they remained disfranchised along with their black brothers. Nevertheless, women remained in the vanguard of racial uplift. In the 1930s, the National Council of Negro Women (NCNW), led by Mary McLeod Bethune, proclaimed itself the "Voice of Negro Womanhood." It used interest group politics to pressure Franklin D. Roosevelt's New Deal to extend greater access and economic benefits to African Americans, the group hardest hit by the Great Depression. Bethune wielded formal power from her appointment as a high-ranking official of the National Youth Administration and informally from her close association with Eleanor Roosevelt, the president's wife. Both the NACW and the NCNW were composed primarily of middle-class women. Working-class black women found greater representation in the United Negro Improvement Association, the black nationalist movement of Marcus Garvey and his wife Amy Jacques-Garvey, which flourished in the 1920s. In the next decade, the International Ladies' Auxiliary of the Brotherhood of Sleeping Car Porters supported trade unionism and consumer cooperatives. In their roles as wives and mothers, its members strove to promote union activities among their husbands and to feed their families more economically through the formation of consumer cooperatives. All of these groups faced the common dilemma of having to balance issues of race, gender, and class. As Deborah White has shown, African American women bore a very heavy load in defending themselves against racism, sexism, and economic discrimination, while at the same time maintaining racial solidarity with men.

By World War II, whatever progress black women had achieved fell short of restoring freedom to African Americans. In the literature on the civil rights movement, World War II has gained recognition for jumpstarting the modern black freedom struggle. The anti-racist ideology inherent in fighting a war against Nazism furnished African Americans with a potent weapon to explode the United States' smug claim of practicing democracy at home. Pursuing victory abroad as well as within the nation's shores, blacks intensified their campaigns for desegregation of the military, equal employment opportunities, and expansion of the right to vote. Spurred on by growing wartime expectations, the NAACP, the premier civil rights organization of this period, saw its membership skyrocket, and A. Philip Randolph and Bayard Rustin first devised such tactics as mass marches and freedom rides that would be implemented with great success in the 1960s. Moreover, the participation of black men in the military, albeit under segregation, created a group of veterans who returned home after the war intent on asserting constitutional rights that had long been denied them and gaining a fair share of the economic rewards the American Dream promised. In communities throughout the South, many ex-GIs took the lead in mounting court cases and conducting voter registration drives. Community development through moral and economic uplift had paved the way, but it would take direct political pressure to achieve "Freedom Now."

Connecting the rise of the civil rights movement to World War II further increased the focus on men as soldiers and veterans. How, then, do we explain why women played key roles from the outset of the postwar black liberation struggle? If, as this essay argues, women have had a long history of participation and leadership in black emancipation efforts, why have their contributions in the years immediately after 1945 been neglected, in contrast to those of men? The answer lies in the reconstruction of memory in the light of contemporary concerns. For instance, standing alongside male veterans and ministers, black women helped wage voter registration campaigns in the South, spurred on by the Supreme Court's outlawing of the white primary in 1944. Two years later, black women in Atlanta organized their communities and signed up previously disfranchised citizens in record numbers. The actual history, much of which was recognized at the time, is replete with women's involvement. However, as African Americans in Atlanta succeeded in electing mainly black men to office over the next three decades, culminating in the triumph of Maynard Jackson as mayor in 1973, the pioneering role of women faded from public memory. Instead, the official narrative of racial progress featured exclusively the black men who rose to power through the mobilization of African American voters. Consequently, as Kathryn L. Nasstrom has effectively argued, black women who had been the "centerpiece" in first organizing their community around suffrage campaigns "slipped from the prominent place [they]... formerly had in assessments of the voter registration drives, and with it the fortunes of women slipped as well" (1999: 132).

Despite this historical amnesia, it must be emphasized that World War II did encourage women to renew their struggle for first-class citizenship. Inspired by the wartime rhetoric of equality, some 4,000 black women managed to gain admission into the Women's Army Corps and other branches of the military. Moreover, the war whet the appetite of black women for continued progress. Having profited from the greater availability of jobs during the war, many African American women desired to hold onto them in peacetime. As Paula Giddings noted, the postwar period witnessed a rising percentage of black women college graduates and professionals and their entry into the middle class. As their educational and economic achievements escalated, African American women heightened their expectations of attaining the political and constitutional rights that marked full citizenship. Not surprisingly, young women and girls, like Linda Brown, were prominent among the students who took the lead in desegregating southern schools. Reflecting the rising number of black women attending college, Autherine Lucy briefly desegregated the University of Alabama and Vivian Malone made it permanent, while Charlayne Hunter did the same at the University of Georgia.

Other factors besides the war left women poised to seek civil rights. With the NAACP directing strategy in the early postwar period, education topped its legal agenda. Since the end of slavery, education had assumed enormous importance for African Americans. As moral guardians of the family, black mothers remained primarily responsible for getting their children safely to school. As Joanne Meyerowitz has shown, the traditional demands of motherhood could result in unconventional consequences in the 1950s. Thus, black women became very visible on civil rights battlefields as they stood behind their daughters and sons who sought admission to previously segregated schools.

Furthermore, black women – married and single – who worked outside the home at a higher rate than white women experienced other frustrations of racial discrimination. From early in the century, they constituted a large share of the passengers on public transportation and encountered rude treatment and arbitrarily enforced segregation rules. As Giddings pointed out, "there had always been a tinderbox quality to the ill treatment of Black women on public conveyances" (1984: 262). Not only did women who worked in menial jobs in white sections of their communities experience the harshness of racism, but so had more prominent black women such as the turn-of-the-century journalist Ida B. Wells and the North Carolina educator Charlotte Hawkins Brown. With expectations rising for racial equality after World War II, it was only a matter of time before women trained their sights on public transportation to express their grievances.

Montgomery, Alabama, provided the opportunity. If there has been one woman identified with the civil rights movement among the crowd of prominent men, it is Rosa Parks. Despite this recognition, Parks's involvement has been shrouded in myth. Portrayed as returning home from work as a department store seamstress and just too tired to relinquish her bus seat to a white man, Parks appears as a single individual who just happened to ignite spontaneously a history-making boycott. This narrative is constructed in a way that allows the story to reach its true significance only when Dr. King and his fellow ministers take control of the protests. The boycott and the conventional account of it assume added importance because Montgomery marks the opening salvo of the modern civil rights movement, and its portrayal has reinforced the distorted image that men led and women quickly disappeared into the background. Hence it is vital to get the Montgomery chronicle straight. First, Mrs. Parks did not casually get caught up in some larger historical whirlwind. She had been an officer of the local chapter of the NAACP, and as far back as World War II had challenged the actions of biased bus drivers. Earlier in 1955, Parks had received training from the Highlander Folk School in Tennessee, a civil rights movement center that offered intensive interracial sessions in community organizing. Her refusal to give up her seat may have been spontaneous insofar as she had not planned it in advance; but it more accurately reflected Parks's personal history as a longtime civil rights activist.

Not only was Mrs. Parks other than an unwitting agent of a social revolution, but the initial success of the boycott owed a great deal to Montgomery's women. Since the late 1940s, a group of middle-class and professional women had laid the basis for challenging bus discrimination. In the early 1950s, the Women's Political Council petitioned the Montgomery city government to hire African American bus drivers for routes in black neighborhoods, discipline discourteous white drivers, and ease inflexible restrictions on seating arrangements. Buoyed by the decision in *Brown*, the Council eagerly waited for a test case to fulfill its demands. Mrs. Parks provided it, and the Council possessed the organization to spring into action. One of its leaders, Jo Ann Gibson Robinson, an English teacher at the local black college, engineered the printing and distribution of 50,000 leaflets that informed blacks of the planned boycott and the mass meeting that would be held to launch it. Once the boycott began, Robinson remained active in the newly formed Montgomery Improvement Association, headed by the Reverend King. Moreover, women not only walked and carpooled to work, but they filled the church pews at the rallies that sustained the morale of the boycotters. The episode of the *Eyes on the Prize* documentary television series that deals with Montgomery graphically shows that although ministers orated from the pulpits, women provided the energy that infused these meetings through their singing and affirmations of support.

In addition to public conveyances, schools offered a vehicle for women's leadership. Three years after Mrs. Parks's protest, Little Rock, Arkansas, sorely tested the resolve of African Americans seeking equal, desegregated education for their children.

In 1957, armed with a federal court order requiring Central High School to admit nine black students, the NAACP sought compliance. Daisy Bates, the chapter president, took charge of the teenagers attempting to break through the racial barricades. Bates was not a newcomer to civil rights activism. Together with her husband L.C., she edited the local black newspaper and investigated racial injustices, which resulted in white hostility and economic reprisals. Of the nine students, six were young women, and one of them, Elizabeth Eckford, became the poster girl for the harrowing experience. On the first day of trying to attend Central, she found herself alone surrounded by a howling mob of whites attempting to deny her entry. Photographers captured her strength and courage as she remained calm and finally managed, with the help of a couple of sympathetic white bystanders, to make her way to safety. In the end, President Dwight Eisenhower had to send in federal troops and order the Alabama National Guard to protect the Little Rock Nine. Melba Patillo Beals, one of the students, has poignantly written of the experience. She credits her mother and especially her grandmother for providing the encouragement to sustain her through an extremely difficult year, one in which the state militia did little to restrain the often brutal physical and psychological harassment blacks faced inside the school.

In both Montgomery and Little Rock, as would be true in subsequent situations, black activists portrayed themselves as adhering to the highest standards of middle-class respectability. The ideology of white supremacy had included at its core negative sexual stereotypes of African Americans, male and female. Black men were looked upon as bestial, potential rapists, and women were viewed as promiscuous Jezebels eager to give up their bodies for pleasure. The racial uplift philosophy embraced by black club women throughout the century sought to counter these negative images by replacing them with bourgeois notions of morality, sexuality, and cleanliness, which they hoped would prove African Americans worthy of citizenship. However, racial uplift ideology, although frequently conveying conservative connotations, was flexible enough to carry over to the liberationist goals of the civil rights movement. Thus, Rosa Parks and Daisy Bates garnered favorable publicity from all but the most diehard segregationists because they clearly maintained standards of decency and respectability that challenged racist stereotypes of African American women. This can be seen most vividly from still photographs and documentary film footage of the movement in the late 1950s and 1960s that captured images of black women protesters neatly dressed in skirts and blouses and black men in jackets and ties. Wearing their best churchgoing attire, they highlighted the intimate connection between presenting a favorable image of moral correctness and obtaining racial equality.

Indeed, the most solidly middle-class civil rights organization, the NAACP, attracted a number of strong black women to leadership positions. In the 1940s, Ella Baker served as director of branches and set up youth councils. Though she left the association because its hierarchical form of leadership conflicted with her more democratic approach, Baker had accomplished a good deal by spearheading the NAACP's postwar surge in growth. Ruby Hurley, a Washington, DC, activist, replaced Baker as youth council director and in the 1950s was appointed to direct the Southeast region, the site of the most important battles of the civil rights era. During this period, the NAACP's legal team included Constance Baker Motley, who litigated cases in school desegregation hot spots in the South. She later was appointed to the federal bench. What still needs to be written is an analysis of how a top-down, male-centered organization like the NAACP succeeded in utilizing the talents of so many impressive women.

Furthermore, it is generally forgotten that older, gender-based groups like the NCNW adapted their programs to meet the challenges of the civil rights era. Dorothy Height, who led the organization following Bethune, created the Wednesdays in Mississippi project, which dispatched interracial teams of women from the state to promote school desegregation and voting rights. Height also helped organize the historic 1963 March on Washington, and though she did not address the crowd, she sat on the platform alongside the most prominent male leaders. While recognizing the importance of the foremothers of the civil rights movement, it is also noteworthy to remember that even at the national level, prominent women such as Height have not received proper acknowledgment for their contributions, with most of the credit still bestowed upon men.

Few of the women who threw themselves into the black freedom struggle considered themselves feminists, because their concerns primarily centered around the advancement of their race rather than their sex. Yet it is difficult to separate gender from race. It is fair to say that as male civil rights activists were motivated by the need to exert their manhood, female activists pursuing racial equality sought to validate their womanhood. In her description of the late nineteenth-century activist Maggie Lena Walker of Richmond, Virginia, as a "womanist," who viewed race and gender as intimately connected to her personal identity and political commitment, Elsa Barkley Brown has furnished a term that aptly applies to many African American women in the civil rights era. Throughout its long history, the black liberation struggle has not been so much a campaign for individual freedom as it has for collective emancipation. By exerting their womanhood and manhood, black women and men attempted to resist racially embedded, white supremacist notions of their sexual depravity.

Though some black women throughout the twentieth century identified themselves as feminists, they, too, combined struggles for woman's rights with the battle for racial equality. At the same time, although white women have been more closely identified with campaigns for gender equity than racial justice, there were important exceptions. Indeed, the history of white women in the civil rights movement generally remains as unfamiliar as that of black women. The earliest efforts during the first third of the twentieth century centered on campaigns against lynching, though the southern white women who led them did not attack racial segregation directly. Jessie Daniel Ames of Texas, as Jacquelyn Dowd Hall has demonstrated, opposed lynching because it placed southern white women on a hollow pedestal that really kept them subservient to men. Along with black anti-lynching advocates, Ames and her organization, the Association of Southern Women for the Prevention of Lynching, demolished the excuse that murderous retribution was necessary to protect white women from savage black rapists. Marshaling evidence that most lynchings did not involve charges of rape, Ames and her associates argued that women did not need safeguarding through violent reprisals, and in making this argument they helped breach the boundaries of paternalism that operated to reinforce the racial and sexual hegemony of white males.

As lynching began to decline by the late 1930s, the focus of white women's racial activism was aimed more at class than gender concerns. The economic crisis of the Great Depression, which hit the South hardest, underscored the necessity of bringing relief to the poor, white and black alike. The foremost group advocating economic and racial justice was the Southern Conference for Human Welfare (SCHW). Bringing together labor organizers, Communists, African American activists, and white liberals and moderates, in the late 1930s and 1940s the SCHW campaigned for economic reforms and defied norms of racial segregation. The Conference had the support of Eleanor Roosevelt, and one of its leading proponents was Virginia Foster Durr. The daughter of a respected family from Montgomery, Durr moved easily in New Deal liberal circles. She worked tirelessly to reduce the influence of conservative white southern politicians in the Democratic Party, and to this end she helped organize as an offshoot of the SCHW the National Committee to Abolish the Poll Tax. Durr believed that the elimination of this franchise requirement would extend the suffrage to poor whites as well as blacks who might then join together and rescue the Democratic Party from the control of southern oligarchs. In 1948, Durr lined up behind the Progressive Party candidacy of Henry A. Wallace and ran for the U.S. Senate in Virginia. Though neither won, their campaigns addressed integrated crowds and appealed for black votes. In 1955, Durr and her husband Clifford, an attorney, were among the first to come to the assistance of their friend Rosa Parks after her arrest in Montgomery. Along with the Durrs, Anne and Carl Braden of Louisville, Kentucky, agitated for racial and economic justice, and their efforts yielded antagonism from powerful southern politicians who sought to smear them as subversives.

In Virginia Durr and Anne Braden, a younger generation of white, college-educated, southern women found role models. Like their black counterparts, many white women gained inspiration for joining the struggle from their religious values. In her book, *Personal Politics* (1980), Sara Evans writes that although "southern Protestantism in the 1950s was in general as segregated and racist as the rest of southern society, it also nourished elements of egalitarian idealism." Anne Braden recalled that her childhood church had first taught her "that all men are One," a lesson that reinforced her activism throughout her life (Evans 1980: 29). As more young women began to enroll on college campuses in the 1950s, some of them fell under the influence of campus ministers expounding Christian existentialism, whose principles of authenticity and personal witness provided a radical critique of mainstream America and southern racism. Typical of this group was Sandra "Casey" Cason. Attending the University of Texas at Austin as an undergraduate in the late 1950s, Cason became active in the YWCA and the Faith and Life Community, which advocated leading one's life according to principles of brotherhood and respect for others, commitments that were taken seriously. She met like-minded women and men, and Cason's experiences in these groups turned her from " 'a lively bobby soxer' into one of the principal leaders of the interracial movement in Austin" (Evans 1980: 34). Black women such as Ella Baker and Dorothy Height, who worked with the YWCA on interracial projects, mentored Cason and other young whites. From Texas, Cason went on to become one of the most important southern white female staff members of SNCC. After marrying fellow activist Tom Hayden, one of the founders of the Students for a Democratic Society, she continued to work with other women from similar backgrounds, including Mary King, Dorothy Dawson, Joan Browning, and Constance Curry.

Radical Christianity alone does not explain the growing participation of young women in the civil rights movement of the 1950s and 1960s. Deborah Schultz has recently explored women from Jewish backgrounds who flocked to the black freedom struggle. Blacks and Jews historically had an uneasy relationship. Although common objects of discrimination, they frequently clashed in the mundane affairs of daily life. As Jews assimilated into American culture and achieved success as shopkeepers, merchants, and landlords, they came into conflict with blacks and were seen by them as no different than other exploitive whites. Expressions of black anti-Semitism stood side by side with those of Jewish racism. Nevertheless, among the leadership class, blacks and Jews often cooperated in battling discrimination that affected members of both groups. Jews had been among the founders of the NAACP and provided influential lawyers to represent the national association in winning early victories before the Supreme Court. Individual Jews provided financial contributions to fund civil rights activities, and Jewish organizations cooperated in lobbying for civil rights legislation. In similar fashion as young Christian women with a finely honed religious consciousness, college-educated Jewish women also turned to the civil rights movement to bear witness to their moral principles. However, ethnicity more than religious devotion shaped Jewish women's identities as activists. Women who went South in the 1960s to work in the movement, including Dottie Miller Zellner and Elaine DeLott Baker, tended to come from secular Jewish homes; some, like Zellner, had parents who had been Communists. But as Schultz has argued, whatever their personal background, these young women inherited a "Jewish moral framework about social justice" (2001: 4). In addition, they had grown up at a time when American Jews were first trying to make some sense of the Holocaust, and at a basic level these young activists absorbed the lesson that an oppressed people had to "fight back" against racial injustice or perish.

However important their stories, white women and men, Christian and Jewish alike, played a secondary role to that of blacks in leading the movement. The student sit-ins of 1960 galvanized a new generation behind the freedom movement and gave African American women increased opportunities for leadership. Diane Nash, a Fisk University undergraduate, and Ruby Doris Smith Robinson of Spelman College helped direct protests against segregated facilities in Nashville, Tennessee, and Atlanta, Georgia, respectively. In April 1960, along with over one hundred veterans of the fledgling sit-in movement, Nash joined in the creation of SNCC (Robinson entered the group the next year). In May 1961, when the freedom rides stalled in the wake of violence in Birmingham, Alabama, Nash made certain that SNCC members boarded buses to continue the trip. Robinson heeded her call and was one of over three hundred riders jailed in Mississippi. Nash and her husband, James Bevel, moved on to work for SCLC and were instrumental in paving the way for

Dr. King to conduct his famous march from Selma to Montgomery in 1965. That same year, Robinson won election as executive secretary of SNCC.

More than any major civil rights group, SNCC fostered women's participation and leadership. In great measure this was a result of the influence of Ella Baker, who encouraged the young organization to remain independent of existing civil rights associations. Baker's conception of leadership as group centered and her view of decision making as an outgrowth of participatory democracy appealed to women. Middle-class, educated women like Nash and Robinson found it easier to make their voices heard in this kind of political atmosphere and to gain respect for their ideas. The grassroots organizing tactics that SNCC preferred further enhanced the position of women in the group. Women proved adept at organizing projects in the rural South that depended on dealing patiently with local people and winning their trust. They displayed similar courage as men in bearing personal witness to racism in the most hostile areas. As a democratic, nonhierarchical organization, SNCC provided many spaces for black and white women staff to display their leadership skills. Nevertheless, traditional gender norms did not automatically disappear within SNCC (its slogan was "A Band of *Brothers*, A Circle of Trust" [emphasis added]), and with the brief exception of Ruby Doris Smith Robinson, men held the top titled positions. However, as much as possible within the larger male-dominated culture, SNCC women shared leadership responsibilities with men.

Women also gained significant influence within other civil rights organizations. The leadership positions wielded in the NAACP by women such as Ruby Hurley and Daisy Bates have been noted earlier. At the grassroots level, this also included the campaigns that Modjeska Simkins undertook for the South Carolina Conference of the NAACP. In planning strategy, raising money to finance school desegregation cases, and distributing food and clothing to the needy, Simkins came to be considered a "mother-benefactress" by those she assisted (Woods 1990: 114).

Next to the NAACP, the SCLC had the tightest organizational structure, whose hierarchical chain of command led directly to the Reverend King. Eschewing group-centered for charismatic leadership, King and his fellow ministers made it impossible, as Ella Baker had discovered, for women to gain equal authority with men. Nevertheless, strong women did make powerful contributions to the Conference. As mentioned earlier, Diane Nash Bevel was one, Septima P. Clark was another. A teacher in the Charleston, South Carolina, public schools in the 1950s, Clark participated in the YWCA and NAACP and attended leadership training workshops at the Highlander Folk School. After losing her teaching job because of her civil rights activities, Clark was hired by Highlander as educational director, where in 1955, she encountered Rosa Parks. She also worked closely with Baker, and in 1961, the SCLC employed her to supervise workshops on citizenship training and literacy, using innovative techniques that placed nontraditional teachers, recruited from the community, in charge of preparing people to vote.

CORE, which in many ways shared SNCC's approach to organizing in the deep South, also attracted strong women. In her classic autobiography, Anne Moody describes her journey from a racially stifling hometown in Mississippi to her recruitment by CORE to participate in some of the most dangerous civil rights battles in the

Magnolia State. In the local villages and towns that Moody and the other movement women ventured into, they routinely connected with black women who offered them their homes for shelter and their kitchens for meals, thus exposing their families to grave risk. Not only providers of daily sustenance, these local women, affectionately called "Mamas," were at the very heart of civil rights activities and opened doors in their communities that outsiders could not otherwise have entered. Moreover, they furnished vivid examples of independence and courage for young black and white women in the movement to emulate.

Of all the local women, Fannie Lou Hamer perhaps best represents the ability of the civil rights movement to identify and cultivate grassroots female leadership. Her story has been well told in two biographies by Chana Kai Lee and Kay Mills. A timekeeper on a plantation in Ruleville, Mississippi, Hamer became a SNCC staff worker. She lost her job because of her civil rights efforts, but unlike most local women, she gained national fame. A founder of the Mississippi Freedom Democratic Party in 1964, she traveled to the National Democratic Party Convention in Atlantic City, New Jersey, to win recognition and seats for its delegates as replacements for representatives of the white supremacist state party organization. In the plain-spoken, folksy style that reflected her lack of education and poor background, she delivered a widely publicized indictment of white racism in Mississippi and a stirring account as to how it had brutalized her personally. When national party leaders at the behest of President Lyndon Johnson offered a token compromise of representation, Mrs. Hamer forcefully rallied her fellow delegates to reject it. Although Mississippi insurgents did not achieve their immediate demand for seating, the national party instituted nondiscriminatory guidelines that guaranteed Mississippi reformers, including Hamer, seats at the Democratic nominating convention in 1968.

As biographies of key movement women have appeared in the past decade, giving greater visibility to many of the heroines of the struggle, they caution us not to treat these women as one-dimensional figures. Because these activists had not previously received the acclaim they deserved, in bringing them out of obscurity it is tempting to romanticize them. The autobiography of Anne Moody, published in 1968, should make readers aware that black female activists, especially those who lived their entire lives in the South, carried on the struggle at great personal sacrifice. Chana Lee's 1999 biography of Hamer makes this point abundantly clear. Lee poignantly reveals Hamer's distress concerning her grandmother who, like numerous southern black women, was sexually molested by white men. Hamer suffered the pain of an unwanted sterilization procedure while she was in the hospital for an operation for an unrelated stomach ailment, the results of which prevented her from becoming a birth mother. In revering Mrs. Hamer's strength and courage, we forget the physical disabilities she endured on a daily basis and the depression she suffered in the years before her death in 1977. Lee suggests the toll her public life exacted on her husband and family, which was a particularly difficult situation for women who were expected to make domestic affairs their top priority. Many women saw their marriages and personal relationships buckle under the pressure of participating in a stressful and time-consuming political and social revolution.

Despite plentiful evidence of the egalitarian treatment of women in organizations like SNCC, a protracted historical debate has raged about the presence and impact of sexism within the movement. The debate has focused on SNCC because it had the reputation as the most hospitable civil rights group for women's activism. In *Personal Politics*, Sara Evans described the complaint of white women in SNCC that they received second-class treatment within the organization. This incipient feminist consciousness erupted at a SNCC gathering in Waveland, Mississippi, in late 1964 as the group sought to reassess its place in the civil rights movement. An anonymous memo circulated at the retreat and authored by two veteran white staff members, Mary King and Casey Hayden, listed their grievances. Why is it in SNCC, the memo asked, "that women who are competent, qualified, and experienced, are automatically assigned to the 'female' kinds of jobs such as typing, desk work, telephone work, filing, library work, cooking, and the assistant kind of administrative work but rarely the 'executive' kind?" (quoted in Evans 1980: 233–4). Moreover, at a party to unwind after hours of intense discussions, Stokely Carmichael, who the following year would take over as chair of SNCC, jokingly referred to the anonymous manifesto: "The only position for women in SNCC is prone" (quoted in Evans 1980: 87). Carmichael's flippant remark became widely quoted in budding feminist circles and amounted to something of an opening salvo in the emerging women's liberation struggle.

In the wake of Evans's study, most scholars initially accepted the interpretation that women experienced sexism within SNCC and the gap between the group's egalitarian ideals and its practices encouraged the growth of feminism. However, recent scholarship and the publication of several autobiographies of SNCC women have presented a different and more complicated explanation of the memo in particular, and SNCC's attitude toward women in general. It is important to explain the context in which the Waveland Conference was held. It came a few months after the exceedingly stressful Freedom Summer, and SNCC was undergoing an identity crisis. Controversies flared over whether the group should continue to tolerate its hyperdemocratic, loose organizational structure or adopt a more centralized, structured framework. Challenges surfaced as to the extent that white people should participate in a black-centered struggle, especially as many blacks in the organization were beginning to embrace racial nationalism. For many, the influx of northerners during Freedom Summer, most but not all of whom were white, and their desire to continue on staff raised questions about the ability of the organization to remain true to its original principles, including nonviolence and integration. Ironically, the authors of the memo, Hayden and King, despite what appears to be very plain language describing SNCC's sexist character, have claimed that this impression is false. Both have argued that they did not target sexism per se in their 1964 statement, but they were really troubled by the possibility that SNCC would renounce its participatory democratic principles and move toward top-down leadership. Because women in SNCC had flourished within a decentralized structure, Hayden and King asserted they were mainly concerned that women would lose out in the proposed reorganization.

Black women did not join the challenge mounted by SNCC's white women and deny that sexism was a problem for them. They have pointed out that black women worked side by side with men and ran their own field projects in the South. The election of Ruby Doris Smith Robinson as SNCC's executive secretary in 1965 further attests to the acceptance of a strong black woman to occupy one of the two main leadership posts in the organization. In fact, functioning equally with black men, as Cynthia Washington, a SNCC staffer put it, black women were placed "in some category other than female" (quoted in Evans 1980: 239). One result, however, was that white women, who occupied more traditional feminine roles than African American women, often became more suitable for dating by black men, which fostered resentment by black women.

Although King and Hayden's retrospective comments place the issue in larger perspective, they fail to explain the specific complaints against the treatment of women that were presented in 1964. A more complete answer lies in consideration of race rather than gender as the primary explanation of SNCC's attitudes. The sharpest difference in treatment of black and white women occurred during Freedom Summer. Northern white women flocked to the South ready to jump into the fray. Intelligent, strong-minded, and courageous women, nevertheless they had little first-hand experience of southern culture and customs. Intent on openly showing their contempt for racism, some of them flaunted norms against interracial dating without fully realizing the danger they posed to black men. Fannie Lou Hamer, whose commitment to integration remained steadfast, nevertheless sharply criticized white women for acting as if race did not matter in Mississippi. Worried that violation of racial taboos would get black men killed, Mrs. Hamer complained that if young white women continued to hang around black men in full public view and "can't obey the rules, call their mothers and tell them to send their sons instead!" (quoted in Lee 1999: 76). Concern over appearances and the threat to the safety of black men, more than explicitly sexist attitudes, resulted in confining white women volunteers to the kind of traditional female work catalogued by Hayden and King in their provocative memo. Despite the criticism she has received for highlighting SNCC's sexism, Evans recognized that the problem for white women was not just a male/female one, and in this vein she quotes an African American female SNCC staff member: "It was a race problem rather than a woman's problem" (quoted in Evans 1980: 81). In the final analysis, the legacy of SNCC's influence on women may be mixed, but as the leading authority on African American women and the civil rights movement, Belinda Robnett, has concluded: "While SNCC was not completely successful, women were not subjugated to, nor were their contributions predefined by, men" (1997: 205).

Moreover, the story of black women's relationship to racial and gender justice movements continues to evolve. In later years, after the heyday of the civil rights movement passed, many black women recognized that in showing solidarity with African American men, they had diminished the extent to which gender concerns affected them. Yet the brand of feminism they defined and displayed was affected by several considerations. In the late 1960s and 1970s, second-wave feminism, itself shaped and stimulated by the civil rights movement, began to embrace race and class issues that were important to black women. The rise of Black Power and Black Nationalism, with their displays of acute masculinity, raised the consciousness of black female activists to the sexist side of the struggle to achieve equality. Such political radicals as Angela Davis, Black Panthers Elaine Brown and Kathleen Cleaver, and writers Alice Walker and Toni Morrison have all expressed the view that sexism cannot be ignored if black women and men intend to free themselves, their families, and communities from racial, economic, and gender discrimination. By the early 1970s, a number of women with long experience in civil rights founded the National Black Feminist Organization. Others continued to emphasize womanist perspectives, but focused greater attention on the specific concerns of African American women.

In the forty years since the height of the civil rights movement, scholars have produced a rich literature on the people, communities, and organizations that helped reconstruct the South and the nation along more egalitarian lines. Not until the last decade or so have women gained recognition for the central contributions they made. More remains to be explored as researchers move from the first tier of notable female activists to those unsung women whose participation and leadership were so embedded in the daily struggle that they have been hard to distinguish from the movement itself. In the process of further disentangling women's diverse roles, researchers are beginning to pay greater attention to the operation of gendered norms within the civil rights movement. So far we have mostly had a women's history tacked onto a men's history of civil rights, which emphasizes the contributions of each sex rather than the complicated relationship between the two. Future studies should reveal that in the long battle against racism, black men were not merely seeking to exert their manhood, nor were black women their womanhood, but together they sought to affirm their race consciousness and personhood.

BIBLIOGRAPHY

Barnard, Hollinger F. (ed.) (1985) *Outside the Magic Circle: The Autobiography of Virginia Foster Durr.* Alabama: University of Alabama Press.

Bates, Daisy (1962) *The Long Shadow of Little Rock: A Memoir.* New York: David McKay.

Beals, Melba Patillo (1994) *Warriors Don't Cry: A Searing Memoir of the Battle to Integrate Little Rock's Central High.* New York: Washington Square Press.

Bederman, Gail (1995) *Manliness and Civilization: A Cultural History of Gender and Race in the United States, 1880–1917.* Chicago: University of Chicago Press.

Braden, Anne (1999) *The Wall Between*, 2nd ed. Knoxville: University of Tennessee Press.

Brown, Elaine (1992) *A Taste of Power: A Black Woman's Story.* New York: Doubleday.

Brown, Elsa Barkley (1989) "Womanist Consciousness: Maggie Lena Walker and the Independent Order of Saint Luke," *Signs* 14, pp. 610–33.

Chappell, Marisa, Hutchinson, Jenny, and Ward, Brian (1999) " 'Dress Modestly, Neatly... As If You Were Going to Church': Respectability, Class and Gender in the Montgomery Bus Boycott and the Early Civil Rights Movement," in Peter J. Ling and Sharon Monteith (eds.), *Gender in the Civil Rights Movement.* New York: Garland Publishing, pp. 69–100.

Chateauvert, Melinda (1998) *Marching Together: Women of the Brotherhood of Sleeping Car Porters.* Urbana: University of Illinois Press.

Clark, E. Culpepper (1993) *The Schoolhouse Door: Segregation's Last Stand at the University of Alabama.* New York: Oxford University Press.

Clark, Septima (1962) *Echo in My Soul.* New York: E. P. Dutton.

Crawford, Vicki, Rouse, Jacqueline Anne, and Woods, Barbara (eds.) (1990) *Women in the Civil Rights Movement: Trailblazers and Torchbearers, 1941–1965*. Brooklyn: Carlson Publishing.

Curry, Connie (1995) *Silver Rights*. Chapel Hill, NC: Algonquin Books.

Curry, Connie et al. (2000) *Deep in Our Hearts: Nine Women in the Freedom Movement*. Athens: University of Georgia Press.

Davis, Angela Y. (1981) *Women, Race and Class*. New York: Random House.

Evans, Sara (1980) *Personal Politics: The Roots of Women's Liberation in the Civil Rights Movement and the New Left*. New York: Vintage Books.

Eyes on the Prize – America's Civil Rights Years, Awakenings, 1954–56. (1986) Documentary film. Boston: Blackside/PBS-TV.

Fleming, Cynthia Griggs (1998) *Soon We Will Not Cry: The Liberation of Ruby Doris Smith Robinson*. Lanham, MD: Rowman and Littlefield.

Franklin, John Hope and Moss, Alfred A. (1994) *From Slavery to Freedom: A History of African Americans*, 7th ed. New York: McGraw-Hill.

Garrow, David (ed.) (1987) *The Montgomery Bus Boycott and the Women Who Started It: The Memoir of Jo Ann Gibson Robinson*. Knoxville: University of Tennessee Press.

Giddings, Paula (1984) *When and Where I Enter: The Impact of Black Women on Race and Sex in America*. New York: William Morrow.

Gilmore, Glenda Elizabeth (1996) *Gender and Jim Crow: Women and the Politics of White Supremacy in North Carolina, 1896–1920*. Chapel Hill: University of North Carolina Press.

Grant, Joanne (1998) *Ella Baker: Freedom Bound*. New York: John Wiley and Sons.

Greenberg, Cheryl (1998) *A Circle of Trust: Remembering SNCC*. New Brunswick, NJ: Rutgers University Press.

Halberstam, David (1998) *The Children*. New York: Random House.

Hall, Jacquelyn Dowd (1979) *Revolt Against Chivalry: Jessie Daniel Ames and the Women's Campaign Against Lynching*. New York: Columbia University Press.

Hewitt, Nancy A. (2001) *Southern Discomfort: Women's Activism in Tampa, Florida, 1880s–1920s*. Urbana: University of Illinois Press.

Hunter Gault, Charlayne (1992) *In My Place*. New York: Farrar, Straus, and Giroux.

King, Mary (1987) *Freedom Song: A Personal Story of the 1960s Civil Rights Movement*. New York: William Morrow.

Kirk, John A. (1999) "Daisy Bates, the National Association for the Advancement of Colored People, and the 1957 Little Rock School Crisis," in Peter J. Ling and Sharon Monteith (eds.), *Gender in the Civil Rights Movement*. New York: Garland Publishing, pp. 17–40.

Lawson, Steven F. (1997) *Running for Freedom: Civil Rights and Black Politics in America since 1941*, 2nd ed. New York: McGraw-Hill.

Lee, Chana Kai (1999) *For Freedom's Sake: The Life of Fannie Lou Hamer*. Urbana: University of Illinois Press.

Lewis, Abigail Sara (1999) "The Role of the Young Women's Christian Association in Shaping the Gender Consciousness of the Student Non-violent Coordinating Committee, 1960–1965," M.A. thesis, University of California, Los Angeles.

Ling, Peter J. (1999) "Gender and Generation: Manhood in the Southern Christian Leadership Conference," in Peter J. Ling and Sharon Monteith (eds.), *Gender in the Civil Rights Movement*. New York: Garland Publishing, pp. 101–30.

Ling, Peter J. and Monteith, Sharon (eds.) (1999) *Gender in the Civil Rights Movement*. New York: Garland Publishing.

Loveland, Anne C. (1986) *Lillian Smith: A Southerner Confronting the South*. Baton Rouge: Louisiana State University Press.

Lynn, Susan (1992) *Progressive Women in Conservative Times: Racial Justice, Peace, and Feminism, 1945 to the 1960s*. New Brunswick, NJ: Rutgers University Press.

McFadden, Grace Jordan (1990) "Septima P. Clark and the Struggle for Human Rights," in Vicki Crawford, Jacqueline Anne Rouse, and Barbara Woods (eds.), *Women in the Civil Rights Movement: Trailblazers and Torchbearers, 1941–1965*. Brooklyn: Carlson Publishing, pp. 85–97.

Meyerowitz, Joanne (1993) "Beyond the Feminine Mystique: A Reassessment of Postwar Mass Culture, 1946–1958," *Journal of American History* 79, pp. 1455–82.

Mills, Kay (1993) *This Little Light of Mine: The Life of Fannie Lou Hamer*. New York: Dutton.

Moody, Anne (1968) *Coming of Age in Mississippi*. New York: Dell Publishing.

Morris, Aldon (1984) *The Origins of the Civil Rights Movement*. New York: Free Press.

Murray, Pauli (1989) *Pauli Murray: The Autobiography of a Black Activist, Feminist, Lawyer, Priest, and Poet*. Knoxville: University of Tennessee Press.

Nasstrom, Kathryn L. (1999) "Down to Now: Memory, Narrative, and Women's Leadership in the Civil Rights Movement in Atlanta, Georgia," *Gender and History* 11, pp. 113–44.

Norman, Martha Prescod (1997) "Shining in the Dark: Black Women and the Struggle for the Vote, 1955–1965," in Ann Gordon, with Bettye Collier-Thomas et al. (eds.), *African American Women and the Vote, 1837–1965*. Amherst: University of Massachusetts Press, pp. 172–99.

Parks, Rosa, with Jim Haskins (1992) *My Story*. New York: Dial Books.

Payne, Charles (1990) "Men Led, But Women Organized: Movement Participation of Women in the Mississippi Delta," in Vicki Crawford, Jacqueline Anne Rouse, and Barbara Woods (eds.), *Women in the Civil Rights Movement: Trailblazers and Torchbearers, 1941–1965*. Brooklyn: Carlson Publishing, pp. 1–11.

Raines, Howell L. (1977) *My Soul is Rested: Movement Days in the Deep South Remembered*. New York: G. P. Putnam's Sons.

Ransby, Barbara (2003) *Ella Baker and the Black Freedom Movement: A Radical Democratic Vision*. Chapel Hill: University of North Carolina Press.

Robnett, Belinda (1997) *How Long? How Long? African-American Women and the Struggle for Freedom and Justice*. New York: Oxford University Press.

Rossinow, Doug (1998) *The Politics of Authenticity: Liberalism, Christianity, and the New Left in America*. New York: Columbia University Press.

Schultz, Deborah L. (2001) *Going South: Jewish Women in the Civil Rights Movement*. New York: New York University Press.

Spritzer, Lorraine Nelson and Bergmark, Jean B. (1997) *Grace Towns Hamilton and the Politics of Southern Change*. Athens: University of Georgia Press.

Sullivan, Patricia (1996) *Days of Hope: Race and Democracy in the New Deal Era*. Chapel Hill: University of North Carolina Press.

Taylor, Ula Y. (2000) "Negro Women are Great Thinkers as Well as Doers: Amy Jacques-Garvey and Community Feminism," *Journal of Women's History* 12, pp. 104–26.

Trillin, Calvin (1964) *An Education in Georgia*. New York: Viking Press.

White, Deborah Gray (1999) *Too Heavy a Load: Black Women in Defense of Themselves, 1894–1994*. New York: W. W. Norton.

Woods, Barbara A. (1990) "Modjeska Simkins and the South Carolina Conference of the NAACP, 1939–1957," in Vicki Crawford, Jacqueline Anne Rouse, and Barbara Woods (eds.), *Women in the Civil Rights Movement: Trailblazers and Torchbearers, 1941–1965*. Brooklyn: Carlson Publishing, pp. 99–120.

Chapter Twenty-Four

Second-wave Feminism

Rosalyn Baxandall and Linda Gordon

THE women's movement of the 1960s and 1970s was the largest social movement in the history of the United States. Its impact has been felt in every home, school, and business, in every form of entertainment and sport, in all aspects of personal and public life. Like a river overflowing its banks and seeking a new course, it permanently altered the American landscape.

The "second-wave" US women's movement emerged in the late 1960s in two separate streams, with two distinct sets of roots. The first branch, which we call here the equal rights tendency, derived in part from women's activist networks during the New Deal and World War II. Although few women were raising gender issues at that time, some female leaders both in and outside the government were active in social justice and human welfare campaigns. Within the Communist Party, which was itself a large-scale social movement in the 1930s and 1940s, women were disproportionately active in struggles for better housing, day care, consumer rights, and union representation. At the time the Communist Party was the *only* political arena in which women were criticizing what was then called male chauvinism and calling for sex equality. Even at the nadir of McCarthyist repression in the 1950s, many of these progressive women remained active in union and local community campaigns.

Individual women had continued politically active within the two main parties, mainly the Democratic. In 1961 this network persuaded President Kennedy, as a payback for their active support in the very close election of 1960, to establish a Presidential Commission on the Status of Women. It was chaired by Eleanor Roosevelt, herself both a symbolic and a real continuity with first-wave feminism and the New Deal. Women's Bureau chief Esther Peterson served as vice-chair. Kennedy may have expected this commission, like so many others, to keep the women busy talking and out of his hair. But the commission began an ongoing process. Its report, issued in 1963, called for equal pay for *comparable* work (in other words, it understood that equal pay for equal work would not be adequate because jobs were so sex-segregated), childcare services, paid maternity leave, and many other measures still not achieved. Determined not to let its momentum stall or its message reach only small elite circles, the commission built a network among many existing women's organizations, made special efforts to include black women, and convinced Kennedy to establish two continuing federal committees. Most consequential, it stimulated the creation of state women's commissions, created in every state by 1967. The network that formed through these commissions enabled the creation of the National Organization for Women (NOW) in 1966.

Modeled on the National Association for the Advancement of Colored People (NAACP), NOW focused particularly on equal rights for women, in the law and in employment. Although the creation of NOW is often attributed to Betty Friedan, whose bestseller *The Feminine Mystique* (1963) captured the experience of white, suburban, college-educated women, NOW included significant working-class and minority leadership. NOW's founders included black lawyer and minister Pauli Murray, labor union women like Dorothy Haener of the United Auto Workers (UAW) and Addie Wyatt of the Amalgamated Meatcutters, and Betty Friedan, who brought her Old Left and union experience. African American Aileen Hernandez was NOW's second president. NOW's first headquarters was provided by the UAW. Nevertheless, NOW, like other parts of the women's movement, was at first dominated by white middle-class women. After a successful internal affirmative action effort, black and Latina women made up one-third of NOW's national staff and leadership by the mid-1990s.

Primarily an organization representing adult professional women and a few male feminists, NOW did not at first attempt to build a mass movement. Thirty women had attended its founding conference, three hundred its second conference, but from the start NOW effectively created and used the impression that it could mobilize a mass power base – an impression which became reality. At the peak of the campaign for the Equal Rights Amendment (ERA), NOW had approximately 250,000 members in six hundred chapters in all fifty states and the District of Columbia. NOW concentrated heavily on employment issues, reflecting its close ties to the US Women's Bureau – Catherine East of the Women's Bureau and Mary Eastwood of the Justice Department were among NOW's twenty-eight founders. NOW litigated pioneering class-action lawsuits against sex discrimination in employment and campaigned to elect women to local and national political offices. Its members used their professional and political skills to exert pressure upwards to elected or appointed officials.

NOW's initial impetus was anger that the Equal Employment Opportunity Commission (EEOC) was not enforcing the sex-discrimination provisions of the Civil Rights Act of 1964, and it got some immediate results: in 1967 President Johnson issued Executive Order 11375 prohibiting sex discrimination by federal contractors. In the same year, NOW forced the EEOC to rule that sex-segregated want ads were discriminatory (although newspapers ignored this ruling with impunity for years). NOW's legal committee, composed of four high-powered Washington lawyers, three of them federal employees, brought suits against protective legislation which, in the name of protecting women's fragility, in fact kept them out of better jobs. (In arguing one case, the five-foot one-hundred-pound lawyer picked up the equipment which the company claimed was too heavy for women and carried it around with one hand as she argued to the jury.)

NOW's most extensive grassroots campaign was the struggle for an Equal Rights Amendment. Approved by Congress in 1972, this proposed twenty-seventh amendment was ratified only by thirty-five of the required thirty-eight states, thus failing despite endorsement by both major political parties and despite popular approval, which never fell below 54 percent. The "Stop-ERA" campaign was headed by Phyllis Schlafly and generously funded by conservative groups and corporations that stood to lose if the amendment were passed (such as the insurance industry, whose rates discriminated against women). It represented a growing and tightly organized anti-feminist backlash, which was able to wield power disproportionate to its public support.

Just as NOW arose from New Deal Democrats and the Old Left, so women's liberation, the other stream in the revival of feminism, arose from civil rights and the New Left. By the late 1960s, there was a sense of unity among radical campaigns for social justice, expressed in the way participants referred collectively to "the movement," singular. Reflecting the context of relative prosperity, its mood was optimistic, even at times utopian; its members as often from the middle class as from the poor or working class, it was equally critical of commercialization and conformity as of poverty. Its implicit motto was to challenge received wisdoms and hierarchical authorities. It was quintessentially a movement of young people, and it was correspondingly impatient. In dress, in sexual behavior, in its favorite intoxicants, and above all in its beloved music, it distinguished itself sharply from grown-ups.

Within this movement, some women began to examine power relations in areas that the movement's male leaders had not considered relevant to radical politics. The women's self-examination uncovered a deep well of grievances about men's power over women inside this very movement. Women in civil rights, the New Left, and the anti-Vietnam War movement were on the whole less victimized, more respected, and less romanticized than they were in the mainstream culture or the counterculture. But despite women's passionate and disciplined work for social change, they remained typically far less visible and less powerful than the men who dominated the meetings and the press conferences. Women came into greater prominence wherever grassroots organizing went on, as in voter registration in the South and the Students for a Democratic Society (SDS) community projects in northern and midwestern cities. Throughout the civil rights and student movements, women proved themselves typically the better organizers: of course some men excelled and some women did not, but on average women's greater ability to listen and to connect allowed them to reach across class and even race lines, to seek out potential activists, to persevere despite failure and lack of encouragement. Still, they experienced galling frustrations and humiliations. Everywhere and in every organization women were responsible for keeping records, producing leaflets, telephoning, cleaning offices, cooking, organizing social events, and catering to the egos of male leaders, while the men wrote manifestos, talked to the press, negotiated with officials, and made public speeches. This division of labor did not arise from misogyny or acrimony. It was "natural," or so it seemed to most women as well as men – until for some women it began to seem no longer natural at all.

The second branch of the women's movement, known as women's liberation, arose from a rebellion of these civil rights and New Left women. It developed a style, constituency, and politics different from those of NOW: these women were younger, mostly in their twenties, and less professional; they insisted on woman-only, autonomous groups; and they were radical in the sense of working for structural change and skeptical that conventional politics could achieve it. Women's liberation sought not just to redistribute wealth and power in the existing society, but to challenge the private as well as the public, the psychological as well as the economic, the cultural as well as the legal sources of male dominance. Emerging from male-dominated grassroots social justice movements, women's liberation groups formed in 1967 and 1968, and soon attracted women without previous activist experience.

This movement's most important organizational and theoretical contribution was consciousness raising (CR), a form of structured discussion in which women connected their personal experiences to larger structures of gender. Through CR women developed the understanding that many of their "personal" problems – insecurity about appearance and intelligence, exhaustion, physical and sexual abuse – were not individual failings but a result of discrimination. These discussion groups, usually small, sprung up throughout the country among women of all ages and social positions, and they were simultaneously supportive and transforming. Women formed these groups by the hundreds, then by the thousands. Mentions of the women's movement in the national press increased ten times in the ten months from May 1969 to March 1970.

The earliest forms of protest were agitprop: spreading the word through leaflets, pamphlets, letters to newspapers; pasting stickers onto sexist advertisements; verbally protesting being called "girl" or "baby" or "chick"; hollering at guys making vulgar proposals on the streets. Community women's schools were a typical early project of women's liberation groups, offering courses ranging from auto mechanics to de Beauvoir, from Marxism to wicca, from karate to prepared childbirth. Housework was the subject of a great deal of analysis: feminists demanded recognition of housework as labor that could be shared by all members of a household. Soon action groups supplemented and, in some cases, replaced CR groups. Women pressured employers to provide daycare centers, publicized job and school discrimination, opened women's centers and women's schools, agitated for women's studies courses at colleges. Feminist scholarship, once considered illegitimate or even an oxymoron, evolved into a rich and extensive range of intellectual work with conferences, journals, and prizes in virtually all humanities and social science fields. The clerical workers' union 9 to 5 emerged from a socialist feminist organizing campaign. The bestseller *Our Bodies, Ourselves*, which had sold 4.5 million copies in many countries by 1995, emerged from one CR group's critique of sexist medical practices. Feminist skepticism about male-dominated medical practice led to a women's health movement whose victories included the acceptance of alternative childbirth practices involving the use of midwives, birth without anesthesia, and women's right to have partners as coaches in labor and delivery. Women's liberation also revolutionized the common understanding of rape and domestic violence, creating crisis hotlines and shelters, and forcing law enforcement agencies to stop blaming rape and battering victims.

Although black women in civil rights inspired women's liberation in many ways, and although women's liberationists were committed to fighting racism, nevertheless women's liberation was overwhelmingly white. Awareness of this problem did not make it solvable. Good intentions were not enough. Women of color rarely joined, in some cases because they had not been invited and in some cases because they were offended by the whiteness of the agenda as well as the membership. Most white women simply did not see the whiteness of their outlook. Most early CR tended to produce generalizations and even theories about women's oppression which were actually particular to privileged, white, college-educated women. These included antagonism toward the family, which was a traditional refuge from racism for people of color, and idealization of paid work as liberatory, which ignored the fact that poverty and discrimination drove so many women of color into low-paying, monotonous, even dangerous jobs.

But women of color were not latecomers to feminism; rather, they often developed autonomous women's groups from autonomous roots. Within a variety of civil rights organizations – Puerto Rican, Chicano/a, Asian American, and Native American as well as African American – women formed caucuses and persuaded their organizations to include sex oppression and inequality among their concerns. For example, by 1972 women in the Young Lords Party, a militant Puerto Rican group, managed to get the organization to adopt a strongly feminist position paper which condemned *machismo*, violence against women, the belief that women should stay in the home; it also condemned the coercive sterilization program imposed on Puerto Rican women and demanded legal abortion.

After several years the movement grew and, in growing, divided into different theoretical/political tendencies. The women's liberation side further developed its critique of liberal feminism – that seeking equality for women within the existing social and political system was inadequate, that the whole system should become more democratic and participatory. Women's liberation was critical of electoral politics and the lack of choice between the two major parties, and sought social change through changing consciousness. They used media-grabbing theatrical stunts and guerrilla theater, as well as picketing and demonstrations, to provoke changes in consciousness. These provocative actions did not often result in lasting structural change. The younger women's liberation activists lacked the patience of the older NOW insiders, who were prepared for a slower pace of change.

Division also arose within women's liberation. Those committed to a broad New Left agenda typically called themselves socialist feminists (to be distinguished from Marxist feminists, who remained convinced that Marxist theory could explain women's oppression and were not committed to an autonomous women's movement). Socialist feminists weighed issues of race and class equally with those of gender and tried to develop an integrated, holistic theory of the society. Radical feminists, by contrast, prioritized sexual oppression, although they by no means ignored other forms of domination. The radical/socialist opposition is often overstated, but small theoretical differences seemed important at the time. Separatists, often but not exclusively lesbians, attempted to create self-sustaining female communities and to withdraw their energies as much as possible from contact with men. In the late 1970s, some women became cultural feminists, celebrating women's specialness and difference from men and retreating from direct challenges to sexist institutions; they believed, rather, that change could come about through building exemplary female communities.

But the clarity and discreteness of these tendencies should not be exaggerated; there was cross-fertilization, none was sealed off from others, the borderlines and definitions shifted, and there were heated debates *within* tendencies. Most members of women's liberation – especially outside big cities – did not identify with any of these tendencies and considered themselves simply feminists, unmodified.

Feminists of different racial/ethnic groups established independent organizations from the beginning, and within those organizations created somewhat different feminisms. Black feminism was soon joined by Latina feminisms, Asian American feminism, Native American feminism. Feminists of color emphasized the problems with universalizing assumptions about women and with identifying gender as a category autonomous from race and class. Theoretical differences between these feminisms have sometimes been overstated, however, and feminists of color were not more unanimous than white feminists – there were, for example, black liberal feminists, black socialist feminists, black radical feminists, black cultural feminists. But virtually all feminists of color experienced racism within the women's movement. The majority of feminists, white women of middle-class backgrounds, were often oblivious to the lives of women from minority and working-class families.

Critiques of racism from feminists of color precipitated creative expansion of feminist thought and the feminist agenda. For example, many African American feminists have explored Alice Walker's 1983 concept of womanism. Walker originally intended the term to refer to audacious and courageous behavior and commitment to the survival and wholeness of the entire African American people, male and female. Gradually the term was being used by many feminists of color to call attention to differences among women, the multiple axes of women's oppression and strength, and the multiple identities that are united in every individual woman. African American feminism helped generate a spectacular flowering of black women's writing and the recovery of earlier black female artists. Chicana feminism gave rise to an exquisite development of Mexican and Mexican American mural painting. Women of color tended to link issues of race, reproductive rights, and economic injustice, thereby contributing to the feminist project.

The development of lesbian theory and politics was inseparable from the feminist movement. Feminists did not invent lesbianism, but women's liberation did open up protected space and opportunity for exploring a new dimension of relationships with women. Coming out is not always a process of leaping from one identity to another; in fact, the supportive women's movement context made it possible for women to try out new sexual and emotional options and to resist being straitjacketed into a fixed category. Lesbian feminists, and later also bisexual and transgender feminists, contributed much to heterosexual feminists by challenging conventional heterosexual norms, such as conceiving of "the" sex act as missionary position intercourse.

Lesbians sometimes created separate feminist groups, but gay–straight discord has been exaggerated. Although some NOW leaders feared that openly lesbian members would discredit the respectability of the movement, soon the NOW majority came to back gay rights unequivocally, notably helping to litigate on behalf of lesbian mothers' custody rights. As lesbians became more open and vocal, they identified and protested the heterosexual assumptions of many straight feminists, but they were also discriminated against by sexism in the male-dominated gay movement. For the most part, lesbians continued to be active in women's liberation and frequently made important contributions to feminist theory. Lesbians also often participated in and even led campaigns of primary concern to heterosexual women, such as reproductive rights.

Although the majority of feminists were secular, religious feminists played a significant role in the movement. In American Catholicism, Protestantism, and Judaism, women struggled for a feminist theology and for changes in hierarchies and practices, against heavy odds. Womanist theology called for an androgynous view of God and Jesus, gender-neutral language in liturgy, and ceremonies that addressed women's unique experiences. Religious feminists agitated for the inclusion of women as ministers, priests, and rabbis. In fact, spiritual feminists reinvented a number of unorthodox beliefs and practices, such as witchcraft, which women tried to rescue from stigma and to turn into practices that put women in charge.

At the beginning of the movement, feminists tended to create multi-issue organizations, which in turn might create committees to focus on single issues, such as day care, rape, or running a women's center. By the mid-1970s feminist politics was occurring primarily in single-issue organizations focused on, for example, reproductive rights, employment discrimination, health, domestic violence, women's studies. An expanded reproductive rights campaign asserted women's rights to bear children in safe and healthy circumstances as well as to choose not to give birth, so the movement saw day care and child welfare as equal in importance to birth control. The Reproductive Rights National Network (known as R2N2) succeeded in restricting the then widespread practice of coercive sterilization. It investigated and documented thousands of cases of forced sterilization, especially of people of color; of welfare recipients threatened with cutoffs of stipends unless they submitted to sterilization; and of women asked to sign sterilization consent forms while in labor, either in pain or partly anesthetized. In 1974, responding to women's movement pressure, the US Department of Health, Education, and Welfare issued guidelines that required informed consent and prohibited sterilization of women under twenty-one. Although it took over a decade to bring most hospitals into compliance with these guidelines, the R2N2 campaign eventually reduced sterilization abuse significantly.

Whereas reproductive rights tended to create unity among feminists, another issue – pornography – illustrated vividly how deep feminist divisions could be. In 1976 West Coast feminists organized Women Against Violence Against Women (WAVAW) to protest advertising and entertainment imagery featuring abuse of women and suggesting that women liked it. One of WAVAW's first targets was a Rolling Stone record cover and billboard, "I'm Black and Blue from the Rolling Stones and I Like It," showing an ecstatic woman bound and beaten. WAVAW used direct action – demonstrations, a mass letter-writing campaign, painting new slogans on top of ads – and forced Warner/Elektra/Atlantic Records to eliminate this image and to agree not to use other such images. As the anti-violence campaign spread it mutated, targeting porn in general instead of violence and arguing that even nonviolent porn was itself abusive of women. A new organization, Women Against Pornography (WAP), called for state intervention in the form of zoning and censorship laws, rather than direct action and consciousness raising. As a result of these positions, WAP leaders found natural allies among conservatives who were anti-feminist on most issues. Another sector of feminists opposed this strategy and organized the Feminists Against Censorship Taskforce (FACT). By the early 1980s, the disagreements were so hot and hardened that they became known as the "porn wars."

Contrary to the stereotype that the women's movement focused exclusively on sexual issues, feminists in many parts of the country generated a great deal of activism focused on economic, bread-and-butter problems of employed women. Women's wages, which were about 59 percent of men's when women's liberation emerged, were actually losing ground in the 1950s. By 1993 women's wages reached 77 percent of men's, and among unionized workers, women have gained even more equity, earning 84 percent of men's wages on average. Unfortunately, some of women's gains are more apparent than real, resulting from the fact that men's real wages (i.e., wages expressed in terms of actual buying power) have been declining.

Much of the wage decline results from the weakening of labor unions, a decline that would be worse if the women's movement had not reenergized organizing. Unions had shown relatively little interest in organizing clerical and service workers until the civil rights and women's movements pushed them, from both within and without unions. The women's movement initiated organizing projects among clerical workers, bank tellers, janitors, healthcare workers, waitresses, stewardesses, communication workers, and other groups. The movement was particularly successful with clerical workers, because so much of the feminist constituency was employed in that sector. In New York there was WOW (Women Office Workers), in Chicago WE (Women Employed), and in the Bay Area Union WAGE (Women's Alliance to Gain Equality). Today the best-known union of clerical workers is 9 to 5, which grew out of Boston's socialist feminist women's union, Bread and Roses. Using the slogan "Raises not Roses," 9 to 5 published an "office workers' bill of rights," demanding equal pay and promotion opportunities, detailed job descriptions, maternity benefits, overtime pay, and the right to refuse to do personal errands for the employer. The phrase "9 to 5" and the idea behind it gained such prominence that clerical workers' rebellion was featured in a Hollywood hit movie starring Jane Fonda, Dolly Parton, and Lili Tomlin. Its success rested on retaining its independent identity as a women's movement organization even after it joined the AFL-CIO. Like clerical workers, flight attendants became particularly critical of the discriminatory and exploitive aspects of their jobs, which required appearance and weight checks, excluded women of color, fired employees who reached thirty or got married, and advertised stewardesses' looks in ways that invited sexual harassment. Their victories are evident on airplanes today, where there are flight attendants of both sexes and all sizes and appearances; less visibly, they have also won better health benefits, wages, and schedules.

In 1974, 3,200 women from fifty-eight different unions met in Chicago to found the Coalition of Labor Union Women (CLUW). For a brief time CLUW had chapters in many cities, trained women for union leadership, and pressured unions to include women in apprenticeship programs, to make childcare a priority, to fight sexual harassment, to support abortion rights and the ERA. CLUW was largely responsible for transforming the labor movement's family policy from one which had stubbornly assumed the family wage – i.e., that male workers single-handedly supported wives and children – to an approach that recognized women's employment as the norm. In 1986, CLUW promulgated a family bill of rights, arguing that workers and their families should be entitled to jobs and economic security, health-care, child and elder care, family leave, services for the elderly, education, equal opportunity, pay equity, shelter, and a work and home environment safe from health hazards.

In fact, sexual issues, sometimes labeled as exclusively of interest to middle-class women, have been a central and enduring concern of working women. Whenever women have been employed or active outside their homes, they have been vulnerable to unwelcome sexual advances; working women have been protesting such treatment for centuries, as far back as the 1840s, when the Lowell mill "girls" objected to harassment by foremen. But the range of behaviors included in this category – from whistles to "compliments" on women's figures, to indecent exposure and grabbing women, to demanding sex in return for favors – would previously have been considered harmless boys-will-be-boys play, flirtation, or even flattery. There had been little progress before the second-wave women's movement, and working women had little recourse against sexual aggression by co-workers and bosses except to seek other work. In popular literature, sexual harassment was treated as a joke. The actress who "succeeds" by means of the casting couch, the "Fly Me" airline stewardess, and other stereotypes permeated American/male humor.

In 1970, women's liberation advocates in several locales conducted "Ogle-Ins," turning the tables on the guys by directing whistles, animal noises, and evaluations of sexual organs against obnoxious men, even grabbing crotches. Los Angeles feminists were provoked into action by an official Chamber of Commerce "Girl-watching Week." Activists carried tape measures, shouted "too small" and "Hey, fella, can you type, file and make coffee?" In May 1975, Working Women United in Ithaca, New York, held the first Speak-out on Sexual Harassment. At this extraordinary public event women who had never dared complain before – waitresses, administrators, clerks, factory workers, an assistant professor, a filmmaker – told of receiving threats, obscenities, propositions to barter sex for jobs. Civil rights and feminist activist Eleanor Holmes Norton, then New York City's Commissioner on Human Rights, included testimony on sexual harassment in public hearings she was conducting on sex discrimination in employment, and it was because of her doing so that the national press first reported on the issue. Among the first sexual harassment cases to reach the federal courts were those brought by African American women. The consciousness raised in such campaigns made possible Anita Hill's dramatic protest in US Senate hearings in 1991 and the nationwide support she received from women of all groups. It made it possible as well for women in the armed forces to speak out against sexual harassment today.

One of the movement's most ambitious campaigns was in pursuit of pay equity, once known as "comparable worth." By the late 1970s, feminists were aware that the

Equal Pay Act of 1963 and Title VII of the Civil Rights Act of 1964 had failed to equalize male and female wages. It became clear that, because the labor force was so "sexegated," and female jobs were so consistently undervalued, a new strategy was needed. The comparable worth strategy called for equal wages for work of comparable expertise, even when the jobs were different. For example, truck drivers earned much more than registered nurses, whose training and responsibility were so much greater. Most job evaluation studies showed wage gaps of 20 to 30 percent between women and men, affecting 99 percent of women workers.

The comparable worth strategy was initially urged during World War II, when the War Labor Board reported that war-industry managers set wages not by the market but by automatically, possibly even unthinkingly, inflating the value of men's over women's jobs. In the 1970s, the women's movement reopened a challenge to this discrimination through litigation, collective bargaining, and state legislation. This pressure was used in 1979 by Eleanor Holmes Norton, then head of the EEOC, to call for using job evaluations to remedy women's low wages. Unfortunately her successor, Clarence Thomas, opposed even the consideration of comparable worth claims. Although some substantial victories were won in state and union battles – for example, the American Federation of State, County, and Municipal Employees (AFSCME) won wage increases averaging 32 percent and back pay retroactive to 1979 for Washington state employees, 35,000 of whom shared a $482 million settlement – the comparable worth campaign slowed at the end of the century.

Although women's liberationists had little faith in making social change through the electoral process, the equal rights segment of the movement devoted substantial time, energy, and resources to get more women into government. Myriad local, state, and national women's groups promoted female candidates and male candidates who favored a feminist agenda; they tried to defeat anti-feminist politicians; they raised funds, lobbied, and established think tanks; they constructed women's caucuses in Congress and the state legislatures. Women are hardly disinterested in politics. Since 1964 the number of female voters has exceeded the number of male voters in every presidential election. The sex difference in voter turnout rates is greatest among African Americans but holds true for Hispanics and whites as well.

Still, the obstacles are formidable. Perhaps the biggest is the increasing dependence of candidates on expensive media campaigns and therefore on corporate wealth. By and large women have less access to this kind of money, not only because of direct sexism but also because they tend to be more progressive (whether they are Democrats or Republicans) and because they often prioritize different concerns, such as peace, the environment, education, health, housing, and welfare. (Of all public officials, African American women were the most liberal and the most likely to belong to feminist organizations.) The women's movement encouraged women to run for office but could not free women candidates from the sexism of the public gaze. Women in politics have to tread a razor-thin line between appearing too tough or not tough enough, too feminine or not feminine enough, too family-centered or not devoted enough to family. In January 2001, a record 10 percent of the state governors, 13 percent of US Senators, and 13.56 percent of Representatives in the

US House were female. If the proportion of women continued to grow at the current rate, it would take three hundred years to achieve parity. Women have done somewhat better on state and local levels, where huge war chests are not as essential. Twenty-two percent of state legislators are women, but even here it would take fifty years to achieve equality with men. Women's representation in government puts the United States approximately on a par with Iraq. But women's voting power has encouraged some male politicians to adopt "women's issues."

As the movement grew to encompass so many facets of life – home, workplace, love, sex, health, school – emphasis on single-issue campaigns seemed the most expedient way to change sexist practice because it facilitated making broad coalitions. However, single-issue politics tended to deemphasize theory. This approach reduced divisions and had the advantage of making coalitions easier, but it ceded feminist theory construction to academics often divorced from activism. The coalitions and compromises necessitated by single-issue politics made the movement less radical and more practical. Single-issue politics also, of course, lessened the movement's coherence as activists became specialized and sometimes professionalized. But stable organizations with paid staff meant that feminist lobbying could become more continuous, that expertise and contacts could be passed down, that women could be trained and could earn their livings in the political realm.

A coherent mass women's movement began to weaken by the end of the 1970s. Some of this decline was inevitable, because mass social movements never have a long life – they require such intensity of participation that they produce burnout. Moreover, in a movement largely driven by youth, the natural aging process pulls activists into professions, family life, or simply into a more stable and quieter lifestyle. And it was difficult for feminism to thrive outside the context of other progressive social movements, some of which also declined precipitously in the mid-1970s. As a new generation of women emerged into adulthood, they quite naturally took for granted many of the gains made by the previous generation and no longer thought they needed a women's movement. The women's liberation stream, moreover, was temperamentally and ideologically opposed to structure, centralization, and hierarchy and as a result did not develop enduring organizations.

Above all, second-wave feminism underestimated the backlash that its very successes provoked. Always concentrating on what remained to be achieved instead of what had already been accomplished, most of its activists did not grasp how radical and deeply disturbing to many people were the social and personal changes it was initiating. Still, although anti-feminist conservatives found a fertile field in which to win followers, their primary strength came from extraordinary levels of funding and unified organization, which allowed them to saturate the public with their messages. They did not convert many feminists to conservatism, but they moved the mainstream far to the right and forced the women's movement onto the defensive until at least the end of the century.

The most protracted anti-feminist campaign has been against abortion. Its first major victory was discursive: redefining the anti-abortion cause as "right to life" and focusing on the "unborn" helped mobilize massive evangelical Protestant and

Catholic support among people who would not have been comfortable directly challenging women's freedom to choose. Since then it has won many other victories: limiting *Roe v. Wade* through state legislation and judicial decisions which restrict abortion in many ways; prohibiting the use of public funds for abortion both in the United States and in US aid programs abroad; terrorizing clinics and even murdering doctors, which has radically reduced the availability of abortion; preventing medical schools from teaching abortion techniques; keeping RU486 (a non-surgical method of abortion) off the market. Perhaps its biggest victory has been to prevent the women's movement from moving forward on its agenda into other issues.

Right to life was part of a larger new religious Right, which has been able to change political discourse through its focus on "family values." The particularly vehement condemnation of single motherhood allowed a coded attack on poor women, particularly poor women of color and welfare mothers; on lesbians; on career women; and on sexual permissiveness, typically characterized as women's promiscuity. Liberal television and Hollywood have received particularly strong denunciation, as for example in vice-presidential candidate Dan Quayle's 1992 attack on the popular comedian Murphy Brown when she chose to have a child on her own. The historic repeal of Aid to Families with Dependent Children in 1996, making the United States the only economically developed nation to provide no guarantee of help to poor children and their caretakers, was made possible by the vilification of poor single mothers and the racist underpinnings of that portrayal.

The anti-feminist backlash depended on vast funding from right-wing corporate fortunes, fervent support from religious fundamentalists, and considerable media attention. The intensity of the reaction is a measure of how threatened conservatives were by popular backing for women's liberation and the rapid changes it brought about. Even with their billions of dollars, hundreds of lobbyists and public relations men, and whole foundations and magazines dishing out anti-feminist misinformation, compared to the puny amounts of money and volunteer labor available to women's liberation, the striking fact is that public opinion has not shifted much. Although the term "feminist" has been discredited among some groups, polls show overwhelming support for feminist positions on key issues.

Although second-wave feminism arose in a context of anti-imperialist consciousness and conflicts, and although many early US feminists supported anti-colonial struggles (in Vietnam, Cuba, southern Africa, and Ireland, for example), most US feminists remained insular and parochial in their understanding and their agenda. First-wave feminists built links primarily with European feminists, but today's women's movement connections are fully global. Facilitating the new global feminism was the United Nations declaration of 1975–85 as a "decade for women." Conferences in Mexico City (1975), Copenhagen (1980), Nairobi (1985), and Beijing (1995) adopted platforms of action, which then allowed feminist leaders from around the world to use them to pressure their own states and the private sector to advance women's rights. They focused attention, for example, on the impact of war, military occupations, civil wars, poverty, and environmental damage on women and children, and on the importance of education and citizenship to women's welfare.

These conferences, combined with increasing access to the Internet, allowed women from all over the world to create formal and informal networks bringing together those concerned with similar issues. These networks are the characteristic organizational form of transnational feminism. Third world grassroots women's activism, coordinated by networks, has fought against dowry deaths in India, genital mutilation in Africa and the Middle East, rape and "ethnic cleansing" in war zones, forced prostitution in East and Southeast Asia, and austerity programs imposed by the International Monetary Fund which forced governments to cut back on health, education, and welfare. As always, much local women's activism assumed a maternalist form, both because children are often women's highest priority and because speaking as mothers gives legitimacy to women's politics. In Argentina, women challenged the dictator through "Las Madres de Plaza de Mayo," mothers protesting the disappearance (in reality, kidnapping, torture, and murder) of their children. In Ireland, the peace campaign led by Betty Williams and Mairead Corrigan, who won the 1976 Nobel prize, rested on maternalist rhetoric. In Russia, virtually the only protest against the Chechen war came from the organized mothers of soldiers. In Israel, Women in Black jumpstarted the peace movement.

Development of local feminist leadership enabled these grassroots movements to exert significant leverage on international organizations. Women's demands have been recognized, although often only grudgingly, by official governmental organizations. Each of the UN-sponsored conferences included an official government meeting as well as a forum for nongovernmental organizations (NGOs). The powerful American philanthropic foundations, such as Ford and Rockefeller, have funded many woman-empowering projects in the third world. Examples include support of women's education, from basic literacy to women's studies programs in universities, in eastern Europe and the third world; vocational training to enable women to develop some level of economic independence; skills improvement and consciousness raising for midwives and other healthcare workers who deliver services to women; and basic public health measures, from water purification to vaccination to AIDS education.

A major accomplishment of global feminism has been in redefining the concept of human rights so as to include rights specific to women. Crimes such as rape, battering, genital mutilation, denial of education and citizenship, and sexual slavery are now being discussed as violations of human rights. The recent war crimes tribunal in the Hague, considering the atrocities of the Balkan wars, recognized rape for the first time as a war crime – a victory for women of great historical importance. As a result, the US Immigration and Naturalization Service has been forced to consider applications for political asylum that rest on violence and abuse of women. Yet feminists had not hitherto made human rights a political issue within the United States, despite the fact that this country's violations are notorious, including the disproportionate arrest and imprisonment of people of color, the high infant mortality and illness rates among the poor, capital punishment, trying children as adults, depriving the poor of healthcare, corrupt elections, and the repeal of welfare.

Starting in the 1980s, global feminisms have so proliferated that they have begun to influence the American movement and to expand American feminist consciousness to include the majority of the world's women who are poor, hungry, often illiterate, denied equal rights, and frequently the victims of violence, either military or domestic. American feminists today are less likely to think of their own experiences as universal. The globalization of feminism has helped American feminists recognize the diversity of their own country. Moreover, US feminist organizations are increasingly focused on an international agenda. For example, the Women's Economic Development Organization (WEDO) is based in New York, but its leadership group comes from all over the world and its agenda is oriented outside the United States.

American feminist scholarship has also been transformed by the new global awareness. From postcolonial studies to social indicator surveys, from film studies to evaluations of small loan programs, researchers in all fields increasingly focus their studies through international and comparative lenses. Many scholars are collaborating with other feminist scholars across national lines, and there are now books examining many specific topics – for example, prisons, reproductive rights, sex work, law, war, violence, democratization and civil society – with chapters on different parts of the world.

While thousands of women remained active in single-issue and international campaigns throughout the 1980s and 1990s, young women belonged to what some have called a postfeminist generation, that is, they took for granted and benefited from the achievements of feminism, but did not consider themselves part of an ongoing social movement. As Judith Stacey defined it, postfeminism involved the "simultaneous incorporation, revision and depoliticization of many of the central goals of second-wave feminism" (1987: 7). However, by the 1990s an increasing number of younger women were identifying themselves as part of a third wave of feminism.

The phrase "third wave" first appeared in the mid-1980s but took off after 1992. In that year one hundred young feminists met in New York and, using the name Third Wave, organized an activist network. Their first action was Freedom Ride 1992, a bus tour to register voters in poor communities of color. However, the main arena for third-wave feminism has been cultural.

Reclaiming the anger of early women's liberation, a prominent identity of the third wave is Riot Grrls, "girls who wish their gender started with a grrrrowl! . . . and . . . women who are too pissed off, unhappy, tough, geeky, or brainy to do and think what they're told" (http://garnet.berkeley.edu/~annaleen/riot.grrls.html). Riot Grrls and other zap action and affinity groups model themselves on ACT-UP, a militant, theatrical AIDS activist group. They sometimes irritate older feminists because they seem to be reinventing the wheel and rendering second-wave feminism invisible. Yet in many ways the third wave speaks in a voice remarkably similar to that of the early second wave, showing a commitment to collective action, often writing anonymously or signing with pseudonyms; the use of hyperbole, autobiographical accounts, rough and purposely nonslick design; anger at the way mass commercial culture uses women's bodies; appropriation and redefinition of negative epithets for women (bitch, cunt) to assert "girl power" – a kind of "linguistic jujitsu" (Delaney 1999: 9). They differ in their acute awareness of racial and sexual difference, in their strongly prosexual attitudes, their comfort with the term girl (rejecting the more dignified "woman" for which the second wave fought so hard), and their use of the body as a theater, even a weapon. The third wave's major forms of dissemination are the Internet and zines – do-it-yourself publications, typically xeroxed or posted on the Web. At this point it is too early to tell whether the third wave will become an influential social movement.

It is difficult to appraise the accomplishments of the women's movement because so much was changed, and so much of it was personal and cultural in addition to institutional and economic. A 1986 Gallup poll reported that one of every two white women, and two of every three women of color, identified themselves as feminists. In 1972 a *New York Times* reporter studied Hope, Indiana, and found that "Women's Lib is Either a Joke or a Bore" (or so claimed the headline), and that no woman expressed interest in the women's movement. By the end of the 1980s, the town had numerous feminist books and a librarian reported that high school students consulted women's history monographs for school essays; the library displayed a battered women's poster from Columbus, Ohio; and a local women's reading club had devoted a year to books about prominent women.

In fact, few areas of life were untouched by feminism. As regards health, for example, many physicians and hospitals have made major improvements in the treatment of women; at the turn of the twenty-first century about 50 percent of medical students are women; women successfully fought their exclusion from medical research; diseases affecting women, such as breast cancer, now receive better funding thanks to women's efforts. Feminists insisted that violence against women, previously a well-kept secret, become a public political issue; made rape, incest, battering, and sexual harassment understood as crimes; and got public funding for shelters for battered women. Due to feminist pressure, changes in education have been substantial: curricula and textbooks have been rewritten to promote equal opportunity for girls, and students in the universities have access to women's studies programs and feminist instructors. Title IX, passed in 1972 to mandate equal access to college programs, has worked a virtual revolution in sports. To cite but two examples, consider the many women's records broken in track and field, and the professional women's basketball leagues created in 1997. In supporting families, feminists organized daycare centers, developed standards and curricula for early childhood education, demanded daycare funding from government and private employers, and fought for the rights of mothers and for a decent welfare system.

Feminists also struggled for new options for women in employment. They won greater access to traditionally male occupations, from construction to professions to business. They entered and changed the unions, and have been successful at organizing previously nonunion workers such as secretaries, waitresses, hospital workers, and flight attendants. Affirmative action, typically discussed as a measure to help people of color, has actually benefited women (of all racial/ethnic groups) most. As the great majority of American women increasingly need to work for wages throughout their lives, more men are taking more responsibility for housework and childraising. Although women continue to do the bulk of that work, it is still commonplace today to see men in playgrounds, supermarkets, and PTA meetings.

America's poorest women have not shared equally in these economic gains. At the beginning of the movement, feminists in several major cities participated in and supported welfare rights campaigns, and the National Welfare Rights Organization won significant victories in prohibiting household searches, residence requirements, and cutoffs without hearings. With the conservative resurgence of the 1980s, however, poor women lost ground both in welfare and in employment: capital flight, deunionization, outsourcing, cutbacks in benefits, and increasingly authoritarian work rules and supervision have disproportionately disadvantaged women. When, as a culmination of several decades of conservative attacks, welfare was repealed in 1996, what remained of the women's movement did not prioritize the problems of poverty and increasing inequality.

Feminism changed how women look and dress and what is considered attractive. Increasing numbers of women refuse to wear the constricting, uncomfortable clothes that were required in the 1950s (although some are making a comeback) – girdles, garter belts, and stockings; tight, flimsy, pointed and high-heeled shoes; crinolines and cinch belts; tight short skirts. Beauty standards are changing so that women wearing pants, loose jackets, walking shoes, and no make-up feel attractive and are recognized by others as attractive. The Miss America pageant of 2000 earned its lowest television ratings in forty-one years. Mainstream political women such as Senator Hillary Clinton regularly wear pant suits. Women's newfound passion for athletics has made fashionable a look of health and strength, sometimes to an oppressive degree as women feel coerced to reach a new kind of thinness that is muscular and firm. A few older movie stars, such as Susan Sarandon, Olympia Dukakis, and Meryl Streep, are recognized as desirable, and women entertainers in many media and art forms are rejecting simplistic, demeaning, and passive roles, despite the reemergence of misogynist and hypersexualized entertainments. In the fine arts in general women's progress has been slower, illustrating the fallacy of assuming that the elite is less sexist than those of lesser privilege.

Even the way we speak has been altered: new words have been coined, like "sexist" and "Ms." and "gender"; many Americans are at least self-conscious about the use of "he" to mean a human, and textbooks and even sacred texts are being rewritten in inclusive language. Women are being called "women" instead of "ladies" or "girls."

Some of the biggest transformations were personal and familial, and they have been hotly contested. Indeed, even from a feminist perspective, not all of them are positive. Women's relationships with other women are more publicly valued and celebrated, even in the popular commercial media, and lesbianism is more accepted. People are marrying later and some are choosing not to marry. Most women today enter marriage or other romantic relationships with the expectation of equal partnership; since they do not always get this, women seem more willing to live singly than to put up with domineering or abusive men. More women think of marriage as only one possible option, aware that singleness and lesbianism are reasonable alternatives, and as only one aspect of life, supplementing motherhood, work, and self-fulfillment. Despite the conservative backlash, there is a growing sentiment that families come in a variety of forms.

Religion is another arena of feminist success. More women are in the pulpit than ever before: women are one-seventh of Episcopalian clergy and 45 percent of newly ordained Reform rabbis. Some of the largest divinity schools now enroll more than 22 percent women, curricula in these schools have been reshaped to include women, and many religious services now use androgynous language.

Judicial and legislative victories have been considerable, but also vulnerable to attack and erosion. These gains include the legalization of abortion in 1973, federal guidelines against coercive sterilization, rape shield laws which encourage more women to prosecute their attackers, affirmative action programs which aim to correct past discrimination, parental leave, albeit unpaid – but not, however, the Equal Rights Amendment. Feminism was one of the forces behind federal and state hate crime laws and domestic partnership laws. The Violence Against Women Act of 1994 created an unprecedented federal government bureau devoted to combating violence against women.

None of these gains is necessarily permanent. Yet despite major expenditures by foundations, journalism, and lobbying against feminist programs, compared to the small amounts of money and volunteer labor available to women's liberation, the remarkable fact is that public opinion remains strongly in favor of woman's rights and sex equality.

BIBLIOGRAPHY

Anderson, Karen (1996) *Changing Woman: A History of Racial Ethnic Women in Modern America.* New York: Oxford University Press.

Baxandall, Rosalyn and Gordon, Linda (eds.) (2000) *Dear Sisters: Dispatches from the Women's Liberation Movement.* New York: Basic Books.

Boxer, Marilyn Jacoby (1999) *When Women Ask the Questions: Creating Women's Studies in America.* Chicago: University of Chicago Press.

Brownmiller, Susan (1999) *In Our Time: Memoir of a Revolutionary.* New York: Dial Press.

Cobble, Dorothy Sue (1999) " 'A Spontaneous Loss of Enthusiasm': Workplace Feminism and the Transformation of Women's Service Jobs in the 1970s," *International Labor and Working-class History* 56, pp. 23–44.

Collins, Patricia Hill (1990) *Black Feminist Thought: Knowledge, Consciousness, and the Politics of Empowerment.* Boston: Unwin Hyman.

Davis, Flora (1991) *Moving the Mountain: The Women's Movement in America since 1960.* New York: Simon and Schuster.

Delaney, Rebekah (1999) "Girl Power: From Disruption to Consumption," *Phoebe*, pp. 1–25.

Deslippe, Dennis A. (2000) *"Rights, not Roses": Unions and the Rise of Working-class Feminism, 1945–80.* Urbana: University of Illinois Press.

DuPlessis, Rachel Blau and Snitow, Ann (eds.) (1998) *The Feminist Memoir Project.* New York: Three Rivers Press.

Echols, Alice (1989) *Daring to be Bad: Radical Feminism in America, 1967–1975.* Minneapolis: University of Minnesota Press.

Eisenstein, Hester (1983) *Contemporary Feminist Thought.* London: G. K. Hall.

Evans, Sara (1980) *Personal Politics: The Roots of Women's Liberation in the Civil Rights Movement and the New Left.* New York: Vintage Books.

Ferree, Myra Marx and Hess, Beth B. (2000) *Controversy and Coalition: The New Feminist Movement Across Four Decades of Change*, 3rd ed. New York: Routledge.

Gabin, Nancy F. (1990) *Feminism in the Labor Movement: Women and the United Auto Workers, 1935–1975.* Ithaca, NY: Cornell University Press.

García, Alma (ed.) (1997) *Chicana Feminist Thought: The Basic Historical Writings.* New York: Routledge.

Garrison, Ednie Kaeh (2000) "U.S. Feminism – Grrrl Style! Youth (Sub)Cultures and the Technologies of the Third Wave," *Feminist Studies* 26, pp. 141–70.

Harrison, Cynthia (1988) *On Account of Sex: The Politics of Women's Issues, 1945–1968.* Berkeley: University of California Press.

Hartmann, Susan M. (1989) *From Margin to Mainstream: American Women and Politics since 1960.* New York: Alfred A. Knopf.

Hine, Darlene Clark (ed.) (1990) *Black Women in U.S. History: Theory and Practice.* Vols. 9–10: *The Twentieth Century.* Brooklyn: Carlson Publishing.

Howard, Angela and Tarrant, Sasha Ranae Adams (eds.) (1997) *Anti-feminism in America: A Collection of Readings from the Literature of the Opponents to U.S. Feminism, 1948 to the Present.* New York: Garland Press.

Kaplan, Laura (1995) *The Story of Jane: The Legendary Underground Feminist Abortion Service.* Chicago: University of Chicago Press.

Luker, Kristin (1984) *Abortion and the Politics of Motherhood.* Berkeley: University of California Press.

Mathews, Donald G. and De Hart, Jane Sherron (1990) *Sex, Gender and the Politics of the ERA: A State and the Nation.* New York: Oxford University Press.

Moraga, Cherrie and Anzaldua, Gloria (eds.) (1983) *This Bridge Called My Back: Writings by Radical Women of Color.* New York: Kitchen Table Press.

Murray, Pauli (1989) *Pauli Murray: The Autobiography of a Black Activist, Feminist, Lawyer, Priest, and Poet.* Knoxville: University of Tennessee Press.

Petchesky, Rosalind Pollack (1990) *Abortion and Woman's Choice: The State, Sexuality, and Reproductive Freedom.* Boston: Northeastern University Press.

Reagan, Leslie J. (2000) "Crossing the Border for Abortion: California Activists, Mexican Clinics, and the Creation of a Feminist Public Health Agency in the 1960s," *Feminist Studies* 26, pp. 323–48.

Rosen, Ruth (2000) *The World Split Open: How the Modern Women's Movement Changed America.* New York: Viking Books.

Rossi, Alice (ed.) (1973) *The Feminist Papers.* New York: Columbia University Press.

Rowbotham, Sheila (1997) *A Century of Women: The History of Women in Britain and the US.* New York: Viking Books.

Ruíz, Vicki (1998) *From Out of the Shadows: Mexican Women in Twentieth-century America.* New York: Oxford University Press.

Ruíz, Vicki and DuBois, Ellen (eds.) (2000) *Unequal Sisters: A Multicultural Reader in U.S. Women's History*, 3rd ed. New York: Routledge.

Stacey, Judith (1987) "Sexism by a Subtler Name? Postindustrial Conditions and Postfeminist Consciousness in the Silicon Valley," *Socialist Review* 96, pp. 7–28.

Thompson, Becky (2001) *A Promise and a Way of Life: White Antiracist Activism.* Minneapolis: University of Minnesota Press.

Tobias, Sheila (1996) *Faces of Feminism.* New York: Westview.

Watkins, Bonnie and Tothchild, Nina (eds.) (1997) *In the Company of Women: Voices from the Women's Movement.* Minneapolis: University of Minnesota Press.

White, Deborah Gray (1999) *Too Heavy a Load: Black Women in Defense of Themselves, 1894–1994.* New York: W. W. Norton.

Whittier, Nancy (1995) *Feminist Generations: The Persistence of the Women's Movement.* Philadelphia: Temple University Press.

Bibliography: Selected Secondary Sources

Compiled by April de Stefano

Theory and General Interest

Abramovitz, Mimi (1988) *Regulating the Lives of Women: Social Welfare Policy from Colonial Times to the Present.* Boston: South End Press.

Aisenberg, Nadya and Harrington, Mona (1988) *Women of Academe: Outsiders in the Sacred Grove.* Amherst: University of Massachusetts Press.

Amott, Theresa and Matthei, Julie (1996) *Race, Gender and Work: A Multi-cultural Economic History of Women in the United States.* Boston: South End Press.

Anderson, Karen (1996) *Changing Woman: A History of Racial Ethnic Women in Modern America.* New York: Oxford University Press.

Apple, Rima D. and Golden, Janet (eds.) (1997) *Mothers and Motherhood: Readings in American History.* Columbus: Ohio State University Press.

Armitage, Susan and Jameson, Elizabeth (eds.) (1987) *The Women's West.* Norman: University of Oklahoma Press.

Bacon, Margaret Hope (1986) *Mothers of Feminism: The Story of Women in America.* San Francisco: Harper and Row.

Baker, Paula (1984) "The Domestication of Politics: Women and American Political Society, 1780–1920," *American Historical Review* 89, pp. 620–47.

Baron, Ava (ed.) (1991) *Work Engendered: Toward a New History of American Labor.* Ithaca, NY: Cornell University Press.

Basch, Norma (1999) *Framing American Divorce: From the Revolutionary Generation to the Victorians.* Berkeley: University of California Press.

Bay, Mia (2000) *The White Image in the Black Mind: African-American Ideas about White People, 1830–1925.* New York: Oxford University Press.

Bercaw, Nancy (ed.) (2000) *Gender and the Southern Body Politic.* Jackson: University of Mississippi Press.

Berebitsky, Julie (2000) *Like Our Very Own: Adoption and the Changing Culture of Motherhood, 1851–1950.* Lawrence: University Press of Kansas.

Berkhofer, Jr., Robert (1978) *The White Man's Indian: Images of the American Indian from Columbus to the Present.* New York: Alfred A. Knopf.

Berkin, Carol and Norton, Mary Beth (1979a) *The Myth of the Golden Age in Women of America: A History.* Boston: Houghton Mifflin.

Berkin, Carol and Norton, Mary Beth (eds.) (1979b) *Women of America: Original Essays and Documents.* Boston: Houghton Mifflin.

Brodkin, Karen (1998) *How Jews Became White Folks and What That Says about Race in America.* New Brunswick, NJ: Rutgers University Press.

Brown, Elsa Barkley (1989a) "African-American Women's Quilting: A Framework for Conceptualizing and Teaching African-American Women's History," *Signs* 14, pp. 921–9.

Brown, Elsa Barkley (1989b) "Womanist Consciousness: Maggie Lena Walker and the Independent Order of Saint Luke," *Signs* 14, pp. 610–33.

Brumberg, Joan and Tomes, Nancy (1982) "Women and the Professions: A Research Agenda for American Historians," *Reviews in American History* 10, pp. 275–96.

Buhle, Mari Jo (1998) *Feminism and Its Discontents: A Century of Struggle with Psychoanalysis.* Cambridge, MA: Harvard University Press.

Butler, Judith (1997) *Excitable Speech: A Politics of the Performative.* New York: Routledge.

Carby, Hazel V. (1992) "Policing the Black Woman's Body in an Urban Context," *Critical Inquiry* 18, pp. 738–55.

Castañeda, Antonia (1992) "Women of Color and the Rewriting of Western History: The Discourse, Politics, and Decolonization of History," *Pacific Historical Review* 61, pp. 501–35.

Cott, Nancy (1993) *Intercultural and Interracial Relations.* History of Women in the United States, Vol. 14. New Providence, RI: K. G. Saur.

Cott, Nancy F. (2000) *Public Vows: A History of Marriage and the Nation.* Cambridge, MA: Harvard University Press.

D'Emilio, John and Freedman, Estelle B. (1988) *Intimate Matters: A Social History of Sexuality in America.* New York: Harper and Row; 2nd ed., 1997.

Danbom, David B. (1995) *Born in the Country: A History of Rural America.* Baltimore: Johns Hopkins University Press.

Davis, Angela Y. (1981) *Women, Race and Class.* New York: Random House.

de la Torre, Adela and Pesquera, Beatriz (eds.) (1993) *Building with Our Hands: New Directions in Chicana Studies.* Berkeley: University of California Press.

Ehrenreich, Barbara and English, Deirdre (1978) *For Her Own Good: 150 Years of the Experts' Advice to Women.* Garden City, NY: Anchor Press/Doubleday.

Eisenmann, Linda (ed.) (1998) *Historical Dictionary of Women's Education in the United States.* Westport, CT: Greenwood Press.

Engels, Frederick (1942 [1884]) *The Origin of the Family, Private Property and the State in the Light of the Researches of Lewis H. Morgan.* New York: International Publishers.

Etienne, Mona and Leacock, Eleanor (eds.) (1980) *Women and Colonization: Anthropological Perspectives.* New York: Praeger.

Faderman, Lillian (1981) *Surpassing the Love of Men: Romantic Friendship and Love between Women from the Renaissance to the Present.* New York: William Morrow.

Foner, Philip (1979) *Women and the American Labor Movement: From the First Trade Unions to the Present.* New York: Free Press.

Foster, Martha Harroun (1993) "Of Baggage and Bondage: Gender and Status among Hidatsa and Crow Women," *American Indian Culture and Research Journal* 17, pp. 121–52.

Foster, Martha Harroun (1995) "Lost Women of the Matriarchy: Iroquois Women in the Historical Literature," *American Indian Culture and Research Journal* 19, pp. 121–40.

Giddings, Paula (1984) *When and Where I Enter: The Impact of Black Women on Race and Sex in America.* New York: William Morrow.

Gillespie, Michelle and Clinton, Catherine (eds.) (1998) *Taking Off the White Gloves: Southern Women and Women Historians.* Columbia: University of Missouri Press.

Golden, Janet (1996) *A Social History of Wet-Nursing in America.* New York: Cambridge University Press.

Gordon, Linda (1976) *Woman's Body, Woman's Right: A Social History of Birth Control in America.* New York: Grossman. Revised and updated (1990), New York: Penguin.

Graham, Patricia A. (1975) "So Much To Do: Guides for Historical Research on Women in Higher Education," *Teacher's College Record* 76, pp. 421–9.

Graham, Patricia A. (1978) "Expansion and Exclusion: A History of Women in American Higher Education," *Signs* 3, pp. 759–73.

Grewal, Inderpal (1996) *Home and Harem: Nation, Gender, Empire, and the Cultures of Travel.* Durham, NC: Duke University Press.

Griswold, Robert L. (1994) *Fatherhood in America: A History.* New York: Basic Books.

Hall, Jacquelyn and Scott, Anne Firor (1987) "Women in the South," in John Boles and Evelyn Thomas Nolen (eds.), *Interpreting Southern History: Historiographical Essays in Honor of Sanford W. Higginbotham.* Baton Rouge: Louisiana State University Press, pp. 454–509.

Handlin, Oscar (1951) *The Uprooted: The Epic Story of the Great Migrations that Made the American People.* Boston: Little, Brown.

Hansen, Marcus Lee (1961) *The Atlantic Migration, 1607–1860: History of the Continuing Settlement of the United States.* New York: Harper.

Hartmann, Mary and Banner, Lois (eds.) (1974) *Clio's Consciousness Raised.* New York: Harper and Row.

Hartog, Hendrik (2000) *Man and Wife in America: A History.* Cambridge, MA: Harvard University Press.

Hewitt, Nancy A. (1985) "Beyond the Search for Sisterhood: American Women's History in the 1980's," *Social History* 10, pp. 299–321.

Hewitt, Nancy A. (ed.) (1990) *Women, Families, and Communities: Readings in American History.* 2 vols. New York: Longman.

Hewitt, Nancy A. and Lebsock, Suzanne (eds.) (1993) *Visible Women: New Essays on American Activism.* Urbana: University of Illinois Press.

Hine, Darlene Clark (ed.) (1986) *The State of Afro-American History: Past, Present, and Future.* Baton Rouge: Louisiana State University Press.

Hine, Darlene Clark (ed.) (1990) *Black Women in U.S. History: Theory and Practice.* Brooklyn: Carlson Publishing.

Hine, Darlene Clark, King, Wilma, and Reed, Linda (eds.) (1995) *"We Specialize in the Wholly Impossible": A Reader in Black Women's History.* Brooklyn: Carlson Publishing.

Hine, Darlene Clark and Thompson, Kathleen (1998) *A Shining Thread of Hope: The History of Black Women in America.* New York: Broadway Books.

Hodes, Martha M. (ed.) (1999) *Sex, Love, Race: Crossing Boundaries in North American History.* New York: New York University Press.

hooks, bell (1992) *Black Looks: Race and Representation.* Boston: South End Press.

Howe, Irving (1976) *World of Our Fathers.* New York: Harcourt Brace Jovanovich.

Hunt, Nancy Rose (1999) *A Colonial Lexicon of Birth Ritual, Medicalization, and Mobility in the Congo.* Durham, NC: Duke University Press.

Jacobson, Matthew Frye (1998) *Whiteness of a Different Color: European Immigrants and the Alchemy of Race.* Cambridge, MA: Harvard University Press.

Jameson, Elizabeth and Armitage, Susan (eds.) (1997) *Writing the Range: Race, Class and Culture in the Women's West.* Norman: University of Oklahoma Press.

Jensen, Joan M. (1981) *With These Hands: Women Working on the Land.* Old Westbury, NY: Feminist Press.

Jensen, Joan M. (1991) *Promise to the Land: Essays on Rural Women.* Albuquerque: University of New Mexico Press.

Jensen, Joan M. and Miller, Darlis A. (eds.) (1986) *New Mexico Women: Intercultural Perspectives.* Albuquerque: University of New Mexico Press.

Jones, Gareth Stedman (1983) *Languages of Class: Studies in English Working-class History, 1832–1982.* New York: Cambridge University Press.

Jones, Jacqueline (1985) *Labor of Love, Labor of Sorrow: Black Women, Work and the Family from Slavery to the Present.* New York: Basic Books; 2nd ed., 1995.

Kaplan, Caren (1996) *Questions of Travel: Postmodern Discourses of Displacement.* Durham, NC: Duke University Press.

Kelly, Joan (1976) "The Social Relations of the Sexes: Methodological Implications of Women's History," *Signs* 1, pp. 809–23.

Kelly, Joan (1977) "Did Women Have a Renaissance?" in Renate Bridenthal and Claudia Koonz (eds.), *Becoming Visible: Women in European History.* Boston: Houghton, Mifflin, pp. 137–64.

Kenneally, James J. (1981) *Women and American Trade Unionism.* Montreal: Eden Press.

Kerber, Linda K. (1988) "Separate Spheres, Female Worlds, Woman's Place: The Rhetoric of Women's History," *Journal of American History* 75, pp. 9–39.

Kerber, Linda K. (1998) *No Constitutional Right to Be Ladies: Women and the Obligations of Citizenship.* New York: Hill and Wang.

Kessler-Harris, Alice (1975) "Where are the Organized Women Workers?" *Feminist Studies* 3, pp. 92–111.

Kessler-Harris, Alice (1982) *Out to Work: A History of Wage-earning Women in the United States.* New York: Oxford University Press.

Koester, Susan (ed.) (1993) "Gender in the West," Special Issue, *Journal of the West* 32.

Kolodny, Annette (1975) *The Lay of the Land: Metaphors as Experience and History in American Life and Letters.* Chapel Hill: University of North Carolina Press.

Komarovsky, Mirra (1976) *Dilemmas of Masculinity.* New York: W. W. Norton.

Komarovsky, Mirra (1985) *Women in College: Shaping New Feminine Identities.* New York: Basic Books.

Lancaster, Roger N. and Di Leonardo, Micaela (eds.) (1997) *The Gender/Sexuality Reader: Culture, History, Political Economy.* New York: Routledge.

Laqueur, Thomas (1986) "Orgasm, Generation and the Politics of Reproductive Biology," *Representations* 14, pp. 1–41.

Laqueur, Thomas (1990) *Making Sex: Body and Gender from the Greeks to Freud.* Cambridge, MA: Harvard University Press.

Leavitt, Judith Walzer (1985) *Brought to Bed: Childbearing in America, 1750–1950.* New York: Oxford University Press.

Leavitt, Judith Walzer (ed.) (1999) *Women and Health in America: Historical Readings*, 2nd ed. Madison: University of Wisconsin Press.

Lerner, Gerda (ed.) (1972) *Black Women in White America: A Documentary History.* New York: Vintage Books.

Lerner, Gerda (1979) *The Majority Finds its Past: Placing Women in History.* New York: Oxford University Press.

Lightfoot-Klein, Hanny (1989) *Prisoners of Ritual: An Odyssey into Female Genital Circumcision in Africa.* New York: Herrington Park Press.

Ling, Huping (1988) *Surviving on Gold Mountain: A History of Chinese American Women and their Lives.* Albany: State University of New York Press.

Litoff, Judy Barrett (1978) *American Midwives: 1860 to the Present.* Westport, CT: Greenwood Press.

Loudon, Irvine (1992) *Death in Childbirth: An International Study of Maternal Care and Maternal Mortality, 1800–1950.* New York: Oxford University Press.

McCarthy, Kathleen D. (1998) *Women and Philanthropy in the United States, 1790–1990.* New York: Center for the Study of Philanthropy, City University of New York.

McClintock, Anne (1995) *Imperial Leather: Race, Gender, and Sexuality in the Colonial Conquest.* New York: Routledge.

McGerr, Michael (1990) "Political Style and Women's Power, 1830–1930," *Journal of American History* 77, pp. 864–85.

Marsh, Margaret and Ronner, Wanda (1996) *The Empty Cradle: Infertility in America from Colonial Times to the Present.* Baltimore: Johns Hopkins University Press.

Matsumoto, Valerie J. and Allmendinger, Blake (eds.) (1999) *Over the Edge: Remapping the American West.* Berkeley: University of California Press.

Matthei, Julie A. (1982) *An Economic History of Women in America: Women's Work, the Sexual Division of Labor and the Development of Capitalism.* New York: Schocken.

Meyerowitz, Joanne (1992) "American Women's History: The Fall of Women's Culture," *Canadian Journal of American Studies*, Special Issue, pp. 27–52.

Michaelsen, Scott and Johnson, David E. (1997) *Border Theory: The Limits of Cultural Politics.* Minneapolis: University of Minnesota Press.

Milner, Clyde A. (ed.) (1996) *A New Significance: Re-envisioning the History of the American West.* New York: Oxford University Press.

Mintz, Sidney and Price, Richard (1976) *An Anthropological Approach to the Afro-American Past: A Caribbean Perspective.* Philadelphia: Institute for the Study of Human Issues.

Nash, Gary B. (1995) "The Hidden History of Mestizo America," *Journal of American History* 82, pp. 941–64.

Oakley, Ann (1985) *The Captured Womb: A History of the Medical Care of Pregnant Women.* London: Oxford University Press.

Oates, Mary J. (ed.) (1987) *Higher Education for Catholic Women: An Historical Anthology.* New York: Garland Publishers.

Ong, Walter (1982) *Orality and Literacy.* New York: Methuen.

Parker, Andrew, Russo, Mary, Sommer, Doris, and Yaeger, Patricia (eds.) (1992) *Nationalisms and Sexualities.* New York: Routledge.

Pateman, Carole (1988) *The Sexual Contract.* Stanford, CA: Stanford University Press.

Peiss, Kathy and Simmons, Christina, with Robert Padgug (eds.) (1989) *Passion and Power: Sexuality in History.* Philadelphia: Temple University Press.

Pfeffer, Naomi (1993) *The Stork and the Syringe: A Political History of Reproductive Medicine.* Cambridge: Polity Press.

Pleck, Elizabeth (1987) *Domestic Tyranny: The Making of American Social Policy Against Family Violence from Colonial Times to the Present.* New York: Oxford University Press.

Pratt, Mary Louise (1992) *Imperial Eyes: Travel Writing and Transculturation.* New York: Routledge.

Pratt, Mary Louise (1988) "Arts of the Contact Zone," *Profession* 91, pp. 33–40.

Prentice, Alison, Bourne, Paula, Brandt, Gail Cuthbert, Lights, Beth, Mitchinson, Wendy, and Black, Naomi (eds.) (1996) *Canadian Women: A History*, 2nd ed. Toronto: Harcourt Brace and Company.

Rabinow, Paul (ed.) (1984) *The Foucault Reader.* New York: Pantheon Books.

Reilly, Philip R. (1991) *The Surgical Solution: A History of Involuntary Sterilization in the United States.* Baltimore: Johns Hopkins University Press.

Rich, Adrienne (1976) *Of Woman Born: Motherhood as Experience and Institution.* New York: W. W. Norton.

Roberts, Dorothy (1997) *Killing the Black Body: Race, Reproduction, and the Meaning of Liberty.* New York: Vintage Books.

Robertson, Claire and Klein, Martin (eds.) (1983) *Women and Slavery in Africa.* Madison: University of Wisconsin Press.

Roediger, David R. (1991) *The Wages of Whiteness: Race and the Making of the American Working Class.* New York: Verso.

Ruíz, Vicki and DuBois, Ellen (eds.) (2000) *Unequal Sisters: A Multicultural Reader in U.S. Women's History,* 3rd ed. New York: Routledge.

Ruíz, Vicki, Monk, Janice, and Schlissel, Lillian (eds.) (1988) *Western Women: Their Lands, Their Lives.* Albuquerque: University of New Mexico Press.

Scanlon, Jennifer (ed.) (2000) *The Gender and Consumer Culture Reader.* New York: New York University Press.

Schiebinger, Londa (1993) *Nature's Body: Gender in the Making of Modern Science.* Boston: Beacon Press.

Scott, Anne Firor (1992) *Natural Allies: Women's Associations in American History.* Urbana: University of Illinois Press.

Scott, Joan C. (1986) "Gender: A Useful Category of Historical Analysis," *American Historical Review* 91, pp. 1053–75.

Scott, Joan C. (1988) *Gender and the Politics of History.* New York: Columbia University Press.

Snitow, Ann, Stansell, Christine, and Thompson, Sharon (eds.) (1983) *Powers of Desire: The Politics of Sexuality.* New York: Monthly Review Press.

Solomon, Barbara Miller (1985) *In the Company of Educated Women: A History of Women and Higher Education in America.* New Haven, CT: Yale University Press.

Stanton, Domna C. (1992) *Discourses of Sexuality: From Aristotle to Aids.* Ann Arbor: University of Michigan Press.

Stanton, Elizabeth Cady, Anthony, Susan B., and Gage, Matilda Joslyn (eds.) (1881–1906) *The History of Woman Suffrage,* 6 vols. Rpt. (1985), Salem, NH: Ayer.

Stearns, Peter and Lewis, Jan (eds.) (1998) *An Emotional History of the United States.* New York: New York University Press.

Stoler, Ann L. (1989) "Making Empire Respectable: The Politics of Race and Sexual Morality in Twentieth-century Colonial Empires," *American Ethnologist* 16, pp. 634–60.

Stoler, Ann L. (1991) "Sexual Affronts and Racial Frontiers: European Identities and the Cultural Policies of Exclusion in Colonial Southeast Asia," *Comparative Studies in Society and History* 34, pp. 514–51.

Stoler, Ann L. (2001) "Tense and Tender Ties: Intimacies of Empire in North American History and (Post)Colonial Studies," *Journal of American History* 88, pp. 829–65.

Strasser, Susan (1982) *Never Done: A History of American Housework.* New York: Pantheon.

Thompson, E. P. (1963) *The Making of the English Working Class.* New York: Pantheon.

Wertheimer, Barbara (1977) *We Were There: The Story of Working Women in America.* New York: Pantheon.

White, Shane and White, Graham (1998) *Stylin': African American Expressive Culture from its Beginnings to the Zoot Suit.* Ithaca, NY: Cornell University Press.

Colonial

Amussen, Susan D. (1988) *An Ordered Society: Gender and Class in Early Modern England.* London: Oxford University Press.

Anderson, Karen (1991) *Chain Her By One Foot: The Subjugation of Women in Seventeenth-century New France.* New York: Routledge.

Andrews, William (ed.) (1990) *Journeys in New Worlds: Early American Women's Narratives.* Madison: University of Wisconsin Press.

Axtell, James (1997) *The Indians' New South: Cultural Change in the Colonial Southeast.* Baton Rouge: Louisiana State University Press.

Bailyn, Bernard (1960) *Education in the Forming of American Society: Needs and Opportunities for Study.* Chapel Hill: University of North Carolina Press.

Barr, Juliana (1999) "The 'Seductions' of Texas: The Political Language of Gender in the Conquests of Texas, 1609–1803," Ph.D. dissertation, University of Wisconsin.

Bartels, Emily (1992) "Imperialist Beginnings: Richard Hakluyt and the Construction of Africa," *Criticism* 34, pp. 517–38.

Bay, Edna G. (1995) "Belief, Legitimacy and the Kpojito: An Institutional History of the 'Queen Mother' in Precolonial Dahomey," *Journal of African History* 36, pp. 1–27.

Beckles, Hilary M. (1989) *Natural Rebels: A Social History of Enslaved Black Women in Barbados.* New Brunswick, NJ: Rutgers University Press.

Berlin, Ira (1998) *Many Thousands Gone: The First Two Centuries of Slavery in North America.* Cambridge, MA: Harvard University Press.

Berlin, Ira and Hoffman, Ronald (eds.) (1983) *Slavery and Freedom in the Age of the American Revolution.* Charlottesville: University Press of Virginia.

Berlin, Ira and Morgan, Philip D. (eds.) (1993) *Cultivation and Culture: Labor and the Shaping of Slave Life in the Americas.* Charlottesville: University Press of Virginia.

Biemer, Linda Briggs (1983) *Women and Property in Colonial New York: The Transition from Dutch to English Law, 1643–1727.* Ann Arbor, MI: UMI Research Press.

Bloch, Ruth H. (1987) "The Gendered Meanings of Virtue in Revolutionary America," *Signs* 13, pp. 37–58.

Bonomi, Patricia (1986) *Under the Cope of Heaven: Religion, Society, and Politics in Colonial America.* New York: Oxford University Press.

Bouvier, Virginia (2001) *Women and the Conquest of California, 1542–1840.* Tucson: University of Arizona Press.

Bowler, Clara Ann (1977) "Carted Whores and White Shrouded Apologies: Slander in the County Courts of Seventeenth-century Virginia," *Virginia Magazine of History and Biography* 85, pp. 411–26.

Branson, Susan (2001) *These Fiery Frenchified Dames: Women and Political Culture in Early National Philadelphia.* Philadelphia: University of Pennsylvania Press.

Brasseaux, Carl A. (1986) "The Moral Climate of French Colonial Louisiana," *Louisiana History* 27, pp. 27–41.

Braund, Kathleen E. Holland (1990) "Custodians of Tradition and Handmaidens to Change: Women's Role in Creek Economic and Social Life During the Eighteenth Century," *American Indian Quarterly* 14, pp. 239–58.

Breen, T. H. (1993) "The Meaning of Things: Interpreting the Consumer Economy in the Eighteenth Century," in John Brewer and Roy Porter (eds.), *Consumption and the World of Goods.* New York: Routledge, pp. 249–60.

Brekus, Catherine A. (1998) *Strangers and Pilgrims: Female Preaching in America, 1740–1845.* Chapel Hill: University of North Carolina Press.

Breslaw, Elaine G. (1996) *Tituba, Reluctant Witch of Salem: Devilish Indians and Puritan Fantasies.* New York: New York University Press.

Brooks, James F. (1996) "'This Evil Extends Especially... To the Feminine Sex': Negotiating Captivity in the New Mexico Borderlands," *Feminist Studies* 22, pp. 279–309.

Brown, Chandos Michael (1995) "Mary Wollstonecraft, or, the Female Illuminati: The Campaign Against Women and 'Modern Philosophy' in the Early Republic," *Journal of the Early Republic* 15, pp. 389–424.

Brown, Jennifer S. H. (1980) *Strangers in Blood: Fur Trade Company Families in Indian Country.* Norman: University of Oklahoma Press.

Brown, Judith K. (1975) "Iroquois Women: An Ethnohistoric Note," in Rayna R. Reiter (ed.), *Toward an Anthropology of Women.* New York: Monthly Review Press, pp. 235–51.

Brown, Kathleen M. (1993) "Brave New Worlds: Women's and Gender History," *William and Mary Quarterly*, 3rd ser., 50, pp. 310–28.

Brown, Kathleen M. (1996) *Good Wives, Nasty Wenches, and Anxious Patriarchs: Gender, Race, and Power in Colonial Virginia.* Chapel Hill: University of North Carolina Press.

Butterfield, L. H. et al. (eds.) (1963–) *Adams Family Correspondence.* Cambridge, MA: Harvard University Press.

Carney, Judith (1996) "Rice Milling, Gender, and Slave Labour in Colonial South Carolina," *Past and Present* 153, pp. 108–34.

Carr, Lois Green and Walsh, Lorena S. (1977) "The Planter's Wife: The Experience of White Women in Seventeenth-century Maryland," *William and Mary Quarterly*, 3rd ser., 34, pp. 543–71.

Castiglia, Christopher (1996) *Bound and Determined: Captivity, Culture-crossing, and White Womanhood from Mary Rowlandson to Patty Hearst.* Chicago: University of Chicago Press.

Castillo, Edward (1994) "Gender Status Decline, Resistance and Accommodation among Female Neophytes in the Missions of California: A San Gabriel Case Study," *American Indian Culture and Research Journal* 18, pp. 67–93.

Cayton, Andrew L. and Teute, Fredrika J. (eds.) (1998) *Contact Points: American Frontiers from the Mohawk Valley to the Mississippi, 1750–1830.* Chapel Hill: University of North Carolina Press.

Chaplin, Joyce E. (1997) "Natural Philosophy and an Early Racial Idiom in North America: Comparing English and Indian Bodies," *William and Mary Quarterly*, 3rd ser., 54, pp. 229–52.

Clinton, Catherine and Gillespie, Michele (eds.) (1997) *The Devil's Lane: Sex and Race in the Early South.* New York: Oxford University Press.

Conklin, Alice (1998) "From World Systems to Post-coloniality: Teaching the History of European Encounters in the Modern Age," *Radical History Review* 71, pp. 150–63.

Cott, Nancy (1976) "Eighteenth-century Family and Social Life Revealed in Massachusetts Divorce Records," *Journal of Social History* 10, pp. 20–43.

Curtin, Phillip (1969) *The Atlantic Slave Trade: A Census.* Madison: University of Wisconsin Press.

Daunton, Martin and Halpern, Rick (eds.) (1999) *Empire and Others: British Encounters with Indigenous Peoples, 1600–1850.* Philadelphia: University of Pennsylvania Press.

Davis, David Brion (1997) "Constructing Race: A Reflection," *William and Mary Quarterly*, 3rd ser., 54, pp. 7–18.

Davis, Natalie Zemon (1995) *Women on the Margins: Three Seventeenth-century Lives.* Cambridge, MA: Harvard University Press.

Dayton, Cornelia Hughes (1991) "Taking the Trade: Abortion and Gender Relations in an Eighteenth-century New England Village," *William and Mary Quarterly*, 3rd ser., 48, pp. 19–49.

Dayton, Cornelia Hughes (1995) *Women Before the Bar: Gender, Law, and Society in Connecticut, 1639–1789.* Chapel Hill: University of North Carolina Press.

DeBerg, Betty (1990) *Ungodly Women: Gender and the First Wave of American Fundamentalism.* Minneapolis: University of Minnesota Press.

Demos, John (1970) *A Little Commonwealth: Family Life in Plymouth Colony.* New York: Oxford University Press.

Demos, John (1982) *Entertaining Satan: Witchcraft and the Culture of Early New England.* New York: Oxford University Press.

Demos, John (1994) *The Unredeemed Captive: A Family Story from Early America.* New York: Alfred A. Knopf.

Derounian-Stodola, Kathryn Zabelle and Levernier, James Arthur (1993) *The Indian Captivity Narrative, 1550–1900.* Boston: Twayne.

Devens, Carol (1986) "Separate Confrontations: Gender as a Factor in Indian Adaptation to European Colonization in New France," *American Quarterly* 38, pp. 461–80.

Devens, Carol (1992) *Countering Colonization: Native American Women and Great Lakes Missions, 1630–1900.* Berkeley: University of California Press.

Dickason, Olive Patricia (1984) *The Myth of the Savage and the Beginnings of French Colonialism in the Americas.* Edmonton: University of Alberta Press.

Dowd, Gregory Evans (1992) *A Spirited Resistance: The North American Indian Struggle for Unity, 1745–1815.* Baltimore: Johns Hopkins University Press.

Dunn, Mary Maples (1978) "Saints and Sisters: Congregational and Quaker Women in the Early Colonial Period," *American Quarterly* 30, pp. 582–601.

Eltis, David (2000) *The Rise of African Slavery in the Americas.* Cambridge: Cambridge University Press.

Eltis, David and Engerman, Stanley (1993) "Was the Slave Trade Dominated by Men?" *Journal of Interdisciplinary History* 23, pp. 237–57.

Fage, J. D. (1989) "African Societies and the Atlantic Slave Trade," *Past and Present* 125, pp. 97–115.

Fischer, Kirsten (2002) *Suspect Relations: Sex, Race, and Resistance in Colonial North Carolina.* Ithaca, NY: Cornell University Press.

Foreman, Carolyn T. (1943) *Indians Abroad, 1493–1938.* Norman: University of Oklahoma Press.

Galenson, David W. (1986) *Traders, Planters, and Slaves: Market Behavior in Early English America.* Cambridge: Cambridge University Press.

Gaspar, David Barry and Hine, Darlene Clark (eds.) (1996) *More Than Chattel: Black Women and Slavery in the Americas.* Indianapolis: Indiana University Press.

Geggus, David P. (1989) "Sex Ratio, Age, and Ethnicity in the Atlantic Slave Trade: Data from French Shipping and Plantation Records," *Journal of African History* 30, pp. 23–44.

Gomez, Michael A. (1998) *Exchanging Our Country Marks: The Transformation of African Identities in the Colonial and Antebellum South.* Chapel Hill: University of North Carolina Press.

Gordon-Reed, Annette (1997) *Thomas Jefferson and Sally Hemings: An American Controversy.* Charlottesville: University Press of Virginia.

Green, Rayna (1980) "Native American Women," *Signs* 6, pp. 248–67.

Greven, Jr., Philip J. (1970) *Four Generations: Population, Land, and Family in Colonial Andover, Massachusetts.* Ithaca, NY: Cornell University Press.

Greven, Jr., Philip J. (1977) *The Protestant Temperament: Patterns of Child-rearing, Religious Experience, and the Self in Early America.* New York: Alfred A. Knopf.

Gutiérrez, Ramón A. (1991) *When Jesus Came, the Corn Mothers Went Away: Marriage, Sexuality, and Power in New Mexico, 1500–1846.* Stanford, CA: Stanford University Press.

Hall, David and Allen, David Grayson (eds.) (1984) *Seventeenth-century New England.* Boston: Colonial Society of Massachusetts.

Hall, David D. (1968) *The Antinomian Controversy, 1636–1638: A Documentary History.* Middletown, CT: Wesleyan University Press.

Hall, Kim F. (1995) *Things of Darkness: Economies of Race and Gender in Early Modern England.* Ithaca, NY: Cornell University Press.

Handler, Jerome S. and Corruccinni, Robert S. (1986) "Weaning among West Indian Slaves: Historical and Bioanthropological Evidence from Barbados," *William and Mary Quarterly,* 3rd ser., 43, pp. 111–17.

Harkin, Michael and Kan, Sergei (eds.) (1996) "Native Women's Responses to Christianity," Special Issue, *Ethnohistory* 43.

Hendricks, Margo and Parker, Patricia (eds.) (1994) *Women, "Race," and Writing in the Early Modern Period.* New York: Routledge.

Heyrman, Christine (1997) *Southern Cross: The Beginnings of the Bible Belt.* Chapel Hill: University of North Carolina Press.

Hoffman, Ronald and Albert, Peter (eds.) (1989) *Women in the Age of the American Revolution.* Charlottesville: University Press of Virginia.

Hulme, Peter (1986) *Colonial Encounters: Europe and the Native Caribbean, 1492–1797.* New York: Methuen.

Humez, Jean M. (1981) *Gifts of Power: The Writings of Rebecca Jackson, Black Visionary, Shaker Eldress.* Amherst: University of Massachusetts Press.

Innes, Stephen (ed.) (1988) *Work and Labor in Early America.* Chapel Hill: University of North Carolina Press.

Jordan, Winthrop D. (1968) *White Over Black: American Attitudes Toward the Negro, 1550–1812.* Chapel Hill: University of North Carolina Press.

Juster, Susan (1989) "In a Different Voice: Male and Female Narratives of Religious Conversion in Post-Revolutionary America," *American Quarterly* 41, pp. 34–62.

Juster, Susan (1994) *Disorderly Women: Sexual Politics and Evangelicalism in Revolutionary New England.* Ithaca, NY: Cornell University Press.

Juster, Susan (1997) "The Spirit and the Flesh: Gender, Language, and Sexuality in American Protestantism," in Harry S. Stout and Daryl G. Hart (eds.), *New Directions in American Religious History.* New York: Oxford University Press, pp. 334–61.

Juster, Susan (2000) "Mystical Pregnancy and Holy Bleeding: Visionary Experience in Early Modern Britain and America," *William and Mary Quarterly,* 3rd ser., 57, pp. 249–88.

Kamensky, Jane (1997) *Governing the Tongue: The Politics of Speech in Early New England.* New York: Oxford University Press.

Karlsen, Carol F. (1987) *The Devil in the Shape of a Woman: Witchcraft in Colonial New England.* New York: W. W. Norton.

Karttunen, Frances (1994) *Between Worlds: Interpreters, Guides, and Survivors.* New Brunswick, NJ: Rutgers University Press.

Kerber, Linda K. (1976) "The Republican Mother: Women and the Enlightenment – an American Perspective," *American Quarterly* 28, pp. 187–205.

Kidwell, Clara Sue (1992) "Indian Women as Cultural Mediators," *Ethnohistory* 39, pp. 97–107.

Klein, Herbert S. and Engerman, Stanley (1978) "Fertility Differentials between Slaves in the United States and the British West Indies; A Note on Lactation Practices and their Possible Implications," *William and Mary Quarterly*, 3rd ser., 35, pp. 357–74.

Klepp, Susan F. (1998) "Revolutionary Bodies: Women and the Fertility Transition in the Mid-Atlantic Region, 1760–1820," *Journal of American History* 85, pp. 910–45.

Klinghoffer, Judith Apter and Elkis, Lois (1992) "'The Petticoat Electors': Women's Suffrage in New Jersey, 1776–1807," *Journal of the Early Republic* 12, pp. 159–93.

Koehler, Lyle (1980) *A Search for Power: The "Weaker Sex" in Seventeenth-century New England*. Urbana: University of Illinois Press.

Kolodny, Annette (1984) *The Land Before Her: Fantasy and Experience of the American Frontiers, 1630–1860*. Chapel Hill: University of North Carolina Press.

Kulikoff, Allan (1986) *Tobacco and Slaves: The Development of Southern Cultures in the Chesapeake, 1680–1800*. Chapel Hill: University of North Carolina Press.

Kupperman, Karen Ordahl (ed.) (1995) *America in European Consciousness, 1493–1750*. Chapel Hill: University of North Carolina Press.

Kupperman, Karen Ordahl (1997) "Presentment of Civility: English Reading of American Self-presentation in the Early Years of Colonization," *William and Mary Quarterly*, 3rd ser., 54, pp. 193–228.

Kupperman, Karen Ordahl (2000) *Indians and English: Facing Off in Early America*. Ithaca, NY: Cornell University Press.

Landes, Joan (1988) *Women and the Public Sphere in the Age of the French Revolution*. Ithaca, NY: Cornell University Press.

Lang, Amy Schrager (1987) *Prophetic Women: Anne Hutchinson and the Problem of Dissent in the Literature of New England*. Berkeley: University of California Press.

Laslett, Peter (1965) *The World We Have Lost: England Before the Industrial Age*. New York: Charles Scribner's Sons.

Lavrin, Asuncion (ed.) (1989) *Sexuality and Marriage in Colonial Spanish America*. Lincoln: University of Nebraska Press.

Law, Robin (1991) *The Slave Coast of West Africa, 1550–1750: The Impact of the Atlantic Slave Trade on an African Society*. Oxford: Clarendon Press.

Levy, Barry (1988) *Quakers and the American Family: British Settlement in the Delaware Valley*. New York: Oxford University Press.

Little, Ann M. (n.d.) "Abraham in Arms: Gender and Power on the New England Frontier, 1620–1760," manuscript in progress.

Littlefield, Daniel (1991) *Rice and Slaves: Ethnicity and the Slave Trade in Colonial South Carolina*. Urbana: University of Illinois Press.

Lockridge, Kenneth (1993) *On the Sources of Patriarchal Rage*. New York: New York University Press.

McCartney, Martha W. (1989) "Cockacoeske, Queen of the Pamunkey: Diplomat and Suzeraine," in Peter H. Wood, Gregory Waselkov, and M. Thomas Hatley (eds.), *Powhatan's Mantle: Indians in the Colonial Southeast*. Lincoln: University of Nebraska Press, pp. 173–95.

Mack, Phyllis (1992) *Visionary Women: Ecstatic Prophecy in Seventeenth-century England*. Berkeley: University of California Press.

Mandell, Daniel R. (1998) "Shifting Boundaries of Race and Ethnicity: Indian–Black Intermarriage in Southern New England, 1760–1880," *Journal of American History* 85, pp. 466–501.

Monaghan, E. Jennifer (1988) "Literacy Instruction and Gender in New England," *American Quarterly* 40, pp. 18–41.

Monaghan, E. Jennifer (1990) "'She Loved to Read in Good Books': Literacy and the Indians of Martha's Vineyard, 1643–1725," *History of Education Quarterly* 30, pp. 493–521.

Montrose, Louis (1991) "The Work of Gender in the Discourse of Discovery," *Representations* 33, pp. 1–41.

Morgan, Edmund (1944) *The Puritan Family: Religion and Domestic Relations in Seventeenth-century New England.* New York: Harper and Row.

Morgan, Jennifer L. (1997) "'Some Could Suckle Over Their Shoulder': Male Travelers, Female Bodies, and the Gendering of Racial Ideology, 1500–1770," *William and Mary Quarterly,* 3rd ser., 54, pp. 167–92.

Mozumbdar, Chandana (1995) "The Role of Mixed Bloods among the Southeastern Indians during the Colonial Period," *New England Journal of History* 51, pp. 2–9.

Murray, Judith Sargent (1995) *Selected Writings of Judith Sargent Murray,* ed. Sharon M. Harris. New York: Oxford University Press.

Namias, June (1993) *White Captives: Gender and Ethnicity on the American Frontier.* Chapel Hill: University of North Carolina Press.

Narrett, David E. (1992) *Inheritance and Family Life in Colonial New York City.* Ithaca, NY: Cornell University Press.

Nash, Gary B. (1972) "The Image of the Indian in the Southern Colonial Mind," *William and Mary Quarterly,* 3rd ser., 29, pp. 197–230.

Nash, Gary B. (1995) "The Hidden History of Mestizo America," *Journal of American History* 82, pp. 941–64.

Neumann, Klaus (1994) "'In Order to Win Their Friendship': Renegotiating First Contact," *The Contemporary Pacific* 6, pp. 111–45.

Noel, Jan (1998) *Women in New France.* Ottowa: Canadian Historical Association.

Norton, Mary Beth (1976) "'My Resting Reaping Times': Sarah Osborn's Defense of her 'Unfeminine' Activities, 1767," *Signs* 2, pp. 515–29.

Norton, Mary Beth (1980) *Liberty's Daughters: The Revolutionary Experience of American Women, 1750–1800.* New York: Little, Brown.

Norton, Mary Beth (1984) "The Evolution of White Women's Experience in Early America," *American Historical Review* 89, pp. 593–619.

Norton, Mary Beth (1987) "Gender and Defamation in Seventeenth-century Maryland," *William and Mary Quarterly,* 3rd ser., 44, pp. 3–39.

Norton, Mary Beth (1996) *Founding Mothers and Fathers: Gendered Power and the Forming of American Society.* New York: Alfred A. Knopf.

Nussbaum, Felicity A. (1995) *Torrid Zones: Maternity, Sexuality, and Empire in Eighteenth-century English Narratives.* Baltimore: Johns Hopkins University Press.

Page, Hilary and Lesthaeghe, Ron (eds.) (1981) *Child-spacing in Tropical Africa: Traditions and Change.* New York: Academic Press.

Parmenter, Jon (1999) "Isabel Montour: Cultural Broker on the Frontiers of New York and Pennsylvania," in Ian K. Steele and Nancy L. Rhoden (eds.), *The Human Tradition in Colonial America.* Wilmington, DE: Scholarly Resources, pp. 141–59.

Perdue, Theda (1997) "Pocahontas Meets Columbus in the American South," *Southern Cultures* 3, pp. 4–21.

Perdue, Theda (1998) *Cherokee Women: Gender and Culture Change, 1700–1835.* Lincoln: University of Nebraska Press.

Perdue, Theda (ed.) (2001) *Sifters: Native American Women's Lives.* New York: Oxford University Press.

Perlmann, Joel and Shirley, Dennis (1991) "When Did New England Women Acquire Literacy?" *William and Mary Quarterly,* 3rd ser., 48, pp. 50–67.

Perry, Ruth (1991) "Colonizing the Breast: Sexuality and Maternity in Eighteenth-century England," *Journal of the History of Sexuality* 2, pp. 204–34.

Pestana, Carla (1991) *Quakers and Baptists in Colonial Massachusetts.* New York: Cambridge University Press.

Peterson, Jacqueline (1985) "Many Roads to Red River: Métis Genesis in the Great Lakes Region, 1680–1815," in Jacqueline Peterson and Jennifer S. H. Brown (eds.), *The New Peoples: Being and Becoming Métis in North America.* Lincoln: University of Nebraska Press.

Plane, Ann Marie (2000) *Colonial Intimacies: Indian Marriage in Early New England.* Ithaca, NY: Cornell University Press.

Porterfield, Amanda (1991) *Female Piety in Puritan New England.* New York: Oxford University Press.

Reis, Elizabeth (1997) *Damned Women: Sinners and Witches in Puritan New England.* Ithaca, NY: Cornell University Press.

Richardson, David (1989) "Slave Exports from West and West-Central Africa, 1700–1810: New Estimates of Volume and Distribution," *Journal of African History* 30, pp. 1–22.

Richter, Daniel K. (1983) "Whose Indian History?" *William and Mary Quarterly* 50, 3rd ser., pp. 379–93.

Robertson, Karen (1996) "Pocahontas at the Masque," *Signs* 21, pp. 551–83.

Rodney, Walter (1970) *A History of the Upper Guinea Coast 1545–1800.* London: Oxford University Press.

Roper, Lyndal (1989) *The Holy Household: Women and Morals in Reformation Augsburg.* London: Oxford University Press.

Salmon, Marylynn (1986) *Women and the Law of Property in Early America.* Chapel Hill: University of North Carolina Press.

Salmon, Marylynn (1994) "The Cultural Significance of Breastfeeding and Infant Care in Early Modern England and America," *Journal of Social History* 28, pp. 247–70.

Saunt, Claudio (1999) *A New Order of Things: Property, Power, and the Transformation of the Creek Indians, 1733–1816.* New York: Cambridge University Press.

Sayre, Gordon M. (1997) *Les Sauvages Américains: Representations of Native Americans in French and English Colonial Literature.* Chapel Hill: University of North Carolina Press.

Scholten, Catherine M. (1977) "'On the Importance of the Obsterick Art': Changing Customs of Childbirth in America, 1760–1825," *William and Mary Quarterly,* 3rd ser., 34, pp. 426–45.

Schwartz, Stuart B. (ed.) (1994) *Implicit Understandings: Observing, Reporting, and Reflecting on the Encounters between Europeans and Other Peoples in the Early Modern Era.* Cambridge: Cambridge University Press.

Seed, Patricia (1988) *To Love, Honor and Obey in Colonial Mexico: Conflicts Over Marriage Choice, 1547–1821.* Stanford, CA: Stanford University Press.

Shammas, Carole (1980) "The Domestic Environment in Early Modern England and America," *Journal of Social History* 14, pp. 3–24.

Shammas, Carole (1985) "Black Women's Work and the Evolution of Plantation Society in Virginia," *Labor History* 26, pp. 5–28.

Shammas, Carole (1995) "Anglo-American Household Government in Comparative Perspective," *William and Mary Quarterly*, 3rd ser., 52, pp. 104–44.

Sheehan, Bernard W. (1980) *Savagism and Civility: Indians and Englishmen in Colonial Virginia*. New York: Cambridge University Press.

Shields, Richard (1981) "The Feminization of American Congregationalism, 1730–1835," *American Quarterly* 33, pp. 46–62.

Shoemaker, Nancy (1997) "How Indians Got to be Red," *American Historical Review* 102, pp. 625–44.

Silverblatt, Irene (1987) *Moon, Sun, and Witches: Gender Ideologies and Class in Inca and Colonial Peru*. Princeton, NJ: Princeton University Press.

Sleeper-Smith, Susan (2000) "Women, Kin, and Catholicism: New Perspectives on the Fur Trade," *Ethnohistory* 47, pp. 423–52.

Slotkin, Richard (1973) *Regeneration through Violence: The Mythology of the American Frontier, 1600–1860*. Middletown, CT: Wesleyan University Press.

Smith, Daniel Blake (1980) *Inside the Great House: Planter Family Life in Eighteenth-century Chesapeake Society*. Ithaca, NY: Cornell University Press.

Smith, Daniel Scott (1975) "Parental Power and Marriage Patterns: An Analysis of Historical Trends in Hingham, Massachusetts," *Journal of Marriage and the Family* 35, pp. 419–28.

Smith, Daniel Scott and Hindus, Michael (1975) "Premarital Pregnancy in America, 1640–1671," *Journal of Interdisciplinary History* 5, pp. 537–70.

Smith, Merril D. (ed.) (1998) *Sex and Sexuality in Early America*. New York: New York University Press.

Smith-Rosenberg, Carroll (1993) "Captured Subjects/Savage Others: Violently Engendering the New American," *Gender and History* 5, pp. 177–95.

Smits, David D. (1982) "The 'Squaw Drudge': A Prime Index of Savagism," *Ethnohistory* 29, pp. 281–306.

Smits, David D. (1987a) "'Abominable Mixture': Toward the Repudiation of Anglo-Indian Intermarriage in Seventeenth-century Virginia," *Virginia Magazine of History and Biography* 95, pp. 157–92.

Smits, David D. (1987b) "'We Are Not To Grow Wild': Seventeenth-century New England's Repudiation of Anglo-Indian Intermarriage," *American Indian Culture and Research Journal* 11, pp. 1–31.

Sobel, Mechal (1987) *The World They Made Together: Black and White Values in Eighteenth-century Virginia*. Princeton, NJ: Princeton University Press.

Spear, Jennifer Michel (1999) "'Whiteness and the Purity of Blood': Race, Sexuality, and Social Order in Colonial Louisiana," Ph.D. dissertation, University of Minnesota.

Stout, Harry S. and Brekus, Catherine (1991) "Declension, Gender, and the 'New Religious History,'" in Philip R. VanderMeer and Robert P. Swierenga (eds.), *Belief and Behavior: Essays in the New Religious History*. New Brunswick, NJ: Rutgers University Press, pp. 15–37.

Sweet, David G. and Nash, Gary B. (eds.) (1981) *Struggle and Survival in Colonial America*. Berkeley: University of California Press.

Syrett, Harold et al. (eds.) (1961–79) *The Papers of Alexander Hamilton*. 26 vols. New York: Columbia University Press.

Tate, Thad W. and Ammerman, David L. (eds.) (1979) *The Chesapeake in the Seventeenth Century: Essays on Anglo-American Society*. Chapel Hill: University of North Carolina Press.

Taves, Ann (1999) *Fits, Visions, and Trances: Experiencing Religion and Explaining Experience from Wesley to James*. Princeton, NJ: Princeton University Press.

Thompson, Roger (1986) *Sex in Middlesex: Popular Mores in a Massachusetts County, 1649–1699.* Amherst: University of Massachusetts Press.

Thornton, John (1988) "On the Trail of Voodoo: African Christianity in Africa and the Americas," *The Americas* 44, pp. 261–78.

Thornton, John (1992) *Africa and Africans in the Making of the Atlantic World, 1400–1680.* New York: Cambridge University Press.

Ulrich, Laurel Thatcher (1982) *Goodwives: Image and Reality in the Lives of Women in Northern New England, 1650–1750.* New York: Alfred A. Knopf.

Ulrich, Laurel Thatcher (1990) *A Midwife's Tale: The Life of Martha Ballard, Based on Her Diary, 1785–1812.* New York: Alfred A. Knopf.

Van Kirk, Sylvia (1980) *Many Tender Ties: Women in Fur Trade Society, 1670–1870.* Norman: University of Oklahoma Press.

Wall, Helena (1990) *Fierce Communion: Family and Community in Early America.* Cambridge, MA: Harvard University Press.

Waselkov, Gregory A. and Braund, Kathryn E. Holland (eds.) (1995) *William Bartram on the Southeastern Indians.* Lincoln: University of Nebraska Press.

Wells, Robert V. (1980) "Illegitimacy and Bridal Pregnancy in Colonial America," in Peter Laslett (ed.), *Bastardy and its Comparative History.* Cambridge, MA: Harvard University Press, pp. 349–61.

Westerkamp, Marilyn J. (1999) *Women and Religion in Early America, 1600–1850: The Puritan and Evangelical Traditions.* New York: Routledge.

White, Richard (1991) *The Middle Ground: Indians, Empires, and Republics in the Great Lakes Region, 1650–1815.* Cambridge: Cambridge University Press.

Wilson, Lisa (1999) *Ye Heart of a Man: The Domestic Life of Men in Colonial New England.* New Haven, CT: Yale University Press.

Wood, Betty and Frey, Sylvia (1998) *Come Shouting to Zion: African American Protestantism in the American South and British Caribbean to 1830.* Chapel Hill: University of North Carolina Press.

Wood, Peter H. (1974) *Black Majority: Negroes in Colonial South Carolina, from 1670 through the Stono Rebellion.* New York: W. W. Norton.

Wright, Louis B. (ed.) (1966) *The Elizabethans' America.* Cambridge, MA: Harvard University Press.

Wulf, Karin A. (2000) *Not All Wives: Women of Colonial Philadelphia.* Ithaca, NY: Cornell University Press.

Yazawa, Melvin (1985) *From Colonies to Commonwealth: Familial Ideology and the Beginnings of the American Republic.* Baltimore: Johns Hopkins University Press.

Zamora, Margarita (1990/1991) "Abreast of Columbus: Gender and Discovery," *Cultural Critique* 17, pp. 127–50.

From 1780 to 1880

Allgor, Catherine (2000) *Parlor Politics: In Which the Ladies of Washington Help Build a City and a Government.* Charlottesville: University Press of Virginia.

Als, Hilton (2000) "GWTW," in James Allen et al. (eds.), *Without Sanctuary: Lynching Photographs in America.* Santa Fe, NM: Twin Palms Publishing, pp. 38–44.

Altschuler, Glenn C. and Saltzgaber, Jan M. (1983) *Revivalism, Social Conscience and Community in the Burned-over District: The Trial of Rhoda Bement.* Ithaca, NY: Cornell University Press.

Anderson, Bonnie (2000) *Joyous Greetings: The First International Women's Movement, 1830–1860.* New York: Oxford University Press.

Ash, Stephen V. (1995) *When the Yankees Came: Conflict and Chaos in the Occupied South, 1861–1865.* Chapel Hill: University of North Carolina Press.

Attie, Jeannie (1998) *Patriotic Toil: Northern Women and the American Civil War.* Ithaca, NY: Cornell University Press.

Barron, Hal S. (1984) *Those Who Stayed Behind: Rural Society in Nineteenth-century New England.* New York: Cambridge University Press.

Basch, Norma (1982) *In the Eyes of the Law: Women, Marriage, and Property in Nineteenth-century New York.* Ithaca, NY: Cornell University Press.

Bellows, Barbara (1993) *Benevolence among Slaveholders: Assisting the Poor in Charleston, 1670–1860.* Baton Rouge: Louisiana State University Press.

Berlin, Ira et al. (eds.) (1982) *Freedom: A Documentary History of Emancipation, 1861–1867.* Ser. II: *The Black Military Experience.* New York: Cambridge University Press.

Blackmar, Elizabeth (1989) *Manhattan for Rent, 1785–1850.* Ithaca, NY: Cornell University Press.

Bleser, Carol (ed.) (1991) *In Joy and Sorrow: Women, Family, and Marriage in the Victorian South.* New York: Oxford University Press.

Blewett, Mary H. (1998) *Men, Women, and Work: A Study of Class, Gender, and Protest in the Nineteenth-century New England Shoe Industry, 1780–1910.* Urbana: University of Illinois Press.

Boydston, Jeanne (1990) *Home and Work: Housework, Wages, and the Ideology of Labor in the Early Republic.* New York: Oxford University Press.

Boydston, Jeanne (1996) "The Woman Who Wasn't There: Market Labor and the Transition to Capitalism in the United States," *Journal of the Early Republic* 16, pp. 183–206.

Boydston, Jeanne, Kelley, Mary, and Margolis, Anne (eds.) (1988) *The Limits of Sisterhood: The Beecher Sisters on Women's Rights and Woman's Sphere.* Chapel Hill: University of North Carolina Press.

Boylan, Anne (1986) "Timid Girls, Venerable Widows, and Dignified Matrons: Life Cycle Patterns among Organized Women in New York and Boston, 1787–1840," *American Quarterly* 38, pp. 779–98.

Braude, Ann (1989) *Radical Spirits: Spiritualism and Women's Rights in Nineteenth-century America.* Boston: Beacon Press.

Breault, Judith C. (1974) *The World of Emily Howland: Odyssey of a Humanitarian.* Millbrae, CA: Les Femmes Press.

Brockett, L. P. and Vaughan, Mary C. (1867) *Woman's Work in the Civil War: A Record of Heroism, Patriotism, and Patience.* Philadelphia: Zeigler, McCurdy.

Brodie, Janet Farrell (1994) *Contraception and Abortion in Nineteenth-century America.* Ithaca, NY: Cornell University Press.

Brown, Elsa Barkley (1994) "Negotiating and Transforming the Public Sphere: African American Political Life in the Transition from Slavery to Freedom," *Public Culture* 7, pp. 107–46.

Brown, Elsa Barkley and Kimball, Gregg D. (1996) "Mapping the Terrain of Black Richmond," in Kenneth W. Goings and Raymond A. Mohl (eds.), *The New African American Urban History.* Thousand Oaks, CA: Sage, pp. 66–115.

Brown, Gillian (1990) *Domestic Individualism: Imagining Self in Nineteenth-century America.* Berkeley: University of California Press.

Butchart, Ronald (1980) *Northern Schools, Southern Blacks and Reconstruction: Freedmen's Education, 1862–1875.* Westport, CT: Greenwood Press.

Butler, Anne (1989) "Still in Chains: Black Women in Western Prisons, 1865–1910," *Western Historical Quarterly* 20, pp. 19–35.

Bynum, Victoria E. (1987) " 'War Within a War': Women's Participation in the Revolt of the North Carolina Piedmont," *Frontiers* 9, pp. 43–9.

Bynum, Victoria E. (1992) *Unruly Women: The Politics of Social and Sexual Control in the Old South.* Chapel Hill: University of North Carolina Press.

Campbell, Edward D. C. and Rice, Kym (eds.) (1996) *A Woman's War: Southern Women, Civil War, and the Confederate Legacy.* Richmond and Charlottesville: Museum of the Confederacy and University of Virginia Press.

Cashin, Joan E. (1991) *A Family Venture: Men and Women on the Southern Frontier.* Baltimore: Johns Hopkins University Press.

Cashin, Joan E. (1995) "Black Families in the Old Northwest," *Journal of the Early Republic* 15, pp. 449–75.

Castañeda, Antonia (1998) "Engendering the History of Alta California, 1769–1848," in Ramón Gutiérrez and Richard J. Orsi (eds.), *Contested Eden: California Before the Gold Rush.* Berkeley: University of California Press, pp. 230–59.

Cayleff, Susan E. (1987) *Wash and Be Healed: The Water-cure Movement and Women's Health.* Philadelphia: Temple University Press.

Censer, Jane Turner (1984) *North Carolina Planters and their Children, 1800–1860.* Baton Rouge: Louisiana State University Press.

Chmielewski, Wendy E., Kern, Louis J., and Klee-Hartzell, Marlyn (eds.) (1993) *Women in Spiritual and Communitarian Societies in the United States.* Syracuse, NY: Syracuse University Press.

Clark, Christopher (1990) *The Roots of Rural Capitalism: Western Massachusetts, 1780–1860.* Ithaca, NY: Cornell University Press.

Clark, Elizabeth B. (1990) "Matrimonial Bonds: Slavery and Divorce in Nineteenth-century America," *Law and History Review* 8, pp. 25–54.

Clinton, Catherine (1982) *The Plantation Mistress: Woman's World in the Old South.* New York: Pantheon.

Clinton, Catherine (1995) *Tara Revisited: Women, War, and the Plantation Legend.* New York: Abbeville Press.

Clinton, Catherine and Silber, Nina (eds.) (1992) *Divided Houses: Gender and the Civil War.* New York: Oxford University Press.

Cogan, Jacob Katz and Ginzberg, Lori D. (1997) "Archives: 1846 Petition for Woman's Suffrage, New York State Constitutional Convention," *Signs* 22, pp. 427–39.

Cohen, Patricia Cline (1998) *The Murder of Helen Jewett: The Life and Death of a Prostitute in Nineteenth-century New York.* New York: Alfred A. Knopf.

Coleman, Willi (1990) "Travelling Black Women: Spreading the Anti-slavery Message Beyond Hearth and Home," in Frances Richardson Keller (ed.), *Views of Women's Lives in Western Traditions.* New York: Edwin Mellin Press, pp. 547–68.

Conrad, Susan Phinney (1976) *Perish the Thought: Intellectual Women in Romantic America, 1830–1860.* New York: Oxford University Press.

Cott, Nancy F. (1977) *The Bonds of Womanhood: "Woman's Sphere" in New England, 1780–1835.* New Haven, CT: Yale University Press.

Cott, Nancy F. (1978) "Passionlessness: An Interpretation of Victorian Sexual Ideology, 1790–1850," *Signs* 4, pp. 219–36. Rpt. (1984) in Judith W. Leavitt (ed.), *Women and*

Health in America: Historical Readings. Madison: University of Wisconsin Press, pp. 57–69.

Culpepper, Marilyn Mayer (1991) *Trials and Triumphs: Women of the American Civil War*. East Lansing: Michigan State University Press.

Dannett, Sylvia (1959) *Noble Women of the South*. New York: Thomas Yoseloff.

Davidoff, Leonore and Hall, Catherine (1987) *Family Fortunes: Men and Women of the English Middle Class, 1780–1850*. London: Hutchinson.

de Graaf, Lawrence B. (1980) "Race, Sex, and Region: Black Women in the American West, 1850–1920," *Pacific Historical Review* 49, pp. 285–313.

Diffendal, Anne P. (1994) "The La Flesche Sisters: Victorian Reformers in the Omaha Tribe," *Journal of the West* 33, pp. 37–44.

Diffley, Kathleen (1992) *Where My Heart is Turning Ever: Civil War Stories and Constitutional Reform, 1861–1876*. Athens: University of Georgia Press.

Diner, Hasia R. (1983) *Erin's Daughters in America: Irish Immigrant Women in the Nineteenth Century*. Baltimore: Johns Hopkins University Press.

Donegan, Jane B. (1986) *"Hydropathic Highway to Health": Women and Water-cure in Antebellum America*. Westport, CT: Greenwood Press.

Dorsey, Bruce (2002) *Reforming Men and Women: Gender in the Antebellum City*. Ithaca, NY: Cornell University Press.

Douglas, Ann (1977) *The Feminization of American Culture*. New York: Alfred A. Knopf.

Dublin, Thomas (1979) *Women at Work: The Transformation of Work and Community in Lowell, Massachusetts, 1826–1860*. New York: Columbia University Press.

Dublin, Thomas (ed.) (1981) *Farm to Factory: Women's Letters, 1830–1860*. New York: Columbia University Press; 2nd ed., 1993.

Dublin, Thomas (1994) *Transforming Women's Work: New England in the Industrial Revolution*. Ithaca, NY: Cornell University Press.

DuBois, Ellen (1978) *Feminism and Suffrage: The Emergence of an Independent Women's Movement in America, 1848–1869*. Ithaca, NY: Cornell University Press.

DuBois, W. E. B. (1935) *Black Reconstruction*. New York: Russell and Russell.

Dudden, Faye E. (1983) *Serving Women: Household Service in Nineteenth-century America*. Middletown, CT: Wesleyan University Press.

Dunaway, Wilma (1997) "Rethinking Cherokee Acculturation: Agrarian Capitalism and Women's Resistance to the Cult of Domesticity, 1800–1838," *American Indian Culture and Research Journal* 21, pp. 155–92.

Edgar, Walter (1998) *South Carolina: A History*. Columbia: University of South Carolina Press.

Edmondston, Catherine Ann Devereaux (1979) *Journal of a Secesh Lady: The Diary of Catherine Ann Devereaux Edmondston*, ed. Beth G. Crabtree and James W. Patton. Raleigh: North Carolina Division of Archives and History.

Edwards, Laura F. (1997) *Gendered Strife and Confusion: The Political Culture of Reconstruction*. Urbana: University of Illinois Press.

Edwards, Laura F. (2000) *Scarlett Doesn't Live Here Anymore: Southern Women in the Civil War Era*. Urbana: University of Illinois Press.

Fahs, Alice (2001) *The Imagined Civil War: Popular Literature of the North and South, 1861–1865*. Chapel Hill: University of North Carolina Press.

Faragher, John Mack (1979) *Women and Men on the Overland Trail*. New Haven, CT: Yale University Press.

Faragher, John Mack (1986) *Sugar Creek: Life on the Illinois Prairie*. New Haven, CT: Yale University Press.

Farnham, Christie Anne (1994) *The Education of the Southern Belle: Higher Education and Student Socialization in the Antebellum South.* New York: New York University Press.

Faust, Drew Gilpin (1996) *Mothers of Invention: Women of the Slaveholding South in the American Civil War.* Chapel Hill: University of North Carolina Press.

Faust, Drew Gilpin (1998) "'Ours As Well As That of the Men': Women and Gender in the Civil War," in James M. McPherson and William J. Cooper, Jr. (eds.), *Writing the Civil War: The Quest to Understand.* Columbia: University of South Carolina Press, pp. 228–40.

Fields, Barbara Jeanne (1985) *Slavery and Freedom on the Middle Ground: Maryland During the Nineteenth Century.* New Haven, CT: Yale University Press.

Fischer, Gayle V. (2001) *Pantaloons and Power: Nineteenth-century Dress Reform in the United States.* Kent, OH: Kent State Press.

Flexner, Eleanor (1959) *Century of Struggle: The Woman's Rights Movement in the United States.* Cambridge, MA: Harvard University Press.

Foote, Cheryl J. (1990) *Women of the New Mexico Frontier, 1846–1912.* Niwot: University Press of Colorado.

Forbes, Ella (1998) *African American Women During the Civil War.* New York: Garland Publishing.

Forten, Charlotte L. (1981) *The Journal of Charlotte Forten*, ed. Ray Allen Billington. New York: W. W. Norton.

Fox-Genovese, Elizabeth (1988) *Within the Plantation Household: Black and White Women of the Old South.* Chapel Hill: University of North Carolina Press.

Frankel, Noralee (1999) *Freedom's Women: Black Women and Families in Civil War Era Mississippi.* Bloomington: Indiana University Press.

Freedman, Estelle B. (1981) *Their Sisters' Keepers: Women's Prison Reform in America, 1830–1930.* Ann Arbor: University of Michigan Press.

Friedman, Jean E. (1985) *The Enclosed Garden: Women and Community in the Evangelical South, 1830–1900.* Chapel Hill: University of North Carolina Press.

Gallagher, Gary (1997) *The Confederate War.* Cambridge, MA: Harvard University Press.

Gallman, J. Matthew (1990) *Mastering Wartime: A Social History of Philadelphia During the Civil War.* New York: Cambridge University Press.

Gardiner, Martha Mabie (1999) "Working on White Womanhood: White Working Women in the San Francisco Anti-Chinese Movement, 1877–1890," *Journal of Social History* 33, pp. 73–95.

Giesberg, Judith Ann (2000) *Civil War Sisterhood: The U.S. Sanitary Commission and Women's Politics in Transition.* Boston: Northeastern University Press.

Gilfoyle, Timothy J. (1992) *City of Eros: New York City, Prostitution and the Commercialization of Sex.* New York: W. W. Norton.

Gilfoyle, Timothy J. (1994) "The Hearts of Nineteenth-century Men: Bigamy and Working-class Marriage in New York City, 1800–1890," *Prospects* 19, pp. 135–60.

Ginzberg, Lori D. (1990) *Women and the Work of Benevolence: Morality, Politics, and Class in the Nineteenth-century United States.* New Haven, CT: Yale University Press.

Ginzberg, Lori D. (1994) "'The Hearts of Your Readers Will Shudder': Fannie Wright, Infidelity, and American Free Thought," *American Quarterly* 46, pp. 195–226.

Ginzberg, Lori D. (2000) *Women in Antebellum Reform.* Wheeling, IL: Harlan Davidson.

Glatthaar, Joseph T. (1985) *The March to the Sea and Beyond: Sherman's Troops on the Savannah and Carolinas Campaigns.* Baton Rouge: Louisiana University Press.

Glymph, Thavolia (2000) "African-American Women in the Literary Imagination of Mary Boykin Chestnut," in Robert Louis Paquette and Louis A. Ferleger (eds.), *Slavery, Secession and Southern History.* Charlottesville: University Press of Virginia, pp. 140–59.

González, Deena (1999) *Refusing the Favor: The Spanish-Mexican Women of Santa Fe, 1820–1880.* New York: Oxford University Press.

Gordon, Ann (ed.) (1997) *The Selected Papers of Elizabeth Cady Stanton and Susan B. Anthony.* Vol. 1: *In the School of Anti-slavery, 1840–1866.* New Brunswick, NJ: Rutgers University Press.

Gordon, Beverly (1998) *Bazaars and Fair Ladies: The History of the American Fundraising Fair.* Knoxville: University of Tennessee Press.

Gordon, Lynn D. (1989) "Race, Class, and the Bonds of Womanhood at Spelman Seminary, 1881–1923," *History of Higher Education Annual* 9, pp. 7–32.

Griffin, Farah Jasmine (ed.) (1999) *Beloved Sisters and Loving Friends: Letters from Rebecca Primus of Royal Oak, Maryland, and Addie Brown, of Hartford, Connecticut, 1854–1868.* New York: Alfred A. Knopf.

Grossberg, Michael (1983) "Who Gets the Child? Custody, Guardianship, and the Rise of a Judicial Patriarchy in Nineteenth-century America," *Feminist Studies* 9, pp. 235–50.

Grossberg, Michael (1985) *Governing the Hearth: Law and the Family in Nineteenth-century America.* Chapel Hill: University of North Carolina Press.

Gutman, Herbert (1976) *The Black Family in Slavery and Freedom, 1750–1925*, 1st ed. New York: Pantheon Books.

Gutman, Herbert (1977) *Work, Culture and Society in Industrializing America.* New York: Alfred A. Knopf.

Haag, Pamela (1992) "The 'Ill-use' of a Wife: Patterns of Working-class Violence in Domestic and Public New York City, 1860–1880," *Journal of Social History* 25, pp. 447–77.

Haas, Lisbeth (1995) *Conquests and Historical Identities in California, 1769–1936.* Berkeley: University of California Press.

Hahn, Steven and Prude, Jonathan (eds.) (1985) *The Countryside in the Age of Capitalist Transformation: Essays in the Social History of Rural America.* Chapel Hill: University of North Carolina Press.

Hall, Catherine (1992) *White, Male, and Middle-class: Explorations in Feminism and History.* New York: Routledge.

Haller, Jr., J. S. and Haller, R. M. (1974) *The Physician and Sexuality in Victorian America.* Urbana: University of Illinois Press.

Handlin, Oscar (1941) *Boston's Immigrants, 1790–1865: A Study in Acculturation.* Cambridge, MA: Harvard University Press.

Hansen, Deborah Gold (1993) *Strained Sisterhood: Gender and Class in the Boston Female Anti-slavery Society.* Amherst: University of Massachusetts Press.

Hansen, Karen V. (1994) *A Very Social Time: Crafting Community in Antebellum New England.* Berkeley: University of California Press.

Hareven, Tamara K. (1982) *Family Time and Industrial Time: The Relationship between the Family and Work in a New England Industrial Community.* New York: Cambridge University Press.

Harris, Katherine (1993) *Long Vistas: Women and Families on Colorado Homesteads.* Niwot: University Press of Colorado.

Hartog, Hendrik (1997) "Lawyering, Husbands' Rights, and the Unwritten Law in Nineteenth-century America," *Journal of American History* 84, pp. 67–96.

Hersh, Blanche Glassman (1978) *The Slavery of Sex: Feminist-Abolitionism in America.* Urbana: University of Illinois Press.

Hershberger, Mary (1999) "Mobilizing Women, Anticipating Abolition: The Struggle against Indian Removal in the 1830s," *Journal of American History* 86, pp. 15–40.

Hesseltine, William B. (1936) *A History of the South, 1607–1936.* New York: Prentice-Hall.

Hewitt, Nancy A. (1984) *Women's Activism and Social Change: Rochester, New York, 1822–1872.* Ithaca, NY: Cornell University Press.

Higonnet, Margaret Randolph et al. (eds.) (1987) *Behind the Lines: Gender and the Two World Wars.* New Haven, CT: Yale University Press.

Hill, Marilynn Wood (1993) *Their Sisters' Keepers: Prostitution in New York City, 1830–1870.* Berkeley: University of California Press.

Hinkley, Ted C. (1993) "Glimpses of Societal Change among Nineteenth-century Tlingit Women," *Journal of the West* 32, pp. 12–24.

Hodes, Martha M. (1993) "The Sexualization of Reconstruction Politics: White Women and Black Men in the South after the Civil War," *Journal of the History of Sexuality* 3, pp. 402–17.

Hodes, Martha M. (1997) *White Women, Black Men: Illicit Sex in the Nineteenth-century South.* New Haven, CT: Yale University Press.

Hoffert, Sylvia D. (1995) *When Hens Crow: The Woman's Rights Movement in Antebellum America.* Bloomington: Indiana University Press.

Holmes, Kenneth (ed.) (1989) *Covered Wagon Women: Diaries and Letters from the Western Trails, 1862–1865.* Lincoln: University of Nebraska Press.

Horton, James Oliver (1986) "Freedom's Yoke: Gender Conventions among Antebellum Free Blacks," *Feminist Studies* 12, pp. 51–76.

Horton, James Oliver and Horton, Lois E. (1997) *In Hope of Liberty: Culture, Community, and Protest among Northern Free Blacks, 1700–1860.* New York: Oxford University Press.

Hudspeth, Robert N. (ed.) (2001) *"My Heart is a Large Kingdom": Selected Letters of Margaret Fuller.* Ithaca, NY: Cornell University Press.

Hunter, Tera W. (1997) *To 'Joy My Freedom: Southern Black Women's Lives and Labors After the Civil War.* Cambridge, MA: Harvard University Press.

Hurtado, Alberto L. (1988) *Indian Survival on the California Frontier.* New Haven, CT: Yale University Press.

Hurtado, Alberto L. (1999) *Intimate Frontiers: Sex, Gender, and Culture in Old California.* Albuquerque: University of New Mexico Press.

Isenberg, Nancy (1998) *Sex and Citizenship in Antebellum America.* Chapel Hill: University of North Carolina Press.

Jeffrey, Julie Roy (1979) *Frontier Women: The Trans-Mississippi West, 1840–1880.* New York: Hill and Wang.

Jeffrey, Julie Roy (1998) *The Great Silent Army of Abolitionism: Ordinary Women in the Antislavery Movement.* Chapel Hill: University of North Carolina Press.

Jensen, Joan M. (1986) *Loosening the Bonds: Mid-Atlantic Farm Women, 1750–1850.* New Haven, CT: Yale University Press.

Jensen, Joan M. and Miller, Darlis A. (eds.) (1980) "The Gentle Tamers Revisited: New Approaches to the History of Women in the American West," *Pacific Historical Review* 49, pp. 173–213.

Johnson, Susan Lee (2000) *Roaring Camp: The Social World of the California Gold Rush.* New York: W. W. Norton.

Johnson, Walter (1999) *Soul By Soul: Life Inside the Antebellum Slave Market.* Cambridge, MA: Harvard University Press.

Jones, Jacqueline (1980) *Soldiers of Light and Love: Northern Teachers and Georgia Blacks, 1865–1873.* Chapel Hill: University of North Carolina Press.

Kan, Sergei (1996) "Clan Mothers and Godmothers: Tlingit Women and Russian Orthodox Christianity, 1840–1940," *Ethnohistory* 43, pp. 613–41.

Kelley, Mary (1984) *Private Woman, Public Stage: Literary Domesticity in Nineteenth-century America.* New York: Oxford University Press.

Kelly, Catherine E. (1999) *In the New England Fashion: Reshaping Women's Lives in the Nineteenth Century.* Ithaca, NY: Cornell University Press.

Kennon, Donald R. (ed.) (1999) *A Republic for the Ages: The United States Capitol and the Political Culture of the Early Republic.* Charlottesville: United States Capitol Historical Society and the University of Virginia Press.

Kerber, Linda K. (1980) *Women of the Republic: Intellect and Ideology in Revolutionary America.* Chapel Hill: University of North Carolina Press.

Kern, Kathi (2001) *Mrs. Stanton's Bible.* Ithaca, NY: Cornell University Press.

Kerns, Kathryn (1986) "Farmers' Daughters: The Education of Women at Alfred Academy and University Before the Civil War," *History of Higher Education Annual* 6, pp. 11–28.

Kerr, Andrea Moore (1992) *Lucy Stone: Speaking Out for Equality.* New Brunswick, NJ: Rutgers University Press.

Kirschmann, Anne T. (1999) "A Vital Force: Women Physicians and Patients in American Homeopathy, 1850–1930," Ph.D. dissertation, University of Rochester, Rochester, New York.

Krowl, Michelle A. (1998) "Dixie's Other Daughters: African-American Women in Virginia, 1861–1868," Ph.D. dissertation, University of California, Berkeley.

Lasser, Carol (1987) "The Domestic Balance of Power: Relations between Mistress and Maid in Nineteenth-century New England," *Labor History* 28, pp. 5–22.

Lawes, Carolyn J. (2000) *Women and Reform in a New England Community, 1815–1860.* Lexington: University of Kentucky Press.

Lebsock, Suzanne (1984) *The Free Women of Petersburg: Status and Culture in a Southern Town, 1784–1860.* New York: W. W. Norton.

Leonard, Elizabeth D. (1994) *Yankee Women: Gender Battles in the Civil War.* New York: W. W. Norton.

Leonard, Elizabeth D. (1999) *All the Daring of the Soldier: Women of the Civil War Armies.* New York: W. W. Norton.

Lerner, Gerda (1969) "The Lady and the Mill Girl: Changes in the Status of Women in the Age of Jackson," *Midcontinent American Studies Journal* 10, pp. 5–15.

Lerner, Gerda (1977) *The Grimké Sisters from South Carolina: Pioneers for Woman's Rights and Abolition.* New York: Schocken Books.

Levy, Jo Ann (1990) *They Saw the Elephant: Women in the California Gold Rush.* Norman: University of Oklahoma Press.

Lewis, Jan (1983) *The Pursuit of Happiness: Family and Values in Jefferson's Virginia.* New York: Cambridge University Press.

Lewis, Jan (1987) "The Republican Wife: Virtue and Seduction in the Early Republic," *William and Mary Quarterly*, 3rd ser., 44, pp. 689–721.

Lewis, Jan (1995) "'Of Every Age Sex & Condition': The Representation of Women in the Constitution," *Journal of the Early Republic* 15, pp. 359–87.

Lewis, Jan and Lockridge, Kenneth (1988) "'Sally Has Been Sick': Pregnancy and Family Limitation among Virginia Gentry Women, 1780–1830," *Journal of Social History* 22, pp. 5–19.

Lindsay, Matthew J. (1988) "Reproducing a Fit Citizenry: Dependency, Eugenics, and the Law of Marriage in the United States, 1860–1920," *Law and Social Inquiry* 23, pp. 541–85.

Lubin, David M. (1994) *Picturing a Nation: Art and Social Change in Nineteenth-century America*. New Haven, CT: Yale University Press.

Lystra, Karen (1989) *Searching the Heart: Women, Men, and Romantic Love in Nineteenth-century America*. New York: Oxford University Press.

McClymer, John F. (ed.) (1999) *This High and Holy Moment: The First National Woman's Rights Convention, Worcester, 1850*. Fort Worth, TX: Harcourt, Brace College Publishers.

McCurry, Stephanie (1995) *Masters of Small Worlds: Yeoman Households, Gender Relations, and the Political Culture of the Antebellum South Carolina Low Country*. New York: Oxford University Press.

McGregor, Deborah K. (1998) *From Midwives to Medicine: The Birth of American Gynecology*. New Brunswick, NJ: Rutgers University Press.

McLaughlin, William G. (1986) *Cherokee Renascence in the New Republic*. Princeton, NJ: Princeton University Press.

McMahon, Lucia (2002) "Gender, Education, and Sociability in the Early Republic," Ph.D. dissertation, Rutgers University, New Brunswick, NJ.

McMillen, Sally G. (1990) *Motherhood in the Old South: Pregnancy, Childbirth, and Infant Rearing*. Baton Rouge: Louisiana State University Press.

McMurry, Sally Ann (1995) *Transforming Rural Life: Dairying Families and Agricultural Change, 1820–1885*. Baltimore: Johns Hopkins University Press.

McMurry, Sally Ann (1997) *Families and Farmhouses in Nineteenth-century America: Vernacular Design and Social Change*. Knoxville: University of Tennessee Press.

McPherson, James and Cooper, Jr., William A. (1998) *Writing the Civil War: The Quest to Understand*. Columbia: University of South Carolina Press.

Mahoney, Kathleen A. (2003) "American Catholic Colleges for Women: Historical Perspectives," in Tracy Schier and Cynthia Russett (eds.), *Catholic Women's Colleges in America*. Baltimore: Johns Hopkins University Press.

Mason, Michael (1994) *The Making of Victorian Sexuality*. New York: Oxford University Press.

Massey, Mary Elizabeth (1964) *Refugee Life in the Confederacy*. Baton Rouge: Louisiana State University Press.

Massey, Mary Elizabeth (1966) *Bonnet Brigades: American Women in the Civil War*. New York: Alfred A. Knopf.

Melder, Keith E. (1977) *Beginnings of Sisterhood: The American Woman's Rights Movement, 1800–1850*. New York: Schocken Books.

Mihesuah, Devon Abbott (1993) *Cultivating the Rosebuds: The Education of Women at the Cherokee Female Seminary, 1851–1909*. Urbana: University of Illinois Press.

Mitchell, Reid (1993) *The Vacant Chair: The Northern Soldier Leaves Home*. New York: Oxford University Press.

Mohr, Clarence L. (1986) *On the Threshold of Freedom: Master and Slaves in Civil War Georgia*. Athens: University of Georgia Press.

Mohr, James C. (1978) *Abortion in America: The Origins and Evolution of National Policy, 1800–1900*. New York: Oxford University Press.

Montoya, María (2000) "Dividing the Land: The Taylor Ranch and the Case for Preserving the Limited Access Commons," in William G. Robbins and James C. Foster (eds.), *Land in the American West: Private Claims and the Common Good*. Seattle: University of Washington Press, pp. 121–44.

Morantz, Regina M. (1977) "Making Women Modern: Middle-class Women and Health Reform in 19th-century America," *Journal of Social History* 10, pp. 490–507.

Morton, Patricia (ed.) (1996) *Discovering the Women in Slavery.* Athens: University of Georgia Press.

Moynihan, Ruth, Armitage, Susan, and Dichamp, Christiane Fischer (eds.) (1990) *So Much to be Done: Women Settlers on the Mining and Ranching Frontier.* Lincoln: University of Nebraska Press.

Murphy, Teresa Anne (1992) *Ten Hours' Labor: Religion, Reform, and Gender in Early New England.* Ithaca, NY: Cornell University Press.

Myres, Sandra L. (1982) *Westering Women and the Frontier Experience, 1800–1915.* Albuquerque: University of New Mexico Press.

Nash, Margaret A. (1997) "Rethinking Republican Motherhood: Benjamin Rush and the Young Ladies' Academy of Philadelphia," *Journal of the Early Republic* 17, pp. 171–91.

Nee, Victor and Nee, Brett de Bary (1973) *Longtime Californ': A Documentary Study of an American Chinatown.* New York: Pantheon Books.

Nissenbaum, Stephen (1980) *Sex, Deity, and Debility in Jacksonian America: Sylvester Graham and Health Reform.* Westport, CT: Greenwood Press.

Novak, Michael (1972) *The Rise of the Unmeltable Ethnics: Politics and Culture in the Seventies.* New York: Macmillan.

O'Leary, Cecelia Elizabeth (1999) *To Die For: The Paradox of American Patriotism.* Princeton, NJ: Princeton University Press.

Oates, Stephen B. (1994) *A Woman of Valor: Clara Barton and the Civil War.* New York: Free Press.

Osterud, Nancy Grey (1991) *Bonds of Community: The Lives of Farm Women in Nineteenth-century New York.* Ithaca, NY: Cornell University Press.

Painter, Nell Irvin (1996) *Sojourner Truth: A Life, A Symbol.* New York: W. W. Norton.

Palladino, Grace (1990) *Another Civil War: Labor, Capital, and the State in the Anthracite Regions of Pennsylvania, 1840–68.* Urbana: University of Illinois Press.

Palmer, Beverly Wilson (ed.) (2001) *Selected Letters of Lucretia Coffin Mott.* Urbana: University of Illinois Press.

Paludan, Phillip Shaw (1988) *"A People's Contest": The Union and the Civil War.* Lawrence: University Press of Kansas.

Park, Robert E. and Miller, Herbert A. (1969) *Old World Traits Transplanted.* New York: Arno Press.

Perdue, Theda (1989) "Cherokee Women on the Trail of Tears," *Journal of Women's History* 1, pp. 14–30.

Peterson, Carla L. (1995) *"Doers of the Word": African-American Women Speakers and Writers in the North, 1830–1880.* New York: Oxford University Press.

Prude, Jonathan (1985) *The Coming of the Industrial Order: Town and Factory Life in Rural Massachusetts, 1810–1860.* New York: Cambridge University Press.

Quarles, Benjamin (1953) *The Negro in the Civil War.* Boston: Little, Brown.

Rable, George C. (1989) *Civil Wars: Women and the Crisis of Southern Nationalism.* Urbana: University of Illinois Press.

Raboteau, Albert (1978) *Slave Religion: The "Invisible Institution" in the Antebellum South.* New York: Oxford University Press.

Ramsdell, Charles W. (1944) *Behind the Lines in the Southern Confederacy.* Baton Rouge: Louisiana State University Press.

Ransom, Roger (1989) *Conflict and Compromise: The Political Economy of Slavery, Emancipation and the American Civil War.* New York: Cambridge University Press.

Reed, James (1978) *From Private Vice to Public Virtue: The Birth Control Movement and American Society since 1830.* New York: Basic Books.

Reese, William J. (1995) *The Origins of the American High School.* New Haven, CT: Yale University Press.

Rhodes, Jane (1998) *Mary Ann Shadd Cary: The Black Press and Protest in the Nineteenth Century.* Bloomington: Indiana University Press.

Riley, Glenda (1984) *Women and Indians on the Frontier, 1825–1915.* Albuquerque: University of New Mexico Press.

Riley, Glenda (1988) *The Female Frontier: A Comparative View of Women on the Prairie and the Plains.* Lawrence: University Press of Kansas.

Riley, Glenda (1998) "The Myth of Female Fear of Western Landscapes," *Journal of the West* 37, pp. 33–41.

Roberson, Susan (ed.) (1998) *Women, America, and Movement: Narratives of Relocation.* Columbia: University of Missouri Press.

Robertson, Stacey M. (2000) *Parker Pillsbury: Radical Abolitionist, Male Feminist.* Ithaca, NY: Cornell University Press.

Russett, Cynthia E. (1989) *Sexual Science: The Victorian Construction of Womanhood.* Cambridge, MA: Harvard University Press.

Ryan, Mary P. (1981) *The Cradle of the Middle Class: The Family in Oneida County, New York, 1780–1865.* New York: Cambridge University Press.

Ryan, Mary P. (1990) *Women in Public: Between Banners and Ballots, 1825–1880.* Baltimore: Johns Hopkins University Press.

Sachs, Carolyn E. (1983) *The Invisible Farmers: Women in Agricultural Production.* Totowa, NJ: Rowman and Allenheld.

Sahli, Nancy (1979) "Smashing: Women's Relationships Before the Fall," *Chrysalis* 17, pp. 679–703.

Sander, Kathleen Waters (1998) *The Business of Charity: The Woman's Exchange Movement, 1832–1900.* Urbana: University of Illinois Press.

Saville, Julie (1994) *The Work of Reconstruction: From Slave to Wage Laborer in South Carolina, 1860–1870.* New York: Cambridge University Press.

Schiebinger, Londa (1986) "Skeletons in the Closet: The First Illustrations of the Female Skeleton in Nineteenth-century Anatomy," *Representations* 14, pp. 42–82.

Schlissel, Lillian (1982) *Women's Diaries of the Westward Journey.* New York: Schocken Books.

Schwalm, Leslie A. (1997) *A Hard Fight for We: Women's Transition from Slavery to Freedom in South Carolina.* Urbana: University of Illinois Press.

Scott, Anne Firor (1970) *The Southern Lady: From Pedestal to Politics, 1830–1930.* Chicago: University of Chicago Press.

Scott, Anne Firor (1979) " 'The Ever-widening Circle': The Diffusion of Feminist Values from the Troy Female Seminary, 1822–1872," *History of Education Quarterly* 19, pp. 3–25.

Shoemaker, Nancy (1991) "The Rise or Fall of Iroquois Women," *Journal of Women's History* 2, pp. 39–57.

Siegel, Reva (1994) "Home as Work: The First Woman's Rights Claims Concerning Wives' Household Labor, 1850–1880," *Yale Law Journal* 103, pp. 1073–1217.

Silber, Nina (1993) *The Romance of Reunion: Northerners and Southerners, 1865–1900.* Chapel Hill: University of North Carolina Press.

Simkins, Francis Butler and Patton, James Welch (1936) *The Women of the Confederacy.* Richmond: Garrett and Massie.

Sklar, Kathryn Kish (1973) *Catharine Beecher: A Study in American Domesticity.* New Haven, CT: Yale University Press.

Sklar, Kathryn Kish (1993) "The Schooling of Girls and Changing Community Values in Massachusetts Towns, 1750–1820," *History of Education Quarterly* 33, pp. 511–42.

Sklar, Kathryn Kish (1995) *Florence Kelley and the Nation's Work: The Rise of Women's Political Culture, 1830–1900.* New Haven, CT: Yale University Press.

Sklar, Kathryn Kish (2000) *Women's Rights Emerges Within the Antislavery Movement, 1830–1870.* Boston: Bedford/St. Martin's.

Smith, Daniel Scott (1973) "Family Limitation, Sexual Control, and Domestic Feminism in Victorian America," *Feminist Studies* 1, pp. 40–57.

Smith-Rosenberg, Carroll (1971) "Beauty, the Beast, and the Militant Woman: A Case Study of Sex Roles and Social Stress in Jacksonian America," *American Quarterly* 23, pp. 562–84.

Smith-Rosenberg, Carroll (1975) "The Female World of Love and Ritual: Relations between Women in Nineteenth-century America," *Signs* 1, pp. 1–29.

Smith-Rosenberg, Carroll (1985) *Disorderly Conduct: Visions of Gender in Victorian America.* New York: Alfred A. Knopf.

Speicher, Anna M. (2000) *The Religious World of Antislavery Women: Spirituality in the Lives of Five Abolitionist Lecturers.* Syracuse, NY: Syracuse University Press.

Spurlock, John C. (1988) *Free Love: Marriage and Middle-class Radicalism in America, 1825–1860.* New York: New York University Press.

Stanley, Amy Dru (1996) "Home Life and the Morality of the Market," in Melvyn Stokes and Stephen Conway (eds.), *The Market Revolution in America.* Charlottesville: University of Virginia Press, pp. 74–96.

Stanley, Amy Dru (1998) *From Bondage to Contract: Wage Labor, Marriage, and the Market in the Age of Slave Emancipation.* New York: Cambridge University Press.

Stanley, Amy Dru (1999) "'We Did Not Separate Man and Wife, But All Had to Work': Freedom and Dependence in the Aftermath of Slave Emancipation," in Stanley L. Engerman (ed.), *Terms of Labor: Slavery, Serfdom, and Free Labor.* Stanford, CA: Stanford University Press, pp. 188–212.

Stansell, Christine (1986) *City of Women: Sex and Class in New York City, 1789–1860.* New York: Alfred A. Knopf.

Sterling, Dorothy (ed.) (1984) *We Are Your Sisters: Black Women in the Nineteenth Century.* New York: W. W. Norton.

Sterling, Dorothy (1991) *Ahead of Her Time: Abby Kelly and the Politics of Antislavery.* New York: W. W. Norton.

Sterx, H. E. (1970) *Partners in Rebellion: Alabama Women in the Civil War.* Rutherford, NJ: Farleigh Dickinson University Press.

Stevenson, Brenda E. (1996) *Life in Black and White: Family and Community in the Slave South.* New York: Oxford University Press.

Stratton, Joanna L. (1981) *Pioneer Women: Voices from the Kansas Frontier.* New York: Simon and Schuster.

Terborg-Penn, Rosalyn (1998) *African American Women and the Struggle for the Vote, 1850–1920.* Bloomington: Indiana University Press.

Todd, Jan (1998) *Physical Culture and the Body Beautiful: Purposive Exercise in the Lives of American Women, 1800–1870.* Macon, GA: Mercer University Press.

Tong, Benson (1994) *Unsubmissive Women: Chinese Prostitutes in Nineteenth-century San Francisco.* Norman: University of Oklahoma Press.

Turbin, Carol (1992) *Working Women of Collar City: Gender, Class and Community in Troy, New York, 1864–86.* Urbana: University of Illinois Press.

Varon, Elizabeth R. (1998) *We Mean to be Counted: White Women and Politics in Antebellum Virginia.* Chapel Hill: University of North Carolina Press.

Vrettos, Athena (1995) *Somatic Fictions: Imagining Illness in Victorian Culture.* Stanford, CA: Stanford University Press.

Waldstreicher, David (1997) *In the Midst of Perpetual Fetes: The Making of American Nationalism, 1776–1820.* Chapel Hill: University of North Carolina Press.

Walters, Ronald G. (ed.) (1974) *Primers for Prudery: Sexual Advice to Victorian America.* Englewood Cliffs, NJ: Prentice-Hall.

Walters, Ronald G. (ed.) (1997) *American Reformers, 1815–1860.* New York: Hill and Wang.

Ward, Geoffrey, C. (1996) "Refighting the Civil War," in Robert Brent Toplin (ed.), *Ken Burns' The Civil War: Historians Respond.* New York: Oxford University Press.

Watkins, Sam (1994 [1882]) "*Co. Aytch.*" Wilmington, NC: Broadfoot Publishing.

Weiner, Marli F. (1998) *Mistresses and Slaves: Plantation Women in South Carolina, 1830–1880.* Urbana: University of Illinois Press.

Wellman, Judith (1991) "The Seneca Falls Woman's Rights Convention: A Study of Social Networks," *Journal of Women's History* 3, pp. 9–37.

Wells-Barnett, Ida B. (1969) *On Lynchings: Southern Horrors* (1892), *A Red Record* (1895), and *Mob Rule in New Orleans* (1900). Rpt., New York: Arno Press.

Welter, Barbara (1966) "The Cult of True Womanhood, 1820–1860," *American Quarterly* 18, pp. 151–74.

Welter, Barbara (1976) *Dimity Convictions: The American Woman in the Nineteenth Century.* Athens: Ohio State University Press.

Wesley, Charles H. (1937) *The Collapse of the Confederacy.* Washington, DC: Associated Publishers.

White, Bruce (1999) "The Woman Who Married a Beaver: Trade Patterns and Gender Roles in the Ojibwa Fur Trade," *Ethnohistory* 46, pp. 109–47.

White, Deborah Gray (1985) *Ar'n't I a Woman?: Female Slaves in the Plantation South.* New York: W. W. Norton.

Whites, LeeAnn (1995) *The Civil War as a Crisis in Gender: Augusta, Georgia, 1860–1890.* Athens: University of Georgia Press.

Wiley, Bell Irvin (1943) *The Plain People of the Confederacy.* Baton Rouge: Louisiana State University Press.

Wiley, Bell Irvin (1975) *Confederate Women.* Westport, CT: Greenwood Press.

Winegarten, Ruth (ed.) (1995) *Black Texas Women.* Austin: University of Texas Press.

Yee, Shirley J. (1992) *Black Women Abolitionists: A Study in Activism, 1828–1860.* Knoxville: University of Tennessee Press.

Yellin, Jean Fagan (1989) *Women and Sisters: The Antislavery Feminists in American Culture.* New Haven, CT: Yale University Press.

Yellin, Jean Fagan and Van Horne, John C. (eds.) (1994) *The Abolitionist Sisterhood: Women's Political Culture in Antebellum America.* Ithaca, NY: Cornell University Press.

Young, Agatha B. (1959) *The Women and the Crisis: Women of the North in the Civil War.* New York: McDowell, Obolensky.

Zagarri, Rosemarie (1992) "Morals, Manners, and the Republican Mother," *American Quarterly* 44, pp. 192–215.

Zagarri, Rosemarie (1998) "The Rights of Man and Woman in Post-Revolutionary America," *William and Mary Quarterly*, 3rd ser., 55, pp. 203–30.

Zboray, Ronald J. and Zboray, Mary Saracino (1997) "Whig Women, Politics, and Culture in the Campaign of 1840: Three Perspectives from Massachusetts," *Journal of the Early Republic* 17, pp. 277–315.

Ziegler, Sara L. (1996) "Wifely Duties: Marriage, Labor, and the Common Law in Nineteenth-century America," *Social Science History* 20, pp. 63–96.

From 1880 to 1990

Abelson, Elaine (1989) *When Ladies Go A-Thieving: Middle-class Shoplifters in the Victorian Department Store.* New York: Oxford University Press.

Adams, David Wallace (1995) *Education for Extinction: American Indians and the Boarding School Experience, 1875–1928.* Lawrence: University Press of Kansas.

Alexander, Ruth M. (1995) *The "Girl Problem": Female Sexual Delinquency in New York, 1900–1930.* Ithaca, NY: Cornell University Press.

Anderson, Karen (1981) *Wartime Women: Sex Roles, Family Relations and the Status of Women During World War II.* Westport, CT: Greenwood Press.

Anderson, Karen (1982) "Last Hired, First Fired: Black Women Workers During World War II," *Journal of American History* 69, pp. 82–97.

Anderson, Karen (1996) *Changing Woman: A History of Racial Ethnic Women in Modern America.* New York: Oxford University Press.

Antler, Joyce (1980) "After College, What? New Graduates and the Family Claim," *American Quarterly* 32, pp. 409–34.

Antler, Joyce (1986) *Lucy Sprague Mitchell: The Making of a Modern Woman.* New Haven, CT: Yale University Press.

Apple, Rima D. (1987) *Mothers and Medicine: A Social History of Infant Feeding, 1890–1950.* Madison: University of Wisconsin Press.

Bailey, Beth (1999) *Sex in the Heartland.* Cambridge, MA: Harvard University Press.

Bailey, Beth and Farber, David (1992) *The First Strange Place: The Alchemy of Race and Sex in World War II Hawaii.* New York: Free Press.

Baker, Jeffrey P. (1996) *The Machine in the Nursery: Incubator Technology and the Origins of Newborn Intensive Care.* Baltimore: Johns Hopkins University Press.

Barnard, Hollinger F. (ed.) (1985) *Outside the Magic Circle: The Autobiography of Virginia Foster Durr.* Alabama: University of Alabama Press.

Barrett, James (1992) "Americanization from the Bottom Up: Immigration and the Remaking of the Working Class in the United States, 1880–1930," *Journal of American History* 79, pp. 996–1020.

Bates, Daisy (1962) *The Long Shadow of Little Rock: A Memoir.* New York: David McKay.

Baxandall, Rosalyn and Gordon, Linda (eds.) (2000) *Dear Sisters: Dispatches from the Women's Liberation Movement.* New York: Basic Books.

Beals, Melba Patillo (1994) *Warriors Don't Cry: A Searing Memoir of the Battle to Integrate Little Rock's Central High.* New York: Washington Square Press.

Beasley, Maurine (1987) *Eleanor Roosevelt and the Media: A Public Quest for Self-fulfillment.* Urbana: University of Illinois Press.

Bederman, Gail (1989) " 'The Women Have Had Charge of the Church-work Long Enough': The Men and Religion Forward Movement of 1911–1912 and the Masculinization of Middle-class Protestantism," *American Quarterly* 41, pp. 432–65.

Bederman, Gail (1995) *Manliness and Civilization: A Cultural History of Gender and Race in the United States, 1880–1917.* Chicago: University of Chicago Press.

Benson, Susan Porter (1986) *Counter Cultures: Saleswomen, Managers, and Customers in American Department Stores, 1890–1940.* Urbana: University of Illinois Press.

Bentley, Amy (1998) *Eating for Victory: Food Rationing and the Politics of Domesticity.* Urbana: University of Illinois Press.

Bernstein, Alison (1984) "A Mixed Record: The Political Enfranchisement of American Indian Women During the Indian New Deal," *Journal of the West* 23, pp. 13–20.

Bishop, Elizabeth (1983) *The Complete Poems, 1927–1979.* New York: Farrar, Straus, and Giroux.

Blackwelder, Julia Kirk (1984) *Women of the Depression: Caste and Culture in San Antonio, 1939–1949.* College Station: Texas A & M Press.

Blair, Karen (1980) *The Clubwoman as Feminist: True Womanhood Redefined, 1868–1914.* New York: Holmes and Meier.

Bledstein, Burton (1976) *The Culture of Professionalism: The Middle Class and the Development of Higher Education in America.* New York: W. W. Norton.

Blee, Kathleen (1991) *Women of the Klan: Racism and Gender in the 1920s.* Berkeley: University of California Press.

Bookman, Ann and Morgen, Sandra (eds.) (1988) *Women and the Politics of Empowerment.* Philadelphia: Temple University Press.

Bordin, Ruth (1981) *Women and Temperance: The Quest for Power and Liberty, 1873–1900.* Philadelphia: Temple University Press.

Bordin, Ruth (1986) *Frances Willard: A Biography.* Chapel Hill: University of North Carolina Press.

Boris, Eileen (1994) *Home to Work: Motherhood and the Politics of Industrial Homework in the United States.* New York: Cambridge University Press.

Boris, Eileen (1998) " 'You Wouldn't Want One of 'Em Dancing with Your Wife': Racialized Bodies on the Job in World War II," *American Quarterly* 50, pp. 77–108.

Borst, Charlotte G. (1995) *Catching Babies: The Professionalization of Childbirth, 1870–1920.* Cambridge, MA: Harvard University Press.

Boxer, Marilyn Jacoby (1999) *When Women Ask the Questions: Creating Women's Studies in America.* Chicago: University of Chicago Press.

Braden, Anne (1999) *The Wall Between*, 2nd ed. Knoxville: University of Tennessee Press.

Breazeale, Kenon (1994) "In Spite of Women: Esquire Magazine and the Construction of the Male Consumer," *Signs* 20, pp. 1–22.

Breines, Wini (1992) *Young, White, and Miserable: Growing Up Female in the Fifties.* Boston: Beacon Press.

Brennan, Timothy (1989) "Cosmopolitans and Celebrities," *Race and Class* 31, pp. 1–20.

Brennan, Timothy (1997) *At Home in the World: Cosmopolitanism Now.* Cambridge, MA: Harvard University Press.

Brickman, Jane Pacht (1983) "Public Health, Midwives, and Nurses, 1880–1930," in Ellen Condliffe (ed.), *Nursing History: New Perspectives, New Possibilities.* New York: Teacher's College Press, pp. 65–88.

Briggs, L. J. (1998) "Reproducing Empire: Race and Sex, Science and Reform in Puerto Rico and the Mainland United States, 1880–1960," Ph.D. dissertation, Brown University.

Brody, David (1979) "The Old Labor History and the New: in Search of an American Working Class," *Labor History* 20, pp. 111–26.

Brown, Elaine (1992) *A Taste of Power: A Black Woman's Story.* New York: Doubleday.

Brownmiller, Susan (1999) *In Our Time: Memoir of a Revolutionary.* New York: Dial Press.

Brumberg, Joan Jacobs (1982) "Ruined Girls: Changing Community Responses to Illegitimacy in Upstate New York, 1890–1920," *1984, Journal of Social History* 18, pp. 247–72.

Buhle, Mari Jo (1981) *Women and American Socialism, 1870–1920.* Urbana: University of Illinois Press.

Bullard, Robert (ed.) (1993) *Confronting Environmental Racism: Voices from the Grassroots.* Boston: South End Press.

Burman, Barbara (ed.) (1999) *The Culture of Sewing: Gender, Consumption and Home Dressmaking.* New York: Berg Publishers.

Cahn, Susan K. (1994) *Coming on Strong: Gender and Sexuality in Twentieth-century Women's Sports.* Cambridge, MA: Harvard University Press.

Cameron, Ardis (1993) *Radicals of the Worst Sort: Laboring Women in Lawrence, Massachusetts, 1860–1912.* Urbana: University of Illinois Press.

Carby, Hazel V. (1986) "'It Jus' Be's Dat Way Sometime': The Sexual Politics of Women's Blues," *Radical America* 20, pp. 9–24.

Casper, Monica J. (1998) *The Making of the Unborn Patient: A Social Anatomy of Fetal Surgery.* New Brunswick, NJ: Rutgers University Press.

Cayleff, Susan E. (1995) *Babe: The Life and Legend of Babe Didrikson Zaharias.* Urbana: University of Illinois Press.

Chafe, William H. (1972) *The American Woman: Her Changing Social, Economic and Political Roles, 1929–1970.* New York: Oxford University Press.

Chafe, William H. (1991) *The Paradox of Change: American Women in the 20th Century.* New York: Oxford University Press.

Chan, Sucheng (ed.) (1991) *Entry Denied: Exclusion and the Chinese Community in America, 1882–1943.* Philadelphia: Temple University Press.

Chateauvert, Melinda (1998) *Marching Together: Women of the Brotherhood of Sleeping Car Porters.* Urbana: University of Illinois Press.

Chauncey, George (1982) "From Sexual Inversion to Homosexuality: Medicine and the Changing Conceptualization of Female Deviance," *Salmagundi* 58/59, pp. 114–46.

Chauncey, George (1994) *Gay New York: Gender, Urban Culture, and the Making of the Gay Male World, 1890–1940.* New York: Basic Books.

Chesler, Ellen (1992) *Woman of Valor: Margaret Sanger and the Birth Control Movement in America.* New York: Simon and Schuster.

Clark, Adele E. (1998) *Disciplining Reproduction: Modernity, American Life Sciences, and the Problems of Sex.* Berkeley: University of California Press.

Clark, E. Culpepper (1993) *The Schoolhouse Door: Segregation's Last Stand at the University of Alabama.* New York: Oxford University Press.

Clark, Septima (1962) *Echo in My Soul.* New York: E. P. Dutton.

Clark-Lewis, Elizabeth (1996) *Living In, Living Out: African American Domestics and the Great Migration.* New York: Kodansha International.

Clifford, Geraldine Joncich (ed.) (1989) *Lone Voyagers: Academic Women in Coeducational Institutions, 1870–1937.* New York: Feminist Press.

Clifford, James (1988) *The Predicament of Culture: Twentieth-century Ethnography, Literature, and Art.* Cambridge, MA: Harvard University Press.

Clifford, James (1997) *Routes: Travel and Translation in the Late Twentieth Century.* Cambridge, MA: Harvard University Press.

Cobble, Dorothy Sue (1991) *Dishing It Out: Waitresses and their Unions in the Twentieth Century.* Urbana: University of Illinois Press.

Cobble, Dorothy Sue (1999) " 'A Spontaneous Loss of Enthusiasm': Workplace Feminism and the Transformation of Women's Service Jobs in the 1970s," *International Labor and Working-class History* 56, pp. 23–44.

Cohen, Lizabeth (1990) *Making a New Deal: Industrial Workers in Chicago, 1919–1939.* New York: Cambridge University Press.

Cohen, Lizabeth (1996) "From Town Center to Shopping Center: The Reconfiguration of Community Marketplaces in Postwar America," *American Historical Review* 101, pp. 1050–81.

Cohen, Miriam (1992) *Workshop to Office: Two Generations of Italian Women in New York City, 1900–1950.* Ithaca, NY: Cornell University Press.

Collins, Patricia Hill (1990) *Black Feminist Thought: Knowledge, Consciousness, and the Politics of Empowerment.* Boston: Unwin Hyman.

Conable, Charlotte (1977) *Women at Cornell: The Myth of Equal Education.* Ithaca, NY: Cornell University Press.

Cook, Blanche Weisen (1992) *Eleanor Roosevelt*, 2 vols. New York: Penguin.

Cookingham, Mary E. (1984a) "Bluestockings, Spinsters, and Pedagogues: Women College Graduates, 1865–1910," *Population Studies* 38, pp. 349–64.

Cookingham, Mary E. (1984b) "Combining Marriage, Motherhood and Jobs Before World War II: Women College Graduates, Classes of 1905–1935," *Journal of Family History* 9, pp. 349–64.

Cookingham, Mary E. (1984c) "Working After Childbearing in Modern America," *Journal of Interdisciplinary History* 14, pp. 773–92.

Cooper, Patricia (1987) *Once a Cigar Maker: Men, Women and Work Culture in American Cigar Factories, 1900–1919.* Urbana: University of Illinois Press.

Cott, Nancy (1987) *The Grounding of Modern Feminism.* New Haven, CT: Yale University Press.

Cowan, Ruth Schwartz (1983) *More Work for Mother: The Ironies of Household Technology from the Open Hearth to the Microwave.* New York: Basic Books.

Crain, Marion (1994) "Gender and Union Organizing," *Industrial and Labor Relations Review* 47, pp. 227–48.

Crawford, Vicki, Rouse, Jacqueline Anne, and Woods, Barbara (eds.) (1990) *Women in the Civil Rights Movement: Trailblazers and Torchbearers, 1941–1965.* Brooklyn: Carlson Publishing.

Crow, Barbara A. (ed.) (2000) *Radical Feminism: A Documentary History.* New York: New York University Press.

Curry, Connie et al. (2000) *Deep in Our Hearts: Nine Women in the Freedom Movement.* Athens: University of Georgia Press.

Curry, Lynne (1999) *Modern Mothers in the Heartland: Gender, Health, and Progress in Illinois, 1900–1930.* Columbus: Ohio State University Press.

Daniels, Cynthia R. (1997) "Between Fathers and Fetuses: The Social Construction of Male Reproduction and the Politics of Fetal Harm," *Signs* 22, pp. 584–88.

Davidson, James West and Lytle, Mark Hamilton (1986) "From Rosie to Lucy: The Mass Media and Images of Women in the 1950s," in West and Hamilton (eds.), *After the Fact: The Art of Historical Detection*, 2nd ed. New York: Alfred A. Knopf, pp. 364–94.

Davis, Allen F. (1967) *Spearheads for Reform: The Social Settlements and the Progressive Movement, 1890–1914.* New Brunswick, NJ: Rutgers University Press.

Davis, Angela Y. (1998) *Blues Legacies and Black Feminism: Gertrude "Ma" Rainey, Bessie Smith and Billie Holiday.* New York: Pantheon Books.

Davis, Flora (1991) *Moving the Mountain: The Women's Movement in America since 1960.* New York: Simon and Schuster.

Davis, Simone Weil (2000) *Living Up to the Ads: Gender Fictions of the 1920s.* Durham, NC: Duke University Press.

De Grazia, Victoria and Furlough, Ellen (eds.) (1996) *The Sex of Things: Essays on Gender and Consumption.* Berkeley: University of California Press.

Declerq, Eugene R. (1985) "The Nature and Style of Practice of Immigrant Midwives in Early Twentieth-century Massachusetts," *Journal of Social History* 19, pp. 113–29.

Delaney, Rebekah (1999) "Girl Power: From Disruption to Consumption," *Phoebe*, pp. 1–25.

Delegard, Kirsten (1999) "Women Patriots: Female Activism and the Politics of American Anti-radicalism, 1919–1935," Ph.D. dissertation, Duke University.

Deslippe, Dennis A. (2000) *"Rights, Not Roses": Unions and the Rise of Working-class Feminism, 1945–80.* Urbana: University of Illinois Press.

Deutsch, Sarah (1987) *No Separate Refuge: Culture, Class, and Gender on an Anglo-Hispanic Frontier in the American Southwest, 1880–1940.* New York: Oxford University Press.

Deutsch, Sarah (2000) *Women and the City: Gender, Space, and Power in Boston, 1870–1940.* New York: Oxford University Press.

Di Leonardo, Micaela (1987) "The Female World of Cards and Holidays: Women, Families, and the Work of Kinship," *Signs* 12, pp. 440–54.

Douglas, Susan J. (1994) *Where the Girls Are: Growing Up Female with the Mass Media.* New York: Times Books.

Drachman, Virginia G. (1998) *Sisters in Law: Women Lawyers in Modern American History.* Cambridge, MA: Harvard University Press.

DuBois, Ellen (1997) *Harriet Stanton Blatch and the Winning of Woman Suffrage.* New Haven, CT: Yale University Press.

Duggan, Lisa (2000) *Sapphic Slashers: Sex, Violence and American Modernity.* Durham, NC: Duke University Press.

DuPlessis, Rachel Blau and Snitow, Ann (eds.) (1998) *The Feminist Memoir Project.* New York: Three Rivers Press.

Dye, Nancy Schrom (1980) *As Equals and Sisters: Feminism, Unionism and the Women's Trade Union League of New York.* Columbia: University of Missouri Press.

Dzuback, Mary Ann (1993) "Women and Social Research at Bryn Mawr College, 1915–1940," *History of Education Quarterly* 33, pp. 579–608.

Echols, Alice (1989) *Daring to be Bad: Radical Feminism in America, 1967–1975.* Minneapolis: University of Minnesota Press.

Ehrenreich, Barbara (1983) *The Hearts of Men: American Dreams and the Flight from Commitment.* New York: Doubleday.

Eisenmann, Linda (1996) "Befuddling the Feminine Mystique: Academic Women and the Creation of the Radcliffe Institute, 1950–1965," *Educational Foundations* 10, pp. 5–26.

Eisenstein, Hester (1983) *Contemporary Feminist Thought.* London: G. K. Hall.

Enstad, Nan (1999) *Ladies of Labor, Girls of Adventure: Working Women, Popular Culture and Labor Politics at the Turn of the Twentieth Century.* New York: Columbia University Press.

Erenberg, Lewis (1980) *Steppin' Out: New York Nightlife and the Transformation of American Culture, 1890–1930.* Westport, CT: Greenwood Press.

Etzioni, Amitai (1969) *The Semi-professions and their Organizations: Teachers, Nurses, and Social Worker.* New York: Free Press.

Evans, Sara (1980) *Personal Politics: The Roots of Women's Liberation in the Civil Rights Movement and the New Left.* New York: Vintage Books.

Ewen, Elizabeth (1985) *Immigrant Women in the Land of Dollars: Life and Culture on the Lower East Side, 1890–1925.* New York: Monthly Review Press.

Eyes on the Prize – America's Civil Rights Years, Awakenings, 1954–56. (1986) Documentary film. Boston: Blackside/PBS-TV.

Faderman, Lillian (1991) *Odd Girls and Twilight Lovers: A History of Lesbian Life in Twentieth-century America.* New York: Columbia University Press.

Fass, Paula S. (1977) *The Damned and the Beautiful: American Youth in the 1920s.* New York: Oxford University Press.

Fass, Paula S. (1989) *Outside In: Minorities and the Transformation of American Education.* New York: Oxford University Press.

Faue, Elizabeth (1991) *Community of Suffering and Struggle: Women, Men, and the Labor Movement in Minneapolis, 1915–1945.* Chapel Hill: University of North Carolina Press.

Feldstein, Ruth (2000) *Motherhood in Black and White: Race and Sex in American Liberalism, 1930–1965.* Ithaca, NY: Cornell University Press.

Felsenthal, Carol (1981) *The Sweetheart of the Silent Majority: The Biography of Phyllis Schlafly.* Garden City, NY: Doubleday.

Ferree, Myra Marx and Hess, Beth B. (2000) *Controversy and Coalition: The New Feminist Movement Across Four Decades of Change*, 3rd ed. New York: Routledge.

Fields, Mamie Garvin and Fields, Karen (1983) *Lemon Swamp and Other Places: A Carolina Memoir.* New York: Free Press.

Filene, Peter S. (1974) *Him/Her/Self: Sex Roles in Modern America.* New York: New American Library.

Finnegan, Margaret (1999) *Selling Suffrage: Consumer Culture and Votes for Women.* New York: Columbia University Press.

Fitzpatrick, Ellen (1990) *Endless Crusade: Women Social Scientists and Progressive Reform.* New York: Oxford University Press.

Fleming, Cynthia Griggs (1998) *Soon We Will Not Cry: The Liberation of Ruby Doris Smith Robinson.* Lanham, MD: Rowman and Littlefield.

Flexner, Eleanor (1959) *Century of Struggle: The Woman's Rights Movement in the United States.* Cambridge, MA: Harvard University Press.

Foley, Neil (1997) *The White Scourge: Mexicans, Blacks and Poor Whites in Texas Cotton Culture.* Berkeley: University of California Press.

Foreman, Joel (ed.) (1997) *The Other Fifties: Interrogating Midcentury American Icons.* Urbana: University of Illinois Press.

Formanek-Brunell, Miriam (1993) *Made to Play House: Dolls and the Commercialization of American Girlhood, 1830–1930.* New Haven, CT: Yale University Press.

Fousekis, Natalie Marie (2000) "Fighting for Our Children: Women's Activism and the Battle for Child Care in California, 1940–1965," Ph.D. dissertation, University of North Carolina, Chapel Hill.

Fout, John C. and Tantillo, Maura Shaw (eds.) (1993) *American Sexual Politics: Sex, Gender and Race since the Civil War.* Chicago: University of Chicago Press.

Fox, Richard Wightman and Lears, T. J. Jackson (eds.) (1983) *The Culture of Consumption: Critical Essays in American History, 1880–1980.* New York: Pantheon.

Frank, Dana (1985) "Housewives, Socialists and the Politics of Food: The 1917 Cost of Living Protests," *Feminist Studies* 11, pp. 255–85.

Frank, Dana (1994) *Purchasing Power: Consumer Organizing, Gender, and the Seattle Labor Movement, 1919–1929*. Cambridge, MA: Harvard University Press.

Frankel, Noralee and Dye, Nancy Shrom (eds.) (1991) *Gender, Class, Race, and Reform in the Progressive Era*. Lexington: University of Kentucky Press.

Franklin, John Hope and Moss, Alfred A. (1994) *From Slavery to Freedom: A History of African Americans*, 7th ed. New York: McGraw-Hill.

Freedman, Estelle B. (1979) "Separatism as Strategy: Female Institution Building and American Feminism, 1870–1930," *Feminist Studies* 5, pp. 512–29.

Freedman, Estelle B. (1996) *Maternal Justice: Miriam Van Waters and the Female Reform Tradition*. Chicago: University of Chicago Press.

Freeman, Jo (1975) *The Politics of Women's Liberation*. New York: McKay.

French, Brandon (1978) *On the Verge of Revolt: Women in American Films of the Fifties*. New York: Frederick Ungar.

Fuller, Kathryn H. (1996) *At the Motion Picture Show: Small-town Audiences and the Creation of Movie-fan Culture*. Washington, DC: Smithsonian Institution Press.

Gabaccia, Donna R. (1984) *From Sicily to Elizabeth Street: Housing and Social Change among Italian Immigrants, 1880–1930*. Albany: State University of New York Press.

Gabin, Nancy F. (1990) *Feminism in the Labor Movement: Women and the United Auto Workers, 1935–1975*. Ithaca, NY: Cornell University Press.

Gaines, Kevin (1996) *Uplifting the Race: Black Leadership, Politics, and Culture in the Twentieth Century*. Chapel Hill: University of North Carolina Press.

García, Alma (ed.) (1997) *Chicana Feminist Thought: The Basic Historical Writings*. New York: Routledge.

Garrison, Dee (1979) *Apostles of Culture: the Public Librarian and American Society, 1876–1920*. New York: Free Press.

Garrison, Dee (1989) *Mary Heaton Vorse: The Life of an American Insurgent*. Philadelphia: Temple University Press.

Garrison, Ednie Kaeh (2000) "U.S. Feminism – Grrrl Style! Youth (Sub)Cultures and the Technologies of the Third Wave," *Feminist Studies* 26, pp. 141–70.

Garrow, David (ed.) (1987) *The Montgomery Bus Boycott and the Women Who Started It: The Memoir of Jo Ann Gibson Robinson*. Knoxville: University of Tennessee Press.

Garrow, David J. (1994) *Liberty and Sexuality: The Right to Privacy and the Making of Roe v. Wade*. New York: Macmillan.

Garvey, Ellen Gruber (1996) *The Adman in the Parlor: Magazines and the Gendering of Consumer Culture, 1880s to 1910s*. New York: Oxford University Press.

Gilmore, Glenda Elizabeth (1996) *Gender and Jim Crow: Women and the Politics of White Supremacy in North Carolina, 1896–1920*. Chapel Hill: University of North Carolina Press.

Glazer, Nathan and Moynihan, Daniel Patrick (1970) *Beyond the Melting Pot: The Negroes, Puerto Ricans, Jews, Italians, and Irish of New York City*. Cambridge, MA: MIT Press.

Glazer, Penina Migdal and Slater, Miriam (1987) *Unequal Colleagues: The Entrance of Women into the Professions, 1890–1940*. New Brunswick, NJ: Rutgers University Press.

Glenn, Evelyn Nakano (1986) *Issei, Nissei, War Bride: Three Generations of Japanese American Women in Domestic Service*. Philadelphia: Temple University Press.

Glenn, Susan A. (1990) *Daughters of the Shtetl: Life and Labor in the Immigrant Generation*. Ithaca, NY: Cornell University Press.

Glenn, Susan A. (1998) "'Give an Imitation of Me': Vaudeville Mimics and the Play of the Self," *American Quarterly* 50, pp. 47–76.

Glenn, Susan (2000) *Female Spectacle: The Theatrical Roots of Modern Feminism.* Cambridge, MA: Harvard University Press.

Glickman, Lawrence (1997) *A Living Wage: American Workers and the Making of Consumer Society.* Ithaca, NY: Cornell University Press.

Goldberg, Michael Lewis (1997) *An Army of Women: Gender and Politics in Gilded Age Kansas.* Baltimore: Johns Hopkins University Press.

Golden, Janet (1999) " 'An Argument that Goes Back to the Womb': The Demedicalization of Fetal Alcohol Syndrome, 1973–1992," *Journal of Social History* 33, pp. 269–98.

Goodwin, Joanne L. (1997) *Gender and the Politics of Welfare Reform: Mothers' Pensions in Chicago, 1911–1929.* Chicago: University of Chicago Press.

Gordon, Ann, with Bettye Collier-Thomas et al. (eds.) (1997) *African American Women and the Vote, 1837–1965.* Amherst: University of Massachusetts Press.

Gordon, Linda (1988) *Heroes of their Own Lives: The Politics and History of Family Violence, Boston, 1880–1960.* New York: Viking Books.

Gordon, Linda (ed.) (1990) *Women, the State, and Welfare.* Madison: University of Wisconsin Press.

Gordon, Linda (1991) "Black and White Visions of Welfare: Women's Welfare Activism, 1890–1945," *Journal of American History* 78, pp. 559–90.

Gordon, Linda (1994) *Pitied But Not Entitled: Single Mothers and the History of Welfare.* New York: Free Press.

Gordon, Linda (1999) *The Great Arizona Orphan Abduction.* Cambridge, MA: Harvard University Press.

Gordon, Lynn D. (1987) "The Gibson Girl Goes to College: Popular Culture and Women's Higher Education in the Progressive Era, 1890–1920," *American Quarterly* 39, pp. 211–30.

Gordon, Lynn D. (1990) *Gender and Higher Education in the Progressive Era.* New Haven, CT: Yale University Press.

Gordon, Sarah Barringer (1996) "The Liberty of Self-degradation: Polygamy, Women's Suffrage and Consent in Nineteenth-century America," *Journal of American History* 44, pp. 815–47.

Graham, Sarah Hunter (1996) *Woman Suffrage and the New Democracy.* New Haven, CT: Yale University Press.

Grant, Joanne (1998) *Ella Baker: Freedom Bound.* New York: John Wiley and Sons.

Grant, Nicole J. (1992) *The Selling of Contraception: The Dalkon Shield Case, Sexuality, and Women's Autonomy.* Columbus: Ohio State University Press.

Green, Elna (1997) *Southern Strategies: Southern Women and the Woman Suffrage Question.* Chapel Hill: University of North Carolina Press.

Green, Nancy L. (1997) *Ready-to-Wear and Ready-to-Work: A Century of Industry and Immigrants in Paris and New York.* Durham, NC: Duke University Press.

Greenberg, Cheryl (1997) *Or Does It Explode? Black Harlem in the Great Depression.* New York: Oxford University Press.

Greenberg, Cheryl (1998) *A Circle of Trust: Remembering SNCC.* New Brunswick, NJ: Rutgers University Press.

Gullett, Gayle (2000) *Becoming Citizens: The Emergence and Development of the California Women's Movement, 1880–1911.* Urbana: University of Illinois Press.

Halberstam, David (1998) *The Children.* New York: Random House.

Hall, Jacquelyn Dowd (1979) *Revolt Against Chivalry: Jessie Daniel Ames and the Women's Campaign Against Lynching.* New York: Columbia University Press.

Hall, Jacquelyn Dowd (1986) "Disorderly Women: Gender and Labor Militancy in the Appalachian South," *Journal of American History* 73, pp. 354–82.

Hall, Jacquelyn Dowd, Jones, LuAnn, Korstad, Robert, Leloudis, James, and Murphy, Mary (1987) *Like a Family: The Making of a Southern Cotton Mill World*. Chapel Hill: University of North Carolina Press.

Hansen, Karen (1989) *Distant Companions: Servants and Employers in Zambia, 1900–1985*. Ithaca, NY: Cornell University Press.

Hansen, Miriam (1991) *Babel and Babylon: Spectatorship in American Silent Film*. Cambridge, MA: Harvard University Press.

Harley, Sharon and Terborg-Penn, Rosalyn (eds.) (1978) *The Afro-American Woman: Struggles and Images*. Port Washington, NY: Kennikat Press.

Harris, Neil (1990) *Cultural Exclusions: Marketing Appetites and Cultural Tastes in Modern America*. Chicago: University of Chicago Press.

Harrison, Cynthia (1988) *On Account of Sex: The Politics of Women's Issues, 1945–1968*. Berkeley: University of California Press.

Hartmann, Susan M. (1982) *The Home Front and Beyond: American Women in the 1940s*. Boston: Twayne.

Hartmann, Susan M. (1989) *From Margin to Mainstream: American Women and Politics since 1960*. New York: Alfred A. Knopf.

Heinze, Andrew R. (1990) *Adapting to Abundance: Jewish Immigrants, Mass Consumption, and the Search for American Identity*. New York: Columbia University Press.

Helmbold, Lois Rita (1987) "Beyond the Family Economy: Black and White Working-class Women During the Great Depression," *Feminist Studies* 13, pp. 629–55.

Hepler, Allison L. (1999) "Shaping the Life of the Pre-natal: Labor Laws, Liability, and Lead Poisoning of Women in Industry in Twentieth-century United States," *Social Politics* 6, pp. 54–75.

Hepler, Allison L. (2000) *Women in Labor: Mothers, Medicine, and Occupational Health in the United States, 1890–1980*. Columbus: Ohio State University Press.

Herbst, Jurgen (1989) *And Sadly Teach: Teacher Education and Professionalization in American Culture*. Madison: University of Wisconsin Press.

Hewitt, Nancy A. (2001) *Southern Discomfort: Women's Activism in Tampa, Florida, 1880s–1920s*. Urbana: University of Illinois Press.

Higginbotham, Evelyn Brooks (1993) *Righteous Discontent: The Women's Movement in the Black Baptist Church, 1880–1920*. Cambridge, MA: Harvard University Press.

Hine, Darlene Clark (1989) *Black Women in White: Racial Conflict and Cooperation in the Nursing Profession, 1890–1950*. Bloomington: Indiana University Press.

Hobson, Barbara (1987) *Uneasy Virtue: The Politics of Prostitution and the American Reform Tradition*. New York: Basic Books.

Hoffman, Nancy (ed.) (1979) *Woman's True Profession: Voices from the History of Teaching*. New York: Feminist Press.

Hoff-Wilson, Joan and Lightman, Marjorie (eds.) (1984) *Without Precedent: The Life and Career of Eleanor Roosevelt*. Bloomington: Indiana University Press.

Holland, Dorothy C. and Eisenhart, Margaret A. (1990) *Educated in Romance: Women, Achievement, and College Culture*. Chicago: University of Chicago Press.

Holz, Rosemarie (2002) "The Birth Control Clinic: Women, Planned Parenthood, and the Birth Control Manufacturing Industry, 1923–1973," Ph.D. dissertation, University of Illinois, Urbana-Champaign.

Honey, Maureen (1984) *Creating Rosie the Riveter: Class, Gender, and Propaganda During World War II.* Amherst: University of Massachusetts Press.

Honig, Emily (1996) "Women at Farah Revisited: Political Mobilization and its Aftermath among Chicano Workers in El Paso, Texas, 1972–1992," *Feminist Studies* 22, pp. 425–52.

Horowitz, Daniel (1985) *The Morality of Spending: Attitudes toward the Consumer Society in America, 1875–1940.* Baltimore: Johns Hopkins University Press.

Horowitz, Helen Lefkowitz (1984) *Alma Mater: Design and Experience in the Women's Colleges from their Nineteenth-century Beginnings to the 1930s.* New York: Alfred A. Knopf.

Horowitz, Helen Lefkowitz (1994) *The Power and Passion of M. Carey Thomas.* New York: Alfred A. Knopf.

Horowitz, Roger and Mohun, Arwen (eds.) (1998) *His and Hers: Gender, Consumption, and Technology.* Charlottesville: University of Virginia Press.

Howard, Angela and Tarrant, Sasha Ranae Adams (eds.) (1997) *Antifeminism in America: A Collection of Readings from the Literature of the Opponents to U.S. Feminism, 1948 to the Present.* New York: Garland Press.

Hummer, Patricia M. (1979) *The Decade of Elusive Promise: Professional Women in the United States, 1920–1930.* Ann Arbor, MI: University Microfilms Research Press.

Hunter Gault, Charlayne (1992) *In My Place.* New York: Farrar, Straus, and Giroux.

Hyman, Paula (1980) "Immigrant Women and Consumer Protest: The New York City Kosher Meat Boycott of 1902," *American Jewish History* 70, pp. 126–40.

Jeansonne, Glen (1996) *Women of the Far Right: The Mother's Movement and World War II.* Chicago: University of Chicago Press.

Jellison, Katherine (1993) *Entitled to Power: Farm Women and Technology, 1913–1963.* Chapel Hill: University of North Carolina Press.

Jensen, Joan and Scharf, Lois (eds.) (1983) *Decades of Discontent: The Women's Movement, 1920–1940.* Westport, CT: Greenwood Press.

Jetter, Alexis, Orleck, Annelise, and Taylor, Diana (eds.) (1997) *The Politics of Motherhood: Activist Voices from Left to Right.* Hanover: University Press of New England.

Joffe, Carole (1995) *Doctors of Conscience: The Struggle to Provide Abortion Before and After Roe v. Wade.* Boston: Beacon Press.

Kahn, Susan Martha (2000) *Reproducing Jews: A Cultural Account of Assisted Reproduction in Israel.* Durham, NC: Duke University Press.

Kaledin, Eugenia (1984) *Mothers and More: American Women in the 1950s.* Boston: Twayne.

Kammen, Michael (1999) *American Culture, American Tastes: Social Change in the Twentieth Century.* New York: Alfred A. Knopf.

Kaplan, Laura (1995) *The Story of Jane: The Legendary Underground Feminist Abortion Service.* Chicago: University of Chicago Press.

Kauffman, Linda (ed.) (1993) *American Feminist Thought at Century's End: A Reader.* Cambridge, MA: Blackwell.

Kennedy, Elizabeth Lapovsky and Davis, Madeline D. (1993) *Boots of Leather, Slippers of Gold: The History of a Lesbian Community.* New York: Routledge.

Kerber, Linda K., Kessler-Harris, Alice, and Sklar, Kathryn Kish (eds.) (1995) *U.S. History as Women's History: New Feminist Essays.* Chapel Hill: University of North Carolina Press.

Kessler-Harris, Alice (1990a) *A Woman's Wage: Historical Meanings and Social Consequences.* Lexington: University of Kentucky Press.

Kessler-Harris, Alice (1990b) "Gender Ideology in Historical Reconstruction: A Case Study from the 1930s," *Gender and History* 2, pp. 31–9.

Kibler, M. Alison (1999) *Rank Ladies: Gender and Cultural Hierarchy in American Vaudeville*. Chapel Hill: University of North Carolina Press.

Kidwell, Claudia B. and Christman, Margaret C. (1974) *Suiting Everyone: The Democratization of Dress in America*. Washington, DC: Smithsonian Institution Press.

King, Charles R. (1991) "The New York Maternal Mortality Study: A Conflict of Professionalization," *Bulletin of the History of Medicine* 65, pp. 476–80.

King, Mary (1987) *Freedom Song: A Personal Story of the 1960s Civil Rights Movement*. New York: William Morrow.

Klatch, Rebecca (1988) *Women of the New Right*. Philadelphia: Temple University Press.

Klaus, Alisa (1993) *Every Child a Lion: The Origins of Maternal and Infant Health Policy in the United States and France, 1890–1920*. Ithaca, NY: Cornell University Press.

Kleinberg, Susan J. (1989) *The Shadow of the Mills: Working-class Families in Pittsburgh, 1870–1917*. Pittsburgh: University of Pittsburgh Press.

Kornbluh, Joyce and Frederickson, Mary (eds.) (1984) *Sisterhood and Solidarity: Worker's Education for Women, 1914–1984*. Philadelphia: Temple University Press.

Koven, Seth and Michel, Sonya (1990) "Womanly Duties: Maternalist Politics and the Origins of Welfare States in France, Germany, Great Britain and the United States, 1880–1920," *American Historical Review* 95, pp. 1076–1108.

Koven, Seth and Michel, Sonya (eds.) (1993) *Mothers of a New World: Maternalist Politics and the Origins of Welfare States*. New York: Routledge.

Kraditor, Aileen (1965) *The Ideas of the Women's Suffrage Movement, 1890–1920*. New York: Columbia University Press.

Kraut, Alan M. (1982) *The Huddled Masses: The Immigrant in American Society, 1880–1921*. Arlington Heights, IL: Harlan Davidson.

Kunzel, Regina G. (1993) *Fallen Women, Problem Girls: Unmarried Mothers and the Professionalization of Social Work, 1890–1945*. New Haven, CT: Yale University Press.

Kunzel, Regina G. (1995) "Pulp Fictions and Problem Girls: Reading and Rewriting Single Pregnancy in the Postwar United States," *American Historical Review* 100, pp. 1465–87.

Ladd-Taylor, Molly (1986) *Raising a Baby the Government Way: Mothers' Letters to the Children's Bureau, 1915–1932*. New Brunswick, NJ: Rutgers University Press.

Ladd-Taylor, Molly (1994) *Mother-work: Women, Child Welfare, and the State, 1890–1930*. Urbana: University of Illinois Press.

Ladd-Taylor, Molly (1997) "Saving Babies and Sterilizing Mothers: Eugenics and Welfare Politics in the Interwar United States," *Social Politics* 4, pp. 136–53.

Ladd-Taylor, Molly and Umansky, Lauri (eds.) (1998) *Bad Mothers: The Politics of Blame in Twentieth-century America*. New York: New York University Press.

Lamphere, Louise (1987) *From Working Daughters to Working Mothers: Immigrant Women in a New England Industrial Community*. Ithaca, NY: Cornell University Press.

Lash, Joseph P. (1971) *Eleanor and Franklin: The Story of their Relationship*. New York: W. W. Norton.

Lawson, Steven F. (1997) *Running for Freedom: Civil Rights and Black Politics in America since 1941*, 2nd ed. New York: McGraw-Hill.

Leach, William (1984) "Transformations in a Culture of Consumption: Women and Department Stores, 1890–1925," *Journal of American History* 71, pp. 311–42.

Leach, William (1993) *Land of Desire: Merchants, Power, and the Rise of a New American Culture*. New York: Pantheon.

Lears, T. J. Jackson (1994) *Fables of Abundance: A Cultural History of Advertising in America*. New York: Basic Books.

Leavitt, Judith Walzer (1987) "The Growth of Medical Authority, Technology, and Morals in Turn-of-the-century Obstetrics," *Medical Anthropology Quarterly* 1, pp. 230–55.
Leavitt, Judith Walzer (1996) *Typhoid Mary: Captive to the Public's Health.* Boston: Beacon Press.
Lee, Chana Kai (1999) *For Freedom's Sake: The Life of Fannie Lou Hamer.* Urbana: University of Illinois Press.
Leeder, Elaine (1993) *The Gentle General: Rose Pesotta, Anarchist and Labor Organizer.* Albany: State University of New York Press.
Lemke-Santangelo, Gretchen (1996) *Abiding Courage: African American Migrant Women and the East Bay Community.* Chapel Hill: University of North Carolina Press.
Lemons, J. Stanley (1973) *The Woman Citizen: Social Feminism in the 1920s.* Urbana: University of Illinois Press.
Lever, Janet and Schwartz, Pepper (1971) *Women at Yale: Liberating a College Campus.* Indianapolis, IN: Bobbs-Merrill.
Levine, Susan (1991) "Workers' Wives: Gender, Class, and Consumerism in the 1920s United States," *Gender and History* 3, 45–64.
Lewis, Abigail Sara (1999) "The Role of the Young Women's Christian Association in Shaping the Gender Consciousness of the Student Non-violent Coordinating Committee, 1960–1965," M.A. thesis, University of California, Los Angeles.
Lindenmeyer, Kriste (1997) *A Right to Childhood: The U.S. Children's Bureau and Child Welfare, 1912–46.* Urbana: University of Illinois Press.
Ling, Huping (1998) *Surviving on the Gold Mountain: A History of Chinese American Women and their Lives.* Albany: State University of New York Press.
Ling, Peter J. and Monteith, Sharon (eds.) (1999) *Gender in the Civil Rights Movement.* New York: Garland Publishing.
Logan, Onnie Lee, as told to Katherine Clark (1989) *Motherwit: An Alabama Midwife's Story.* New York: E. P. Dutton.
Loveland, Anne C. (1986) *Lillian Smith: A Southerner Confronting the South.* Baton Rouge: Louisiana State University Press.
Lowe, Lisa (1996) *Immigrant Acts: On Asian American Cultural Politics.* Durham, NC: Duke University Press.
Luker, Kristin (1984) *Abortion and the Politics of Motherhood.* Berkeley: University of California Press.
Lunbeck, Elizabeth (1987) "A New Generation of Women: Progressive Psychiatrists and the Hypersexual Female," *Feminist Studies* 13, pp. 513–43.
Lunbeck, Elizabeth (1994) *The Psychiatric Persuasion: Knowledge, Gender, and Power in Modern America.* Princeton, NJ: Princeton University Press.
Lynn, Susan (1992) *Progressive Women in Conservative Times: Racial Justice, Peace, and Feminism, 1945 to the 1960s.* New Brunswick, NJ: Rutgers University Press.
McBee, Randy D. (2000) *Dance Hall Days: Intimacy and Leisure among Working-class Immigrants in the United States.* New York: New York University Press.
McCandless, Amy Thompson (1987) "Preserving the Pedestal: Restrictions on Social Life at Southern Colleges for Women, 1920–1940," *History of Higher Education Annual* 7, pp. 45–67.
McCandless, Amy Thompson (1999) *The Past in the Present: Women's Higher Education in the Twentieth-century American South.* Tuscaloosa: University of Alabama Press.
McCann, Carole R. (1994) *Birth Control Politics in the United States, 1916–1945.* Ithaca, NY: Cornell University Press.

McEnaney, Laura (2000) *Civil Defense Begins at Home: Militarization Meets Everyday Life in the Fifties.* Princeton, NJ: Princeton University Press.

McGovern, James (1968) "The American Woman's Pre-World War I Freedom in Manners and Morals," *Journal of American History* 58, pp. 315–33.

MacLean, Nancy (1991a) "The Leo Frank Case Reconsidered: Gender and Sexual Politics in the Making of Reactionary Populism," *Journal of American History* 78, pp. 917–48.

MacLean, Nancy (1991b) "White Women, Klan Violence in the 1920s: Agency, Complicity, and the Politics of Women's History," *Gender and History* 3, pp. 285–303.

MacLean, Nancy (1994) *Behind the Mask of Chivalry: The Making of the Second Ku Klux Klan.* New York: Oxford University Press.

McMurry, Linda O. (1998) *To Keep the Waters Troubled: The Life of Ida B. Wells.* New York: Oxford University Press.

Maines, Rachel P. (1999) *The Technology of Orgasm: "Hysteria," The Vibrator and Women's Sexual Satisfaction.* Baltimore: Johns Hopkins University Press.

Marchand, Roland (1985) *Advertising the American Dream: Making Way for Modernity.* Berkeley: University of California Press.

Mark, Joan (1988) *A Stranger in Her Native Land: Alice Fletcher and the American Indians.* Lincoln: University of Nebraska Press.

Markowitz, Ruth Jacknow (1993) *My Daughter the Teacher: Jewish Teachers in the New York City Schools.* New Brunswick, NJ: Rutgers University Press.

Marti, Donald B. (1991) *Women of the Grange: Mutuality and Sisterhood in Rural America, 1866–1920.* New York: Greenwood Press.

Martin, Emily (1987) *Woman in the Body: A Cultural Analysis of Reproduction.* Boston: Beacon Press.

Martin, Theodora Penny (1987) *The Sound of Our Own Voices: Women's Study Clubs, 1860–1910.* Boston: Beacon Press.

Mathews, Donald G. and De Hart, Jane Sherron (1990) *Sex, Gender and the Politics of the ERA: A State and the Nation.* New York: Oxford University Press.

Matsumoto, Valerie (1993) *Farming the Home Place: A Japanese American Community in California, 1919–1982.* Ithaca, NY: Cornell University Press.

May, Elaine Tyler (1988) *Homeward Bound: American Families in the Cold War Era.* New York: Basic Books.

May, Elaine Tyler (1995) *Barren in the Promised Land: Childless Americans and the Pursuit of Happiness.* Cambridge, MA: Harvard University Press.

Meckel, Richard A. (1990) *Save the Babies: American Public Health Reform and the Prevention of Infant Mortality, 1850–1929.* Baltimore: Johns Hopkins University Press.

Mehaffy, Marilyn Maness (1997) "Advertising Race/Raceing Advertising: The Feminine Consumer(-Nation), 1876–1900," *Signs* 23, pp. 131–74.

Melosh, Barbara (1982) *The Physician's Hand: Work Culture and Conflict in American Nursing.* Philadelphia: Temple University Press.

Melosh, Barbara (1991) *Engendering Culture: Manhood and Womanhood in the New Deal Public Art and Theater.* Washington, DC: Smithsonian Institution Press.

Mettler, Suzanne (1998) *Dividing Citizens: Gender and Federalism in New Deal Public Policy.* Ithaca, NY: Cornell University Press.

Meyer, Leisa D. (1992) "Creating G. I. Jane: The Regulation of Sexuality and Sexual Behavior in the Women's Army Corps During World War II," *Feminist Studies* 18, pp. 581–601.

Meyer, Leisa D. (1996) *Creating G. I. Jane: Sexuality and Power in the Women's Army Corps During World War II.* New York: Columbia University Press.

Meyerowitz, Joanne J. (1988) *Women Adrift: Independent Wage-earners in Chicago, 1880–1930.* Chicago: University of Chicago Press.

Meyerowitz, Joanne (1993) "Beyond the Feminine Mystique: A Reassessment of Postwar Mass Culture, 1946–1958," *Journal of American History* 79, pp. 1455–82.

Meyerowitz, Joanne (ed.) (1994) *Not June Cleaver: Women and Gender in Postwar America, 1945–1960.* Philadelphia: Temple University Press.

Meyerowitz, Joanne (1996) "Women, Cheesecake, and Borderline Material: Responses to Girlie Pictures in the Mid-twentieth-century United States," *Journal of Women's History* 8, pp. 9–35.

Meyerowitz, Joanne (2001) "Sex, Gender, and the Cold War Language of Reform," in James Gilbert and Peter Kuznick (eds.), *Rethinking Cold War Culture.* Washington, DC: Smithsonian Institution Press, pp. 106–23.

Michel, Sonya (1999) *Children's Interests/Mothers' Rights: The Shaping of America's Child Care Policy.* New Haven, CT: Yale University Press.

Michel, Sonya and Rosen, Ruth (1992) "The Paradox of Maternalism: Elizabeth Lowell Putnam and the American Welfare State," *Gender and History* 4, pp. 364–86.

Milkman, Ruth (1979) "Women's Work and the Economic Crisis: Some Lessons from the Great Depression," in Nancy F. Cott and Elizabeth H. Pleck (eds.), *A Heritage of Her Own: Toward a New Social History of American Women.* New York: Simon and Schuster, pp. 507–41.

Milkman, Ruth (ed.) (1985) *Women, Work and Protest: A Century of Women's Labor History.* London: Routledge and Kegan Paul.

Milkman, Ruth (1987) *Gender at Work: The Dynamics of Job Segregation by Sex During World War II.* Urbana: University of Illinois Press.

Mills, Kay (1993) *This Little Light of Mine: The Life of Fannie Lou Hamer.* New York: Dutton.

Mink, Gwendolyn (1995) *The Wages of Motherhood: Inequality in the Welfare State, 1917–1942.* Ithaca, NY: Cornell University Press.

Mohr, James (1978) *Abortion in America: The Origins and Evolution of National Policy.* New York: Oxford University Press.

Moody, Anne (1968) *Coming of Age in Mississippi.* New York: Dell Publishing.

Moraga, Cherrie and Anzaldua, Gloria (eds.) (1983) *This Bridge Called My Back: Writings by Radical Women of Color.* New York: Kitchen Table Press.

Moran, Michelle (2002) "Leprosy and American Imperialism: Patient Communities and the Politics of Public Health in Hawai'i and Louisiana, 1888–1959," Ph.D. dissertation, University of Illinois, Urbana-Champaign.

Morantz-Sanchez, Regina (1985) *Sympathy and Science: Women Physicians in American Medicine.* New York: Oxford University Press.

Morantz-Sanchez, Regina (1999) *Conduct Unbecoming a Woman: Medicine on Trial in Turn-of-the-century Brooklyn.* New York: Oxford University Press.

Morgan, Francesca (1998) " 'Home and Country': Women, Nation and the Daughters of the American Revolution, 1890–1939," Ph.D. dissertation, Columbia University.

Morgan, Lynn M. and Michaels, Meredith W. (1999) *Fetal Subjects, Feminist Positions.* Philadelphia: University of Pennsylvania Press.

Morris, Aldon (1984) *The Origins of the Civil Rights Movement.* New York: Free Press.

Moskowitz, Eva (1996) " 'It's Good to Blow Your Top': Women's Magazines and a Discourse of Discontent, 1945–1965," *Journal of Women's History* 8, pp. 66–98.

Mumford, Kevin (1977) *Interzones: Black/White Sex Districts in Chicago and New York in the Early Twentieth Century.* New York: Columbia University Press.

Muncy, Robyn (1991) *Creating a Female Dominion in American Reform, 1890–1935.* New York: Oxford University Press.

Murphy, Marjorie (1990) *Blackboard Unions: The AFT and the NEA, 1900–1980.* Ithaca, NY: Cornell University Press.

Murray, Pauli (1987) *Song in a Weary Throat: An American Pilgrimage.* New York: Harper and Row.

Murray, Pauli (1989) *Pauli Murray: The Autobiography of a Black Activist, Feminist, Lawyer, Priest, and Poet.* Knoxville: University of Tennessee Press.

Myers-Shirk, Susan E. (2000) "'To Be Fully Human': U.S. Protestant Psychotherapeutic Culture and the Subversion of the Domestic Ideal, 1945–1965," *Journal of Women's History* 12, pp. 112–36.

Nasaw, David (1993) *Going Out: The Rise and Fall of Public Amusements.* New York: Basic Books.

Nasstrom, Kathryn L. (1999) "Down to Now: Memory, Narrative, and Women's Leadership in the Civil Rights Movement in Atlanta, Georgia," *Gender and History* 11, pp. 113–44.

Neth, Mary (1995) *Preserving the Family Farm: Women, Community, and the Foundations of Agribusiness in the Midwest, 1900–1940.* Baltimore: Johns Hopkins University Press.

Neverdon-Morton, Cynthia (1989) *Afro-American Women of the South and the Advancement of the Race, 1895–1925.* Knoxville: University of Tennessee Press.

Newcomer, Mabel (1959) *A Century of Higher Education for American Women.* New York: Harper Brothers.

Newman, Karen (1996) *Fetal Positions: Individualism, Science, Visuality.* Stanford, CA: Stanford University Press.

Newman, Louise M. (1999) *White Women's Rights: The Racial Origins of Feminism in the United States.* New York: Oxford University Press.

Nielsen, Kim (2001) *Un-American Womanhood: Antiradicalism, Antifeminism, and the First Red Scare.* Columbus: Ohio State University Press.

Noble, Jeanne (1956) *The Negro Woman's College Education.* New York: Teacher's College Press.

Norwood, Stephen (1990) *Labor's Flaming Youth: Telephone Operators and Worker Militancy, 1878–1923.* Urbana: University of Illinois Press.

Odem, Mary E. (1995) *Delinquent Daughters: Protecting and Policing Adolescent Female Sexuality in the United States, 1885–1920.* Chapel Hill: University of North Carolina Press.

Orleck, Annelise (1993) "We Are That Mythical Thing Called the Public: Militant Housewives in the Great Depression," *Feminist Studies* 19, pp. 147–72.

Orleck, Annelise (1995) *Common Sense and a Little Fire: Women and Working-class Politics in the United States, 1900–1965.* Chapel Hill: University of North Carolina Press.

Ownby, Ted (1999) *American Dreams in Mississippi: Consumers, Poverty, and Culture, 1830–1998.* Chapel Hill: University of North Carolina Press.

Painter, Nell Irvin (1976) *Exodusters: Black Migration to Kansas After Reconstruction.* New York: Alfred A. Knopf.

Palmieri, Patricia A. (1995) *In Adamless Eden: The Community of Women Faculty at Wellesley.* New Haven, CT: Yale University Press.

Parker, Alison M. (1997) *Purifying America: Women, Cultural Reform and Pro-censorship Activism, 1873–1933.* Urbana: University of Illinois Press.

Parks, Rosa, with Jim Haskins (1992) *My Story.* New York: Dial Books.

Pascoe, Peggy (1990) *Relations of Rescue: The Search for Female Moral Authority in the American West, 1874–1939.* New York: Oxford University Press.

Peiss, Kathy (1986) *Cheap Amusements: Working Women and Leisure in Turn-of-the-century New York*. Philadelphia: Temple University Press.

Peiss, Kathy (1998) *Hope in a Jar: The Making of America's Beauty Culture*. New York: Metropolitan Books.

Petchesky, Rosalind Pollack (1987) "Fetal Images: The Power of Visual Culture in the Politics of Reproduction," *Feminist Studies* 13, pp. 263–92.

Petchesky, Rosalind Pollack (1990) *Abortion and Woman's Choice: The State, Sexuality, and Reproductive Freedom*. Boston: Northeastern University Press.

Petrik, Paula (1987) *No Step Backward: Women and Family on the Rocky Mountain Mining Frontier, 1865–1900*. Helena: Montana Historical Society Press.

Phillips, Kimberly L. (1999) *Alabama North: African-American Migrants, Community and Working-class Activism in Cleveland, 1915–1945*. Urbana: University of Illinois Press.

Pleck, Elizabeth H. (1979) *Black Migration and Poverty, Boston, 1865–1900*. New York: Academic Press.

Pleck, Elizabeth H. (2000) *Celebrating the Family: Ethnicity, Consumer Culture, and Family Rituals*. Cambridge, MA: Harvard University Press.

Quinn, Elizabeth Lasch (1993) *Black Neighbors: Race and the Limits of Reform in the American Settlement House Movement, 1890–1945*. Chapel Hill: University of North Carolina Press.

Rabinovitz, Lauren (1998) *For the Love of Pleasure: Women, Movies, and Culture in Turn-of-the-century Chicago*. New Brunswick, NJ: Rutgers University Press.

Rafter, Nicole Hahn (1988) *White Trash: The Eugenic Family Studies, 1877–1919*. Boston: Northeastern University Press.

Raines, Howell L. (1977) *My Soul is Rested: Movement Days in the Deep South Remembered*. New York: G. P. Putnam's Sons.

Ransby, Barbara (2003) *Ella Baker and the Black Freedom Movement: A Radical Democratic Vision*. Chapel Hill: University of North Carolina Press.

Rapp, Rayna (1999) *Testing Women, Testing the Fetus: The Social Impact of Amniocentesis in America*. New York: Routledge.

Reagan, Leslie J. (1997) *When Abortion Was a Crime: Women, Medicine, and Law in the United States, 1867–1973*. Berkeley: University of California Press.

Reagan, Leslie J. (2000) "Crossing the Border for Abortions: California Activists, Mexican Clinics, and the Creation of a Feminist Public Health Agency in the 1960s," *Feminist Studies* 26, pp. 323–48.

Reverby, Susan (1987) *Ordered to Care: The Dilemma of American Nursing, 1850–1945*. New York: Cambridge University Press.

Reverby, Susan M. (ed.) (2000) *Tuskegee's Truths: Rethinking the Tuskegee Syphilis Study*. Chapel Hill: University of North Carolina Press.

Robnett, Belinda (1997) *How Long? How Long? African-American Women and the Struggle for Freedom and Justice*. New York: Oxford University Press.

Rosen, Ruth (1982) *The Lost Sisterhood: Prostitution in America*. Baltimore: Johns Hopkins University Press.

Rosen, Ruth (2000) *The World Split Open: How the Modern Women's Movement Changed America*. New York: Viking Books.

Rosenberg, Clifford (1998) "Beyond the Melting Pot?" *Contemporary European History* 7, pp. 421–9.

Rosenberg, Emily S. (1994) "'Foreign Affairs' after World War II: Connecting Sexual and International Politics," *Diplomatic History* 18, pp. 59–70.

Rosenberg, Rosalind (1982) *Beyond Separate Spheres: Intellectual Roots of Modern Feminism.* New Haven, CT: Yale University Press.

Rosenberg, Rosalind (1992) *Divided Lives: American Women in the Twentieth Century.* New York: Hill and Wang.

Ross, Ellen (1993) *Love and Toil: Motherhood in Outcast London, 1870–1918.* New York: Oxford University Press.

Rossi, Alice (ed.) (1973) *The Feminist Papers.* New York: Columbia University Press.

Rossinow, Doug (1998) *The Politics of Authenticity: Liberalism, Christianity, and the New Left in America.* New York: Columbia University Press.

Rossiter, Margaret (1982) *Women Scientists in America: Struggles and Strategies to 1940.* Baltimore: Johns Hopkins University Press.

Rossiter, Margaret (1995) *Women Scientists in America: Before Affirmative Action, 1940–1972.* Baltimore: Johns Hopkins University Press.

Rothman, Barbara Katz (1989) *Recreating Motherhood: Ideology and Technology in a Patriarchal Society.* New York: W. W. Norton.

Rouse, Jacqueline (1989) *Lugenia Burns Hope: Black Southern Reformer.* Athens: University of Georgia Press.

Rousmaniere, John (1970) "Cultural Hybrid in the Slums: The College Woman and the Settlement House, 1889–1894," *American Quarterly* 22, pp. 45–66.

Rowbotham, Sheila (1997) *A Century of Women: The History of Women in Britain and the US.* New York: Viking Books.

Ruíz, Vicki (1987) *Cannery Women, Cannery Lives: Mexican Women, Unionization, and the California Food Processing Industry, 1930–1950.* Albuquerque: University of New Mexico Press.

Ruíz, Vicki (1998) *From Out of the Shadows: Mexican Women in Twentieth-century America.* New York: Oxford University Press.

Rupp, Leila (1978) *Mobilizing Women for War: German and American Propaganda, 1939–1945.* Princeton, NJ: Princeton University Press.

Rupp, Leila (1997) *Worlds of Women: The Making of an International Women's Movement.* Princeton, NJ: Princeton University Press.

Rupp, Leila J. and Taylor, Verta (1987) *Survival in the Doldrums: The American Women's Rights Movement, 1945 to the 1960s.* New York: Oxford University Press.

Rury, John L. (1991) *Education and Women's Work: Female Schooling and the Division of Labor in Urban America, 1870–1930.* Albany: State University of New York Press.

Sadker, Myra and Sadker, David (1995) *Failing at Fairness: How Our Schools Cheat Girls.* New York: C. Scribner's Sons.

Salem, Dorothy (1990) *To Better Our World: Black Women in Organized Reform, 1880–1920.* Brooklyn: Carlson Publishing.

Salyer, Lucy E. (1995) *Law Harsh as Tigers: Chinese Immigrants and the Shaping of Modern Immigration Law.* Chapel Hill: University of North Carolina Press.

Sanchez, George (1993) *Becoming Mexican American: Ethnicity, Culture, and Identity in Chicano Los Angeles.* New York: Oxford University Press.

Sanday, Peggy Reeves (1990) *Fraternity Gang Rape: Sex, Brotherhood, and Privilege on Campus.* New York: New York University Press.

Scanlon, Jennifer (1995) *Inarticulate Longings: The Ladies' Home Journal, Gender, and the Promises of Consumer Culture.* New York: Routledge.

Scarborough, Elizabeth and Furumoto, Laurel (1987) *Untold Lives: The First Generation of Women Psychologists.* New York: Columbia University Press.

Scharf, Lois (1980) *To Work and to Wed: Female Employment, Feminism, and the Great Depression.* Westport, CT: Greenwood Press.

Schoen, Johanna (1996) "A Great Thing for Poor Folks: Birth Control, Sterilization and Abortion in Public Health and Public Welfare," Ph.D. dissertation, University of North Carolina, Chapel Hill.

Schoen, Johanna (1997) "Fighting for Child Health: Race, Birth Control, and the State in the Jim Crow South," *Social Politics* 4, pp. 90–113.

Schultz, Deborah L. (2001) *Going South: Jewish Women in the Civil Rights Movement.* New York: New York University Press.

Schwager, Sally (1987) "Educating Women in America," *Signs* 12, pp. 333–72.

Scott, Anne Firor (1970) *The Southern Lady: From Pedestal to Politics, 1830–1930.* Chicago: University of Chicago Press.

Scott, Anne Firor (1984) *Making the Invisible Woman Visible.* Urbana: University of Illinois Press.

Sharpless, Rebecca (1999) *Fertile Ground, Narrow Choices: Women on Texas Cotton Farms, 1900–1940.* Chapel Hill: University of North Carolina Press.

Shaw, Stephanie J. (1996) *What a Woman Ought to Be and to Do: Black Professional Women Workers During the Jim Crow Era.* Chicago: University of Chicago Press.

Showalter, Elaine (ed.) (1978) *These Modern Women: Autobiographical Essays from the Twenties.* New York: Feminist Press.

Sicherman, Barbara (ed.) (1984) *Alice Hamilton: A Life in Letters.* Cambridge, MA: Harvard University Press.

Sidel, Ruth (1982) *Women and Children Last: The Plight of Poor Women in Affluent America.* New York: Viking Books.

Simmons, Christina (1979) "Companionate Marriage and the Lesbian Threat," *Frontiers* 4, pp. 54–9.

Sklar, Kathryn Kish (1985) "Hull House in the 1890s: A Community of Women Reformers," *Signs* 19, pp. 658–77.

Sklar, Kathryn Kish (1995) *Florence Kelley and the Nation's Work: The Rise of Women's Political Culture, 1830–1900.* New Haven, CT: Yale University Press.

Skold, Karen Beck (1989) "The Job He Left Behind: American Women in the Shipyards During World War II," in Carol R. Berkin and Clara M. Lovett (eds.), *Women, War and Revolution.* New York: Holmes and Meier, pp. 55–75.

Smith, Judith E. (1985) *Family Connections: A History of Italian and Jewish Immigrant Lives in Providence, Rhode Island, 1900–1940.* Albany: State University of New York Press.

Smith, Susan L. (1995) *Sick and Tired of Being Sick and Tired: Black Women's Health Activism in America, 1890–1950.* Philadelphia: University of Pennsylvania Press.

Smith, Susan L. (2004) *Japanese American Midwives: Culture, Community and Health Politics, 1880–1950.* Urbana: University of Illinois Press.

Snyder, Robert W. (1989) *The Voice of the City: Vaudeville and Popular Culture in New York.* New York: Oxford University Press.

Solinger, Rickie (1992) *Wake Up Little Susie: Single Pregnancy and Race Before Roe v. Wade.* New York: Routledge.

Solinger, Rickie (1994) *The Abortionist: A Woman Against the Law.* New York: Free Press.

Somerville, Siobhan B. (2000) *Queering the Color Line: Race and the Invention of Homosexuality in American Culture.* Durham, NC: Duke University Press.

Spritzer, Lorraine Nelson and Bergmark, Jean B. (1997) *Grace Towns Hamilton and the Politics of Southern Change.* Athens: University of Georgia Press.

Stacey, Judith (1987) "Sexism by a Subtler Name? Postindustrial Conditions and Postfeminist Consciousness in the Silicon Valley," *Socialist Review* 96, pp. 7–28.

Stolberg, Benjamin (1944) *Tailor's Progress: The Story of a Famous Union and the Men Who Made It*. New York: Doubleday.

Strasser, Susan, McGovern, Charles, and Judt, Matthias (eds.) (1998) *Getting and Spending: European and American Consumer Societies in the Twentieth Century*. New York: Cambridge University Press.

Stricker, Frank (1976) "Cookbooks and Law Books: The Hidden History of Career Women in 20th-century America," *Journal of Social History* 10, pp. 1–19.

Strom, Sharon Hartman (1983) "Challenging Women's Place: Feminism, the Left and the Industrial Unionism of the 1930s," *Feminist Studies* 9, pp. 359–86.

Strom, Sharon Hartman (1992) *Beyond the Typewriter: Gender, Class, and the Origins of Modern American Office Work, 1900–1930*. Urbana: University of Illinois Press.

Sullivan, Patricia (1996) *Days of Hope: Race and Democracy in the New Deal Era*. Chapel Hill: University of North Carolina Press.

Swerdlow, Amy (1993) *Women Strike for Peace: Traditional Motherhood and Radical Politics in the 1960s*. Chicago: University of Chicago Press.

Swiencicki, Mark A. (1998) "Consuming Brotherhood: Men's Culture, Style, and Recreation as Consumer Culture, 1880–1930," *Journal of Social History* 31, pp. 773–808.

Tax, Meredith (1980) *The Rising of the Women: Feminist Solidarity and Class Conflict, 1880–1917*. New York: Monthly Review Press.

Taylor, Ula Y. (2000) "Negro Women are Great Thinkers as Well as Doers: Amy Jacques-Garvey and Community Feminism," *Journal of Women's History* 12, pp. 104–26.

Tentler, Leslie Woodcock (1979) *Wage-earning Women: Industrial Work and Family Life in the United States, 1900–1930*. New York: Oxford University Press.

Terborg-Penn, Rosalyn (1998) *African American Women and the Struggle for the Vote, 1850–1920*. Bloomington: University of Indiana Press.

Thomas, William I. and Znaniecki, Florian (1958) *The Polish Peasant in Europe and America*. New York: Dover.

Thompson, Becky (2001) *A Promise and a Way of Life: White Antiracist Activism*. Minneapolis: University of Minnesota Press.

Tidball, M. Elizabeth et al. (1999) *Taking Women Seriously: Lessons and Legacies for Educating the Majority*. Phoenix, AZ: Oryx Press.

Tilly, Louise and Gurin, Patricia (eds.) (1990) *Women, Politics, and Change*. New York: Russell Sage Foundation.

Tobias, Sheila (1996) *Faces of Feminism*. New York: Westview.

Tone, Andrea (1996) "Contraceptive Consumers: Gender and the Political Economy of Birth Control in the 1930s," *Journal of Social History* 29, pp. 485–506.

Toth, Emily (1997) *Ms. Mentor's Impeccable Advice to Academic Women*. Philadelphia: University of Pennsylvania Press.

Trillin, Calvin (1964) *An Education in Georgia*. New York: Viking Press.

Turner, Elizabeth Hayes (1997) *Women, Culture and Community: Religion and Reform in Galveston, 1880–1920*. New York: Oxford University Press.

Tyack, David and Hansot, Elisabeth (1990) *Learning Together: A History of Coeducation in American Public Schools*. New Haven, CT: Yale University Press.

Van Kleeck, Mary (1994) *Life's America: Family and Nation in Postwar Photojournalism*. Philadelphia: Temple University Press.

Walsh, Margaret (1979) "The Democratization of Fashion: The Emergence of the Women's Dress Pattern Industry," *Journal of American History* 66, pp. 299–313.

Wandersee, Winifred D. (1980) *Women's Work and Family Values, 1920–1940.* Cambridge, MA: Harvard University Press.

Wandersee, Winifred D. (1988) *On the Move: American Women in the 1970's.* Boston: Twayne.

Ware, Susan (1981) *Beyond Suffrage: Women in the New Deal.* Cambridge, MA: Harvard University Press.

Ware, Susan (1982) *Holding Their Own: American Women in the 1930s.* Boston: Twayne.

Ware, Susan (1997) *Partner and I: Mollie Dewson, Feminism and New Deal Politics.* New Haven, CT: Yale University Press.

Watkins, Bonnie and Tothchild, Nina (eds.) (1997) *In the Company of Women: Voices from the Women's Movement.* Minneapolis: University of Minnesota Press.

Watkins, Elizabeth Siegel (1998) *On the Pill: A Social History of Oral Contraceptives, 1960–1970.* Baltimore: Johns Hopkins University Press.

Weigand, Kate (1992) "The Red Menace, the Feminine Mystique, and Ohio Un-American Activities Commission: Gender and Anti-Communism in Ohio, 1951–1954," *Journal of Women's History* 3, pp. 70–94.

Weigand, Kate (2000) *Red Feminism: American Communism and the Making of Women's Liberation.* Baltimore: Johns Hopkins University Press.

Weiner, Lynn (1985) *From Working Girl to Working Mother: The Female Labor Force in the United States, 1820–1980.* Chapel Hill: University of North Carolina Press.

Weiner, Lynn Y. (1994) "Reconstructing Motherhood: The La Leche League in Postwar America," *Journal of American History* 80, pp. 1357–81.

Weisbord, Robert G. (1975) *Genocide? Birth Control and the Black American.* Westport, CT: Greenwood Press.

Weiss, Jessica (2000) *To Have and to Hold: Marriage, the Baby Boom, and Social Change.* Chicago: University of Chicago Press.

Wexler, Laura (2001) *Tender Violence: Domestic Images in an Age of U.S. Imperialism.* Chapel Hill: University of North Carolina Press.

Wheeler, Marjorie Spruill (1993) *New Women of the New South: The Leaders of the Woman's Suffrage Movement in the Southern States.* New York: Oxford University Press.

White, Deborah Gray (1996) "Private Lives, Public Personae: A Look at Early Twentieth-century African-American Clubwomen," in Nancy A. Hewitt, Jean O'Barr, and Nancy Rosebaugh (eds.), *Talking Gender: Public Images, Personal Journeys, and Political Critiques.* Chapel Hill: University of North Carolina Press, pp. 106–23.

White, Deborah Gray (1999) *Too Heavy a Load: Black Women in Defense of Themselves, 1894–1994.* New York: W. W. Norton.

Whittier, Nancy (1995) *Feminist Generations: The Persistence of the Women's Movement.* Philadelphia: Temple University Press.

Wilkinson, Patrick (1999) "The Selfless and the Helpless: Maternalist Origins of the U.S. Welfare State," *Feminist Studies* 25, pp. 571–97.

Willett, Julie A. (2000) *Permanent Waves: The Making of the American Beauty Shop.* New York: New York University Press.

Wu, Chia-Ling (1997) "Women, Medicine, and Power: The Social Transformation of Childbirth in Taiwan," Ph.D. dissertation, University of Illinois, Urbana-Champaign.

Yans-McLaughlin, Virginia (1977) *Family and Community: Italian Immigrants in Buffalo, 1880–1930.* Ithaca, NY: Cornell University Press.

Yung, Judy (1995) *Unbound Feet: A Social History of Chinese Women in San Francisco.* Berkeley: University of California Press.

Zelizer, Viviana A. (1985) *Pricing the Priceless Child: The Changing Social Value of Children.* New York: Basic Books.

Index

Abelove, Henry, 222
abolitionism, 111, 119, 122, 123, 124, 125–7
abortion, 351–2, 360–1; nineteenth-century increase in, 208, 210; restricted, 209, 368, 377; movement against, 424–5; *see also* birth control
activism, women's, 236, 253, 328–44, 384–5; middle-class white, 109–10, 119–21, 123–6, 229–30, 332–4, 336, 337, 338–43, 404–6, 409–10, 415, 417–18; African American, 111, 122–3, 259, 335, 400–1; in the South, 119, 121, 160; working-class, 122, 251, 253, 260–1, 263, 267–8, 337, 385, 400–1, 421; and religion, 122–3, 125; and Civil War, 176–8; and consumption, 289–90; immigrant, 321, 386–7, 418; post-World War II, 384–7; grassroots, 386–7, 398, 408, 415–17, 426; *see also* civil rights movement; conservative women; feminism
Adams, Abigail, 88–9
Adams, John, 88–9
Addams, Jane, 232, 332, 337
adoption, 358–9
advertising, 279–80, 286, 306–7
affirmative action, 245, 247, 430
Africa: *see* West Africa; West African women
African Americans, 94; middle-class, 108; in North, 108–9; and politics of respectability, 109, 114, 198; colleges and universities, 236; and consumption, 278, 284–5, 286–7, 289; *see also* African American women; civil rights movement; enslaved persons; enslaved women
African American women: and American Revolution, 62, 93–5; and work, 106, 108, 152, 198–9, 236, 243, 258–60, 262, 374, 375; domesticity of, 108–9, 337; and sexual violence, 109, 214–15; and politics of respectability, 109, 114, 284, 330, 403; activism of, 111, 122–3, 125, 259, 267–8, 335, 400–1, 408; and abolitionism, 122, 126–7; and religion, 122–3; in West, 141–2, 155; and Civil War, 167–9, 172, 179–81, 186–8; and Reconstruction, 187–8, 197–9, 214–15; and childbirth, 218; and education, 228–9, 242, 245; professional, 236–7, 238, 245, 401; and sex, 242; and "matriarchy," 259; and migration to North, 264–5; and popular culture, 303, 306; and suffrage, 341–2, 399; and reproduction, 353–4, 356; and World War II, 374, 401; feminism of, 404, 409–10, 417–18, 419; in politics, 423; *see also* civil rights movement; enslaved women
Africans, 9, 10, 11, 16, 22, 24; *see also* African women; West Africa; West African women
African women, 3, 9, 10; *see also* African American women; enslaved women; West African women
Aid to Dependent Children (ADC), 369, 370–1, 389
Aid to Families with Dependent Children, 425
Alaska, 44

Alexander, Ruth, 303–4
Algonquians, 3
Altschuler, Glenn, 124
American Association of University Women (AAUW), 228
American Birth Control League, 368
American Federation of Teachers, 235
American Female Moral Reform Society, 118
Americanization, 238, 283, 300, 307, 318, 322
American Revolution, 62, 83–97
Ames, Jessie Daniel, 404–5
Amussen, Susan, 55
Anglo-American women, 12, 14, 38, 55, 138–9, 324
Anthony, Susan B., 176, 177
anti-Communism, 245, 255, 340, 384–5
anti-feminism, 424–5
Antinomian crisis, 72–3
Apaches, 143
Asian immigrants, 142, 230; *see also* Chinese immigrant women
Asian immigrant women, 264, 319
assimilation, 317–18, 323
Association of Southern Women for the Prevention of Lynching, 404–5
athletics, 246, 428, 429
Atlanta, 262, 295, 306, 307–8, 337, 386, 400–1
Atlanta Baptist Female Seminary, 229

baby boom, 244–5, 383
Baker, Ella, 264, 398, 403, 405–6, 407
Bao, Xiaolan, 266–7
Baptists, 71–2
Barbados, 21, 22, 31
Barr, Juliana, 43
Barton, Clara, 177–8
Bass, Charlotta, 237
Bates, Daisy, 403, 407
beauty shops, 287–8
Beecher, Catharine, 118, 119, 162, 216
Bethune, Mary McLeod, 229, 399–400
birth control, 241, 350–1, 368, 425; sexual abstinence, 29; "voluntary motherhood," 120, 350; among Indians, 135; misinformation about, 207, 279; nineteenth-century, 209, 210, 212; *see also* abortion
Birth of a Nation, The, 168
Black Power, 410
Blewett, Mary, 101–2
blues, 305
Boris, Eileen, 268–9
boycotts, 85, 289, 386, 397, 402
Boydston, Jeanne, 200
Braden, Anne, 405
breastfeeding, 10, 13, 28, 212
Brodie, Janet Farrell, 210
Brookwood Labor College, 254, 255
Brotherhood of Sleeping Car Porters, International Ladies' Auxiliary, 400
Brown, Elsa Barkley, 128, 289
Brown, Kathleen, 59
Brown, Linda, 397
Brown, Margaret Wise, 234
Brown v. Board of Education, 397
Bryn Mawr Summer School for Women Workers, 243, 254, 255
Buhle, Mari Jo, 255, 257, 391
Bunting, Mary, 245
Bureau of Indian Affairs (BIA), 229–30, 369–70

Cadet Nurse Corps, 236–7
California, 132–3, 135, 139–42, 342
Cameron, Ardis, 261–2
Canada, 37–8, 43
captivity narratives, 14–16, 38–9, 51–2, 58
Carby, Hazel, 302, 305
Carp, Wayne, 358
Carr, Lois, 55
Cason, Sandra "Casey," 405–6, 409, 410
Castiglia, Christopher, 14–15
Catholicism, 119, 243; and female authority, 43; and Indians, 51–2, 136; and education, 230, 242; and movement for women priests, 246; and abortion, 424–5
Chafe, William, 372, 373
Cherokee women, 121–2, 134
Chesapeake, 52–3, 55, 56–7
Chesler, Ellen, 351
Chicanas, 145, 419
childbirth, 11, 28, 93, 218, 354–5
childcare, 378, 428
childrearing, 52, 53, 55, 156, 356–7, 428
Children's Bureau, 334, 358
Chinese Exclusion Law (1882), 141
Chinese immigrant women, 133, 140–1, 230, 266–7, 319, 324, 387

Christianity, 37, 42, 75, 78, 240, 405–6; *see also* churches; evangelicalism; religion; specific denominations
churches, 76–7, 119, 122, 157, 246, 398; *see also* evangelicalism; religion; specific denominations
circumcision, female, 27–8, 29
Civil Rights Act of 1964, 245, 415, 423
civil rights movement, 386, 397–411, 416
Civil Rights Restoration Act, 245
Civil War, 167–8; and popular memory, 167–9, 178–9; and African American women, 167–9, 179–81, 186–8; image of southern lady in, 168, 175; women's narratives of, 169; and white women, 172, 176–8, 179, 181–2, 183; home front, 173–4, 178, 181–3; women's work in, 173–4, 175–6; and slavery, 184, 186
Clark, Christopher, 103
Clarke, Edward, 231
Clark-Lewis, Elizabeth, 264
class: and whiteness, 8; and sexuality, 9, 207, 208, 263–4; and consumption, 84, 113, 265–6, 278–9, 301; in the South, 160, 196–7; in rural areas, 163–4; and marriage, 193, 201–2, 203; social construction of, 193, 202–3, 255; identity, 194, 265; and language, 194–5; and fertility, 207, 208; and women's education, 231, 241; consciousness, 255, 300; *see also* middle class; working class; working-class women
class formation, 100–14, 119, 120, 199, 275
clerical work, 235, 417, 421
Clifford, James, 315
clothing, 286–7, 288, 429
Coalition of Labor Union Women (CLUW), 256, 421–2
Cobble, Dorothy Sue, 263
Cohen, Miriam, 320
Cold War, 245, 385–6
Cole, Johnnetta, 236
colleges and universities, 236, 240–1, 244, 246; *see also* education, women's; women's colleges
Collier, John, 369–70
colonialism, xv–xvi, 3–17, 35–45; naturalization of, 6, 41; and white women, 12–13, 14, 38; and cultural exchange, 36, 38, 40–2, 43–4; and disease, 37; and regional history, 39–40; and identity, 40; Spanish, 36, 38, 40, 42–3, 44; and Christianity, 37, 40, 42, 43; French, 43, 44, 60–1; and women, 314, 425
Committee on Fair Employment Practice (FEPC), 374
Communist Party, 406, 414
Community Service Organization, 386–7
Congress of American Women, 385
Congress of Industrial Organizations (CIO), 263, 372
Congress of Racial Equality (CORE), 407–8
Connecticut River Valley, 103
conquest, xvi, 35–6, 38, 40, 41, 43; and eroticization, 6, 8; Spanish, 42, 44, 132, 135, 136; US, of West, 44, 136, 143–4, 145; gender politics of, 133–7; *see also* colonialism
consciousness raising (CR), 417
conservative women, xv, 126, 331, 338–40, 387
consumption: and sexuality, 71; of enslaved persons, 84; and class, 84, 113, 275–6, 278–9, 301; and identity, 113–14, 296–7; and working-class women, 263–4, 288; and farm women, 275–6, 281–3; and individualism, 276, 280; family-oriented, 276, 280, 284, 285, 320; and middle-class white women, 277, 283, 383; and Indian women, 277; and gender differences, 277–8; and leisure, 278, 283, 285–6, 295–6; and immigrant women, 280–1, 283, 286–7, 300, 320; and African Americans, 284–5, 286–7, 289; politics of, 289, 322; and activism, 261, 289–90
Cooke, Marvel, 264
cosmetics, 286, 287, 306–7
Cott, Nancy, 100, 119, 196, 207–8
country music, 295, 296
coverture, 54, 56, 57, 60, 87, 195, 199
Cowan, Ruth Schwartz, 276, 288
"cult of true womanhood," 100, 117; *see also* domesticity
cultural exchange, 36, 38, 40–2, 43–4

Daughters of Bilitis, 389
Davis, Natalie Zemon, 43
Davis, Simone Weil, 279
daycare: *see* childcare
Dayton, Cornelia Hughes, 57
Democratic Party, 112, 372
Demos, John, 51–2

department stores, 278–9, 289
Deutsch, Sarah, 276
Dill, Bonnie Thornton, 264
Diner, Hasia, 320
disfranchisement, 399
disorderly women: *see* unruly women
divorce, 91, 139, 239, 244–5, 337, 368
domesticity, 100, 107–8, 118; and African American women, 108–9, 337; as a check on men's behavior, 138–9; and rural women, 157–8; regional differences in, 184–5; and working class, 257; and reform, 332; postwar images of, 382–3, 390–2
domestic science: *see* home economics
domestic service, 29, 94, 106, 108, 142, 264–5, 366–7
domestic violence, 417
Dorris, Michael, 361
Dorsey, Bruce, 127
Douglas, Ann, 113
Douglass, Frederick, 123
Dublin, Thomas, 101
DuBois, Ellen, 120, 343
DuBois, W. E. B., 169
Dunn, Mary Maples, 73
Dunnigan, Alice Allison, 237
Durr, Virginia Foster, 405
Dutch immigrant women, 60
Dye, Nancy Shrom, 335

education: and Enlightenment ideals, 85–7; in rural areas, 156; African American, 228–9; Indian, 229–30; Jewish, 230; reform of, 234–5, 428; vocational, 235; "feminization" of, 240; girls', 244; *see also* colleges and universities; education, women's; women's colleges; specific schools
education, women's: purpose of, 85, 86, 104, 118, 227; fears concerning, 86, 207, 227, 231, 239, 241, 244–5; higher, 227–8, 239, 240, 244, 246–8; teacher training, 227–8, 234; regional differences in, 227–8; African American, 228, 229, 242, 245; Catholic, 230, 242; and class, 231, 241; coeducational, 231; graduate and professional, 232–4, 236, 237, 244; business, 235; and World War II, 244; *see also* home economics; women's colleges
Edwards, Laura, 197, 214
emancipation, 93–5, 171–2, 185–8, 193, 198–9
Enlightenment, 85–7, 301–2
enslaved persons: cost of, 20, 24; mortality of, 20–1, 22, 23, 30–1; families of, 58–9, 95; and Christianity, 75; consumption, 84; and American Revolution, 87, 93–5, 97; runaways, 94; Indians, 136; and work, 153, 154, 160–1; and Civil War, 171–2, 186; marriage of, 196–7
enslaved women, 3, 180–1; subversion of slavery, 21, 30, 31, 122; and reproduction, 22, 23, 31; and work, 29, 95, 152; and markets, 30; and religion, 74, 75; and American Revolution, 93–5; and sexual relations with masters, 95; and Civil War, 174, 175, 178, 179, 183–4, 185, 187; rape of, 214–15
Enstad, Nan, 263, 307
entrepreneurship, 287
environmental racism, 259
Equal Employment Opportunity Commission (EEOC), 415
Equal Pay Act of 1963, 423
Equal Rights Amendment (ERA), 242, 384, 415–16, 430
ethnicity: *see* immigrant women; immigration
eugenics, 352–3
evangelicalism, 73–6, 77–8, 119–21, 124, 161, 424–5
Evans, Sara, 405, 409
Ewen, Elizabeth, 299–301, 307
exercise, 216

Faderman, Lillian, 213–14
Fair Labor Standards Act of 1938, 369
family: hierarchies within, 49–50, 51, 54, 55, 102, 104; and the state, 49–50, 54–8; plantation, 52–3; in New England, 53–4; Indian, 58; enslaved, 58–9, 95; educational functions of, 86; women's influence in, 90, 93, 154; and work, 102–3; and wage work, 199–200, 321, 368, 370
"family values," 382, 425
family wage, 102, 201–2, 370, 371, 422
Faragher, John Mack, 138
farm women, 102–3, 153–4, 155, 159, 281–3; *see also* rural women
Fass, Paula, 243

Faue, Elizabeth, 262
Faust, Drew, 176, 187
female "delinquency," 302–3, 353
femes covert, 53
femes soles, 53, 57–8
"feminine mystique," 244, 382, 390
feminism: origins of, 118, 119–20, 342; and spiritualism, 123–4; strands of, 237, 241, 260, 263, 418–19; decline of, 242, 247; associated with "manhating," 242; second-wave, 250, 409–10, 414–30; and women of color, 404, 409–11, 417–18, 419; equal rights branch, 414–15; women's liberation, 416–20; global, 425–7; third-wave, 427–8; *see also* anti-feminism
Feminists Against Censorship Taskforce (FACT), 421
fertility, 103, 349; and class, 207, 208; decline in, 209–10, 217, 219, 239; baby boom, 244–5, 383; and medical intervention, 359–60
fetal alcohol syndrome (FAS), 361
Finnegan, Margaret, 304
Flexner, Eleanor, 332, 341
Foley, Neil, 265
Foner, Philip, 256
4-H Clubs, 287
Fox-Genovese, Elizabeth, 180
Frankel, Noralee, 335
freedom rides, 406
Freedom Summer, 410
Freedmen's Bureau, 199
free love, 120, 351
French Canadian immigrant women, 319
Friedan, Betty, 245, 390, 415
fur trade, 36, 37–8, 43, 44, 135

Gabin, Nancy, 378
Gage, Matilda J., 176, 177
Garrow, David, 351
Garvey, Ellen, 285–6
Garvey, Marcus, 400
"gaze," the, 4, 5, 7, 13, 16–17, 302
General Federation of Women's Clubs, 340
GI Bill, 244, 377–8
Giesberg, Judith Ann, 176–7, 178
Ginzberg, Lori, 110, 125
Glenn, Susan, 305, 307, 321–2
globalization, 268
Goldberg, Michael, 342
gold rush (1848), 132–3, 139–40
Gone With the Wind (movie), 168, 179
González, Rosalinda, 265
Gordon, Linda, 120, 350, 358, 370–1
"Grange," the, 163
Great Awakening, 73–4; Second, 75, 109, 119
Great Depression, 340, 367–76; and married women's work, 243, 257, 367, 371; and African American women, 243, 366–7
Great Lakes region, 40, 41, 43
Greven, Jr., Philip J., 53–4
Grimké, Sarah and Angelina, 121
Griswold v. Connecticut, 351
Gullett, Gayle, 342
Gutiérrez, Ramón, 40
Gutman, Herbert, 255

Haley, Margaret, 235
Hall, Jacquelyn Dowd, 214, 263–4, 337, 404–5
Haller, John and Robin, 218
Hamer, Fannie Lou, 408, 410
Handlin, Oscar, 315–16
Hansen, Miriam, 301
Harley, Sharon, 265
Hayden, Casey: *see* Cason, Sandra "Casey"
health care, 207; in rural areas, 156–7; in Civil War, 175–6; prenatal, 360–1; feminist critique of, 417
Height, Dorothy, 404, 405–6
Hembold, Lois, 368
Henry, Alice, 253
Henry Street Settlement, 298
Hernandez, Aileen, 415
Hesseltine, William B., 183
Hewitt, Nancy, 321, 335, 338
Highlander Folk School, 402, 407
Hill, Anita, 422
home demonstration agents, 286–7
home economics, 164, 235, 245
Homestead Act (1862), 154–5
homework: *see* outwork
homosexuality, 212, 388–9; *see also* lesbians, lesbianism
homosociability, 112–13, 212–14, 239–40
Honey, Maureen, 376
honor, 136, 207
Horowitz, Daniel, 278
Horton, James Oliver, 108–9
Horton, Lois, 108–9

household: as basis for political organization, 88; economy, 100, 101, 102, 103, 106, 107, 108, 277; and politics, 261; power relations in, 266–7; production, 281–2, 367
Housewives' Leagues, 289
housework, 106–8, 392; devalued, 107; on farms, 153; and industrial capitalism, 200–2, 258; meaning of, 201–2; and consumption, 288; and feminism, 417, 428
Howes, Ethel Puffer, 243
Huerta, Dolores, 387
Hunter, Charlayne, 401
Hunter, Tera, 262, 303, 306, 307–8
Hurley, Ruby, 403, 407
Hutchinson, Anne, 72–3
hysteria, 211, 217, 218–19

identities, 300, 307–8, 313, 315, 323; *see also* subjectivity
immigrant women: and work, 250–1, 320–1; and consumption, 280–1, 283, 286–7; and popular culture, 307, 321–2; daughters, 320; and respectability, 330; *see also* specific ethnic groups
immigration, 132–3, 163, 312–13, 315–20, 323–4, 387
Immigration Restriction League, 324
imperialism: *see* colonialism
indentured servants, 59
Independent Order of St. Luke, 289
Indian men, 4–5, 7, 13, 38; *see also* Indians; Indian women; specific tribes
Indian Removal, 132, 134, 139
Indians, 44; European images of, 5–6, 14; sexuality of, 6; and Christianity, 37, 51–2; families, 58–9; and American Revolution, 95–6; and sexual division of labor, 96; and gender equality, 96, 133–4; assimilation of, 96, 133, 134, 136, 229–30; enslaved, 136; and missionaries, 139, 153; on reservations, 145; education of, 229–30; and fetal alcohol syndrome, 361; and the New Deal, 369–70; *see also* Indian men; Indian women; specific tribes
Indian wars, 133, 143
Indian women: white images of, 3, 7, 13; as symbol of America, 4; and sexuality, 7, 8; rape of, 36; and European intermarriage, 36, 37, 40, 43, 60–1, 135; and cultural exchange, 36, 38, 42, 43, 134, 135, 136; economic production of, 36, 134, 135, 136, 144, 152–3, 159, 370; and religion, 37; and interracial relationships, 42; power of, 134, 144; and consumption, 277; and World War II, 374–5; *see also* specific tribes
industrial capitalism, 83, 84, 100–1, 102–4; and marriage, 195; and housework, 200–2
Inman, Mary, 258
International Ladies' Garment Workers' Union (ILGWU), 254, 263, 267
interracial marriage: between Europeans and Indians, 8, 36, 37, 40, 43, 136–7; in West, 142
interracial relationships: and colonialism, 42, 51–2, 59–60; and families, 59; and the law, 208; in civil rights movement, 410; *see also* interracial marriage; miscegenation laws
Irish immigrant women, 320, 321
Italian immigrant women, 318–19, 320

Jacques-Garvey, Amy, 400
Japanese American women, 387
Jensen, Joan, 103
Jewish women, 321–2, 406
Jews, 230, 243
Johnson, Lyndon B., 245, 408, 415
Jones, Beverly, 266
Jones, Jacqueline, 258–9
Jordan, Winthrop, 9
journalists, 234, 237, 244, 252–3, 264

Kamensky, Jane, 70
Kansas, 342
Kaplan, Caren, 314, 315
Karlsen, Carol, 57
Kelley, Mary, 105
Kelly, Joan, 257
Kennedy, John F., 145
Kerber, Linda, 62, 109
Kessler-Harris, Alice, 256, 257, 258
Kibler, M. Alison, 305
King, Jr., Martin Luther, 397
King, Mary, 409, 410
Kinsey reports, 388
Kobrin, Frances, 355
Koehler, Lyle, 57
Ku Klux Klan, 339
Kulikoff, Allan, 58–9

labor, 84, 101; child, 102; sexual division of, 103, 108; and nativism, 141; education, 254–5, 260; and immigration, 324–5; *see also* domestic service; strikes; unions; work (women's)
labor movements, 121, 124–5, 185; *see also* strikes; unions
Ladd-Taylor, Molly, 334
Landes, Joan, 301
Laqueur, Thomas, 220
Lasser, Carol, 106
Lathrop, Julia, 334
Lawrence, Mass., 321
Lawson, John, 8, 13
lawyers, 233–4
Leach, William, 301
Leacock, Eleanor, 37
Lears, Jackson, 275
Leavitt, Judith Walzer, 354–5
Lebsock, Suzanne, 121
legal system, 55; in New England, 54; and slavery, 59; and slander, 70, 71; and racial inequality, 133; in Spanish territories, 137; and marriage, 139, 194; and interracial sex, 207–8, 215
Leonard, Elizabeth, 176, 177
Leopold, Alice, 385
Lerner, Gerda, 122, 335
lesbians, lesbianism, 377, 389, 418, 419–20; *see also* homosexuality
Levy, Barry J., 52
librarians, 235–6
Life and Labour, 253
literacy, 86–7, 118, 157, 159–60
Litoff, Judy Barrett, 355–6
Little Rock, Ark., 402–3
Locke, John, 85–6
Lucy, Autherine, 401
Lunbeck, Liz, 263
Lundberg, Ferdinand, 388
lynching, 215, 399, 404
Lystra, Karen 213

McCurry, Stephanie, 185, 196–7
Maines, Rachel P., 217–18
March on Washington (1963), 404
marriage: romantic notions of, 93, 299; and legal system, 139, 194; egalitarian, 158, 392, 429; and class, 193, 199, 201–2, 203; property rights of, 194–203, 207; "Boston," 213–14, 239–40, 242, 337; and college-educated women, 240, 241, 242; and women's careers, 243
masculinity, xv; in New England, 61–2; and religion, 78; and politics, 112; in West, 133, 140; working-class, 262; hedonistic, 278; and whiteness, 324; post-World War II, 384
Massey, Elizabeth, 176, 179–80
maternalism, 118, 140, 253, 337, 339
maternity leave, 253
matriarchy, 27
May, Elaine Tyler, 384, 390
mental illness, 67
Methodists, 77
Mettler, Suzanne, 369
mexicanas, 38
Mexicans: racial status of, 142; segregation of, 230
Mexican women, 265, 266, 280, 283, 307, 367; activism of, 386–7
Meyer, Leisa, 376–7
Meyerowitz, Joanne, 299–301
middle class: white women, 104–6, 109–10, 216, 277, 283; antebellum, 112–13; consumption, 113–14; and separate spheres, 195–6; and sexual self-control, 208; *see also* class; class formation
middle passage, 20–2
midwives, 354–6
military: women's exclusion from, 90, 236; women in, 177–8, 376–7, 401; nurses, 233, 236–7
Milkman, Ruth, 366–7, 373–4
miscegenation laws, 133, 142
missionaries, 12; and gender, 37, 135; Catholic, 40, 43; and sexuality, 135; and Indians, 139, 153; and Chinese, 141, 230; Yankee, 199; and African Americans, 228–9
Mississippi, 277–8, 286–7, 407–8, 410
Mississippi Freedom Democratic Party, 408
Mitchell, Lucy Sprague, 234
modernity, 307
Modern Woman: The Lost Sex (1947), 388
Mohr, James, 210
Montgomery, Ala., 386, 397, 402
Montgomery bus boycott, 397, 402
Moody, Anne, 407–8
"moral panics," 303
moral reform, 118, 119, 120, 139; *see also* activism, women's; reform movements

Morantz, Regina Markell, 216
Morgan, Edmund, 50, 51
Moynihan Report, 258
Murray, Judith Sargent, 86
Murray, Pauli, 245, 415

Narrett, David E., 60
Nash, Diane, 406–7
National Association for the Advancement of Colored People (NAACP), 386, 399, 401, 402–4, 407
National Association of Colored Graduate Nurses (NACGN), 236–7
National Association of Colored Women (NACW), 399
National Black Feminist Organization, 411
National Black Nurses Association, 237
National Conference on Charities and Corrections, 232
National Consumer's Leagues, 289
National Council of Negro Women (NCNW), 384, 399–400, 404
National Education Association (NEA), 235
National Organization for Women (NOW), 415–16, 419–20
National Woman's Party, 384
National Women's Trade Union League (NWTUL), 253, 384
National Youth Administration, 400
Native Americans: *see* Indians
Navajo, 144
neurasthenia, 218–19; *see also* hysteria
New Deal, 243, 369–72, 399–400
New England, 42, 50–2, 53, 54, 56–7, 92
New France, 60–1
New Jersey, 88
New Left, 416, 418
Newman, Louise, 342
New Mexico, 132, 136, 144
New York City, 101–2, 124–5, 199–200, 267
"New Woman," 213, 240
Nineteenth Amendment: *see* woman suffrage
"noble savage" ideology, 7, 11
Noel, Jan, 60–1
North Carolina, 12, 354
Northeast, 159–60
Norton, Eleanor Holmes, 422, 423
Norton, Mary Beth, 56–7
Norwood, Stephen, 304
nurses, 232–3, 236–7, 243–4

Odem, Mary, 302–3
O'Hara, Scarlett, 179
Old Left, 415
Oliver, Patsy Ruth, 259
Omaha (Indians), 139
O'Neill, William L., 237
Our Bodies, Ourselves, 417
outwork (putting-out), 101–2, 153, 159, 268–9
Overland trail, 132–3, 137–8
Ownby, Ted, 277–8, 285

Page Law of 1875, 319, 325
Paine, Thomas, 86, 91
Pallodino, Grace, 185
Parks, Rosa, 386, 397
patriarchy, 13, 52, 53, 55, 56, 92, 154, 262, 321
Payne, Ethel, 237
peace movements, 127
Peiss, Kathy, 286, 287, 299–301, 306–7
Perdue, Theda, 121–2
Peterson, Esther, 414
Philadelphia, 123, 127
Philadelphia Female Anti-Slavery Society, 123
philanthropy, 127
phrenology, 216
physicians, 217, 232, 349–50, 355, 428
Planned Parenthood, 350–1
plantations, 29–30, 52–3
planter women: work of, 160–1, 180; as symbol of southern women, 178; and home front, 183–4, 187
politics: and relationship to domestic order, 12–13; and economic action, 85; partisan, 111–12; reconceptualization of, 128, 331; women in electoral, 423–4; single-issue, 424
popular culture: and wage-earning women, 250–1, 263, 307, 376; and commercial leisure, 278, 281, 285–6, 295–6, 300; and the "self," 297–8, 300, 307–8, 322; and reformers, 298; and oppression of women, 300; and African American women, 303, 306; performers, 304–5; seen as passive, 306; and immigrant women, 307, 320–2; and domesticity, 390–2; and alternate images of women, 391–2
population control, 350–1
pornography, 420–1

postmodernism, 314
power relations: analysis of, 3–4, 61–2; as gendered, 5–6, 12; and sexual labels, 208; and travel, 315
Pratt, Mary Louise, 41
pregnancy: *see* childbirth; reproduction
Presidential Commission on the Status of Women, 414
primogeniture, 91
private sphere, 90; *see also* domesticity; public sphere; "separate spheres"
Progressive Party, 237
progressivism, 234, 252, 333, 335
property rights, 60, 61; of women, 91, 124, 137, 139, 143, 154–5, 195; *see also* marriage, property rights of
prostitutes, 120, 140–1, 301–2
public housing, 375
public space, 296–7, 298, 301–2, 304
public sphere, 86, 100, 301–2; *see also* private sphere
publishing, 118
Pueblos, 38, 40
Puerto Rican women, 418
Puritans, 12–13, 50, 53, 68, 69, 71, 72–3
putting-out: *see* outwork

Quakers (Society of Friends), 52, 53, 76, 103, 121, 123, 124
Quarles, Benjamin, 169
quotas, 232, 243, 246

Rabinovitz, Lauren, 302
race, 12, 238; and Indians, 7–8, 9; and slavery, 16, 22; social construction of, 59–60; and legal system, 133; and Mexicans, 142; and women's rights, 145; and sexuality, 208; and immigration, 323; and adoption, 358–9; and the New Deal, 369–70; *see also* whiteness
"race suicide," 219, 240, 241, 324
racial uplift, 109, 399, 403
Radcliffe Institute, 245
radio, 295, 296
rape, 36, 214–15, 417, 430
Reagan, Leslie, 368
Reagan, Ronald, 245
Reconstruction, 187–8, 197–8, 214–15
reform movements, 243; justifications for, 90; antebellum, 109; and women's sphere, 109–10; and maternalism, 118; interracial, 122, 123, 126–7; legal, 124; and class divisions, 124–5; and rural women, 160, 162; *see also* activism, women's; moral reform
reformers: response to commercial leisure, 283, 298, 301, 302–3; in federal government, 372
Reis, Elizabeth, 68
religion, 66–78; in West Africa, 27; and Indian women, 37; and Puritan families, 50; and childrearing, 52, 53; and possession by the devil, 67, 68–9; and the body, 67, 73; and women sinners, 68, 69; and sexuality, 71–2; and unruly women, 72–3; Antinomian crisis, 72–3; and enslaved women, 74–5; and women preachers, 76, 77; "feminization" of, 77–8, 119, 240; and masculinity, 78; and radicalism, 123–4; and feminism, 420, 430; *see also* Christianity; churches; evangelicalism; specific denominations
reproduction, 348–67; as a colonial concern, 13; and white women, 13, 216; of enslaved women, 22, 23, 31; and physicians, 207; and feminism, 420; *see also* birth control
Reproductive Rights National Network (R2N2), 420
Republicanism, 86, 88–9, 90, 112, 124–5, 219
Republican Motherhood, 62, 150
respectability: and work, 104; African American politics of, 109, 114, 284, 330, 403; and public space, 301–2; and whiteness, 323–4; and immigrant women, 330; and woman suffrage, 342
Richards, Ellen, 235
Richmond, Mary, 232
Richmond, Va., 289
Riot Grrls, 427–8
riots, food, 85, 184, 321
Roberts, Dorothy, 353
Robinson, Jo Ann Gibson, 386, 402
Robinson, Ruby Doris Smith, 406–7, 410
Robnett, Belinda, 410
Rochester, NY, 123, 124
Rodrique, Jessie, 353–4
Roe v. Wade, 351, 425
Roosevelt, Eleanor, 236, 244, 400, 405, 414
Roper, Lyndal, 56
Rosie the Riveter, 250, 251, 376

Ross, Ellen, 356
Rowlandson, Mary, 15–16, 39
Rowson, Susanna, 39, 87
Royal African Company, 21, 24
Ruíz, Vicki, 263–4, 266, 280, 307
rural women, 150–64; *see also* farm women; planter women
Ryan, Mary P., 104, 106, 119–20, 196, 277

Salmon, Marylynn, 54–5
Saltzgaber, Jan M., 124
same-sex relationships, 242; *see also* homosexuality; homosociability; lesbians, lesbianism
San Antonio, Tex., 367
Sanger, Margaret, 351, 353
Saville, Julie, 198
Scanlon, Jennifer, 279
Schaw, Janet, 16
Schlafly, Phyllis, 387, 416
Schlissel, Lillian, 138
Schoen, Johanna, 354
Schultz, Deborah, 406
science, 216–22, 246
Scott, Anne Firor, 118–19, 180, 332
Scott, Joan, 194
segregation, 142, 228, 230, 289
Seneca Falls Woman's Rights Convention (1848), 124, 128, 160
"separate spheres," 100, 107–8, 241–2; in South, 53, 121; and African Americans, 109, 199; questioned as a theory, 109, 110, 213; as ideology for reform, 109–10, 117–18, 139; shaped by political culture, 112; religious belief in, 119–20; and middle class, 195–6; and women's education, 227; *see also* domesticity
settlement houses, 232, 253, 298
Seven Sisters Colleges, 228, 241, 245
sewing machines, 282, 286–7
sex, 12; premarital, 72, 92, 241–2; extramarital, 72, 95, 207–8, 388; as source of emotional intimacy, 208; as source of physical pleasure, 209, 220, 388; interracial (consensual), 215; regulation of, by the state, 215; and college women, 241–2; and African American women, 242
sexual harassment, 109, 250, 264, 374, 422
sexuality, xiv, 6, 7, 40, 120; and class, 9, 207, 208, 263–4; female, images of, 71, 92, 207, 217, 220; and consumption, 71; and religion, 71–2; and "passionlessness," 92–3, 207, 208, 214, 217–18, 221; double standard, 118, 120, 207, 377; of single women, 200, 357; and race, 208, 214–15; and science, 216–22; control of, 217, 302–4, 377, 388; and public space, 298, 300; and autonomy, 308; and popular culture, 388
sexual violence, 109, 214, 246, 264, 426, 428; *see also* domestic violence; rape
Sheppard-Towner Act, 243, 334
Simkins, Modjeska, 407
sit-in movement, 406
Sklar, Kathryn Kish, 118
slander, 70–1
slavery, 16, 20–31, 59, 94, 184, 186, 196–8, 202; *see also* emancipation; enslaved persons; enslaved women
slaves: *see* enslaved persons; enslaved women
Sleeper-Smith, Susan, 43
Smith, Daniel Blake, 52–3
Smith, Daniel Scott, 209
Smith, Ola Delight, 337
Smith, Susan L., 356
Smith College, 243
Smith-Hughes Act, 235
Smith Lever Act, 235
Smith-Rosenberg, Carroll, 112, 213
Snyder, Robert W., 301
social scientists (women), 252–3
social security, 264, 369, 370
social welfare, 258–9, 333–4, 354, 369, 370–1, 429; *see also* the state, welfare
social work, 232, 243
Society of Friends: *see* Quakers
sororities, 242, 243, 245
South, 119, 121–2, 160–1, 228, 296
South Carolina, 29–30
Southern Association of College Women, 288
Southern Christian Leadership Conference (SCLC), 398
Southern Conference for Human Welfare (SCHW), 405
Southwest, 38, 39, 132–3, 136–7, 143, 282
Spain, 135, 136
Spelman College, 229, 236, 242, 406
spiritualism, 123–4
Stanley, Amy Dru, 202
Stansell, Christine, 101–2, 124–5, 199–200
Stanton, Elizabeth Cady, 176, 177

Starr, Mary Rozet, 337
state, the: and the family, 49–50, 54–8; and regulation of sexual behavior, 215, 303; welfare, 334–5; and reproduction, 348–9, 352; and childrearing, 357
Staupers, Mabel K., 236–7
Stedman Jones, Gareth, 194–5
sterilization, 352–3, 408, 420, 430
Strasser, Susan, 288
strikes, 124, 254, 261, 288, 304, 321; shoe factory (1860), 101, 102; Lawrence mill (1912), 261–2; Atlanta washerwomen, 262; Joaquin Valley agricultural workers (1933), 266; Duke University hospital workers (1970s), 267
Student Nonviolent Coordinating Committee (SNCC), 406–7, 409
subjectivity, 297–8, 307–8, 321–2; *see also* identities
suffrage, 87, 405; *see also* woman suffrage
Survey, 232
sweatshops, 268

Talbot, Marion, 235
Tampa, Fla., 321, 337, 338, 341
Tax, Meredith, 257
teachers, 104–5, 227–8, 234–5, 236, 243
Tentler, Leslie Woodcock, 298–9
Terrell, Mary Church, 399
Texas, 43, 132, 282
Thomas, Clarence, 423
Thompson, E. P., 193–4, 255
Title IX, 245, 428
trade unions: *see* unions
Trafzer, Clifford, 277
transnational history, xv–xvi
travel, 313–15
Treaty of Guadalupe Hidalgo, 142, 143

Ulrich, Laurel Thatcher, 61, 62, 354
unions, 253–4, 329, 373, 378; teachers', 235; organizing, 251, 421; radicals purged from, 254–5; gender relations in, 261, 262–3, 267, 372, 374; clerical and service workers', 267–8, 417, 421; women's activism in, 385, 400; and feminism, 415, 428; *see also* labor movements; strikes
UNITE, 268
United Auto Workers (UAW), 385, 415
United Farm Workers' Union, 387
United Negro Improvement Association (UNIA), 400
University of Chicago, 233
unruly women, 12–13, 67–73
unwed mothers, 357–8, 389
US Employment Service, 378
US Sanitary Commission, 176–7, 178
US Women's Bureau, 415
utopian communalism, 120, 121, 127

Van Kirk, Sylvia, 37–8
vaudeville, 301, 305
violence, 6, 140, 420–1, 430; *see also* domestic violence; rape; sexual violence
Violence Against Women Act (1994), 430
voluntary organizations: *see* activism, women's
voter registration, 400–1

Wald, Lillian, 298, 299
Walker, Alice, 419
Walker, Maggie Lena, 289, 404
Walsh, Lorena, 55
Ware, Susan, 371–2
Weiss, Jessica, 392
"Wellesley marriages": *see* marriage, "Boston"
Wells-Barnett, Ida B., 215, 237, 399
Welter, Barbara, 117–18
Wertheimer, Barbara, 256
West, 132–46; as a multi-ethnic society, 44, 161; migration to, 132–3, 137–8, 155, 162; masculinity in, 133; US conquest of, 136; legal rights of women in, 139; African Americans in, 141–2, 155; and miscegenation laws, 142; and women's property rights, 154–5; political rights of women in, 162–3, 342
West Africa, 20, 23, 24, 25–9
West African women, 26–8, 29–30
Whigs, 111–12
White, Deborah Gray, 180
White, Lynn, 245
White, Richard, 41
Whitefield, George, 73
whiteness, 8, 9, 257–8, 265–6, 323–4
white women: and colonialism, 12–13, 14, 38; and reproduction, 13, 216; and interracial relationships, 51–2; middle class, 104–6, 109–10, 277; activism of, 109–10, 119–21, 123–6, 229–30, 332–4,

white women (*cont'd*)
336, 337, 338–43, 404–6, 409–10, 415, 417–18; and Civil War, 172, 176–8, 179, 181–2, 183; and consumption, 277, 283, 383
Wilkinson, Patrick, 334
Willard, Frances, 215
Willett, Julie, 287–8
Wilson, Lisa, 61–2
witchcraft, 12–13, 57, 66, 67–9, 70
Wolfson, Theresa, 253–4
Wollstonecraft, Mary, 86
womanism, 419
"womanist," 404
woman suffrage, 332; and property ownership, 87–8; in eighteenth-century New Jersey, 88; radicals vs. moderates, 120; African American, 127, 341–2, 399; in the West, 162–3, 342–3; for school board elections, 236; and popular culture, 304; and race, 343
Women's Christian Temperance Union, 215, 333
woman's rights movement, 119, 120, 127–8; and abolitionism, 124, 126, 127; international connections of, 128; *see also* feminism
Women Against Pornography (WAP), 421
Women Against Violence Against Women (WAVAW), 420–1
Women's Army Corps (WAC), 377, 401
women's clubs: *see* activism, women's; specific clubs and organizations
women's colleges, 228, 230, 231, 241, 242, 247; *see also* education, women's; Seven Sisters Colleges; specific colleges
Women's Economic Development Organization (WEDO), 427
Women's International League for Peace and Freedom, 385
women's liberation, 416–20
Women's Political Council (Montgomery, Ala.), 402
Women's Relief Corps (WRC), 188
women's sphere: *see* private sphere; "separate spheres"
women's studies, 246
work (women's): unpaid, 100, 106–7, 200–1, 258, 375; as a family endeavor, 102–3, 266, 281, 370; and respectability, 104; and middle-class women, 104–6; and African American women, 108, 152, 199, 236, 243, 258–60, 262, 374, 375; of rural women, 152–6; wartime, 173–4, 175, 373–6, 401; professional, 232–8, 243–5, 246, 401; clerical and service workers, 235, 251, 421; "feminization" of, 235–6; and immigrant women, 320–1; and gender segregation, 367, 373–4; and discrimination, 378; postwar, 383; and pay equity, 422–3; *see also* housework
working class: formation of, 84, 102, 199–200; consciousness of, 193, 265–6; structure of, 193; studies of, 255–6
working-class women: and popular culture, 110, 263–4, 307; activism of, 122, 251, 253, 260–1, 263, 267–8, 337, 385, 400–1, 421; domesticity of, 257; consciousness of, 257, 298–9; politics of, 261; and World War II, 373–6
workplace, regulation of, 253, 260
World War I, 233
World War II: and women's education, 244; and food rationing, 290; and African American women, 236–7, 374, 401; and women's work, 372–7; and Indian women, 374–5; and Japanese American women, 375; and civil rights movement, 400, 401

Yakimas, 277
Young Women's Christian Association (YWCA), 387, 405